Understanding Global Cooperation

Understanding Global Cooperation

Twenty-Five Years of Research on Global Governance

Edited by

Kurt Mills
Kendall Stiles

BRILL

LEIDEN | BOSTON

Cover illustration: Image from Shutterstock.

The Library of Congress Cataloging-in-Publication Data is available online at http://catalog.loc.gov
LC record available at http://lccn.loc.gov/2021909043

Typeface for the Latin, Greek, and Cyrillic scripts: "Brill". See and download: brill.com/brill-typeface.

ISBN 978-90-04-46259-5 (hardback)
ISBN 978-90-04-46260-1 (e-book)

Printed by Printforce, the Netherlands

Contents

Twenty-Five Years of Global Governance

Charting the Development of International Responses to Global Problems

Kurt Mills and Kendall Stiles[1]

Twenty-five years ago, the journal *Global Governance* was established as the voice of the Academic Council on the United Nations System, intended to speak to both academic and practitioner audiences. This was 50 years after the founding of the United Nations, and the fact that the title of the journal did not mention the UN was a reflection of both the reality of, and the need for, international governance structures to address an increasingly interconnected but also fractured international system that included the UN but also looked far beyond this global organization for leadership. The editors noted that it was "a time of great hope and great hopelessness, a time when ideological fault lines have disappeared, while the global rifts of wealth and power have widened." This description of the period immediately after both the fall of the Berlin Wall on the one hand and the Rwandan genocide on the other seems particularly apt today. *Governance* at the global level has expanded dramatically in the last quarter century while *governments* continue to challenge this expansion.

The pages of *Global Governance* have served as a kind of historical record over the past 25 years, documenting both this hope and hopelessness, the promises and challenges of attempts to address issues that cross national boundaries. Unlike most academic journals, while *Global Governance* has always aimed at the audience of scholars in their efforts to develop theory and concepts, it has also reached out to—and included—policy-making and policy-makers in its pages. A number of the pieces included in this work were written by senior officials and activists who sought to engage broader theoretical arguments in their own work. And this broader voice makes the work found in the journal all the more relevant. Those who publish in *Global* Governance

---

1   Kurt Mills is Professor of International Relations and Human Rights at the University of Dundee. His research focuses on human rights, responsibility to protect, international criminal justice, and humanitarianism, with a regional focus on sub-Saharan Africa. His most recent book is *International Responses to Mass Atrocities in Africa: Responsibility to Protect, Prosecute, and Palliate* (Pennsylvania/London). Kendall Stiles is Professor of Political Science at Brigham Young University, where he teaches courses on international relations, including international organization and law. His most recent book is *Trust and Hedging in International Relations* (Michigan).

generally support the ideals of the UN and global governance more generally as a way to tackle common global problems, but approach their subject with an unflinching critical eye.

For the 25th anniversary, we asked the former editors of the journal to nominate an article from each year that exemplified this critical approach to the formal institutions and other actors in global governance. What emerged is a rich and fascinating mixture of issues, theoretical approaches, and methodologies which chart the development of global governance over a quarter of a century via a range of both academic and more policy-oriented pieces. It reveals both optimism and pessimism. It describes development of concepts sitting side by side with confusion over the meaning and best way to brings those concepts to life. The majority of the articles featured here appear rooted in liberal traditions which identify cooperation as the best way to address global problems while at the same time seeing self-interested realist constraints on such development, as well as constructivist approaches which, to paraphrase Alexander Wendt, argue that global governance is what states make of it. While at times there appears to be a sense of progress in the liberal, enlightened sense, there is plenty to draw in the sceptic who sees much nuance and multidirectional movement in global governance efforts.

This introduction will highlight some of the main themes running through these pieces, while allowing each piece to speak for itself. We see a few main analytical and topical themes which bind these pieces together but which also point to diversity of perspective. There is discussion of the concept of global governance and its place within international relations more broadly. We see analysis of the UN and other IOs as organizations themselves, set with broader international relations contexts. We see a significant focus on security, from peacekeeping to key issues of international security. Human rights features prominently, as do the environment and key issues surrounding economics, development, and business. In other words, we see the full range of issues that the UN has grappled with for 75 years, but which other IOs have also tackled as specialized and regional organizations have developed and expanded their competency and reach.

1   Global Governance as Concept

In his contribution to the very first issue of *Global Governance*, James Rosenau, in "search[ing] for order in disorder, for coherence in change" identifies global governance not as "command" but as "steering." This is a recognition that governance does not necessarily imply hierarchy. In an interdependent world, governance is about systems of rule which may exist "even in the absence of established legal or political authority." The UN and other formal intergovernmental organizations are obviously part of the picture, but they do not necessarily "command" (although the EU perhaps more so than the UN). Other formal and informal institutions and organizations contribute to governance, and state-level mechanisms of command are increasingly embedded within regional and global governance arrangements. The locus and mechanism of control or "steering" evolves, and there has been a relocation of authority away from the state, upwards but also downwards in parallel processes of globalization and localization. Governance in the 21st century, he argues, will be polyarchal.

David Held investigates the processes of globalization to highlight the challenge of global governance. He identifies a paradox of democracy at the national level when there are so many issues that are and must be addressed at the regional and global levels (the current Covid-19 pandemic illustrates all too perfectly an issue which by its very nature cannot be addressed by any single country within its own borders). Instead of confining democracy to individual states, he argues for a cosmopolitan democracy which recognizes the "overlapping communities of fate" which characterize the global condition. While accepting state-level democracy, this would incorporate "a layer of governance to constitute a limitation on national sovereignty" in order to address transboundary issues at the regional and global levels, a version, perhaps, of Rosenau's polyarchy.

2   The Multiple United Nations and the Broader Terrain of International Organization

Inis Claude identifies two United Nations. The first is comprised of the staff who advocate for principle over power. This UN is represented by the Secretary-General who speaks for the UN and, in one sense, for the world. The second UN is made up of states who act on the basis of self-interest—power over principle in many cases. The Secretary-General is thus both commander, or perhaps chief "steerer," of a large bureaucratic organization that tries to steer the global political scene, as well as an employee of the state members of the UN who want him (or her as must be the case in the not too distance future) to do their bidding. Given the contradictions between principle and power, and the fact that the employers do not agree on what their employees should be doing, it is not surprising that, for example, the considerable efforts of the first UN to bring about peaceful settlement of disputes or engage in peacekeeping, for example (or, one might add, pursue a multitude of other urgent global agendas), do not always bear fruit.

Where Claude sees two UNs, Roger Coate identifies three. In addition to the Secretariat and state members, Coate sees civil society, including "NGOs, academics, consultants, experts, and independent commissions" as a key component of UN deliberations and vital for the success of the UN. He identifies a number of avenues of engagement and influence for civil society actors, including "networking and coalition building," "global campaigns," "parallel conferencing," and "partnerships." He cites the Cardoso Report on UN-civil society relations to argue that "'Civil society is now so vital to the United Nations that engaging with it well is a necessity, not an option. It must also engage with others, including the private sector, parliaments and local authorities.'" This ties in directly to Rosenau who identified social movements as a key element of global governance, empowered by a "skill revolution."

The serving UN Secretary-General at the time, Kofi Annan, noted a "quiet revolution" of increased cooperation, with the UN a pivotal player in helping states govern themselves better. Like Rosenau, he notes that central authority has been undermined, which in turns undermines good governance. But he also argues that in order to promote good governance in states, the UN also requires good governance, and identified the need for reform of UN mechanisms to make them more responsive and coherent. Indeed, UN reform has been a perennial concern which is not likely to go away anytime soon. And, like Coate, he argues for effective partnerships with civil society, thus reaffirming the necessity of nongovernmental actors in Rosenau's global governance "steering."

Ngaire Woods highlights the necessity of good governance within international organizations as well as within the broader realm of global governance—i.e. "links between individuals, peoples, groups, and international organizations." The principles of good governance include competent administration, as well as participation, accountability, fairness (procedural and substantive), transparency. These give IOs legitimacy and effectiveness. Yet, too often IOs (and broader global governance mechanisms) lack many elements of good governance, allowing key states to control decision making. Some organisations will include external stakeholders—such as aid recipients—a seat at the table, while implementing procedures such as supermajorities to prevent powerful actors from imposing their will. She notes that one measure to ensure everybody has a voice—unanimity—can impede effectiveness of an organization, while consensus decision making which avoids votes, may be a better alternative. Yet, the way a form of consensus decision making is embedded within the working practices of the UN Security Council, for example, under-mines participation and transparency. Woods also notes that while changes in voting procedures—such as double qualified majorities—might not nec-essarily substantively change outcomes, but could significantly affect per-ceptions of the legitimacy of decisions. Organizations also face the issue of democratic deficit—the lack of direct popular participation in decision mak-ing. She uses the example of the European Union (EU) which introduced the directly elected European Parliament to address this issue. Yet, 20 years later, the democratic deficit is still a hotly debated issue (and featured heavily in the campaign for the United Kingdom to leave the EU with characterizations of "unelected bureaucrats" in Brussels making decisions).

Craig Warkentin and Karen Mingst highlight how technological change—and in particular the World Wide Web—have enabled and empowered NGOs and the emerging "global civil society" to set agendas and control outcomes in global decision making. This is an example of Rosenau's "skill revolution" where individuals and groups are better able to understand issues and have a voice as a result of technological change. NGOs are able to reframe (or even block) treaties, for example, and they argue that this represents an irreversible change in global political dynamics.

If much scholarship on global governance takes a liberal or neo-liberal insti-tutional approach to studying international organizations, Peter Haas takes a constructivist approach, examining how UN conferences—and specifically environmental conferences—provide space for complex dynamics between interests and norms. He examines the dynamics of socialization, education, persuasion, discourse, and norm inculcation as mechanisms by which states derive meaning and acquire identity and interests. While the effectiveness of UN conferences is not always clear, they allow actors to share information, including technical facts. They can also set progressive agendas and secure public support for certain policy options. They can also advance monitoring and early-warning mechanisms.

Michele Betsill and Harriet Bulkeley argue that global governance should not be separated into "local" and "global" categories since the various levels of governance interact in important ways. Regime theory is far too state-centric to capture a variety of actors which are increasingly prominent addressing diverse global issues, such as climate change. On the other hand, work on transnational networks tends to ignore civil authorities as well. And so we need to emphasize multilevel governance which brings together all varieties of actors in an issue-area, whether public or private, for-profit or not, national, supra-national or sub-national.

3   **International Security**

Preventing and stopping wars has been at the heart of global governance
since the creation of the current international system in 1945. While the initial
focus was on interstate conflict, it is now clear that most organized violent
conflict is internal (although frequently with an internationalized component). Mats Berdal examines these "new wars," which are internal but connected to broader international economic and political dynamics. Specifically,
he asks whether globalization has substantially altered the nature of civil
wars. He examines several civil wars to better measure the economic activities and interests of the states, belligerent groups, and civilian actors involved.
Globalization has increased inequality between North and South and transnational economic actors have increasingly inserted themselves into domestic
conflicts. Intensified interdependence is thus inseparably connected to civil
warfare. It is therefore imperative to focus on the potential economic gains of
the various actors in the context of globalization. Many guerilla movements
take advantage of abandoned natural resources such as diamond deposits to
prosecute the war and enrich themselves. Likewise, corrupt officials see their
government positions as opportunities for profiteering. These individuals on
both sides of the conflicts often form economic ties with their counterparts in
neighboring countries, creating regional economic networks that profit from
warfare. Of course, this is not entirely new—and there exist non-financial reasons for civil war. But as history, identity, and greed interact, warfare begins to
make sense. Add to this the fuel provided by state and non-state arms providers and it is easier to see how these wars can endure.

Where Berdal examines how civil wars are fueled and extended, Michael
Barnett, Hunjoon Kim, Madalene O'Donnell, and Laura Sitea look at a key area
of UN and other IO action in conflict situations—peacebuilding—and how
such activities have been incorporated into their wider mandates. They note
that the many state and IGO actors involved in its implementation actually
have very different conceptions of its meaning. We can see clustering of particular conceptions in the UN Secretariat, in UN specialized agencies, in the
European Union, and among particular member-states. The UN stresses the
effort to improve capacity and policies in states that have experienced conflict
in order to prevent it in the future. On the other hand, while the IMF emphasizes recovery, the World Bank focuses on prevention—all under the banner
of peacebuilding. The EU tends to disaggregate the term and treat each component as deserving of its own focus. Individual states not only disagree with
each other, but the various agencies within states tend to emphasize those
issues that match up with their primary missions. Because the basic aim of

peacebuilding is so multifaceted, almost anything can be included. Looking across the spectrum, democratization and reconstruction are the most popular programs, while most others are only addressed by a few agencies. For the most part, international and domestic agencies have simply expanded their normal mission to incorporate some aspects of peacebuilding.

As noted below, Paul Williams, Alex Bellamy, and Mateja Peter examine recent developments in military responses to internal conflicts by the UN. Williams and Bellamy look at the first real use of the responsibility to protect principle, where the UN Security Council authorized military intervention to stop atrocities in Libya. Peter looks at the evolution of peacekeeping to include more robust uses of force to stop violence between warring parties—although frequently in favor of one side, namely governments. They are different types of uses of power, but both raise significant questions about UN positionality vis-à-vis particular conflicts and actors.

Returning to interstate conflict, Jessica Tuchman Mathews examines what she argues is an unrecognized success story in UN conflict prevention and arms reduction/elimination—the elimination of weapons of mass destruction—and in particular the dismantling of a nuclear weapons program—in Iraq. UN agencies were at the heart of successful attempts to find and destroy Iraq's unconventional weapons during the 1990s, supported by effective UN sanctions. In fact, they had better information on Iraq's nuclear weapons programs than key states. The fact that this success went unrecognized and thus was not able to prevent the US invasion of Iraq in 2003 is perhaps a reflection of the political weakness of the UN vis-à-vis the most powerful global actors. Further strengthening weapons inspection mechanisms will be key in preventing the spread and use of weapons of mass destruction.

4 Economic Governance

Economic governance is a key component of global governance more widely, addressing the fundamental contradiction of increasing global economic interdependence even as states fight to keep control of their economies. It also engages with the challenge of global inequality—both between states and within states—via development and trading regimes which can either exacerbate or decrease inequality. And, as noted by Berdal, global economic dynamics—globalization—can exacerbate violent internal conflict. Much governance happens at the macroeconomic level, while some recent innovations have operated at a more microeconomic level, attempting to persuade individual businesses to operate in different ways. John Ruggie argues that the UN Global Compact attempts to induce corporations to operate in a more socially responsible manner (drawn from international human rights, labor, and environmental norms and standards) not by conventional regulation but by asking corporations to sign up to voluntary codes of practice. Businesses are to learn from each other and other actors via a networked approach. It is not binding law, but there is hope that stronger norms and laws will develop over time. Structurally, the GC consists of a dense web of interorganizational networks at many levels of governance. These are primarily voluntary, private, interconnected associations. Corporations are motivated to burnish their reputations in an age of increased scrutiny and expectations. It may not satisfy those who want a hard regulatory approach to corporate conduct while businesses may resist any intrusion on how they operate as private, profit-making entities, but instead represents a compromise approach to changing behavior.

5   Environmental Governance

The environment (and in particular climate change) has become a key touchstone of global politics today, but Peter Haas demonstrates that environmental issues have featured in global deliberations—especially via the UN—for decades. He traces how UN environmental conferences have created new frameworks and agendas which have helped to drive consideration of environmental issues forward, even as the effectiveness of such conferences in terms of direct, positive impacts on protecting the environment is frequently difficult to measure or discern.

Beyond the global UN conferences, Michele Betsill and Harriet Bulkeley identify other loci of concern for, and action on, climate change. They argue that cities have become key players in addressing key environmental issues and are embedded in multi-level global networks of local and global, state and non-state actors which have developed to deal with climate change. They note that while it is states that make commitments to reduce greenhouse gas emissions, local governments have significant authority over land use, waste management, transportation, and energy consumption, which makes them key actors in national and global efforts to address climate.

While policy-makers have tended to look at the management of water in terms of discrete regimes, Claudia Pahl-Wostl, Joyeeta Gupta, and Daniel Petry argue that a multi-level global approach is called for. This is easier said than done, since local and regional governance structures are powerful and territorial, and each agency and network has adopted different principles and structures. International law provides a framework for many aspects of water policy, along with international agencies and regimes. The EU and other regional bodies have also been active in this area, along with multi-stakeholder public-private networks such as the World Water Council. Add to this private control of certain waterways and the role of scientists and advocates, and we find a governance structure that resembles a Mobius strip.

6   Human Rights

Human rights are mentioned seven times in the UN Charter and have been the focus of broad and deep global and regional norms and institutional structures intended to regulate how states treat their people. The very mixed success of these norms and institutions—and their uneven effects in different regions—indicate the challenge human rights pose to state sovereignty and the impediment sovereignty poses to human rights protection even as the state is and will remain the primary locus of actual human rights protection. Yet, is also undeniable that over the last quarter of a century, protecting human rights has come to be one of the main concerns of global governance. The question of whether human rights are truly global and universal poses an ongoing challenge to efforts to protect human, as arguments about Western imposition of human rights bolster assertions of cultural relativism which are used by authoritarian governments to undermine human rights. However, as argued by Kathryn Sikkink, non-"Western" voices—in particular from Latin America—have featured prominently in developing human rights norms.

Rosemary Foot documents the challenges for human rights protection when they become entangled with key state security concerns. The response by the US and other states to the terrorist attacks on September 11 2001 highlights the weakness of international human rights norms when security becomes states' primary concern. She sees continuing concern for international reputation in human rights protection as even as states undermine human rights norms in the pursuit of national security—such as engaging in torture of suspected terrorists—thus exposing "the patchiness of the actual implementation of human rights norms." She sees a resurgence of sovereignty sitting alongside global institutions dedicated to ensuring that human rights are not sacrificed on the altar of sovereignty.

The creation of the International Criminal Court (ICC) to prosecute those who commit the worst violations of human rights in conflict also directly challenges state sovereignty. While a majority of the world's countries have come together to support the development of the ICC, some countries have worked to undermine it. While the United States (US) originally supported the idea of the new court, it quickly drew back on its support as it became clear that most countries would not allow it to control the operation of the court via its position on the UN Security Council. Since then, the US has had a complicated relationship with the court. Andrea Birdsall traces the souring of this relationship as the US took action to undermine its independence and efficacy and sought to insulate itself from its reach, reflecting yet again how the post-9/11 so called "War on Terror" has undermined support for human rights norms and institutions by powerful states. The threats against court personnel and their families by the previous US Secretary of State—after a warming of relations under the previous administration—indicates the fickle relationship the US has with international norms and institutions—a relationship more often driven by traditional state interests than normative concerns.

7   The Waxing and Waning of New Norms

Running through much of the work in Global Governance has been a topic that has fascinated liberal and constructivist alike: the rise and fall of new international norms and rules. In recent years this has been particularly important as global institutions have been formed to instantiate and enforce new norms, failing in the effort as often as they have succeeded. This is particularly true with respect to the Responsibility to Protect, as well as more robust peacekeeping efforts, discussed by Williams and Bellamy on the one hand and Peter on the other.

Williams and Bellamy argue that the Responsibility to Protect (R2P) has empowered the international community to intervene to protect victims of atrocities and created an expectation of intervention. This is not to say political consensus in particular cases is always possible. In the case of Libya, UN Security Council members reached agreement on the Muammar Gaddafi regime's threat to civilians and imposed sanctions, underscoring the government's duty to protect its people. While NATO mobilized, the Secretary-General spoke directly with Gaddafi, to no avail. Despite skepticism and concerns, the major powers on the Council felt pressured to support (or refrain from opposing) UN action in part because the Council had previously endorsed international engagement and the UN Secretariat had said atrocities were imminent. Resolution 1973 calling for intervention therefore passed by 10-0-5. This represented a breakthrough in R2P. This is not to say that external intervention is likely to recur—or be effective. Historically, atrocities have typically ended as a result of internal factors. Military intervention is typically constrained by disagreement over basic principles, considerations regarding domestic politics, and prudential considerations of risk and reward. Yet, there is reason to be hopeful that the R2P norm is becoming independently significant in state decision-making.

On the other hand, Peter discusses the facts on the ground where UN peace-keepers work to mitigate internal violence—particularly in Africa. UN peace-keepers are engaged in a wide range of novel offensive operations aimed at strengthening state power—best conceived as "enforcement peacekeeping". Many of these actions violate the basic principles of peacekeeping, such as neutrality and non-use of force. The result is a disconnect between principles and practices that are generally not acknowledged in New York. UN peace-keepers fight alongside government forces in the DRC and the operations in Mali are explicitly designed to help the government fight Islamists. In Somalia peacekeepers are essentially fighting Al-Shabaab in a conventional war. These types of operations generally use troops from other African countries in places where open warfare is on-going and peacekeepers are always in harm's way. There is no effort to secure the consent of the warring parties before deploying troops. The troops clearly takes sides in the conflicts and use force offensively—not just to protect themselves. All of this risks undermining the legitimacy of and support for peacekeeping and even escalating the conflicts they are being directed to end.

On a related note, John Karlsrud argues that individuals assigned by the UN Secretary-General to oversee peace programs often have considerable autonomy and adopt new norms on the fly. While empowered by the S-G, these Special Representatives also operate far from New York. As a result, they can bring about new interpretations of international norms, thereby becoming "norm arbiters". Faced with an untenable situation in Côte d'Ivoire, the SRSG authorized the use of force to protect civilians unilaterally. On the other hand, the SRSG in Afghanistan communicated regularly with the Taliban along with other key players. The authority of the SRSG is tied to delegated powers from the S-G, expertise, moral authority, charisma and prestige (meaning an independent career and status). SRSG autonomy can actually increase the odds of success and allow them to inject novel interpretations and applications of international norms.

Sikkink drew our attention to the origins of many human rights norms by focusing on the role of early Latin American advocates. For example, they adopted the American Declaration of the Rights and Duties of Man before the Universal Declaration was adopted. This history turns on its head the conventional wisdom that human rights advocacy was primarily an invention of the

Global North. Several key Latin American governments became democratic in the 1940s and played essential roles in the drafting of the human rights elements of the UN Charter and of various human rights initiatives.

Finally, Kjølv Egeland explores whether emerging rhetoric regarding the elimination and criminalization of nuclear weapons, while perhaps aspirational, is having a direct effect on debates at the highest levels. In 2017 the UN Treaty on the Prohibition of Nuclear Weapons was opened for signature (the vote was 122-1-1). While some may dismiss this as mere "cheap talk", there is something significant about it. It represents a repudiation of the notion that a few elite states deserve to have nuclear weapons. Now that the treaty has come into effect with the required 50 ratifications, it is hoped that it will stigmatize the possession of nuclear weapons and nudge nuclear weapons states to explore alternatives. The first steps toward this end were accomplished when nuclear weapons states were unable to provide convincing arguments against the treaty. At this point, supporters of the ban hold the moral high ground. It also shows that international norms can be effectively challenged by small- and medium-sized states. Its effect remains to be seen, of course.

8   Global Leadership

While Global Governance was founded in a period of considerable optimism—tempered by caution—the emergence of Trump, Putin, Xi and Brexit have undercut much of that early hope. Some have noted that the policies of the powerful are not easily constrained by norms, and that even the most mature and capable international institutions will struggle to resist a concerted effort at manipulation and even corruption by the world's great powers. At the same time, some find a silver lining in the fact that even as they attempt to undermine global governance, great power policy-makers must make use of the very rhetoric they oppose in making their arguments. And many smaller and middle powers demonstrate a more consistent commitment to global governance and resist attempts to undermine it.

Matthew Stephen acknowledges the discontent of emerging powers such as Russia, China and India, but imagines a wide range of possible scenarios as they challenge existing institutions. He find they are both reinforcing and complicating their functioning. Institutions are "sticky", but power politics is unrelenting and so we can expect a new form of global governance that is more contested and fragmented and less liberal and universal. It is important to note that the emerging powers are generally less committed to liberal values of individualism and self-expression, which means there will be less consensus regarding the aims of international institutions. Since their wealth and power depends on collective goods created by the UN and Bretton Woods systems, we should not expect obstinate defiance or wholesale attacks. Rather, we can anticipate several possible scenarios: contestation over leadership and privilege, deemphasizing liberal values, institutional paralysis, a turn toward informal arrangements, and fragmentation with the creation of new arrangements that compete with existing ones.

Gregory Chin argues that there is evidence that, despite China's apparent contempt for Bretton Woods institutions, it must invoke such principles as liberalism and tolerance even as it erects new, rival economic institutions. The new Asian Infrastructure Investment Bank (AIIB) has the potential of opening new possibilities for development lending, structured as it is to encourage creativity and accountability. In some ways it resembles the World Bank in that China, as the principal contributor, can veto key decisions through a system of weighted voting. But it has promised to exercise restraint. The first director is Chinese, and the Board resembles that of the World Bank—except that its members do not live near the organization's headquarters. This will likely give the staff and management more sway and autonomy. Thus far, China's willingness to support Asian infrastructure growth has been welcomed by its counterparts, low- and medium-income alike. China promises that loans will be provided on the basis of objective economic analysis rather than politics. At this point, it appears that the AIIB will likely change how development lending happens in Asia.

Caroline Fehl and Johannes Thimm focus on the relative withdrawal of the Trump administration and the resulting power vacuum in most global institutions. They ask whether governance can survive the loss of the hegemon. Looking more closely at the issues of nuclear arms control, climate change, and trade policies, they conclude that US leadership is likely indispensable. While NGOs, epistemic communities, and social movements can play a key role in creating and sustaining international regimes, states are still essential to bring it all to fruition. At this point, the EU is not strong enough (although it probably could do more), China is too ambivalent (and often contrarian), and Russia lacks global influence. That said, Trump's obstinacy may have the effect of unifying the world in opposition to his anti-multilateral agenda—which means non-hegemonic cooperation may yet emerge.

9 Eclecticism

While most articles in Global Governance are squarely focused on the ways global institutions emerge and operate, the journal has also welcomed pieces that address yet other issues—including the implementation of eclectic governance arrangements to address local problems.[2] For example, Gilles Carbonnier, Fritz Brugger, and Jana Krause consider how the multiplicity of local, regional, and global stake-holders influence democratization in resource-rich states. Sometimes these arrangements are expected to establish new centers of power, to legitimize certain actors and norms, alter the power relations between actors, and otherwise behave as regimes. In Nigeria and Azerbaijan, these arrangements are intended to shift power away from rent-seeking and corrupt officials toward the people. However, civil society in these countries have a hard time constraining the actions of state actors. Not only are they often excluded from decision-making, their members are sometimes persecuted by the state.

This raises the more general question of the evolving focus of Global Governance and whether global institutions and international governmental organizations in particular ought to still take center-stage. There is always some risk in defining one's subject-matter in terms of certain key actors since this is a defining feature of theory in international relations. To deemphasize the state almost invariably means discounting power, while focusing on what takes place in New York at UN headquarters may distract us from changes that are taking place in bars, pubs, shebeens, and tea houses around the world. Stepping back and looking at new actors may enable scholars of global governance to better understand essential dynamics while better anticipating new forces that will end up having a direct bearing on whether governance will continue or decay.

10   Conclusions

As should be clear, while there is general agreement on the importance of global governance, debates persist about its meaning, mechanisms, durability, and significance. While liberal concepts serve as a starting point, scholars are also prone to ask whether governance is always fair, impartial, and professional. In recent years, they have even asked whether governance can persist where powerful states have walked away from its founding principles. Interestingly, this raises the very liberal question: should it? Can global governance ignore the preferences of the states that crafted IOs' founding documents or who fund and otherwise support their day-to-day operations? As mentioned, is it appropriate or ethical for IO to staff be more deeply committed to the bylaws of their institutions rather than the—perhaps—extra-legal demands of their

---

2 Weiss and Wilkinson 2018.

member-states? What is leadership in today's world? Does it mean a powerful state should abandon what it considers a rogue international regime and set up a rival structure? Should the staff follow it out the door? And if it stays, how does one cope with a renegade principal? When Russia and China continue to assert territorial claims even after they are rejected by international tribunals and other bodies does global governance provide any other avenues for recourse, or does this demonstrate the limits of global governance? And what is to be done when the United States and Great Britain repudiate liberal international trade agreements they had a hand in crafting?

Answers to these questions are offered and implied in the essays found in this volume. They help to explain the rise and fall of institutions and norms, shifts in how key terms are defined, and how leadership is expressed. They address developments across a wide range of issues and in many different regions. They even anticipate some of today's questions. They can help us prepare to understand what may one day be a transformed international environment with, for example, post-Bretton Woods or pre-cold war characteristics. As you read this collection, we hope you will see how thinking about global governance has evolved and be inspired to add your own voice to the literature.

Bibliography

Weiss, Thomas G., and Rorden Wilkinson. "The Globally Governed—Everyday Global Governance." *Global Governance* Vol. 24 (2) (2018), 193–210.

CHAPTER 1

Governance in the Twenty-First Century

James N. Rosenau[1]

To anticipate the prospects for global governance in the decades ahead is to discern powerful tensions, profound contradictions, and perplexing paradoxes. It is to search for order in disorder, for coherence in contradiction, and for continuity in change. It is to confront processes that mask both growth and decay. It is to look for authorities that are obscure, boundaries that are in flux, and systems of rule that are emergent. And it is to experience hope embedded in despair.

This is not to imply that the task is impossible. Quite to the contrary, one can discern patterns of governance that are likely to proliferate, others that are likely to attenuate, and still others that are likely to endure as they always have. No, the task is not so much impossible as it is a challenge to one's appreciation of nuance and one's tolerance of ambiguity.

1   Conceptual Nuances

In order to grasp the complexities that pervade world politics, we need to start by drawing a nuanced set of distinctions among the numerous processes and structures that fall within the purview of global governance. Perhaps most important, it is necessary to clarify that global governance refers to more than the formal institutions and organizations through which the management of international affairs is or is not sustained. The United Nations system and national governments are surely central to the conduct of global governance, but they are only part of the full picture. Or at least in this analysis global governance is conceived to include systems of rule at all levels of human

---

*   This chapter was originally published in Global Governance, Volume 1, Issue 1, 1995.

1   James N. Rosenau was University Professor of International Affairs at George Washington University. He was the author or editor of numerous publications, including, *Global Voices: Dialogues in International Relations* (1993), *The United Nations in a Turbulent World* (1992), *Governance Without Government* (1992), and *Turbulence in World Politics: A Theory of Change and Continuity* (1990).

The author is grateful to Walter Truett Anderson and Hongying Wang for their reactions to an early draft of this article.

activity—from the family to the international organization—in which the
pursuit of goals through the exercise of control has transnational repercussions. The reason for this broad formulation is simple: in an ever more interdependent world where what happens in one corner or at one level may have
consequences for what occurs at every other corner and level, it seems a mistake to adhere to a narrow definition in which only formal institutions at the
national and international levels are considered relevant. In the words of the
Council of Rome,

> We use the term governance to denote the command mechanism of a
> social system and its actions that endeavor to provide security, prosper-
> ity, coherence, order and continuity to the system.... Taken broadly, the
> concept of governance should not be restricted to the national and inter-
> national systems but should be used in relation to regional, provincial
> and local governments as well as to other social systems such as educa-
> tion and the military, to private enterprises and even to the microcosm
> of the family.[2]

Governance, in other words, encompasses the activities of governments, but it
also includes the many other channels through which "commands" flow in the
form of goals framed, directives issued, and policies pursued.

1.1   *Command and Control*

But the concept of commands can be misleading. It implies that hierarchy,
perhaps even authoritarian rule, characterizes governance systems. Such an
implication may be descriptive of many forms of governance, but hierarchy
is certainly not a necessary prerequisite to the framing of goals, the issuing of
directives, and the pursuit of policies. Indeed, a central theme of this analysis
is that often the practices and institutions of governance can and do evolve
in such a way as to be minimally dependent on hierarchical, command-based
arrangements. Accordingly, while preserving the core of the Council of Rome
formulation, here we shall replace the notion of command mechanisms
with the concept of *control* or *steering* mechanisms, terms that highlight the

---

2   Alexander King and Bertrand Schneider, *The First Global Revolution: A Report of the Council of
    Rome* (New York: Pantheon Books, 1991), pp. 181–182 (italics added). For other inquiries that
    support the inclusion of small, seemingly local systems of rule in a broad analytic framework,
    see John Friedmann, *Empowerment: The Politics of Alternative Development* (Cambridge,
    Mass.: Blackwell, 1992), and Robert Huckfeldt, Eric Plutzer, and John Sprague, "Alternative
    Contexts of Political Behavior: Churches, Neighborhoods, and Individuals," *Journal of Politics*
    55 (May 1993): 365–381.

purposeful nature of governance without presuming the presence of hierarchy. They are terms, moreover, informed by the etymological roots of *governance*: the term "derives from the Greek 'kybenan' and 'kybernetes' which means 'to steer' and 'pilot or helmsman' respectively (the same Greek root from which 'cybernetics' is derived). The process of governance is the process whereby an organization or society steers itself, and the dynamics of communication and control are central to that process."[3]

To grasp the concept of control one has to appreciate that it consists of relational phenomena that, taken holistically, constitute systems of rule. Some actors, the controllers, seek to modify the behavior and/or orientations of other actors, the controllees, and the resulting patterns of interaction between the former and the latter can properly be viewed as a system of rule sustained by one or another form of control. It does not matter whether the controllees resist or comply with the efforts of controllers; in either event, attempts at control have been undertaken. But it is not until the attempts become increasingly successful and compliance with them increasingly patterned that a system of rule founded on mechanisms of control can be said to have evolved. Rule systems and control mechanisms, in other words, are founded on a modicum of regularity, a form of recurrent behavior that systematically links the efforts of controllers to the compliance of controllees through either formal or informal channels.[4]

It follows that systems of rule can be maintained and their controls successfully and consistently exerted even in the absence of established legal or political authority. The evolution of intersubjective consensuses based on shared fates and common histories, the possession of information and knowledge, the pressure of active or mobilizable publics, and/or the use of careful planning, good timing, clever manipulation, and hard bargaining can—either separately

---

3 Steven A. Rosell et al., *Governing in an Information Society* (Montreal: Institute for Research on Public Policy, 1992), p. 21.

4 Rule systems have much in common with what has come to be called the "new institutionalism." See, for example, Robert O. Keohane, "International Institutions: Two Approaches," *International Studies Quarterly* 32 (December 1988): 379–396; James G. March and Johan P. Olsen, "The New Institutionalism: Organizational Factors in Political Life," *American Political Science Review* 78 (September 1984): 734–749; and Oran R. Young, "International Regimes: Toward a New Theory of Institutions," *World Politics* 39 (October 1986): 104–122. For an extended discussion of how the concept of control is especially suited to the analysis of both formal and informal political phenomena, see James N. Rosenau, *Calculated Control as a Unifying Concept in the Study of International Politics and Foreign Policy*, Research Monograph No. 15 (Princeton: Center of International Studies, Princeton University, 1963).

or in combination—foster control mechanisms that sustain governance without government.[5]

1.2   *Interdependence and Proliferation*

Implicit in the broad conception of governance as control mechanisms is a
premise that interdependence involves not only flows of control, consequence,
and causation within systems, but that it also sustains flows across systems.
These micro-macro processes—the dynamics whereby values and behaviors
at one level get converted into outcomes at more encompassing levels, outcomes that in turn get converted into still other consequences at still more
encompassing levels—suggest that global governance knows no boundaries—
geographic, social, cultural, economic, or political. If major changes occur in
the structure of families, if individual greed proliferates at the expense of
social consciences, if people become more analytically skillful, if crime grips
neighborhoods, if schools fail to provoke the curiosity of children, if racial or
religious prejudices become pervasive, if the drug trade starts distributing its
illicit goods through licit channels, if defiance comes to vie with compliance as
characteristic responses to authority, if new trading partners are established, if
labor and environmental groups in different countries form cross-border coalitions, if cities begin to conduct their own foreign commercial policies—to
mention only some of the more conspicuous present-day dynamics—then the
consequences of such developments will ripple across and fan out within provincial, regional, national, and international levels as well as across and within
local communities. Such is the crazy-quilt nature of modern interdependence.
And such is the staggering challenge of global governance.

The challenge continues to intensify as control mechanisms proliferate at
a breathtaking rate. For not only has the number of UN members risen from
51 in 1945 to 184 a half-century later, but the density of nongovernmental organizations (NGOs) has increased at a comparable pace. More accurately, it has
increased at a rate comparable to the continuing growth of the world's population beyond five billion and a projected eight billion in 2025. More and more
people, that is, need to concert their actions to cope with the challenges and
opportunities of daily life, thus giving rise to more and more organizations to

---

5   Cf. Rosenau and Ernst-Otto Czempiel, eds., *Governance Without Government: Order and
    Change in World Politics* (Cambridge: Cambridge University Press, 1992). Also see the formu-
    lations in Peter Mayer, Volker Rittberger, and Michael Zürn, "Regime Theory: State of the
    Art and Perspectives," in Volker Rittberger, ed., *Regime Theory and International Relations*
    (New York: Oxford University Press, 1993), and Timothy J. Sinclair, "Financial Knowledge
    as Governance," a paper presented at the Annual Meeting of the International Studies
    Association, Acapulco, 23–27 March 1993.

satisfy their needs and wants. Indeed, since the needs and wants of people are most effectively expressed through organized action, the organizational explosion of our time is no less consequential than the population explosion. Hastened by dynamic technologies that have shrunk social, economic, political, and geographic distances and thereby rendered the world ever more interdependent, expanded by the advent of new global challenges such as those posed by a deteriorating environment, an AIDS epidemic, and drug trafficking, and further stimulated by widespread authority crises within existing governance mechanisms, the proliferation of organizations is pervasive at and across all levels of human activity—from neighborhood organizations, community groups, regional networks, national states, and transnational regimes to international systems.

Not only is global life marked by a density of populations, it is also dense with organized activities, thereby complicating and extending the processes of global governance. For while organizations provide decision points through which the steering mechanisms of governance can be carried forward, so may they operate as sources of opposition to any institutions and policies designed to facilitate governance. Put in still another way, if it is the case, as many (including myself) argue, that global life late in the twentieth century is more complex than ever before in history, it is because the world is host to ever greater numbers of organizations in all walks of life and in every corner of every continent. And it is this complexity, along with the competitive impulses that lead some organizations to defy steerage and resort to violence, that makes the tasks of governance at once so difficult and so daunting.

1.3   *Disaggregation and Innovation*

An obvious but major conceptual premise follows from the foregoing: There is no single organizing principle on which global governance rests, no emergent order around which communities and nations are likely to converge. Global governance is the sum of myriad—literally millions of—control mechanisms driven by different histories, goals, structures, and processes. Perhaps every mechanism shares a history, culture, and structure with a few others, but there are no characteristics or attributes common to all mechanisms. This means that any attempt to assess the dynamics of global governance will perforce have multiple dimensions, that any effort to trace a hierarchical structure of authority that loosely links disparate sources of governance to each other is bound to fail. In terms of governance, the world is too disaggregated for grand logics that postulate a measure of global coherence.

Put differently, the continuing disaggregation that has followed the end of the Cold War suggests a further extension of the anarchic structures that have long pervaded world politics. If it was possible to presume that the absence of hierarchy and an ultimate authority signified the presence of anarchy during the era of hegemonic leadership and superpower competition, such a characterization of global governance is all the more pertinent today. Indeed, it might well be observed that a new form of anarchy has evolved in the current period—one that involves not only the absence of a highest authority but that also encompasses such an extensive disaggregation of authority as to allow for much greater flexibility, innovation, and experimentation in the development and application of new control mechanisms.

In sum, while politicians and pundits may speak confidently or longingly about establishing a new world order, such a concept is meaningful only as it relates to the prevention or containment of large-scale violence and war. It is not a concept that can be used synonymously with global governance if by the latter is meant the vast numbers of rule systems that have been caught up in the proliferating networks of an ever more interdependent world.

1.4   *Emergence and Evolution*

Underlying the growing complexity and continuing disaggregation of modern governance are the obvious but often ignored dynamics of change wherein control mechanisms emerge out of path-dependent conditions and then pass through lengthy processes of either evolution and maturation or decline and demise. In order to acquire the legitimacy and support they need to endure, successful mechanisms of governance are more likely to evolve out of bottom-up than top-down processes. As such, as mechanisms that manage to evoke the consent of the governed, they are self-organizing systems, steering arrangements that develop through the shared needs of groups and the presence of developments that conduce to the generation and acceptance of shared instruments of control.

But there is no magic in the dynamics of self-organization. Governance does not just suddenly happen. Circumstances have to be suitable, people have to be amenable to collective decisions being made, tendencies toward organization have to develop, habits of cooperation have to evolve, and a readiness not to impede the processes of emergence and evolution has to persist. The proliferation of organizations and their ever greater interdependence may stimulate felt needs for new forms of governance, but the transformation of those needs into established and institutionalized control mechanisms is never automatic and can be marked by a volatility that consumes long stretches of time. Yet at each stage of the transformation, some form of governance can be said to exist, with a preponderance of the control mechanisms at any moment evolving somewhere in the middle of a continuum that runs from nascent to fully institutionalized mechanisms, from informal modes of framing goals, issuing directives, and pursuing policies to formal instruments of decisionmaking, conflict resolution, and resource allocation.

In other words, no matter how institutionalized rule systems may be, governance is not a constant in these turbulent and disaggregated times. It is, rather, in a continuous process of evolution, a becoming that fluctuates between order and disorder as conditions change and emergent properties consolidate and solidify. To analyze governance by freezing it in time is to ensure failure in comprehending its nature and vagaries.

2   The Relocation of Authority

Notwithstanding the evolutionary dynamics of control mechanisms and the absence of an overall structural order, it is possible to identify pockets of coherence operating at different levels and in different parts of the world that can serve as bases for assessing the contours of global governance in the future. It may be the case that "processes of governance at the global level are inherently more fragile, contingent, and unevenly experienced than is the case within most national political systems,"[6] but this is not to deny the presence of central tendencies. One such tendency involves an "upsurge in the collective capacity to govern": despite the rapid pace of ever greater complexity and decentralization—and to some extent because of their exponential dynamics—the world is undergoing "a remarkable expansion of collective power," an expansion that is highly disaggregated and unfolds unevenly but that nevertheless amounts to a development of rule systems "that have become 1) more intensive in their permeation of daily life, 2) more permanent over time, 3) more extensive over space, 4) larger in size, 5) wider in functional scope, 6) more constitutionally differentiated, and 7) more bureaucratic."[7] Global governance in the twenty-first century may not take the form of a single world order, but it will not be lacking in activities designed to bring a measure of coherence to the multitude of jurisdictions that is proliferating on the world stage.

---

6   Anthony G. McGrew, "Global Politics in a Transitional Era," in Anthony G. McGrew, Paul G. Lewis, et al., eds., *Global Politics: Globalization and the Nation-State* (Cambridge: Polity Press, 1992), p. 318.

7   Martin Hewson, "The Media of Political Globalization," a paper presented at the Annual Meeting of the International Studies Association, Washington, D.C., March 1994, p. 2.

Perhaps even more important, a pervasive tendency can be identified in which major shifts in the location of authority and the site of control mechanisms are under way on every continent and in every country, shifts that are as pronounced in economic and social systems as they are in political systems. Indeed, in some cases the shifts have transferred authority away from the political realm and into the economic and social realms even as in still other instances the shifts occur in the opposite direction.

Partly these shifts have been facilitated by the end of the Cold War and the lifting of the constraints inherent in its bipolar global structure of superpower competition. Partly they have been driven by a search for new, more effective forms of political organization better suited to the turbulent circumstances that have evolved with the shrinking of the world by dynamic technologies. Partly they have been driven by the skill revolution that has enabled citizens to identify more clearly their needs and wants as well as to empower them more thoroughly to engage in collective action. Partly they have been stimulated and sustained by "subgroupism"—the fragmenting and coalescing of groups into new organizational entities—that has created innumerable new sites from which authority can emerge and toward which it can gravitate. Partly they have been driven by the continuing globalization of national and local economies that has undermined long-established ways of sustaining commercial and financial relations. And, no less, the shifts have been accelerated by the advent of interdependence issues—such as environmental pollution, AIDS, monetary crises, and the drug trade—that have fostered new and intensified forms of transnational collaboration as well as new social movements that are serving as transnational voices for change.

In short, the numerous shifts in the loci of governance stem from interactive tensions whereby processes of globalization and localization are simultaneously unfolding on a worldwide scale. In some situations these foregoing dynamics are fostering control mechanisms that extend beyond national boundaries, and in others the need for the psychological comfort of neighborhood or ethnic attachments is leading to the diminution of national entities and the formation or extension of local mechanisms. The combined effect of the simultaneity of these contradictory trends is that of lessening the capacities for governance located at the level of sovereign states and national societies. Much governance will doubtless continue to be sustained by states and their governments initiating and implementing policies in the context of their legal frameworks—and in some instances national governments are likely to work out arrangements for joint governance with rule systems at other levels—but the effectiveness of their policies is likely to be undermined by the proliferation of emergent control mechanisms both within and outside their jurisdictions. In the words of one analyst, "The very high levels of interdependence and vulnerability stimulated by technological change now necessitate new forms of global political authority and even governance."[8]

Put more emphatically, perhaps the most significant pattern discernible in the crisscrossing flow of transformed authority involves processes of bifurcation whereby control mechanisms at national levels are, in varying degrees, yielding space to both more encompassing and narrower, less comprehensive forms of governance. For analytic purposes, we shall refer to the former as transnational governance mechanisms and the latter as subnational governance mechanisms, terms that do not preclude institutionalized governmental mechanisms but that allow for the large degree to which our concern is with dynamic and evolving processes rather than with the routinized procedures of national governments.

While transnational and subnational mechanisms differ in the extent of their links across national boundaries—all the former are by definition boundary-spanning forms of control, while some of the latter may not extend beyond the jurisdiction of their states—both types must face the same challenges to governance. Both must deal with a rapidly changing, ever more complex world in which people, information, goods, and ideas are in continuous motion and thus endlessly reconfiguring social, economic, and political horizons. Both are confronted with the instabilities and disorder that derive from resource shortages, budgetary constraints, ethnic rivalries, unemployment, and incipient or real inflation. Both must contend with the ever greater relevance of scientific findings and the epistemic communities that form around those findings. Both are subject to the continuous tensions that spring from the inroads of corrupt practices, organized crime, and restless publics that have little use for politics and politicians. Both must cope with pressures for further fragmentation of subgroups on the one hand and for more extensive transnational links on the other. Both types of mechanisms, in short, have severe adaptive problems and, given the fragility of their legal status and the lack of long-standing habits of support for them, many of both types may fail to maintain their essential structures intact. Global governance, it seems reasonable to anticipate, is likely to consist of proliferating mechanisms that fluctuate between bare survival and increasing institutionalization, between considerable chaos and widening degrees of order.

---

8   John Vogler, "Regimes and the Global Commons: Space, Atmosphere and Oceans," in McGrew, Lewis, et al., *Global Politics*, p. 118.

3   Mechanisms of Global Governance

Steering mechanisms are spurred into existence through several channels: through the sponsorship of states, through the efforts of actors other than states at the transnational or subnational levels, or through states and other types of actors jointly sponsoring the formation of rule systems. They can also be differentiated by their location on the aforementioned continuum that ranges from full institutionalization on the one hand to nascent processes of rule making and compliance on the other. Although extremes on a continuum, the institutionalized and nascent types of control mechanisms can be caus- ally linked through evolutionary processes. It is possible to trace at least two generic routes that link the degree to which transnational governance mecha- nisms are institutionalized and the sources that sponsor those developments. One route is the direct, top-down process wherein states create new institu- tional structures and impose them on the course of events. A second is much more circuitous and involves an indirect, bottom-up process of evolutionary stages wherein nascent dynamics of rule making are sponsored by publics or economies that experience a need for repeated interactions that foster habits and attitudes of cooperation, which in turn generate organizational activities that eventually get transformed into institutionalized control mechanisms. Stated more generally, whatever their sponsorship, the institutionalized mech- anisms tend to be marked by explicit hierarchical structures, whereas those at the nascent end of the continuum develop more subtly as a consequence of emergent interaction patterns which, unintentionally, culminate in fledgling control mechanisms for newly formed or transformed systems.

Table 1.1 offers examples of the rule systems derivable from a combination of the several types of sponsors and the two extremes on the continuum, a matrix that suggests the considerable variety and complexity out of which the processes of global governance evolve. In the table, moreover, are hints of the developmental processes whereby nascent mechanisms become institution- alized: as indicated by the arrows, some of the control mechanisms located in the right-hand cells have their origins in the corresponding left-hand cells as interdependence issues that generate pressures from the nongovernmental world for intergovernmental cooperation which, in turn, lead to the formation of issue-based transnational institutions. The history of more than a few con- trol mechanisms charged with addressing environmental problems exempli- fies how this subtle evolutionary path can be traversed.

However they originate, and at whatever pace they evolve, transna- tional governance mechanisms tend to be essentially forward-looking. They may be propelled by dissatisfactions over existing (national or subnational) arrangements, but their evolution is likely to be marked less by despair over the past and present than by hope for the future, by expectations that an expansion beyond existing boundaries will draw upon cooperative impulses that may serve to meet challenges and fill lacunae that would otherwise be left unattended. To be sure, globalizing dynamics tend to create resistance and opposition, since any expansion of governance is bound to be detrimental to those who have a stake in the status quo. Whether they are explicitly and formally designed or subtly and informally constructed, however, transnational systems of governance tend on balance to evolve in a context of hope and progress, a sense of breakthrough, an appreciation that old problems can be circumvented and moved toward either the verge of resolution or the edge of obsolescence. But relatively speaking, subnational mechanisms are usually (though not always) energized by despair, by frustration with existing systems that seems best offset by contracting the scope of governance, by a sense that large-scale cooperation has not worked and that new subgroup arrangements re bound to be more satisfying. That distinction between transnational and subnational governance mechanisms can, of course, be overstated, but it does suggest that the delicacies of global governance at subnational levels may be greater than those at transnational levels.

TABLE 1.1   The sponsorship and institutionalization of control mechanisms

		Nascent	Institutionalized
Not state-sponsored	Transnational	– nongovernmental organizations – social movements ⟶ – epistemic communities – multinational corporations	– internet – European Environmental Bureau – credit rating agencies
	Subnational	– ethnic minorities ⟶ – microregions ⟶ – cities	– American Jewish Congress – the Greek lobby – crime syndicates
State-sponsored		– macroregions – European community ⟶ – GATT ⟶	– United Nations System – European Union – World Trade Organization
Jointly sponsored		– cross-border coalitions – issue regimes ⟶	– election monitoring – human-rights regime

To highlight the variety of forms transnational governance may take in the twenty-first century, the following discussion focuses on examples listed in Table 1.1. Due to space limitations, only some of the listed examples are subjected to analysis, and even the discussion of those is far from exhaustive. But hopefully both the table and its elaboration convey a sense of the degree to which global governance is likely to become increasingly pervasive and disaggregated in the years ahead.

3.1   *Transnational Nascent Control Mechanisms*
Private volunteer and profit-making organizations. Irrespective of whether they are volunteer or profit-making organizations, and quite apart from whether their structures are confined to one country or span several, NGOs may serve as the basis for, or actually become, nascent forms of transnational governance. Why? Because in an ever more interdependent world, the need for control mechanisms outstrips the capacity or readiness of national governments to provide them. There are various types of situations in which governments fear involvement will be counterproductive, or where they lack the will or ability to intrude their presence. (And, as noted below, there are also numerous circumstances where governments find it expedient to participate in rule systems jointly with organizations from the private sector.)

Put more specifically, just as at the local level "community associations are taking over more of the functions of municipal governments,"[9] and just as in diplomatic situations distinguished individuals from the private sector are called upon when assessments are made that assert, in effect, that "I don't think any governments wanted to get involved in this,"[10] so are NGOs of all kinds to be found as the central actors in the deliberations of control mechanisms relevant to their spheres of activity. Whether the deliberations involve the generation and allocation of relief supplies in disaster situations around the world or the framing of norms of conduct for trade relationships—to mention only two of the more conspicuous spheres in which transnational governance occurs—volunteer associations or business corporations may make the crucial decisions. In the case of alliances fashioned within and among multinational corporations, for example, it has been found that "transnational actors, unlike purely domestic ones, have the organizational and informational resources

---

9   Diana Jean Schemo, "Rebuilding of Suburban Dreams," *New York Times*, 4 May 1994, p. A11.
10   Steven Greenhouse, "Kissinger Will Help Mediate Dispute Over Zulu Homeland," *New York Times*, 12 April 1994, p. A8.

necessary to construct private alternatives to governmental accords."[11] And even if only a small proportion of NGOs preside over steering mechanisms, their contribution to global governance looms as substantial when it is appreciated that more than 17,000 international nongovernmental organizations (INGOs) in the nonprofit sector were active in the mid-1980s and that in excess of 35,000 transnational corporations with some 150,000 foreign subsidiaries were operating in 1990.[12]

Furthermore, in their activities both volunteer and profit-making organizations are not unmindful of their role in nascent control mechanisms. That can be discerned in the charters of the former and in the public pronouncements of the latter. An especially clear-cut expression along this line was made by the chairman and CEO of the Coca-Cola Company: "four prevailing forces— the preeminence of democratic capitalism, the desire for self-determination, the shift in influence from regulation to investment, and the success of institutions which meet the needs of people—reinforced by today's worldwide communications and dramatic television images, ... all point to a fundamental shift in global power. To be candid, I believe this shift will lead to a future in which the institutions with the most influence by-and-large will be businesses."[13]

Social movements. Much less structured but no less important, social movements have evolved as wellsprings of global governance in recent decades. Indeed, they are perhaps the quintessential case of nascent control mechanisms that have the potential to develop into institutionalized instruments of governance. Their nascency is conspicuous: they have no definite memberships or authority structures; they consist of as many people, as much territory, and as many issues as seem appropriate to the people involved; they have no central headquarters and are spread across numerous locales; and they are all-inclusive, excluding no one and embracing anyone who wishes to be part of the movement. More often than not, social movements are organized around a salient set of issues—like those that highlight the concerns of feminists,

11   Peter B. Evans, "Building an Integrative Approach to International and Domestic Politics: Reflections and Projections," in Peter B. Evans, Harold K. Jacobson, and Robert D. Putnam, eds., *Double-Edged Diplomacy: International Bargaining and Domestic Politics* (Berkeley: University of California Press, 1993), p. 419. For interesting accounts of how multinational corporations are increasingly inclined to form transnational alliances, see "The Global Firm: R.I.P.," *Economist*, 6 February 1993, p. 69, and "The Fall of Big Business," *Economist*, 17 April 1993, p. 13.

12   Jan Aart Scholte, *International Relations of Social Change* (Philadelphia: Open University Press, 1993), pp. 44–45.

13   Roberto C. Goizueta, "The Challenges of Getting What You Wished For," remarks presented to the Arthur Page Society, Amelia Island, Florida, 21 September 1992.

environmentalists, or peace activists—and as such they serve transnational needs that cannot be filled by national governments, organized domestic groups, or private firms. Social movements are thus constituent parts of the globalizing process. They contribute importantly to the noneconomic fabric of ties facilitated by the new communications and transportation technologies. They pick up the pieces, so to speak, that states and businesses leave in their wake by their boundary crossing activities. Just as the peace movement focuses on the consequences of state interactions, for example, so has the ecological movement become preoccupied with the developmental excesses of transnational corporations. Put even more strongly, "The point about these anti systemic movements is that they often elude the traditional categories of nation, state, and class. They articulate new ways of experiencing life, a new attitude to time and space, a new sense of history and identity."[14]

Despite the lack of structural constraints that allow for their growth, however, social movements may not remain permanently inchoate and nascent. At those times when the issues of concern to their members climb high on the global agenda, they may begin to evolve at least temporary organizational arrangements through which to move toward their goals. The International Nestlé Boycott Committee is illustrative in this regard: it organized a seven-year international boycott of Nestlé products and then was dismantled when the Nestlé Company complied with its demands. In some instances, moreover, the organizational expression of a movement's aspirations can develop enduring features. Fearful that the development of organizational structures might curb their spontaneity, some movement members might be aghast at the prospect of formalized procedures, explicit rules, and specific role assignments, but clearly the march toward goals requires organizational coherence at some point. Thus have transnational social movement organizations (TSMOS) begun to dot the global landscape. Oxfam and Amnesty International are two examples among many that could be cited of movement spinoffs that have evolved toward the institutionalized extreme of the continuum. The European Environmental Bureau (EEB), founded in 1974, has moved less rapidly toward that extreme, but it now has a full-time staff quartered in a Brussels office and shows signs of becoming permanent as the environmental movement matures.[15]

---

14   Joseph A. Camilleri, "Rethinking Sovereignty in a Shrinking, Fragmented World," in R.B.J. Walker and Saul H. Mendlovitz, eds., *Contending Sovereignties: Redefining Political Community* (Boulder: Lynne Rienner, 1990), p. 35.

15   Janie Leatherman, Ron Pagnucco, and Jackie Smith, "International Institutions and Transnational Social Movement Organizations: Challenging the State in a Three-Level Game of Global Transformation," a paper presented at the Annual Meeting of the International Studies Association, Washington, D.C., March 1994, p. 20.

3.2   *Subnational Nascent Mechanisms: Cities and Microregions*

The concept of regions, both the macro and micro variety, has become increasingly relevant to the processes of global governance. Although originally connotative of territorial space, it is a concept that has evolved as a residual category encompassing those new patterns of interaction that span established political boundaries and at the same time remain within a delimited geographic space. If that space embraces two or more national economies, it can be called a macroregion, whereas a space that spans two or more subnational economies constitutes a microregion.[16] As can be inferred from Table 1.1, both types of regions can emerge out of bottom-up processes and thus evolve out of economic foundations into political institutions. This evolutionary potential makes it "difficult to work with precise definitions. We cannot define regions because they define themselves by evolving from objective, but dormant, to subjective, active existence."[17]

Abstract and elusive as it may be, however, the notion of micro- and macroregions as residual categories for control mechanisms that span conventional boundaries serves to highlight important features of transnational governance. In the case of microregions, it calls attention to the emergent role of certain cities and "natural" economic zones as subtle and nascent forms of transnational rule systems that are not sponsored by states and that, instead, emerge out of the activities of other types of actors—which at least initially may foster a relocation of authority from the political to the economic realm. To be sure, some microregions may span conventional boundaries within a single state and thus be more logically treated as instances of subnational control mechanisms, but such a distinction is not drawn here because many such regions are, as noted in the ensuing paragraphs, transnational in scope. Indeed, since they "are interlinked processes,"[18] it is conceivable that the evolution of microregions contributes to the emergence of macroregions, and vice versa.

An insightful example along these lines is provided by the developments that have flowed from the success of a cooperation pact signed in 1988 by Lyon, Milan, Stuttgart, and Barcelona, developments that have led one analyst to observe that "a resurrection of 'city states' and regions is quietly transforming Europe's political and economic landscape, diminishing the influence of

---

16   Robert W. Cox, "Global Perestroika," in Ralph Milband and Leo Panitch, eds., *Socialist Register* (London: Merlin Press, 1992), p. 34.

17   Björn Hettne, "The New Regionalism: Implications for Development and Peace," in Björn Hettne and Andras Inotai, eds., *The New Regionalism: Implications for Global Development and International Security* (Helsinki: UNU World Institute for Development Economics Research, 1994), p. 2.

18   Hettne, "The New Regionalism," p. 6.

national governments and redrawing the continental map of power for the 21st century."[19] All four cities and their surrounding regions have an infrastructure and location that are more suited to the changes at work in Europe. They are attracting huge investment and enjoying a prosperity that has led to new demands for greater autonomy. Some argue that, as a result, the emerging urban centers and economies are fostering "a new historical dynamism that will ultimately transform the political structure of Europe by creating a new kind of 'Hanseatic League' that consists of thriving city-states."[20] One specialist forecasts that there will be nineteen cities with at least twenty million people in the greater metropolitan area by the year 2000, with the result that "cities, not nations, will become the principal identity for most people in the world."[21] Others offer similar interpretations, anticipating that these identity shifts will have profound implications for nationhood and traditional state boundaries.[22]

And what unit is evolving in the place of the nation-state as a natural unit for organizing activity within the economic realm? Again the data point to the emergence of control mechanisms that are regional in scope. These regional control mechanisms are not governmentally imposed but "are drawn by the deft but invisible hand of the global market for goods and services."[23] This is not to say, however, that region states are lacking in structure. On the contrary, since they make "effective points of entry into the global economy because the very characteristics that define them are shaped by the demands of that economy."[24] Needless to say, since the borders of regional states are determined by the "naturalness" of their economic zones and thus rarely coincide with the boundaries of political units, the clash between the incentives induced

---

19   William Drozdiak, "Revving Up Europe's 'Four Motors,'" *Washington Post*, 27 March 1994, p. C3.

20   Ibid.

21   Pascal Maragall, quoted in ibid. For extensive inquiries that posit the transnational roles of cities as increasingly central to the processes of global governance, see Saskia Sassen, *The Global City: New York, London, Tokyo* (Princeton: Princeton University Press, 1991), and Earl H. Fry, Lee H. Radebaugh, and Panayotis Soldatos, eds., *The New International Cities Era: The Global Activities of North American Municipal Governments* (Provo, Utah: Brigham Young University Press, 1989).

22   See, for example, Thomas P. Rohlem, "Cosmopolitan Cities and Nation States: A 'Mediterranean' Model for Asian Regionalism," a paper presented at the Conference on Asian Regionalism, Maui, 17–19 December 1993; Ricardo Petrilla, as quoted in Drozdiak, "Revving Up Europe's 'Four Motors,'" p. C3. For an analysis by the same author that indicates concern over the trend to citylike states, see Petrilla, "Techno-racism: The City-States of the Global Market Will Create a 'New Apartheid,'" *Toronto Star*, 9 August 1992; and Kenichi Ohmae, "The Rise of the Region State," *Foreign Affairs* 72 (Spring 1993): 78.

23   Ohmae, "The Rise of the Region State," pp. 78–79.

24   Ibid., p. 80.

by markets and the authority of governments is central to the emergence of transnational governance mechanisms. Indeed, it is arguable that a prime change at work in world politics today is a shift in the balance between those two forces, with political authorities finding it increasingly expedient to yield to economic realities. In some instances, moreover, political authorities do not even get to choose to yield, as "regional economic interdependencies are now more important than political boundaries."[25] Put differently, "The implications of region states are not welcome news to established seats of political power, be they politicians or lobbyists. Nation states by definition require a domestic political focus, while region states are ensconced in the global economy."[26]

This potential clash, however, need not necessarily turn adversarial. Much depends on whether the political authorities welcome and encourage foreign capital investment or whether they insist on protecting their noncompetitive local industries. If they are open to foreign inputs, their economies are more likely to prosper than if they insist on a rigorous maintenance of their political autonomy. But if they do insist on drawing tight lines around their authoritative realms, they are likely to lose out.

It seems clear, in short, that cities and microregions are likely to be major control mechanisms in the world politics of the twenty-first century. Even if the various expectations that they replace states as centers of power prove to be exaggerated, they seem destined to emerge as either partners or adversaries of states as their crucial role becomes more widely recognized and they thereby move from an objective to an intersubjective existence.

3.3   State-Sponsored Mechanisms

Although largely nursed into being through the actions of states, macroregions may be no less nascent than cities and microregions. And like their micro counterparts, the macroregions, which span two or more states, are deeply ensconced in a developmental process that may, in some instances, move steadily toward institutionalization, while in others the evolutionary

---

25   Michael Clough and David Doerge, *Global Changes and Domestic Transformations: New Possibilities for American Foreign Policy: Report of a Vantage Conference* (Muscatine, Iowa: The Stanley Foundation, 1992), p. 9. For indicators that a similar process is occurring in the Southwest without the approval of Washington, D.C., or Mexico City, see Cathryn L. Thorup, *Redefining Governance in North America: The Impact of Cross-Border Networks and Coalitions on Mexican Immigration into the United States* (Santa Monica: The Rand Corporation, 1993). Although using a different label ("tribes"), a broader discussion of regional states can be found in Joel Kotkin, *Tribes: How Race, Religion and Identity Determine Success in the New Global Economy* (New York: Random House, 1993).

26   Ohmae, "The Rise of the Region State," p. 83.

process may either move slowly or fall short of culminating in formal institutions. Movement toward institutionalization—or in Hettne's felicitous term, "regionness"—occurs the more a region is marked by "economic interdependence, communication, cultural homogeneity, coherence, capacity to act and, in particular, capacity to resolve conflicts."[27]

Whatever their pace or outcome, those processes have come to be known as the "new" regionalism, which is conceived to be different from the "old" regionalism in several ways. While the latter was a product of Cold War bipolarity, the former has come into being in the context of present-day multipolarity. The old regionalism was, in effect, created on a top-down basis from the outside by the superpowers. The new regionalism, on the other hand, consists of more spontaneous processes from within that unfold largely on a bottom-up basis as the constituent states find common cause in a deepening interdependence. As one observer puts it,

> The process of regionalization from within can be compared with the historical formation of nations states with the important difference that a coercive centre is lacking in processes of regionalization which presuppose a shared intention among the potential members.... The difference between regionalism and the infinite process of spontaneous integration is that there is a politically defined limit to the former process. The limitation, however, is a historical outcome of attempts to find a transnational level of governance which includes certain shared values and minimizes certain shared perceptions of danger. Like the formation of ethnic and national identities, the regional identity is dependent on historical context and shaped by conflicts. And like nations and ethnies, regional formations which have a subjective quality ... [are] "imagined communities." ... Despite enormous historical, structural, and contextual differences, there is an underlying logic behind contemporary processes of regionalization.[28]

---

27   Hettne, "The New Regionalism," p. 7.
28   Ibid., pp. 2–3. For another formulation that also differentiates between the old and new regionalism, see Kaisa Lahteenmaki and Jyrki Kakonen, "Regionalization and Its Impact on the Theory of International Relations," paper presented at the Annual Meeting of the International Studies Association, Washington, D.C., March 1994, p. 9. For a contrary perspective, see Stephen D. Krasner, "Regional Economic Blocs and the End of the Cold War," paper presented at the International Colloquium on Regional Economic Integration, University of Sao Paulo, December 1991.

Currently, of course, the various new regions of the world are at very different stages of development, with some already having evolved the rudiments
of control mechanisms while others are still at earlier stages in the process. As
noted below, Europe has advanced the most toward institutionalized steering
mechanisms, but the decline of hegemons, the advent of democracies, and the
demise of governmentally managed economies throughout the world has fostered the conditions under which the new regionalism can begin to flourish.
Pronounced movements in this direction are discernible in the Nordic region,
in the Caribbean, in the Andean Group, and in the Southern Cone of South
America. Lesser degrees of regionness are evident in the three Asia-Pacific
regions—East Asia, Southeast Asia, and the European Pacific—and the former Soviet Union, while the regionalization process has yet to become readily
recognizable in South Asia, the Middle East, and Africa.

Whatever the degree to which the new regionalism has taken hold in various parts of the world, however, it seems clear that this macrophenomenon
is increasingly a central feature of global governance. Indeed, the dynamics
of macroregions can be closely linked to those of microregions in the sense
that as the former shift authority away from national states, so do they open
up space for the latter to evolve their own autonomous control mechanisms.
"This can be seen all over Europe today."[29] The dynamics of globalization and
localization are intimately tied to each other.

3.4   *Jointly Sponsored Mechanisms*

Issue regimes. Despite a mushrooming of literature around the concept of
international regimes—as the rules, norms, principles, and procedures that
constitute the control mechanisms through which order and governance in
particular issue areas are sustained—there has been little convergence around
a precise and shared notion of the essential attributes of regimes. Indeed,
"scholars have fallen into using the term regime so disparately and with such
little precision that it ranges from an umbrella for all international relations to
little more than a synonym for international organizations."[30] Notwithstanding
this conceptual disarray, however, the conception of governance used here as
steering mechanisms that are located on a nascent-to-institutionalized continuum serves to highlight regimes as important sources of global governance.
Most notably, since they allow for the evolution of a variety of arrangements

---

29   Hettne, "The New Regionalism," p. 11.
30   Arthur Stein, "Coordination and Collaboration: Regimes in an Anarchic World," in
        David A. Baldwin, ed., *Neorealism and Neoliberalism: The Contemporary Debate* (New
        York: Columbia University Press, 1993), p. 29.

whereby nongovernmental as well as governmental actors may frame goals and pursue policies in particular issue areas, regimes meet the need for "a wider view" that includes not only states, international organizations, and international law "but also the often implicit understandings between a whole range of actors, some of which [are] not states, which [serve] to structure their cooperation in the face of common problems."[31] In some instances the control mechanisms of issue areas may be informal, disorganized, conflictful, and often ineffective in concentrating authority—that is, so rudimentary and nascent that governance is spasmodic and weak. In other cases the control mechanisms may be formalized, well organized, and capable of effectively exercising authority—that is, so fully institutionalized that governance is consistent and strong. But in all regimes, regardless of their stage of development, "the interaction between the parties is not unconstrained or is not based on independent decision making."[32] All regimes, that is, have control mechanisms to which their participants feel obliged to accede even if they do not do so repeatedly and systematically.

It is important to stress that whether they are nascent or institutionalized, the control mechanisms of all regimes are sustained by the joint efforts of governmental and nongovernmental actors. This shared responsibility is all too often overlooked in the regime literature. More accurately, although the early work on regimes allowed for the participation of NGOs, subsequent inquiries slipped into treating regimes as if they consisted exclusively of states that were more or less responsive to advice and pressures from the nongovernmental sector. However, from a global governance perspective in which states are only the most formalized control mechanisms, the original conception of regime membership as open to all types of actors again becomes compelling. And viewed in that way, it immediately becomes clear that issue regimes evolve through the joint sponsorship of state and nonstate actors. To be sure, as regimes evolve from the nascent toward the institutionalized extreme of the continuum, the more intergovernmental organizations will acquire the formal authority to make decisions; but movement in that direction is likely to be accompanied by preservation of the joint sponsorship of state and nonstate actors through arrangements that accord formal advisory roles to the relevant NGOs. No issue regime, it seems reasonable to assert, can prosper without control mechanisms that allow for some form of participation by all the interested parties. As one observer puts it with respect to several specific issue regimes,

---

31   Vogler, "Regimes and the Global Commons," p. 123.
32   Stein, "Coordination and Collaboration," p. 31.

Increasingly, this transnationalization of civic participation is redefining the terms of governance in North America, not only in the commercial arena but also on issues such as the environment, human rights, and immigration. Nongovernmental organizations, particularly grassroots groups, located throughout these societies are playing a growing role in setting the parameters of the North American agenda, limiting the ability of public officials to manage their relationship on a strict government-to-government basis, and setting the stage for a much more complete process of interaction.[33]

As indicated in Table 1.1, it follows that not all the steering mechanisms of issue regimes are located at the nascent end of the continuum. Some move persistently toward institutionalization—as was recently the case in the human rights regime when the United Nations created a high commissioner for human rights—while others may be stalemated in an underdeveloped state for considerable periods of time. However, given the ever greater interdependence of global life, it seems doubtful whether any issue area that gains access to the global agenda can avoid evolving at least a rudimentary control mechanism. Once the problems encompassed by an issue area become widely recognized as requiring attention and amelioration, it can hardly remain long without entering at least the first stage of the evolutionary process toward governance. On the other hand, given the disaggregated nature of the global system, it also seems doubtful whether any regime can ever become so fully institutionalized that its rule system evolves a hierarchy through which its top leadership acquires binding legal authority over all its participants. Rather, once a regime acquires a sufficient degree of centralized authority to engage in a modicum of regulatory activities, it undergoes transformation into an international organization, as is suggested in Table 1.1 by the evolution of GATT into the World Trade Organization.

How many issue regimes are there? Endless numbers, if it is recalled that issue areas are essentially a conglomeration of related smaller issues and that each of the latter evolves identifiable mechanisms for governance that are at some variance with other issues in the same area. The global agenda is conceived in terms of large-issue areas only because those are more easily grasped and debated, but it is on the smaller issues that particularistic activities requiring special governance arrangements focus.

---

33   Cathryn L. Thorup, "Redefining Governance in North America: Citizen Diplomacy and Cross-Border Coalitions," *Enfoque* (Spring 1993): 1, 12.

Cross-border coalitions. Some issue regimes, moreover, are so disaggregated as to encompass what have been called "cross-border coalitions."[34] These can be usefully set aside for separate analysis as instances of jointly sponsored, nascent control mechanisms. The emphasis here is on the notion of coalitions, on networks of organizations. As previously noted, INGOs are by definition cross-border organizations, but their spanning of boundaries tends to occur largely through like-minded people from different countries who either share membership in the same transnational organization or who belong to national organizations that are brought together under umbrella organizations that are transnational in scope. Cross-border coalitions, on the other hand, consist of organizations that coalesce for common purposes but do not do so under the aegis of an umbrella organization. Some of these may form umbrella INGOs as they move on from the nascent stage of development, but at present most of the new coalitions are still in the earliest stage of formation. They are networks rather than organizations, networks that have been facilitated by the advent of information technologies such as E-mail and electronic conferencing and that thus place their members in continuous touch with each other even though they may only come together in face-to-face meetings on rare occasions. Put more dramatically, "rather than be represented by a building that people enter, these actors may be located on electronic networks and exist as 'virtual communities' that have no precise physical address."[35]

It is noteworthy that some cross-border coalitions may involve local governments located near national boundaries that find it more expedient on a variety of issues to form coalitions with counterparts across the border than to work with their own provincial or national governments. Such coalitions may even be formed deliberately in order to avoid drawing "unnecessary or premature attention from central authorities to local solutions of some local problems by means of informal contacts and 'good neighborhood' networks. Often it [is] not a deliberate deception, just an avoidance of unnecessary complications."[36]

That cross-border coalitions are a nascent form of issue regimes is indicated by the fact that they usually form around problems high on the agendas of their communities. During the 1993 debate over the North American Free Trade Agreement (NAFTA), for example, a number of advocacy groups

---

34   For a valuable attempt to explore this concept theoretically and empirically, see Thorup, "The Politics of Free Trade and the Dynamics of Cross-Border Coalitions in U.S.-Mexican Relations," *Columbia Journal of World Business* 26 (Summer 1991): 12–26.

35   David Ronfeldt and Cathryn L. Thorup, "North America in the Era of Citizen Networks: State, Society, and Security," (Santa Monica: RAND 1993), p. 22.

36   Ivo D. Duchachek, "The International Dimension of Subnational Government," *Publius* 14 (Fall 1984): 25.

concerned with environmental, human rights, labor, and immigration issues linked up with their counterparts across the U.S.-Mexican boundary, and in some instances the networks spanned the sectoral issue areas as the implications of NAFTA were discovered to have common consequences for otherwise disparate groups. This is not to say that the advent of cross-border coalitions reduced the degree of conflict over the question of NAFTA's approval. As can be readily expected whenever a control mechanism is at stake, coalitions on one side of the issue generated opposing coalitions.

In short, "the new local and cross-border NGO movements are a potential wild card. They may be proactive or reactive in a variety of ways, sometimes working with, sometimes against, state and market actors who are not accustomed to regarding civil society as an independent actor."[37]

3.5   Transnational Institutionalized Control Mechanisms: Credit Rating Agencies

Turning now to transnational control mechanisms that are located more toward the institutionalized extreme of the governance continuum, the dimension of the global capital markets in which risk is assessed and creditworthiness legitimated offers examples of both discernible rule systems that came into being through the sponsorship of states and others that evolved historically out of the private sector.[38] The International Monetary Fund (IMF) and the World Bank are illustrative of the former type of mechanism, while Moody's Investors Service and Standard & Poor's Ratings Group (S&P) dominate the ratings market in the private sector. Although the difference between the two types is in some ways considerable—unlike the agencies in the private sector, the IMF and the World Bank derive much of their capacity for governance from the sponsorship and funding by the state system that founded them—they are in one important respect quite similar: in both cases their authority derives at least partially from the specialized knowledge on which their judgments are based and the respect they have earned for adhering to explicit and consistent standards for reaching their conclusions as to the creditworthiness of enterprises, governments, and countries. And in both cases the judgments they

---

37   Ronfeldt and Thorup, "North America in the Era of Citizen Networks," p. 24.

38   This brief discussion of the credit rating agencies in the private sector is based on Timothy J. Sinclair, "The Mobility of Capital and the Dynamics of Global Governance: Credit Risk Assessment in the Emerging World Order," a paper presented at the Annual Meeting of the International Studies Association, Washington, D.C., March 1994, and Sinclair, "Passing Judgment: Credit Rating Processes as Regulatory Mechanisms of Governance in the Emerging World Order," Review of International Political Economy (April 1994).

render are authoritative in the sense that the capital markets acquiesce to and conduct themselves on the basis of their ratings. To be sure, fierce debates do break out over the appropriateness of the standards employed to make the risk assessments of debt security, but the credibility of the private rating agencies has not been so effectively challenged as to diminish their status as control mechanisms.

That the private agencies are transnational in scope is indicated by the fact that both Moody's and S&P have branches in London, Paris, Frankfurt, Tokyo, and Sydney. Most of the other agencies in this trillion-dollar market are domestically focused and confine their assessments to the creditworthiness of borrowers in the countries where they are located, albeit there are signs that a Europewide agency is in the process of evolving.

In sum, the private ratings agencies are a means through which key parts of national and transnational economies are, relatively speaking, insulated from politics. By presiding over that insulation, the agencies have become, in effect, control mechanisms. Put differently, "rating agencies seem to be contributing to a system of rule in which an intersubjective framework is created in which social forces will be self-regulating in accord with the limits of the system."[39]

3.6   Subnational Institutionalized Mechanisms: Crime Syndicates
It is a measure of the globalization of governance that crime syndicates have evolved institutional forms on a transnational scale, that they can properly be called "transnational criminal organizations" (TCOs). Their conduct, of course, violates all the norms that are considered to undergird the proper exercise of authority, but their centrality to the course of events is too conspicuous not to note briefly their role among the diverse control mechanisms that now constitute global governance. Indeed, upon reflection it seems clear that, "with the globalization of trade and growing consumer demands for leisure products, it is only natural that criminal organizations should become increasingly transnational in character," that they have been "both contributors to, and beneficiaries of, ... a great increase in transactions across national boundaries that are neither initiated nor controlled by states,"[40] and that

---

39   Sinclair, "The Mobility of Capital and the Dynamics of Global Governance," p. 16.

40   Phil Williams, "Transnational Criminal Organizations and International Security," Survival 36 (Spring 1994): 97. See also Williams, "International Drug Trafficking: An Industry Analysis," Low Intensity Conflict and Law Enforcement 2 (Winter 1993): 397–420. For another dimension of transnational criminality, see Victor T. Levine, "Transnational Aspects of Political Corruption," in Arnold J. Heidenheimer, Michael Johnston, and Victor T. LeVine, eds., Political Corruption: A Handbook (New Brunswick, N.J.: Transaction, 1989), pp. 685–699.

not only is transnational activity as open to criminal groups as it is to legitimate multinational corporations, but the character of criminal organizations also makes them particularly suited to exploit these new opportunities. Since criminal groups are used to operating outside the rules, norms and laws of domestic jurisdictions, they have few qualms about crossing national boundaries illegally. In many respects, therefore, TCOS are transnational organizations *par excellence*. They operate outside the existing structures of authority and power in world politics and have developed sophisticated strategies for circumventing law enforcement in individual states and in the global community of states.[41]

A good measure of how new opportunities have facilitated the explosiveness of TCOs in the present era is provided by the pattern of criminal activities that has evolved in the former Soviet Union since the collapse of the Soviet empire. "More than 4,000 criminal formations comprising an estimated 100,000 members now operate in Russia alone," and of these, some "150 to 200 ... have international ties."[42]

While TCOs operate outside the realm of established norms, and while they are marked by considerable diversity in size, structure, goals, and membership, they are nevertheless institutionalized in the sense that they control their affairs in patterned ways that often involve strategic alliances between themselves and national and local criminal organizations, alliances that "permit them to cooperate with, rather than compete against, indigenously entrenched criminal organizations."[43] Yet TCOs have not succumbed to excessive bureaucratization. On the contrary, "they are highly mobile and adaptable and able to operate across national borders with great ease ... partly because of their emphasis on networks rather than formal organizations."[44] It is interesting and indicative of the dynamics of globalization that legitimate multinational corporations have recently come to resemble TCOs in two ways: first, by developing more fluid and flexible network structures that enable them to take advantage of local conditions and, second, by resorting to strategic alliances that facilitate development on a global scale.

---

41   Williams, "Transnational Criminal Organizations and International Security," p. 100.
42   Rensselaer W. Lee III, "Post-Soviet Organized Crime and Western Security Interests," testimony submitted to the Subcommittee on Terrorism, Narcotics and International Operations, Senate Committee on Foreign Relations, Washington, D.C., 21 April 1994.
43   Williams, "Transnational Criminal Organizations and International Security," p. 106.
44   Ibid., p. 105.

3.7   State-Sponsored Mechanisms

The United Nations system. The United Nations is an obvious case of a steering mechanism that was sponsored by states and that took an institutional form from its founding. To be sure, its processes of institutionalization have continued to evolve since 1945 to the point where it is now a complex system of numerous associate agencies and subunits that, collectively, address all the issues on the global agenda and that amount to a vast bureaucracy. The institutional histories of the various agencies differ in a number of respects, but taken as a whole they have become a major center of global governance. They have been a main source of problem identification, information, innovation, and constructive policies in the fields of health, environment, education, agriculture, labor, family, and a number of other issues that are global in scope.

This is not to say that the collective history of the United Nations depicts a straight-line trajectory toward ever greater effectiveness. Quite to the contrary, not only have its many agencies matured enough to be severely and properly criticized for excessive and often misguided bureaucratic practices, but also— and even more important—its primary executive and legislative agencies (the secretary-general, the General Assembly, and the Security Council) have compiled a checkered history with respect to the UN's primary functions of preventive diplomacy, peacekeeping, and peacemaking under Chapter VII of its charter. For the first four decades, its record was that of a peripheral player in the Cold War, an era in which it served as a debating arena for major conflicts, especially those that divided the two nuclear superpowers, but accomplished little by way of creating a new world order that provided states security through the aggregation of their collective strength. Then, at the end of the Cold War, the United Nations underwent both a qualitative and quantitative transformation, one that placed it at the very heart of global governance as states turned to the Security Council for action in a number of the major humanitarian and conflict situations that broke out with the end of superpower competition. The inclination to rely on the United Nations, to centralize in it the responsibility for global governance, reached a peak in 1991 with the successful multilateral effort under UN auspices to undo Iraq's conquest of Kuwait.

It is not difficult to demonstrate the quantitative dimensions of the UN's transformation at the end of the Cold War. In 1987, the United Nations had assigned some ten thousand peacekeepers—mostly troops in blue helmets who were supposed to resort to force only if attacked—to five operations around the world on an annual budget of about $233 million. Seven years later the number of troops had risen to seventy-two thousand in eighteen different situations at an annual cost of more than $3 billion. Similarly, whereas the Security Council used to meet once a month, by 1994 its schedule involved meeting every day, and often twice a day. Put differently, during the first forty-four years of its history, the Security Council passed only six resolutions under Chapter VII in which "threats to the peace, breaches of the peace, acts of aggression" were determined to exist. Between 1990 and 1992, on the other hand, the Security Council adopted thirty-three such resolutions on Iraq (twenty-one), the former Yugoslavia (eight), Somalia (two), Liberia (one), and Libya (one).

Even more impressive are the qualitative changes that underlay the UN's transformation: as the cold war wound down and ended, two remarkable developments became readily discernible. One was the advent of a new consensus among the five permanent members of the Security Council with respect to the desirability of the United Nations's involvement in peacekeeping activities, and the other was the extension of that consensus to the nonpermanent members, including virtually all of the nonaligned states elected to the council. These changes are evident in the fact that the number of unanimously adopted Security Council resolutions jumped from 61 percent (72 of 119) in 1980–1985 to 84 percent in 1986–1992 (184 of 219). In 1993 alone, the Security Council passed more than 181 resolutions and statements, all of which high-mindedly addressed peacekeeping issues (such as a demand for the end of ethnic cleansing in the former Yugoslavia).

Furthermore, those transformations rendered the United Nations into a control mechanism in the military sense of the term. The organization's operations in both Somalia and Bosnia found the secretary-general conducting himself as commanding general and making the final decisions having to do with the application of air power, the disposition of ground forces, and the dismissal of commanding officers.

Despite those transformations in its role and orientations, in its performances the United Nations has not lived up to the surge of high hopes for it that immediately followed the end of the Cold War. Rather than sustaining movement toward effective global governance, it foundered in Somalia, dawdled in Bosnia, and cumulatively suffered a decline in the esteem with which it is held by both governments and publics. The reasons for this decline are numerous—ranging from a lack of money to a lack of will, from governments that delay paying their dues to publics that resist the commitment of troops to battle—but they add up to a clear-cut inability to carry out and enforce the resolutions of the Security Council. Consensus has evolved on the desirability of the UN's intervening in humanitarian situations, but there is a long distance between agreement on goals and a shared perspective on the provision of the necessary means: the readiness to implement multilateral goals and thereby enhance the UN's authority so as to achieve effective governance is woefully lacking, leading one analyst to describe the organization's activities in the peacekeeping area as "faint-hearted multilateralism."[45]

But the checkered history of the UN's institutionalization suggests that its present limitations may undergo change yet again. The organization continues to occupy a valued and critical position in the complex array of global control mechanisms. The need for collective action in volatile situations is bound to continue, so that it is likely that the world will seek to fill this vacuum by again and again turning to the United Nations as the best available means of achieving a modicum of governance. And in the processes of doing so, conceivably circumstances will arise that swing faint-hearted commitments back in the direction of a more steadfast form of multilateralism.

The European Union. Much more so than the United Nations, the history of the European Union (EU) is a record of the evolutionary route to institutionalization. Even a brief account of this history is beyond the scope of this analysis, but suffice it to say that it is one macroregion that has passed through various stages of growth to its present status as an elaborately institutionalized instrument of governance for the (increasing number of) countries within its jurisdiction. Sure, it was states that formalized the institutionalization, but they did so as a consequence of transformations that culminated in the member countries holding referenda wherein the establishment of the EU was approved by citizenries. In this sense the EU offers a paradigmatic example of the dynamics that propel evolutionary processes from nascent to institutionalized steering mechanisms. As one observer puts it, this transformation occurred through "the gradual blurring of the distinction made between the 'Community' and the 'nation-states' which agreed to form that community in the first place.... Although the two are by no means linked as tightly as are subnational units to the center in the traditional state, the Community-state entanglement is such that the Community is very far from being a traditional regional organization."[46] Indeed, such is the evolution of the European Union that it

---

45   Thomas Risse-Kappen, "Faint-Hearted Multilateralism: The Re-Emergence of the United Nations in World Politics," a paper presented at the Annual Meeting of the International Studies Association, Washington, D.C., March 1994.

46   Alberta Sbragia, "From 'Nation-State' to 'Member-State': The Evolution of the European Community," a paper presented at the Europe After Maastrict Symposium, Washington University, Saint Louis, 1–3 October 1993, pp. 1–2.

is now better conceptualized as a union of states rather than as an organization. The international law doctrine that actors are either states or
organizations has become unrealistic.... In [a 1992] decision the Court of
Justice established that Community law within its sphere is equal in status to national law. Further, the court has successfully maintained that,
because law should be uniform, Community law must take precedence
over conflicting national law.[47]

In short, while the EU does not have "federal law because Community legislation suffers from the defect that its statutes are not legitimized by a democratic
legislature,"[48] it does have a rule system in the combination of its executive
and judicial institutions.

3.8   *Jointly Sponsored Institutionalized Mechanisms*
A good illustration of how control mechanisms can evolve toward the institutionalized end of the governance continuum through the sponsorship of both
states and NGOs is provided by the emergence of clear-cut patterns wherein
it has become established practice for external actors to monitor the conduct
of domestic elections in the developing world. Indeed, the monitoring process has become quite elaborate and standardized, with lengthy instructional
booklets now available for newcomers to follow when they enter the host
country and shoulder their responsibilities as monitors. And no less indicative
of the degree of institutionalization is that some of the monitors, such as the
United Nations or the National Democratic Institute, send representatives to
observe virtually all elections in which outside monitors are present.

   But does external monitoring constitute a control mechanism? Most certainly. Whatever hesitations the host countries may have about the presence
of outsiders who judge the fairness and propriety of their election procedures,
and irrespective of their attempts to circumvent the monitors and load the
electoral outcome, now they yield both to the pressure for external monitoring and to the judgments the outsiders make during and after election day.
Elections have been postponed because of irregularities in voter lists detected
by the external monitors, "dirty tricks" uncovered during the balloting have
been terminated at the insistence of monitors, and the verdict of outsiders that
the final tallies were fraudulent has resulted in the holding of new elections.

---

47   Christopher Brewin, "The European Community: A Union of States Without Unity of
      Government," in Friedrich Kratochwil and Edward D. Mansfield, eds., *International
      Organization: A Reader*, (New York: HarperCollins, 1994), pp. 301–302.
48   Ibid., p. 302.

To be sure, a few countries still adamantly refuse admission to outside monitors or do not allow them to be present on a scale sufficient to allow for legitimation of the electoral outcome, but the monitoring process has become so fully institutionalized that normally the host countries overcome their reluctance as they begin to recognize the problems they cause for themselves by refusing to acquiesce to the monitoring process. Put differently, the advent of established procedures for the external monitoring of elections demonstrates the large extent to which control mechanisms derive their effectiveness from information and reputation even if their actions are not backed up by constitutional authority. It might even be said that governance in an ever more complex and interdependent world depends less on the issuance of authoritative directives and more on the release of reliable information and the legitimacy inherent in its detail.

As for the presence of both state and NGO actors, the spreading norm that the establishment of democracy justifies the international community's involvement in domestic elections attracts both official and unofficial groups to train and send monitors. Whatever organizations may have led the negotiations that result in the acceptance of outside observers, a number of others (such as the Organization of American States [OAS], the Socialist International, and the Latin American Studies Association in the case of Paraguay's 1993 election) find reasons important to their memberships to be present, and there are few precedents for denying admission to some monitoring teams while accepting others. Although the monitoring process may not be free of friction and competition among the numerous teams, the more procedures have been institutionalized, the greater has been the collaboration among the teams. It is not stretching matters to conclude that not only does the international community turn out in force for domestic elections in distant countries, but it does so with representatives from many of its diverse segments. In the 1990 Nicaraguan election, for example, 2,578 accredited observers from 278 organizations were present on election day.[49]

3.9   Continuing and Changing Forms of Governance
The above observations suggest that a full picture of what are likely to be the contours of global governance in the decades ahead requires attention to the

---

49   Of these, 278 organizations were present on election day, with 435 observers fielded by the OAS visiting 3,064 voting sites (some 70 percent of the total) and 237 UN monitors visiting 2,155 sites. In addition, some 1,500 members of the international press corps were on the scene. Cf. Robert A. Pastor, "Nicaragua's Choice," in Carl Kaysen, Robert A. Pastor, and Laura W. Reed, eds., Collective Responses to Regional Problems: The Case of Latin America and the Caribbean (Cambridge: American Academy of Arts and Sciences, 1994), pp. 18, 21.

dynamics of localization and how they are in part responses to the dynamics of globalization, responses that give rise to what can be called "distant prox-imities" that may well become systems of rule with diverse types of control mechanisms. Although some localizing dynamics are initiated by national governments—as when France decided to decentralize its steering apparatus and reduce Paris's control over policy and administrative issues—perhaps the preponderance of them are generated at subnational levels, some with the help and approval of national agencies but many in opposition to national pol-icies, which then extend their scope abroad. The tendencies toward strength-ened ethnic subgroups that have surfaced since the end of the Cold War are a case in point. Even though these actors may not have direct ties to supporters in other countries, their activities on the local scene can foster repercussions abroad that thereby transform them into aspects of global governance. The recent struggles in Bosnia, Somalia, and Rwanda are examples. Similarly, since so many of the world's resource, water, and air quality problems originate in subnational communities, and since this level is marked by a proliferation of both governmental and nongovernmental agencies that seek to control these problems within their jurisdiction and to do so through cooperative efforts with transnational counterparts, the environmental area offers another array of local issues that are central to the conduct of global governance.

The emphasis here on transnational and subnational mechanisms is not, of course, to imply that national governments and states are no longer cen-tral loci of control in the processes of global governance; they are very central indeed. No account of the global system can ignore them or give them other than a prominent place in the scheme of things. Nevertheless, states have lost some of their earlier dominance of the governance system, as well as their abil-ity to evoke compliance and to govern effectively. This change is in part due to the growing relevance and potential of control mechanisms sustained by transnational and subnational systems of rule.

4   Governance in the Twenty-First Century

If the analysis were deemed complete here, the reader, like the author, would likely feel let down, as if the final chapter of this story of a disaggregated and fragmenting global system of governance has yet to be written. It is an unfinished story, one's need for closure would assert. It needs a conclusion, a drawing together of the "big picture," a sweeping assessment that offers some hope that somehow the world can muddle through and evolve techniques of cooperation that will bridge its multitude of disaggregated parts and achieve a measure of coherence that enables future generations to live in peace, achieve sustainable development, and maintain a modicum of creative order. Assess the overall balance, one's training cries out, show how the various emergent centers of power form a multipolar system of states that will manage to cope with the challenges of war within and among its members. Yes, that's it— depict the overall system as polyarchical and indicate how such an arrangement can generate multilateral institutions of control that effectively address the huge issues that clutter the global agenda. Or, perhaps better, indicate how a hegemon will emerge out of the disaggregation and have enough clout to foster both progress and stability. At the very least, one's analytic impulses demand, suggest how worldwide tendencies toward disaggregation and localization may be offset by no less powerful tendencies toward aggregation and globalization.

Compelling as these alternative interpretations may be, however, they do not quell a sense that it is only a short step from polyarchy to Pollyanna and that one's commitment to responsible analysis must be served by not taking that step. The world is clearly on a path-dependent course, and some of its present outlines can be discerned if, as noted at the outset, allowance is made for nuance and ambiguity. Still, in this time of continuing and profound transformations, too much remains murky to project beyond the immediate present and anticipate long-term trajectories. All one can conclude with confidence is that in the twenty-first century the paths to governance will lead in many directions, some that will emerge into sunlit clearings and others that will descend into dense jungles.

CHAPTER 2

Peace and Security: Prospective Roles for the Two United Nations

Inis L. Claude, Jr.[1]

The world's celebration of the ending of the Cold War was quickly and rudely interrupted by the realization that stability and order, justice and welfare, and peace and security remain objectives by no means achieved and not readily achievable on a global scale. Although the threat of universal destruction by a dash of superpowers has been relieved, the multistate system continues to produce its usual quota of frictions and conflicts among members. Moreover, the post-Cold War world is beset by an epidemic of serious difficulties within states: persecutions, civil wars, rebellions, secessionist movements, genocidal campaigns, and other such horrors. The chaos, privation, and instability generated by despotic regimes, failed and failing states, and dissolving societies are prominent features of our time.

These internal problems of states are now generally regarded as an integral part of the business of international relations; they have, indeed, come to dominate the agenda of the UN. We no longer assume, for better or for worse (and the merits of this change are debatable), that the UN should or will abstain from involvement in the domestic affairs of states and confine its attention to the relationships between those entities. With regard to the internal crises of states, the UN is now less likely to be upbraided for exceeding its authority than to be criticized for failing to meet its responsibilities. For example, a recent column in the *Washington Post* begins: "One of the tragedies of Rwanda's civil war was the failure of the United Nations to prevent widespread slaughter."[2] The world's quest for peace and security is now treated as having intranational no less than international aspects.

---

* This chapter was originally published in Global Governance, Volume 2, Issue 3, 1996.

1 Inis L. Claude, Jr., was professor emeritus at the University of Virginia. The editors wish to thank Professor Claude for permitting *Global Governance* to publish this article, which has been derived from the paper he presented at the UNU Global Seminar '95 on "The UN at 50: Building Peace," coorganized with Kanagawa Foundation for Academic and Cultural Exchange.

2 Morris B. Abram, "Libya? On the Security Council?" *Washington Post*, 12 July 1995, p. A19.

The first post-Cold War crisis to capture the world's attention was Iraq's conquest of Kuwait and its putative threat to Saudi Arabia. This action generated condemnation by the UN, resolve by the United States to mobilize a coalition to roll back Iraqi aggression, and UN authorization followed by successful military action to achieve that result. This episode was widely hailed as evidence of a new multilateral will and capability to control international aggression, and it gave rise to a revival of enthusiastic rhetoric about the transformation of the UN into a genuine collective security system. At long last, so it was proclaimed, the Wilsonian ideal of an international agency that would reliably protect every state against aggression could be and would be realized in the UN.

As had always happened before, support for and expectation of the establishment of such a system quickly dwindled. Throughout the twentieth century, the terminology of collective security has been appropriated, its ideology has been recurrently endorsed, and its implementation has been persistently rejected. Neither governments nor peoples have ever genuinely accepted the view that every act of international aggression deserves condemnation and necessitates their paying the price of involvement in collective coercive efforts. We would welcome the promised benefits of a collective security system, but we are not prepared to do what states must do if such a system is to be a reality. Clearly, this rejection of the responsibilities of collective security was not overturned by the termination of the Cold War, nor by satisfaction at the multilateral liberation of Kuwait. Very soon, there came to the fore the familiar and prudent conviction of national leaders that their duty is to avoid military involvements except when security considerations appear to leave them no alternative. The notion that the UN should serve as the world's guardian against any and every aggressor gave way to the understanding that the organization might, in some selected instances, find it both desirable and possible to sponsor collective reaction to acts of international aggression. Multilateral resistance to aggression will continue to be, as it always has been, selective, unpredictable, and, therefore, unreliable. This is to say that collective security, in the comprehensive Wilsonian sense, is no less an impossible dream today than in earlier postwar periods.

But let us consider seriously and soberly the issue of the tasks related to promoting peace, stability, and order that we can reasonably assign to the UN. In what ways can we realistically expect the UN to be useful in the quest for world order? What problems are of such urgent importance and are sufficiently amenable to solution or alleviation by the UN that they deserve to be the focal points of its attention and expenditure of resources?

To answer these questions, it is first necessary to distinguish between the two identities of the UN, which I shall call the "First UN" and the "Second

UN." These two "institutions" are closely intertwined and mutually dependent, but they are nonetheless quite different and have distinctive capabilities. It is therefore of the greatest importance to be clear about which of them we have in mind when we discuss their appropriate tasks.

The First UN is constituted by its staff, an international secretariat or bureaucracy located in New York, Geneva, and other regional headquarters. Its leader and chief, and most authoritative official spokesperson, is the secretary-general. Most discussions of the intentions, hopes, and plans of the UN refer in fact to the will of this First UN, as expressed by the secretary-general or his or her subordinate officials. Thus, for instance, it was reported some months ago that the UN had abandoned efforts to raise a large peacekeeping force to protect Rwandan refugees, after the secretary-general's appeal to sixty governments for the necessary troops and equipment had failed; the UN wished to act in this case, but its members rejected its proposal.[3] This report introduces the all-important topic of the relationship between the First UN and its member states. States hold the power of life and death over the organization: they created and sustain it, and they can starve or destroy it. Theoretically, states control this UN, although the extent of their actual control and direction is limited and variable. At the least, however, the member states exercise very considerable influence. The UN's member states are the First UN's sponsors, suppliers, supporters, and directors, its clients and customers, the beneficiaries of most of its activities. But they are not, and cannot be, this First UN. It is a corporate entity, existing alongside the member states, something other than and different from a state, separate from but dependent on and useful to the states that are listed as its members.

The Second UN is a collectivity formed by almost all the states of the world; it consists of its member states, who employ an international secretariat to support their joint deliberations and activities. Various states exercise leadership from time to time, in particular areas of policy. Most notably, the major powers tend to be its leaders, and for many of its most important functions the world's most prominent state, the United States, is the indispensable leader of this Second UN, while the secretary-general is its chief employee. (One might say that the secretary-general is the general in command of the First UN and the secretary of the Second UN.) The roles of the Secretariat and the member states are reversed in the two organizations: the staff constitutes the First UN and works for the Second UN, while the states support the First UN and constitute the Second UN. From the point of view of the member states, the First UN

---

3 Julia Preston, "Force to Aid Rwandans Abandoned," *Washington Post*, 24 January 1995, p. A12.

requires the third-person pronoun and the Second UN takes the first-person—the former is "they" or possibly "it," while the latter is "we."

Having argued that there are, in effect, two UN organizations, I now suggest that there are two equally distinctive types of activity closely related to the objectives of global peace and security. It then remains to determine how the two organizations are related to the two functional categories.

The first category of activity is noncoercive, consensual, and neutral. It entails the rendering of impartial assistance to all of the parties involved in a troubled and potentially explosive situation, at their request or with their consent, with a view to helping them avoid the degeneration of the relationship into violent conflict. It assumes—and requires for its success—that each of the parties is sufficiently decent and prudent to place the prevention of armed conflict high on its agenda. It also assumes and requires that all of the parties have confidence in the impartiality, evenhandedness, and integrity of the organization offering assistance, as well as of its agents. This kind of activity cannot usefully be pursued when any of the parties is intent upon winning a war and is determined to achieve its aims by force if necessary. The essential resources for the intervening agency, if it is to be acceptable to the parties and effective in its work, are not military or other coercive capability but moral capital, reputation for fairness and freedom from political bias, and diplomatic skill.

The second category is essentially judgmental, partisan, and coercive. Action under this heading starts with the rejection of neutrality, the denial of the moral equivalence of the claims or behavior of the parties, and the identification of one or more parties whose efforts should be defeated and of others who deserve to be assisted in their resistance. The essence of the matter is to take sides and use whatever form and degree of pressure may be required, including possible military action, to frustrate the efforts of parties indulging in culpable conduct. Clearly, the resources needed for this sort of activity are the political and physical capabilities for decisive action—firmness and resoluteness, willingness to take risks and pay heavy costs, substantial military forces and equipment, and skill in the command and control of military operations.

Let me now introduce the central thesis of my presentation. It is quite simply that the activities in the first category I have described are the province of the First UN, while those in the second category are appropriate to the Second UN.

The quintessential activity in the first category, and a primary responsibility of modern international organization, is the promotion of the pacific settlement of disputes. At least since the Hague Conferences of 1899 and 1907, this tradition has called for multilateral agencies to provide third parties whose help in arranging and conducting negotiations and formulating possible terms of settlement may be welcomed by the states engaged in dispute, so that an agreed and voluntarily accepted solution to the issue at hand may obviate the danger of resort to a military solution. Today, the scope of this function has been broadened to include disputes and volatile situations within states and among nonstate entities whose potential clashes may disrupt either domestic or international order. Effective third-party involvement requires negotiating skills and persuasive techniques that are not the monopoly of a single professional group—be it national diplomats, statesmen, international jurists, or secretariat officials. The First UN is a potentially invaluable supplier of honest brokers and facilitators of peaceful settlement. In many instances, its own chief, the secretary-general, may be the ideal mediator; the status of the secretary-general as an internationally oriented figure, a spokesperson for the organized community rather than for any state or bloc, enhances his or her suitability for this role.

Unfortunately, this is not an area in which the record of the UN has been particularly impressive. This deficiency is attributable in part to the fact that not all disputes are susceptible of such settlement and that not all parties are genuinely receptive to aid in preventing armed conflict. A major problem has been the tendency of disputants and their supporters to exploit the political forum of the UN, usually the General Assembly, as a venue for achieving political victory instead of using the settlement-promoting potential of the organization—that is, they have treated the UN as a battlefield rather than as a peace conference. Such behavior is, in effect, resorting to the Second UN in preference to the First UN. A crucial ingredient of the possible usefulness of the First UN in this work is its internationalism—its image as an agency of humankind, guardian of the common interests, and evenhanded advocate of justice and decency. This key resource has in some measure been squandered, as the Secretariat has been somewhat politicized and the political organs have become tools of political and ideological blocs. The Second UN is largely responsible for this wastage of the First UN's most valuable asset—its status as a neutral in a world be set by political tensions.

The pacific settlement of disputes is potentially the most useful world order function of the First UN. That organization will require the support, cooperation, and forbearance of the Second UN if it is to realize this potential. The First UN will have to work at restoring its reputation for impartiality and fairmindedness in dealing with contentious situations and at expanding its resources as an agency for supplying and supporting third parties. It must strive to gain the opportunity for service to disputants at the optimal stage of their difficulties, before violent clashes and public recriminations have hardened opposing positions. Even so, not all disputes will yield to the ministrations of UN peace facilitators. The goal of increasing its effectiveness in this area is nevertheless a worthy objective for the First UN.

The second major item in the category of noncoercive, consensual, and neutral activities is a relatively new one, a function not foreseen by the framers of the UN Charter but invented during the Cold War. I refer to peacekeeping, which began as an improvised reaction to the Suez crisis of 1956 and was subsequently given theoretical elaboration by Secretary-General Dag Hammarskjöld. This function, as its early practitioners understood it, entailed the UN's undertaking to assist in the stabilization of a precarious peace in a troubled situation, when the parties want to avoid war, lack confidence in their ability to avoid it unaided, and are willing to invoke or to accept the help of the UN. Its mechanism is an intervention organized and directed by the secretary-general, using contingents largely of military personnel supplied voluntarily by member states acceptable to the parties. The mission of such a peacekeeping force more closely resembles that of a police patrol than that of an army: it is not to fight or defeat or compel but to act impartially and, without judging the merits of the case, to help hold the line against the potential flaring-up of conflict. A peacekeeping force can serve only so long as all parties want its help in maintaining peace; if any party decides to make war, its proper action is to withdraw (as UNEF I withdrew from the Sinai in 1967). Clearly, the First UN cannot exercise this function without the collaboration of the Second UN. The secretary-general is dependent on personnel, equipment, and funds available only from member states, but peacekeeping is, I would argue, fundamentally the secretary-general's mission. It is the responsibility of an international statesman, acting on behalf of the world's central organization, in pursuit of the general interest in world order.

In the future, as in the past forty years, there will be occasions for peacekeeping, both within and among states. It should be—and, in principle, can be—a valuable contribution to peace under the aegis of the First UN. As in the case of pacific settlement of disputes, however, the eligibility of the First UN for this service depends on its capacity to inspire confidence in its neutrality. This essential asset of the Secretariat has been endangered, as have other crucial requirements of the function, by the recent proliferation of UN forces that are designated as peacekeepers—even though many of them have been sent into situations where there is no peace to be kept, and parties are intent on waging war rather than negotiating peace, and when they have been assigned missions incompatible with the original understanding of the peacekeeping function. If peacekeepers turn out to be combatants, attempting to influence the outcome of military conflict or to impose solutions on unwilling parties, it is unlikely that when volatile situations arise in the future, the parties involved will be willing to receive—or the member states to provide—peacekeeping forces. The value of peacekeeping for world order depends on the restoration of its integrity; field operations bearing the seal of the UN must be distinguished according to their missions, and the peacekeeping label must no longer be misapplied.

We turn now to the second category of world order functions. Clearly, the world is and will continue on occasion to be confronted by actual hostilities—situations in which the parties, be they states or other organized entities, wage war against each other in efforts to defeat or to resist, to take or to keep, to hold or to regain. In some of these cases, a consensus may emerge to the effect that some variety of forcible intervention on behalf of the organized society of states is necessary and feasible. This action may take the form of participation in combat to defeat the party deemed culpable and to defend its victims, efforts to limit the scope or mitigate the effects of the struggle by enforcing restraints upon the conduct of hostilities by one or more of the parties, or attempts to impose upon the parties—against the will of some or all of them—the cessation of fighting and possibly terms of settlement dictated by the outside world. Some of these measures involve the overt taking of sides, as in the tradition al idea of collective security action to oppose aggressors. Others are ostensibly neutral and humanitarian: one wishes merely to restrict the spread of war, minimize its impact on innocent populations, and restore the blessings of peace to all. These latter measures, however, almost inevitably have non-neutral consequences and therefore engender armed reaction. When we designate cities as safe areas and try to meet the needs of their populations, we interfere in the efforts of some party to achieve victory by waging siege warfare or a war of attrition. When we demand the termination of hostilities, we seek to frustrate the determination of some or all of the parties to improve their relative situations by continued combat. When we try to impose terms of settlement, we demand that at least one of the parties settle for less than it hopes to gain by continued fighting. The point is that states and other entities rarely engage in hostilities for the joy of fighting. They tend to take their objectives seriously; they think the issues at stake are worth dying for, and they are unlikely to welcome interference with their efforts. They are inclined to welcome peace when, but only when, they have achieved as much as they think possible by war, and they look forward to a settlement that reflects their military achievements—not the sentiments of the outside world. In short, interventions in armed conflicts, for whatever declared purposes, entail the very high probability of active military involvement.

This is equally true of interventions within states to counter the behavior of their ruling regimes toward some or all of the inhabitants, compelling the rulers to change their policies and perhaps even deposing those rulers. The threat or exercise of international coercion—whether intended to defeat an aggressor, circumscribe the behavior of belligerents, force an end to fighting, defend the human rights of a population, or oust a tyrant—obviously requires the will and the resources for engagement in armed conflict.

These, I suggest, are tasks for the Second UN, not for the First UN. The UN over which the secretary-general presides has neither a military establishment nor the social and economic base on which such a force could rest. It has very limited expertise in the management of armed forces or the command and control of military operations. I do not think it is possible to convert this organization into a military power analogous to, and equal or superior to, say, the United States. The effort to transform the First UN in that way would undermine its capacity to carry out the important missions of pacific settlement and peacekeeping. Moreover, such an effort seems unnecessary because—let us not forget—we have another UN, the Second UN, the one consisting of all the major powers and most of the other states. The Second UN is well equipped, indeed, with military power and professional skill in using it.

UN missions that require readiness to use force fall within the province of the member states, particularly the most powerful ones. Decisions regarding such missions properly belong to those whose contributions are most likely to be needed and whose interests are therefore most heavily engaged. The Security Council, designed to give special weight to such states, is the normal locus of these decisions. The Security Council is to the UN of states as the secretary-general is to the UN of staff officers, and it is, no less than the secretary-general, entitled to express the will and dispense the authorization of the organization—to speak and act in the name of the UN. Primary responsibility for taking coercive action under the aegis of the UN falls on the great powers. In past practice, the Second UN has been capable of effective military action only when the United States has mobilized a coalition of states and managed its performance—as in the Korean and Gulf Wars. I am aware of no evidence that such U.S. leadership will not be essential in the near future, although the initiative of other major powers should also be encouraged.

In my view, the most pressing requirement for the future effectiveness of the UN in promoting peace and security is a stern insistence on clarity and honesty with regard to the nature of its field operations. Those purporting to represent the organization—whether the secretary-general or a subordinate official of the First UN, or members of the Security Council acting as the

Second UN—must observe certain restraints. They must refrain from putting peacekeepers into situations that call for combat troops. They must not declare "safe havens" or "no-fly zones," or promise to protect civilians and punish malefactors unless the appropriate states are clearly prepared to enforce such commitments—that is, to engage in war-making rather than peacekeeping missions.

There can be no guarantee that the states composing the effective core of the Second UN will make the decisions and take the actions required for dealing with all the crises that will make for disorder and injustice in the world of the future. Those states may sometimes abuse their power, involving the UN in actions incompatible with its proper goals. There is a substantially greater probability that they will be guilty of nonfeasance rather than of malfeasance, condemning the UN to passivity or feeble response to crises. There is no doubt that this UN will respond selectively. Indeed, the plethora of trouble spots leaves no alternative to the rationing of attention and resources. There is equally no doubt that decisions to intervene in or abstain from situations will sometimes deserve, and even more often will receive, criticism. No formula can infallibly guide decisions in these matters. In the end, the world will have to rely on the good judgment, wisdom, prudence, courage, and decency of the governments representing the states that constitute the Second UN. If this reliance provides less than perfect reassurance to those of us who care about world order, we might remind ourselves that there is no alternative. We might also reflect on the fact that, even if world government were a reality rather than an impossible dream, there is no reason to assume that the makers and implementers of its decisions would be superior to the statesmen upon whom we must rely in the Second UN.

Finally, I should emphasize the importance of contributions to peace and stability that take effect well before there are armed conflicts to be controlled, cease-fires to be monitored, or disputes to be negotiated. I refer to UN activities aimed at promoting the development of good societies, effective and responsible governments, and constructive cooperation between states. These noncrisis activities are not glamorous and media-worthy, but they are the meat and potatoes (or the rice and fish) of the international menu. Given the reciprocal impact of political and security matters, on the one hand, and economic, social, and cultural matters, on the other, it may well be that the best service international organizations can render for world order is to assist in the development of thriving and stable national states. Both the UNs are, and should be, deeply involved in programs aimed at such objectives. The First UN provides a nonstate agency to work alongside states, while the Second UN provides a multistate agency that facilitates cooperation between states. For the long term, the potential contribution of the Economic and Social Council and its related agencies may rival that of the Security Council.

In conclusion, let me suggest that the UN should be conceived, and valued, as an instrument of the multistate system, a device for making that system workable. In its two aspects—as an organization *for* states and as an organization *of* states—the UN's role is to help in remedying the deficiencies of the pluralistic state system, in coping with the problems that the system presents, and in exploiting the opportunities that it provides. The UN bears the responsibility of nurturing its members, helping states to develop and function effectively and decently and facilitating their interactions.

There are people, of course, who despair of achieving a decent world order comprising independent states and who yearn for—and insist that the UN should strive for—the abolition of international relations in favor of the politics of a world government that would preside over a global state. Let us not forget, however, that there are virtues as well as vices in pluralism, and that most human beings value the freedom and diversity that are nourished by the multistate system at its best. In any case, the mission assigned to the UN by its founders and endorsed by its members is not to promote integration but to make the world safe for pluralism—and pluralism safe for the world.

CHAPTER 3

Democracy and Globalization

David Held[1]

There is a striking paradox to note regarding the contemporary era: from Africa to Eastern Europe, Asia to Latin America, more and more nations and groups are championing the idea of democracy; but they are doing so at just that moment when the very efficacy of democracy as a national form of political organization appears open to question. As substantial areas of human activity are progressively organized on a regional or global level, the fate of democracy, and of the independent democratic nation-state in particular, is fraught with difficulty.

Throughout the world's major regions, there has been a consolidation of democratic processes and procedures. In the mid-1970s, more than two-thirds of all states could reasonably be called authoritarian. This percentage has fallen dramatically; less than a third of all states are now authoritarian, and the number of democracies is growing rapidly.[2] Democracy has become the fundamental standard of political legitimacy in the current era. Events such as the release of Nelson Mandela from prison and the tearing down of the Berlin Wall are symbolic of changes indicating that, in more and more countries, citizen voters are, in principle, able to hold public decisionmakers to account. Yet, at the same time, the democratic political community is increasingly challenged by regional and global pressures and problems. How can problems such as the spread of AIDS, the debt burden of many countries in the "developing world," the flow of financial resources that escape national jurisdiction, the drugs trade, and international crime be satisfactorily brought within the sphere of democracy? What kind of accountability and control can citizens of a single nation-state have over international actors, e.g., multinational corporations (MNCS), and over international organizations, e.g., the World Bank? In the context of trends toward regionalization, European integration, fundamental

---

* This chapter was originally published in Global Governance, Volume 3, Issue 3, 1997.

1 David Held was professor of politics and sociology at Open University. This paper is based on a lecture delivered at the conference, "The Fate of Democracy in the Era of Globalization," Wellesley College, Wellesley, Massachusetts, 14–17 March 1996. The author would like to thank Joel Krieger and Craig Murphy for the initial invitation and for their generous hospitality, intellectual and social.

2 See David Potter et al., eds., *Democratization* (Cambridge: Polity, 1997).

transformations in the global economy, mass communications and information technology, how can democracy be sustained? Are new democratic institutions necessary to regulate and control the new international forces and processes? How can citizens participate as citizens in a new, more complex, internationally organized world? In a world organized increasingly on regional and global lines, can democracy as we know it survive?

Of course, there is nothing new about the emergence of global problems. Although their importance has grown considerably, many have existed for decades, some for centuries. But now that the old confrontation between East and West has ended, many regional and global issues have come to assume an urgent place on the international political agenda. Nonetheless, profound ambiguity still reigns as to where, how, and according to what criteria decisions about these matters can be made.

Democratic theory's exploration of emerging regional and global problems is still in its infancy. While students of democracy have examined and debated at length the challenges to democracy that emerge from within the boundaries of the nation-state, they have not seriously questioned whether the nation-state itself can remain at the center of democratic thought; the questions posed by the rapid growth of complex interconnections and interrelations between states and societies, and by the evident intersection of national and international forces and processes, remain largely unexplored.[3] By contrast, this paper seeks to address these questions by, first, examining the nature of globalization and, second, laying out a novel conception of democratic options in the face of the new global circumstances.[4]

1   Globalization

"Globalization" is a much-contested word. On the one hand, there are those who claim that we live in an integrated global order. According to this view, social and economic processes operate predominantly at a global level and

---

3   For an elaboration of this theme, see my *Democracy and the Global Order: From the Modern State to Cosmopolitan Governance* (Cambridge: Polity, 1995).

4   In focusing on processes of globalization, I would like to acknowledge my debt to David Goldblatt, Anthony G. McGrew, and Jonathan Perraton, with whom I have collaborated over the last four years on a research project investigating the changing enmeshment of states in global flows and transformations. The conception of globalization along with many of the examples in the following section are drawn from our joint work. See *Global Flows, Global Transformations: Concepts, Evidence and Arguments* (Cambridge: Polity, 1998).

national political communities are inevitably "decision takers."[5] This development represents a fundamental break in the organization of human affairs—a shift in the organizational principle of social life. On the other hand, there are those people who are very skeptical about the extent of globalization and who still think the national state is as integrated and robust as it ever was. They point out, for instance, that contemporary forms of international economic interaction are not without precedent and that nation-states continue to be immensely powerful with an impressive range of political options.[6]

Both these views are misleading in significant respects. We live in a world that is changing due to processes of globalization. The interconnectedness of different peoples today is more extensive and intensive than it has ever been. But globalization is not a new phenomenon; societies have always been connected with one another to some degree. Conceptions of globalization need to be sensitive to the historical variation in forms of globalization as well as to their variable impact on politics. It is easy to exaggerate the extent to which globalization signals "the end of the nation-state." Global processes should not be assumed to represent either a total eclipse of the states system or the simple emergence of a global society. Accordingly, before we proceed further, the concept of globalization needs clarification.

Globalization is best understood as a spatial phenomenon, lying on a continuum with "the local" at one end and "the global" at the other. It denotes a shift in the spatial form of human organization and activity to transcontinental or interregional patterns of activity, interaction, and the exercise of power. It involves a stretching and deepening of social relations and institutions across space and time such that, on the one hand, day-to-day activities are increasingly influenced by events happening on the other side of the globe and, on the other, the practices and decisions of local groups or communities can have significant global reverberations.[7]

Globalization today implies at least two distinct phenomena. First, it suggests that many chains of political, economic, and social activity are becoming interregional or intercontinental in scope and, second, it suggests that there has been an intensification of levels of interaction and interconnectedness within and between states and societies.[8] What is noteworthy about the

5 See, for example, Kenichi Ohmae, *The Borderless World* (London: Collins, 1990); Robert Reich, *The Work of Nations* (New York: Simon & Schuster, 1991).

6 See Paul Hirst and Grahame Thompson, *Globalization in Question* (Cambridge: Polity, 1996).

7 See Anthony Giddens, *The Consequences of Modernity* (Cambridge: Polity, 1990).

8 See Anthony G. McGrew, "Conceptualizing Global Politics," in McGrew, P.G. Lewis, et al., *Global Politics* (Cambridge: Polity, 1992).

modern global system is the stretching of social relations in and through new dimensions of activity and the chronic intensification of patterns of interconnectedness mediated by such phenomena as modern communication networks and new information technology. It is possible to distinguish different historical forms of globalization in terms of: (1) the extensiveness of networks of relations and connections, (2) the intensity of flows and levels of enmeshment within the networks, and (3) the impact of these phenomena on particular communities.

Globalization is neither a singular condition nor a linear process. Rather, it is best thought of as a multidimensional phenomenon involving diverse domains of activity and interaction including the economic, political, technological, military, legal, cultural, and environmental. Each of these spheres involves different patterns of relations and activity. A general account of globalization cannot simply predict from one domain what will occur in another. It is important, therefore, to build a theory of globalization from an understanding of what is happening in each one of these areas.

The significance of globalization, of course, differs for individuals, groups, and countries. The impact of various global flows on, for instance, policymaking in the economic domain will alter considerably depending on whether the country in question is the United States, Peru, or Spain. For individuals and groups as well, variable enmeshment in global flows is the norm. The elites in the world of politics, law, business, and science are often quite at home in the global capitals, the leading hotels, and in the major cultural centers. Their access to and use of these different facilities are clearly in marked contrast to those peoples, for example, villagers in sub-Saharan Africa, who live at the margin of some of the central power structures and hierarchies of the global order. But the latter are by no means unaffected by changing processes and forms of globalization. On the contrary, they are often in the position of being profoundly influenced by these processes and forms, even if they cannot control them. What often differentiates the position of these peoples from what some have called the new "cosmopolitan elite," is differential, unequal, and uneven access to the dominant organizations, institutions, and processes of the new emerging global order.

At the heart of this "differential access" is power, where power has to be conceptualized as the capacity to transform material circumstances—whether social, political, or economic—and to achieve goals based on the mobilization of resources, the creation of rule systems, and the control of infrastructures and institutions. The particular form of power that is of concern to a theory of globalization is comprised of *hierarchy* and *unevenness*. Hierarchy connotes the asymmetrical access to global networks and infrastructures, while unevenness refers to the asymmetrical effects of such networks on the life chances and the well-being of peoples, classes, ethnic groupings, and the sexes.[9]

In order to elaborate a theory of globalization, it is necessary to turn from a general concern with its conceptualization to an examination of the distinctive domains of activity and interaction in and through which global processes evolve. This task cannot be pursued here at any length. But some significant changes can be highlighted. An obvious starting point is the world economy and, in particular, trade, financial flows, and the spread of multinational corporations.

1.1   Trade

There are those who are skeptical about the extent of the globalization of trade in the contemporary period and they sometimes point out that trade levels in the late twentieth century have only recently reached the same levels as in 1914. This skeptical view is open to doubt. First, using constant price data, it can be shown that the proportion of trade to gross domestic product (trade-GDP ratios) surpassed that of the gold-standard era (that is, the period from 1875 to 1914) by the early 1970s and was considerably higher by the late 1970s and 1980s. In other words, trade has continued to expand as a proportion of GDP. Export- and import-GDP ratios were around 12–13 percent for advanced industrial countries during the gold-standard era but rose to 15–20 percent—or even higher for some developed countries—from the late 1970s onward. Second, if one removes government expenditure from the inquiry, and focuses on trade in relation to the size of national economic activity, it can be demonstrated that the proportion of trade to such activity has grown particularly rapidly, by as much as a third. Technological developments have made many classes of goods, particularly those in the service sector, tradable where previously they were not. Finally, the evidence also shows that there has not been a simple increase in intraregional trade around the world. Measures of the intensity of trade reveal sustained growth between regions as well (albeit concentrated among Europe, North America, and Pacific Asia). Growth in trade within regions and growth among regions are not contradictory developments; rather, they appear to be complementary.

What these points suggest is that trade has grown rapidly, reaching unprecedented levels today. More countries are involved in trading arrangements—e.g., India and China—and a great number of people and nations are affected by such trade. In the context of lowering tariff barriers across the world, one can

---

9   See Richard Falk, *On Humane Governance: Toward a New Global Politics* (Cambridge: Polity, 1995).

reasonably expect these trends to continue. Any argument suggesting that the world's three key trading blocs—the EU, NAFTA, and Pacific Asia—are becoming more inward-looking and protectionist is not supported by the evidence. Although contemporary trading arrangements stop far short of a perfectly open global market, national economies are enmeshed in a pattern of increasingly dense and competitive international trade. When linked to changes in finance and the organization of production and banking, this has significant political implications.

1.2 *Finance*

The expansion of global financial flows around the world has been staggering in the last ten to fifteen years. The growth of foreign-exchange turnover is now more than a trillion dollars a day. The volume of turnover of bonds, securities, and other assets on a daily basis is also without precedent. A number of things can be said about these flows. First, the proportion of foreign-exchange turnover to trade has mushroomed from eleven dollars to one to more than fifty-five dollars to one in the last thirteen to fourteen years; that is, for every fifty-five dollars turned over in the foreign-exchange markets, one dollar is turned over in real trade. Second, a great deal of this financial activity is speculative—it generates fluctuations in values in excess of those that can be accounted for by changes in the underlying fundamentals of asset values. Third, while the *net* movement of capital relative to GDP is smaller for some countries today than in earlier periods, this has nothing to do with diminishing levels of globalization—i.e., lower levels of capital-market integration. The liberalization of capital markets in the 1980s and early 1990s has created a more integrated financial system than has ever been known. Lastly, the effects of global financial flows on economic policy are profound. Among the most important are:

1. The increased possibility of rapid and dramatic shifts in the effective valuation of economies as illustrated, for instance, in Mexico in January 1995.
2. The increasing difficulty for countries of pursuing independent monetary policies and independent exchange-rate strategies in the face of the current volume of international turnover in currencies and bonds.
3. The erosion of the option to pursue Keynesian reflationary strategies in a single country; the costs and benefits of these strategies have shifted against the pursuit of such options in many places.
4. Finally, as can be seen in the growing macroeconomic policy convergence across political parties in the present period, a deepening acknowledgment of the decline in the economic maneuverability of individual governments. Recent examples of this can be found in the reshaping

of economic policy among the social democratic parties of Europe; the transformation of the economic policy of the Labour Party in Britain—from policy emphasizing demand management to policy prioritizing supply-side measures (above all, in education and training) to help meet the challenges of increased competition and the greater mobility of capital—is a particular case in point.

Many of these changes might not be of concern if financial-market operators had a monopoly of economic expertise, but they clearly do not. Their actions can precipitate crises and can help contribute to making sound policies unworkable. In addition, they can erode the very democratic quality of government. This does not lead necessarily to political impotence—although it has done so in some countries in some respects—but it creates new political questions.

1.3   *Multinational Corporations*

The globalization of production and the globalization of financial transactions are organized in part, familiarly enough, by fast-growing multinational companies. Two central points need to be made about them. First, MNCs account for a quarter to a third of world output, 70 percent of world trade, and 80 percent of direct international investment. They are essential to the diffusion of technology and they are key players in international money markets. Second, although evidence indicates that many of the largest MNCs still generate most of their sales and profits from domestic business, this is largely due to the influence of U.S. companies—which have, of course, a particularly large home market.[10] The proportion of sales and profits generated domestically is much lower for non-U.S. companies and, significantly, for higher-tech companies. Moreover, although a company like Ford or General Motors may well have the majority of its assets in one particular country—in these cases, the United States—it would be wrong to suggest that their performance is not substantially affected by their overseas activities. Even if a minority of assets is held overseas—say, 20–30 percent—this still represents a significant interlocking of a company's assets into overseas market conditions and processes. Companies are highly vulnerable to changes in economic conditions, wherever they are. Marginal decreases in demand can profoundly affect the operations of a company.

Multinational corporations in general have profound effects on macroeconomic policy; they can respond to variations in interest rates by raising

---

10   For a fuller account of these points see Jonathan Perraton, David Goldblatt, David Held, and Anthony McGrew, "The Globalization of Economic Activity," *New Political Economy* 2, no. 2 (1997).

finance in whichever capital market is most favorable. They can shift their demand for employment to countries with much lower employment costs. And, in the area of industrial policy, they can move their activities to where the maximum benefits accrue. Irrespective of how often MNCs actually take advantage of these opportunities, it is the fact that they *could* do so in principle that influences government policy and shapes economic strategies. But the impact of MNCs should not be measured by these indicators alone. They have a significant influence on an economy even when their levels of capitalization are not particularly high. For example, in Zimbabwe, the Coca-Cola bottling plant is not a big factory by global standards; yet, it has a major influence on local management practices and on aspects of economic policy more broadly.

Economic globalization has significant and discernible characteristics that alter the balance of resources, economic and political, within and across borders. Among the most important of these is the tangible growth in the enmeshment of national economies in global economic transactions (i.e., a growing proportion of nearly all national economies involves international economic exchanges with an increasing number of countries). This increase in the extent and intensity of economic interconnectedness has altered the relation between economic and political power. One shift has been particularly significant: "the historic expansion of exit options for capital in financial markets relative to national capital controls, national banking regulations and national investment strategies, and the sheer volume of privately held capital relative to national reserves. Exit options for corporations making direct investments have also expanded ... the balance of power has shifted in favour of capital *vis-à-vis* both national governments and national labour movements."[11] As a result, the autonomy of democratically elected governments has been, and is increasingly, constrained by sources of unelected and unrepresentative economic power. These have the effect of making adjustment to the international economy (and, above all, to global financial markets) a fixed point of orientation in economic policy and of encouraging an acceptance of the "decision signals" of its leading agents and forces as a, if not the, standard of rational decisionmaking. The options for political communities, and the costs and benefits of them, ineluctably alter.

---

11   David Goldblatt, David Held, Anthony McGrew, and Jonathan Perraton, "Economic Globalization and the Nation-State: Shifting Balances of Power," *Alternatives* 22, no. 3 (1997), pp. 269–288.

1.4   *Cultural and Communication Trends*

Interlinked changes in trade, finance, and the structure of multinational corporations are somewhat easier to document and analyze—even if their implications remain controversial—than is the impact of globalization in the sphere of the media and culture. Evidence of globalization in this domain is complex and somewhat uncertain. A great deal of research remains to be carried out. Nonetheless, a number of remarkable developments can be pointed to, for instance:

1.   English has spread as the dominant language of elite cultures; it is the dominant language in business, computing, law, science, and politics.
2.   The internationalization and globalization of telecommunications have been extraordinarily rapid as manifest in the growth of, e.g., international telephone traffic, transnational cable links, satellite links, and the Internet.
3.   Substantial multinational media conglomerates have developed, such as the Murdoch empire, but there are many other notable examples as well, including Viacom, Disney, and Time Warner.
4.   There has been a huge increase in tourism: for example, in 1960 there were 70 million international tourists, while in 1995 there were nearly 500 million.
5.   The transnationalization of television programs and films is also striking: 60–90 percent of box-office receipts in Europe, for instance, came from foreign movies (although this is largely the story of U.S. dominance).

None of these examples—or the accumulated impact of parallel instances—should be taken to imply the development of a single global, media-led culture—far from it. But taken together, these developments do indicate that many new forms of communication and media range in and across borders, linking nations and peoples in new ways. Accordingly, national political communities by no means simply determine the structure and processes of cultural life in and through which their citizens are formed. Citizens' values and judgments are now influenced by a complex web of national, international, and global cultural exchange. The capacity of national political leaders to sustain a national culture has become more difficult. For example, China sought to restrict access and use of the Internet but has found it extremely difficult to do so.

1.5   *The Environment*

Contemporary environmental problems are perhaps the clearest and starkest examples of the global shift in human organization and activity, creating some of the most fundamental pressures on the efficacy of the nation-state and of state-centric politics.

There are three types of problems at issue:

1. Shared problems involving the global commons, i.e., fundamental elements of our ecosystem, the clearest examples of which are the atmosphere, the climate system, and the oceans and seas; and among the most fundamental challenges here are global warming and ozone depletion.

2. Interlinked challenges of demographic expansion and resource consumption, an example of the profoundest importance of which is desertification; other examples include questions of biodiversity and challenges to the very existence of certain species.

3. Transboundary pollution of various kinds such as acid rain or river pollutants; more dramatic examples arise from the siting and operation of nuclear power plants—for instance, Chernobyl.

In response to the progressive development of, and publicity surrounding, environmental problems, there has been an interlinked process of cultural and political globalization, as illustrated by: the emergence of new cultural, scientific, and intellectual networks; new environmental movements with transnational organizations and transnational concerns; and new institutions and conventions such as those agreed in 1992 at the Earth summit in Brazil. Not all environmental problems are, of course, global. Such an implication would be quite false. But there has been a striking shift in the physical and environmental circumstances—that is, in the extent and intensity of environmental problems—affecting human affairs in general. These processes have moved politics dramatically away from an activity that crystallizes simply around state and interstate concerns. It is clearer than ever that the political fortunes of communities and peoples can no longer be understood in exclusively national or territorial terms.

1.6   *Politics, Law, and Security*

The sovereign state now lies at the intersection of a vast array of international regimes and organizations that have been established to manage whole areas of transnational activity (trade, the oceans, space, and so on) and collective policy problems. The growth in the number of these new forms of political organization reflects the rapid expansion of transnational links, the growing interpenetration of foreign and domestic policy, and the corresponding desire by most states for some form of international governance and regulation to deal with collective policy problems.

One illustration of these developments is that new forms of multilateral and multinational politics have been established and with them distinctive styles of collective decisionmaking involving governments, IGOs, and a wide variety of transnational pressure groups and international nongovernmental organizations (INGOS). In 1909, there were 37 IGOS and 176 INGOS, while in

1989 there were nearly 300 IGOS and 4,624 INGOS. In the middle of the nineteenth century, there were two or three conferences or congresses per annum sponsored by IGOS; today the total number is close to four thousand annually. Against this background, the range and diversity of the participants at the Earth Summit in Rio de Janeiro in 1992 or the women's conference at Beijing in 1995 may not seem quite as remarkable as the occasions initially suggested.

Second, all this has helped engender a shift away from a purely state-centered international system of "high politics" to new and novel forms of geogovernance. Perhaps one of the most interesting examples of this can be drawn from the very heart of the idea of a sovereign state—national security and defense policy. There is a documentable increase in emphasis on collective defense and cooperative security. The enormous costs, technological requirements, and domestic burdens of defense are contributing to the strengthening of multilateral and collective defense arrangements as well as international military cooperation and coordination. The rising density of technological connections between states now challenges the very idea of national security and national arms procurement. Some of the most advanced weapons systems in the world today—e.g., fighter aircraft—depend on components that come from many countries. There has been a globalization of military technology linked to a transnationalization of defense production.

Moreover, finally, the proliferation of weapons of mass destruction makes all states insecure and problematizes the very notion of "friends" and "enemies."

Even in the spheres of defense and arms production and manufacture, the notion of a singular, discrete, and delimited political community appears problematic. As a result, the proper home and form of politics and of democracy become a puzzling matter.

2   Rethinking Democracy

The developments documented above have contributed to the transformation of the nature and prospects of democratic political community in a number of distinctive ways.

First, the locus of effective political power can no longer be assumed to be national governments—effective power is shared and bartered by diverse forces and agencies at national, regional, and international levels. Second, the idea of a political community of fate—of a self-determining collectivity—can no longer be meaningfully located within the boundaries of a single nation-state alone. Some of the most fundamental forces and processes that determine the nature of life chances within and across political communities are now beyond the reach of individual nation-states.

The system of national political communities persists of course, but it is articulated and rearticulated today with complex economic, organizational, administrative, legal, and cultural processes and structures that limit and check its efficacy. If these processes and structures are not acknowledged and brought into the political process themselves, they may bypass or circumvent the democratic state system.

Third, it is not part of my argument that national sovereignty today, even in regions with intensive overlapping and divided political and authority structures, has been wholly subverted—not at all. However, it *is* part of my argument that the operations of states in increasingly complex global and regional systems affects both their autonomy (by changing the balance between the costs and benefits of policies) and their sovereignty (by altering the balance between national, regional, and international legal frameworks and administrative practices). While massive concentrations of power remain features of many states, these are frequently embedded in, and articulated with, fractured domains of political authority. Against this background, it is not fanciful to imagine, as Bull once observed, the development of an international system that is a modern and secular counterpart of the kind of political organization found in Christian Europe in the Middle Ages, the essential characteristic of which was a system of overlapping authority and divided loyalties.[12]

Fourth, the late twentieth century is marked by a significant series of new types of "boundary problems." If it is accepted that we live in a world of overlapping communities of fate—where, in other words, the trajectories of each and every country are more tightly entwined than ever before—then new types of boundary problems follow. In the past, of course, nation-states principally resolved their differences over boundary matters by pursuing reasons of state, backed, ultimately, by coercive means. But this power logic is singularly inadequate and inappropriate to resolve the many complex issues—from economic regulation to resource depletion and environmental degradation—that engender an intermeshing of "national fortunes." In a world where transnational actors and forces cut across the boundaries of national communities in diverse ways, and where powerful states make decisions not just for their peoples but for others as well, the questions of who should be accountable to whom, and on what basis, do not easily resolve themselves. Overlapping

---

12   Hedley Bull, *The Anarchical Society* (London: Macmillan, 1997), pp. 254–255.

spheres of influence, interference, and interest create dilemmas at the center of democratic thought.

In the liberal democracies, consent to government and legitimacy for governmental action are dependent on electoral politics and the ballot box. Yet the notions that consent legitimizes government and that the ballot box is the appropriate mechanism whereby the citizen body as a whole periodically confers authority on government to enact the law and regulate economic and social life become problematic as soon as the nature of a "relevant community" is contested. What is the proper constituency, and proper realm of jurisdiction, for developing and implementing policy with respect to health issues such as AIDS or BSE (Bovine Spongiform Encephalopathy), the use of nuclear energy, the harvesting of rainforests, the use of nonrenewable resources, the instability of global financial markets, and the reduction of the risks of nuclear warfare? National boundaries have demarcated traditionally the basis on which individuals are included and excluded from participation in decisions affecting their lives; but if many socioeconomic processes, and the outcomes of decisions about them, stretch beyond national frontiers, then the implications of this are serious, not only for the categories of consent and legitimacy but for all the key ideas of democracy. At issue are the nature of a constituency, the role of representation, and the proper form and scope of political participation. As fundamental processes of governance escape the categories of the nation-state, the traditional national resolutions of the key questions of democratic theory and practice are left open to doubt.

Against this background, the nature and prospects of the democratic polity need reexamination. The idea of a democratic order can no longer be defended simply as an idea suitable to a particular closed political community or nation-state. We are compelled to recognize that we live in a complex interconnected world where the extensity, intensity, and impact of issues (economic, political, or environmental) raise questions about where those issues are most appropriately addressed. Deliberative and decisionmaking centers beyond national territories are appropriately situated when those significantly affected by a public matter constitute a cross-border or transnational grouping, when "lower" levels of decisionmaking cannot manage and discharge satisfactorily transnational or international policy questions, and when the principle of democratic legitimacy can only be properly redeemed in a transnational context. If the most powerful geopolitical interests are not to settle many pressing matters simply in terms of their objectives and by virtue of their power, then new institutions and mechanisms of accountability need to be established.

It would be easy to be pessimistic about the future of democracy. There are plenty of reasons for pessimism; they include the fact that the essential political units of the world are still based on nation-states while some of the most powerful sociopolitical forces of the world escape the boundaries of these units. In reaction to this, in part, new forms of fundamentalism have arisen along with new forms of tribalism—all asserting the a priori superiority of a particular religious or cultural or political identity over all others—and all asserting their sectional aims and interests. But there are other forces at work that seem to create the basis for a more optimistic reading of democratic prospects. An historical comparison might help to provide a context for this consideration.

In the sixteenth and seventeenth centuries, Europe was marked by civil conflict, religious strife, and fragmented authority; the idea of a secular state, separate from ruler and ruled, as well as from the church, seemed an unlikely prospect. Parts of Europe were tearing themselves to pieces, and yet, within 150–200 years, a new concept of politics became entrenched, that was based around a new concept of the state. Today we live at another fundamental point of transition, but now to a more transnational, global world. There are forces and pressures that are engendering a reshaping of political cultures, institutions, and structures. First, one must obviously note the emergence, however hesitating, of regional and global institutions in the twentieth century. The UN is, of course, weak in many respects, but it is a relatively recent creation and is an innovative structure that can be built on. It is a normative resource that provides—for all its difficulties—an enduring example of how nations might (and sometimes do) cooperate better to resolve, and to resolve fairly, common problems. In addition, the development of a powerful regional body such as the European Union (EU) is a remarkable state of affairs. Just over fifty years ago, Europe was at the point of self-destruction. Since that moment, Europe has created new mechanisms of collaboration, human rights enforcement, and new political institutions in order not only to hold member states to account across a broad range of issues but also to pool aspects of their sovereignty. Furthermore, there are, of course, new regional and global transnational actors contesting the terms of globalization—not just corporations but new social movements such as the environmental movement, the women's movement, and so on. These are the "new" voices of an emergent "transnational civil society," heard, for instance, at the Rio Conference on the Environment, the Cairo Conference on Population Control, and the Beijing Conference on Women. In short, there are tendencies at work seeking to create new forms of public life and new ways of debating regional and global issues. These are, of course, all in early stages of development, and there are no guarantees that the balance of political contest will allow them to develop. But they point in the direction of establishing new ways of holding transnational power systems to account— that is, they help open up the possibility of a cosmopolitan democracy.

Cosmopolitan democracy involves the development of administrative capacity and independent political resources at regional and global levels as a necessary complement to those in local and national polities. At issue would be strengthening the administrative capacity and accountability of regional institutions like the EU along with developing the administrative capacity and forms of accountability of the UN system itself. A cosmopolitan democracy would not call for a diminution per se of state power and capacity across the globe. Rather, it would seek to entrench and develop democratic institutions at regional and global levels as a necessary complement to those at the level of the nation-state. This conception of democracy is based on the recognition of the continuing significance of nation-states, while arguing for a layer of governance to constitute a limitation on national sovereignty.

The case for cosmopolitan democracy is one for the creation of new political institutions that would coexist with the system of states but that would override states in clearly defined spheres of activity where those activities have demonstrable transnational and international consequences, require regional or global initiatives in the interests of effectiveness, and depend on such initiatives for democratic legitimacy. At issue, in addition, would not merely be the formal construction of new democratic mechanisms and procedures but also the construction, in principle, of broad "access avenues" of civic participation at national and regional levels. Table 3.1 (p. 266) provides an outline of some of the constitutive features of cosmopolitan democracy.[13]

3   In Sum

The theory of cosmopolitan democracy is one of the few political theories that examines systematically the democratic implications of the fact that nation-states are enmeshed today in complex interconnected relations. Our world is a world of *overlapping communities of fate*, where the fate of one country and that of another are more entwined than ever before. In this world, there are many issues stretching beyond the borders of countries and challenging the relevance of those borders in key respects. Many of these issues have already been referred to—pollutants, resource use questions, the regulation of global networks of trade, finance, etc. Can these be brought within the sphere of democracy? The theory of cosmopolitan democracy suggests this is not only a real necessity but also a real possibility.

---

13   For further discussion and elaboration of these and related features see Daniele Archibugi and David Held, eds., *Cosmopolitan Democracy: An Agenda for a New World Order* (Cambridge: Polity, 1995); Held, *Democracy and the Global Order.*

TABLE 3.1   Cosmopolitan democracy

Illustrative institutional features

Polity/ governance	Short-term	Long-term
	Reform of leading UN governing institutions such as the Security Council (to give developing countries a significant voice and effective decisionmaking capacity)	New Charter of Rights and Obligations locked into different domains of political, social, and economic power
	Creation of a UN second chamber (following an international constitutional convention)	Global parliament (with limited revenue-raising capacity) connected to regions, nations, and localities
	Enhanced political regionalization (EU and beyond) and the use of transnational referenda	Separation of political and economic interests; public funding of deliberative assemblies and electoral processes
	Creation of a new, international Human Rights Court, compulsory jurisdiction before the International Court	Interconnected global legal system, embracing elements of criminal and civil law
	Establishment of an effective, accountable, international, military force	Permanent shift of a growing proportion of a nation-state's coercive capability to regional and global institutions
Economy/ civil society	Short-term	Long-term
	Enhancement of nonstate, nonmarket solutions in the organization of civil society	Creation of a diversity of self-regulating associations and groups in civil society
	Systematic experimentation with different democratic organizational forms in the economy	Multisectoral economy and pluralization of patterns of ownership and possession
	Provision of resources to those in the most vulnerable social positions in order to defend and articulate their interests	Social framework investment priorities set through public deliberation and government decision, but extensive market regulation of goods and labor remain

TABLE 3.1   Cosmopolitan democracy (*cont.*)

Principle justification
−   In a world of intensifying regional and global relations, with marked overlapping "communities of fate," democracy requires entrenchment in regional and global networks as well as in national and local polities. Without such a development, many of the most powerful regional and global forces will escape democratic mechanisms of accountability and legitimacy.

General conditions
−   Continuing development of regional, international, and global flows of resources and networks of interaction.
−   Recognition by growing numbers of peoples of increasing interconnectedness of political communities in diverse domains including the social, cultural, economic, and environmental.
−   Development of an understanding of overlapping "collective fortunes" that require collective democratic solutions—locally, nationally, regionally, and globally.
−   Enhanced entrenchment of democratic rights and obligations in the making and enforcement of national, regional, and international law.
−   Transfer of increasing proportion of a nation's military coercive capability to transnational agencies and institutions, with the ultimate aim of demilitarization and the transcendence of the states' war system as a means of resolving conflicts of national interest.

CHAPTER 4

The Quiet Revolution

Kofi Annan[1]

The past ten years have been tumultuous for the United Nations, with difficult challenges and, occasionally, painful setbacks. But they have also been years of promise, years in which a quiet revolution—a revolution of good governance and of cooperation, within the UN, among citizens of different countries, and between citizens organizations and the UN—has enhanced the prospects for achieving many of the world's shared goals. I want to use this opportunity to reflect on those changes and, at the end of those reflections, to suggest further ways in which the international academic community and the UN might cooperate to achieve goals we share.

Despite the setbacks of the last decade, it has become apparent to all that the United Nations remains as much in demand as in need of change. That is our momentous challenge but also our great promise. In our efforts to fulfill that promise, we are learning new ways to do what we do better, and we are finding new strategies to suit a changed environment. We are focusing on the importance of sustainability—on "sustainable development"—in all aspects of our work, including peace and security. Above all, we are directing more of our energies toward ensuring adequate institutional frameworks in developing countries and within reformed international institutions. We are seeking to bring the stability, the trust, the legitimacy, and the accountability of good governance to all parts of the world.

Without good governance—without the rule of law, predictable administration, legitimate power, and responsive regulation—no amount of funding, no amount of charity will set the developing world on the path to prosperity.

---

* This chapter was originally published in Global Governance, Volume 4, Issue 2, 1998.
1 Kofi Annan was the seventh secretary-general of the United Nations and the first to have emerged from the ranks of the international civil service. He had a remarkably varied UN career spanning three decades. Among his numerous appointments, he served as: both under-secretary-general and assistant secretary-general for peacekeeping operations; special envoy in the former Yugoslavia; assistant secretary-general for program planning, budget, and finance and controller; assistant secretary-general in the Office of Human Resources Management and security coordinator for the UN system; director of budget in the Office of Financial Services; and deputy director of administration and head of personnel at the Office of the UN High Commissioner for Refugees.

Member states have increasingly recognized that good governance is indispensable for building peaceful, prosperous, and democratic societies. They are turning to the United Nations because, since the end of the Cold War, our knowledge and our experience in this field have expanded greatly. UN programs now target virtually all the key elements of good governance: safeguarding the rule of law; verifying elections; training police; monitoring human rights; fostering investments; and promoting accountable administration. Good governance is also a component of our work for peace. It has a strong preventive aspect; it gives societies sound structures for economic and social development. In postconflict settings, good governance can promote reconciliation and offer a path for consolidating peace.

Promoting good governance within societies requires good governance in the United Nations. It requires more than ever a UN that is focused, coherent, responsive, and cost-effective. This has been the goal of the recent program of UN reform. Reform is not simply an exercise in cutting costs or reducing staff. It is desired to assure the organization's relevance in a changing world and to make sure that those mandates that are given to it by its 185 member states are performed effectively and efficiently within the resources that are appropriate for those ends. The purpose of reforming the UN is to strengthen an indispensable institution and to prepare it to meet the challenges of the future, and those challenges are numerous and complex.

Let me say something about those challenges and about the current round of UN reform before returning to my main theme: the citizen partnerships with the UN family that are at the center of the hopeful, quiet revolution of our time.

1   Challenges of the New Global Era

At both the international and national levels, fundamental forces are reshaping patterns of social organization, structures of opportunities and constraints, objects of aspiration, and sources of fear. Globalization envelops the world even as fragmentation and the assertion of differences are on the rise. Zones of peace expand while outbursts of horrific violence intensify; unprecedented wealth is being created but large pockets of poverty remain endemic; the will of the people and their integral rights are increasingly both celebrated and violated; science and technology enhance human life at the same time as their by-products threaten planetary life-support systems.

We live in an era of realignment. A decade ago the cessation of superpower rivalry and military confrontation set in motion a whole host of progressive changes within and among countries. But we are also still struggling with the adverse consequences of bipolarity's collapse. The interethnic conflicts that followed the breakup of several multiethnic states, whether in Central Asia or the former Yugoslavia, are tragic cases in point. Some of the former proxy battlegrounds of the Cold War in Asia and Africa continue to reel from instability. States that were held together by their perceived strategic utility to one side or the other in some instances have suffered grievously.

Realignment is taking place along with globalization, which is, perhaps, the most profound source of international transformation since the Industrial Revolution. Beginning in the 1960s, with the limited lifting of capital controls and the gradual emergence of multinational manufacturing firms, financial markets have become increasingly integrated and the production of goods and services transnationalized. Globalization and the liberalization that produced it have generated a sustained period of economic expansion, together with the most rapid reconfiguration of international economic geography ever. Unprecedentedly high standards of living exist in the industrialized world. Elsewhere, some countries that struggled with poverty a mere generation ago are now growth poles in their own right. Over the course of the next generation, a majority of the world's most rapidly growing economies will be located in what is now the developing world.

Yet, globalization poses numerous policy challenges, among them the inherent risks created by financial markets lacking critical regulatory safeguards. Globalization erodes the efficacy of the policy instruments by which the industrialized countries pursued full employment and social stability after World War II, while in the developing world the promise of globalization has so far been fulfilled in only a very few countries. Some 40 percent of the direct foreign investment that flows to developing countries is accounted for by China alone; East Asia as a whole absorbs nearly two thirds. In contrast, Africa is the recipient of a meager 4 percent. Among the countries bypassed by global capital flows are those that are experiencing the most enduring poverty.

Furthermore, all developing countries, even the most successful, are in the difficult position of being forced by globalization to realign the character of their state apparatus in several directions simultaneously. The growing recognition that the state is not the exclusive, or often the principal, creator of wealth has led to widespread privatization and deregulation, but even in market-oriented developing countries the state has critical roles to play in providing an enabling environment for sustainable development. The World Bank's 1997 *World Development Report* shows systematically how crucial an effective state is in this regard. Finding the appropriate balance, however, especially in contexts where civil society is weak and transnational forces overpowering, is an exceedingly complex task. (I might add that the various UN "good governance" programs are designed to assist individual governments in defining the balance that best meets their needs.)

Globalization rests on and is sustained by a remarkable revolution in its own right in information technology, particularly the integration of increasingly powerful computers with telecommunication systems that permit high volume and high quality real-time voice and data transmissions. Indeed, the adjective "global" refers less to a place than to a space defined by electronic flows and a state of mind. World currency markets are the most global of all in this sense, and what has come to be known as the global factory relies similarly on such electronic infrastructure.

The information revolution has unfolded most extensively in the industrialized world, but it also holds enormous potential for the developing countries. It diminishes the constraints of distance in manufacturing industries and many services, and offers new tools in the form of administrative capacities, long-distance learning, telemedicine, the more effective management of microcredit systems, agricultural production, and a variety of other applications.

The intensification of global environmental interdependencies constitutes an additional, simultaneous transformative force. At the UN Conference on Environment and Development (UNCED) held at Rio de Janeiro in 1992, the international community endorsed the concept of sustainable development as the key to reconciling economic and social progress, which all desire, with safeguarding the planet's ecosystems, on which all depend. Many of these systems are under increasing stress, however, with adverse consequences that range from the local destructiveness of flash floods resulting from deforestation, to the slower but globally indivisible atmospheric warming that results from increased emissions of greenhouse gases. Progress since UNCED has been disappointing, whether in meeting targets for controlling environmental degradation or providing technological and financial assistance to developing countries. Negotiation in this area is very difficult, as witnessed in the recent Kyoto session of the Conference of the Parties to the United Nations Framework Convention on Climate Change.

Environmental negotiations have at times been facilitated by another new international force: the pronounced transnational expansion of civil society, a major factor in the quiet revolution. This is of great significance for the United Nations. Private investment capital exceeds by a factor of six the available official development assistance and must be further mobilized for development purposes. In recent years, the UN has found that much of its work at the country level, be it in humanitarian affairs, economic and social development, public health, or the promotion of human rights, intimately involves the diverse and dedicated contributions of nongovernmental organizations and groups.

A closely related trend is the move toward democratization and respect for human rights. Countries in all parts of the world are voluntarily limiting the arbitrary powers of state agencies together with the abuses and the social and economic costs they engender. Some 120 countries now hold generally free and fair elections, the highest total in history. The social, economic, and political benefits of basing systems of rule on the principles of human dignity and the will of the people are felt in domestic as well as regional peace and prosperity, although the transition to democracy itself is often fraught with difficulty.

Moreover, the same technologies that foster democratization and the expansion of civil society along with globalization also provide the infrastructure for expanding global networks of "uncivil society"—organized crime, drug traffickers, money launderers, and terrorists who corrupt politics at all levels, undermine judiciaries, and pose security threats even to the most powerful states. Uncivil society is one aspect of the fragmentation that has come along with the integrative aspects of globalization. Indeed, the broad uncertainties and insecurities engendered by fundamental change frequently result in a heightened quest to redefine and reassert collective identities.

At their best, identity politics provide a robust sense of social coherence and civic pride, which have salutary effects for economic development and the peaceful resolution of disputes at home and abroad. At their worst, however, identity politics result in the vilification of "the other," whether that other is a different ethnic or tribal group, a different religion, or a different nationality. This particularistic and exclusionary form of identity politics has intensified in recent years within and among countries. It is responsible for some of the most egregious violations of international humanitarian law and, in several instances, of elementary standards of humanity: genocidal violence; the conscious targeting of civilian populations, often women and children, by factional combatants; rape as a deliberate instrument of organized terror; and attacks on emergency relief workers and missions. Negative forms of identity politics are a potent and potentially explosive force. Great care must be taken to recognize, confront, and restrain them lest they destroy the potential for peace and progress that the new era holds in store.

Times of transformation can be times of confusion. The policymaking process can easily get caught in transition traps, moments of discontinuity when taking the wrong step can have severe long-term consequences. The international community has an obligation to itself and to succeeding generations to strengthen the available multilateral mechanisms, among which the United

Nations is a unique instrument of concerted action, so as to successfully harness the mutual benefits of change while managing its adverse effects.

2   Renewing the United Nations

These numerous competing forces and tensions of this era of transition are daunting. Yet it is not beyond our power to tip the scale toward a more secure and predictable peace, greater economic well-being, social justice, and environmental sustainability. No country can achieve these global public goods on its own. Multilateral diplomacy was invented and has been sustained because political leaders as well as the people they represent have recognized this simple fact. The United Nations with its near-universal membership, its comprehensive mandate, a span of activities that ranges from the normative to the operational, and an institutional presence that is at once global, regional, and country-based can and should be at the very center of this endeavor.

Often this is difficult. The recent fiscal precariousness of the United Nations is unprecedented and debilitating. For too many years we have been forced to "borrow" from the peacekeeping account to cover regular budget shortfalls caused by nonpayment of dues by some members. Now that source, too, is depleted. I hope and trust that we shall soon be able to put this problem behind us, and that in the future all member states will fulfill their legal obligations to the organization and one another by paying their dues in full and on time. This is the essential foundation on which good multilateral governance can be built.

Even apart from the specific fiscal problems caused by arrears, we must accept that the resources available to multilateral organizations, including the UN, are declining relative to the magnitude of the tasks they face and to the capacities of other actors, especially the private sector. What is more, the very concept of intergovernmentalism as we know it is being altered as a result of the redefinition of the role of government and the means of governance now under way throughout the world.

In this transformed context, the UN's past pattern of incremental adaptations will not suffice. To succeed in the new century the United Nations must unleash its own major resource: the complementarities and synergies that exist within it. In other words, the UN must undergo fundamental, not piecemeal, reform. That is why I have made reform one of my highest priorities. That is why I have launched a quiet revolution at the United Nations.

The fundamental objective of this reform effort is to narrow the gap between aspiration and accomplishment. It seeks to do so by establishing a new leadership culture and management structure at the UN that will lead to greater unity of purpose, coherence of efforts, and agility in responding to the pressing needs of the international community. The major source of institutional weakness in the United Nations is the fact that over the course of the past half century certain of its organizational features had become fragmented, duplicative, rigid, in some areas ineffective, in others superfluous. The Cold War and the system of bloc politics that was its consequence made it extremely difficult and in some cases impossible for the organization to implement the Charter conceptions of its many roles, especially in the area of peace and security. In this hostile environment, the numerous new initiatives that the UN was able to launch throughout the Cold War years all too often were simply layered onto previous activities. Even previous reform efforts were constrained by these same forces. Often they produced parallel mechanisms or created additional bodies that were intended to coordinate, rather than instituting effective management structures.

Once the Cold War ended, the United Nations rushed and was pushed to respond to a vast increase in demand for its services. We made many mistakes, often because the means given to the organization did not match the demands made on it. Now that the frenzy of the immediate post-Cold War years has passed, we can and must step back to reassess which are the most effective means to realize the UN's enduring goals.

We know, for example, that over the course of the next generation a majority of the world's most rapidly growing economies will be located in what is now the developing world, while many of the least developed countries risk being bypassed by this process of economic expansion. We know that most of the policy issues in which the UN is involved have become, or are now better understood to be, intersectoral or transsectoral in character. We know that information age technologies have transformed the temporal context of policymaking, putting a premium on agility and flexibility of any organization that operates within it. Finally, we know that the institutional context in which all international organizations now operate is much more densely populated by other international actors, both public and private, than it was in the past. Today intergovernmental organizations at all levels number in the thousands. The resources of several of these organizations far exceed those of the United Nations. Moreover, the expanding transnational network of nongovernmental organizations (NGOs) encompasses virtually every sector of public concern, from the environment and human rights to the provision of microcredit, and is active at virtually every level of social organization, from villages on up to global summits. And the private sector continues to expand transnationally.

These developments demand, first, that the UN focus within its overall Charter mission on those intersectoral activities, or on those aspects of activities, that it does better than others, and, second, that we devise effective means by which to collaborate with other international organizations and institutions of civil society, thereby amplifying the effect of its own moral, institutional, and material resources. In sum, the very organizational features that are now most demanded by the UN's external context in some respects are in shortest supply: strategic deployment of resources, unity of purpose, coherence of effort, agility and flexibility. The current reform effort aims at redressing this imbalance.

In January 1997, I took my first steps by reorganizing the management of the Secretariat's work program around the five areas that comprise the core missions of the United Nations: peace and security; economic and social affairs; development cooperation; humanitarian affairs; and human rights. This process involved all UN departments, programs, and funds. I established executive committees in the first four areas, designating human rights as a cross-cutting focus participating in each of the other four core groups. The conveners of the four executive committees along with several other senior officials have become the UN's Senior Management Group, which functions like a cabinet. While this may be standard operating procedure for most governments, the UN has never had such an arrangement before. The members of the Senior Management Group consult on work programs as well as other substantive and administrative matters of collective concern, to identify and exploit ways of pooling resources. In March 1997, I announced a further set of administrative and budgetary measures, integrating and rationalizing a number of departments.

It was in July 1997, however, that the main platform of the quiet revolution within the UN was laid out in a report to the General Assembly.[2] Some proposals, dealing primarily with the reorganization of the Secretariat's leadership and management structure, the consolidation of UN operations at the country level, and a thorough overhaul of human resources policies, were things I could do on my own initiative, although, of course, I was pleased when they were unanimously endorsed in November 1997.[3]

The second set of reforms complemented the first, but required General Assembly approval. That was given for most of the proposals in a ten-part resolution adopted without a vote in December 1997.[4] The Assembly established the post of deputy secretary-general to assist the secretary-general in managing the Secretariat's operations and to support me in ensuring intersectoral

2   *Renewing the United Nations: A Programme for Reform.* UN Doc. A/51/ 950, 14 July 1997, and Add 1–7.
3   UN Doc. A/RES/52/12, 12 November 1997.
4   UN Doc. A/52/L.72/Rev. 1, 19 December 1997.

and interinstitutional coherence of activities and programs, and in elevating the organization's profile and leadership in the economic and social spheres, including further efforts to strengthen the United Nations as a leading center for development policy and assistance. On 12 January 1998, Louise Fréchette of Canada was appointed to the position. In regard to economic and social affairs, the Assembly began a process that should lead to the rationalization of operations and to more predictable, continuous, and assured resources for development.

In the peace and security area, the Assembly began the work of rationalizing and streamlining agencies. It invited member states to improve the supply of information to the secretary-general that could assist the organization in preventing conflict. It recommended a procedure to the Security Council that would assure a status-of-forces agreement would be made in a timely manner between the United Nations and the host government for an operation. Relative to humanitarian affairs, the Assembly rationalized some responsibilities, established a humanitarian affairs segment of the Economic and Social Council (ECOSOC), and designated the emergency relief coordinator as the UN humanitarian assistance coordinator.

Regarding the financing of the organization, the Assembly asked me to submit detailed proposals for the possible establishment of a Revolving Credit Fund and took note of my recommendation that any unspent balances under the regular budget at the end of the fiscal period be retained. The Assembly decided to include a development account in the program budget for 1998/99, to be funded from reductions in administration and other overhead costs, and it continued to study my recommendation on initiating a review of the International Civil Service Commission (ICSC). Finally with regard to the second type of reform measures, the Assembly took note of my recommendation to shift UN program budgeting toward a system of results-based budgeting and asked me to submit a more detailed report; and the Assembly agreed to expedite its consideration of the draft code of conduct that I had submitted.

A third type of reform proposal deals with even more fundamental change and will require very serious consideration on longer deliberation by members. I have argued that member states should refocus the work of the General Assembly on issues of highest priority and should reduce the length of its sessions. I have called for a ministerial-level commission to examine the need for fundamental change through review of the UN Charter and the legal instruments from which the specialized agencies derive their constitutions. I have proposed transforming the Trusteeship Council into a forum through which member states exercise their collective trusteeship for guaranteeing the integrity of the global environment and common areas such as the oceans, atmosphere, and outer space. This reconstituted Trusteeship Council would serve to link the United Nations and civil society in addressing those areas of global concern that require the active contribution of public, private, and voluntary sectors. I also suggested that the session of the General Assembly to be held in the year 2000 be designated as "a Millennium Assembly" to focus on preparing the UN to meet the major challenges and needs of the world community in the twenty-first century. It would be accompanied by a companion people's assembly, the "Millennium Forum," a model, perhaps, for subsequent linked topically focused sessions of a Trusteeship Council-based forum and the General Assembly. The last General Assembly asked for more details about these proposals, which I provided in a March 1998 report.

These actions and the extensive deliberations that preceded and have followed them, as well as the Assembly's consideration of its own reform proposals emanating from the five working groups that it set up in 1992, highlight the extent to which reform is an ongoing process. The mind-set of reform is the mind-set of good governance. It should become an essential part of the way we do business. However, no matter how vital reform is for our future, we must remember that "reform" is not an abstract end in itself. It should facilitate, not eclipse, our substantive work. We should not allow the process to obscure the broader picture—our work to promote human security and peace. That is what the world's people demand of us; not that we become eternally inward looking. Organizational self-obsession on reform is unhealthy, not to mention uncaring. Reform should be outward looking. The reform process is about enhancing and ensuring the capacity of the world organization to respond effectively to the challenges to human security.

3   A New UN for the New Century: Creating Effective Partnerships
       with Civil Society

A prerequisite for the ultimate success of the quiet revolution within the UN is a unity of purpose within the world organization and the larger system of international agencies of which it is a central part. The UN's five core missions—peace and security, economic and social affairs, development cooperation, humanitarian affairs, and human rights—must have an unambiguous unifying focus that forges coherence among them. That unifying focus, of course, must be grounded in the primary raison d'être of the world organization: the promotion and maintenance of peace and security.

As the global order has transformed over the last half century, however, so too has the meaning of peace and security. Peace has come to be viewed as meaning much more than the absence of armed conflict, and security has been transformed to encompass the broad notion of human security. To respond effectively and creatively to the challenges of the twenty-first century, the UN must stress the security of people, not just the security of states. As stated in the 1993 UNDP *Human Development Report*, "The concept of security must change from an exclusive stress on national security to a much greater stress on people's security, from security through armaments to security through human development, from territorial security to food, employment, and environmental security."[5] It is a phenomenon that encompasses sustainable human development, social justice, environmental protection, democratization, disarmament, and respect for human rights. These elements constitute the pillars of peace and are inseparable from human security. Human security requires democratic rule, respect for human rights, and sustainable development.

To take root, sustainable development requires an enabling environment for economic growth and prosperity. It also requires major policy initiatives at the national level. Democratization and the rule of law, including respect for human rights, are indispensable. Good domestic governance is essential. Getting economic fundamentals right is axiomatic, but sustainable development requires more. It needs to provide all members of society with access to development opportunities. It must ensure that the property of the farmer, the shop owner, and the manufacturer is secure. It requires that education be prized, health care provided. It implies that renewable resources be managed, not depleted. Part of the role of the state is to support the provision of good health services and educational opportunities for its citizens either directly or by coordinating its provision by the private sector or by the institutions of civil society. Education is vital. Knowledge and skills will be the driving force in development in the twenty-first century. It is becoming clear that in today's world knowledge and skills are the decisive factors in giving countries or corporations their competitive edge.

A recent World Bank study found that close to 65 percent of growth can be attributed, not to natural resources, finance, or infrastructure, but to human and social capital. Increasingly, major corporations are investing heavily in the human and social capital of their organizations. They are thinking in terms of structures and policies that can attract, retain, develop, motivate, and make effective use of high-caliber staff. Top managers are discovering the importance of their organizations' knowledge base. Old-style centralized management styles are giving way to more collegial forms of management.

---

5   UNDP, *Human Development Report 1993* (New York: Oxford University Press, 1993), p. 2.

There is a lesson here for the UN. As soon as we identify the larger goal of the United Nations as human security requiring a sustainable form of development, we begin to recognize the connection between our own processes of reform and the larger forces to which we seek to respond. The UN is becoming more collegial and more attentive to the formation of its own "human capital" in recognition that we must match our means to our ends. To do so requires the humbling recognition that the UN can do little by itself to achieve its aims. In fact, we must accept the perhaps even more humbling recognition that even UN member governments can do little by themselves as well.

In part, this is due to the emergence and proliferation of nonstate actors who have a growing influence on global governance, many of whom, in their own way, are taking part in the larger quiet revolution of good governance. The UN has been responding accordingly. NGOs have traditionally been the most visible manifestation in multilateral relations of what is referred to as "civil society," that is, the sphere in which social movements organize themselves around objectives, constituencies, and thematic interests. These movements include specific groups such as women, youth, and indigenous people. More recently, however, other actors have also taken on an increasingly important role in shaping national and international agendas. They include local authorities, mass media, business and industry, professional associations, religious and cultural organizations, and the intellectual and research communities.

The emergence or, in several parts of the world, the reemergence of civil society is linked to two interlocking processes: the quest for a more democratic, transparent, accountable, and enabling governance and the increasing preponderance of market-based approaches to national and global economic management. These processes have resulted in redefining the role of the state and vested new and broader responsibilities in market and civil society actors in the pursuit of growth and well-being. In this overall context, a vibrant civil society is critical to processes of democratization and empowerment.

Here my focus is more on the groups that provide public participation in world events, especially, for example, at the major conferences convened by the United Nations in the 1990s, where the concept of "international civil society" has acquired true meaning, with tens of thousands of organizations from around the world being involved in the identification of priorities and issues and avenues for addressing them. No area of UN involvement, either at the policy or operational level, has been left unchanged by this process. Overall, civil society's increasing influence is contributing to a process of enlargement of international cooperation and spurring the UN system and other intergovernmental structures toward greater transparency and accountability and closer linkages between national and international levels of decisionmaking and implementing.

NGOs and other civil society actors are now perceived not only as disseminators of information or providers of services but also as shapers of policy, be it in peace and security matters, in development, or in humanitarian affairs. The involvement of NGOs and other actors, such as parliamentarians, local authorities, and business leaders, in the UN global conferences demonstrates this. It would now be difficult to imagine organizing a global event and formulating multilateral agreements and declarations without the active participation of NGOs. In fact, NGOs are often on the ground before the international community gives the UN the mandate to act.

NGOs are thus particularly crucial in preventive diplomacy, humanitarian work, development, and human rights. The relationship is complementary, as in the best human relationships. Each contributes something unique, producing a result that is greater than the sum of its parts. It is a relationship based on trust, because partnership is both a privilege and a responsibility.

In a vast range of activities, the United Nations and NGOs are now also *operational* partners. Let me give some examples. In mine-clearance efforts in Afghanistan, the UN has been working with six Afghan NGOs, one international NGO, and a relief agency from the Islamic Republic of Iran. We are engaged in a new dialogue with the private sector. An exchange of expertise, knowledge, advice, and data is under way. Nongovernmental organizations dealing with human rights have been essential partners with the United Nations in the rebuilding of civil society after conflict in such countries as Cambodia, El Salvador, and Guatemala. The involvement of local government leaders, of mayors, and of officials of provincial administrations from many countries has been vital in UN programs on governance. There is an important ongoing dialogue with them. The crucial importance of elected parliamentarians as partners in the realization of our common goals has been recognized by the close relationship now established between the United Nations and the Inter-Parliamentary Union.

Of particular importance is the relationship of the United Nations and the organizations of the UN system with the business community. The impact of the private sector, in both developing and developed countries, is of growing importance; and it would be timely to develop better means of consultation between the UN and the business community. Such consultations would enable the concerns and interests of both sides to be more fully understood. The International Chamber of Commerce and the World Economic Forum have both taken the initiative to establish mechanisms for this purpose, a move I applaud.

One of my major priorities as secretary-general has been to establish a new partnership for development between the United Nations and the private sector. I see such a partnership as involving a joint program of cooperation with governmental and nongovernmental organizations, in both the developing and the transitional economies. The aim will be to bring more of the world's poor into the expanding zone of opportunity, by increasing the conditions for domestic and international investment, job creation, and people-driven and people-centered development. I see the partnership as working in the following fields: twinning companies in developed and developing countries to undertake joint public concern initiatives, such as training, technological development, and environmental conservation; helping to develop financial markets, including appropriate regulatory frameworks; strengthening national and provincial chambers of commerce and industry, patent offices, technology parks, business incubators, and other private-sector support institutions; developing market-based incentives for environmental management; supporting international and regional institutions for promotion of business; supporting nongovernmental and other community-based nonprofit organizations; and providing physical infrastructure.

Some will say that emphasizing the importance of the private sector means neglecting the millions in developing countries who lack capital. It is true that for millions of people with meager resources, obtaining credit is either fraught with danger or simply impossible—the money lenders and their exorbitant charges are prohibitive. But new ways are being devised for ordinary, poor people to have access to credit on affordable terms. The microcredit movement is a new way of empowering women, especially rural women. It is rising to the challenge of extending small loans to people who lack collateral and a credit history.

These partnerships with diverse elements of civil society are more necessary than ever as the world faces a daunting agenda of global challenges. Such partnerships are vital because we face new enemies, especially the forces of "uncivil society." They are the enemies of civil society. These new global enemies include drug traffickers, gunrunners, the exploiters of young people for prostitution, and fraudulent currency dealers. They all move in the netherworld between state sovereignty and international cooperation. They are part of the dark side of the process of globalization. To combat them, international civil society must be mobilized to support human security and sustainable human development.

4   Toward a Global Partnership with the Academy

For all the reasons mentioned above, and as an essential part of reforming the UN, the organization needs to review and update the ways in which it interacts with civil society, as it seeks to serve both the governments and the peoples of the world. One of the most important relationships is the one the UN has with members of the global academic community. The ideas and research findings and methods of scholars from nearly all disciplines have, of course, been incorporated into the substantive work of UN agencies since their inception. That interactive process, however, has tended to be narrowly compartmentalized along disciplinary and sectoral lines. Far too seldom has integrative, holistic thinking capable of bringing the larger picture of global governance and intersectoral linkages been brought to bear on dealing with specific issues and problems.

The new United Nations of the twenty-first century cannot afford to perpetuate such narrow nonintegrative thinking and approaches. The global environment is too complex and interdependent. The challenges and demands are too great. Institutional resources and capacities are too limited.

The conceptualization of human security as the unifying concept in the UN, the acknowledgment of the central role of sustainable human development in providing that security, the redefinitions of the state and of international cooperation to good governance, and the imperative of building partnerships with "civil society" all call for a rethinking of multilateralism and global governance. New patterns of multilateralism are, of course, continuously evolving, and multilateral agencies are involved in a wide variety of ways with diverse elements of civil society. However, little systematic knowledge exists about such relationships, their nature, scope, origins, costs, benefits, and other implications. If we are to bring out managed change for improving the effectiveness of multilateral institutions as mechanisms for global governance, a more systematic and comprehensive understanding of such phenomena is required. The need is clear and critical.

It is precisely for this reason that an expanded partnership between the United Nations and students of international organization and global governance is needed now more than ever. Over the past decade, great strides have been made in linking and stimulating a continuing dialogue between practitioners and students of multilateralism. Some of the success for this special partnership is due to the activities of the Academic Council on the United Nations System (ACUNS), of which I am proud to have been a member since its very beginning. Through ACUNS and its numerous programs, conferences, fellowships, publications, and other activities, scholarly interest and research in multilateralism and international organization has been revitalized. An academic subject that a few prominent scholars two decades ago had pronounced as being dead is again alive and well.

It is now time, I believe, to expand ACUNS-like activities to every region of the world. A main goal would be to establish a constructive partnership between academia and the UN system for producing new knowledge about how to build and sustain effective international organization—"civil society" partnerships for promoting human security. Reliance on existing institutional mechanisms within the organization, like the UNU which acts as a bridge between policymakers, the international academic community, and the UN, would be important. Special emphasis might be placed on linking scholars in remote locations to larger regional and global intellectual and professional communities as well as with UN agencies and staff. There is an important need to build and nurture interdisciplinary research networks among international organization scholars from different nationalities, cultures, professions, and disciplines, with a particular focus on young scholars and professionals from regions with emergent or reemergent civil societies. Moreover, to the extent possible and practicable without undermining international civil service provisions, it is important to provide opportunities for those young scholars to gain firsthand experience in the operations of UN agencies through a program of fellowships as well as through direct involvement in ongoing research activities in UN agencies.

Good policies and effective programs must be built on sound knowledge and good models. There is much to be known and scholars could be very helpful in providing new knowledge about the dynamics of global governance, especially as related to the evolving global discourse and practice over human security, the dynamic interplay of agents and forces that threaten or degrade human security, and ways that multilateral institutions might better promote security. Furthermore, scholars could assist in producing new knowledge about what international institutions have done and are currently doing to promote partnerships with diverse elements of international civil society. It would be welcome, for example, to have a comprehensive, comparative picture of the way in which various groups within international civil society have gone about influencing and working with the entire UN family. Scholars could also assist in identifying institutional reforms that would be needed to enhance multilateral institutions' capabilities for facilitating the development of open societies and promoting human security as well as the initiatives that are necessary, sufficient, and politically plausible for stimulating and bringing about such managed institutional change.

There is a great deal of experience of NGOs working with the UN system to promote human security. In some fields this seems to have been more successful than in others. We know from the 1995 *Human Development Report*, for example, that gender inequality is diminishing, that democratization is increasing, and that the range of environmental international governance is increasing. We also know that there are some similarities between the ways in which women's groups, environmental NGOs, and democratizing/human rights NGOs work with each other and with the UN. But there are differences as well. There has been less success, for example, in achieving quality across occupational lines; in fact, such inequality is growing and the social services sectors are somewhat weak. We know that labor groups and employers groups do not organize in the same ways and do not yet cooperate as successfully within the UN system. It would be useful if scholars could study such questions and propose better ways for collaboration among UN agencies, NGOs, the private sector, and the local public sector, based on the best practices revealed by recent history.

In sum, the importance of UN partnerships with academia cannot be overemphasized. As we approach the new century, the international community has some way to go to realize the hopes and commitments of the UN Charter. But the UN as "they" cannot do it alone. "We the Peoples of the United Nations" means just that: global governance for the twenty-first century is a truly collective enterprise, one in which effective partnerships with academia and other important elements of society are likely to make all the difference. But, as secretary-general, I have every confidence that we will succeed. When we measure our progress against the state of the world a century ago, we can only be impressed by how far we have come. Indeed, one of the most significant differences between that fin de siècle and this is precisely the more robust and more universal set of international organizations that now exist to remind, and enable, the world to do better. That is why it is our solemn and historic obligation to make the United Nations the most effective instrument possible for the achievement of peace and progress for our children, and for theirs.

CHAPTER 5*

Good Governance in International Organizations

Ngaire Woods[1]

Good governance moved onto the agenda of many international organizations at the end of the Cold War when calls for democracy and better government became louder and as expectations were heightened as to what international organizations might do to further this aim. Many multilateral agencies—from the UN to multilateral development banks—took up the summons. They are now part of a chorus of voices urging governments across the world to heed higher standards of democratic representation, accountability, and transparency.

Much more slowly, multilateral organizations have begun to question what *good governance* means for the way in which they themselves are structured and in which they make and implement decisions. They have been very slow to set down a standard for themselves—and there is little precedent in the international system for doing so. To quote former UN Secretary-General Boutros Boutros-Ghali: "Democracy has not featured in the history of the international system of states. Sovereignty, rather than democracy, has been its guiding principle…. [Today,] the democratization of the international system can be seen as both necessary and possible."[2]

Yet if international organizations are going to become more participatory, accountable, and transparent, what standards are relevant to them? In this article, I set out to provide one part of an answer to this question, primarily probing what good governance means for relations among states in multilateral organizations. The first section of the article explores the concept of good governance, how it has emerged, and what its core principles mean. I draw a distinction between applying principles of good governance

---

* This chapter was originally published in Global Governance, Volume 5, Issue 1, 1999.

1 Ngaire Woods is dean of the Blavatnik School of Government and professor of Global Economic Governance at Oxford University. Her recent publications include *The Globalizers: the IMF, the World Bank, and their Borrowers* (Cornell University Press 2006), *Inequality, Globalization and World Politics* (Oxford University Press, 1999), *Explaining International Relations Since 1945* (Oxford University Press, 1996), and several articles on the international financial institutions.

2 Boutros Boutros-Ghali, "Democracy: A Newly Recognized Imperative," *Global Governance* 1, no. 1 (winter 1995): 3–11.

to relations among states within international organizations (*international governance*) and applying the principles more broadly to links between individuals, peoples, groups, and international organizations (*global governance*). My emphasis in the following sections is on international governance. I have chosen several institutions to illustrate the tensions and trade-offs. These include the regional development banks, the UN Security Council, the General Agreement on Tariffs and Trade (GATT) and World Trade Organization (WTO), the International Fund for Agricultural Development, the Global Environment Facility of the UN Development Programme/World Bank, and the European Union.[3] By looking at the actual practices of organizations, I highlight existing problems of governance and the scope for improvement even among interstate relations. In the conclusion, I relate the article's findings on international governance to the broader questions and issues raised by global governance.

1   The Emergence of the Good Governance Agenda

Scholars and practitioners of development expressed real concern at the end of the 1980s about the failure of structural adjustment and the failure of so many countries to reap the fruits of a decade of stringent reforms.[4] By the early 1990s, the answer widely agreed on was that countries taking on reforms simply did not have adequate institutional depth and capacity.[5] This finding coincided with a renewed interest in institutions flourishing in the social sciences—from Nobel Prize-winning economists to international relations experts.[6] Furthermore, the concern with institutions and governance emerged amid increasing worldwide interest in democracy and democratization in

---

3   Here the article draws on research completed for the Group of Twenty-Four and published as Ngaire Woods, "Governance in International Organizations: The Case for Reform in the Bretton Woods Institutions," in UNCTAD/Group of Twenty-Four, *International Monetary and Financial Issues for the 1990s*, vol. 9 (Geneva: United Nations, 1998).

4   Joan M. Nelson, ed., *Economic Crisis and Policy Choice: The Politics of Adjustment in the Third World* (Princeton: Princeton University Press, 1990).

5   M. Dos Santos and M. Natalicchio, *Democratización, ajuste y gobernabilidad en América Latina: Una guía analítica y documental* (Buenos Aires: IDIN/CLASCO, 1993); Joan Nelson, ed., *Intricate Links: Democratization and Market Reforms in Latin America and Eastern Europe* (Washington, D.C.: Overseas Development Council, 1994).

6   Douglass North, *Institutions, Institutional Change and Economic Performance* (New York: Cambridge University Press, 1990); Robert Keohane, *International Institutions and State Power* (Boulder: Westview, 1989); John Mearsheimer, "The False Promise of International Institutions," *International Security* 19, no. 3 (1995): 5–49; Robert Keohane and Lisa Martin, "The Promise of Institutionalist Theory," *International Security* 20, no. 1 (1995): 39–51.

the wake of the end of the Cold War.[7] It is not surprising that scholars and practitioners started to see good governance not just as a necessary condition for effective reforms but also as fitting with a new rhetoric about democratic participation and accountability. Against this background, a whole new literature and set of prescriptions about good governance were unleashed.

In some agencies, the new idea of governance or good governance, borrowing from U.S. corporate language, came simply to mean good quality management.[8] This narrow definition of governance envisages limiting the role of the state while ensuring it provides the necessary framework of policy and institutions for markets to flourish. Institutions, in this view, exist to iron out imperfections in the marketplace and to provide a limited range of what economists define as *public goods*. A slightly broader version of this definition emphasizes the need to strengthen the "institutional capacity of the state" through the enhancement of autonomy, efficiency, rationality, and training.[9]

An alternative understanding of good governance links institutions and society with a wider conception of government. Within this broader view, governance is concerned, as Oran Young defines it, with the "establishment and operation of ... the rules of the game that serve to define social practices, assign roles, and guide interactions."[10] In order to understand this broader notion of governance, scholars are now drawing on political and sociological literature about the conditions and institutions needed to represent and mediate the vast and competing array of interests in any society.[11] At the same time, international institutions such as the World Bank and agencies of the UN are

---

7   Larry Diamond, *Promoting Democracy in the 1990s: Actors, Instruments, Issues and Imperatives* (New York: Carnegie, 1995); Doll Chull Shin, "On the Third Wave of Democratization: A Synthesis and Evaluation of Recent Theory and Research," *World Politics* 47, no. 1 (1994): 135–170.

8   IMF, *Good Governance: The IMF's Role* (Washington, D.C.; IMF, 1997); Edgardo Boeninger, "Governance and Development: Issues and Constraints," *Proceedings of the World Bank Annual Conference on Development Economics* (Washington, D.C.: World Bank, 1991).

9   P. Landell-Mills and I. Serageldin, "Governance and the External Factor," *Proceedings of the World Bank Annual Conference on Development Economics* (Washington, D.C.: World Bank, 1991); A. Israel, "The Changing Role of the State: Institutional Dimensions," PPR Working Papers WPS 495 (Washington, D.C.: World Bank, 1990).

10   Oran Young, *International Governance: Protecting the Environment in a Stateless Society* (Ithaca, N.Y.: Cornell University Press, 1994), p. 15.

11   Leila Frischtak, "Governance Capacity and Economic Reform in Developing Countries," World Bank Technical Paper no. 254 (Washington, D.C.: World Bank, 1994); Fernando Calderón, "Governance, Competitiveness and Social Integration," *CEPAL Review* (December 1995): 45–46; G. Hyden, "Creating an Enabling Environment" and "The Changing Context of Institutional Development in Sub-Saharan Africa," in *The Long-Term Perspective Study of Sub-Saharan Africa: Institutional and Socio-political Issues*, vol. 3 (Washington, D.C.: World Bank, 1990).

deriving a checklist of factors that, in their experience, are useful indicators of good governance. These factors include key principles such as participation, accountability, and fairness (on which I elaborate below).[12]

Surprisingly few attempts have been made during the same period to link the emerging literature about good governance and institutions in a specific way to international organizations.[13] Yet the time is ripe for such a linkage. International institutions are besieged with new problems arising from both globalization and the impact of the end of the Cold War. The recent financial crisis in East Asia, the humanitarian and security crisis around the Great Lakes of Africa, and the problems of climate change and ozone depletion are but a few of these problems.

In dealing with new issues, international organizations are being challenged in terms both of their legitimacy and their effectiveness. This challenge takes two forms. At the global level, institutions are being challenged by nonstate actors and domestic lobbies—raising broad issues of global democracy. The good governance agenda translates into questions about the very foundations of world order and the place of sovereignty within it.[14] At a more modest level, the legitimacy of international institutions is being contested by states who feel inadequately consulted or represented within organizations. The old hierarchy of states within multilateral forums is being challenged and their effectiveness and legitimacy questioned by smaller or weaker states. Here, the good governance agenda can be applied to prescribe greater participation, accountability, and fairness among states within organizations.

Applying good governance to arrangements among states in international organizations may seem a rather old-fashioned idea. Indeed, in the 1980s and in the early 1990s, scholars began a full-fledged assault on state-centered international politics based on sovereignty. Since that time, new rationales for intervention and expanded conditionalities have been opened up,[15] the increased participation of nongovernmental organizations (NGOs) has been encouraged,

---

12   World Bank, *Governance and Development* (Washington, D.C.: World Bank, 1992); World Bank, *Governance: The World Bank's Experience* (Washington, D.C.: World Bank, 1994); United Nations Development Programme, *Human Development Report* (New York: UNDP, 1993).

13   The clearest attempt is probably Commission on Global Governance, *Our Global Neighbourhood* (Oxford: Oxford University Press, 1995).

14   For example, Meghnad Desai and Paul Redfern, eds., *Global Governance: Ethics and Economics of the World Order* (London: Pinter, 1995); Daniele Archibugi and David Held, *Cosmopolitan Democracy: An Agenda for a New World Order* (Cambridge, England: Polity Press, 1995).

15   Devesh Kapur, "The New Conditionalities of the International Financial Institutions," in UNCTAD, *International Monetary and Financial Issues for the 1990s*, vol. 8 (Geneva: United Nations, 1997).

and concepts of "global civil society" have been developed.[16] There has been a tendency, in other words, to move away from the older, more state-centered views of international relations and toward a more global approach. This new approach has made an important contribution to thinking about democracy at the global level. As regards international organizations, however, the tendency to dismiss sovereignty as anachronistic and illegitimate needs a further rethinking.

At the end of the 1990s, many states participating in international forums have undergone or are undergoing democratization. As these states become more democratic, so too their claims to being the legitimate representatives of people are bolstered. For international organizations, this means that *the state* remains an important—if no longer exclusive—way to represent people all over the world. At the same time, however, the principles on which power and influence are distributed among states within institutions need to be rethought.

2   State-Centered Organizations and Good Governance

The effectiveness of international organizations has for a long time been presumed to derive from the commitment and actions of their most powerful members. In other words, institutions are effective so long as they reflect the hierarchy of power among states.[17] This assumption underpinned the organization of both the League of Nations (in which the most powerful took up permanent seats in the executive—the Council) and the UN Security Council (in which the Permanent Five members enjoy what amounts to a veto on all substantive issues). Likewise, in earlier international organizations, voting power was determined purely by financial contributions, ensuring that the most economically powerful members would prevail. This was the case in the International Telegraphic Union established in 1865 and, subsequently, in the Universal Postal Union, the International Wine Office, and the International Institute of Agriculture, all of which were created by 1914.

In the second half of the twentieth century, however, questions of legitimacy began more strongly to influence the core structure of international

---

16   L. MacDonald, "Globalizing Civil Society: Interpreting International NGOs in Central America," *Millennium—Journal of International Studies* 23 (1994): 267–285; Peter Evans, "The Eclipse of the State? Reflections on Stateness in an Era of Globalization," *World Politics* 50 (1997): 62ff; S. Turner, "Global Civil Society, Anarchy and Governance: Assessing an Emerging Paradigm," *Journal of Peace Research* 35 (1998): 25–42.

17   Robert Tucker, *The Inequality of Nations* (London: Martin Robertson, 1977).

organizations. In the first place, equality among states has developed as an important principle that borrows from ideas about equality and the "rights of man."[18] By analogy, individual states should be treated as equal members of international society. And further bolstering this argument is the view that we should respect the sovereign equality of states because each is a unit within which humans can express political rights and consent to be governed. The principle of equality has been applied in many organizations that have accorded every state an equal vote, such as the GATT, its successor the WTO, and the UN General Assembly. The principle has also underpinned the alloca-tion of an equal number of basic votes to otherwise unequal members in the International Monetary Fund (IMF) and the World Bank.[19]

However, for most of this century, equality among states has been recognized only in formal rights of representation. In reality, in the name of effectiveness, these formal rights have given way to structures that reflect the hierarchy of power among states. Yet today, for practical reasons, this top-down, hierarchi-cal vision of management is being reevaluated.[20] Certainly in the short term, effectiveness requires that an institution be able to make the relevant or neces-sary decisions, to muster the necessary resources and capabilities, and to apply resources to implementing and enforcing decisions. And these qualities can all be met by the most powerful states running an organization. However, effec-tiveness in the longer term requires more.

The long-term effectiveness of an institution requires agreement among members about rules, identity, and decisionmaking. Scholars working on the effectiveness of institutions point out that an institution must be able to show that it can fulfill its allotted role and thereby prove to its members that it is necessary. It needs an ongoing raison d'être that is recognized by the mem-bership. It needs a coherent underlying system of ideas for defining problems and their solutions, a system that members perceive as valid. And it needs a capacity to absorb new systems of ideas when its own are seen to be failing.[21] An effective institution must also be able to retain its identity while adapting

---

18   Bengt Broms, "The Doctrine of Equality of States as Applied in International Organiza-
      tions" (Ph.D. diss., University of Helsinki, 1959).

19   Joseph Gold, *Voting and Decisions in the International Monetary Fund* (Washington, D.C.:
      IMF, 1972), p. 18; William N. Gianaris, "Weighted Voting in the International Monetary
      Fund and the World Bank," *Fordham International Law Journal* 14 (1990–1991): 919.

20   Ngaire Woods, "Inequality, Globalization and Order," in Andrew Hurrell and Ngaire
      Woods, eds., *Inequality, Globalization and World Politics* (Oxford: Oxford University Press,
      1999).

21   See Oran Young, "The Effectiveness of International Institutions: Hard Cases and Critical
      Variables," in James Rosenau and Ernst-Otto Cziempel, *Governance Without Government:
      Order and Change in World Politics* (Cambridge: Cambridge University Press, 1992).

to change, so that it can plan overall strategic directions and policy choices in conditions of stress and change yet at the same time ensure, through rigid transformation rules, that it retains its character and status.[22] Furthermore, organizations need procedures to determine policies that the membership can and will implement.

More profoundly, it has been argued that for an institution to be effective, a symmetry of power must exist within the institution because it is unlikely to endure over time if powerful states or groups of states can simply flout the rules. As one academic argues, "the more symmetrical the distribution of power, the harder it is to establish institutional arrangements initially but the more effective they are once formed."[23]

These longer-term considerations of effectiveness require a more active and participatory membership than the traditional hierarchical vision, and herein lies a powerful reason for applying lessons of good governance to international institutions. The core lessons of good governance, as defined by multilateral organizations, include three often overlapping principles: participation, accountability, and fairness. Below, I discuss each principle in turn.

3   Core Principles of Good Governance

Participation has become a core issue not just because of the attractiveness of the idea in an era of democratization.[24] There are powerful practical reasons for an increased emphasis on participation. For example, the World Bank has found that projects are more successful where those most affected by the particular project participate directly in its design and operation.[25] The logic is that participation in decisionmaking and implementation gives people a sense of *ownership* in a project and a very real stake in its success. Yet applying this principle is not easy. On the one hand, it may be desirable to empower locals in this way; on the other hand, organizations need to control their operations spread all over the world. As a result, participation is often rendered in a watered-down form, as described by two analysts from the World Bank:

---

22   Ian D. Clark, "Should the IMF Become More Adaptive?" IMF Working Paper WP/96/17 (Washington, D.C.: IMF, 1996).

23   Oran Young, *International Governance*, p. 15.

24   UNDP, *Human Development Report*, declares that—in an era of democratic transitions in developing and formerly socialist countries—"people's participation is becoming the central issue of our time" (p. 1).

25   World Bank, *The World Bank Participation Source Book* (Washington, D.C.: World Bank, 1996).

Participation has often been equated with explaining the project to key stakeholders (individuals and groups who stand to gain or lose from the project), instead of involving them in decision-making. Borrowers are not committed to project goals. Their ownership has been sought by making them responsible for preparation and implementation, instead of ensuring that the impetus for the project is local and that the process provides explicit opportunities for consensus building.[26]

Participation requires more than involvement in an institution. It requires that affected parties have access to decisionmaking and power so that they acquire a meaningful stake in the work of the institution. In other words, affected parties must come to see the decisions of the institution as their own decisions—the success or failure of which relies on their actions. This is what is meant by the term *ownership*, or references to owning particular policies. The next section examines problems in ensuring ownership and participation in international organizations through formal structures of voting and funding, using regional development banks to illustrate how formal control of decisionmaking structures does not necessarily lead to the kind of participation and ownership I describe above.

A second and equally important way of binding members to an institution is to ensure appropriate lines or forms of *accountability*. In the narrow sense of the term, accountability requires that institutions inform their members of decisions and also of the grounds on which decisions are taken. Practically, this means having procedures that ensure transparency and flows of information. As will be seen later in this article, even this narrowly defined requirement is not yet met in many international organizations. However, there is a further, deeper meaning to accountability.

Institutions make decisions on behalf of or for other actors, be they states, regions, or individuals. Accountability requires clarity about for whom or on whose behalf the institution is making and implementing decisions. Furthermore, it demands clarity about who has the power to limit or sanction the institution's work. If organizations were simply run "by the most powerful, for the most powerful," lines of accountability would be easy to draw. Today, however, the demands of effectiveness require less obvious hierarchy, and principles of democracy demand a rethinking about to whom institutions are accountable. For example, where an organization is to be accountable to its member states, decisions need to be made about how the accountability (such

---

26   Robert Piciotto and Rachel Weaving, "A New Project Cycle for the World Bank?" *Finance and Development* 3, no. 4 (December 1994): 42–44.

as through voting or representation) should be apportioned: by economic weight or some other contribution to the institution; by population size so as to be more democratic; or according to which members are most affected by policies. These questions are now being posed in most international organizations. Furthermore, international institutions are increasingly being called to account for their actions not only by their member states but by NGOs, individuals, and other nonstate actors.

Nongovernmental organizations pose a challenge to the accountability of multilateral organizations. The latter are created and formally accountable to their members, who are states. Yet NGOs argue that states are merely vehicles for representing people and that in fact institutions are accountable to people. Hence, NGOs claim their right to represent people and issues that states are neglecting and to hold international organizations accountable to NGO constituencies and issues. Here, undoubtedly, some NGOs have done some excellent work, empowering otherwise marginalized people, promoting participation, and forcing governments and international organizations to be more accountable to some of the most powerless groups that they affect.[27] However, there are serious issues about good governance and accountability that are raised by the claims of NGOs.

There is a tendency in much of the existing literature to assume that most NGOs act in the above-described optimal manner.[28] Yet NGOs are a vast and largely unregulated spectrum of organizations—some legitimate, some self-serving and corrupt. For this reason, within the framework of good governance, NGOs themselves need to be subjected to standards of accountability and good governance. Accountability, for example, has often meant NGOs working in developing countries being answerable to donors in the industrialized countries.[29] Yet good governance surely requires that these NGOs become accountable to those most affected by their work and on whose behalf they are advancing claims. If not, NGOs might themselves be accused of falling into the same hierarchical structures of governance as the institutions they accuse of lacking accountability.

A further problem arising from the participation of NGOs is that they act for particular constituencies and in relation to particular issues. This is acceptable as a second-best solution where, as I mention above, NGOs give voice to

---

27   See the discussion in UNDP, *Human Development Report*, in note 23.

28   Ibid. Other arguments for extending the role of NGOs in international organizations include Robert Housman, "Democratizing International Trade Decision-Making," *Cornell International Law Journal* 27 (1994): 699–754; Thomas Weiss and Leon Gordenker, *NGOs, the United Nations and Global Governance* (Boulder: Lynne Rienner, 1996).

29   David Hulme and Michael Edwards, *NGOs, States and Donors: Too Close for Comfort?* (London: Macmillan, 1997).

marginalized and disempowered people, neglected by the state. It is second best in the sense that it substitutes for the imperfect way in which states represent their own peoples. However, even if they are accountable to their own particular constituencies, NGOs are not being subjected to a scrutiny that distinguishes those fulfilling this second-best solution from those engaged in special pleading and rent seeking for already powerful groups. Hence, rather than ensuring good governance, unregulated NGOs risk distorting the accountability of international organizations, skewing their responsibility yet further away from principles of good governance and toward an unevenly selected set of groups or issues.

In the sections below, problems of accountability will be examined in the context of particular structures and decisionmaking processes within organizations. It will be seen that accountability needs to reflect not just in formal representation but equally in decisionmaking procedures and rules and also in the implementation of decisions. Surprisingly, where consensus decisionmaking has been adopted in organizations, often on the grounds that it would ensure greater participation of all parties, in practice it has often reduced accountability. By contrast, carefully constructed voting requirements might enhance accountability.

Finally, a third principle of good governance is *fairness*, which has two aspects: procedural and substantive. Procedural fairness is a legalistic notion requiring that rules and standards be created and enforced in an impartial and predictable way. In other words, procedural fairness requires the processes of representation, decisionmaking, and enforcement in an institution to be clearly specified, nondiscretionary, and internally consistent. All members should be able to understand and predict the processes by which an institution will take decisions and apply them. Such requirements bolster those of transparency and accountability discussed above. Yet, as will be seen below, in existing international organizations, procedural fairness is often circumvented by procedures that privilege informal meetings and decisionmaking.

A more stringent requirement of fairness is substantive fairness, which concerns a more contested terrain. Here, fairness refers both to how equitable the outcomes of an institution are and to general equality and the distribution of power, influence, and resources within an organization. Although during the 1970s, debates about the structure of international organizations drew heavily on arguments about fairness and equality, in the 1990s, many aspects of substantive fairness lie beyond the ambit of good governance.[30] However, some elements are in fact implicit in the principles of participation and accountability

---

30   Independent (Brandt) Commission, *North-South: A Programme for Survival* (London: Pan Books, 1989).

already discussed. That is to say, for reasons of effectiveness and democracy, more equality of treatment, wider participation, and greater access to decisionmaking are all now on the agenda of international organizations.

Overall, in this section I have outlined the principles of participation, accountability, and fairness. In the sections below, I examine practical aspects of applying these principles to institutions. In the first place, I use the experience of regional development banks to illustrate some of the pitfalls of trying to achieve participation or ownership through formal representation, voting, or control of an institution. In the second place, I address the issues of accountability and fairness in decisionmaking, invoking the experiences of the UN Security Council and the GATT to illustrate the way the dominant consensus mode of decisionmaking can preclude accountability within an institution. Subsequently, I analyze different ways of distributing votes and voting requirements within institutions so as to reflect the various stakes of members within the institution and promote good governance. This latter section draws respectively on the experience of the International Fund for Agricultural Development and the Global Environment Facility. Finally, I examine the experience of the European Union to open up and contrast issues of global governance that are not addressed in the previous sections.

4   Participation, Ownership, and the Limits of Formal Control

More than three decades ago, regional development banks were created to work alongside the multilateral development banks such as the World Bank. For example, the Inter-American Development Bank (IDB) was established in 1959 and the African Development Bank (AfDB) in 1966. These agencies were structured so as to ensure that developing countries in each region would feel that the institutions were their own and take responsibility for their policies—ownership, in the jargon. The regional development banks would give countries more of a voice in matters of development assistance and provide a forum for more solidarity and cooperation among members. It was assumed that these aims could be met by ensuring that developing countries from each region had a controlling share of votes, of capital, and over staffing within their respective organization. Yet the subsequent experience of these institutions has been mixed and poses a sharp question as to how it is that real ownership—as opposed to formal control—by a particular group can in fact be ensured in an institution.

The Inter-American Development Bank was deliberately structured to ensure a strong regional character and a responsiveness to Latin American needs. For this reason, the bank's regional members hold a majority of its capital and votes; its president is always from South America or Central America; and until 1972, only members of the Organization of American States could apply for membership in the bank. As a result of its structure, the bank is said to be more in touch with the region than other multilateral funding agencies, and it has a greater presence there in the form of field offices (although it has been criticized for underutilizing them).[31] Furthermore, it is the largest international lender to the smallest, poorest countries of the region.

However, an inspection of how the IDB works as an institution reveals that the formal structure of ownership does not reflect in how influence is actually wielded or used within the institution. In the first place, in spite of the South and Central American voting power within the bank, the United States enjoys enormous dominance. This is explained by both formal and informal decision-making practices within the institution.

Formally, the United States has a veto on constitutional decisions that require either a three-fourths majority or a two-thirds majority of regional members, and it used to be the case that the board's quorum required the presence of the U.S. executive director. Even in the concessional window of the bank (the fund for special operations)—where the United States now contributes only 8.22 percent—it retains a veto power. Less formally, although the United States does not have a blocking minority in the ordinary capital account of the bank, it has nevertheless negotiated a procedure to ensure that it retains a power to delay loans that it disapproves of.

At the informal level, members of the board say that the United States has tremendous influence because of the resources the U.S. mission to the bank have at their disposal—to present, argue, and lobby for particular positions or policies. In addition, the U.S. position is further strengthened by the location of the bank's headquarters (in Washington, D.C.) and by the fact that one-quarter of its top management, its executive vice-president, and usually also the financial manager and general counsel are from the United States.

The experience of the IDB suggests that control of an institution is strongly affected by informal influence and the decisionmaking rules. The leverage wielded by the United States goes beyond that suggested by the ownership and voting structure of the institution. Yet U.S. dominance is not the only hindrance to Central American and South American participation and ownership of policies. A further issue of governance emerges from an examination of relations between the political executive of the organization (the board) and its operational staff and management. Here, one finds that the governments

---

31   Diana Tussie, *The Inter-American Development Bank* (Boulder: Lynne Rienner, 1995), p. 10.

represented on the board of the IDB exercise very little control over the overall objectives and policies of the institution. Although the IDB was created as an institution in which Central and South American governments would define core objectives and articulate broad policy directions, in fact they do not. However, this is *not* due to a lack of formal power. Rather, it is due to what the 1993 Task Force on Portfolio Management called a "culture of control"—the extent to which the board spends all of its time constantly exercising a detailed control of loans and thereby neglecting the broader tasks of governance.[32]

Similar problems have emerged within the African Development Bank. In 1994, a task force inquiring into the management of the bank reported "paralysing mistrust, suspicion and resentment" within the bank and between its board and management. The board interfered too much in the wrong kinds of issues, scrutinizing details in the budget process and sometimes even usurping the powers of the president.[33] In a similar vein, other analysts have argued the bank needs to delegate more effectively to its management and staff.[34] This repeats the story of relations between management and board in the IDB. In the AfDB, the powerful majority position of African members on the board has not translated into control and responsibility for the overall direction and policy of the organization. Rather, the board spends its time scrutinizing individual projects and micromanaging.

The failure of African board members to participate in and take responsibility for the broad strategic decisions of the organization is further exacerbated by the low level of engagement and concern on the part of African members in questions of the institution's financial and operational strength, the quality of its work, and its contribution to African development. Here, nonregional members of the bank (who hold a minority of votes) have informally set the directions of the institution because of their involvement in analyzing, monitoring, and evaluating the bank's performance and in defining new policies and directives and budgetary and commitment objectives.

In summary, in spite of the fact that the AfDB has a structure of capital, voting, and staff designed to ensure African participation and responsibility for

---

32   Inter-American Development Bank, *Managing for Effective Development* (Washington, D.C.: IDB, 1993).

33   African Development Bank, *The Quest for Quality: Report of the Task Force on Project Quality for the African Development Bank* (Abidjan: African Development Bank, 1994), pp. 26, 31.

34   Philip E. English and Harris M. Mule, *The African Development Bank* (Boulder: Lynne Rienner, 1996).

the institution,[35] this has not translated into African ownership: African members have not made the institution their own by setting the overall direction of the institution and taking responsibility for it. Indeed, even at the operational level, it has been said that "the Bank is absent when it should be present" and that it has "no systematic relations" with the African countries who are its majority shareholders.[36]

Seen in overview, formal ownership in the IDB and the AfDB (through the holding of votes and shares) has not translated into the hoped-for levels of participation and responsibility for the institution. Yet this original aim has not been thwarted purely by realpolitik or a background dominance of the most powerful states. Rather, it has been thwarted by insufficient commitment of members to the institution's core purposes and by insufficient institutional resources with which they might have backed up their own participation. Overall, the lesson for good governance is that principles and formal structures need to be backed up by resources and members' commitments.

5   Consensus and Problems of Accountability

Participation and accountability within institutions are not affected only by action (and inaction) within the overall structure of voting and ownership. Equally important, the decisionmaking procedures operating within an institution determine how members participate and who is responsible for different kinds of decisions. Formal decisionmaking rules also offer a rough guide to accountability within an institution.

In an interstate organization, the most straightforward way to ensure that all states have a voice in decisions is to enforce a rule of unanimity—since unanimity gives every state a veto. However, this approach can greatly impede the effectiveness of an organization. Even the smallest state can hold the others to ransom. Consensus decisionmaking, by contrast, is often held out as a more workable requirement. Unanimity requires every member of an institution to vote affirmatively (or to abstain in instances where this is defined as a positive

---

35   The African Development Bank is located in Abidjan, Côte d'Ivoire. Its president and most of its staff are African. It did not initially admit nonregional members. Today, African countries hold twelve of the eighteen seats and a 50 percent voting share in the concessional window of the bank (which is 98 percent funded by nonregionals).

36   African Development Bank, The Quest for Quality, p. 2. Paradoxically, shortly after the completion of the task force's report, the bank closed the few field offices that it had in order to cut expenditures.

vote). But consensus decisionmaking avoids voting and thus requires a less formal expression of agreement among the parties to a decision.

It is often assumed that consensus gives more voice to those with less voting power and that it ensures a peaceable and constructive atmosphere within institutions. For these reasons, it is often simply asserted that consensus decisionmaking contributes unproblematically to good governance. Yet the experience of consensus decisionmaking in international organizations does not bear this out, as we see below in examining the case of the UN Security Council and of the GATT/WTO.

The experience of the UN Security Council is particularly interesting, given that some have propounded it as a model for global economic governance on the grounds that it would be more representative and more accountable than the IMF or the World Bank.[37] Yet such arguments underplay the negative aspects of governance raised by the working practices of the Security Council and, in particular, the effect of consensus decisionmaking on governance within that organization.

The Security Council is made up of fifteen members, five of whom are permanent (China, France, Russia, the U.K., the United States) and ten of whom are nonpermanent representatives of various groupings of countries. A minimum of nine votes is required for any decision, which must include the concurring vote of all five permanent members. Yet most of the Security Council's business is not carried out by formal voting. Rather, it is conducted in informal consultations of the whole, in which consensus decisionmaking replaces voting. Although undoubtedly this improves the capacity of the council to dispatch its business, it has negative effects nevertheless on participation and transparency within the organization, which are worth highlighting.

In the first place, according to members of the council, consensus decisionmaking has bred a much higher level of informal consultations, private straw votes, and meetings of small groups. Key decisions, in other words, are taken outside formal meetings. Even on procedural matters, when votes are taken they "are, so to speak, pre-cooked in informal consultations,"[38] and whereas

---

37   Maurice Bertrand, "Some Reflections on Reform of the United Nations," JIU/REP/85/9 (Geneva: United Nations, 1985); United Nations Development Programme, *Human Development Report* (New York: United Nations, 1994); Commission on Global Governance, *Our Global Neighbourhood*; Frances Stewart and Sam Daws, "Global Challenges: The Case for a United Nations Economic and Social Security Council," *Viewpoint* 10 (London: Christian Aid, January 1996); Mahbub Ul Haq, *The UN and the Bretton Woods Institutions: New Challenges for the Twenty-First Century* (London: Macmillan, 1995).

38   Michael Wood, "Security Council: Procedural Developments," *International and Comparative Law Quarterly* 45 (1996): 150–161.

there used to be frequent votes on the adoption of the agenda, "nowadays agendas are always agreed in advance ... in informal consultations."[39] This means that only a restricted number of members get to participate in the process of real decisionmaking. This is not the only adverse effect on good governance.

A further, deeper problem with informal processes is that they are unrecorded. This means that the *reasoning* for a decision is not open to scrutiny by other states, *nor is the position taken by each member*. In these ways, the council is not accountable to states who are not party to the informal processes even if they are directly affected by the council's decisions (e.g., for budgetary reasons). Aware of this problem, the council has recently instituted some procedures for briefing a wider group of states.[40] Obviously, the lack of any record also means that the business of the council is also not open to wider public scrutiny.

The experience of the Security Council also highlights that reliance on informal negotiations, which take place behind the scenes, magnifies the unequal resources available to members in order to work effectively to push their own preferences. Those with the greatest staffing and research capabilities are much better placed to use the "informal negotiations" such that, in the words of one commentator, "delegations ... can simply be overwhelmed by delegations of members such as the U.S."[41]

Consensus decisionmaking, then, can have adverse consequences on good governance. We find that the practices within the Security Council have not only sharpened the argument for a wider membership of the council (to include Germany, Japan, and developing countries) but have also catalyzed more insistent calls for greater transparency and accountability in the council's procedures. Yet at the same time, the accountability of the Security Council has been eroded in other ways. In particular, the General Assembly's control over the Security Council's budget has been altered. After strong U.S. lobbying in the 1980s,[42] the passage of Resolution 41/213 requires critical budget decisions to be adopted by consensus at the stage of the committee for program

---

39 Ibid.
40 In October 1994, the council agreed that the president would give informal oral briefings to inform nonmembers of the council about the informal consultations of the whole; in February 1994, the council members decided to make draft resolutions *in blue* (i.e., in near-final form) available to nonmembers of the council; and a 1995 presidential statement (S/PRST/1995/234) sets out a list of "improvements to make the procedures of the Sanctions Committee more transparent."
41 David Caron, "The Legitimacy of the Collective Authority of the Security Council," *American Journal of International Law* 87 (1993): 552–588.
42 Benjamin Rivlin, "UN Reform from the Standpoint of the United States," *UN University Lectures*, no. 11 (Tokyo: United Nations University Press, 1996).

and coordination (as opposed to the UN Charter requirement of a two-thirds majority of the General Assembly).[43]

The analysis of the Security Council highlights problems of transparency and participation that arise from consensus decisionmaking. It also underlines, as we saw in the case of the regional development banks, that members who wish to influence decisions must commit high levels of staff and resources so as to generate proposals and lobby for them both outside and inside formal meetings.

The findings about the impact of consensus are all endorsed by the experience of the decisionmaking that took place within the GATT, the predecessor of the World Trade Organization. In the GATT (as in the WTO), every member had one vote, and decisions required either a simple or a specified special majority of votes. Consensus decisionmaking prevailed, however, and the result was to undermine the equal power of states to vote. Within the GATT, the requirement of consensus encouraged powerful states to offer concessions and to use retaliatory threats. As participants explain, these countries could push negotiations behind the scenes, apply bilateral pressures, and simply not hold meetings until a consensus had been reached. The effect was to concentrate negotiations among a small group of powerful members (usually the Quad: the United States, the European Union, Japan, and Canada) who tended to present decisions virtually as a fait accompli to the other (and particularly developing country) contracting parties.

Perhaps the clearest case of abuse of consensus lay in the GATT's dispute resolution procedure, which many regarded as both unworkable and highly political. When consensus was required for the council to accept panels' rulings, countries adversely affected would simply use delaying tactics. Panel decisions themselves were also often seen as unfair and partial in their treatment of different countries, since they would reflect the desire to reach consensus rather than the application of rules.

An important change in governance has been made in the new World Trade Organization, which—like the GATT—is an equal-voting institution. The WTO, however, is a stronger institution. In particular, it has a dispute settlements procedure that—unlike that of the GATT—can make rulings that are automatically accepted by the organization, unless there is a consensus *against*

---

43   Gene M. Lyons, "Competing Visions: Proposals for UN Reform," in Chadwick F. Alger, Gene M. Lyons, and John Trent, eds., *The United Nations System: The Policies of Member States* (Tokyo: United Nations University Press, 1995).

acceptance. Already, this seems to have improved the legitimacy of the organization. Whereas the GATT mechanisms tended to be used mainly by the Quad, the WTO is now being used by a wide range of countries: of all the requests before the WTO in mid-1996, about half were from developing countries.

There are two final issues about the use of consensus that are highlighted by the experience of the WTO. In the first place, the scope for using consensus needs to be clarified. At present within the WTO, consensus is overriding other rule-making procedures. In lower councils that have rules of procedure of their own, for example, these are ignored when consensus is not reached and decisions are *bumped up* until consensus is reached at a higher level, if necessary going as far as the general council. In other words, consensus has become an all-pervasive practice that overrides other decisionmaking rules. This risks spreading some of the problems of consensus decisionmaking already alluded to above.

A second problem relates to who is formally included in the consensus process and whether or not a meeting might decide, by consensus, to ignore a voting requirement. This is no arcane matter because consensus decisions reflect the mood of those *present at the meeting*. It is therefore a procedure that excludes those who cannot be present or who cannot afford to have a permanent delegation in Geneva. In 1996, only 72 of the 124 members of the WTO had delegations at the organization. For this reason, consensus is a procedure that can detract from the requirements of good governance.

In summary, the experience of both the Security Council and the GATT/WTO highlight several dangers of consensus decisionmaking. First, it can encourage decisionmaking in informal forums and thus exclude groups of members who are not part of the core group of powerful members. Second, the process of consensus decisionmaking is unrecorded, and the accountability of members contributing to the decision is therefore reduced. Third, formal decisionmaking rules that do ensure particular kinds of accountability or representation can be superseded by the operation of consensus. Finally, consensus decisionmaking involves only those present at a meeting and not necessarily all those who should be included in a particular decision.

Although consensus is often applauded as a step toward good governance, it can have the opposite effect, reducing transparency and accountability and thereby increasing the challenge of improving governance. How, then, can particular groups and stakeholders in an institution be assured of inclusion and participation? In the next sections, I examine the experience of other kinds of decisionmaking procedures.

6   Voting Structures, Stakeholders, and Good Governance

In the previous section, I argue that consensus decisionmaking can operate to exclude particular groups from decisionmaking. Yet good governance requires the inclusion of particular groups or states. Expressed another way, there are a range of stakes in the institution that need to be balanced in its governance. The stakeholders of international organizations include member governments who contribute resources, members whose compliance is required for the institution to be effective, and members who represent groups affected by the institution's policies. The key question for any institution is how to reflect and balance the various stakes in the institution and how to adapt when those stakes change. In recent times, international organizations have used or reformed their voting structures and voting requirements to achieve an appropriate balance. In this section, I investigate what their experience suggests for how voting systems might be used to alter or to contribute to good governance in an institution.

The International Fund for Agricultural Development offers an example of how an institution can adapt to changing stakes. It was established in 1977 to channel oil earnings from the Organization of Petroleum Exporting Countries (OPEC) toward neighbors most affected by the increase in oil prices, hence assisting agricultural development and food production in developing countries. The voting structure of the organization was planned so as to reflect the stakes of the various members. Its eighteen hundred votes were split among three groups of countries, giving six hundred votes each to category one (the developed countries), category two (OPEC countries), and category three (developing countries). Each group was then left to decide how it would allocate votes among its members. Each did so in a way that reflected its relationship to the institution and its aims. Developed countries distributed 82.5 percent of votes according to each member's contribution and only 17.5 percent equally among members. OPEC countries distributed 75 percent of votes by contribution and the other 25 percent equally. Developing countries distributed all votes equally among the members.

The main contributors to the fund (developed countries) had their influence in the institution protected not by a majority of votes but by special majorities and quorum requirements. Most major decisions (including lending policies, criteria and regulations regarding financing, and approval of the budget) required a special majority of two-thirds or more. This gave category one countries a veto power over the combined strength of OPEC and developing nations. Furthermore, a strict quorum requirement in both the council and the executive board specified that members representing at least one-half of the votes in each of the three categories and two-thirds of all the votes must be present.

Yet today stakes in the organization have changed. Developed countries, as opposed to oil-producing countries, have now become the major donors, and they have demanded more say within the institution, having already pushed for internal changes in the institution to improve accountability and efficiency in delivering projects. As a result, the basic structure of votes was revised in 1997 so as to distribute votes among all members in part on the basis of membership (i.e., basic votes) and in larger part on the basis of contributions to the fund.[44] The result is a voting structure that reflects a new balance of stakeholders. It bears noting that this is not simply a change in a theoretical voting requirement. Rather, as officials within agencies are quick to point out, even though formal votes are seldom called, voting structures underpin all decision-making within organizations: they provide a weighting of influence and power that is felt throughout all parts of the agency. This is equally true in a more recently created institution.

The Global Environment Facility (GEF) was deliberately structured to reflect a particular range of stakeholders. Launched as a pilot program in 1991 and then restructured in 1994, the institution's charter reflects the good governance and democracy agenda of the international community mentioned above, pledging "to ensure a governance that is transparent and democratic in nature, to promote universality in its participation and to provide for full cooperation in its implementation among the UNDP [UN Development Programme], UNEP [UN Environment Programme] and the World Bank."[45]

Beneath the rhetoric, there are essentially two sets of stakes reflected in the GEF. On the one hand, the organization was created because industrialized countries wished to do something about environmental degradation. On the other hand, it was quickly acknowledged that effective action to moderate global environmental degradation required the cooperation and participation of developing countries. From the outset, developing countries made it clear that they would not participate in the GEF if it were structured in the same way as the World Bank or the IMF.[46] The voting structure of the restructured GEF reflects these aims.

---

44   See the Fourth Replenishment Resolution at the Twentieth Session of the Governing Council of the International Fund for Agricultural Development, February 1997, Resolution 86/XVIII.

45   Global Environment Facility, *Instrument for the Establishment of the Restructured Global Environment Facility* (Washington, D.C.: Global Environment Facility, 1994), preamble.

46   Helen Sjoeberg, *From Idea to Reality: The Creation of the Global Environment Facility*, UNDP-UNEP, Working Paper no. 10, Washington, D.C., 1994.

Within the GEF, the voting structure requires a 60 percent majority of the total number of participants in the GEF (whose votes are placed by their representative members on the council) and also a majority representing 60 percent of total contributions to the fund. This voting rule is only invoked when decision cannot be reached by consensus. However, as I mention above, the voting requirement implicitly weights the structuring of consensus within a meeting because, when votes are not taken, consensus is deemed to be reached when an informal tally of would-be votes around the table reflects an appropriate majority.

It is unclear how successfully the structure of the GEF functions. The institution has been the subject of a barrage of criticism from various quarters, including critiques of its inadequate funds and calls for it to make less agonizing disbursements. From these broader judgments about the effectiveness and resources of the organization, it is difficult to discern clear views about it as a model of governance. However, for the more modest purposes of this article, the example helps to illustrate the way in which stakeholding can be reflected in the formal structure of an institution so as to structure the weight of influence that lies behind any consensus decisionmaking process.

A further significant element of the governance of the GEF is its openness to the participation of grassroots and nongovernmental organizations at all levels—not just in projects but also in policy and program development. When the institution was created, its founding members debated at length the arguments for and against the inclusion of NGOs (including the arguments I address in the first section of this article). In the end, some participation by NGOs was accepted.[47] In practice, the organization has permitted an approved set of NGOs to participate in its work. I have already noted problems that arise from such practices (in the discussion of core principles of good government). The wider concern being reflected here is how an institution can create links to societies and groups who are not adequately represented by its member states. Such concerns have been more fully debated in the context of the European Union, which is the subject of the next section.

7   Beyond Interstate Structures of Governance

Increasing integration in the European Union has led to a lively debate about issues of governance. At stake is how best to ensure that peoples in Europe are represented in institutions that are taking decisions that increasingly

---

47   Ibid.

affect their everyday lives. Furthermore, how can these institutions be made accountable to the people they affect?

At the most state-centered level, the issue of representation has been taken up by large states. They argue that their populations are inadequately represented in the council of the union, which places more premium on equality among its member states than on equality among differently sized populations. The addition of new small states to the union is exacerbating this problem. Here, two kinds of solutions are being considered: reweighting votes or introducing a double-qualified majority vote, which would require a majority of votes also to reflect a majority of the EU's population.[48] The object of double-qualified majorities would be to enhance the representation of large, populous states without touching the existing voting rights of states within the union. This resembles the double majority required in the GEF (above).

Interestingly, existing studies have examined what impact double-qualified majorities would have on voting power among states in the council. These studies suggest that a double majority of 66 percent would shift some voting power to the larger members; a double-qualified majority of 50 percent would simultaneously increase the power of both the largest and smallest members.[49] Overall, the studies highlight that the results of double-qualified majorities would be rather ambiguous. At the same time, however, scholars agree that the most important result of any alteration in voting would be on perceptions of the legitimacy of the council. That is, a change in the formal voting structure would enhance the perceived *representativeness* of the council.

A second issue of representation within the European Union concerns the links between international organizations and political arrangements within countries. Regional governments have been concerned that the institutions of the EU would reinforce the power of central governments. For this reason, the Treaty on European Union (the Maastricht Treaty) set up a committee of the regions, which held its first session in 1994 and is emerging as the guardian of the principle of subsidiarity (i.e., that decisions should be taken by those public authorities that stand as close to the citizen as possible). The committee is also contributing through its special commission on institutional affairs to the debate about the reform of the EU institutions. The Maastricht Treaty also opened up the possibility for regional governments to head delegations to

---

48   Commission of the European Union, *Commission Opinion: Reinforcing Political Union and Preparing for Enlargement* (Brussels: European Commission, 1996).

49   Philip Morris Institute for Public Policy Research, *In a Larger EU Can All Member States Be Equal?* (Brussels: PMI, 1996); Madeleine Hosli, "The Balance Between Small and Large: Effects of a Double-Majority System of Voting Power in the European Union," *International Studies Quarterly* 39 (1995): 351–370.

the Council of Ministers. Previously, only national-level ministers could take seats in the council. However, since this reform, both Germany and Belgium have had regional leaders head delegations on issues such as education and culture. Importantly, these changes underline the shifting of sovereignty on some issues simultaneously *up* to the EU level and *down* to the regional level. This is a kind of change to which other international organizations increasingly will have to adapt.

A further global governance problem illustrated by the European Union is that of the *democratic deficit*. This refers to the lack of direct representation and accountability for decisions taken at an international—here European—level. The problem for the European Union is exacerbated by the shift to qualified majority voting on a number of issues, which empowers a majority (rather than unanimity) of the members of the council to make decisions that directly affect voters across all the states of the union. Aware of the problem of accountability, the council introduced a procedure in the 1992 Maastricht Treaty that included the directly elected European Parliament more closely in decision-making. Under a new "co-decision" procedure, some forty-nine instruments had been adopted by 1996.[50] The 1997 Treaty of Amsterdam subsequently extended the scope of co-decision to new areas, including employment, social policy, and transport. Skeptics point out, however, that the European Parliament has yet to attract public confidence and support such that its inclusion will be seen as legitimating the council's decisions. Their opponents argue that if the parliament were further empowered, it would attract more interest and this would reverse the very low voter turnout for elections to the European Parliament.

The debate over democratizing Europe's institutions reflects the concern that as European institutions make more and more decisions that affect the everyday lives of EU citizens, so too they must be made more democratically accountable. In the language of good governance, the widening jurisdiction of intergovernmental institutions demands a rethinking of participation, accountability, and fairness within them. This rethinking needs to include yet also to go beyond the issues of international governance emphasized in this article.

8   Conclusion

I started out in this article by introducing the debate about good governance and the principles expounded in this debate. I drew a distinction between

---

50   Commission of the European Union, *Report by the Council and the Commission to the Reflection Group* (Brussels: European Commission, 1995).

international governance, used to refer to arrangements among states, and global governance, which envisages a broader set of links among individuals, groups, states, and institutions. My primary focus has been on the challenge of international governance, using specific examples to illustrate the problems and possibilities for applying principles of ownership, participation, inclusion, and accountability to relations among states within multilateral organizations. These examples highlighted three points. First, ownership by particular states within a multilateral organization is not necessarily achieved through formal control of the management and voting structure of the institution. Second, consensus does not necessarily foster the basic elements of good governance among states. Finally, specific voting requirements can be used in order to bolster perceptions of accountability, transparency, and representation among states within an organization.

These arguments are important because they highlight the need to rethink intergovernmental relations within institutions so as to ensure greater and more universal participation and accountability. This form of interstate good governance cannot be sidestepped by opening up participation to a broader group of nonstate actors and NGOs. Indeed, it could be argued that similar principles need to be applied to the participation of nonstate actors because otherwise there is a risk that institutions will simply increase access to representatives of U.S.-based and European-based groups and further skew institutional participation and accountability away from the broader, more universal set of members.

Nevertheless, the final example invoked—the European Union—highlights the importance of the broader global governance agenda. The democratic deficit emerging in the European Union has its parallels in several other international institutions. Indeed, international institutions today exercise influence over many policy areas that were once considered the purview of state sovereignty. The World Bank and the International Monetary Fund, for example, are each involved in advising and monitoring economic policies and arrangements within states. Indeed, these institutions themselves have put good governance on the agenda because they realize the extent to which their programs need to be at least understood and perceived as legitimate not just by governments but by a wider range of actors within states. Equally, virtually all international institutions have accepted that a purely state-centered system of representation in world politics is imperfect, and hence many have opened up some scope for participation by NGOs. I argue here that the good governance agenda also requires that organizations rethink the way in which relations among their state members are organized.

CHAPTER 6*

International Institutions, the State, and Global Civil Society in the Age of the World Wide Web

Craig Warkentin and Karen Mingst[1]

On 3 December 1998, the Organization for Economic Cooperation and Development (OECD) announced that talks on the Multilateral Agreement on Investment (MAI)—a legal instrument intended to codify and protect liberal transnational investment practices—had been halted permanently. Three months later, on 1 March 1999, an international treaty to ban landmines—under which signatories agree to stop using, producing, stockpiling, and transferring the antipersonnel (AP) devices—entered into effect. Each of these events, the former a failure of multilateralism and the latter a success, represented the culmination of a political process begun years earlier that was initiated and driven primarily by the activities of international nongovernmental organizations (NGOs). Despite their variant outcomes, both processes were characterized by the same political context and constitutive dynamics. In both cases, the nature and possibilities of the World Wide Web combined with those of an emergent global civil society to create a new international political environment, one in which state sovereignty was constrained and NGOs—as key actors in civil society—were able to work in novel and notably effective ways.

In this essay, we present a comparative case study of the protest against the MAI and the campaign to ban landmines, with an eye toward examining some of the implications of a global civil society and the World Wide Web for NGO activity in the contemporary era. We begin by presenting our analytical framework, which focuses on NGOs as political actors in their own right, agents of change whose effectualness increasingly is facilitated by the dynamics of the Web and a global civil society. Then, through the lens of a global civil society, we briefly examine the campaigns against the MAI and for a ban on landmines. Our emphasis, in each of these two sections, is on how NGO activities were

---

* This chapter was originally published in Global Governance, Volume 6, Issue 2, 2000.

1 Craig Warkentin is associate professor and chair of the Department of Political Science at the State University of New York, Oswego. Karen Mingst is professor emeritus in the Department of Political Science at the University of Kentucky. This article is based on a paper presented at "International Institutions: Global Processes, Domestic Consequences," a conference at Duke University, 9–11 April 1999.

facilitated by the Web and how these organizations interacted with key state and nonstate actors as they worked to realize their political objectives. In a final section, we expand our analysis and suggest avenues for further research, by suggesting some implications of our findings for an enlarged multilateralism.

1   NGOs, Change, and a Global Civil Society

Analyses of NGOs conventionally have been state-centric in their orientation, in that the state has provided the starting point (or point of reference) for scholarly examination. Peter Willetts's seminal work, in which he portrays NGOs as "pressure groups" seeking to influence state behavior, provides a good example of this.[2] Much of the subsequent work on NGOs has followed Willetts's lead by maintaining—to a greater or lesser degree and more or less explicitly—this state-referential perspective. Some scholars have moved beyond state-centric analysis per se by adding intergovernmental organizations (IGOs) such as the UN to the analytical mix;[3] yet despite their sometimes different emphases, all these studies essentially consign NGOs to the role of lobbying or interest groups forced to work through mediators (i.e., states or international institutions) in their efforts to realize organizational objectives and influence global politics.

In this essay, we take a different conceptual tack, one that focuses on NGOs as effectual political actors in their own right capable of acting independently of international institutions and states. Studies addressing NGOs in this light have become increasingly prevalent since the mid-1990s, with scholars using a variety of different labels to identify the phenomenon. We are most interested in those works that analyze NGOs in terms of their orientation toward social change and that place these organizations and their activities in the broader context of a global civil society.

---

2 Peter Willetts, *Pressure Groups in the Global System: The Transnational Relations of Issue-Oriented Non-Governmental Organizations* (New York: St. Martin's Press, 1982).

3 See, for example, Ann Marie Clark, "Non-Governmental Organizations and Their Influence on International Society," *Journal of International Affairs* 48, no. 2 (1995): 507–525; Ann Marie Clark, Elisabeth J. Friedman, and Kathryn Hochstetler, "The Sovereign Limits of Global Civil Society: A Comparison of NGO Participation in UN World Conferences on the Environment, Human Rights, and Women," *World Politics* 51, no. 1 (1998): 1–35; Peter J. Spiro, "New Global Communities: Nongovernmental Organizations in International Decision-Making Institutions," *Washington Quarterly* 18, no. 1 (1995): 45–56; Thomas Weiss and Leon Gordenker, eds., *NGOs, the UN, and Global Governance* (Boulder: Lynne Rienner, 1996); Peter Willetts, *"The Conscience of the World": The Influence of Non-Governmental Organizations in the U.N. System* (Washington, D.C.: Brookings Institution Press, 1996).

Jackie Smith, Charles Chatfield, and Ron Pagnucco offer perhaps the clearest articulation of NGOs as agents of social change. They focus their attention on social movement organizations (SMOs)—"formal groups explicitly designed to promote specific social changes"—and, more particularly, on transnational social movement organizations (TSMOs) that "incorporate members from more than two countries, have some formal structure, and coordinate strategy through an international secretariat." The "transnational membership structures" of such organizations, which include those discussed in this article, "facilitate communication and action across national borders as well as in intergovernmental institutions."[4] As such, within the broader context of world politics, TSMOs help to shape global policy and influence domestic politics in significant ways.[5]

Other work by international relations scholars is similar to that of Smith, Chatfield, and Pagnucco but places greater emphasis on conceptualizing the nature of the international political environment within which NGOs and other political actors increasingly operate. This analytical orientation has been motivated, in large part, by the end of the Cold War and driven by a perceived need on the part of international relations scholars to make sense of the changing dynamics and processes that characterize contemporary world politics. In the early to mid-1990s, Chris Brown, Richard Shapcott, and others revived the notion of "international society," while scholars such as M.J. Peterson, Ann Marie Clark, and Paul Ghils extended this discussion to include an explicit focus on NGO activities within this broad context.[6] More recently, scholarly attention has turned to the notion of an emergent global civil society and an examination of the implications of this for international politics.

---

4   Jackie Smith, Ron Pagnucco, and Charles Chatfield, "Social Movements and World Politics: A Theoretical Framework," in Jackie Smith, Charles Chatfield, and Ron Pagnucco, eds., *Transnational Social Movements and Global Politics: Solidarity Beyond the State* (Syracuse, N.Y.: Syracuse University Press, 1997), p. 61.

5   As described by Kreisberg, TSMOs are international NGOs "that seek to bring about a [progressive] change in the status quo." Louis Kreisberg, "Social Movements and Global Transformation," in Smith, Chatfield, and Pagnucco, *Transnational Social Movements and Global Politics*, p. 12.

6   Chris Brown, *International Relations Theory: New Normative Approaches* (New York: Harvester/ Wheatsheaf, 1992); Chris Brown, "International Theory and International Society: The Viability of the Middle Way?" *Review of International Studies* 21, no. 2 (1995): 183–196; Clark, "Non-Governmental Organizations"; Paul Ghils, "International Civil Society: International Non-Governmental Organizations in the International System," *International Social Science Journal* 44, no. 3 (1992): 417–431; M.J. Peterson, "Transnational Activity, International Society and World Politics," *Millennium: Journal of International Studies* 21, no. 3 (1992): 371–388; Richard Shapcott, "Conversation and Coexistence: Gadamer and the Interpretation of International Society," *Millennium: Journal of International Studies* 23, no. 1 (1994): 57–83.

Although widely used, the notion of a global civil society has yet to be systematically examined or clearly articulated. Among the most useful treatments in this regard is Ronnie Lipschutz's. Firmly grounding his discussion in a critique of state-centered approaches to the study of international relations, Lipschutz argues that there is emerging a global civil society—that is, "a parallel arrangement of political interaction, one that does not take anarchy or self-help as central organising principles but is focused on the self-conscious constructions of networks of knowledge and action, by decentred, local actors, that cross the reified boundaries of space as though they were not there."[7] According to Lipschutz, of the actors that play pivotal roles in the construction of a global civil society's constitutive networks, NGOs are among the most important.

Lipschutz's conceptualization of global civil society is helpful but remains ambiguous; and little scholarly effort has been dedicated to remedying this problem. In this essay, we use a conceptualization of global civil society forwarded by Craig Warkentin. He builds on Lipschutz's idea by arguing that a global civil society can be understood, at the most fundamental level, as a transnationally defined "set of ideologically variable mechanisms or channels of opportunity for political involvement" and, more broadly, as an ongoing phenomenon that exhibits certain (elemental) characteristics.[8]

Warkentin's definition of a global civil society carries a number of important implications for the nature and conduct of international politics, three of which are particularly relevant to the cases discussed in this essay. First, the notion of a global civil society, so defined, shifts the analytical focus from formal, state-based institutions to social and political relations. This move highlights the nature and political significance of NGOs' (networked) relationships with each other, as well as their interactions with other actors. Second, within this conceptual scheme of a global civil society, NGOs become significant and effectual political actors. This change in focus helps to demonstrate the ways in which NGOs play increasingly crucial roles in particular multilateral endeavors or transnationally defined issue areas. Third, based on Warkentin's articulation of its elemental characteristics (which include "inclusivity"), a global civil society inherently facilitates a more "people-centered" politics and, concomitantly, a conceptual shift toward more democratically oriented transnational political processes. This analytical focus carries with it not only the idea that

---

7   Ronnie Lipschutz, "Reconstructing World Politics: The Emergence of Global Civil Society," *Millennium: Journal of International Studies* 21, no. 3 (1992): 389–420.
8   See Craig Warkentin, "Framing a Global Civil Society: NGOs and the Politics of Transnational Activity" (Ph.D. diss., University of Kentucky, 1998), pp. 48–53.

people, either individually or collectively organized, "matter"; it also implies that states will find their "sovereignty" increasingly constrained and that multilateral endeavors and transnational politics will be characterized by increasingly participatory processes.

Developing alongside a global civil society has been the World Wide Web, an inherently dynamic medium of international communication. Although there is not yet sufficient empirical evidence to prove causal connections between a global civil society and the Web, there are sufficient grounds to argue that the dynamics of both phenomena often play off of and reinforce one another in important ways.[9] In the present context, the Web's multimedia capabilities, interactivity, and immediacy have proven to be invaluable tools in facilitating the transnational communication, networked social relationships, and participatory politics that characterize a global civil society. Thus, to the three implications of a global civil society mentioned above, we add a related fourth point: that, in the context of a global civil society and its constitutive actors, the World Wide Web is becoming an increasingly important political tool. Specifically, the Web facilitates networked sociopolitical relationships in important new ways, it (potentially) increases NGOs' organizational effectiveness and political significance, and it helps to foster more broadly participatory (transnational) political processes.

The dynamics of a global civil society and the World Wide Web proved particularly instrumental in both of the cases we discuss later. In each, NGOs used the channels of opportunity provided by a global civil society, the sociopolitical dynamics that ensue from these, and the communicative potential of the World Wide Web to help them accomplish their particular political objectives. With this in mind, we present each case—the campaign against the MAI and the campaign to ban landmines—in terms of the implications mentioned earlier, illustrating specific ways in which each of these four theoretical points was realized in practice. We also suggest that certain aspects of the MAI and landmine cases point to the development of an enlarged multilateralism.

2 The Campaign against the Multilateral Agreement on Investment

Among the effects of the Uruguay Round of the General Agreement on Tariffs and Trade (GATT) were participants' increased realization of the truly globalized nature of the contemporary international economy and the further institutionalization of liberal economic principles. Thus, as part of the Uruguay Round

---

9   See ibid. for illustrative case studies.

negotiations in the early 1990s, the United States and the European Union (EU) jointly proposed that member countries use the newly created World Trade Organization (WTO) to negotiate a much broader, enforceable multilateral investment agreement. Strong objections from a number of developing countries squelched further action on such an agreement within the WTO; but in May 1995, formal discussions on the Multilateral Agreement on Investment began in the OECD. The delegates' plan was to make the MAI a free-standing agreement open to accession once completed. For nearly two years after the talks were initiated, negotiations on the MAI were conducted behind closed doors at the OECD and beyond public scrutiny.[10] The MAI Negotiating Group, chaired by a Dutch official, met twenty-three times between September 1995 and April 1998. By January 1997, a first draft of the MAI text was concluded. Although the negotiating group deftly borrowed texts from other agreements in drafting the MAI, it did not directly address the hard issues.[11]

Everything changed in February 1997, however, when "an early draft of the treaty, replete with numerous contradictions, was leaked to Public Citizen, a Washington-based public interest group founded by Ralph Nader, and then immediately published on the Web.... Suddenly, what had been a working document among 29 parties became available to anyone with a computer and a modem." What ensued appropriately has been described as an "ambush," in which "more than 600 organizations in 70 countries [began] expressing vehement opposition to the treaty, often in apocalyptic terms."[12] Among the strange bedfellows that opposed the MAI were the American Federation of Labor and Congress of Industrial Organizations (AFL-CIO), Amnesty International, the Australian Conservation Foundation, the Council of Canadians, Friends of the Earth, Oxfam, Public Citizen, the Sierra Club, Third World Network, the United Steelworkers of America, the Western Governors' Association, and the World Development Movement. The battle was waged primarily on the World Wide

10   Preamble Center, "The Multilateral Agreement on Investment: Timeline of Negotiations," fact sheet, updated 6 November 1998, online at http://www.preamble.org/MAI/maihist. html (24 November 1999).

11   William A. Dymond, "The MAI: A Sad and Melancholy Tale," in Fen Osler Hampson, Michael Hart, and Martin Rudner, eds., *Canada Among Nations 1999: A Big League Player?* (Don Mills, Ont.: Oxford University Press, 1999), p. 29.

12   See, for example, Public Citizen, "Public Citizen's Global Trade Watch Backgrounder: The Alarming Multilateral Agreement on Investment (MAI) Now Being Negotiated at the OECD," online at http://www.citizen.org/pctrade/mai/What%20is/maibg.html (24 November 1999). Despite such outcry, the MAI largely was ignored by the mainstream press, prompting Project Censored to name the Multilateral Agreement on Investment the "Top Censored Story" of 1998. Project Censored, "Project Censored's Top 25 1999," online at http://www.sonoma.edu/ProjectCensored/t2599.html (10 June 1999).

Web, where not only successive drafts of the MAI but also accompanying analyses, position papers, fact sheets, and calls to action were posted on websites. But protesting NGOs also supplemented these "new media" tools with tactics from their standard repertoire, including letter-writing campaigns, petitions, and public demonstrations.[13]

It was the MAI's key provisions that elicited such broad-based and passionate opposition. These included, but were not limited to, broad implementation of the nondiscrimination principles of "national treatment" and "most favored nation" for investors; prohibitions of performance requirements (e.g., local content or employment stipulations); "rollback" and "standstill" measures forcing states to reduce or eliminate national laws that failed to conform to MAI standards; bans on the uncompensated expropriation of assets, restrictions on the repatriation of profits, and other restraints on the movement of capital; an investor-state dispute mechanism particularly favorable to investors; and the absence of any legally binding measures to ensure investor responsibility or accountability.[14]

In defense of the MAI, proponents cited the conventional wisdom on the benefits of trade liberalization, arguing that the agreement was needed to reduce obstacles to overseas investment and economic inefficiencies caused by regulation, to increase exports, and to spur economic growth in both host and home countries. To this, opponents countered that, among other things, the lack of environmental standards in the MAI would encourage a "race to the bottom," as countries lowered living standards and weakened regulations in an effort to attract capital; that the MAI's rollback and standstill measures, as well as its dispute resolution mechanisms, would undermine state sovereignty; and that the MAI's legal protections for the rights of investors were not balanced by corresponding safeguards for the interests of host states and citizens.[15]

---

13   Stephen J. Kobrin, "The MAI and the Clash of Globalizations," *Foreign Policy* 112 (fall 1998): 97–98.

14   See Preamble Center, "The Multilateral Agreement on Investment: Key Provisions," fact sheet, Washington, D.C., online at http://www.preamble.org/MAI/keyprovs.html (24 November 1999); Oxfam GB, "Update on the Proposed Multilateral Agreement on Investment," briefing paper, April 1998, online at http://www.oxfam.org.uk/policy/papers/maiapr98.htm (24 November 1999); Oxfam GB, "Oxfam GB Update on the MAI (Multilateral Agreement on Investment)," briefing paper, December 1998, online at http://www.oxfam.org.uk/policy/papers/mai_update/mai_update.htm (24 November 1999).

15   Preamble Center, "The Multilateral Agreement on Investment: Views Pro and Con," fact sheet, online at http://www.preamble.org/MAI/procon.html (24 November 1999); Oxfam GB, "Oxfam GB Update."

Negotiations for the MAI went well at first but increasingly encountered problems as the discussions moved from broad principles to specific provisions. By January 1997, delegates had reached a rough consensus on the MAI and, given their working draft, had set May 1997 as the target date for completing the agreement. However, in April 1997, the OECD announced a six-month halt to the negotiations to allow participants a "period of assessment" and moved the target completion date to May 1998. By the time negotiations resumed in October 1997, prospects for a successfully completed agreement had dimmed considerably. An OECD ministers' meeting in April 1998 produced a second one-year extension and another new target date (May 1999), but an October 1998 consultation did little more than shore up skepticism that the MAI would reach fruition. Perhaps not surprisingly, then, December 1998 marked the end of the OECD's negotiations on a Multilateral Agreement on Investment.

NGOs played an important role in the OECD's failure to successfully negotiate the MAI. In the following paragraphs, we evaluate NGOs' involvement in this regard, presenting our analysis in terms of the four broad assertions presented above. First, the nature of a global civil society—within which the MAI negotiations took place—encourages an analytical shift in focus from formal institutions to social and political relationships among actors. In the case of the MAI, NGOs' networking relationships with each other were relatively weak and loosely defined at best. However, although each organization essentially pursued its own "MAI agenda" and engaged the agreement on its own terms, implicit cross-pollination of ideas did occur. This was evidenced particularly by the way in which information and analysis produced by the various protesting NGOs was extensively linked via their websites.

More important in the MAI case than NGOs' relationships with each other were their relationships with states and with the public. We further explore both of these later. But at this point, it should be noted that NGOs generally played "traditional" roles in their dealings with states and with the public. For example, the protesting organizations lobbied states to change their positions and held them accountable for their actions by disseminating information about their activities with regard to the MAI. Somewhat less conventionally, NGOs worked to defend the interests of states they felt would be affected negatively by the agreement and, later in the process, were able to secure a consultation with OECD negotiators that proved instrumental to the MAI's demise. What was different about NGOs' relationships with each other and with states were the methods the organizations employed in realizing their objectives. Most significantly, NGOs used the Web extensively to network with each other, provide information, and mobilize the public. Given the inherent nature of the

World Wide Web, NGOs were able to do this with unprecedented speed and on a global scale.

States' relationships with each other were also an important factor in the MAI's failure. As Stephen J. Kobrin notes, "the anti-MAI forces could not take all the credit for tabling the talks; the participants' inability to agree also played an important role. The short preamble to the treaty, for example, contains 17 footnotes expressing the concerns of one or more delegations. The [April 1998] draft contains almost 50 pages of country-specific exceptions."[16] State positions beyond the OECD's formal negotiating circles also proved significant. A number of Southern states were highly critical of the MAI, and even some Northern states opposed it. New Zealand pledged not to sign the MAI, France withdrew its support under a new government, and the U.K. rethought its position under similar institutional circumstances. Eventually, these state positions and the relationships they spawned took their toll on the MAI negotiating process.

Second, in the context of a global civil society, NGOs increasingly are significant, effectual, and often key players in political processes. This certainly was the case with the MAI negotiating process (although not in the same way or to the extent that it was true in the landmine case). Perhaps most obviously, and as acknowledged by participating governments, pressure from civil society was an important factor in stalling, and eventually halting, the negotiations. Less noticeable but more important, NGOs played a key role in framing the MAI discourse on two levels. In the broader sense, NGOs shaped the way the debate played out in the public arena. Whereas the MAI was discussed within the OECD and other state-based institutional forums in "economic" or "financial investment" terms, NGOs switched the focus of the language to highlight the implications of the agreement for the environment, global development, human rights, and democratic governance. By speaking about the MAI in terms of a loss of state sovereignty and democratic control and as a purveyor of environmental degradation and a form of neocolonialism, NGOs effectively "set the rules" for how the MAI would be presented to the public. As a "side effect," framing the MAI discourse in this particular way also prompted shifts in the attitudes and positions of some countries.

NGOs also were involved in framing on another level—that is, as the term is used by social movement theorists. Certain of these scholars have articulated what they call "frame theory," a construct that is intended to explain why individuals with different normative orientations and experiences become involved in collective action or social movement organizations. According to

---

16   Kobrin, "The MAI," p. 98.

David Snow and his colleagues, the first to articulate the idea of "frame align-ment," individuals' "participation in SMO activities is contingent in part on alignment of individual and SMO interpretive frames."[17] That is, individuals will not participate in an SMO (or TSMO) unless their own experientially based perspective corresponds to the interpretive orientation of the organization. In the present context, this means that individuals will not become involved in a campaign against the MAI or for a ban on landmines unless, based on their per-sonal experiences and values, the language and activities of the participating NGOs "ring true" to them. In the MAI case, NGOs successfully framed the MAI discourse in a way that made sense to large numbers of the public. The inten-tional erosion of democratic processes and sovereignty are not taken lightly by most, and multinational corporations' disdain for environmental and human rights standards are popular targets in the media and public discussion. Thus, by framing the MAI in such terms, NGOs were able to "make real" to the public the agreement's potential threat.

Third, a global civil society inherently facilitates a more "people-centered" politics and, more specifically, increasingly democratized and participatory political processes. This dynamic also is played out in the MAI case. Here, as noted above, hundreds of NGOs—presumably representing thousands of individual citizens in a variety of countries—became involved in the anti-MAI campaign. Each organization became a participant, in some sense, in the MAI deliberations, prompting increased public participation by encouraging its members to take action. This increased participation, in turn, strength-ened calls for a more "democratically oriented" MAI. On these grounds, not only the principles and provisions of the MAI but also the manner in which it was being negotiated came under fire. In this regard, Oxfam's criticisms were representative of many NGOs' charges against the agreement. In addition to criticizing the MAI's provisions—the "undemocratic nature of the standstill and roll-back clauses," the potential threats to "legitimate national legislation on the environment, taxation, health and safety, consumer and labour rights," and the "secret tribunals" that would ensue from the agreement's investor-state dispute settlement mechanism—Oxfam also denounced the negotiation pro-cess as undemocratic. Specifically, the organization cited the "lack of trans-parency and involvement of all relevant actors (including NGOs) and agencies

---

17   David A. Snow, E. Burke Rochford, Jr., Steven K. Worden, and Robert D. Benford, "Frame Alignment Processes, Micromobilization, and Movement Participation," *American Sociological Review* 51 (1986): 475. See also David A. Snow and Robert D. Benford, "Ideology, Frame Resonance, and Participant Mobilization," in Bert Klandermans, Hanspeter Kriesi, and Sidney Tarrow, eds., *From Structure to Action: Comparing Social Movement Research Across Cultures* (Greenwich, Conn.: JAI Press, 1988), pp. 197–217.

at intergovernmental and governmental levels"; the "exclusion of developing countries from the negotiations even though they were key targets of the eventual treaty"; the "top-down negotiating model, instead of a bottom-up sector-by-sector ('positive list') approach"; and the "lack of adequate, timely and transparent independent reviews of the social and environmental implications of the draft MAI for OECD and developing countries."[18]

The increased public participation was duly noted by MAI negotiators and their respective governments. Belgium's Foreign Trade Ministry observed that "the growing pressure from civil society further exacerbated the differences of opinion within the OECD"; and another "European official observed [that] the wave of protest elevated the question of the MAI from the 'level of civil servants' to the 'ministerial level.'"[19] The report justifying France's withdrawal of support for the MAI went even further by asserting that "more than any other international economic agreement, the MAI has created opposition and tension within civil society. The extent and strength of the opposition and the speed with which it developed were surprising." Citing some of the particular forms taken by this opposition, the report concluded that "the organizations representing civil society have become aware of the stakes involved in international economic negotiations and are determined to leave their mark on them."[20]

Finally, as we noted at the beginning of this essay, the campaign of protest against the MAI was facilitated by—and arguably would not have been possible without—the World Wide Web. The Web provided a new tool for anti-MAI activists, with which they could disseminate information quickly and effectively as well as communicate with each other and with the broader public. As Kobrin observes, "The reason that opposition to the MAI has been so successful is that the treaty has been presented on the Internet in terms that are immediate, meaningful, and threatening to a very large number of disparate individuals and groups.... The Internet allows anti-MAI activists to reach large numbers of people, at little or no cost, who normally would never hear of an investment treaty negotiated in a far away place and would never think that it might affect them directly."[21]

It should also be noted, at this point, that the Web can play a "destructive" role as well. Writing shortly before the OECD halted the MAI negotiations in

18   Oxfam GB, "Oxfam GB Update."
19   Kobrin, "The MAI," p. 99.
20   Council of Canadians, "France's Official Position on Withdrawing from the MAI Negotiations," online at http://www.canadians.org/campaigns/campaigns-maipub03.html
      (24 November 1999).
21   Kobrin, "The MAI," p. 107.

December 1998, Kobrin contended: "Much of the anti-MAI sentiment on the Internet presents barely credible worst-case scenarios as fact. As the OECD discovered, much to its chagrin, there are no controls on the Net over who can 'publish' or what they can say. Although some of the arguments ... are balanced and reasoned, most of the rest are neither. The MAI deals with difficult and often technical issues, and considerable disagreement remains among the parties to the treaty. The Internet is a medium where the most extreme statements attract attention; where an argument scrolling down a computer screen may garner authority it does not deserve."[22]

Despite such drawbacks, we argue that the Web can be not only a constructive but also a powerful political tool. In the case of the MAI, the OECD was "forced" to establish an "official" MAI site in an effort to counter the plethora of anti-MAI sites that populated the Web.[23] The French also noted the power of the Internet when explaining their withdrawal of support for the MAI: "The development of the Internet is shaking up the world of negotiation. It allows for the instantaneous distribution of texts under discussion, the confidentiality of which is increasingly theoretical, and for the sharing of knowledge and expertise across borders." In a comment that may belie Kobrin's contention about the negative aspects of the MAI debate on the Web, they observed that "on a subject that is very technical, representatives of civil society appear to be fully informed, with critiques that are legally well-argued."[24]

3   The International Campaign to Ban Landmines

The campaign to ban landmines represents a "victory" of global civil society in favor of a multilateral approach. The December 1997 Treaty Signing Conference and Mine Action Forum in Ottawa joined representatives of 156 states and the NGO community. By 1 March 1999, the Convention on the Prohibition of the Use, Stockpiling, Production and Transfer of Anti-personnel Mines and on Their Destruction had been signed by 131 states and ratified by 65 (25 more than the 40 states required). What explains this rapid turn of events?

---

22   Ibid.
23   The OECD's "MAI Home Page" has since been replaced by its "International Investment," 19 November 1999, online at http://www.oecd.org/daf/cmis/fdi/index.htm (24 November 1999). However, the organization's MAI documentation remains available online at OECD, "MAI Documentation," 25 February 1999, http://www.oecd.org/daf/cmis/mai/reports.htm (24 November 1999).
24   Council of Canadians, "France's Official Position."

It is well documented that members of civil society, particularly nongovernmental organizations, played a key role in advocating the delegitimization and delegalization of landmines.[25] In the early stages, the lead role was played by the International Committee of the Red Cross (ICRC), an organization uniquely positioned because of its special responsibility in enforcing international humanitarian law. Released from the constraints of the Cold War, during which its neutrality was tested constantly, the ICRC played an advocacy role critical to the initial 1993 meetings. For the first time in its history, the ICRC developed a public advertising campaign and disseminated both specialist and nonspecialist literature, framing the issue of landmines in humanitarian terms.[26]

By 1993, the umbrella network known as the International Campaign to Ban Landmines (ICBL) had assumed leadership under a closely knit steering committee of NGOs. The ICBL comprised organizations from a number of different countries, including France's Handicap International, Germany's Medico International, and the Mines Advisory Group in the U.K.; and Human Rights Watch, Physicians for Human Rights, and Vietnam Veterans of America Foundation (VVAF) in the United States. Jody Williams, of VVAF, served as coordinator. With no staff and no central office, this loosely structured group's early approach was to encourage each respective NGO to pursue its own particular strategy appropriate to banning landmines. By 1996, 600 NGOs from more than forty countries had signed on, the beginning of a coalition that eventually would see more than a thousand NGOs participate in more than sixty countries.[27] These actors functioned as "norm entrepreneurs," focusing attention on the issue by appropriately shaping the public discourse on landmines.[28]

Among the plethora of NGOs—some forming for this specific purpose and many others grafting the landmine issue to their traditional focus on children, health and safety, human rights, social welfare, or disarmament—one NGO was particularly unique and correspondingly effective: the Landmine Survivors

25   Richard Price, "Reversing the Gun Sights: Transnational Civil Society Targets Land Mines," *International Organization* 52, no. 3 (1998): 613–644.

26   Stuart Maslen, "The Role of the International Committee of the Red Cross," in Maxwell A. Cameron, Robert J. Lawson, and Brian W. Tomlin, eds., *To Walk Without Fear: The Global Movement to Ban Landmines* (Toronto: Oxford University Press, 1998), pp. 80–98.

27   Jody Williams and Stephen Goose, "The International Campaign to Ban Landmines," in Cameron, Lawson, and Tomlin, *To Walk Without Fear*, pp. 20–47.

28   Martha Finnemore and Kathryn Sikkink, "International Norm Dynamics and Political Change," *International Organization* 52, no. 4 (1998): 896–897; see also Margaret E. Keck and Kathryn Sikkink, *Activists Beyond Borders: Advocacy Networks in International Politics* (Ithaca, N.Y.: Cornell University Press, 1998).

Network. That group was established to ensure that relief, monetary and otherwise, was provided to those maimed by landmines. Beginning in 1995, these victims' voices, each a living reminder of the devastation of landmines, pushed the agenda ahead, providing an emotive appeal not often seen in international political circles.[29]

NGOs, however, did not act alone. U.S. senator Patrick Leahy, himself a key participant, stated the reality: "Never before have representatives of civil society collaborated with governments so closely, and so effectively, to produce a treaty to outlaw a weapon."[30] NGOs were able to work closely and effectively with a core group of supportive states. Virtually all of these major supporters were small or medium-sized states that took a progressive stance on international aid and related security issues and were secure from threats to their borders. The group included Denmark, Norway, Austria, Belgium, the Netherlands, and Canada. In each of these countries, relevant NGOs were highly influential in pushing the national government to stake a position that largely was consistent with the state's own political and social posture. (For example, with the exception of Belgium, in no case were the states producers or users of landmines.) Since these states were not obligated to change their behavior, this was a relatively easy case of NGO influence.

More critical was the process that brought the larger states to support the ban. Garnering support from Germany, and from especially key UN Security Council members France and Great Britain, proved essential. In both cases, NGOs were well organized and highly influential. For example, the French campaign to ban landmines was organized around Handicap International, Médecins sans Frontières, UNICEF, Greenpeace, the Catholic Committee Against Hunger and for Development, and Agir Ici. A turning point proved to be the appointment of a new French secretary of state for humanitarian affairs, Xavier Emmanuelli, well known in humanitarian circles and a friend of many of these NGO leaders. He declared the landmine ban one of his top priorities and, for the first time, a representative of an NGO actually was invited to join the delegation to the 1996 Ottawa conference. But a strong French position against landmines was not forthcoming until a new government took power and, seeing the Canadian and British commitment, came out in favor of a total ban. The new prime minister, an announced ban advocate, appointed several other pro-ban individuals to positions such as minister for defense and minister for

29   Jerry White and Ken Rutherford, "The Role of the Landmine Survivors Network," in Cameron, Lawson, and Tomlin, *To Walk Without Fear*, pp. 99–117.

30   U.S. senator Patrick Leahy, "Oslo N.G.O. Forum on the Landmine Treaty," 8 September 1997, online at http://www.senate.gov/~leahy/s970908.html (24 November 1999).

cooperation and development.[31] The support of France and Great Britain was viewed as crucial since both states were members of the prestigious Security Council and, more important, producers and users of landmines.

Of all the states, Canada provided the most critical leadership internationally; but leadership there was shared between the NGOs on the one hand and Foreign Minister Lloyd Axworthy on the other. The formation of the NGO coalition known as Mines Action Canada coincided with a major foreign policy initiative in Canada that obligated the government to democratize foreign policy by consulting on a more regularized basis with NGOs. Operating under this mandate, Canada hosted the international strategy conference in October 1996, a conference where NGOs, notably the ICBL, participated at the table, and governments that had not given their commitment were admitted as observers, sitting in the back of the room. Although this seating provided a symbol of newfound NGO power, it was Axworthy's gambit at the end of the conference that mobilized the international community. He challenged governments to negotiate a treaty banning mines and return to Ottawa in just a year, stating unequivocally that he would work closely with the ICBL to make that a reality. He effectively dedicated the Canadian government to the task.[32] As Jessica Mathews remarked at the time, "The new power of NGOs and other nonstate actors gives a much larger role to small and medium-sized governments that decide to seize the baton."[33] Canada and other core states, working together with the NGOs, thus were able to seize this opportunity.

IGOs played a much less critical, albeit still instrumental, role in this ongoing process. UNICEF played a key early role in legitimizing the issue, tying the landmine issue to that of the health and safety of children as indiscriminate victims. Once the process started, the UN General Assembly served as an arena for condemnation. Yet the speed of the process, as set in motion by the suite of ad hoc conferences, essentially left out the UN as a key player. Although Secretary-General Boutros Boutros-Ghali voiced his support for the ban, the UN's role became much more defined after the ban was established and UN demining activities were systematically undertaken.

Notable individuals, including Boutros-Ghali, also were important actors, lending their moral authority to the movement to ban the weapons. Boutros-Ghali was joined by Archbishop Desmond Tutu of South Africa (a key heavily

---

31   See Philippe Chabasse, "The French Campaign," in Cameron, Lawson, and Tomlin, *To Walk Without Fear*, pp. 60–67.

32   Valerie Warmington and Celina Tuttle, "The Canadian Campaign," in Cameron, Lawson, and Tomlin, *To Walk Without Fear*, pp. 48–59; Williams and Goose, "International Campaign."

33   Jessica Mathews, "The New, Private Order," *Washington Post*, 21 January 1997, p. A11.

mined state), Pope John Paul, and the Dalai Lama. However, one not-so-notable individual became notable in the process. The organizer of the ICBL, Jody Williams, and her NGO network won the Nobel Peace Prize in 1997, lending another stamp of international legitimacy to nongovernmental actors. These individuals operating with NGOs created substantial peer pressure, a "norm cascade" supporting the prohibition against landmines.[34]

The channels of opportunity that the ICBL and NGOs utilized included both traditional and newer diplomatic techniques. The NGOs were able to take advantage of the environment spawned by an emergent global civil society. One of the most traditionally recognized and widely touted strengths of NGOs is the generation and dissemination of information. With respect to landmines, NGOs unleashed the full panoply of tools geared toward information dispersion: radio, TV, documentary films, comic books, "stunts" at international conferences, and appeals to reason in elite media like the *Washington Post, New York Times*, and *The Economist*. The information was designed to show not only the proliferation of deployed landmines but also, most vividly, their indiscriminate and devastating effects on unsuspecting civilians. The emotive images were, and continue to be, electrifying: children in wheelchairs, the devil carrying away victims, people with missing limbs, and truckloads of crutches being disseminated to victims. Visual media, including the Web, substantively increased NGOs' effectiveness in addressing the landmine issue.[35]

NGOs also personalized the campaign, as exemplified in UNA-USA's Adopt-a-Minefield Program. "Parents" would "adopt" an active minefield and raise funds to return the land to local populations.[36] Alternative views to the conventional wisdom on the weapons were widely disseminated as well. Most notably, the ICRC commissioned a military assessment of landmines written by a former military officer. The study showed that landmines have had little effect on the outcome of conflicts, thus undermining military arguments for their criticality to battle. The NGOs also effectively were able to build influence through their traditional organizing skills, which they used to hold

---

34   Finnemore and Sikkink, "International Norm Dynamics," p. 901.

35   See, for example, "Seven Days in a Minefield," accessible from International Committee of the Red Cross (ICRC), "Landmines," 17 November 1999, online at http://www.icrc.org/eng/mines (24 November 1999); OneWorld Online, "Killing Fields," online at http://www.oneworld.org/media/gallery/cambodia/1.html (24 November 1999); and OneWorld Online, "Landmines—The Hidden Enemy," online at http://www.oneworld.org/media/gallery/landmines/1.html (24 November 1999).

36   United Nations Association of the United States of America (UNA-USA), "UNA-USA Adopt-A-Minefield Program," online at http://www.unausa.org/programs/aam/adoptamine.htm (24 November 1999).

workshops for activists and training sessions for those going to inspect and report on landmines.

But NGOS and states also were able to do more by using new channels of opportunity. As Robert Lawson, Mark Gwozdecky, Jill Sinclair, and Ralph Lysyshyn point out, "The middle-power/civil society coalition forged by Canada around the AP mine issue was successful in harnessing a number of these new sources of influence—providing a dramatically expanded 'diplomatic tool-kit' for officials developing strategies to influence key decision-makers at state, regional, and global levels."[37]

Three of these "new sources of influence"—or, in terms of a global civil society, channels of opportunity—are critical. First, NGOS and states were able to frame the issue discourse, transforming what many have seen as a security issue to a more nuanced one of human security or humanitarianism. The ICRC clearly made the link between landmines and international humanitarian law. It pointed out that more than 80 percent of the victims were civilians, that many were injured long after war had ceased, and that the injuries suffered were of a horrific nature. It was under this rubric that many of the human rights organizations participated. They did not see international humanitarian law as being exclusively the domain of states.[38] Axworthy provided a frame that was designed to appeal more to traditional states and realist interests by arguing that "with the end of the Cold War, the threat of major conflicts between states has lessened.... Threats to human security—human rights abuses, inter-ethnic tension, poverty, environmental degradation and terrorism—have grown, fueling recurring cycles of violence. Civilians are their primary victims. In these circumstances, to safeguard individual citizens, it is no longer enough to ensure the security of the nation. Security is found in the conditions of daily life ... rather than primarily in the military strength of the state."[39] Thus, the innovation was the ability of both NGOS and state leaders like Axworthy to frame the issue in a way so that groups with various interests would be able to graft their interests to that of landmines and make the heretofore "inaccessible" security

37   Robert J. Lawson, Mark Gwozdecky, Jill Sinclair, and Ralph Lysyshyn, "The Ottawa Process and the International Movement to Ban Anti-Personnel Mines," in Cameron, Lawson, and Tomlin, *To Walk Without Fear*, pp. 160–184.

38   Ramesh Thakur and William Maley, "The Ottawa Convention on Landmines: A Landmark Humanitarian Treaty in Arms Control?" *Global Governance* 5, no. 3 (July–September 1999): 273–302.

39   Canada, Department of Foreign Affairs and International Trade, "An Address by the Honourable Lloyd Axworthy, Minister of Foreign Affairs, to the Opening of the Mine Action Forum," Ottawa, 2 December 1997, online at http://www.dfait-maeci.gc.ca/english/news/statements/97_state/97_057e.htm (24 November 1999).

issue "ring true" to civil society by arguing for the treaty in the name of human security.

Second, NGOs were able to forge closer relationships with states than they ever had in the past. Rather than simply rejoicing at being able to be outside the conference room disseminating information to governmental delegates, NGOs participated as active members of a global civil society. Representatives sat on official delegations, in many cases for the first time. Some, like the ICBL, were given a front seat at the Ottawa table rather than a back-of-the-room position. Many NGOs participated in their government's official deliberations, helped organize the conference, or focused activity at substate or municipal levels. The Italian NGOs seeking landmine bans lobbied municipal governments where landmine manufacturers were located and presented information to the trade unions about the harm their product brought to victims. They effectively brought the global issue to the local level, in this case focusing at the substate level.[40] Nascent NGOs in the South played key roles in organizing two conferences held in the mine-affected countries of Cambodia and Mozambique and in mobilizing the new NGO community in these areas.

NGOs were able to forge such relationships partly because the prohibition of landmines did not challenge major economic or political interests. More than 100 companies in 52 countries produce 344 different types of landmines. For many companies, landmines are just one product among many. Thus, the military-industrial complex did not mount much of a campaign against the treaty, even though certain firms did make their position known.[41] Since the economic interests of most companies were not seriously jeopardized, states were more easily able to support the ban.

Third, NGOs were able to take advantage of new communication technologies to their fullest effect. In the early days of the movement, the phone and fax machine proved most effective. The latter was a step-level improvement in the speed of communication that transformed the dissemination of information to core constituencies. But by late 1995 and early 1996, e-mail and the World Wide Web had transformed information dissemination yet again. Not only could the written word be disseminated via the Internet, but visual images could be transmitted as well. Internet-based technology also aided in the establishment of effective networks; and it provided, and continues to relay, technical information to those in the field doing surveillance and enforcement work. As Richard Price concluded, "'hypermedia'—the global web of electronic media,

---

40   Williams and Goose, "International Campaign."
41   Alex Vines, "The Crisis of Anti-Personnel Mines," in Cameron, Lawson, and Tomlin, *To Walk Without Fear*, pp. 118–135.

including telecommunications, fax machines, and especially the Internet and World Wide Web—have played an unprecedented role in facilitating the growth of a global network of concerned individuals and groups around the landmines issue. Web sites and e-mail have proliferated around the landmines issue, providing a wealth of instantaneously available information that focuses the spotlight on recalcitrants, whether combatants using mines or industries producing them."[42]

Most important, the Web allowed people to act on this information, sending messages to governmental leaders and supporting other NGOS' activities in faraway lands.[43] In providing a critical channel that allows individuals and groups to participate in international and state relations, the Web has expanded the "democratic space" of a global civil society. It is to the implications of this "people-centered" development that we now turn.

4   An Enlarged Multilateralism?

In both the MAI and landmine cases, NGOS were able to take advantage of a global civil society's constitutive dynamics, in combination with the communicative potential of the World Wide Web, to accomplish substantive political objectives. In each case, NGOS assumed important new roles and adopted novel approaches in their interactions with each other, with states, and with international institutions. These dynamics and outcomes are important, in and of themselves, but the two cases also raise broader implications for the future of international relations. Specifically, the landmine and MAI cases suggest that the nature of world politics may be changing in ways that are helping to create an enlarged multilateralism.

Five points provide the contours of an enlarged multilateralism. First, the success or failure of multilateral diplomacy in any given issue area will be affected by how an issue is framed in the public discourse. In each of our cases, NGOS presented and discussed their subject issue in language that "rang true" to key states, groups, and individuals, who then influenced the political process in a variety of important ways. In the MAI case, NGOS were able to tap into public concerns about globalization, a loss of democratic control over political processes, environmental degradation, and the mistreatment of poor

---

42   Richard Price, "Compliance with International Norms and the Mines Taboo," in Cameron, Lawson, and Tomlin, *To Walk Without Fear*, p. 343.

43   See, for example, OneWorld Online, "Landmines—Campaigns," online at http://www .oneworld.org/guides/landmines/landmines_campaigns.html (24 November 1999).

individuals, groups, and countries. As we mentioned earlier, Public Citizen and Oxfam provide notable examples in this regard. In the landmine case, NGOs framed use of the "antipersonnel devices" not as a national security or military security issue but as a humanitarian and human security issue, a personal security issue. This effectively defined each issue participant's position in terms of a simple moral choice for or against the treaty, with exceptions not permitted.[44] In both the MAI and the landmine case, the World Wide Web contributed dramatically to the success of involved NGOs' efforts to frame their issues. Specifically, the Web provided the means to communicate with each other, as well as a relatively inexpensive means to offer immediately available and easily revised information to a wider audience. In the landmine case, the Web's multimedia format also provided the opportunity to help shape issue discourse through the use of visual images and audio clips.

Second, the success or failure of multilateral endeavors will be dependent on effective leadership, the specific form of which may differ from issue to issue. As discussed above, NGOs clearly were primary players in our two subject cases. The World Wide Web allowed NGOs to be more effective leaders— and, in the landmine case, initiators of the political process—by facilitating the gathering and dissemination of information, as well as the building of transnational coalitions. Organizational websites also provided a means for individuals to communicate with others around the world, both private citizens and key government officials, thereby broadening public participation in each issue.

However, particularly in the landmine case, leaders from a group of core states also made several significant decisions and took important steps toward helping NGOs realize their objectives. The landmine treaty was initially drafted by Austrians, with the instructions that it be kept simple and uncomplicated, and was put on a fast track made possible by the Web. The speed at which the World Wide Web allowed information about the treaty to be disseminated and the wide audience that this information reached created a momentum for the treaty process that threatened to leave "slow" states behind. The Web also facilitated speed and organization that, when combined with the no-compromise attitude adopted by key states and NGOs, also left any opposition "out of the loop."

Third, states will continue to play important roles in an enlarged multilateral diplomacy but with new "twists." Key states increasingly will take on different roles in their relationships with other actors. In both the MAI and

---

44   Maxwell A. Cameron, Robert J. Lawson, and Brian W. Tomlin, "To Walk Without Fear," in
      Cameron, Lawson, and Tomlin, *To Walk Without Fear*, pp. 1–17.

landmine cases, states established relationships with NGOs and drew on their insights and skills at certain points throughout the process. Although these relationships were more explicit and extensive in the landmine case than in the MAI case, both cases exhibited similar dynamics in this respect. Key states also will vary from issue to issue, and clearly these states will not always be so-called great powers or hegemons. This reflects a shift similar to the devolution from state to nonstate actors. In the landmine case, Canada and Austria—both middle powers—played key roles. In the MAI case, France similarly played an important role, as did a number of lesser powers and smaller states from the South. Finally, states' importance in multilateral political processes and their influence over the outcomes also will vary, depending on the issue at hand. In the MAI case, states played a relatively more important role in relation to NGOs than was true in the landmine case; and states arguably had a greater influence over the outcome in the MAI case than they did in the landmine case. Such twists may increasingly "muddy the waters" of multilateralism, as changing roles affect the political legitimacy of both states and NGOs in future negotiations and endeavors.

Fourth, an enlarged multilateralism may become more democratized at both the state and international levels, increasingly a bottom-up process that relies for its success on the capabilities and support of nonstate actors. At the state level, this already can be seen in the encroachment of democratic processes on individual countries' foreign policy processes. Both of our subject cases exhibited a similar pattern in this regard. In framing the discourse used to discuss their subject issue, involved NGOs retooled the language in ways that corresponded more closely to their organizational strengths and experiences. Practically speaking, this meant moving away from the detached, objectively framed language widely employed by states and institutions in their discussion of foreign investment and landmine use, in favor of a more frankly stated and emotionally based discourse. It also involved redefining the primary issue areas into which landmines and trade liberalization processes traditionally had been placed, from the more abstract (military security and economics, respectively) to the more practical and publicly accessible (human security and democracy/development/environment). The effect of these shifts, particularly combined with NGOs' extensive use of the Web, was to open to public scrutiny and participation private discussions and political processes conventionally considered the (foreign policy) domain of states. Although arguably few governments recognize that this process is occurring, some (e.g., Canada) have moved to capitalize on it.

Fifth, given the dynamics of the Web and recent advances in transnational communication technologies generally, conventionally negotiated multilateral responses increasingly will lag behind the demand—and the need—for appropriate policy interventions. As illustrated by both the MAI and landmine cases, technological developments (e.g., satellites, faxes, e-mail, mobile phones, the World Wide Web) essentially have collapsed political time by allowing exchanges and processes that once took weeks or months to now be accomplished in hours or days. For example, in the landmine case, norms of prohibition were developed and reproduced with relative speed, in years rather than the decades or centuries of the past. Yet these changes have not been accompanied by appropriately responsive mechanisms on the part of states and international institutions. In both of our subject cases, traditional state-based actors were caught off guard by the speed with which a global civil society used the Web to effectively mobilize people, raise issue awareness, and lobby for particular policy responses. Barring substantive and formalized institutional reforms, this gap between political demands (or needs) and policy responses will continue to widen.

The evolvement of an enlarged multilateralism is not assured, nor are its particulars clearly defined yet. The MAI was under consideration for a long time before it was forced into the open. This confirms the ability of some actors to keep certain discussions out of the public eye and suggests that the movement toward democratization may not be inevitable (at least across all issue areas). Even when issues do enter the public discourse, better-resourced actors—either governments or multinational corporations—may be able to use information, technology, or institutions more effectively. Alternatively, NGOs may find it difficult to collaborate on a given issue—for political or other reasons—or be unable to frame the debate in a way that galvanizes broad public participation.[45] These and other possibilities raise important questions for multilateralism in the coming century: Will trends toward greater centralization of power in some issue areas, such as global finance, be counteracted by the activities of NGOs? Will mechanisms for NGO participation and accountability in multilateral processes become more developed and, possibly, institutionalized? And will NGOs be able to (continue to) use the World Wide Web in ways that will not only facilitate effective political action but also further reinforce the dynamics and processes of an emergent global civil society? The answers to these questions remain unclear for now, but our analysis suggests an affirmative response to each.[46]

---

45   Such has been the case, one might argue, with the campaign to establish a permanent International Criminal Court.

46   Key insights for this paragraph were provided by an anonymous reviewer, to whom we extend our thanks. For further discussion of power and information issues, see

Notwithstanding such uncertainties, the dynamics and processes that characterized the MAI and landmine campaigns are becoming a permanent part of world politics. The French conceded this when they withdrew their support of the MAI, stating: "The MAI ... marks a[n important] step in international ... negotiations. For the first time, we are witnessing the emergence of a 'global civil society' represented by nongovernmental organizations, which are often active in several countries and communicate across borders. This is no doubt an irreversible change."[47] Consistent with this position, we believe that a global civil society and the inherently dynamic communication medium that is the World Wide Web will continue to develop, often hand in hand; that NGOs and nonstate actors increasingly will participate in transnational political processes; and that the effects of these changes will be felt ever more strongly in international relations, both in the relationship between international institutions and states and in the politics of multilateralism.

Robert O. Keohane and Joseph S. Nye, Jr., "Power and Interdependence in the Information Age," *Foreign Affairs* 77, no. 5 (1998): 81–94; and Saskia Sassen's work on globalization, including "Losing Control? The State and the New Geography of Power," *Global Dialogue* 1 (1999): 78–88.

47   Council of Canadians, "France's Official Position."

global_governance.net: The Global Compact as Learning Network

John Gerard Ruggie[1]

Kofi Annan's Global Compact (GC) has attracted wide acclaim in the world's press. In the United States, the venerable *Washington Post* praised it in an editorial, and the *Christian Science Monitor* lauded it as his "most creative reinvention" yet of the United Nations.

At the same time, the initiative has generated suspicion and in some instances sharp criticism by many nongovernmental organizations (NGOs). "The UN's positive image is vulnerable to being sullied by corporate criminals," claims Corpwatch, "while companies get a chance to 'bluewash' their image by wrapping themselves in the flag of the United Nations."[2]

Thus, what the mainstream press views as highly innovative, critics decry as "fatally flawed," reflecting their differing attitudes toward the corporate sector and globalization.

But more subtle factors are also involved in reaching these conflicting assessments. The GC has adopted a learning model for inducing corporate change, in contrast to a more conventional regulatory approach; and it is a network form of organization rather than the traditional hierarchical or bureaucratic form. The upshot of these distinctive (and, for the UN, highly unusual) features is twofold: critics seriously underestimate the GC's potential, while supporters may hold excessive expectations.

1 Objectives

The GC engages the private sector to work with the UN, in partnership with international labor and NGOs, to identify, disseminate, and promote good

---

* This chapter was originally published in Global Governance, Volume 7, Issue 4, 2001.

1 John Gerard Ruggie is Berthold Beitz Professor in Human Rights and International Affairs at Harvard University's Kennedy School of Government and Affiliated Professor in International Legal Studies at Harvard Law School. From 1997 to 2001 he was assistant secretary-general and chief adviser for strategic planning to UN Secretary-General Kofi Annan.

2 *Tangled Up in Blue: Corporate Partnerships at the United Nations* (San Francisco: Transnational Resource and Action Center, 2000), p. 2.

corporate practices based on nine universal principles. These are drawn from the Universal Declaration of Human Rights, the International Labour Organization's (ILO) Fundamental Principles and Rights at Work, and the Rio Declaration on Environment and Development.[3]

Companies are challenged to move toward good corporate practices as understood by the broader international community, rather than relying on their often superior bargaining position vis-à-vis national authorities, especially in small and poor states, to get away with less.

Specifically, companies are asked to undertake three commitments:

1. To advocate the GC in mission statements, annual reports, and similar public venues—on the premise that their doing so will raise the level of attention paid to, and the responsibility for, these concerns within firms.

2. To post on the GC website at least once a year concrete steps to act on any or all of the nine principles, discussing both positive and negative lessons learned, thereby triggering a structured dialogue among the various participants about what is deemed to constitute a good practice.

3. To join with the UN in partnership projects to benefit developing countries largely marginalized by globalization, particularly the least developed.

Companies initiate participation by having their chief executive officer send a letter to the secretary-general expressing their commitment, a step that typically requires board approval. Since a kickoff event in July 2000, some 400 companies worldwide have engaged—from Europe, the United States, Japan, Hong Kong, India, Brazil, and elsewhere. The target is 1,000 firms within three years.

2   Learning Forum

The GC's critics wish it were something that it is *not*: a regulatory arrangement, specifically a legally binding code of conduct with explicit performance criteria and independent monitoring and enforcement of company compliance. Just how does the GC propose to induce corporate change?

---

3   The nine principles are: support and respect for the protection of internationally proclaimed human rights; noncomplicity in human rights abuses; freedom of association and the effective recognition of the right to collective bargaining; the elimination of all forms of forced and compulsory labor; the effective abolition of child labor; the elimination of discrimination in respect of employment and occupation; a precautionary approach to environmental challenges; greater environmental responsibility; and encouragement of the development and diffusion of environmentally friendly technologies.

Its core is a learning forum. Companies submit case studies of what they have done to translate their commitment to the GC principles into concrete corporate practices. This occasions a dialogue among GC participants from all sectors—the UN, labor, and civil society organizations.[4] A research network, led by the Corporate Citizenship Unit of Warwick University, facilitates the dialogue. Its aim is to reach broader, consensus-based definitions of what constitutes good practices than any of the parties could achieve alone. Those definitions, together with illustrative case studies, are then publicized in an online learning bank, which will become a standard reference source on corporate social responsibility. The hope and expectation is that good practices will help drive out bad ones through the power of dialogue, transparency, advocacy, and competition.

Why did the secretary-general choose this approach rather than propose a regulatory code, complete with monitoring and compliance mechanisms? First, the probability of the General Assembly's adopting a meaningful code anytime soon approximates zero. The only countries eager to launch such an effort at this time are equally unfriendly to the private sector, human rights, labor standards, and the environment.

Second, the logistical and financial requirements for the UN to monitor global companies and their supply chains, let alone small and medium-sized enterprises at national levels, far exceed its capacity. For example, Nike, whose past labor practices have made it a frequent target of protesters, has more than 750 suppliers in fifty-two countries, and it is at the lower end among comparable firms in the number of factories as a fraction of its revenue base.[5] When it comes to effective regulation, there simply is no substitute for stronger national action.

---

4   In addition to the five UN participants, they include the International Confederation of Free Trade Unions (ICFTU), an association of national and sectoral labor federations; and more than a dozen transnational NGOs in the three areas covered by the GC, such as Amnesty International and the World Wildlife Fund.

5   The following calculation will illustrate the full magnitude of the task. A Hong Kong-based firm performs social audits (Social Accountability 8000) for a number of U.S. specialty and retail chains that source their products in China. Approximately 250 field technicians manage the export of $1 billion in products. Multiplying that ratio for all U.S. consumer products imports yields a field staff requirement of 55,000 technicians. That already is larger than the worldwide staff of the entire United Nations and all of its specialized agencies combined— and bear in mind that this would cover only the United States and only consumer products, excluding, for example, the extractive industries. The escalating costs of monitoring Central American suppliers experienced by the Gap, a large clothing chain, is reported by Leslie Kaufman and David Gonzalez, "Labor Standards Clash with Global Reality," New York Times, 24 April 2001.

Third, any UN attempt to impose a code of conduct not only would be opposed by the business community but would also drive progressive business leaders into a more uniform anticode coalition.

But these strictly pragmatic reasons imply that a learning-based approach is merely a second-best solution. In fact, there is a far stronger intellectual case.

Many of the GC's principles cannot be defined at this time with the precision required for a viable code of conduct. No consensus exists on what "the precautionary principle" is—that in the face of environmental uncertainty the bias should favor avoiding risk—even though it was enshrined at the 1992 Rio conference. Similarly, no consensus exists, even among advocates, on where to draw the boundaries around corporate "noncomplicity" in human rights abuses. Accumulated experience—through trial, error, and social vetting—will gradually fill in the blanks. The GC learning forum provides that experience.

Moreover, the extraordinary pace of change in corporate strategies, structures, and production processes makes it exceedingly difficult to specify ex ante the full range of performance criteria and desired practices that a code should include. In contrast, the GC learning forum helps companies to internalize the relevant principles so that they can shape and reshape corporate practices as external conditions change. Employees are turning out to be vital allies in this process.[6]

Finally, the accumulation of experience itself is likely to lead gradually to a desire for greater codification, benchmarking, and moving from "good" to "best" practices—including by industry leaders wanting to protect themselves against any possible competitive disadvantage. Laggards will have a harder time opposing actual achievements by their peers than a priori standards.

Thus, there are both pragmatic and principled reasons why the GC adopted a learning model rather than regulation to induce corporate change. Nevertheless, there are certain things that such an approach cannot achieve. The fact that the GC recognizes and promotes a company's "good practice" provides no guarantee that the same company does not engage in "bad" ones elsewhere. Indeed, it may even invite a measure of strategic behavior. Nestlé's recent interest in the GC, for instance, undoubtedly reflects a desire to balance criticism on the breast milk substitute. Moreover, a learning model has no direct leverage over determined laggards. They require other means, ranging from legislation to direct social action.

---

6   A number of participating companies have set up internal websites or other discussion forums enabling employees to comment on company practices in relation to the Global Compact. A corporate-led Scandinavian workshop on diversity in the workplace resulted from one of these. On "internal branding" of this sort, see Bernard Stamler, "Companies Are Developing Brand Messages as a Way to Inspire Loyalty Among Employees," *New York Times*, 5 July 2001.

In sum, the GC's strengths and weaknesses both stem from its having adopted a model that promotes learning by recognizing and reinforcing leadership. It helps create and build momentum toward its universal principles, but it is unlikely to get there by itself.

3   Interorganizational Networks

Organizationally, the GC is an expanding set of nested networks. The five participating UN entities constitute one: the Secretary-General's Office, the UN High Commissioner for Human Rights (UNHCHR), the International Labour Organization (ILO), the UN Environment Programme (UNEP), and the UN Development Programme (UNDP). The Global Compact office in New York is by far the smallest component; its main functions are to provide strategic direction, policy coherence, and quality control.

The core network comprises the UN and the other participants: companies, international labor, transnational NGOs, and university-based research centers. Most of the heavy lifting gets done here.

The Global Compact has triggered several complementary regional, national, and sectoral initiatives. Typically, they take a subset of interested GC participants beyond the subset's minimum commitments. For example, Norway's Statoil and the International Federation of Chemical, Energy, Mine and General Workers' Unions recently reached an agreement within the GC framework whereby Statoil will extend the same labor rights as well as health and safety standards to all overseas operations that it applies in Norway— including Vietnam, Venezuela, Angola, and Azerbaijan.

Finally, a number of initiatives intended for other purposes have associated themselves with the GC. Such business associations as the International Chamber of Commerce, Prince of Wales Business Leadership Forum, International Organization of Employers, and World Business Council for Sustainable Development support the GC in various ways. The most unusual of these partnerships is with the multistakeholder Committee for Melbourne, which is incorporating the GC into the strategic plan it is developing for that Australian city.

Accordingly, the Global Compact exhibits many of the defining attributes of interorganizational networks (IONs), which should be better understood by critics and advocates alike.[7]

---

7   See Rupert F. Chisholm, *Developing Network Organizations* (Reading, Mass.: Addison-Wesley, 1998), chap. 1. For a discussion of network-based organizations in the context of global public policy, see Wolfgang Reinicke and Francis Deng, *Critical Choices: The United Nations,*

- IONs are formed by autonomous organizations combining their efforts voluntarily to achieve goals they cannot reach as effectively or at all on their own. They rest on a bargain, not coercion. The GC's underlying "bargain" is that the UN provides a degree of legitimacy and helps solve coordination problems, while the companies and other social actors provide the capacity to produce the desired changes.
- IONs typically come into being to help their participants understand and deal with complex and ambiguous challenges. They are inherently experimental, not routine and standardized. Few challenges are more complex and ambiguous than internalizing the GC's principles into corporate management practices.
- IONs "operate" as shared conceptual systems within which the participating entities perceive, understand, and frame aspects of their behavior. But the existing actors do all the doing that needs to be done. The GC creates no new entities but is a framework for normatively coordinated behavior to produce a new collective outcome.
- IONs must be guided by a shared vision and common purpose. In the Global Compact, the secretary-general is responsible for sustaining that vision and ensuring that network values and activities are compatible with it.
- IONs are loosely coupled organizational forms, resting on non-directive horizontal organizing principles. Its participants meet when and in formats required to conduct their work.

The major advantage of the GC's network approach is its capacity to respond to the complex and rapidly changing environments that the UN seeks to affect. The UN otherwise lacks that capacity, as do governments, firms, and civil society organizations acting alone or in a different format.[8]

Again, the GC's chief weakness is the same as its main strength. It *is* a network of autonomous actors, each with different interests and needs that intersect only partially. Criticism of the GC for partnering with business fails to appreciate the advantages of interorganizational networks. But by the same token, anyone who sees in the GC the cure for globalization's many ills does not sufficiently grasp the fragile basis of all such networks.

Networks, and the Future of the Global Governance (Ottawa: International Development Research Centre, 2000).

8 For example, the Global Sullivan Principles for corporate social responsibility, a partnership of U.S. firms and some NGOs, lacks the social legitimacy of the UN. As a result, it has picked up virtually no support beyond the United States.

4   The Business of Business

Skeptics still might ask why businesses would take such an arrangement seriously and not treat it as a mere public relations exercise. The most basic rationale is the protection and promotion of a company's brand in the face of new
social expectations, illustrated by the fact that major NGO "brands" now often
dominate companies' brands in public trust.[9] Therefore, it pays for companies to do "good" things—and to be seen to do them.

Some companies have done "bad" things in the past. They have paid the
price in public embarrassment, and even diminished sales or stock values, and
now want to pursue a different path. Others want to ensure that they don't
repeat the errors their peers have committed. Thus, BP is striving in Angola to
avoid Shell's errant ways in Nigeria.

Some companies have come to view global corporate social responsibility as
a natural extension of practices in their home countries, as a rule of the game
in the new global marketplace. Scandinavian-based firms are at the forefront
of this trend.

Still others—particularly companies in knowledge-based industries, where
attracting and retaining absolutely the best personnel worldwide is the key to
success—have found that they cannot sufficiently motivate the very best people, nor meld them into a coherent corporate culture, with monetary rewards
alone. In these cases, more elevated social purposes and principles can help
contribute the necessary incentive and cultural cohesion.[10]

Finally, business has collective interests that are furthered by adopting an
active posture of global corporate social responsibility. The more effective that
is, the less the pressure to accomplish the same ends by other—and potentially far less friendly—ways. Alternatives include throwing the whole bundle
of social and environmental issues into the World Trade Organization (WTO),
regional trade pacts, or national trade legislation where they inevitably would
become part and parcel of the tit-for-tat of a new protectionism.

---

9   The public relations firm Richard Edelman, Inc., conducting research among "thought
       leaders" in the United States, Europe, and Australia, found that NGOs dominate firms
       in terms of public trust in issues related to the environment, human rights, and health.
       Richard Edelman, "The Relationship Among NGOs, Government, Media and Corporate
       Sector," presentation at the Harvard Club of New York, 12 January 2001.
10   Jeffrey Garten also found this to be the case in interviews with global CEOs in Garten, *The
       Mind of the CEO* (New York: Basic Books, 2001).

5   **Conclusion**

The GC seeks to weave universal principles into global corporate behavior. And it brings together all the relevant social actors in doing so: governments, who defined the principles on which the initiative is based; companies, whose behavior it seeks to shape; labor, in whose hands the concrete process of global production takes place; NGOs, reflecting a wider community of stakeholders; and the UN, the world's only truly global political entity.

The Global Compact is a voluntary initiative intended to induce corporate change through identifying and promoting good practices. It is not the only way to achieve those aims, but it is a prototype of one way. Analysts and activists alike should better understand its strengths and weaknesses because it will become a more prevalent response to the challenge of closing global governance gaps in the years ahead.

CHAPTER 8

UN Conferences and Constructivist Governance of the Environment

Peter M. Haas[1]

In this article I review the history of global environmental conferences and draw political lessons about their broader role in constructing efforts at global environmental governance. I also examine the future of global conference diplomacy for the environment, in particular Rio+10 in Johannesburg in 2002 and the prospects of reaching the goals for sustainable development set at the UN Conference on Environment and Development (UNCED). Global conferences are oft-used policy instruments, thus deserving careful evaluation and assessment. Jacques Fomerand expresses justifiable skepticism that most global conferences are momentary media events that provide sound bite opportunities without lasting effects on policies or the quality of the environment.[2] Guilio Gallarotti, and Michael Barnett and Martha Finnemore, offer similar skeptical judgments about the potential for effective state-based international governance.[3] Yet Fomerand also points out, as do I, that many conferences provide indirect effects that may be beneficial for inducing states to take more progressive steps toward governance and sustainable development.

---

* This chapter was originally published in Global Governance, Volume 8, Issue 1, 2002.

1 Peter M. Haas is professor of political science at the University of Massachusetts at Amherst. His recent work focuses on the interplay between international institutions and scientific involvement in the creation and enforcement of international regimes addressing transboundary and global environmental risks. He has consulted for the United Nations Environment Programme, the Commission on Global Governance, and various U.S. agencies and private foundations.

2 Jacques Fomerand, "UN Conferences: Media Events or Genuine Diplomacy?" *Global Governance* 2, no. 3 (1996): 361–375.

3 Michael N. Barnett and Martha Finemore, "The Politics, Power, and Pathologies of International Organizations," *International Organization* 53, no. 4 (1999): 699–732; Guilio Gallaroti, "The Limits of International Organization," *International Organization* 45, no. 2 (1991): 183–220.

1   Governance and Constructivism

Governance has recently become a popular catchphrase of international relations. Without the prospects of hegemonic leadership, and in light of the substantial growth of influence of international institutions and non-state actors,
international rule making has become the domain of multiple overlapping
actors and regimes, rather than the clearcut leadership by one state or multilateral conformity with a small and homogeneous set of shared rules backed
by enforcement mechanisms. Anne Marie Slaughter defines it as "the formal
and informal bundles of rules, roles and relationships that define and regulate the social practices of states and nonstate actors in international affairs."[4]
Sustainable development requires multilateral governance, because without
well-defined rules and expectations most countries are incapable of unilaterally protecting themselves from transboundary and global environmental risks.

   Constructivist scholars of international relations (IR) have been focusing on
the institutional, discursive, and intersubjective procedures by which international governance develops. John Ruggie writes that

> social constructivism rests on an irreducibly intersubjective dimension
> of human action ... constructivism is about human consciousness and its
> role in international life.... Constructivists hold the view that the building
> blocks of international reality are ideational as well as material; that ide-
> ational factors have normative as well as instrumental dimensions; that
> they express not only individual but also collective intentionality; and
> that the meaning and significance of ideational factors are not indepen-
> dent of time and place.[5]

Constructivists look at the mechanisms and consequences by which actors,
particularly states, derive meaning from a complex world, and how they identify their interests and policies for issues that appear new and uncertain.

   It is now widely accepted by most IR scholars that governance increasingly
occurs in a decentralized manner, through a loosely tied network of multiple

---

4 Anne-Marie Slaughter, et al., "International Law and International Relations Theory,"
   American Journal of International Law (July 1998): 371.
5 John Gerard Ruggie, "The Social Constructivist Challenge," *International Organization* 53,
   no. 4 (1998): 856, 879. For other presentations of social constructivism in IR, see Emanuel
   Adler, "Constructivism in International Relations," in Walter Carlsnaess, Thomas Risse, and
   Beth A. Simmons, eds., *Handbook of International Relations* (Beverly Hills: Sage, 2001); and
   Peter M. Haas, "Policy Knowledge and Epistemic Communities," *Encyclopedia of the Social
   and Behavioral Sciences* (London: Elsevier Science, 2001).

actors, states, functional state agencies, and nonstate actors who interact frequently, sometimes at global conferences.[6] Governance of the environment is no different.

Constructivists focus on such distinctive processes as socialization, education, persuasion, discourse, and norm inculcation to understand the ways in which international governance develops. Typically these are complex procedures involving multiple interacting actors that accrue over time and contribute to transformational shifts in perceptions of national identity, international agendas, and the presumptive ways by which national interests are to be attained.

UN conferences contribute to governance and sustainable development by establishing and reinforcing some of these constructivist themes in international relations. As I argue in greater length below, international conferences seldom have direct causal influences on member states' behavior, but their outputs are part and parcel of this broader process of multilateral governance and may contribute to stronger and more effective environmental governance by states.

Accumulated global environmental conferences over the last thirty years have contributed to an aggregate shift in international politics by extending participation and access to environmental diplomacy to national environmental agencies and to nongovernmental organizations (NGOs) and networks of scientists—a process that Fomerand describes as a "large-scale process of social mobilization."[7] Over the last thirty years, governments have added the inspirational norm of ecological integrity to the traditional goals of wealth and power.

The most successful conferences have promoted broader processes of social learning and the construction of new, more comprehensive conceptual frameworks for global environmental governance through issue clarification, popularization of issues, and the introduction of new environmental policymaking approaches to governmental officials. Through this institutionalized constructivist process of participation and education, new norms for environmental protection have been diffused, and participating states have been encouraged to endorse them and to apply them nationally. Gradually, many of these norms have been converted to new institutionalized practices by states. Many states

---

6 Anne-Marie Slaughter "The Real New World Order," *Foreign Affairs* (September–October 1997): 183–197; David Held and Anthony McGrew, David Goldblatt and Jonathan Perraton, *Global Transformations* (Stanford: Stanford University Press, 1999): pp. 53–58; Robert O. Keohane and Joseph S. Nye, *Power and Interdependence*, 3d ed., (New York: Longman, 2001).

7 Fomerand, "UN Conferences," p. 364.

were socialized to appreciate new styles of understanding of relations between economics and ecology and were encouraged to apply new policies to achieve economic development that is more environmentally sustainable than past doctrines.[8] Global environmental conferences have contributed to aggregate substantive changes in environmental governance. The Founex preparations for the UN Conference on the Human Environment (UNCHE) contributed to transcending the environment/development dichotomy in the framing of international environmental policy. As scientific consensus has crystallized around comprehensive forms of ecological management doctrines, the frames and dominant discourses of the environmental conferences have shifted from concern about resource scarcity and depletion to efforts to understand and protect ecosystem integrity. The new consensus over sustainable development that was forged at the 1994 population conference in Cairo states that population growth cannot be considered in isolation of social issues shaping family planning choices, such as women's roles in society, a clear example of the development and application of a new policy discourse at an international conference.[9]

Later, UNCED's Agenda 21 was organized and designed around a matrix of issues, so that policies would be developed to address the interconnections between human activities (industry, agriculture, styles of decisionmaking, consumption patterns, technology) and the environment, as well as between global ecosystems (the atmosphere, fresh water, oceans, land) with chapters of Agenda 21 designed to capture the intersections located in each cell of the matrix.[10] The earlier UNCHE frame work was organized around the more traditional tripartite administrative framework of environmental assessment (evaluation and review, research, monitoring, information exchange), environmental management (goal setting and planning, international consultation and agreements), and supporting measures (education and training, public

---

8   Peter M. Haas, "Social Constructivism and the Evolution of Multilateral Environmental Governance," in Aseem Prakash and Jeffrey A. Hart, eds., *Globalization and Governance* (London: Routledge, 1999); Hart and Prakash, *Globalization and Governance*, pp. 103–133; Peter M. Haas, "Institutionalized Knowledge and International Environmental Politics," in John Ikenberry and Vittorio Parsi, eds., *Manuale di relazaioni internazionale*, (Rome: Gius, Laterza & Figlie, 2001); and Peter M. Haas, "International Environmental Governance," in Chantal de Jonge Oudraat and P.J. Simmons, eds., *Managing a Globalizing World* (Washington, D.C.: Brookings Institution Press, 2001).

9   Fomerand, "UN Conferences," p. 370, Mukul Sanwal, "Sustainable Development, the Rio Declaration, and Multilateral Cooperation," *Colorado Journal of International Environmental Law and Policy* 4, no. 1 (1993): 45–68.

10   "Structure and Organization of Agenda 21," A/CONF.151/Pc/42 9 July 1991.

information, organization, financing, technical cooperation).[11] This had the effect of establishing programs and activities that were not administratively associated with the specific functional issue or international problem that justified their creation. Environmental monitoring, for example, would be a free-standing activity, unrelated to the specific contaminants warranting monitoring. Similarly, problems were defined in isolation, and management responses were associated with each distinct problem. While UNCHE was organized around a conceptual framework of traditional administrative functions, UNCED was set up to capture the newly appreciated analytic attributes of the issues being addressed.

Thus, internationally endorsed policies and responses were designed to address the interplay of environmental problems, including their underlying causes. At UNCED, problems were delimited in terms of the interacting array of social forces that caused them, and thus policies were designed to address the social causes—in contrast to the UNCHE approach, which devised a standard set of monitoring and administrative reforms for problems that were addressed individually and outside of their social context.

Consequently, when combined with the other array of institutional and participatory reforms introduced at various UN environmental conferences over the last thirty years, these new frameworks and agendas have led to a much broader shift in discourse, as new institutions were established to address the new policy components of the agenda. These institutions also serve to popularize the language and policy ingredients for the policy communities worldwide.

Ultimately, international conferences are weak institutional features of international relations that lack many of the properties that constructivists expect to contribute to transformed state beliefs and practices. Constructivists have identified a number of institutional design features that may induce states to recognize new interests and embark upon new patterns of practice. Notable among these features are iterated inter-actions, autonomous secretariats staffed with professionals recruited on merit, independent and capable executive heads, free and easy access to independent experts, significant institutional resources for carrying out meaningful technological and resource transfers, and adequate institutional budgets. Few international conferences are endowed with these properties by sponsoring states. The most successful conferences emerged from repeated preparatory meetings; were supported by secretariats recruited on merit, led by adroit and experienced UN diplomats, such as Maurice Strong; maintained a porous flow of information with

11   "Report of the United Nations Conference on the Human Environment," A/Conf.48/14
      3 July 1972, p. 23; UNEP, *In Defense of the Earth* (Nairobi: UNEP, 1981).

independent experts outside the UN system; and had sufficient resources to support the preparations. Few international conferences had the ability to provide resource transfers to encourage states to participate, although some of the more successful conferences created institutions that had that capability.

Governments generally follow the preparatory activities to ensure that they are not confronted with any unpleasant political surprises at the actual conferences. Because they are one-time events, there is limited access to top-level officials, and it is difficult to maintain long-term pressure on governments through national reporting, information circulation, oversight, or lobbying. Thus, it is difficult for transnational policy networks to organize and consolidate influence through global environmental conferences. Global environmental conferences usually lack significant political or financial resources for inducing change on states and lack any lock-in mechanisms by which decisions become deeply institutionalized within the legal and political systems of attending countries. Occasionally, though, some conferences are able to generate significant outputs or mobilize individual forces that have long-term repercussions internationally.

UN conferences, though, are quite different from the G-8 summits in this regard. Unlike the one-shot nature of UN conferences, the G-8 summits are part of smaller institutionalized discussions among trade and finance ministers and bureaucrats, who maintain frequent interactions at G-8 summits, Organization for Economic Cooperation and Development (OECD) working groups, International Monetary Fund (IMF) working groups, Bank for International Settlements (BIS) working groups, and private conferences. Unlike these small ongoing private group meetings, UN conferences enjoy greater and broader political legitimacy by virtue of their universal representation and the opportunity for middle-level powers and small powers to have a say.

The effects of the most successful conferences have been to increase national concern and to increase government capacity to address problems politically and technically by means of agenda setting, consciousness raising, expanded participation, monitoring, knowledge generation and diffusion, target setting, norm development and diffusion, and administrative reforms. In addition, they have helped to channel financial, technological, and scientific resources to needy countries.[12]

---

12   Peter M. Haas, Robert O. Keohane, and Marc A. Levy, eds., *Institutions for the Earth* (Cambridge: MIT Press, 1993); Fomerand, "UN Conferences," pp. 361–375; Wolfgang H. Reinecke and Francis M. Deng, *Critical Choices* (Toronto: IDRC, 2000).

2   The UN Conferences on the Environment

Global UN conferences on the environment are widely understood as an institutional innovation of the 1970s. With mounting concern about the degradation of the physical environment, governments approached the UN to convene a number of global conferences to address the host of human activities with transboundary and global environmental consequences. These environmental conferences became part of a broader effort at global problem solving that addressed a new class of challenges associated with international interdependence. As global interdependence became increasingly politicized in the 1970s, the UN system turned to global conferences to highlight the interconnections between issues that had previously been treated in isolation. The topics of the global conferences were new to the international agenda, as previous multilateral conferences had principally addressed issues of international economics, human rights, and arms control.[13] The UN, as the only venue with global participation, was the logical forum for such meetings.

The 1972 UNCHE and the 1992 UNCED directly addressed the subject of environmental protection, but special UN conferences devoted to different aspects of human impact on the environment became commonplace in the 1970s. The frequency of such global conferences diminished in the 1980s and 1990s. What has remained constant are the decadal meetings of conferences on population, women, and food, as well as the follow-up annual reviews on UNCED commitments and the more comprehensive and high-profile UNCED+5 meeting in 1997 and the UNCED+10 meeting to be held in 2002.

These global conferences performed multiple functions. They were intended to mobilize concern about new problems, to coordinate national actions to study and monitor environmental quality and human activities with environmental consequences, and to develop joint measures to prevent various sources of environmental degradation and attenuate the effects of human actions on the environment. Economic and equity concerns cut across most of the other specialized conferences.

Typically a conference lasts for several weeks, with high-level diplomatic attendance during the last two or three days to overcome political deadlocks and to sign legally binding resolutions and other commitments developed at the conference. Decisions are generally reached by consensus, so negotiations

---

13   On the previous generation of global conferences, see Johan Kaufmann, *Conference Diplomacy*, 2d ed. (New York: UNITAR, 1988); and Peter Willetts, "The Pattern of Conferences," in Paul Taylor and A.J.R. Groom, eds., *Global Issues in the United Nations' Framework* (New York: St. Martin's Press, 1989).

are slow. Preceding a conference, though, are often several rounds of ad hoc Preparatory Committee sessions ("Prep Coms"), often spread over one to two years, at which national delegations are presented with background papers and preliminary negotiations are conducted on the documents intended for approval at the conference. Most of the arduous work of reconciling political differences occurs during the Preparatory Committee sessions.

Generally the global UN conferences on the environment have produced declarations and action plans for subsequent activities. The most influential conferences endorsed new policy doctrines and policy targets for the international community, authorized the creation of new international organizations, approved legal commitments, and generated new financial resources. The most productive, in terms of their administrative accomplishments, have been UNCHE, the 1974 World Food Conference, UNCED, and the 1994 International Conference on Population and Development.[14] Others, such as the 1977 Conference on Desertification, the 1979 Conference on Science and Technology for Development, and the Conferences on Human Settlements, have failed to spark international concern or to catalyze robust international commitments and action.

The 1972 UNCHE, held in Sweden, was the first major global environmental conference. Sponsored by the UN, it convened 113 countries to discuss contemporary environmental issues. UNCHE adopted the Stockholm Declaration, establishing twenty-six principles of behavior and responsibility to serve as the basis for future legally binding multilateral accords; and the Action Plan for the Human Environment that specified 109 recommendations in the areas of environmental assessment, environmental management, and supporting institutional measures.[15] Implementation was intended for governments and international organizations (IOs).

The 1992 UNCED, held in Rio de Janeiro, marks the high-water mark of these outputs. UNCED adopted the Framework Convention on Climate Change, the Convention on Biological Diversity, and the Statement of Forest Principles. In addition to those three pieces of hard law, UNCED adopted the Rio Declaration, with 287 principles of guiding action, and Agenda 21, a sweeping action plan to promote sustainability, with 2,509 specific recommendations applying to states, international institutions, and members of civil society. The Commission on Sustainable Development was created to ensure effective follow-up of UNCED;

---

14   Thomas G. Weiss and Robert S. Jordan, *The World Food Conference and Global Problem Solving* (New York: Praeger, 1976); Lynton Caldwell, *International Environmental Policy* (Durham: Duke University Press, 1996).
15   *The Results from Stockholm* (Berlin: Erich Schmidt Verlag, 1973).

to enhance international cooperation and rationalize intergovernmental decisionmaking capacity; and to examine progress in Agenda 21 implementation at the local, national, regional, and international levels.[16]

The variation in the degree of influential outputs from conferences is due to a number of factors. The more productive conferences were free of profound political schisms or geopolitical tensions among major parties, including Cold War tensions. The environment was not nested in a politically irreconcilable frame of profound North-South cleavages. The issue at hand appealed to the immediate interests of the industrialized countries because of either popular concern within the countries or perceived linkages between the subject and material national interests, leading major donor states to commit resources to the issues. Robert Putnam and Nicholas Bayne inferred a number of similar background conditions from successful G-7 summits.[17]

UNCHE, for instance, was held at a fortuitous moment. Domestic environmental movements were just becoming active in the United States and Europe. Potential North-South disagreements were avoided by prior high-level discussions that rejected the conceptual dichotomy between economic growth and environmental protection; extended the international agenda to include environmental concerns of the South regarding natural resource policy as well as the pollution concerns of the industrialized countries; and provided a notional commitment to "additionality" and financial assistance on behalf of the North.[18] Environmental protection was not seen as inconsistent with other established goals in international negotiations, including national security and economic liberalization. UNCHE also provided the first opportunity, following U.S. recognition, for China to stake out a position in international diplomacy. North-South relations became more acrimonious with the New International Economic Order (NIEO) discussions in the late 1970s, making it harder to forge consensus at international conferences. Even with these factors, Cold War divides still modestly influenced the conference, as the Soviet Union and the Eastern bloc countries withdrew at the last minute over the participation of West Germany; yet, because the superpowers were in a period of détente, such tactical linkages were not perceived as provocative and freighted with Cold War significance.

---

16   Michael Grubb et al., *The Earth Summit Agreements: A Guide and Assessment* (London: Earthscan and Royal Institute of International Affairs, 1993).

17   Robert D. Putnam and Nicholas Bayne, *Hanging Together* (Cambridge: Harvard University Press, 1987).

18   Wade Rowland, *The Plot to Save the Earth* (Toronto: Clarke, Irwin, 1973); Maurice Strong, "One Year After Stockholm," *Foreign Affairs* 51, no. 4 (1973).

2.1   Effectiveness of International Conferences

It is difficult to evaluate the effectiveness of many of these conferences, in part because of weaknesses and gaps in our ability to monitor progress in achieving conference goals. The record is generally mixed, at best, in terms of achieving the targets and aspirations expressed in the action plans and declarations of the conferences. It is difficult to measure directly the effects on the environment, and the record of states in complying is mixed or uncertain. The goals are often ambiguous. State reporting about compliance is generally weak and incomplete, and few provisions for verification of state compliance are made at the conferences. Most assessments of conference successes remain impressionistic and anecdotal, although some conferences generated new doctrinal consensus or new institutions to help advance the conference goals (such as UNCHE, with the UN Environment Programme [UNEP]; the 1974 World Food Conference, with the World Food Programme and the International Fund for Agricultural Development [IFAD]; the 1994 World Population Conference, with its strong endorsement of new population policy albeit without strong institutional support; and UNCED, with its support for the new doctrine of sustainable development but still with a weak Commission on Sustainable Development). At UNCED+5 the General Assembly and the Commission on Sustainable Development tried to evaluate overall progress achieved since UNCED. It determined, among many observations, that production and consumption patterns had become more energy efficient in industrialized countries; that land use conflicts were more acute in developing countries between competing demands for agriculture, forest cover, and urban uses; and that water scarcity remains a major threat to development and human health in developing countries.[19]

In short, it is difficult to evaluate the effectiveness of the conferences on state policies and on observable environmental impacts. It would be unreasonable to expect such conferences to yield lasting and clear effects on states and on the environment. It is equally unreasonable to assign blame to conferences for failing to reverse environmental decline.

A full list of global environmental conferences is presented in Table 8.1.

2.2   Functions of Conference Diplomacy

Global environmental conferences also have a number of indirect effects with longer-term effects on national policies that affect international governance and the prospects for sustainable development. Without a strong theory of

---

19   "Overall Progress Achieved Since the United Nations Conference on Environment and Development," E/CN.17/1997/2.

state interests, it is not possible to draw clear causal inferences about the influence of international conferences on state interests and practices. Theorists across paradigmatic divides, with the exception of staunch rational choice theorists, should be able to agree that conferences that are able to mobilize more of the functions I discuss later in this article will have a stronger impact on member states than will conferences unable to mobilize as many. Some variables are of interest to neoliberal institutionalists because they influence state assessments of the economic cost of environmental pollution, the ecological benefits of its solution, and the political coalitions associated with each functional issue on the agenda. Conferences thus influence international linkage politics. For constructivists, important variables are the information channels and actual pieces of information that shape states' appreciation of how their citizens are affected by environmental degradation and the political coalitions that support environmental protection. The causal mechanisms by which institutional factors influence state choice are highly contingent upon national administrative characteristics and domestic state/society relations. Moving beyond a systemic level of analysis, variation in an individual state's sensitivity to these functions of conference diplomacy would probably vary by at least the following national level factors: freedom of the press, literacy, access to the media, and democratic institutions that enable citizens to express concern to governments (state/society relations).[20]

While it is not possible to directly stop human activities that degrade the environment through universal declarations or at conferences, global UN conferences can enhance governments' concern about the environment and strengthen their willingness to commit scarce political and financial resources to its protection.

Agenda setting. Global environmental conferences can place new issues on the global agenda and galvanize national concern by publicizing these issues. The conferences often have the effect of reframing issues for decisionmakers, locating the issue within a new political matrix, and thus making possible new tactical and substantive linkages by which policies may be developed.[21] For instance, environmental protection was firmly placed on the international agenda at the UNCHE conference, and the preliminary Founex meeting

---

20   Peter M. Haas, "Compliance with EU Directives," *Journal of European Public Policy* 5, no. 1
      (1998): 38–65; Peter M. Haas, "Choosing to Comply," in Dinah Shelton, ed., *Compliance
      with Soft Law* (Oxford: Oxford University Press, 2000).

21   Ernst B. Haas, "Why Collaborate," *World Politics* 32, no. 3 (1980); Vinod K. Aggarwal, ed.,
      Institutional Designs for a Complex World (Ithaca: Cornell University Press, 1998).

TABLE 8.1   Global environmental and sustainable conferences since 1972

Year	Name, location	Product/outcome
1972	United Nations Conference on the Human Environment, Stockholm	Declaration of Principles Action Plan UNEP
1974	World Food Conference, Rome	Universal Declaration on the Eradication of Hunger and Malnutrition World Food Council IFAD
1974	World Population Conference, Bucharest	World Population Plan of Action
1975	World Conference on Women	
1977	UN Water Conference, Mar del Plata, Argentina	International Drinking Water Supply and Sanitation Decade (1981–1991)
1977	UN Conference on Desertification, Nairobi	Plan of Action to Combat Desertification
1978	UN Conference on Human Settlements, Vancouver	UN Centre for Human Settlements Global Strategy for Shelter to the Year 2000
1979	UN Conference on Science and Technology for Development, Vienna	Vienna Programme of Action on Science and Technology for Development
1979	World Climate Conference, Geneva	
1981	UN Conference on New and Renewable Sources of Energy, Nairobi	Nairobi Programme of Action for the Development and Utilization of New and Renewable Sources of Energy
1984	World Conference on Agrarian Reform and Rural Development, Rome	Programme of Action on Agrarian Reform and Rural Development
1984	Second World Population Conference, Mexico City	
1985	World Conference on Women	
1990	Second World Climate Conference, Geneva	Intergovernmental Panel on Climate Change (IPCC)

TABLE 8.1   Global environmental and sustainable conferences since 1972 (*cont.*)

Year	Name, location	Product/outcome
1992	UNCED, Rio de Janeiro	Rio Declaration Agenda 21 Framework Convention on Climate Change Convention on Biodiversity Statement of Forest Principles UN Commission on Sustainable Development
1994	International Conference on Population and Development, Cairo	Programme of Action
1995	Fourth World Conference on Women, Beijing	Beijing Declaration and Platform of Action
1996	Habitat II, Istanbul	The Habitat Agenda and Istanbul Declaration on Human Settlements
1996	World Food Summit, Rome	Rome Declaration on World Food Security and the World Food Summit Plan of Action
1997	UNGA Special Session on Sustainable Development	

SOURCE: JACQUES FOMERAND, "UN CONFERENCES: MEDIA EVENTS OR GENUINE DIPLOMACY?" *GLOBAL GOVERNANCE* 2, NO. 3 (1996): 361–375; THOMAS G. WEISS, DAVID P. FORSYTHE, AND ROGER A. COATE, *THE UNITED NATIONS AND CHANGING WORLD POLITICS*, 2D ED. (BOULDER: WESTVIEW, 1997), ESP. CHAP. 9; LYNTON CALDWELL, *INTERNATIONAL ENVIRONMENTAL POLICY* (DURHAM: DUKE UNIVERSITY PRESS, 1996)

effectively reconciled North-South differences about the priority accorded to environmental considerations in economic planning. The meeting established the principle that the two goals could be compatible, especially with concessionary finance from the North to pay for incremental pollution control costs in the developing countries. UNCHE also helped inform Northern governments of Southern countries' concern about resource deterioration, deforestation and water quality, and the underlying problems of insufficient money for sewage treatment and effective resource management. The North gradually came to appreciate the possibility of an alternate agenda that would include the South's concerns and still supplement the North's primary focus on industrial pollution, waste management, and transboundary environmental threats.

The 1994 International Conference on Population and Development shifted public debate and discourse on population issues to a focus on the underlying social, political, and economic forces that influence population growth. The Programme of Action marked a distinctive shift in population policy toward promoting cooperation to eradicate poverty, encouraging universal access to health care services, and empowering women.[22]

Popularizing issues and raising consciousness. Conferences provide a brief window of opportunity for educating the mass public and government officials about environmental issues. Conferences spawn publicity about the declarations and statements of principles the meetings produce. Because many journalists attend the conferences, they provide an opportunity for NGOs and the media to publicize issues and to educate members of the media about environmental issues. For instance, at UNCED the Natural Resource Defense Council (NRDC) sent one person whose responsibility was to court the media and frame the presentation of the daily reporting in a way that would be critical of the United States. NRDC hoped to provoke the United States into taking a more environmentally sympathetic role at the conference.

Generating new information and identifying new challenges for governments. Preparation for conferences often generates information for countries about their environmental problems, the array of policies available for addressing such issues, and the political coalitions organized around them. States are invited to submit in advance of the conference national reports about conditions in their countries. This process can lead states to learn of new problems, clarify recognition of their national interest, and identify the political landscape potential for compromise. These reports are often synthesized by the secretariats for subsequent dissemination.[23]

Providing general alerts and early warning of new threats. Conferences help focus attention on new problems and also help identify institutional gaps and needs in addressing such problems. The "Assessment of the World Food

---

22   Lori S. Ashford March, "New Perspectives on Population," *Population Bulletin* 50, no. 1 (1995); Gita Sen, "The World Programme of Action: A New Paradigm for Population Policy," *Environment* (January–February, 1995).

23   For instance, International Conference on Population and Development, "Synthesis of National Reports on Population and Development," UN Document A/49/489 (6 October 1994).

Situation," presented to the 1984 World Food Conference, helped focus attention on the "world food gap" that threatened developing countries. UNCHE helped identify the urgency of addressing land-based marine pollution and the institutional need to create a global environmental monitoring system, which subsequently became one of UNEP's core activities.[24]

Galvanizing administrative reform. Conferences also prompt governments to create or reform national bodies responsible for forms of environmental protection. National administrative bodies serve as the nodes of transnational environmental policy networks. At the time of UNCHE, only 26 governments had administrative agencies responsible for environmental protection (15 in developed, 11 in developing countries). The preparation for UNCHE led many governments to recognize the need for creating national environmental agencies. By 1982, the total number was up to 144 (34 in developed, 110 in developing countries). UNCED led to the establishment of Sustainable Development (SD) committees and bodies in nearly 150 countries.[25]

Adopting new norms, certifying new doctrinal consensus, and setting global standards. Global conferences are sites of doctrinal contestation. UNCHE developed new principles of soft law that have been interpreted and applied by international lawyers to inform a generation of international environmental lawyers.[26] Specific programmatic action, such as the 2,509 specific proposals in Agenda 21, set the stage for legitimate responses to international conferences. The identification of the number of people at risk from malnutrition and targets for official development assistance (ODA) and hunger reduction stipulated at World Food Conferences similarly established standards and aspirations for subsequent governmental practices.

Promoting mass involvement of new actors. International environmental conferences contribute to the participation of new actors in international environmental politics by inviting new groups of actors to attend international conferences. Environmental conferences have been leaders in the introduction of NGOs to international diplomacy. These meetings developed the practice,

---

24   Branislav Gosovic, *The Quest for World Environmental Cooperation* (London: Routledge, 1992).

25   E/CN 17/1997/2, p. 24.

26   Edith Brown Weiss, "The Emerging Structure of International Environmental Law," in Norman J. Vig and Regina S. Axelrod, eds., *The Global Environment* (Washington, D.C.: CQ Press, 1999); Edith Brown Weiss, Daniel Barstow, and Paul C. Szasz, *International Environmental Law* (Dobbs Ferry, N.Y.: Transnational, 1992).

introduced at UNCHE, of holding parallel NGO conferences and governmental conferences and admitting NGO participants as observers at the governmental conferences. Roughly 178 NGOs participated at UNCHE.[27] Over 1,400 were represented at UNCED.

Despite the vast increase in the number of NGOs attending international environmental conferences, the participation is still heavily tilted toward the North, where NGOs have greater financial support and are better able to find resources to attend conferences. At UNCED, 70 percent of the registered NGOs came from industrialized countries.

Conferences provide the potential for networking and developing transnational issue networks to coordinate international campaigns, and NGOs may subsequently provide information to governments and apply pressure on governments.

Conferences often invite participation from major nonstate groups, including NGOs, the transnational scientific community, and, since UNCED, multinational corporations.[28] Such groups are invited to attend expert group meetings in advance of the conference, participate in parallel NGO events, and even attend governmental meetings as observers. Participation is often, particularly in preliminary meetings, by expert advisory groups of specialists such as the Joint Group of Experts on Scientific Aspects of Marine Environmental Protection (GESAMP), the International Council of Scientific Unions (ICSU), and umbrella industry NGOs, such as the International Chamber of Commerce (ICC). Mass public NGOs tend not to participate in the early stages.

Global environmental conferences may be deliberately designed to foster new coalitions more generally and to build support for environmental protection at the national level by including the political influence of transnational policy networks. Maurice Strong, secretary-general of UNCHE and UNCED, coined the phrase "the process is the policy" to capture the idea that through conference diplomacy more actors and perspectives could be introduced to international environmental policymaking.

There is still a wide variation in the extent of NGO influence at conferences. The rules of participation remain set by states' decisions in ECOSOC, and the organizations are continually constrained (if not totally hamstrung) by state choices to allocate resources and set rules of behavior for the organizational dealings with NGOs. NGOs are often more influential at national

---

27   Anne Thompson Feraru, "Stockholm and Vancouver: The Role of ISPAs at UN Conferences," in William M. Evan, *Knowledge and Power in a Global Society* (Beverly Hills: Sage, 1981).

28   Stephan Schmidheiny, *Changing Course* (Cambridge: MIT Press, 1992).

and community levels, but participation and recognition at international conferences reinforces or establishes their domestic claims to authority. Yet even while states cling to formal sovereignty, the exercise of practical sovereignty erodes with NGO participation.[29] Still, Realists would be quick to point out that the willingness to extend participation to NGOs is given by states and is always subject to being reversed.

2.3   Prospects for Rio+10 and Sustainable Development

The aggregation of UN conferences and constructivist forces has been to create a diffuse array of pressures on states militating for forms of sustainable development. Rio+10 provides the next major opportunity for reforming and streamlining multilateral environmental governance. It is intended to refocus international attention on sustainable development and to assess accomplishments since 1992.

Yet, as with the writing of this piece, it lacks most of the properties of conferences that led to productive outputs that contributed to improved international environmental governance. Rio+5 was widely regarded as a failure in this regard, as it did not mobilize any long-standing interest. Mass public interest in sustainable development remains weak, and the United States appears to be developing a new global diplomatic posture of skeptical multilateralism, at best, as seen by the abandonment of the Kyoto Protocol and the Anti-Ballistic Missile (ABM) Treaty. Consequently, there is little political impulse for a productive conference. Multilateral financial and technological transfers for sustainable development have dwindled since the early 1990s. Moreover, there is growing disenchantment with UNEP's remote location in Kenya and its lack of resources. The Commission for Sustainable Development lacks the administrative autonomy or financial resources to be able to reach out to civil society to develop any of the conference functions discussed above that could potentially influence state policies and environmental quality. States also appear increasingly concerned about controlling NGO participation at the meetings.

The best prospects for products from the Rio+10 are probably institutional reforms. The international environmental governance system has not been significantly overhauled in three decades. After UNCHE, UNEP was the only

---

29   See the following articles in *World Politics* 51, no. 1 (1998): Konrad von Moltke, "The Organization of the Impossible," pp. 23–28; John Whalley and Ben Zissimos, "What Could a World Environmental Organization Do?" pp. 29–34; Peter Newell, "New Environmental Architectures and the Search for Effectiveness," pp 35–44; Frank Biermann, "The Emerging Debate on the Need for a World Environment Organization," pp. 45–55. See also Kathryn Hochstettler, Ann Marie Clark, and Elisabeth J. Freidman, "Sovereignty in the Balance," *International Studies Quarterly* 44, no. 4 (2000): 591–614.

international institution responsible for environmental protection. Since then, however, most international institutions have assumed some environmental responsibilities. Recent evaluations suggest that there are administrative overlaps in the system and inefficiencies, as institutions have assumed new responsibilities for the environment.[30] Suggestions for improvements focus on reforming UNEP and on creating a Global Environmental Organization (GEO).

A GEO should be established to fulfill the policy and technology-based functions that provide institutional support for multilateral environmental governance. A GEO would consolidate environmental policy research, technology databases, and clearinghouses; conduct training; and centralize the secretariats that administer current environmental regimes. Centralizing these secretariats would facilitate the creation of a broader global policy network across specific environmental issues and justify the creation of national environmental embassies to represent states and participate in future negotiations. A GEO could also serve as a legal advocate for environmental protection and regulations to counter-balance the World Trade Organization (WTO) by collecting a roster of international environmental lawyers to participate in WTO panels. The GEO should have high-profile annual ministerial meetings to address all environmental issues to ensure widespread involvement in environmental policy networks and galvanize rapid responses to new alerts. Ongoing efforts would continue to be addressed through the existing secretariats and conferences of parties. The GEO could even have a panel of environmental inspectors available to verify compliance by states and firms with multilateral environmental agreements. UNEP would be retained as the monitoring and research hub of the UN system, as it was initially intended by its architects at UNCHE. The UN Commission on Sustainable Development, as well as some other institutional bodies within the UN and Bretton Woods systems, could be absorbed into the GEO.

---

30   For a review of these proposals, see *Global Environmental Politics* 1, no. 1 (2001); Frank Biermann, "The Case for a World Environment Organization," *Environment* 42, no. 9 (2000): 22–31; Calestous Juma, "The UN's Role in the New Diplomacy," *Issues in Science and Technology* 17, no. 1 (2000): 37–38; Dan Esty, "The Case for a Global Environmental Organization," in Peter B. Kenen, ed., *Managing the World Economy: Fifty Years after Bretton Woods* (Washington, D.C.: Institute for International Economics, 1994), pp. 287–309; David Downie and Marc A. Levy, "UNEP," in Pamela S. Chasek, ed., *The Global Environment in the Twenty-First Century* (Tokyo: UN University Press, 2000).

3 Conclusion

UN environmental conferences have helped contribute to a broader shift in international environmental governance through educating governmental elites, exposing them to new agendas and discourses, and providing them with added resources to pursue sustainable development. While Rio+10 lacks many of the conditions that have accompanied successful conferences, Rio+10 may at the least encourage multilevel participation, improve contact between civil society and states, and streamline institutional responsibilities within the UN and Bretton Woods systems for sustainable development.

While the political preconditions appear modest for any dramatic achievements and cognitive transformations at Rio+10, we must remember that the conference is part of a thirty-year-long era of multilateral environmental protection. The conference can continue to legitimate the participation of NGOs and scientists in international environmental governance, improve contact between civil society and states, and streamline institutional responsibilities within the UN and Bretton Woods systems for sustainable development. Even in the absence of strong political support by member governments for significant multilateral commitments, progressive governments and other conference participants can still press for reforms to existing arrangements that will ensure more national reporting on their movement toward sustainable development, create information clearinghouses about green technologies, and endow UNEP, a new GEO, or another international institution with verification authority to monitor international movement toward sustainable development.

CHAPTER 9

How "New" Are "New Wars"? Global Economic Change and the Study of Civil War

Mats Berdal[1]

Attempts to comprehend, through empirical inquiry and philosophical reflection, the likely effects of deeper, seemingly unstoppable processes of socioeconomic change on patterns of violent conflict within and across societies are not new. Indeed, the relationship between the momentous transformations wrought by industrialization and the long-term prospects for war and peace was a prominent theme of political and sociological thought in nineteenth-century Europe. In a celebrated lecture, delivered at the London School of Economics in 1957, Raymond Aron observed how thinkers such as Auguste Comte and Herbert Spencer, both profoundly conscious of "living in a period of transition," had been prepared to make prophecies about the future of war "whose boldness and dogmatism astound us."[2] By the time Aron himself came to reflect on the subject, the horrors of two world wars and the terrifying prospect of another even more destructive conflict ensured that "long-range historical predictions" were decidedly out of fashion. Instead, the Cold War came to be marked by an acute concern with the present; a concern that shaped and, in important respects, also distorted thinking about war and peace. The latter was true in particular for the study of civil or intrastate wars, wars whose local sources and regional dynamic were often overshadowed by a preoccupation with the central strategic balance and the competition for influence between East and West.

The end of the Cold War, then, involved more than just a release from the balance of terror. It also had a liberating impact on the study of conflict, causing a "strong feeling of living in a period of transition" to again permeate much of the writings and debates about sources of war and peace in the international

---

* This chapter was originally published in Global Governance, Volume 9, Issue 4, 2003.

1 Mats Berdal is professor of security and development in the Department of War Studies in the School of Social Science and Public Policy and Director of the Conflict, Security and Development Research Group at King's College London (University of London). An earlier version of this article was presented at the Annual Conference of the International Institute for Strategic Studies (IISS) in Geneva in September 2001.

2 Raymond Aron, *War and Industrial Society* (London: Oxford University Press, 1958), p. 3.

system. While the emergence of industrial society had preoccupied an earlier generation of thinkers, "globalization" has, to many, assumed a similar role of describing the sense that we are living through a period of universal, far-reaching, and irreversible changes.

1 Structure, Qualifications, and Argument in Brief

Of special interest to this article is the more specific suggestion that processes of globalization have contributed to changes in the nature of war so profound that one is justified in talking of "New Wars."[3] This claim to newness rests, in part, on the assertion that changes in the nature and workings of the global economy, especially in the 1980s and 1990s, are impacting uniquely on the patterns and character of intrastate and/or region-wide conflict around the world. This article examines this assertion in greater detail. It does so, however, against the backdrop of a wider debate, one that has focused on the economic agendas of belligerents, local populations caught up in conflict, and external actors in the emergence and consolidation of contemporary wars. There are two reasons for thus widening the debate. In the first place, the salience of economic agendas in contemporary wars is considered by many to be directly and causally connected to changes in the global economic environment over the past quarter century or so. Secondly, by assessing the comparative importance of one set of factors, the article hopes to contribute to a broader discussion, which the New Wars debate has helped to stimulate, about the nature of contemporary wars.

It is a basic premise of the article that this can most usefully be done by drawing upon the actual knowledge, however incomplete and fragmentary, that we now have of individual conflicts. As such, what follows is not an exercise in grand theorizing about global economic change and war. It represents a more modest, though necessary, effort to test generalizations, unspoken assumptions, and implied causal connections that are often made about contemporary forms of warfare, against our understanding of individual cases. To this end, special attention is given throughout the article to what we know (and,

---

3   Mary Kaldor and Basker Vashee, eds., *New Wars* (London: Pinter, 1998); and Mary Kaldor, *New and Old Wars: Organized Violence in the Global Era* (Cambridge, Mass.: Polity Press, 2001). It should be noted at the outset that the argument for "New Wars" does not rest solely, or even principally, on the claim that global economic processes have transformed the nature of warfare. This is, however, one of its more interesting claims, and, crucially for the purpose of this article, it is the one that lends itself, at least in theory, to further empirical investigation.

indeed, what we do not fully comprehend) about wars in West and Central Africa, Algeria, and the former Yugoslavia.[4]

With these qualifications and considerations in mind, the article has been divided into three parts. The first places the study of war briefly within the broader context of debates on globalization. It emphasizes the limited utility of globalization as an analytical category and argues that a more precise focus on economic globalization is required if anything of value is to be said about the so-called global economic underpinnings of contemporary wars. Even so, this still leaves the question of just how global economic processes—including the effects of financial liberalization, partial industry deregulation, speed and ease of transactions, the growing importance of private actors, and private capital flows—relate to the outbreak and dynamics of armed conflict. The relationship cannot simply be assumed. There are two, distinct but related, ways in which the connections between economic globalization and contemporary wars have been approached.

The first, of a more *indirect* kind, revolves around the linkages that are said to exist between globalization, poverty, inequality, and war. Specifically, it has been argued that rapid economic globalization is contributing to a growing "cleavage between rich and poor [that] represents a deep form of structural violence."[5] This in turn, so the argument runs, helps to explain the growth of intrastate war and violent conflict in many parts of the developing world. It is an argument that will be examined here only briefly. Instead, the principal concern of this article is with the second approach alluded to above, that is, with evidence pointing toward a more *direct* relationship between global economic processes and ongoing intrastate wars. The attempt to establish these more direct connections cannot easily be separated from the wider discussion that has taken place, especially since the mid-1990s, about the precise role of economic agendas in civil wars. These agendas are examined more fully in the second part of the article.

Part three steps back to look at the limitations of explanations that privilege the role of economic factors and, in particular, it explores critically the view that global economic processes now play a crucial role in sustaining wars. In doing so, it also offers a broader critique of those who have stressed the "newness" of contemporary wars. In brief, it argues that the attention given to

---

4 Stathis Kalyvas argues persuasively that much of the writings that seek to establish the "newness" of contemporary civil wars are based on information that is "incomplete and biased." See "'New' and 'Old' Civil Wars: A Valid Distinction?" *World Politics* 54 (October 2001): 99.

5 Susan Willett, "Globalization and Insecurity," in Susan Willet, ed., *Structural Conflict in the New Global Disorder*, IDS Bulletin, vol. 32, no. 2, April 2001, p. 5 (henceforth *New Global Disorder*).

economic agendas and their global underpinnings represents a necessary and valuable addition to the study of civil wars. These elements, however, must be placed in a proper historical perspective and carefully balanced against a wider range of human motivations and explanatory factors. As the concluding section makes clear, an appreciation of continuity as well as change, of material as well as nonmaterial incentives, of the unique as well as the common characteristics of conflict, are all required if external actors—be they governments, international organizations, or nongovernmental organizations—are to be more effective in addressing the roots and mitigating the consequences of armed conflict.

2   Globalization and the Study of Contemporary Civil Wars

The lack of precision with which the term *globalization* is typically used presents a serious obstacle to a better understanding of the way in which the workings of the world economy, or parts of it, may or may not be influencing patterns of armed conflict. At one level, the term is no more than a "*metaphor* for the sense that a number of universal processes are at work generating increased interconnection and interdependence between states and between societies."[6] In theory these processes can be quantified and their impact assessed, though this usually leads to endless (mostly inconclusive) debates about the interpretation of data and the kind of inferences that can legitimately and meaningfully be drawn from what is, inevitably, a limited and random selection of indices. Certainly, the view that we now live in an inescapably interdependent world is hardly novel. Reinhold Niebuhr may not have spoken of global interdependence in 1944 but he did talk of a "technical civilization" whose "instruments of production, transport and communication [had] reduced the space-time dimensions of the world to a fraction of their previous size and [had] led to a phenomenal increase in the interdependence of all national communities."[7]

To others, the term *globalization* is entirely divorced from any heuristic purpose, concealing instead ideological predispositions and political biases. At one end of the spectrum, terms such as *global village* or *global neighborhood* do little more than express an aspiration, perfectly noble, to a better world. At

---

6   Andrew Hurrell, "Explaining the Resurgence of Regionalism in World Politics," *Review of International Studies* 21, no. 4 (1995): 345 (emphasis in original).

7   Reinhold Niebuhr, *The Children of Light and the Children of Darkness* (New York: Charles Scribner's Sons, 1944), p. 158.

the other extreme, the term is sometimes no more than a convenient byword for an aspect of the modern world of which one disapproves or is especially concerned, as in the equation by some French intellectuals of *mondialisation* with an insidious cultural onslaught on home-grown values and aesthetic sensibilities. Either way, whether globalization is treated as a source of unbridled hope or the deepest gloom, it cannot serve as a starting point for analysis.

Although these considerations highlight the limited utility of the term as an analytical category, this has not deterred social scientists, including those engaged in the study of war, from resorting to its use. Indeed, much of the writings on the so-called New Wars of the 1990s typically proceed from a loose understanding of globalization as "the widening and deepening of economic, political, social and cultural interdependence and interconnectedness."[8] The difficulty with this is not whether changes have occurred or not in each of these areas, nor whether there is greater continuity with the past than is sometimes supposed. From an analytical viewpoint, the deeper problem lies in the term's "totalising pretensions" and the deeply distorting effect this invariably has on any effort to understand individual cases and specific mechanisms at work.[9] To understand these, as Frederick Cooper has perceptively remarked, we need "concepts that are less sweeping, more precise ... which seek to analyze change with historical specificity rather than in terms of a vaguely defined and unattainable endpoint."[10]

While much of the writing on New Wars suffers from this lack of precision, it has nevertheless drawn attention to distinctive aspects of global change whose possible links to war and conflict do lend themselves, at least in theory, to more systematic empirical investigation. The most obvious of these, and the principal focus of this article, are the processes (themselves in need of further definition) subsumed under "economic globalization."[11]

The core features and principal drivers of economic globalization in the late twentieth and early twenty-first century are not fundamentally in dispute. Assessing their significance, either in historical, political, or even economic

---

8   Willett, "Globalization and Insecurity," p. 1. Likewise, Kaldor speaks of "globalization" as the "intensification of global interconnectedness—political, economic, military and cultural." Kaldor, *New and Old Wars*, p. 3.

9   Frederick Cooper, "What is the Concept of Globalization Good For? An African Historian's Perspective," *African Affairs* 100, no. 399 (April 2001): 193.

10   Ibid., p. 192.

11   There are, of course, other global connections to conflict that merit attention but which are beyond the scope of this article. See, for example, Paul Richards, *Fighting for the Rain Forest: War, Youth and Resources in Sierra Leone* (Oxford: James Curry, 1996), and David Turton, ed., *War and Ethnicity: Global Connections and Local Violence* (Rochester, N.Y.: Rochester University Press, 1997).

terms, is more contentious. In brief, technological change and financial liberalization have—with accelerating speed since the late 1970s—worked in tandem to stimulate a marked growth in the "relative weight of transactions and organizational connections that cross national boundaries."[12] Financial liberalization was initially boosted by the wave of deregulation in the 1980s and has since been powerfully reinforced by revolutions in the field of communications and information technology, and by further efforts to reduce regulatory obstacles to cross-border flows of capital and services. Alongside and closely related to these all-important changes in the global financial architecture, has been the internationalization of production, evidenced in the growth of foreign direct investment (FDI) and a more prominent role for multinational or "transnational" (Susan Strange's preferred term) corporations in the world economy.[13] International trade has also grown rapidly in recent decades, while, more significantly, its character has changed away from merely the movement of goods between countries toward "a flow of goods within production networks that are organized globally rather than nationally."[14]

The extent to which these developments have resulted in a world economy that is more truly integrated is a subject of continuing debate. Robert Wade suggests that a careful reading of the data points to processes that are more international than global.[15] Razeen Sally has argued that there are elements distinctive to late twentieth-century globalization and emphasizes "the phenomenal rise of North-North intra-industry trade and the vertically integrated cross-border networks of multinational enterprises."[16] He firmly rejects, however, the proposition that economic globalization itself is "novel and unprecedented," and that we live in an increasingly borderless world.[17] Finally, there is the argument that the picture of economic globalization presented above

12   Peter Evans, "The Eclipse of the State? Reflections of Stateness in an Era of Globalization," *World Politics* 50, no. 1 (October 1997): 65.

13   David Held, Anthony McGrew, David Goldblatt, and Jonathan Perraton, *Global Transformations: Politics, Economics and Culture* (Cambridge, Mass.: Polity Press, 1999), pp. 236–282; and Susan Strange, *The Retreat of the State: the Diffusion of Power in the World Economy* (Cambridge: Cambridge University Press, 1996), p. 44.

14   Evans, "The Eclipse of the State?" p. 66.

15   Robert Wade, "Globalization and Its Limits: Reports of the Death of the National Economy are Greatly Exaggerated," in Suzanne Berger and Ronald Dore, eds., *National Diversity and Global Capitalism* (Ithaca, N.Y.: Cornell University Press, 1996), pp. 60–88.

16   Razeen Sally, "Globalization and Policy Response: Three Perspectives," *Government and Opposition* 35, no. 2 (Spring 2000): 241.

17   Ibid. For the view that we live in an increasingly borderless world, see Kenichi Ohmae, *The Borderless World: Power and Strategy in the Interlinked Economy* (New York: Harper Collins, 1990).

is only really recognizable as an "OECD plus" phenomenon, and that to speak of greater interconnectedness and integration on a global scale is strictly misleading. These may all be considered legitimate criticisms of what has been dubbed the hyperglobalization thesis. As such, however, they do not deny the reality of change in the world economy, including the greater mobility and ease of access to capital and finance, improved communication and transportation links, partial deregulation of industries, and, more generally, a greater density of transnational processes of production and exchange.

The question, then, becomes how do these developments relate to the nature and prevalence of contemporary intrastate conflict? There are two ways in which the question may be approached.

The first of these is concerned with what is left out of the description above, that is, with those parts of the world economy that have not benefited from economic globalization. Specifically, the growth and prosperity that economic globalization has unquestionably brought to developed economies have been contrasted with an increase in poverty in developing economies and a widening of inequalities globally. This, it has been argued, provides an important explanation for the rise in intrastate conflict, with the implication that there is a relatively clear-cut and unambiguous causal connection between economic globalization, socioeconomic dislocation, and the outbreak of violence. The second approach draws attention, more directly, to the manner in which contemporary wars tie into and are sustained by global processes, and, in particular, how the mechanisms of a more open and deregulated international economy have enabled belligerents not only to maintain but also to develop a vested economic interest in continued conflict. This article concentrates on the latter of these approaches. A brief observation on the debate (and much of the literature) on the broader connection between global economic change and the outbreak of armed conflict is nevertheless in order.

There is no doubt that once war has broken out, it feeds on and is nourished by economic deprivation and underdevelopment, often giving the war in question a difficult-to-break logic of its own. There is also some evidence indicating that greater openness in the world economy (encouraged by the partial removal of policy barriers to cross-border financial movements and other restrictions on access to domestic markets) combined with new technologies that allow for instantaneous trading have, in some cases, facilitated the rapid transmission of social and economic tensions, leading *in extremis* to political destabilization and large-scale civil violence.[18] The most obvious and oft-cited

---

18   See Raphael Kaplinsky, "Globalization and Economic Insecurity," in Susan Willet, ed., *New Global Disorder*, pp. 15–16, and "Global Financial Flows and their Impact on Developing

example is that of Indonesia in 1997 and 1998, whose financial and political turmoil appears to suggest that the rapidity and ease with which capital now moves in response to market and other signals (often leading to speculative attacks on currencies) can be highly destabilizing in politically fragile, ethnically divided, and economically weak economies. Yet it is a major leap from these observations to the much more sweeping assertion that economic globalization is somehow inherently conflict generating, an assertion found in much of what may loosely be described as the antiglobalization literature. The causal connections between economic globalization, socioeconomic dislocation, and the outbreak of war are in fact far from unambiguous. In a thoughtful and carefully researched piece examining the efforts of scholars to link environmental stress and demographic pressures to violent conflict, Morris Miller has drawn attention to the persistent failure to explain "when, where, and how the tension and resultant stress become transmuted into armed violence on a societal scale."[19] This, indeed, is also a basic problem with much of the globalization literature that has sought to establish a crude causal relationship between global economic change and intrastate war in the early twenty-first century.

3   The Economics of Civil Wars

It is commonplace to assert that the period since the end of the Cold War has witnessed a marked rise in the number and intensity of civil wars, and that international conflict is increasingly a relic of the past. The perfunctory, uncritical, and ahistorical manner in which this claim is often presented hides a more complex reality. Civil wars are far from unique to the post-Cold War period. Moreover, the very distinction between "civil" and "international" tends, on closer inspection, to be less than clear-cut. What is beyond doubt, however, is that the international community has taken greater interest in conflicts that would in the past more readily have been classed as falling within the domestic jurisdiction of a given state. Such interest, while fragile and highly selective in application, has stimulated the study of contemporary civil wars, wars whose

---

Countries: Addressing the Matter of Volatility," Report of the UN Secretary General, 1998, reprinted (in part) in Barry Herman, *Global Financial Turmoil and Reform* (Tokyo: UNU Press, 1999), pp. 29–42.

19   Morris Miller, "Poverty as a Cause of Wars?" *Interdisciplinary Science Review* 25, no. 4 (2000): 282.

horrors and apparent intractability have all too often confounded the efforts of
outside actors to bring violence to an end.

Understanding why these wars have tended to persist, in spite of external
efforts to resolve them, has been aided by the increased attention given to the
role of economic motivations or agendas in the emergence and perpetuation
of violence.[20] By posing the question of what *functional utility* violence may
be serving to participants in wars—to elites, ordinary people caught up in war,
and external actors that stand to gain from conflict—it becomes possible to
discern how a set of vested interests in the continuation of war may emerge.
Over time, such interests will crystallize into a distinctive war economy, usually forming part of a regional pattern of informal economic activity. While
these war economies are costly and catastrophic for societies as a whole,
they may be highly profitable and lucrative for individuals and groups within
society. The characteristics of these economies, the role played by economic
agendas, and the specific claims to "newness" resting on the presumed link
between wars and global economic processes, are best examined in relation to
individual cases.

3.1   The Economic Logic of War

A striking example of how the calculations of disparate actors add up to a war
economy with a logic of its own is provided by the case of Angola in the 1990s,
perhaps the most carefully researched modern war economy.[21] Whereas
both the Movimento Popular de Libertação de Angola (MPLA) and the late
Jonas Savimbi's União Nacional para Independência Total de Angola (UNITA)
benefited substantially from external patronage in the earlier phase of their
long, drawn-out confrontation—the MPLA supported by the Soviet Union and
Cuba, UNITA receiving aid from apartheid-era South Africa and the United
States—the end of the Cold War required a readjustment of support strategies,
especially for UNITA, whose international backing was withdrawn once the
UN Security Council identified it as primarily responsible for the resumption
of civil war in 1992. Jonas Savimbi, at one stage lauded by Jeanne Kirkpatrick

---

20   See *Greed and Grievance: Economic Agendas in Civil Wars*, Mats Berdal and David Malone,
      eds., (Boulder: Lynne Rienner, 2000). See also David Keen, *The Economic Functions of
      Violence in Civil Wars*, Adelphi Paper 320 (Oxford: Oxford University Press/IISS, 1998).
21   See Philippe Le Billon, "Angola's Political Economy of War: The Role of Oil and Diamonds,
      1975–2000," *African Affairs* 100, no. 38 (January 2001); Jakkie Cilliers and Christian
      Dietrich, eds., *Angola's War Economy: The Role of Oil and Diamonds* (Pretoria: Institute for
      Security Studies, 2000); and Tony Hodges, *Angola from Afro-Stalinism to Petro-Diamond
      Capitalism* (Oxford: James Currey, 2001).

as "one of the few authentic heroes of our time,"[22] was able to regroup, in large part, because of UNITA's capture and control of key diamond production areas. Control of these, which fluctuated in the 1990s but is thought to have peaked in 1996 when UNITA was able to exploit key diamond fields in the Cuango Valley and eastern Lundas, allowed Savimbi to finance his war effort.[23] Not only that, during the comparative lull in fighting following the signing of the Lusaka Protocol in November 1994, and subject to UN sanctions, UNITA was able to emerge, by mid-1998, as a more resilient and formidable military force than it had arguably ever been.[24] At the same time, the exploitation of widely dispersed alluvial deposits, much less capital-intensive than kimberlite deposits, created the conditions for local traders, middlemen, and regional UNITA commanders to accumulate considerable fortunes. For President José Eduardo Dos Santos and the government side in the war, often neglected in Western policy discussions about Angola, revenues associated with the exploitation of Angola's considerable oil wealth provided the main source of economic security and personal enrichment for the MPLA elite. Benefiting handsomely from the clientist reallocation of oil revenues, Dos Santos's inner circle and state *nomenklatura* had little interest in peace. In sum, the abundance of natural resources in Angola enabled the MPLA and UNITA to consolidate their respective military positions throughout the 1990s and to keep the war going at a terrible price.[25]

Angola's war economy throughout the 1990s is not the only one to be based on the exploitation of natural resources. It has been suggested, most explicitly in a report by a UN-appointed panel of experts in April 2001, that the war that has raged with fluctuating intensity since 1996 in the Democratic Republic of Congo (DRC), has come to be driven largely by economic agendas and interests. In fact, the report concludes that the war is "mainly about access, control and trade of five key mineral resources: coltan, diamonds, copper, cobalt and gold," and it details exploitation of these by means of confiscation, extraction,

---

22   Backcover quote in Fred Bridgland, *Jonas Savimbi: A Key to Africa* (New York: Paragon Publishers, 1987).

23   Estimates of the value of diamond production in UNITA-controlled territory between 1992 and 2000 cannot be established with any degree of certainty. The most widely used estimate is between U.S.$3 and 4 billion, unevenly distributed by year reflecting the military fortunes of the movement. See also Christian Dietrich, "UNITA's Diamond and Exporting Capacity," in Cilliers and Dietrich, eds., *Angola's War Economy*, pp. 274–290.

24   See Jakkie Potgieter, "'Taking Aid from the Devil Himself'—UNITA's Support Structures," Cilliers and Dietrich, eds., in *Angola's War Economy*, p. 263.

25   Le Billon, "Angola's Political Economy of War," p. 79.

forced monopoly, and price-fixing.[26] It highlights the opportunistic behavior of private companies and influential individuals, focusing on the role played by Burundi, Rwanda, and Uganda.[27] And, significantly, it seeks to establish a firm link between economic exploitation of resources and the continuation of war. William Reno's suggestion that conditions of modern warfare might in some cases be better understood as "an instrument of enterprise and violence as a mode of accumulation" was made, not surprisingly in light of the above, with the conflict in Central Africa in mind.[28]

Similar processes of accumulation and predatory economic activity can be found in the interrelated wars that, for much of the 1990s, have engulfed Liberia and Sierra Leone.[29] In both countries a struggle among warlords for control of the state has carried with it substantial and direct economic benefits for some; economic opportunities for others previously excluded from established and corrupt patronage networks; an expansion of the informal and criminalized sectors of the economy; and new alliances between warlords and external actors (including neighboring states, traders, and businesses based in and outside West Africa). In the character and career of Charles Taylor, the Liberian civil war has also provided an example of the warlord par excellence and a particularly persuasive case for the need to integrate economic analysis into the study of contemporary civil wars. Indeed, by one definition, "warlords are, quite literally, businessmen of war" wielding "violence as the main instrument of their economic activity."[30] Between 1990 and 1994, Taylor is believed by one estimate to have made U.S.$75 million per year by levying taxes on Liberian diamond, gold, iron ore, rubber, and timber exports organized from territory

---

26   "Report of the Panel of Experts on the Illegal Exploitation of Natural Resources and Other Forms of Wealth of the Democratic Republic of Congo," UN Doc. 2/2001/357 (12 April 2001), para. 213, (henceforth "UN Report on Illegal Exploitation in the DRC"), available online at http://www.eldis.org/static/DOC10939.htm.

27   The report largely ignores the role of Zimbabwe that came to the aid of the DRC government under President Joseph Kabila and whose military also helped itself to the riches of Congo (Zimbabwean troops deployed to the copper and cobalt rich areas in Katanga). See "Branching Out: Zimbabwe's Resource Colonialism in DRC," *A Report by Global Witness* (Global Witness: London, February 2002).

28   William Reno, "Shadow States and the Political Economy of War," in Berdal and Malone, eds., *Greed and Grievance*, p. 57.

29   For background see Adekeye Adebajo, *Liberia's Civil War* (Boulder: Lynne Rienner, 2002); Stephen Ellis, *The Mask of Anarchy: The Destruction of Liberia and the Religious Dimension of an African Civil War* (London: Hurst and Company, 1999); John L. Hirsch, *Sierra Leone: Diamonds and the Struggle for Democracy* (New York: International Peace Academy, 2001).

30   Patrick Chabal and Jean-Pascal Daloz, *Africa Works: Disorder as Political Instrument* (Oxford: James Curry, 1999), p. 85.

under his control.[31] This was when he was still technically a rebel. Part of the income from his highly lucrative business deals was used to purchase weapons originating in former Warsaw Pact countries and brought in through the neighboring states of Côte d'Ivoire and Burkina Faso. It was also used to pay senior commanders, thus securing their loyalty and also ensuring that his ethnic and regional base of support remained intact.[32]

Angola, Congo, Liberia, and Sierra Leone all illustrate how, in the context of acute state weakness or state collapse, war and violence give rise to economic opportunities for a range of actors, both at the level of elites and among populations adjusting to the dislocations and stresses of war. For warlords the demand for resources, and for people the demands for survival, give rise to new and, even, expanding forms of economic activity. Indeed, Liberia offers an example of "how a country may collapse but extend its economic influence as an informal economy comes to dominate."[33] But state collapse does not provide the only set of circumstances in which economic motives come to play a significant role. The Algerian civil war, which erupted soon after the military coup of January 1992, and the cancellation of the second round of parliamentary elections that might otherwise have brought the main Islamist movement, the Front Islamique du Salut (FIS), to power, also created economic opportunities, chances for plunder, and the accumulation of wealth. These were seized upon by leaders of *both* the armed Islamic groups and the military, and help explain local patterns of violence and the persistence of the war. Indeed, as Luis Martinez shows, the war as a whole, savage and immensely costly in human terms, presents a paradox: "an intense degree of violence has been accompanied by job creation (especially in the profession of arms), by considerable investment in the oil and gas sector, and by lively activity in the commercial sector."[34]

3.2   *Collusion, Fragmentation, and Regionalization*
The logic at work in the Algerian and other cases is connected to a further paradox evident, to varying degrees, in civil wars where economic agendas have played a prominent part: the tendency for opposing parties to acquire a shared interest in reaping the benefits of war and, if local conditions permit, avoid costly and drawn-out battles. Where chains of command are weak and the

---

31   Ellis, *The Mask of Anarchy*, pp. 90–91.

32   Ibid. See also Keen, *The Economic Functions of Violence*, p. 32, and John Mackinlay, "War Lords," *RUSI Journal* 143, no. 2 (April 1998): 24–32.

33   Ellis, *The Mask of Anarchy*, p. 166.

34   Luis Martinez, *The Algerian Civil War* (London: Hurst and Company, 2000), pp. 16, 119–146.

scope for plunder is particularly great, fighting may assume an almost ritualistic quality serving instead as a cover for looting and plunder. Between 1993 and 1997, commanders and officers of the murderous Khmer Rouge, Cambodian government officials, and Thai army officers cooperated without much difficulty in illegal logging and the trade in gems.[35] In this and other cases, "the point of war" is not to win but rather to confer "legitimacy on actions that in peacetime would be punishable as crimes."[36] Cooperative arrangements, reflecting an implicit or even explicit understanding between warring parties, are usually highly localized and often coexist with fierce fighting elsewhere along the "front" (a term that, strictly speaking, ceases to have much meaning). In Angola, for example, trade and local business deals between UNITA and government forces, including the sale of weapons, coexisted with periods of fighting.[37] Even the wars of Yugoslav succession—wars characterized by deep-seated conflicts of identity and fueled by exclusionary and racist visions of ethnic unity—were certainly not free from instances of adversarial cooperation, much of it highly organized and of long duration. In Bosnia between 1992 and 1995, alliances emerged on the ground that were held together not so much by blood and ethnic kinship as by the promise of profit and loot. The practices of ethnic cleansing and the siege conditions that existed in Sarajevo, Bihac, and enclaves in eastern Bosnia, provided their own business opportunities, through plunder, monopolistic control of vital supplies (notably gasoline, which led to the emergence of "petrol barons" in Serbia and Croatia), and informal economic activity on a large scale.[38]

In situations where participants become preoccupied primarily with economic gain, a process of fragmentation typically sets in, with major armed factions splintering into smaller groups and units. The result is a mutation of the original conflict to the point where "immediate agendas assume an increasingly important role," which in turn "feed into economically-motivated violence."[39] In the case of Liberia, the initial insurrection against the hated and

---

35   See Mats Berdal and David Keen, "Violence and Economic Agendas in War: Some Policy Implications," *Millennium* 26, no. 3 (1997).

36   Keen, *The Economic Functions of Violence*, p. 12.

37   Alex Vines, *Angola and Mozambique: The Aftermath of Conflict*, Conflict Studies 280 (London: RISCT, 1996), p. 14.

38   See David Rohde, *A Safe Area: Srebrenica* (London: Simon and Schuster, 1997), pp. 107–109; Brendan O'Shea, *Crisis at Bihac: Bosnia's Bloody Battlefield* (Basingstoke: Sutton Publishing Limited, 1998); Tim Judah, *The Serbs: History, Myth and the Destruction of Yugoslavia* (New Haven: Yale University Press, 1997), pp. 242–258; Final Report of UN Commission of Experts Established Pursuant to Security Council Resolution 780 (1992), S/1994/674/Annexes, Annex Summaries and Conclusions, UN Document, 1994.

39   Keen, *The Economic Functions of Violence*, p. 24.

oppressive regime of Samuel Doe was quickly followed by the proliferation of armed factions, by one estimate as many as eight in 1994.[40] In Algeria, the "gradual distancing of the 'Emirs' from their initial struggle against the regime, to concentrate on economic rather than military activity, was one of the major turning points in the urban guerrilla war."[41] Once the first generation of district emirs, those that had been motivated principally by political and ideological grievances, had been eliminated, "new fighters attracted more by the profits of the enterprise than by the original objective" came to the fore.[42]

The actual process of mutation and the resulting political economy of conflict can also be stimulated by the chosen policies of the international community toward the conflict in question. In the particular case of Yugoslavia, evidence suggests that sanctions had the paradoxical effect of strengthening (at least for some time) President Milosevic's hold on power, and that the sanctions regime resulted not so much in the collapse of the country's economy as in its transformation into a criminalized war economy. The components of that economy included a variety of moneymaking schemes that grew up around sanctions: monopolistic control of trade in oil and other strategic goods subject to sanctions, the selective granting by the regime of lucrative licenses for exports/imports and foreign exchange dealings, and dramatic growth in corruption and the criminalization of the state as a result of the weakening of the formal economy.

An important aspect of the process of mutation outlined above lies in the transnational or transborder characteristics that many modern war economies have acquired, especially over time.[43] This is one reason why the terms "intrastate," "civil," or "internal" used to describe conflicts are often so problematic. Region-wide networks of informal economic activity provide the connecting tissue that links different countries and a diverse set of official and unofficial actors together. In the case of Sierra Leone's war, Nigeria, Guinea, and Liberia have all been directly drawn into the conflict, while other West African countries have played a significant though more indirect role in that war's continuation. Angola, although torn by its own internal struggle, was also caught up in the war in neighboring Democratic Republic of Congo; a war in which no fewer than five other countries have, at various times, been directly engaged (Rwanda, Uganda, Burundi, Namibia, and Zimbabwe). Transborder

---

40   Anthony Clayton, *Frontiersmen: Warfare in Africa Since 1950* (London: UCL Press, 1999), p. 195.

41   Martinez, *The Algerian Civil War*, p. 139.

42   Ibid.

43   Mark Duffield, "Globalization, Transborder Trade and War Economies," in Berdal and Malone, eds., *Greed and Grievance*, pp. 69–91.

networks and linkages, especially of a criminal kind, were also essential to the continuing violence and instability in the Balkans.[44] Yet another example is provided by Afghanistan, where, as Barnett Rubin has shown, more than two decades of war gave rise to a region-wide "political economy of war and peace" whose constituent parts and geographical scope included Dubai and Iran to the west, Pakistan to the east, and the Central Asian republics to the north.[45]

3.3   The Claim to Newness: Local Wars, Global Connections

How, then, do these wars relate to processes of economic globalization over the past quarter century or so, and what, if anything, is new about them? The link to global processes has in fact been alluded to in several of the aforementioned cases. Jeroen de Zeeuw and Georg Frerks provide a succinct summary of the implied relationship, relating it specifically to the issue of resource extraction:

> Globalization has opened up new opportunities for individual nonstate actors within weak states to link to global trading networks and potential partners without state interference. Improved communication technology, fast capital movements and increased deregulation in Western economies have created the necessary preconditions for coalitions between local warlords, private business, intermediary agents and emerging private security companies to capitalise upon the lack of states control on resource extraction.[46]

The importance of global networks and access to world markets derives, in other words, from the observation that war economies are not self-sustaining (indeed, quite the opposite where formal state structures have all but collapsed) and that warring parties, while they may control assets and resources, remain dependent on external support for their realization, and procurement of arms and other supplies.

There is clearly some evidence in support of the general proposition that many contemporary civil wars have been sustained by virtue of their

44   Thomas Köppel and Agnes Székely, "Transnational Organized Crime and Conflict in the Balkans," in Mats Berdal and Mónica Serrano, eds., *Transnational Organized Crime and International Security: Business as Usual?* (Boulder: Lynne Rienner, 2002).

45   Barnett R. Rubin, "The Political Economy of War and Peace in Afghanistan," *World Development* 28, no. 10 (2000): 1790.

46   Jeroen de Zeeuw and Georg Frerks, Proceedings, Seminar on the Political Economy of Internal Conflict, 22 November 2000, Netherlands Institute of International Relations (Clingendael), December 2000, p. 5. (Henceforth, "Proceedings Political Economy Seminar"), p. 10.

integration into world markets of various sorts. With respect to Angola, the readiness of the diamond industry to address the issue of conflict diamonds is partly a reflection of the ease with which international sales were plowed back into UNITA's war chest. Likewise, the Angolan government's exploitation of its country's oil wealth has relied on the technological capacity and investment of foreign oil corporations for extraction, and close and politically delicate relations between these and the regime of President dos Santos have long existed. Of the other cases, Stephen Ellis notes how, right through the civil war, "each Liberian warlord of any substance had alliances with foreign businessmen and at least one foreign government."[47] In Afghanistan, the indomitable fighter and Tajik warlord Ahmad Shah Massoud reached agreement with a Polish firm in 1999 for the marketing of the precious gems (lapis lazuli and emeralds) from the territory he controlled in northeast Afghanistan.[48] As Rubin shows for Afghanistan as a whole, the transit, drug, gem trade, and their associated service industries fit into a pattern of regional economic activity with global connections.[49]

Insofar as global connections can be shown to have assumed a more critical role in recent times, and that they have heightened the salience of economic agendas in war, they also provide the most interesting claim to "newness" for contemporary wars. It is to this wider issue I now turn.

4   The Not-So-New Aspects of New Wars

An awareness of the economic self-interest of local elites, vulnerable populations concerned with survival, and external actors in pursuit of profit helps correct earlier and more simplistic explanations of the prevalence of intrastate wars in the 1990s. In particular, it challenges those who have seen a "new barbarism" at work in many of today's war zones, and those who have prioritized, supposedly primordial, ethnic divisions and tensions at the exclusion of other factors.

And yet a sense of proportion must be maintained in evaluating the economic underpinnings of contemporary wars. Indeed, one-sided attention to economic motives and the global character of conflict also runs the risk of creating a distorted picture of what is driving actors to violence and war. The principal source of distortion is the tendency of some policymakers and academics,

---

47   Ellis, *The Mask of Anarchy*, p. 164.
48   Rubin, "War and Peace in Afghanistan," p. 1796.
49   Ibid., p. 1797.

while generalizing across different cases, to focus excessively on the material and greed-inspired motivations of actors. More specifically, there are three sets of difficulties with the way in which the so-called greed-and-grievance debate has been framed. These also apply more broadly to the argument that we are faced with regarding so-called New Wars as distinct from those of an earlier era, be it "old wars," "Clausewitzean wars," or "wars of classical modernity":

- The failure to account for the full range of motives that inspire or incite violent behavior; the coexistence of such motives at different levels (that is, elite, grassroots, and external) during conflict; and, critically, their interaction over time to produce a distinctive dynamic of conflict.
- The absence of a proper historical perspective; one that draws both on the insights and scope for comparison offered by the history of warfare and, at the same time, is mindful of the specific historical context in which a given armed conflict occurs.
- The tendency to simplify and, in many cases, exaggerate the relative importance of global economic process in sustaining civil wars.

Again, each of these abstract categories is most meaningfully explored by reference to specific cases and examples.

4.1   *Motives and Agendas in Civil Wars*

The juxtaposition of greed and grievance in relation to which much of the debate on civil wars has been conducted, has diverted attention away from the fact that economic motives can only be meaningfully examined in the context of, and in interaction with, a range of different motives that drive men and women to resort to violence. Indeed, Paul Richards, drawing on his study of the culture, history, and civil war in Sierra Leone, argues that "models of economic causality in general show severe limitations in understanding what was going on in these conflicts," and that the focus on greed alone may be particularly distorting. Other elements include struggles for power, religious dimensions of conflict, and "deep-rooted cultural and ideological complexes."[50] They also include those that are instinctively uncomfortable to many social scientists and conflict researchers—honor, prestige, fear, and pride—but which are difficult to get around in individual cases. Ioan Lewis writes that the Somalis possess "an extraordinarily developed sense of personal and collective superiority [which] informs and powerfully affects dealings with others at the family, clan, and national or ethnic level, for Somalis, despite everything, believe there is no nation superior to theirs."[51] It is too easy to dismiss these kinds of ele-

---

50   "Proceedings Political Economy Seminar," p. 5.
51   Ioan M. Lewis, "Why the Warlords Won," *Times Literary Supplement*, 8 June 2001, p. 3.

ments as being invented or merely instrumental, though clearly their relative importance must be set in context and balanced against other factors. Doing so poses a major challenge for outside observers, and calls for detailed knowledge of individual cases and their complexity.

The influential, though one-sided, attention to the element of greed appears to be closely linked to the popular and much publicized image of the modern warlord as concerned exclusively with plunder for personal enrichment and the conspicuous display of wealth. The life of, and the life stories surrounding, Mobutu Sese Seko, long-term president of Zaire and the "inventor of modern kleptocracy" (though at his peak clearly more than just a warlord), provide the foremost example of this image.[52] "No other leader," in the words of his most recent biographer, has "plundered his economy so effectively or lived the high life to such excess."[53] But there are other examples indicating that predatory economic activity is primarily about financing a war fought for aims other than personal enrichment. Indeed, there is often more evidence in support of another of Raymond Aron's perceptive observations: "By participating in collective power men find satisfactions which sweep aside economic calculations and make sacrifices meaningful. The desire for power and pride in surpassing other men, are no less profound impulses than the desire for worldly goods."[54] There appears, for example, to be agreement among those who followed the long career of Jonas Savimbi that he was interested, above all, in power and was driven less by greed than by a deep conviction that he was fated to rule the whole of Angola. Echoing the views of those who dealt and met with Savimbi over the years, Tony Hodges wrote of his "messianic sense of destiny."[55] The speed with which a comparatively stable ceasefire was concluded after his death in 2001 only appears to confirm the key role played by his personality in keeping the war going throughout the previous decade. This, of course, did not prevent others in Savimbi's movement, including regional and senior UNITA commanders, from being less concerned with the cause than with personal enrichment and plunder. Explaining the dynamics of the Angolan civil war requires an understanding of the interactions of these different sets of motives; economic greed alone does not suffice.

Another example is provided by the case of Jokahr Dudayev, leader of the self-declared republic of Chechnya until his assassination by Russian forces in

---

52   Micheala Wrong, *In the Footsteps of Mr. Kurtz: Living on the Brink of Disaster in the Congo* (London: HarperCollins Publishers), p. 10.

53   Ibid., p. 4.

54   Aron, *War and Industrial Society*, p. 53.

55   Hodges, *Petro-Diamond Capitalism*, p. 18.

1996. His declaration of independence for Chechnya created unique opportunities for personal enrichment, and a "kind of clan warfare" quickly developed among Dudayev's followers with officials effectively seizing different parts of the economy.[56] However, Dudayev (to many another quintessential example of the modern warlord) was "too caught up in his romantic project of Chechen independence and too much of an army officer to bother himself with personal enrichment."[57] With respect to the continuing conflict in Chechnya, Anatol Lieven has argued that it offers in fact a compelling case *against* mono-causal explanations of violent conflict; as in other wars and conflicts on the territory of the former Soviet Union, "social protest, national protest, and brigandage have been mutually reinforcing and cannot easily be disentangled."[58]

Both examples highlight the importance of considering not just one set of motivations but also their interaction. Another example of the vital importance of connecting a wider and more diverse set of agendas is provided by the war in Bosnia, specifically the local mechanisms at work in the process of ethnic cleansing between 1992 and 1995.

The UN Commission of Experts, which in 1994 looked into the military structure, tactics, and strategy of the warring factions in Bosnia, concluded that "most paramilitary units sustained themselves through looting, thefts, ransoms and trafficking in contraband."[59] These findings did not, of course, come as a surprise to many of the journalists, peacekeepers, and NGOs based on the ground, who could not fail to notice that the logic of war and the patterns of confrontation locally often had more to do with economic agendas than with the ethnic visions of nationalist politicians. Yet those visions played a crucial role in providing the framework and the impetus for the cleansing policies and the atrocities that ensued. And they were not held simply for instrumental purposes, whether as an excuse for plunder or the consolidation of power. There is, for example, no reason to believe that Franjo Tudjman and his closest nationalist allies were not deeply committed to the idea of Greater Croatia, however repugnant the convictions on which that idea was based.[60]

---

56   Carlotta Gall and Thomas de Waal, *Chechnya: A Small Victorious War* (London: Pan Books, 1997), p. 126.

57   Ibid., p. 126.

58   See comments in "The Economics of War: The Intersection of Need, Creed and Greed," Woodrow Wilson International Center/International Peace Academy Conference Report, September 2001, p. 27.

59   "Final Report of UN Commission/Warring Parties in Bosnia," paragraph 80.

60   See Warren Zimmermann, *Origins of a Catastrophe* (New York: Random House, 1996) and Drago Hedl, "Living in the Past: Franjo Tudjman's Croatia," *Current History* 99, no. 635 (March 2000).

Nor is there any doubt that the idea provided powerful encouragement for the activities of the Bosnian Croat (HVO) forces in central Bosnia, including those who saw it as a license to loot, plunder, and steal. Here, then, is another example of how local economic agendas feed upon and interact with the ideological and political views of leaders and elites.

4.2   Historical Context

One of the principal difficulties with the New Wars thesis lies in the juxtaposition of "newness" against what is supposedly a distinctive "Clausewitzean" era of warfare.[61] Not only is the notion of such an era deeply problematic, but it also excludes from view historical experiences that offer a rich source of insight and comparison with contemporary wars, not least with regard to their economic underpinnings.[62] These include war in early modern Europe, a period tellingly described by one historian as a time when war was "pervasive but undefined."[63] They also include the various wars and phases of imperial and colonial conquest from the sixteenth through to the twentieth century. And, of special interest, are the conditions of warfare that were usually a permanent feature of life at the edge or borderlands of empires, especially as they expanded and shrunk.[64] In many of these cases, economic interests, private capital, and private actors played key roles as drivers and sources of military activity. For example, the financing requirements of expanding armies, coupled with state weakness (administratively as well as in terms of fiscal resources), gave the military entrepreneur or contractor a vital role during the Thirty Years' Wars (1618 to 1648)—one that provides interesting parallels with

---

61   Kaldor accepts that the "classification of types of wars does not represent hard and fast distinctions." Yet the subsequent analysis remains firmly predicated on the assumption that new wars can be usefully contrasted with those of a historically distinctive era. As Kalyvas shows, disregard for historical research on earlier wars is a distinguishing feature of much of the writings that seek to draw a distinction between older and contemporary civil wars. Kalyvas, "'New' and 'Old' Wars," p. 98.

62   It should be added that those who have contributed to a better understanding of economic agendas have not all been ignorant or dismissive of historical parallels. See, for example, David Keen, "Organized Chaos: Not the New World We Ordered," *The World Today* 52, no. 1 (January 1996): 16.

63   M.S. Anderson, *War and Society in Europe of the Old Regime, 1618–1789* (London: Fontana Paperbacks, 1988), pp. 13–16.

64   R. Brian Ferguson and Neil L. Whitehead, in a rich collection of essays, speak of the "violent edge of empire." See R. Brian Ferguson and Neil L. Whitehead, eds., *War in the Tribal Zone: Expanding States and Indigenous Warfare* (Santa Fe, NM: School of American Research Press, 1992).

the modern warlord phenomenon.[65] Others, looking specifically at the role of private actors in relation to resource extraction, have pointed to the similarities between some contemporary wars and merchant wars of the early colonial period.[66]

In addition to the insights offered by the history of warfare, the analysis of current wars cannot be isolated from the more specific historical settings in which they occur.[67] This point is well illustrated by recent works on wars in West Africa and Algeria, wars where economic agendas and commercial alliances with external actors have also played a key part in explaining the dynamics of conflict. In comments that are of relevance to the study of civil wars more broadly, Stephen Ellis stresses how the Liberian civil war has been fought "in a historically constituted society, one whose attitudes, beliefs and values were rooted in cultural patterns inherited from the past, to constitute Liberia's 'governmentality.'"[68] Indeed, the war and the events of the 1990s, including the war in neighboring Sierra Leone, are only intelligible against the backdrop of the *"longue durée* of West African history," including, in particular, the precolonial history of relations, and the sociopolitical imbalances that have long existed, between coastal-based elites and peoples of the hinterland.[69] Likewise, while economic incentives have played a prominent part in the course of the Algerian war, the bloody events of the 1990s cannot fully be understood without an appreciation of a historical and deeply rooted "image of war," shared by both the military and the armed Islamic groups, whereby social advancement has been achieved, and wealth and prestige obtained, through the use of violence.[70]

---

65   See Frank Tallett, *War and Society in Early Modern Europe, 1495–1715* (London: Routledge, 1992), p. 77, and Geoffrey Parker, *The Military Revolution: Military Innovation and the Rise of the West, 1500–1800* (Cambridge: Cambridge University Press, 1988), pp. 64–68.

66   Le Billon, "The Political Economy of Resource Wars," p. 39.

67   This may seem self-evident, though it is often neglected, especially in accounts that focus on contemporary "global processes." Concerned not merely with war and conflict, Chabal and Daloz, in a tone of despair, note how "it seems to be the enduring fate of Africa to be 'explained' in terms which are so ahistorical as to be risible." See Chabal and Daloz, *Africa Works*, p. xviii.

68   Stephen Ellis, "Liberia's Warlord Insurgency" in Christopher Clapham, ed., *African Guerrillas* (Oxford: James Currey), p. 169.

69   Ibid., p. 169.

70   This is the "central hypothesis" of Martinez's book on the war. See Martinez, *The Algerian Civil War*, pp. 7–14.

4.3   Economic Globalization, External Actors, and Civil Wars

If the importance of economic agendas in wars needs to be balanced against other motives and placed in a proper historical context, what about the relationship between economic globalization and armed conflict? Clearly, many contemporary wars have benefited from greater openness in the world economy, including the expansion of transborder activity that has been stimulated by market deregulation and liberalization.[71] But what are the exact connections and processes at work? Tentative answers to this question are best provided by looking at specific cases, and one which lends itself well to closer scrutiny is the history of UNITA and the Angolan civil war in the 1990s. There are three reasons for this. In the first place, UNITA's ability to emerge by mid-1998 militarily stronger than at any time in its history, despite international isolation and sanctions, is often cited as a particularly successful example of adaptation to a new globalized economic environment. Second, the case sheds light on an aspect of current intrastate conflict that, more than any other, has been linked to global processes: the ease with which arms and military equipment (especially light weapons) can be acquired. Third, not only is Angola a particularly well-researched war economy, but the decision by the UN Security Council in 1999 to investigate how UNITA was able to circumvent the international arms embargo against it has provided valuable new insights into the role of external actors and sources of finance and supplies for warring parties.

Jakkie Potgieter, highlighting the elements of continuity in UNITA's support structures, shows how, since its inception, the movement relied on a strategy of self-reliance and an infrastructure to "ensure its own survival and support."[72] In fact, diamonds already supported UNITA's war effort in the 1970s and 1980s, supplemented by revenues from the sale of hardwood and ivory, and Potgieter (writing before the death of Savimbi) concludes that "much of the UNITA's insurgency [was] largely sustainable from inside Angola."[73] In this sense, there is greater continuity between the Cold War and post-Cold War period than is often supposed. Yet what also happened in the 1990s, as the UN's investigation into UNITA's sanctions-busting found, was a privatization of UNITA's existing supply networks as "former agents ... no longer of use to the [Cold War] networks started their own business relationships with UNITA."[74] In effect, the

---

71   Duffield, "Globalization, Transborder Trade, and War Economies," in Berdal and Malone, eds., *Greed and Grievance*, p. 69.

72   Potgieter, "UNITA's Support Structures," p. 271.

73   Ibid.

74   Johan Peleman, "The Logistics of Sanctions Busting: The Airborne Component," in Cilliers and Dietrich, eds., *Angola's War Economy*, pp. 296–297. Johan Peleman was commissioned by the UN Panel of Experts to produce a study of the UNITA "transportation support

older supply networks were transformed into profitable business schemes, with arms brokers and shipping agents benefiting from, and exploiting to the full, weaknesses in national and international regulatory frameworks. This points to more indirect, though still significant, ways in which globalizing processes can shape the course of local conflict. In relation to UNITA and African conflicts more generally, the supply of arms has been facilitated by two types of global integration.

In the first instance, the "globalization of trade and electronic info-commerce make it easier than ever for experienced arms dealers and operators" to work around porous and weak systems of control.[75] Related to this, the deregulation of certain key industries, in this case the international air transport industry, opens new market realities that may be exploited. Specifically, cross-border mergers, leasing, chartering, franchising, and offshore registration of air fleets, crews, and companies, and the use of registers of convenience have all, according to Brian Wood and Johan Peleman, made it far more "difficult to monitor the airspace and freighting industry."[76] Thus, deregulation has enabled networks of subcontractors and front companies to operate more effectively in locating arms and bringing them to customers. There is a parallel here to the ease with which UNITA and warring groups in West Africa were able to benefit from the highly deregulated workings of the world diamond industry. Moreover, another form of global integration has taken place in Africa. This is the "increasingly active" role of the continent in the "informal trade in illegal substances ... and a vast array of other smuggling operations."[77] This process, which has accompanied the continent's marginalization within the formal world economy, clearly helped UNITA's resupply operations and also helps explain how conflicts in West and Central Africa have been kept alive.

The history of UNITA in the 1990s also shows, however, that its success in re-arming depended critically upon two additional factors. First, not only UNITA but a wide range of warring groups, factions, and governments around the world (including practically every other case referred to in this article) have

---

network." Together with Brian Wood, he has also produced an insightful study of the role of arms brokers and shipping agents. See Brian Wood and Johan Peleman, *The Arms Fixers: Controlling the Brokers and Shipping Agents* (Oslo: Prio Report 3/99, 1999).

75   Wood and Peleman, *The Arms Fixers*, p. 14. On the opportunities offered by economic globalization for arms brokers, see also Small Arms Survey Staff, *Small Arms Survey 2001— Profiling the Problem* (Oxford: Oxford University Press, 2001).

76   Wood and Peleman, *The Arms Fixers*, pp. 14–15. See also "Angola: Sanctions Buster," *Africa Research Bulletin* 37, no. 4 (1999): 14094.

77   Chabal and Daloz, *Africa Works*, p. 87. On the continent's integration into networks of transnational organized crime see also, Jean-François Bayart, Stephen Ellis, and Béatrice Hibou, *The Criminalization of the State in Africa* (Oxford: James Curry, 1999).

benefited from the collapse of—that is, lack of capacity and/or unwillingness to enforce—export control regimes and the ability to monitor surplus stocks of weapons in former Warsaw Pact countries and Soviet republics. Again and again leakages have been uncovered, especially though not exclusively from Ukraine, Bulgaria, Belarus, Slovakia, and Russia.[78] The emergence of large criminal networks in the wake of the collapse of the Soviet Union, making use of global processes and themselves part of transborder networks, has also played a key role in the arms trade. Second, in UNITA's case the role of regional powers, including Congo-Brazzaville, Rwanda, Burkina Faso, Togo, and Zambia as service providers, transit corridors, and suppliers, has been essential to UNITA's success in evading sanctions.[79] And, as Philippe Le Billon makes clear, such "friendships" have been built "as much on pragmatic power politics as on private financial interest."[80]

Understanding of the complex and shady workings of the international market in light weapons—the role of international criminal networks, the effects of industry deregulation, and the role of regional and other powers— has obviously benefited from the special attention given to Angola. Overall, however, more research is required, especially of individual cases, before too unequivocal conclusions are drawn.[81]

There is a final consideration here relating to the question of how civil wars are financed. Although not directly linked to the discussion above, it has figured in much of the debate and writings about civil wars. Specifically, the New Wars literature has suggested that another global dimension of current conflict is the role of diaspora communities and humanitarian aid as sources of finance for warring parties. Although there are many examples of diaspora communities making a contribution through remittances to warring parties— notably the Tamil community's support for the Tamil Tigers in Sri Lanka—this is hardly a new phenomenon. More substantively, the actual importance of

---

78 Jeffrey Boutwell, Michael T. Klare, and Laura W. Reed, eds., *Lethal Commerce: The Global Trade in Small Arms and Light Weapons* (Cambridge, MA: American Academy of Arts and Sciences, 1995); Chris Smith, "Light Weapons Proliferation: A Global Survey," *Jane's Intelligence Review* 011, no. 007 (July 1999): 46.

79 As the "Angolagate" scandal in France has shown, it is not only neighboring states that have been prepared to violate the sanctions regime. See François Misser, "The Angolagate Scandal," *African Business*, no. 265, May 2001, pp. 8–11.

80 Le Billon, "Angola's Political Economy of War," p. 79.

81 For an excellent survey of the state of literature see Karin Ballentine, "Critical Issues in the Political Economy of Civil War: Causes, Dynamics, and Prospects," Paper presented at Swiss Peace Foundation Workshop, 28–29 June 2001, Berne (I am grateful for permission to cite the paper).

diaspora income remains unclear and underresearched.[82] As for the role of humanitarian aid in prolonging war, the particular case of the fifteen-year-old, highly institutionalized, relief operation in Sudan (Operation Lifeline Sudan) provides an example of how humanitarian relief, though well-intentioned, can come to play an integral part in the local war economy.[83] Beyond the case of Sudan, however, the impact of relief aid on the course of civil wars, especially in prolonging them, appears to be exaggerated.[84]

5   Conclusion

The attention given in recent years to the economic agendas of belligerents and external actors in civil wars has unquestionably enhanced our under-standing of the local dynamics at work in a wide range of conflict zones. The role of economic motivations, however, cannot easily be isolated from other factors that drive men and women to resort to violence, and the range of motivations involved (as well as their mutual interaction) needs to be stud-ied. Understanding individual conflicts also requires that greater attention be paid to their historical and cultural roots than either the greed-and-grievance framework or the New Wars thesis has allowed. The obvious implication here is that generalizations about civil wars and, in particular, the effort to iden-tify common or universal characteristics that apply across a range of cases, will always be fraught with difficulty. This is not to deny the importance of a comparative approach to the study of civil wars. The aim of such an approach, however, should not be to find universal patterns among a myriad of diverse cases. That remains a vain hope. A comparative approach, if properly con-ducted, should instead seek to furnish the analyst and the policymaker with

---

82   According to de Zeeuw and Frerks the "flows of remittances, voluntary or forced, gener-ated by diaspora groups have been analyzed by some but little is known about the vol-ume of resources involved. The use of migrant remittances in general and the ways in which such financial transfers impact on internal conflict remain as yet unstudied." See "Proceedings Political Economy Seminar," p. 13.

83   Ken Menkhaus and John Prendergast, "Conflict and Crisis in the Greater Horn of Africa," *Current History* 98, no. 628 (May 1999): 215. See also Frances Stewart and Emma Samman, "Food Aid During Civil War," in Frances Stewart and Valpy Fitzgerald, eds., *War and Underdevelopment, Vol. 1,* (Oxford: Oxford University Press, 2001), pp. 169–179.

84   See David Shearer, "Aiding or Abetting? Humanitarian Aid and Its Economic Role in Civil War," in Berdal and Malone, eds., *Greed and Grievance,* pp. 189–203. See also Jane Hoverd, "Humanitarian Action in Bosnia: A Study of the Office of the United Nations High Commissioner for Refugees, 1991–1999" (Ph.D. diss., Oxford University, 2001).

some basic questions that may usefully be asked when confronted with a given instance of intrastate conflict.

This article has argued that for such policy responses to be successful, an understanding of the political economy of civil wars is essential. Developing such an understanding with respect to individual cases will be aided by the attention given to three sets of issues or questions. The first is the degree and nature of *state weakness and fragmentation* in the country concerned, including socioeconomic, ethnic, religious, and historically contingent sources of division and tension. This may involve, as in the example of West Africa, a legacy of economic exploitation by a dominant group(s) and/or it may be associated with significant geographical fault lines or urban-rural divisions. Second, the nature and patterns of *local and regional economic activity*, both formal and informal, including levels and distribution of natural resources, need to be properly understood and accounted for. The latter opens possibilities, as illustrated by the ongoing wars in Central Africa and West Africa, for systematic and opportunistic exploitation of resources by elites and soldiers at the grassroots. Finally, *forms of integration* and ease of access to *international markets and actors* that may help the utilization of local assets, finance and support the continuation of war, will also need to be understood. The aforementioned case of UNITA's transition from reliance on Cold War patronage to post-Cold War self-sufficiency shows that the nexus between global economic processes and the activities of local actors is more complex than is sometimes suggested. None of these factors, even when looked at together and over time, will provide unambiguous and clear-cut answers about the nature of contemporary wars. They do, however, provide an alternative to some of the cruder explanations that continue to influence public and policy debate about conflict in the early twenty-first century.

CHAPTER 10

Weapons of Mass Destruction and the United Nations

Jessica Tuchman Mathews[1]

1   What Happened in Iraq? The Success Story of UN Inspections

This is an extraordinarily important moment for the United Nations. Before attention is lost in the controversies over the war itself and in the challenges of its aftermath, the UN must capture, clarify, and publicize the record of international inspections in Iraq: for itself, for member governments, and for the public. Was the process encompassing the UN Special Commission (UNSCOM), the International Atomic Energy Agency (IAEA), and the UN Monitoring, Verification and Inspection Commission (UNMOVIC) from 1991 to 2003 a success? Or was it the bumbling embarrassment, the "sham," portrayed by top U.S. officials and still understood that way by the American public—and perhaps by the public elsewhere?

The bottom line is that it was in fact a rather striking international success that stands out in the record of recent decades. However, it is a success studded with weaknesses that need to be understood and corrected and one that, because it is not yet *recognized*, is not fully real. Without a concerted analytical effort, the record of what actually happened, and its very real promise for the future, could easily be lost.

In the surging controversy over British and U.S. intelligence failures in Iraq, a critical fact is still largely unnoticed: while the national intelligence services were getting it wrong, UN inspectors were getting the picture largely right.

In 1991–1998, UNSCOM and the IAEA—while facing unrelenting Iraqi opposition and obstruction—successfully discovered and eliminated most, if not

---

*   This chapter was originally published in Global Governance, Volume 10, Issue 3, 2004.

1   Jessica Tuchman Mathews is a Distinguished Fellow at the Carnegie Endowment for International Peace and coauthor with Joseph Cirincione and George Perkovich of "WMD in Iraq: Evidence and Implications," available online at www.ceip.org/files/Publications/IraqReport3.asp?from=pubdate.

     This article is adapted from the keynote address to the International Peace Academy conference "Weapons of Mass Destruction and the United Nations: Diverse Threats and Collective Response," 5 March 2004.

all, of Iraq's unconventional weapons and production facilities and destroyed or monitored the destruction of most of its chemical and biological weapons agents. Iraq's most secret program—its biological weapons program—was discovered through painstaking detective work and was reported to the Security Council four months before the defection of Saddam Hussein's son-in-law Hussein Kamel. UNSCOM also uncovered covert transactions between Iraq and more than five hundred companies from more than forty countries—a body of work that assumes fresh significance in the light of recent disclosures of the nuclear sales network of Pakistan's A.Q. Khan. Also, inspectors put in place a mechanism to track and block banned exports and imports.

In the months immediately preceding the war, UN inspectors' assessments of Iraq's programs were remarkably close to what has since been found—and far more accurate than U.S. or British prewar beliefs. UNMOVIC was permitted to operate for less than four months, and only for a matter of weeks at full strength. But to the best of present knowledge, the inspectors were in fact in the process of finding and beginning to dismantle what was there.

This record suggests a number of lessons—positive and negative. First, it appears that a package of international restraints—sanctions, the procurement investigations, and the export/import controls combined with core inspections—worked together in a way that is not yet understood, and that this package was considerably more effective than has been appreciated then or since.

Second, even though UNSCOM and the early IAEA inspections operated under a degree of Iraqi obstruction that the Security Council never should have tolerated, the UN inspections' greatest area of weakness lay in New York, not in Iraq. Iraq played a highly effective game of divide and conquer in the Security Council, setting the permanent members against each other until political support was so undermined that inspections were forced to a halt in 1998. The lesson is clear. Political unity in backing inspections is as important as technology and expertise on the ground, and the Security Council is not now set up to provide it. Inspections should not again be launched without more settled political support behind them. And the Security Council should never again allow rules of the game that tilt the playing field so steeply in favor of the miscreant and against its own agents.

Third, the relationship between international inspections and national intelligence agencies needs a thorough review. It is almost a waste of time to embark on such an undertaking if the international effort does not have the technology to protect itself against penetration by the intelligence agencies of the target country. There must be established means set up for two-way communication between the inspectorate and national intelligence agencies—means that will fully protect the information provided, protect against penetration and misuse by the governments providing information as well as by the target, and allow feedback between intelligence providers and inspectors as discoveries are made and defectors come to light. If international inspections are to be undertaken again, there needs to be an established set of rules that do not need to be invented day by day and that allow a much more confident and easy flow of information.

Still pending in the Iraq case is the rather urgent question: How much of what inspectors knew did U.S. intelligence know, and if there was key material the United States did not learn, why not? For example, UNSCOM discovered in 1991 that Iraq's nerve gas weapons were no longer potent enough for battle-field use because Iraqi scientists were incapable of keeping the agent stable for very long. Why then was the United States treating these same weapons as a threat twelve years later? How much of the more than 30 million-page archive produced by the UN and IAEA inspectors was sifted by U.S. analysts before the war?

Fourth, if inspections are to be undertaken again, governments and the public need to better understand the process. In the Iraqi case, inspections were widely perceived as a hopeless chase after easily hidden needles in a haystack and were therefore easily ridiculed and undermined. Before becoming head of the U.S. Iraq Survey Group, David Kay wrote, "When it comes to the United Nations weapons inspection in Iraq, looking for a smoking gun is a fool's mission.... Even the best inspectors have almost no chance of discovering hidden weapons sites such as these in a country the size of Iraq."[2] Yet the perception that inspections consist of running from place to place is not the reality. Lengthy interviews, relationship building with key individuals, story building from individual to individual, procurement investigations, and highly technical analysis—all of this is of the essence. Contrast Kay's earlier comment with one he made after his time in Iraq that suggests this reality. "If there are large stockpiles, they had to be produced by people, they had to be produced in facilities, and they would have left some indelible signs. Where are those people? Where are those facilities? Where are the documents, the importation and the other records of such large production? They have not been found."[3]

Fifth, cost needs to be evaluated—particularly cost for results achieved. UNSCOM's budget was U.S.$25–30 million per year. UNMOVIC's was about

---

2   David Kay, "It Was Never About a Smoking Gun," *Washington Post*, 19 January 2003, sec. B, p. 3.

3   Remarks by David Kay at the Carnegie Endowment for International Peace/Century Foundation/Georgetown University Forum, "Combating Weapons of Mass Destruction," 5 February 2004.

the same for the four months it operated.[4] We do not yet have a firm number, but the announced cost of U.S. inspections over the past year is about $900 million.[5] UNSCOM was definitely underequipped, and the IAEA has been chronically underfunded for a decade; but even making a generous allowance for needed improvements, international inspections look like a high-productivity operation if properly designed and backed, as compared to U.S. inspections and especially as compared to the quarter-trillion-dollar cost of the war and its aftermath.

For these reasons, among others, the following needs to be done now. First, the UN secretary-general should charter a detailed review of the inspections process—an after-action report. The relative value of site visits and analysis needs to be clarified. The various strengths and weaknesses of this pioneering international effort need to be fully understood, including its human resources, access to technology, relations with national intelligence agencies, vulnerability to penetration, and more. It is important to look ahead, but it would be an awful mistake at this moment to fail to look back. We are taught from childhood to learn from our mistakes. Successes have as much to teach.

Second, the United States should collaborate with the UN to produce a complete history and inventory of Iraq's weapons of mass destruction (WMD) and missile programs. To do so, UNMOVIC personnel should be working on the ground with the Iraq Survey Group. Both the United States and the UN deserve criticism for the failure to do so to date. The right people on the ground—a few dozen at most—could make a big difference. An UNMOVIC report released to the Security Council in early March makes clear that it has not been contacted by the Iraq Survey Group and is not in any way working with them.[6] As the UN is reinserted in the political transition process in Iraq, one hopes that the relationship on this front too can be repaired.

---

4 United Nations Special Commission on Iraq, "Basic Facts," available online at www.un.org/Depts/unscom/General/basicfacts.html (accessed 24 March 2004). According to officials, UNMOVIC budgeted approximately $80 million for its first full year of operations, of which about $20 million were start-up costs that could be spread over several years.

5 On 3 November 2003, Congress approved the Bush administration's $87 billion supplemental, which included $600 million for the Iraq Survey Group (ISG). This was in addition to the reported $300 million previously appropriated for the ISG. James Rissen and Judith Miller, "Officials Say Bush Seeks $600 Million to Hunt Iraq Arms," *New York Times*, 2 October 2003, sec. A, p. 1; Helen Dewar, "Senate Approves Spending for Iraq," *Washington Post*, 4 November 2003, sec. A, p. 1; Douglas Jehl, "U.S. to Shift Some Experts from Arms to Antiterror," *New York Times*, 27 November 2003, sec. A, p. 15.

6 United Nations Monitoring, Verification, and Inspections Commission, *16th Quarterly Report to the United Nations Security Council*, 27 February 2004, available online at www.un.org/Docs/journal/asp/ws.asp?m=S/2004/160 (accessed 24 March 2004).

Third, in this joint effort, particular attention should be paid to discovering which of the several international constraints on Iraq were effective (and to what degree) and to determining how they worked as a package.

Finally, an accurate story of the U.S. and British intelligence failures can never be pieced together without the various investigations having full access to the UN archive. None of the more than half-dozen investigations now under way in Washington are taking steps to do this. On its side, the UN should facilitate that access.

2   Learning from the Past, Building Institutions for the Future

Based on the results of these reviews, a number of institutional changes to combat the spread of WMD should be contemplated. Serious consideration should be given to the creation of a permanent UN inspections and monitoring body. Inspections are not a panacea. Indeed, no magic bullet will be found effective against proliferation. But inspections appear to be an invaluable component of a layered defense system. Intelligence from a distance—no matter how good—can never do what a physical presence on the ground, armed with an international writ and unfettered access, can do.

A permanent, international, nonproliferation inspection capability would provide vital enforcement—hence seriousness—to the broader regime and fill the gaps between the various weapons treaties. Iraq, Libya, Iran, Pakistan, and North Korea all point to the need for such an established—not ad hoc—capability.

Because long-term monitoring is just as important as inspections, only a standing, permanent body can do the job. Training, and developing the expertise of, a broadly international corps of experts will have the added benefit of helping build a sense in these individuals' home governments of engagement in and shared responsibility for what must be the global responsibility of preventing proliferation. Success will never be achieved if nonproliferation is seen as the responsibility of one or a handful of like-minded states.

Creating a permanent inspectorate is one element of the broader need to increase the role and the responsibilities of the Security Council, following on its 1992 declaration that proliferation is a threat to international peace and security.

The political weaknesses of the Council have been amply demonstrated over the years in dealing with Iraq, but—with effort—political will can be built. That effort is worth making because no other entity, existing or imagined, commands the Security Council's universal legitimacy or its umbrella mandate for peace and security. Anyone who doubts its importance has only to look at how hard countries work to avoid being taken to the Security Council—North Korea and Iran notably among them.

How could the Security Council's role be built up, beyond the creation of the permanent inspectorate? A 1995 international study, chaired by former U.S. national security adviser McGeorge Bundy,[7] urged that the Security Council create a special rapporteur on nonproliferation to report directly to the Council on trends and developments. The special rapporteur would in effect staff the Security Council and prod it on a constant basis; draw together all the threats stemming from weapons proliferation; deal with countries not members of the various arms control and disarmament treaties; and provide the staff basis for taking action. A standing position like this would lower the bar to action by making consideration of nonproliferation by the Council routine rather than extraordinary.

Beyond strengthening the Council, nonproliferation needs a unifying strategic concept. Universal compliance fits the bill. "Compliance" means more than signatures on treaties or declarations of fine intent—it means actual performance. Attention has been focused for too long on universal membership in treaties without sufficient drive for compliance and without sufficient attention to enforcement. "Universal" means that all states must comply with the norms and terms that apply to them. This includes states suspected of violating safeguard agreements, or abetting proliferation through technology transfers, and equally to nuclear weapons states that are not living up to commitments they have made.

The effort to build a strengthened international nonproliferation regime will be in vain, for example, if the United States fails to eventually ratify the Comprehensive Test Ban Treaty (CTBT) and if it chooses to develop new types of nuclear weapons. The violation of the *spirit* of Article VI inherent in doing so is simply too egregious to be tolerated by non-nuclear states that are being asked to take major steps to move the world in the opposite direction.

The focus on universality has two other crucial aspects. First, it shifts the focus away from the bipolarity of haves and have-nots. In truth, we face a global nuclear proliferation threat that can only be met on a global basis. Also, it provides a means for dealing with the "three-state problem"—India, Pakistan, and Israel. The Nuclear Nonproliferation Treaty (NPT) does not have to be torn apart to find a place for these states within the universal compliance framework. They, like all others, will have their responsibilities to meet.

---

7   *Confronting the Proliferation Danger: The Role of the UN Security Council,* A Report of the UNA-USA Project on the Security Council and Nonproliferation, 1995.

There are literally dozens of individual policies that would need to be adopted to turn this overarching framework into an effective reality. As one example, the IAEA should adopt a rule that prohibits a state that the agency cannot certify to be in full compliance with its transparency and safeguard obligations from receiving foreign assistance for nuclear activities. Equally, the rule would specify that members of the IAEA should adopt national legislation making it illegal for any entity on their territory to facilitate such forbidden assistance.

Such a rule would impede the acquisition of nuclear weapons capabilities by states that the IAEA detected were engaged in dubious activities. It would raise the costs and risks of cheating on transparency and safeguard obligations, and it would extend the burden of compliance not just to recipients of technology and know-how but to providers as well. Finally, the rule would apply to states such as India, Israel, and Pakistan that are not subject to all IAEA transparency and safeguard obligations.

In the event that a state ignores these prohibitions and continues a supply relationship with a noncompliant state, including indirectly by allowing entities on its territory to do so, the IAEA would be required to refer the matter to the Security Council for enforcement.

3   Conclusion

Crises such as those we have lived through in the past few years and months have a silver lining. They jolt the system and create a moment when political will is fluid and can be reshaped.

Admittedly, there are great barriers to change on every front. But it is far too soon to apply the familiar calculus and conclude that nothing can be done to radically strengthen the nonproliferation system. This is a moment when change *is* possible. With sufficient leadership—from the United States, but not just from the United States—exactly that can be achieved.

CHAPTER 11

Human Rights and Counterterrorism in Global Governance: Reputation and Resistance

Rosemary Foot[1]

The terrorist assault on U.S. territory in September 2001 has been instrumental in modifying or redefining certain of the social practices that have guided interactions in world politics among a range of state and nonstate bodies. This is particularly the case in the area of human rights, or more precisely with respect to the right to personal security.[2] Prior to September 11, there had been a reasonably widespread understanding—as opposed to agreement—that governments were expected to protect individual human rights and that failures to protect were of legitimate concern to other state, nonstate, and international institutional actors in global society. A state's reputation no longer rested solely on its ability to exercise authority over territory and the population that resided within it, but it now also embraced the idea of "sovereignty as responsibility,"[3] where a state had a duty to provide for basic human rights in its own land mass and to be concerned about the abuse of rights overseas. Academic writers influenced either by power or by sociological explanations of world politics argued that states accepted this normative understanding because they were coerced or offered positive incentives, because they deemed

---

* This chapter was originally published in Global Governance, Volume 11, Issue 3, 2005.

1 Rosemary Foot is a Senior Research Fellow at the University of Oxford's Department of Politics and International Relations and a Research Associate at the Oxford China Centre at St Antony's College, University of Oxford. Her most recent monograph is *China, the UN, and Human Protection: Beliefs, Power, Image*. Oxford University Press 2020. She is currently writing primarily about the intersection between security and human rights and on regionalism in the Asia Pacific.

2 The abuse of personal security rights encompasses the use of torture, detention without trial, extrajudicial killings, disappearances, and the like.

3 For a discussion of the evolution of sovereignty to a fourth stage describing sovereignty as responsibility, see Francis M. Deng, Sadikiel Kimaro, Terrence Lyons, et al., *Sovereignty as Responsibility: Conflict Management in Africa* (Washington, D.C.: Brookings Institution, 1996), especially chap. 1. See too *The Responsibility to Protect: Report of the International Commission on Intervention and State Sovereignty* (Ottawa: International Development Research Centre, 2001).

the norms to be valid, or because they recognized that this idea of legitimate sovereignty was part of the script of modern statehood.[4]

However, after September 11, this assumption that modern, legitimate statehood increasingly entailed the protection of human rights came under serious challenge in certain parts of the world. An apparent reemphasis on the security of the state and its citizens—as opposed to a concern about the abuse of individuals wherever they might reside—and the perception that antiterrorism requires the introduction of legislation that curtails civil liberties pose part of that challenge. Similarly, the compromises seen as necessary when framing foreign policies toward governments that have poor records in the area of human rights but are deemed important in counterterrorist operations have undercut the weight that has hitherto been accorded the human rights norm in the foreign relations of democratic states. International and regional organizations have passed legislation, instituted monitoring mechanisms, and started to engage in capacity building, all of which reinforces these trends in state behavior. Advocacy groups devoted to human rights promotion find themselves on the defensive, even in danger, and are divided in their assessment of how best to operate or stay relevant in the so-called age of terror.

Many of the political actors affected by these trends seemingly have picked up the signal that building a reputation for resolve and developing an ability to participate effectively in the antiterrorist struggle has become increasingly important, overshadowing human rights matters in the appreciation of their standing as modern states and institutions. As a result, the level of contribution these state and interstate bodies make to the counterterrorist campaign has shown signs of reshaping hierarchies in world politics.

In this article, I develop and explore the argument that a reputation for effectiveness in the counterterrorist campaign is being given more weight than that of human rights defender. To demonstrate this point, I draw on examples from U.S. and Asian state behavior and from UN and Asia Pacific organizations. The United States is key because, through its unilateral actions and its exercise of power in bilateral relationships and in multilateral international institutions, it has been important in the past in defending human rights both at home and abroad; but it also has set in motion the trends that are reshaping reputational goals. Asia is a focus because the United States has designated it a core location in the antiterrorist campaign, containing so-called frontline and second-front states in that struggle. Moreover, prior to September 11, various

---

4 For a useful survey of these arguments, see Hans Peter Schmitz and Kathryn Sikkink, "International Human Rights," in Walter Carsnaes, Thomas Risse, and Beth A. Simmons, eds., *Handbook of International Relations* (London: Sage, 2001).

Asian states had found their human rights records to be under global scrutiny. The UN and Asia Pacific organizations are germane to the discussion, too: as already noted, the United States can exert its influence on organizations, whether it participates in them or not. It has been influential in shaping the counterterrorist actions of both the UN and Asian regional organizations. Thus, Resolution 1373, largely drafted by the Bush administration, led the UN Security Council to set up the Counter-Terrorism Committee (CTC). This prompted Asian regional and subregional organizations to develop antiterrorist measures based on CTC expectations.

A focus on particular governments and international institutions allows for a nuanced conclusion to emerge. My argument attests to the independent capacity of both domestic and global institutions to resist certain well-embedded social practices being overridden. I find that a reputation built on concern for the protection of human rights retains an ability to constrain actions at least among those political bodies where, in the past, human rights issues had established a reasonably firm domestic and international institutional foothold. There is some robustness to the human rights norm as shown by certain governmental actions, in the work of transnational and domestic human rights nongovernmental organizations (NGOs), and at the UN level itself. Perhaps in these instances, therefore, there might be a hybrid form of reputation being established, drawing together the two reputations of human rights defender and antiterrorist fighter. Optimistically, this could lead eventually to the adoption of strategies that realize an acceptable balance between the need to sustain a centralized authority's capacity to protect its people and a commitment to maintain the protection of individual human rights, wherever they are under threat.

Elsewhere, however, in organizations and states where that institutional foothold for human rights was less secure prior to September 11, 2001, then unsurprisingly we are seeing attempts to demonstrate effective counterterrorist action to the neglect, and often the worsening, of human rights protections. Whether this regressive trend continues is open to future investigation.

1   Defining Reputation and Hierarchy

Following Jonathan Mercer, reputation in world politics is defined as a relational concept based on a belief that an actor has an enduring characteristic that creates certain expectations and understandings about behavior in the present and future. This helps to deter or compel in others some forms of behavior, or to induce uncoerced cooperation. Overall, its effects are to reduce costs.[5] In the field of strategic studies, military alliances can have or can build a reputation for treating their mandates seriously and for standing firmly in support of other alliance members, thereby enhancing deterrence. Economic actors are particularly interested in building a reputation for trustworthiness, because this induces cooperation and lowers future transaction costs. Newly democratizing countries view it as valuable to the establishment of their new reputations as law-abiding, democratic states to show that they are willing to take on additional human rights commitments. For example, in 1988, Hungary demonstrated a desire to anchor itself within the democratic community of states by choosing to ratify the optional protocol of the International Covenant on Civil and Political Rights (ICCPR), which allows for individual petition of the UN Human Rights Committee.[6] Even well-established democratic states have been known to recognize the value of recapturing or retaining a reputation for moral authority. In 1976, before his appointment as President Carter's national security adviser, Zbigniew Brzezinski had written that building a concern for human rights into U.S. external relations could help to relegitimate foreign policy both domestically and overseas.[7] Brzezinski understood that a reputation for moral behavior links power with moral authority, which is particularly useful in the absence of enforcement mechanisms or where there is a reluctance to use coercive means.

Hierarchies in world politics—the ranking of state, nonstate, and institutional actors according to how successfully they acquire resources and achieve through material or nonmaterial means their desired outcomes in world politics—can be determined by patterns of political and economic support and the degree to which a state, regional, or global organization is seen as a site of early resort when it comes to problem solving. Thus, Amnesty International (AI), an organization with high standing as a transnational human rights organization, produces authoritative reports that are often drawn on by the various official bodies that work in the human rights field, including the UN Human

---

5   Jonathan Mercer, *Reputation and International Politics* (Ithaca: Cornell University Press, 1996). Other pertinent literature includes C. Reus-Smith, "Politics and International Legal Obligation," *European Journal of International Relations* 9, no. 4 (2003); Robert O. Keohane, *After Hegemony: Cooperation and Discord in the World Political Economy* (Princeton: Princeton University Press, 1984); Robert McElroy, *Morality and American Foreign Policy* (Princeton: Princeton University Press, 1992); and James E. Alt, Randall L. Calvert, and Brian D. Humes, "Reputation and Hegemonic Stability: A Game-Theoretic Analysis," *American Political Science Review* 82, no. 2 (June 1988).

6   Dominic McGoldrick, *The Human Rights Committee: Its Role in the Development of the International Covenant on Civil and Political Rights* (Oxford: Oxford University Press, 1994), pp. 17–18.

7   Daniel C. Thomas, *The Helsinki Effect: International Norms, Human Rights, and the Demise of Communism* (Princeton: Princeton University Press, 2001), p. 135.

Rights Committee, parliamentary committees, and international criminal tribunals. AI, critical in the 1970s and 1980s in launching a worldwide campaign against the use of torture, helped draft a declaration that defined and eventually established the 1984 Convention Against Torture and other Cruel, Inhuman or Degrading Treatment or Punishment (CAT). Among states, the United States is obviously central in this determination of hierarchy because of the attention that is paid to its use of material and symbolic support in its bilateral and multilateral relationships. Important too is its capacity to ignore certain actors or venues as it formulates its policies unilaterally, bilaterally, or through particular multilateral organizations. In America's so-called war on terrorism, Washington has sent a series of powerful signals indicating which political actors are deemed important to the achievement of its counterterrorist goals, in some cases trying patently to turn former virtually "rogue states" into valued partners and moribund organizations into potential problem-solving venues.

2   The Evolving Basis of Reputation

2.1   *Human Rights as the Mark of Legitimate Governance*
The period after 1945 put human rights on the global agenda. Several human rights treaties and declarations were created and were promoted either through the UN or through regional charters. Most significant among these were the ICCPR and the International Covenant on Economic, Social and Cultural Rights, both of which were opened for signature in 1966 and came into effect ten years later. In 1946, the UN created the Commission on Human Rights (UNCHR). Over time, and especially from the late 1970s, this commission and its subcommission became more active in fulfilling their mandates: stepping up the range of their fact-finding activities, appointing new thematic special rapporteurs in such areas as summary or arbitrary executions (1982) and torture (1985), and investigating evidence of abuse in particular countries. Related to this increased activism were developments in democratic states, especially the United States, whose Congress in the early 1970s passed legislation that called for the denial of military or economic aid to any government that grossly violated the human rights of its people. Many other democratic states followed the U.S. lead. Having made such commitments, domestic and transnational activist organizations, which grew substantially in number over this same period, tried to ensure that states and organizations lived up to their obligations.

Despite the obvious difficulties in implementing these policies, human rights standards were set from the mid-1970s, presenting a "summary statement of the minimum social and political guarantees recognized by the international community as necessary for a life of dignity in the contemporary world."[8] Some monitoring of state behavior also resulted from the reporting requirements of several human rights treaties, annual meetings of the UNCHR and its subcommission, record keeping by major human rights NGOs, and the details provided in the annual U.S. State Department *Country Reports on Human Rights Practices*. Much of this human rights activity had emerged as the result of a deeply political, rather than moral, process; yet it proved difficult to disband procedures once they were in place, even though they might in time be used against those that had originated them.[9]

The ending of the Cold War in the late 1980s deepened these trends. Priority could be given to human rights without fear of alienating those countries that could add valuable strategic weight to one side of the Cold War divide at the expense of the other. In 1993, the UN appointed its first High Commissioner for Human Rights (UNHCHR), an office that has grown in stature over time. From then on, UN peacebuilding operations, which grew substantially in number from the 1990s, always included a human rights component. States and interstate bodies increasingly recognized gross violations of human rights as a threat to international peace and security: indeed, during the period 1991 to 1999, the UN Security Council considered on nine occasions whether some external body should, partly or wholly on humanitarian grounds, organize or authorize military action inside a state. In each instance there was, in fact, a humanitarian intervention, not always with UN authorization or host-state consent.[10] Where the United States was concerned, the Clinton administration, although justly criticized for its inconsistency in promoting human rights, nevertheless did appoint credible people to the post of assistant secretary for human rights, afforded unprecedented access to NGOs, and took a decision to make it the responsibility of all executive departments and agencies to be aware of U.S. international human rights obligations.

---

8   Jack Donnelly, *International Human Rights* (Boulder: Westview, 1998), p. 9.

9   A point made in Philip Alston, "The Commission on Human Rights," in Alston, ed., *The United Nations and Human Rights: A Critical Appraisal* (Oxford: Oxford University Press, 1992). Also helpful here is Tom J. Farer and Felice Gaer, "The UN and Human Rights: At the End of the Beginning," in Adam Roberts and Benedict Kingsbury, eds., *United Nations, Divided World* (Oxford: Oxford University Press, 1993); Margaret E. Keck and Kathryn Sikkink, eds., *Activists Beyond Borders* (Ithaca: Cornell University Press, 1998); A. Glenn Mower Jr., *Human Rights and American Foreign Policy* (Westport, Conn.: Greenwood Press, 1987); and Peter R. Baehr, *The Role of Human Rights in Foreign Policy*, 2d ed. (London: Macmillan, 1996).

10   Adam Roberts, "The United Nations and Humanitarian Intervention," in Jennifer M. Welsh, ed., *Humanitarian Intervention and International Relations* (Oxford: Oxford University Press, 2004), p. 81.

This is not to suggest that there was widespread global support for all of these developments. The Asian values argument of the early 1990s, a vivid reminder that some governments—but not necessarily all their citizens— wanted to give priority to political and cultural diversity over universalist claims, projected these normative developments as impositions at a time of post-Cold War Western triumphalism. But even in this region, a number of countries saw the time as ripe to establish national human rights commissions, and some—such as China—started to engage actively in human rights discourse, leading to Beijing's signature of the two major human rights covenants in 1997 and 1998.

Jack Donnelly was surely right, then, when he argued in 1998 that "human rights represent a progressive late twentieth century expression of the important idea that international legitimacy and full membership in international society must rest in part on standards of just, humane or civilized behaviour."[11] Disagreements remained over which rights deserved greatest attention, and on which occasions, as well as about how best to promote human rights. But the expectation that global actors would—indeed should—be concerned about human rights in any part of the world where they might be grossly violated was rarely overtly questioned.

Those states concerned about a reputation for legitimate governance or acceptance by peers as a "civilized" state could be persuaded or shamed into modifying their behavior—at least to the point of signing the major international covenants, submitting to these covenants' reporting obligations, and voicing a rhetorical commitment to the protection of human rights.

2.2   *Institutional Change and Activism after September 11*
The terrorist attacks on the United States in September 2001 have prompted a reconsideration of the worth of a reputation for legitimate governance, or at least have stimulated states and organizations to consider whether there were new priorities to consider in the unprecedented circumstance of a fatal terrorist attack on the most powerful state in the global system. The response of some—encapsulated for a time in the *Le Monde* editorial entitled "We Are All Americans," was to find venues where support for the United States in its hour of need and pain could be demonstrated.[12] The UN Security Council responded uncharacteristically with "rapidity, unanimity, and decisiveness." On September 12, it passed Resolution 1368 condemning the attacks and

---

11   Jack Donnelly, "Human Rights: A New Standard of Civilization?" *International Affairs* 74, no. 1 (January 1998).

12   Jean-Marie Colombani, "Nous sommes tous Américains," *Le Monde*, 13 September 2001.

recognizing the inherent right of collective and self-defense. Resolution 1373, passed sixteen days later, legally obligated all member states to deny terrorists the means to carry on their work. A newly established CTC was set up to monitor compliance with 1373's requirement for states to freeze assets, to prevent the collection or transfer of funds or provision of arms, and to deny safe haven and passage to suspected terrorist groups. Governments are obligated to report to the CTC on steps they are taking to implement the resolution, and the CTC, in turn, acts as a kind of repository of ideas to help states develop a capacity—such as providing model legislation and recommending various forms of training—to meet 1373 obligations.[13] Although the United States drove forward this intergovernmental process, the UN's reputation obviously benefited from being seen to act with decisiveness and competence in extremis. Even if the Security Council left it to the United States to use force against the Taliban and Al-Qaida, the UN could point to the superiority of its multilateral organizational structure when it came to dealing with terrorists by nonmilitary means.[14]

What, though, did the CTC have to say about the human rights implications of the antiterrorist actions and legislation that states were developing? Very little, even though some reports from states swiftly raised concerns in this area (for example, those from Egypt, Estonia, Moldova, New Zealand, Sweden, and the United Kingdom, according to the Human Rights Committee). CTC's first chair, Sir Jeremy Greenstock, noted that the CTC "is not a tribunal for judging states" and thus would not test if state responses were consistent with human rights standards, leaving that to other parts of the UN system to determine.[15] I will say more about the criticisms made of this circumspection later on, but initially the CTC's signals could be read as having given preference to measures that promoted counterterrorism over human rights obligations.

Other regional organizations quickly took a lead from the UN's CTC. In October 2001, the Asia-Pacific Economic Cooperation (APEC) forum met in Shanghai. Prior to September 11, APEC had a rather lackluster record of achievements, including a failure to respond to the Asian financial crisis of

---

13   Edward C. Luck, "Tackling Terrorism," in David M. Malone, ed., *The UN Security Council: From the Cold War to the 21st Century* (Boulder: Lynne Rienner, 2004), p. 96.

14   S. Neil MacFarlane, "Charter Values and the Response to Terrorism," in Jane Boulden and Thomas Weiss, eds., *Terrorism and the UN: Before and After September 11* (Bloomington: Indiana University Press, 2004), especially p. 37.

15   International Peace Academy (IPA), New York, United Nations Office of the High Commissioner for Human Rights, Geneva, and Center on International Organization, Columbia University, New York, *Human Rights, the United Nations, and the Struggle Against Terrorism*, conference report, 7 November 2003, p. 20.

1997–1998 or to make much progress with its core commitment of trade liberalization. It had always eschewed direct involvement with security questions, although security discussions turned out to be indirectly an important part of APEC's latent agenda—for example, the East Timor crisis in 1999. At the October 2001 annual leaders' summit, APEC moved quickly into counterterrorism mode just as the UN Security Council had. Having issued a declaration committing the organization to the antiterrorist struggle, it subsequently created the Counter-Terrorism Task Force to coordinate the implementation of this commitment, established the Secure Trade in the APEC Region (STAR) initiative, and promoted the development of APEC Counter-Terrorism Action Plans. John Ravenhill, though he cautions us not to overestimate the degree of agreement among member states on terrorist issues, still argues: "Post Sept 11, APEC has been revitalized by the new tasks its Leaders have given it through the adoption of a counter-terrorism agenda." Compared with the past, APEC is pursuing this agenda in a more coherent fashion, with greater financial backing and with the support of a more effective secretariat. The various commitments made are still voluntary, but there is an urgency to APEC deliberations that is not characteristic of earlier periods in its history.[16]

There are signs, too, that the Association of Southeast Asian Nations (ASEAN) Regional Forum (ARF), which is the Asia Pacific security organization, has become more energetic as a result of its pursuit of a counterterrorist agenda; its July 2002 "Statement on Measures Against Terrorist Financing" reflects a significant change in language compared with past security communiques. In this document, ARF participants, instead of adopting language that "encouraged" states to implement measures according to national timetables, as it would have in the past, stated that each ARF participant "will aim" to implement the various measures outlined "quickly and decisively." These are not phrases usually associated with Asian regional organizations that have been premised on voluntarism, noninterference, and consensus decisionmaking and consequently have moved at a gradual, if not glacial, pace in implementing all other aspects of their agendas.[17] At an ARF ministerial meeting on counterterrorism in Bali in February 2004, the participants agreed to establish an "ad hoc working group of senior legal officials from around the region" that would "report back to Ministers on the adequacy of regional legal frameworks

---

16   John Ravenhill, "Mission Creep or Mission Impossible? APEC and Security," in Amitav Acharya and Evelyn Goh, eds., *Reassessing Security Cooperation in the Asia-Pacific* (Cambridge: MIT Press, forthcoming 2006).

17   David Capie, "Between a Hegemon and a Hard Place: The 'War on Terror' and Southeast Asian-US Relations," *Pacific Review* 17, no. 2 (2004): 239.

for counter-terrorism cooperation and identify new areas for improvement of cooperation and assistance." For a grouping of states that has been extremely wary of ceding any element of state sovereignty, this represents a notable change in approach.[18]

2.3   *State Actions*

If regional and global institutions have seen it necessary to begin developing reputations for robustness in dealing with terrorists, so have individual governments, even at the expense of civil liberties. The U.S. administration, within one week of the terrorist attacks, brought the U.S. Patriot Act before Congress. The act amended fifteen different federal statutes and awarded sweeping new powers to law enforcement and intelligence agencies, affecting laws relating to immigration, surveillance, and intelligence sharing. It took only six weeks for Congress to pass it. U.S. authorities also locked up roughly 1,200 noncitizens, mostly Muslim men, immediately after September 11.[19] Some U.S. citizens, described as "enemy combatants," have been held without trial. Several hundred prisoners, mostly detained as a result of the fighting in Afghanistan, have been held at the U.S. naval base at Guantánamo Bay, Cuba, but not given prisoner of war status, and few have had their cases reviewed. Well before the shocking revelations of the mistreatment and torture by U.S. military personnel of prisoners held in the Abu Ghraib prison in Iraq, national security officials were reported in the U.S. press as having "defended the use of violence against captives as just and necessary." As one official supervising the capture and transfer of alleged terrorists told a *Washington Post* reporter in December 2002, "If you don't violate someone's human rights some of the time, you probably aren't doing your job."[20]

Washington has also decided to give large-scale financial and symbolic support to states that it believes have key roles to play in the antiterrorist campaign. Nowhere was this shift in U.S. policy more evident than in the case of Pakistan. From being regarded as a virtual failing or "rogue" state—with

---

18   Co-chairs' statement, Bali, 5 February 2004, available online at www.aseansec.org/16000 .htm.

19   David Cole, *Enemy Aliens: Double Standards and Constitutional Freedoms in the War on Terrorism* (New York: New Press, 2003), p. 25.

20   Dana Priest and Barton Gellman, "U.S. Decries Abuse but Defends Interrogations," *Washington Post*, 26 December 2002, p. A1. Some reports indicate that these practices have not been eradicated. See, for example, Frances Williams, "Global Outcry at US Treatment of Prisoners Fails to Stamp Out Abuse," *Financial Times*, 22 December 2004, p. 9. For this section more generally, see Rosemary Foot, "Human Rights and Counter-terrorism in America's Asia Policy," Adelphi Paper No. 363 (Oxford: Oxford University Press, February 2004), especially chap. 1.

fragile institutions, a weak economy, a nuclear weapons capacity, and a military dictatorship—the U.S. executive branch has tried to overlook the attributes it once associated with Islamabad and replace these with that of vital partner. U.S. aid began to flow once the tough U.S. sanctions previously imposed as a result of Pakistan's nuclear test and military coup were lifted in September and October 2001. February 2002 heralded the state visit of Pakistan's president, Pervez Musharraf, to Washington, where Musharraf was described as a "leader of great courage and vision." The accolade of a visit to Camp David came in June 2003, making him the first South Asian leader ever to be invited to the U.S. president's mountain retreat. On that occasion, Musharraf received a further pledge of U.S.$3 billion in aid over five years, half of which is for military assistance. Subsequently, Pakistan was designated a major non-NATO ally of the United States (as was the Philippines—another state closely aligned with the United States in antiterrorist action in Southeast Asia).[21]

Examples of this shift in U.S. perceptions of states that it deems important in the antiterrorist campaign can be found throughout Asia. In the case of Malaysia, the United States now values it as both a source of intelligence on terrorist groupings and effective in arresting terrorist suspects in relatively large numbers. The Bush administration also seeks to project it as a model, moderate, predominantly Islamic country in Southeast Asia that is a "beacon of stability in the region."[22] Malaysia's Internal Security Act (ISA), once regularly criticized in the United States for its arbitrary provisions and use against domestic political opponents, is now seen as essential in a counterterrorism context. Where China is concerned, the Bush administration in August 2002 agreed with the Chinese claim that the East Turkestan Islamic Movement is a terrorist grouping that operates in Xinjiang province and has links with Al-Qaida. This designation has damaged the reputation of the largely peaceful Muslim separatist movement in that area, linking the movement with terrorist activity in support of a clear Chinese attempt to delegitimize the Uighur struggle for religious and cultural autonomy. In Indonesia, the United States had been putting security sector reform relatively high on its policy agenda, in an attempt to help the new post-Suharto leadership reduce the military's role in politics. It had also imposed sanctions to ensure that certain of Indonesia's military leaders were made accountable for past human rights abuses (especially in East Timor). However, U.S. officials have made strong efforts since September 11 to circumvent these sanctions, to strengthen U.S.-Indonesian

---

21   Ibid., chap. 3.
22   "Mahathir Welcome in United States as Washington Shifts Focus," Associated Press, 15 April 2002.

military-to-military relations, and to overlook the need for accountability. Helping Indonesia build a robust reputation for dealing with terrorism has taken precedence in significant parts of the U.S. executive branch over Indonesia's status as a democratizing state that had needed to deal firmly with past human rights transgressions.[23]

What these actions and statements represent are a retreat from the cosmopolitan concern with "saving strangers."[24] They imply reduced attention to security defined as protecting individuals from instances of abuse originating inside states to a more absolutist notion associated with strong central authority in service of continuing statehood. Renewed priority has been given to the ability to police air, sea, and land borders; to arrest terrorist suspects; to focus on their interrogation rather than trial; and to investigate more fully those seeking asylum or relocation. Governments do, of course, have a duty to protect their citizens against terrorists who themselves reject the inviolability of innocent human life and who threaten the right to life. But that duty does not entail the abandonment of fundamental principles and peremptory norms associated with the protection of human rights that had previously gained some purchase at the global and domestic levels.

Security services worldwide have taken advantage of this reputational turn away from human rights protections. On Human Rights Day, 10 December 2001, seventeen special rapporteurs and independent experts of the UNCHR expressed serious concern over the infringements of human rights that were being reported to them on a daily basis due to measures adopted by states after September 11. Antiterrorist legislation, newly passed or amended in many countries, had defined terrorism in terms that were dangerously wide-ranging. A number of government officials also stated explicitly that a concern with human rights and democracy undermined the effective application of a counterterrorism policy. As the Uzbek foreign minister pithily put it, "Let's first bring things in order, then we'll talk about democracy and human rights."[25]

U.S. terminology and behavior have also been used as the benchmark for a number of other Asian governments. Some militaries in Asia have conducted their own "war on terrorism" against domestic opponents of several different

---

23   Foot, "Human Rights and Counter-terrorism," chaps. 4 and 5.

24   Nicholas J. Wheeler, *Saving Strangers: Humanitarian Intervention in International Society* (Oxford: Oxford University Press, 2000).

25   IPA et al., *Human Rights, the United Nations*, especially pp. 17–19. See too the July 2003 statement after the terrorist attack on the Marriott Hotel in Jakarta of the then Indonesian security minister (now president), Susilo Bambang Yudhoyono: "Those who criticize about human rights being breached must understand that all the bombing victims are more important than any human rights issue." Ibid., p. 17.

kinds, emulating in some cases the "shock and awe" tactics of the United States and the idea of embedding friendly journalists during military campaigns— for example, the Indonesian military's actions in Aceh. Where civilian agencies in the security sector have been given a lead, they have taken preventive action on the basis sometimes of flimsy evidence or at least on the basis of evidence that the public is never able to review. A recent Human Rights Watch report on Malaysia, for example, shows that its ISA—which allows for the holding of detainees for sixty days incommunicado, then for two years, with possible renewal of this period without judicial oversight—has led to the arrest of more than a hundred individuals on terror-related grounds. However, the government has not shown that any of those detained has engaged in illegal activity. While in custody, family members and others report that those arrested have suffered serious abuse. The detainees have also apparently been threatened with being sent to Guantánamo Bay's Camp X-Ray if they fail to cooperate— illustrating the latter's status as a symbol that expressed "a new acceptance of human rights violations in the name of fighting terrorism."[26]

There are many examples worldwide where governments appear to believe they have renewed license to abuse human rights in the name of fighting terrorism, on the grounds that this is deemed an acceptable form of behavior and, moreover, emulates the behavior of the most powerful state in the system. The concept of the strong state shows signs of undergoing some redefinition from one based not on the idea of sovereign responsibility but on effectiveness in the antiterrorist struggle, including the ability to act preventively and round up or eliminate suspects.

3   The Robustness of the Human Rights Norm?

What, then, of the power of the human rights norm with which I started this article? Paying attention once again to the same set of state and organizational actors as earlier, it is clear that institutions, domestic and international, can make a difference as to whether the human rights norm retains an ability to constrain.

---

26   Human Rights Watch, *In the Name of Security: Counterterrorism and Human Rights Abuses Under Malaysia's Internal Security Act*, May 2004, p. 4, available online at www.hrw.org. (accessed 20 January 2005).

3.1   The UN and Regional Organizations

Various parts of the UN have been responsible for resurrecting the human rights norm in this inhospitable era for three main reasons: the embeddedness of human rights in the UN's organizational structure; the role of the UNHCHR, which has over time become more visible and active within the UN agencies; and the presence of an outspoken proponent of human rights in the UN secretary-general. To increase the resonance of their arguments, UN human rights advocates make the twin points that, although terrorist actions themselves are a threat to human rights, human rights violations do also increase the population of terrorists.

The CTC came under early pressure to be more assertive in assessing the human rights consequences of the reports that states make as part of obligations associated with Resolution 1373. When the chair of the CTC briefed the UN Security Council on 18 January 2002, he reiterated that monitoring the performance of states in the human rights area was outside the scope of the CTC's mandate. However, on that same occasion, Kofi Annan reminded Council members that there was "no trade-off between effective action against terrorism and the protection of human rights," an argument that he has continued to advance on several subsequent occasions.[27] Both the former UNHCHR, Mary Robinson, and her successor, the late Sergio Vieira de Mello, spoke before the CTC, the latter reminding it in October 2002 that the best and only way to defeat terrorism was by respecting human rights, promoting social justice and democracy, and upholding the rule of law. Sir Nigel Rodley of the UN Human Rights Committee (a body that monitors compliance with the ICCPR) directly stated to the CTC in June 2003: "However inconvenient it may appear, the Council should not leave it wholly to those parts of the UN system that have a specific human rights mandate."[28] This concerted pressure at least has had the effect of promoting regular dialogue between the CTC and the UN's human rights bodies and has led the CTC to refer to expert opinion where there might be human rights consequences flowing from a state's antiterrorist action.

UN General Assembly Resolution 219, passed 18 December 2002, on respect for human rights and fundamental freedoms while combating terrorism, together with Security Council Resolution 1456 of 20 January 2003 on the same theme, declare that states should adopt only those antiterrorist measures that

---

27   For example, before the CTC on 6 March 2003, Kofi Annan stated: "Respect for human rights, fundamental freedoms and the rule of law are essential tools in the effort to combat terrorism—not privileges to be sacrificed at a time of tension." UN General Assembly, 58th session, Report of the Secretary-General, A/58/266, 8 August 2003, p. 7.

28   IPA et al., Human Rights, the United Nations, p. 20.

are in accordance with human rights, refugee, and humanitarian law. Annual UNCHR meetings in Geneva have considered reports of the UN special rapporteur on terrorism and human rights, which included a call to the CTC in the 2004 report to "fully incorporate human rights and humanitarian law obligations into its directives." The Office of the UNHCHR has produced the "Digest of Jurisprudence of the UN and Regional Organizations on the Protection of Human Rights While Countering Terrorism," which, among other matters, clarifies the concept of nonderogable rights under UN and regional human rights conventions. It states categorically, "This publication will help policy makers, including government officials, parliamentarians, judges, lawyers and human rights defenders, in developing counter-terrorism strategies that are fully respectful of human rights." No state can claim to be in ignorance. Similarly, the UN Committee Against Torture has been reminding state parties to the CAT of the nonderogable nature of the obligations they undertook in signing this convention. Nevertheless, the Office of the High Commissioner is under no illusions about the increased threats to virtually all human rights since September 2001, including threats to "human rights defenders ... migrants, refugees and asylum-seekers, indigenous peoples and people fighting for their rights or against the negative effects of economic globalization policies."[29]

However, whereas a number of regional organizations have responded to these signals and have announced a commitment to consider the human rights consequences of the fight against terrorism (European bodies and the Inter-American Commission on Human Rights taking this most seriously), Asian-only regional bodies, such as the ASEAN Plus Three arrangement, ASEAN itself, and the Shanghai Cooperation Organization, have not made reference to the need to respect human rights in the antiterrorist campaign. Only the ARF, APEC, the Asia-Europe meeting (ASEM), and the ASEAN-EU meeting (all of which include extra-Asian members) have nodded in that direction.[30] Against

29   Office of the United Nations High Commissioner for Human Rights, available online at www.ohchr.org/english/issues/terrorism/ (accessed 30 June 2004), p. 6; Counter-Terrorism Committee, available online at www.un.org/Docs/sc/committees/1373/human_rights .html (accessed 30 June 2004); "Terrorism and Human Rights," Final Report of the Special Rapporteur, Kalliopi K. Koufa, UN Doc. E/CN.4/Sub.2/2004/40 (25 June 2004), p. 27.

30   For example, the introductory statement of the ARF Bali Regional Ministerial Meeting on Counter-Terrorism reads: "Ministers agreed that the campaign against terrorism can only be won through comprehensive and balanced measures in full conformity with the purposes and principles of the Charter of the United Nations and human rights covenants" (5 February 2004), available online at www.aseansec.org/16000.htm (accessed 15 April 2004). I am grateful to Dr. Kuniko Ashizawa for research that verifies this section of my argument.

this trend, however, is the "ASEAN-USA Joint Declaration for Cooperation to Combat International Terrorism," signed on 1 August 2002, which makes no reference at all to the need to respect human rights and due process of law. That said, U.S. secretary of state Colin Powell did state at the time that the United States had not "abandoned its insistence upon upholding human rights standards in its dealings in the region."[31] A region that contains states that have tried to hold fast to the norm of nonintervention and have sought to control discussion of human rights or human security has remained wary, with few governments apart from the Japanese feeling under much pressure to respond to arguments to consider the human rights consequences of counterterrorist operations.

3.2   *The United States and Asian Governments*

Individual governments' adherence to human rights norms depends, unsurprisingly, on the vibrancy of a country's civil society and on whether there is rule of law and separation of powers, especially an independent judiciary. Governments can also be reminded of the human rights obligations that inhere as a result of their signature of regional and international human rights agreements.

U.S. mechanisms for challenging the behavior of the Bush administration—concerning, for example, the legal limbo of those in Guantánamo or the incarceration of several thousand Muslim men in the United States itself—have been reasonably far-reaching. It was the U.S. Supreme Court that criticized the Bush administration's claim that those held in Guantánamo were beyond U.S. law. Justice Sandra Day O'Connor, in writing the majority opinion, stated: "It is during our most challenging and uncertain moments that our nation's commitment to due process is most severely tested. It is in those times that we must preserve our commitment at home to the principles that we fight [for] abroad."[32] The U.S. Department of Justice's own Office of the Inspector General wrote a highly critical report on the conditions under which U.S. authorities were holding post-September 11 detainees.[33]

---

31   James Cotton, "Southeast Asia After 11 September," *Terrorism and Political Violence* 15, no. 1 (spring 2003): 161. The Working Group for an ASEAN Human Rights Mechanism made only informal representations to some individual ASEAN members suggesting they should respect human rights while countering terrorism (personal communication via e-mail, 11 June 2004).

32   Edward Alden and Demetri Sevastopuli, "US Supreme Court Says Old Rules Do Apply," *Financial Times*, 29 June 2004, p. 10.

33   "US Inspector General Report Criticizes Significant Problems of Round of Immigrants After 9/11," *New York Times*, 3 June 2003, p. A1.

The strengthening of U.S. bilateral relationships with rights-abusing states is also sometimes disputed, especially where there is a congressional interest in a particular country (Indonesia for example) and where Congress is required to sign off certain funding decisions. Uzbekistan, a country with a very poor human rights record, has been designated a key U.S. antiterrorist ally in Central Asia and has provided a military base useful for the war against the Taliban. However, in July 2002, Congress passed an amendment to the Foreign Operations Appropriations Act that required the administration to report every six months on all security and military assistance to the Uzbek government. In addition, it made all supplementary aid conditional on "substantial and continuing progress" in meeting the democracy and human rights criteria outlined in the U.S.-Uzbek March 2002 "Declaration on the Strategic Partnership and Cooperation Framework."[34] Significantly, human rights conditions appeared in the first section of that declaration. Important too is that, in July 2004, the U.S. State Department for the first time decided not to certify that Tashkent had made sufficient progress to warrant supplemental funding, thus denying President Karimov's government $18 million. Admittedly, this is a very small sum compared with what has been handed over since the start of the war against the Taliban, but it is a sign that human rights requirements can still impose some minor constraints on U.S. relations with a state that the U.S. secretary of defense, Donald Rumsfeld, described in February 2004 as a "key member of the coalition's global war on terror" and thanked for providing "stalwart support" in the antiterrorist campaign.[35]

Separation of powers is a welcome feature of the U.S. political system. In Asia, Japan has had lengthy parliamentary deliberation of antiterrorist legislation against the background of its constitution's human rights provisions. Moreover, elsewhere in the region, domestic and pan-Asian human rights NGOs have been trying to rein in the authoritarian trends by collecting and publicizing information about new antiterrorist legislation or amendments to existing security laws and drawing attention to the way the legislation is being used, including attacks on political opponents, the silencing of human rights activists, and the heightened discrimination against particular ethnic and religious groups.[36]

---

34   Foot, "Human Rights and Counter-terrorism," chap. 3.

35   Statement by Donald Rumsfeld, 25 February 2004, see online at http://usinfo.state/gov/pol/terror/texts/04022501.htm (accessed 2 March 2004); see also "Uzbekistan 'Might Look to China and Russia' After US Cut in Aid," *Financial Times*, 15 July 2004, p. 9.

36   See, for example, "Asian Consultation on the Impact of Terrorism and Antiterrorism Measures in Asia," Bangkok, 19–20 November 2004, organized by FORUM-ASIA (a pan-Asian organization based in Bangkok) and Suara Rakyat SUARAM, Malaysia.

However, as the work of these Asian NGOs attests, a number of Asian governments have taken advantage of the illiberalism associated with the counterterrorist era, especially where judicial and legislative independence is weak or nonexistent and human rights groups—where they have been allowed to operate—can either be intimidated or ignored. Within the most authoritarian of the countries in the region, it is the international human rights NGOs or the international press working clandestinely with local activists that tend to be the sources of information about what is going on. Even among the less authoritarian states of Asia, illiberal trends can garner the support of broad domestic opinion where the mass public has accepted a government's contention that terrorists neither deserve due process nor deserve to be treated in accordance with international human rights law. The Indonesian military campaign against the Gerakan Aceh Merdeka (GAM), or Free Aceh Movement, has been officially projected as a war against separatist-terrorists. The label GAM sympathizer has been tied to human rights activists, students, and journalists with serious consequences for those so labeled. Yet the military's campaign has not been strongly attacked domestically, in part because the armed forces have maintained control over information and have portrayed the operation as a success and as fundamental to maintaining a unified Indonesia.[37]

4   Conclusion

Post-September 11 developments have exposed the patchiness of the actual implementation of human rights norms in ways that mostly are not unfamiliar to us; but in other respects, they are shocking given the alacrity with which states, including the democratic among them, have adopted illiberal legislation and forms of behavior that are illegal and immoral. Nevertheless, evidence suggests that the human rights era is not over; neither does modern, legitimate governance imply the neglect of attention to human rights concerns. Rather, it seems that the twin reputations of defender against terrorism and human rights protector in some settings are in contention, but in others they show signs of being brought together.

Institutions do matter, as shown by the actions of those where the human rights idea has become reasonably well embedded. In some instances, they

---

37   Sidney Jones, "Update on Aceh," remarks before the United States–Indonesia Society, Washington, D.C., 11 June 2003, available online at www.usindo.org/Briefs/2003 (accessed 5 October 2004).

are providing a platform for normative debate and supplying information about the legal implications of human rights commitments already made. In time, they may well constrain more directly certain aspects of this plainly illiberal behavior. Thus, within the UN framework, a great deal of effort is being expended on the argument that the success of the antiterrorist struggle depends on a continuing concern with protecting human rights, and that a reputation for resoluteness in the face of a serious security threat should not come at the expense of the UN's reputation for having built, painstakingly over several decades, the international human rights regime. Unfortunately, however, this effort seems to be absorbing many of the limited resources of the UN's human rights bodies. For Asian state-based regional organizations, there is far less concern about the human rights consequences of antiterrorist campaigns and instead some evidence that regional bodies that have been criticized in the past for considerable inertia have become reinvigorated in the face of counterterrorism.

Some of the Asian states are finding it possible once again to make the argument that order should trump a concern with individual human rights. Moreover, in terms of their relations with the United States, it can make sense for many of these governments to demonstrate a capacity to tackle the terrorist threat because of the largesse that can result. This largesse has the effect of strengthening the security services, thus enhancing authoritarian control and (perhaps in the short term only) regime security. And where terrorist action can be equated with nationalist causes, some governments have garnered local support for actions that deal ruthlessly with those the central authorities have labeled as terrorists. If we accept that the domestic rather than the external realm is primary when it comes to the promotion and protection of human rights, then this finding is sobering.

In consolidated democracies, such as the United States, we are seeing some evidence of the power of domestic structures to rein in various of the executive branch's excesses, especially if there is a congressional interest or a legal question to adjudicate. That said, the continuing reports of abuse, including the use of torture at Guantánamo, at Abu Ghraib, and in detention facilities in Afghanistan, have undermined the U.S. official argument that harsh treatment of detainees has occurred only in a limited number of isolated cases. These reports suggest that strong domestic pressure needs to be maintained in order to root out such behavior.

Overall, therefore, if legitimate governance once had been seen to rest on a reputation for protecting human rights at home and abroad, the script of modern statehood now seems to comprise a wider set of notions. The requirement is for state institutions to build capacity to promote order and deal with transnational and domestic terrorist threats. In some instances, this is being done with considerable ruthlessness, even at the cost of the right to personal security. Sovereignty, defined more straightforwardly in an earlier era as the authority to control territory and peoples, has made something of a comeback. However, it does not have the field entirely to itself where institutions that concern themselves with rights reflect their mandates and retain their vigilance.

CHAPTER 12

Cities and the Multilevel Governance of Global Climate Change

Michele M. Betsill and Harriet Bulkeley[1]

The threat of global climate change is one of the most significant scientific and political challenges of our time. For more than a decade, the need for action to reduce emissions of greenhouse gases (GHGs), the relative responsibilities of different countries, and the means through which action could, or should, be taken have been the subject of fierce debate. Given the global nature of the problem, answers to these questions have been sought through processes of international negotiation between nation-states. However, it is increasingly clear that nation-states will be unable to meet their international commitments for addressing climate change without more explicit engagement with subnational action. GHG emissions originate from processes that are embedded in specific places, and it is often argued that the local is the most appropriate political jurisdiction for bringing about any necessary reductions in these emissions. Many local governments have considerable authority over land use planning and waste management and can play an important role in dealing with transportation issues and energy consumption. Furthermore, local governments have not just responded to predefined policy goals set within national and international arenas, but are also taking initiatives in their own right; this suggests that they represent an important site for the governance of global environmental issues.

In this article, we focus on the Cities for Climate Protection (CCP) program, a transnational network of municipal governments seeking to mitigate the threat of global climate change. We explore how such a network, which is

---

*   This chapter was originally published in Global Governance, Volume 12, Issue 2, 2006.

1   Michele M. Betsill is professor and chair of the Department of Political Science at Colorado State University. Harriet Bulkeley is professor in the Department of Geography at Durham University. For this collaborative project, Bulkeley gratefully acknowledges support from the Leverhulme Trust and the Newton Trust, University of Cambridge, in the form of a research fellowship. Betsill gratefully acknowledges similar support from the Global Environmental Assessment Project at Harvard University (NSF Award BCS-9521910). An earlier version of this paper was presented at the Open Meeting of the Human Dimensions of Global Environmental Change Research Community, Montreal, 16–18 October 2003.

simultaneously global and local, state and nonstate, could be conceptualized as a part of global environmental governance by examining the international relations literature on regime theory and transnational networks. In each case, we find that these approaches fail to adequately engage with the concept of governance, especially the increasingly complex interactions between supranational and subnational state and nonstate actors. Moreover, by distinguishing between "global" processes and actors and those that are "local" in origin and scope on the one hand, and between state and nonstate actors on the other, these approaches obscure how global environmental governance takes place through processes and institutions operating at and between a variety of scales, involving a range of actors with different levels of authority. We contend that a multilevel governance approach captures more fully the social, political, and economic processes that shape global environmental governance, as illustrated by an analysis of the modes of governing invoked through and intersected by the CCP program.

1   The Local Dimension of Climate Change Governance

In international relations theory and practice, global environmental governance is often assumed to take place at the "global" level. We contend that the "local" is also an important site for governing global environmental problems. Here, we use the term *local* primarily to refer to the municipal level. However, many of our points are relevant to discussions about other forms of subnational climate governance involving, for example, states within the United States. The need to address environmental problems at the local level has been a long-standing tenet of green political thought. The 1987 Brundtland Report included a specific chapter on the environmental issues facing cities, arguing that because the majority of the world's future population will live in urban areas, cities should be central to the pursuit of sustainable development.[2] The focus on cities as a means to address environmental issues was subsequently taken up by the European Union[3] and incorporated in Chapter 28

---

2   WCED (World Commission on Environment and Development), *Our Common Future* (Oxford: Oxford University Press, 1987), pp. 235–258.

3   Colin Fudge, "Changing Cities—Transforming Socio-ecological Relations in Bristol and Brussels," in Bettina Blanke and Randall Smith, eds., *Cities in Transition: New Challenges, New Responsibilities* (Basingstoke: Macmillan, 1999), pp. 215–242; Michael Hebbert, "The EU Urban Action Plan," *Town and Country Planning* (April 1999): 123–125; Stephen Ward and Richard Williams, "From Hierarchy to Networks? Sub-central Government and EU Urban Environmental Policy," *Journal of Common Market Studies* 35, no. 3 (1999): 439–464.

of *Agenda 21*, which calls for all local authorities to establish a Local Agenda 21 (LA21) through participation with their communities and encourages the establishment of mechanisms to promote cooperation and coordination between local authorities internationally.[4]

In this context, various commentators have suggested that cities, rather than nation-states, may be the most appropriate arena in which to pursue policies to address specific global environmental problems. For example, on the issue of climate change, cities are seen to be significant for four related reasons.[5] First, in a highly urbanized world, cities are sites of high energy consumption and waste production. The influence of local governments over these processes varies but can include energy supply and management, transport, land use planning, building regulations, and waste management. Second, local governments have been engaging with issues of sustainable development through LA21 in ways that have implications for the mitigation of climate change. Third, local governments can facilitate action by others in response to climate change by fostering partnerships with relevant stakeholders, encouraging public participation, and lobbying national governments. Fourth, some local governments have considerable experience in addressing environmental impacts within the fields of energy management, transport, and planning, and to reduce those impacts, many have undertaken innovative measures and strategies that can serve as demonstration projects or the basis for new experimentation. Through these practices, local governments exercise a degree of influence over GHG emissions in ways that directly impact the ability of national governments to reach targets that they have agreed to internationally. For example, in Australia it has been estimated that local authorities have a degree of influence over half of all GHG emissions.[6]

---

4   Richard Gilbert, Don Stevenson, Herbert Giradet, and Richard Stren, *Making Cities Work: The Role of Local Authorities in the Urban Environment* (London: Earthscan, 1996), p. 69.

5   Ute Collier, "Local Authorities and Climate Protection in the EU: Putting Subsidiarity into Practice?" *Local Environment* 2, no. 1 (1997): 39–57; Benjamin DeAngelo and L.D. Danny Harvey, "The Jurisdictional Framework for Municipal Action to Reduce Greenhouse Gas Emissions: Case Studies from Canada, USA and Germany," *Local Environment* 3, no. 2 (1998): 111–136; Darryn McEvoy, David Gibbs, and James Longhurst, "The Prospects for Improved Energy Efficiency in the UK Residential Sector," *Journal of Environmental Planning and Management* 42, no. 3 (1999): 409–424; Thomas Wilbanks and Robert W. Kates, "Global Change in Local Places: How Scale Matters," *Climatic Change* 43 (1999): 601–628.

6   Intergovernmental Committee on Ecologically Sustainable Development (ICESD), *Future Directions for Australia's National Greenhouse Strategy*, ICESD Discussion Paper, Canberra, 1997; J.M. Lumb, K. Buckley, and K.A. Auty, *Greenhouse Action and Local Government: The New Directions*, report prepared for the National Environmental Law Association (Melbourne: NELA, 1994).

Local authorities have not been conceptualizing and enacting environmental governance in isolation. One of the key features of the post-Rio era has been the growth in transnational networks of subnational governments, with estimates suggesting that there are at least twenty-eight such networks in Europe alone.[7] One of the largest networks, the International Council for Local Environmental Initiatives (ICLEI), was established in 1990 to represent the environmental concerns of local government internationally. ICLEI's CCP program is one vehicle through which local authorities have developed strategies for controlling GHG emissions. The CCP program, which was established in 1993, today includes more than 675 local authorities in Africa, Asia-Pacific, Latin America, Europe, and North America (with the majority in Asia-Pacific and North America), accounting for more than 8 percent of global GHG emissions.[8] Network members commit to passing through a series of five milestones and receive support from ICLEI in the form of software for monitoring GHG emissions and information about best practice. The US CCP program estimated that its members reduced their annual GHG emissions by 7.5 million metric tons in 1999 (an average of 100,000 metric tons per city) with a saving of $70 million in energy and fuel costs.[9] In 2000–2001, Australian councils reduced their emissions by 78,182 metric tons, more than doubling their achievements over the previous year.[10] While GHG emissions in each country have increased, in the context of nation-states that have been reluctant to pursue an agenda of addressing climate change, this is no mean achievement.

Elsewhere, we have discussed the limitations of the CCP program.[11] There is considerable variation in the level of engagement with the network among its members and their ability to access the resources provided by the network. The experience of several local authorities suggests that the process of translating a rhetorical commitment to climate protection into effective policies

---

7   Ward and Williams. "From Hierarchy to Networks?"

8   ICLEI (International Council for Local Environmental Initiatives), *Participants in the Cities for Climate Protection Campaign* (Toronto: ICLEI, 2003), available at www3.iclei. org/co2/ccpmems.htm (accessed 10 May 2005).

9   ICLEI, *U.S. Cities Acting to Protect the Climate: Achievements of ICLEI's Cities for Climate Protection—U.S. 2000* (Berkeley: ICLEI, 2000), pp. 2–3.

10   CCP-Australia, *Cities for Climate Protection Australia: Program Report* (Canberra: Australian Greenhouse Office and ICLEI, 2002), available at www3.iclei.org/ccp-au/ publication/141.pdf (accessed 16 July 2003).

11   Michele M. Betsill and Harriet Bulkeley, "Transnational Networks and Global Environmental Governance: The Cities for Climate Protection Program," *International Studies Quarterly* 48, no. 2 (2004): 471–493; Harriet Bulkeley and Michele M. Betsill, *Cities and Climate Change: Urban Sustainability and Global Environmental Governance* (London: Routledge, 2003), pp. 171–193.

and programs for controlling GHG emissions is far from straightforward. Nevertheless, we contend that the CCP network represents a new form of environmental governance. Moreover, given that such networks are increasingly common, it is imperative to develop a conceptual framework that can capture their role and impact and hence provide a more complete understanding of global environmental governance.

2   Conceptualizing the Local Dimension of Global Environmental
        Governance

While there are many different perspectives and interpretations of the term *governance*, broadly speaking we can say that it involves processes through which collective goals are defined and pursued in which the state (or government) is not necessarily the only or most important actor.[12] Several commentators have noted a shift from government to governance, in which the roles of the public, private, and voluntary sectors are being restructured.[13] The development of a governance perspective involves recognizing the roles of supranational and subnational state and nonstate actors, and the complex interactions between them, in the process of governing.[14] Such an approach is particularly relevant in the context of global environmental issues, where modes of governing are multiple and include processes and institutions that transverse scales as well as networks of actors that cannot be easily characterized by the state/nonstate dichotomy.

---

12   Matthew Paterson, David Humphreys, and Lloyd Pettiford, "Conceptualizing Global Environmental Governance: From Interstate Regimes to Counter-hegemonic Struggles," *Global Environmental Politics* 3, no. 2 (2003): 1–10; Jon Pierre and B. Guy Peters, *Governance, Politics and the State* (Basingstoke: Macmillan, 2000), p. 82; Rod Rhodes, "The New Governance: Governing Without Government," *Political Studies* 44 (1996): 652–667; James N. Rosenau, "Change, Complexity and Governance in Globalizing Space," in Jon Pierre, ed., *Debating Governance* (Oxford: Oxford University Press, 2000), pp. 167–200.

13   Robert Leach and Janie Percy-Smith, *Local Governance in Britain* (Basingstoke: Palgrave, 2001); B. Guy Peters and Jon Pierre, "Developments in Intergovernmental Relations: Towards Multi-level Governance," *Policy and Politics* 29, no. 2 (2001): 131–135.

14   Richard Cowell and Jonathan Murdoch, "Land Use and the Limits to (Regional) Governance: Some Lessons from Planning for Housing and Minerals in England," *International Journal of Urban and Regional Research* 23, no. 4 (1999): 654–669; Andrew Jordan, Rudiger Wurzel, and Anthony Zito, *Has Governance Eclipsed Government? Patterns of Environmental Instrument Selection and Use in Eight States and the EU*, Centre for Social and Economic Research on the Global Environment (CSERGE) Working Paper EDM 03-15 (Norwich: CSERGE, University of East Anglia, 2003); Pierre and Peters, *Governance, Politics and the State*; Rhodes, "The New Governance."

In seeking to conceptualize the role that transnational municipal networks, such as the CCP program, play in global environmental governance, it is necessary to understand the ways in which authority and power are articulated across and between those scales. Within international relations, regime theory and concepts of transnational networks have been developed to analyze processes of global environmental governance. In this section, we argue that these approaches provide limited conceptual space for considering the potential role of transnational municipal networks, and other subnational forms of governing global environmental issues, and thus offer an incomplete understanding of global environmental governance more broadly.

2.1   *International Regimes*
For many international relations scholars, global environmental governance is conducted through the interactions of nation-states, primarily in the formation of international regimes, defined as "social institutions that consist of agreed upon principles, norms, rules and decision-making procedures, and programs that govern the interaction of actors in specific issue areas."[15] Regimes are usually organized around a set of multilateral treaties on a specific issue (e.g., the United Nations Framework Convention on Climate Change and its Kyoto Protocol in the case of global warming). Analysts who view global environmental politics as a problem of collective action over common resources contend that regimes are formed in a specific issue area to facilitate cooperation by providing information and reducing transaction costs. From this perspective, regimes emerge either through the initiative of a hegemon or through interest-based, interstate bargaining.[16] Regime analysis in this tradition has focused on the conditions under which effective regimes are created and maintained, where "effective" is defined in terms of successful cooperation between nation-states and the coherence of the regime.[17]

Alternative accounts of regimes emphasize the role of ideas in shaping the ways that states define their interests. These "knowledge-based" or "constructivist" perspectives view international regimes as a means through which cognitive and normative aspects of the problem in question are constructed

15   Oran R. Young, "Rights, Rules and Resources in World Affairs," in Oran R. Young, ed., *Global Governance: Drawing Insights from the Environmental Experience* (Cambridge: MIT Press, 1997), pp. 5–6.

16   Andreas Hasenclever, Peter Mayer, and Volker Rittberger, *Theories of International Regimes* (Cambridge: Cambridge University Press, 1997), pp. 23–135; Robert O. Keohane, *After Hegemony: Cooperation and Discord in the World Political Economy* (Princeton: Princeton University Press, 1984), pp. 65–84.

17   Oran R. Young, ed., *The Effectiveness of International Environmental Regimes: Causal Connections and Behavioral Mechanisms* (Cambridge: MIT Press, 1999), pp. 1–32.

and in turn shape the ways states perceive their interests.[18] This shift in focus widens the scope of regime theory and reconceptualizes the processes through which regime formation and maintenance take place. In particular, nonstate actors, such as intergovernmental organizations, nongovernmental organizations, multinational corporations, and scientists are seen to have an important role in the formation and maintenance of international regimes.[19]

Despite the growing influence of nonstate actors in environmental regimes, for the most part, the significance of nonstate actors is measured in terms of the extent to which they shape, facilitate, and change the behavior of nation-states.[20] While this is not an unreasonable position—clearly nation-states are critical actors in global environmental governance—it points to fundamental assumptions concerning authority and territoriality underlying this approach that equate political power with the nation-state.[21] In other words, the assumptions of regime theory are more consistent with a government (as opposed to governance) perspective. This has two critical implications. First, the power of nation-states, as territorially bounded entities with a monopoly on the use of (economic or military) force, is seen as most significant on the global stage. Second, given that political power is defined by state boundaries, the internal politics of nation-states is considered to be of little significance. Aside from some interest in the concept of sovereignty,[22] the notion of transgovernmental coalitions,[23] and two-level games,[24] the state remains

18   Hasenclever, Mayer, and Rittberger, *Theories of International Regimes*, pp. 136–210; Karen Litfin, *Ozone Discourses: Science and Politics in Global Environmental Cooperation* (New York: Columbia University Press, 1994).

19   See, for example, Michele Betsill and Elisabeth Corell, "NGO Influence in International Environmental Negotiations: A Framework for Analysis," *Global Environmental Politics* 1, no. 4 (2001): 65–85; Margaret E. Keck and Kathryn Sikkink, *Activists Beyond Borders: Advocacy Networks in International Politics* (Ithaca: Cornell University Press, 1998); Litfin, *Ozone Discourses*; Peter Newell, *Climate for Change: Non-state Actors and the Global Politics of the Greenhouse* (Cambridge: Cambridge University Press, 2000).

20   Matthew Auer, "Who Participates in Global Environmental Governance? Partial Answers from International Relations Theory," *Policy Sciences* 33, no. 2 (2000): 159; Keck and Sikkink, *Activists Beyond Borders*.

21   John Agnew, "Mapping Political Power Beyond State Boundaries: Territory, Identity and Movement in World Politics," *Millennium* 28, no. 3 (1999): 503–507.

22   Karen Litfin, ed., *The Greening of Sovereignty in World Politics* (Cambridge: MIT Press, 1998).

23   Thomas Risse-Kappen, "Bringing Transnational Relations Back In: Introduction," in Thomas Risse-Kappen, ed., *Bringing Transnational Relations Back In: Non-State Actors, Domestic Structures and International Institutions* (Cambridge: Cambridge University Press, 1995), pp. 8–10; Anne-Marie Slaughter, "The Real New World Order," *Foreign Affairs* 76, no. 5 (1997): 183–197.

24   Robert D. Putnam, "Diplomacy and Domestic Politics: The Logic of Two-Level Games," *International Organization* 42 (1988): 429–460.

conceived for the most part as a homogeneous and unitary actor, a "fixed territorial entity … operating much the same over time and irrespective of its place
within the geopolitical order."[25] Implicitly, regime theory assumes that subnational governments act under the (sole) influence and direction of national
government. While a focus on knowledge and the role of nonstate actors has
led to a revision of the nature of interests, politics, and influence operating
within regimes, the state remains defined in terms of national government,
albeit with potential internal conflicts and the roles of domestic actors noted.
Critically, however, the potential role of subnational government is either
ignored or implicitly subsumed within the nation-state.

Given its focus on a fixed and uniform territorial notion of political power,
transnational networks of local governments, such as the CCP program, are
not easily conceptualized within regime theory approaches to global environmental governance. This top-down perspective assumes a vertical relationship
between the international, national, regional, and local scales and ignores the
role of local governments as an important site of global environmental governance in their own right. As noted earlier, many CCP member governments
have initiated policies and programs for managing GHG emissions independent of their national governments. The Australian and US cases are particularly illuminating, given that the national governments in each case have been
vocal opponents to current international efforts to address climate change.
Moreover, regime theory approaches overlook the emergence of network
forms of organization where institutional relationships may bypass levels of
governance, taking place directly between the local and the international.
Not only do CCP members interact directly with one another across national
boundaries, but ICLEI, not national governments, serves as the voice of local
authorities in international climate change negotiations through its observer
status at the Conference of the Parties. This suggests the need to move beyond
traditional concepts of the state as a national entity and assumptions of political power as necessarily territorially bound in order to understand processes of
global environmental governance.

2.2   *Transnational Networks*

Within international relations, there is increasing interest in transnational networks of actors and institutions that operate simultaneously across multiple
scales.[26] Such networks involve "regular interaction across national boundar-

25   John Agnew and Stuart Corbridge, *Mastering Space: Hegemony, Territory and International
       Political Economy* (London: Routledge, 1995), p. 78.
26   See, for example, Susanne Jakobsen, "Transnational Environmental Groups, Media,
       Science and Public Sentiment(s) in Domestic Policy-making on Climate Change," in

ies when at least one actor is a non-state agent or does not operate on behalf of a national government or intergovernmental organization."[27] Three central network concepts have been developed in relation to global environmental governance: epistemic communities, transnational advocacy networks, and global civil society.

The epistemic communities and transnational advocacy networks approaches stress that political authority accrues to transnational networks through their ability to garner and deploy information, knowledge, and values. Epistemic communities, networks of experts who share a common understanding of the scientific and political nature of a particular problem, are seen as gaining influence within international regimes by virtue of their authoritative claims to knowledge and their ability to create a scientific consensus on the issue at hand, to which policymakers turn under conditions of uncertainty.[28] There is some debate as to whether the Intergovernmental Panel on Climate Change constitutes an epistemic community. A transnational advocacy network (TAN) "includes those relevant actors working internationally on an issue, who are bound together by shared values, a common discourse, and dense exchanges of information and services."[29] Such networks operate simultaneously within domestic and international political arenas and are most frequently found in issues where there are easily identified principled positions (the Climate Action Network is an example of a TAN working on the issue of climate change). According to Margaret Keck and Kathryn Sikkink, TANs "use the power of their information, ideas, and strategies to alter the information and value contexts within which states make policies."[30]

These theories offer an alternative to accounts of power focused on the use of economic and military force to direct others and zero-sum concepts in which one actor's gain is another's loss. Instead, power is seen to accumulate from multiple sources of authority, including expertise and moral positions, and to be a relational concept. Nevertheless, in both the epistemic communities and TAN approaches, the power of transnational networks lies in their

<hr />

Richard Higgot, Geoffrey Underhill, and Andreas Bieler, eds., *Non-state Actors and Authority in the Global System* (London: Routledge, 2000), pp. 274–289; Keck and Sikkink, *Activists Beyond Borders*; Sanjeev Khagram, James V. Riker, and Kathryn Sikkink, eds., *Restructuring World Politics: Transnational Social Movements, Networks and Norms* (Minneapolis: University of Minnesota Press, 2002); Robert O'Brien, Anne Marie Goetz, Jan Aart Scholte, and Marc Williams, *Contesting Global Governance: Multilateral Economic Institutions and Global Social Movements* (Cambridge: Cambridge University Press, 2000).

27   Risse-Kappen, "Bringing Transnational Relations Back In," p. 3.

28   Peter M. Haas, *Saving the Mediterranean: The Politics of International Environmental Cooperation* (New York: Columbia University Press, 1990), p. 55.

29   Keck and Sikkink, *Activists Beyond Borders*, p. 2.

30   Ibid., p. 16.

ability to influence nation-states, which remain the location of governance.[31] Thus, these approaches reinforce an interpretation of global environmental governance where "government" is at the heart of the analysis and in which the nature of the state is effectively "black boxed."

In a third approach, sometimes labeled "global civil society," scholars examine the role of transnational networks in a more radical way, which is more in line with a governance perspective.[32] Moving away from state-centered analyses, these approaches consider the multiplicity of actors and institutions that influence the ways in which global environmental issues are addressed across different scales. From this perspective, "governance occurs on a global scale through both the co-ordination of states and the activities of a vast array of rule systems that exercise authority in the pursuit of goals that function outside normal national jurisdictions."[33] Not only are networks considered influential insofar as they shape the range and extent of state action, but also as an important site for governing global environmental issues in their own right.

Collectively, the focus on transnational networks marks a shift within the discipline of international relations from a preoccupation with hierarchical structures toward an appreciation of the importance of network forms of organization. However, these approaches, with their focus on transnational networks as *nonstate* actors, offer only a partial framework for analyzing the CCP program. Network members do undertake the sorts of lobbying and campaigning activities associated with non-governmental organizations. However, transnational municipal networks, like the CCP program, tend to have close links to government administration at local, national, and international levels and to have state agency through their members, so that it is impossible to categorize them as nonstate actors.[34] While many discussions of transnational networks allow for actors with links to the (national) state to be members of such networks, their significance is tied to their ability to alter the behavior of nation-states rather than their role in enhancing the capacity of local authorities to govern issues such as climate change.[35]

31   Auer, "Who Participates in Global Environmental Governance?" p. 159; Rosenau, "Change, Complexity and Governance in Globalizing Space," p. 170.

32   Ronnie Lipschutz and Judith Mayer, *Global Civil Society and Global Environmental Governance* (Albany: State University of New York Press, 1996); Paul Wapner, *Environmental Activism and World Civic Politics* (Albany: State University of New York Press, 1996).

33   Rosenau, "Change, Complexity and Governance in Globalizing Space," p. 172.

34   Harriet Bulkeley, Anna Davies, Bob Evans, David Gibbs, Kristine Kern, and Kate Theobald, "Environmental Governance and Transnational Municipal Networks in Europe," *Journal of Environmental Policy and Planning* 5, no. 3 (2003): 235–254.

35   Risse-Kappen, "Bringing Transnational Relations Back In"; Keck and Sikkink, *Activists Beyond Borders*.

In sum, transnational municipal networks do not fall neatly into such frameworks, suggesting that assumptions about the role of transnational networks in global environmental governance may need more careful scrutiny.[36] Rather than establishing transnational networks as non-state actors, it may be more appropriate to view them as multifaceted, having some of the features of nongovernmental, quasi-governmental, and business organizations.[37]

3   The Multilevel Governance of Global Climate Change

The CCP program, as a transnational municipal network, represents a form of environmental governance not easily captured by the perspectives outlined above. In each case, the assumption is made that global environmental governance is essentially a hierarchical process, so that policies are seen as emanating from the top down, where governing is primarily the responsibility of the state. The CCP program highlights the need for these perspectives to engage more fully with the concept of governance and to account for the changing nature of the state and the links between different levels and spheres of authority.

The concept of multilevel governance, with its emphasis on the connections between vertical tiers of government and horizontally organized forms of governance, provides a useful starting point for understanding the ways in which environmental problems are governed within and across scales. Originally developed to analyze regional policy development within the European Union (EU),[38] the concept has since been elaborated and extended. However, research has tended to focus on the development of multilevel governance within Europe and on sectors related to economic or regional policy.[39] In this section, we introduce the concept of multilevel governance before considering how it can inform an analysis of the CCP program as a part of global environmental governance.

---

36   Betsill and Bulkeley, "Transnational Networks and Global Environmental Governance."

37   Bulkeley et al., "Environmental Governance and Transnational Networks in Europe."

38   Lisbet Hooghe and Gary Marks, "Contending Models of Governance in the European Union," in Alan Cafruny and Carl Lankowski, eds., *Europe's Ambiguous Unity: Conflict and Consensus in the Post-Maastricht Era* (Boulder: Lynne Rienner, 1996), pp. 21–44.

39   For applications to environmental governance, see Jenny Fairbrass and Andrew Jordan, "Protecting Biodiversity in the European Union: National Barriers and European Opportunities?" *Journal of European Public Policy* 8, no. 4 (2001): 499–518; John Vogler, "Taking Institutions Seriously: How Regime Analysis Can Be Relevant to Multilevel Environmental Governance," *Global Environmental Politics* 3, no. 2 (2003): 25–39.

3.1   Types of Multilevel Governance

In its original formulation, proponents of multilevel governance argued that the role of national governments within the EU was diminishing and that a new, multilevel system of governance was taking shape.[40] From this perspective, this system has emerged for several reasons: nation-states no longer monopolize policymaking, given that supranational bodies have an independent influence over these processes; the need for collective decisionmaking over complex problems leads to a loss of control for nation-states; and supranational, national, and sub-national political arenas are interconnected through policy networks.[41] As a result, decisionmaking competencies are increasingly shared between actors operating at different levels of governance. This perspective draws attention to the importance of considering how political authority and processes of policymaking cross traditional divides between state and nonstate actors, domestic and international spheres.

Lisbet Hooghe and Gary Marks argue that two different, and not necessarily exclusive, approaches to multilevel governance have emerged since its original conception.[42] The first (Type 1) "conceives of dispersion of authority to a limited number of non-overlapping jurisdictions at a limited number of levels."[43] Federalism, with its focus on the relationship between central and subnational governments, is the intellectual foundation for this form of multilevel governance.[44] However, "what clearly distinguishes multilevel governance from supranational approaches is that it does not regard the EU as [developing into] a state. The idea is not one of governance *above* the

---

40   Andrew Jordan, "The European Union: An Evolving System of Multilevel Governance ... or Government?" *Policy and Politics* 29, no. 2 (2001): 193–208.

41   Tanja Aalberts, *Multilevel Governance and the Future of Sovereignty: A Constructivist Perspective*, Working Papers Political Science, No. 04/2002 (Amsterdam: Vrije Universiteit, 2002); William D. Coleman and Anthony Perl, "Internationalized Policy Environments and Policy Network Analysis," *Political Studies* 47 (1999): 691–709; Hooghe and Marks, "Contending Models of Governance in the European Union," pp. 21–44; Lisbet Hooghe and Gary Marks, "Unraveling the Central State, But How? Types of Multi-level Governance," *American Political Science Review* 97, no. 2 (2003): 233–243; Charlie Jeffrey, "Sub-national Mobilization and European Integration: Does it Make Any Difference?" *Journal of Common Market Studies* 38, no. 1 (2000): 1–23; Peter John, "The Europeanisation of Sub-national Governance," *Urban Studies* 37, nos. 5–6 (2000): 877–894.

42   Lisbet Hooghe and Gary Marks, "Types of Multi-level Governance," *European Integration Online Papers* 5 (2001), available at http://eiop.or.at/eiop/texte/2001-011.htm (accessed May 2002); Hooghe and Marks, "Unraveling the Central State, But How?" pp. 233–243.

43   Hooghe and Marks, "Types of Multi-level Governance," p. 4.

44   Hooghe and Marks, "Unraveling the Central State, But How?" p. 236.

state … but rather of governance *beyond* the state."[45] In this nested interpretation, a clear hierarchy between different tiers of governance exists; the nation-state retains the central authority in negotiating between the domestic and international levels. State executives and state arenas remain important (if not the most important) components of systems of governance.[46] However, from this perspective, local governments have a degree of independent agency. For example, in the EU, such actors form transnational networks and associations and can outflank the nation-state in order to pursue deeper levels of policy integration.[47] In the US context, scholars have noted the increasing frequency with which local governments engage in foreign policy matters independent of (and sometimes in contradiction to) the federal government.[48]

Type II multilevel governance "captures both the multiple levels at which governance is taking place, and the myriad actors and institutions which act simultaneously across these levels."[49] If the first vision of governance focuses on changes in the *tiers* of authority (e.g., distribution to supranational and subnational levels), the second is equally concerned with new *spheres* of authority[50] resulting from interactions between state and nonstate actors. Spheres of authority may not be defined in a neat hierarchy of scales in which the place of the nation-state is easily identified, but, rather, the territoriality of different forms of political authority is itself a matter of definition and contestation. Hooghe and Marks suggest that it is at the boundaries of formal politics, in relations between state and nonstate actors, and between national and international politics, that such forms of governance are emerging.[51]

While the concept of multilevel governance originated in relation to the EU, it has wider applicability. The Type I model may also be considered in relation to federal states, such as the United States[52] and Australia[53] and, if interna-

45   Tanja Aalberts, "The Future of Sovereignty in Multilevel Governance Europe: A Constructivist Reading," *Journal of Common Market Studies* 42, no. 1 (2004): 28.

46   Hooghe and Marks, "Contending Models of Governance in the European Union," p. 23.

47   Fairbrass and Jordan, "Protecting Biodiversity in the European Union," p. 500.

48   Brian Hocking, "Patrolling the 'Frontier': Globalization, Localization and the 'Actorness' of Non-Central Governments," *Regional and Federal Studies* 9 (spring 1999): 17–39.

49   Bulkeley and Betsill, *Cities and Climate Change*, p. 29.

50   James Rosenau, *Along the Domestic-Foreign Frontier: Exploring Governance in a Turbulent World* (Cambridge: Cambridge University Press, 1997); Rosenau, "Change, Complexity and Governance in Globalizing Space."

51   Hooghe and Marks, "Types of Multi-level Governance," p. 10.

52   Guy Peters, "Administrative Reform and Political Power in the United States," *Policy and Politics* 29, no. 2 (2001): 171–179.

53   Martin Painter, "Multi-level Governance and the Emergence of Collaborative Federal Institutions in Australia," *Policy and Politics* 29, no. 2 (2001): 137–150.

tional regimes are taken as a level of governance "beyond" the state, to other contexts.[54] Moreover, Type II models of multilevel governance can be considered relevant in other contexts where horizontal/transnational networks of governance take shape. Given that the CCP program shows that subnational governments and their networks can act as independent transnational actors, a multilevel governance approach is a useful starting point for developing a new conceptual framework for the analysis of global environmental governance.

3.2   *Multilevel Governance and the CCP Program*

Traditional divisions between state and nonstate, local, national, and global are disrupted by the politics of climate change. Political authority for making decisions related to the mitigation of GHG emissions has been redistributed upward to international organizations and transnational networks, downward to cities and regions, and outward to non-state actors. While the nation-state may be responsible for legitimating and alleviating climate risks, this is a task it cannot complete without addressing the source of risks (energy use) and without the involvement of the institutions and agents responsible for that use (industries and communities).[55] In turn, nonstate actors, which operate at different scales across traditionally discrete policy sectors, share responsibility with the state for defining problems and implementing solutions. The CCP program is one element in the multilevel governance of climate change, where the roles and responsibilities of state and nonstate actors at all levels are being reconfigured.

In one sense, the CCP program could be considered an element of Type I multilevel governance, as a network that mediates between defined political arenas at the local, national, and global levels. However, such an analysis assumes an unwarranted separation and distinction between levels of political authority. We suggest that this transnational network in fact epitomizes the development of Type II multilevel governance, creating a new sphere of authority through which the governance of climate change is taking place and which is not bound to a particular scale. At the international climate change negotiations, ICLEI represents local governments, highlighting the role of CCP members in addressing climate change, which most nation-states fail to fully

---

54   Oran Young's recent work is moving in this direction. See Oran R. Young, *The Institutional Dimensions of Global Environmental Change: Fit, Interplay and Scale* (Cambridge: MIT Press, 2002).

55   Ulrich Beck, *Risk Society: Towards a New Modernity* (London: Sage, 1992); Harriet Bulkeley, "Governing Climate Change: The Politics of Risk Society?" *Transactions of the Institute of British Geographers* 26 (2001): 430–447; Matthew Gandy, "Rethinking the Ecological Leviathan: Environmental Regulation in an Age of Risk," *Global Environmental Change* 9 (1999): 59–69.

appreciate, as evidenced by the fact that few of them report on local actions in their national communications to the climate change secretariat. In this way, the CCP bypasses the nation-state and gives local authorities the opportunity to take a position that may go against that of their national governments, thus illustrating that the nature of climate change governance cannot be read hierarchically. However, the CCP does more than mediate between the formal arenas of local government and the global climate regime; it has created its own arena of governance through the development of norms and rules for compliance with the goals and targets of the network. The CCP network also takes on functions that are typically presumed to rest with national governments, such as setting GHG emissions targets for participants as well as requirements for reporting and monitoring emissions. This suggests that political power and authority not only lie with nation-states, but can accrue to transnational networks operating through a different form of territoriality.

In addition to acting around the state, the CCP program is partly a state-based organization, given that its membership comprises local governments and that it often works closely with national governments and state agencies. In Australia, CCP officials have entered into a partnership with national and local governments and with Environs, a non-governmental organization, to adapt the CCP software to local circumstances and to ensure that local authorities have access to this tool. The CCP program also plays an important role in securing financial resources for local climate protection. Although these resources often come directly or indirectly from the state (national or regional), they would not have been made available to local authorities without lobbying on the part of the CCP. Advocacy from the CCP program has led to the creation of national CCP campaigns in a number of countries, and in many cases, the nation-state plays a central role in coordinating the program. This suggests that spheres of authority are not separate from, or alternative to, state-based power but are inextricably bound up with it.

Although states increasingly rely on nonstate actors and networks such as the CCP program, it is equally clear that the state, operating at multiple scales, has been central in determining how climate change has been interpreted as a policy problem and the extent to which actions have been implemented. Rather than indicating that new forms of "governance" have replaced "government" in the governing of climate change, this suggests that multiple modes of governing are present, and the task is to assess how and to what effect these are articulated. At the local level, the state is sometimes the source of innovation in climate protection.[56] For example, in the United States, the city of Denver's interest in climate protection and its awareness of the link between

---

56   Bulkeley and Betsill, *Cities and Climate Change*, pp. 190–191.

energy use, air quality, and climate change evolved independently from and in advance of the national debate over climate change and is arguably a function of leadership by Mayor Wellington Webb as well as the availability of financial and administrative resources. In Newcastle (Australia) and Newcastle and Leicester (UK), local government research and initiatives on urban responses to climate change took place ahead of the interest of national governments or the CCP program on this issue.

Moreover, nation-states have significant influence over the capacity for the development and implementation of local climate protection policies in the planning, transport, and energy sectors. In the UK, guidance from the national government encourages local planners to consider energy use and the location/design of development. However, since it does not *require* such considerations, local officials feel powerless to deny a development application based solely on these grounds. The case of Newcastle (Australia) demonstrates both the benefits of synergy between federal, state, and local policies and the opportunistic nature through which such circumstances arrive. Legislation in the state of New South Wales required that utilities investigate ways to improve energy efficiency and to promote energy conservation. In Newcastle, these programs have enabled the development of demonstration schemes for renewable energy and created a consumer market for green energy. In turn, Newcastle's initiatives and involvement with the CCP program have provided the federal government with a model upon which to base the further involvement of local governments in addressing climate change and, some might argue, a means through which to displace responsibility for the issue from the federal to subnational states. The effectiveness of the CCP network as a means through which to address climate protection objectives therefore varies considerably from place to place.[57]

A multilevel governance perspective does not necessarily signal a weakening of the state but rather a redefinition of the scope and scale of state activity. As illustrated in the case of climate change, the role of the state is not governed by some determinate and finite notion of capacity, but instead through negotiations in which actors and institutions mutually define their respective roles. In this way, environmental politics is an argumentative struggle in which "actors not only try to make others see problems according to their views but also seek to position other actors in a specific way."[58] Shifts in the scale of state activity and authority should therefore be viewed as a reorganization of the

57   Betsill and Bulkeley, "Transnational Networks and Global Environmental Governance."
58   Maarten Hajer, *The Politics of Environmental Discourse: Ecological Modernization and the Policy Process* (Oxford: Clarendon Press, 1995), p. 53.

social relations between actors, a reorganization that may in some cases reinforce the power of the state.[59] Rather than signaling a shift from "government" to "governance," the multiscalar politics of climate change involves plural modes of governing, which act to reinforce and negate each other. The multilevel governance perspective we have introduced here provides one means of establishing a new conceptual framework for understanding global environmental governance in which both vertical relations between governments and new horizontal spheres of governance can be brought into view. Such a framework is of particular import in the analysis of climate governance where there is growing recognition that "the future of the climate regime may also lie in strong local and regional initiatives."[60]

4   Conclusion

The governance of climate change is a complex, multilevel process. Traditional analytical divisions between international and domestic politics, between local, national, and global scales, and between state and non-state actors no longer suffice. Our analysis of the CCP network demonstrates that global environmental politics are not merely a matter of international negotiation and national policy development, but are also taking place locally. However, the local governance of the global environment is not conducted at a discrete scale, but is constructed by relations of power and influence between subnational and national state and nonstate actors, and through the creation of new spheres of authority.

We have argued that the perspective of multilevel governance offers an alternative analysis to that provided by international regimes and transnational networks. Not only does a multilevel governance approach create conceptual space for considering the role of subnational governments in global environmental governance, it also highlights the multiple forms of government and governance in world politics. Such an approach illuminates the ways

---

59   Bob Jessop, "Post-Fordism and the State," in Ash Amin, ed., *Post-Fordism: A Reader* (Oxford: Blackwell, 1994), pp. 251–279; Gordon Macleod and Mark Goodwin, "Space, Scale and State Strategy: Rethinking Urban and Regional Governance," *Progress in Human Geography* 23, no. 4 (1999): 503–527; Eric Swyngedouw, "Authoritarian Governance, Power, and the Politics of Rescaling," *Environment and Planning D: Society and Space* 18 (2000): 63–76.

60   Rado Dimitrov, Catherine Ganzleben, Kati Kulovesi, Charlotte Salpin, and Christoph Sutter, "A Brief Analysis of the UNFCCC COP-10 Side Events," *ENB on the Side* (Winnipeg: International Institute for Sustainable Development, 2004), available at www.iisd.ca/climate/cop10/enbots.

in which the nature of the state has been taken for granted within much of the literature on global environmental governance, with discussion often limited to whether it does or does not remain center stage in the formation of international regimes. The multilevel governance lens highlights the complexity of the state and the reduced ability of national level state institutions to control the policymaking process. As such, it serves to direct our attention toward other arenas within which the governance of global environmental problems is taking place.

Furthermore, adopting an interpretation of multilevel governance as a polycentric arrangement of overlapping and interconnected spheres of authority shifts the analysis of global environmental governance away from a hierarchical model in which rules, responsibilities, and norms are passed up or down the chain of command from global to local or vice versa, toward a recognition of the ways in which the scaling of political authority is in itself a contested process. The CCP program is but one illustration of how our familiar scales of analysis—international, national, regional and local—are disrupted by emerging forms of environmental governance that transcend or operate beyond these boundaries. As Matthew Paterson and colleagues argue, global environmental governance "is a fundamentally political process involving struggles over who has the authority and legitimacy to propose rules guiding the practices" of different actors and institutions.[61] Such struggles take place within, across, and between spheres and tiers of governance and result in the redefinition of the roles of different actors and their relationships in governance processes.

Future research should examine how these struggles take place and their implications for the effectiveness and legitimacy of global environmental governance.

---

61   Paterson et al., "Conceptualizing Global Environmental Governance," p. 8.

CHAPTER 13

Peacebuilding: What Is in a Name?

Michael Barnett, Hunjoon Kim, Madalene O'Donnell and Laura Sitea[1]

Thirteen years ago, UN Secretary-General Boutros Boutros-Ghali unveiled the concept of postconflict peacebuilding, defining it as "action to identify and support structures which will tend to strengthen and solidify peace in order to avoid relapse into conflict."[2] Since then practitioners, scholars, international and regional organizations, and states have attempted to better identify what institutionalizes peace after war and what the critical ingredients and steps likely to further that goal are. If the success of peacebuilding is measured against how well it has, indeed, institutionalized peace, the picture is very mixed. Nearly 50 percent of all countries receiving assistance slide back into conflict within five years, and 72 percent of peacebuilding operations leave in place authoritarian regimes.[3] If, however, success is measured in terms of the institutionalization of the concept of peacebuilding, then it appears to be a resounding success. An impressive number of organizations contribute to the cause of ending and preventing deadly conflict and use the concept to frame and organize their postconflict activities. Every indication, moreover, is that the demand for peacebuilding will increase further because the long-term

---

[*] This chapter was originally published in Global Governance, Volume 13, Issue 1, 2007.

[1] Michael Barnett is University Professor of International Affairs and Political Science at the Elliott School of International Affairs, George Washington University. His current work focuses on humanitarianism in world affairs. Hunjoon Kim is an associate professor in the Department of Political Science and International Relations, Korea University. His dissertation examines the cause and impact of global diffusion of transitional justice policy. Madalene O'Donnell coordinated a program on postwar state building at New York University's Center on International Cooperation while collaborating on this article. She currently works in the UN Department of Political Affairs. She has held positions with the UN, World Bank, and USAID in Latin America and Eastern Europe, focusing on postconflict governance and anti-corruption. Laura Sitea was a research associate with the program on postwar state building at New York University's' Center on International Cooperation while collaborating on this article. She currently works in the East Africa Team at the United Nations Department of Political Affairs.

[2] UN, *Agenda for Peace*, Report of the Secretary-General, para. 21. Available at http://www.un.org/peace/reports/peace_operations/.

[3] Paul Collier et al., *Breaking the Conflict Trap: Civil War and Development Policy* (New York: Oxford University Press and World Bank, 2003); Charles T. Call and Susan E. Cook, "On Democratization and Peacebuilding," *Global Governance* 9, no. 2 (2003): 233–234.

concern about ending civil wars has now been joined by the fear that weak states pose a major threat to international stability.[4] Perhaps the surest sign of the thriving peacebuilding agenda is the decision by the 2005 World Summit at the UN to endorse UN Secretary-General Kofi Annan's proposals to create a peacebuilding commission, support office, and fund. When implemented, these structures will institutionalize peacebuilding at the highest levels—and increase the incentives for others to join the peacebuilding bandwagon.

Although peacebuilding is generically defined as external interventions that are designed to prevent the eruption or return of armed conflict, there are critical differences among actors regarding its conceptualization and operationalization. This article surveys and analyzes twenty-four governmental and intergovernmental bodies that are currently active in peacebuilding in order to, first, identify critical differences in how they conceptualize and operationalize their mandate and, second, map areas of potential concern. Our survey includes actors who are the largest funders or implementers of international peacebuilding assistance and who are likely to participate in a future UN Peacebuilding Commission.[5] In the first section we briefly outline the various terms used by different actors to describe their peacebuilding activities and correlate these terms with differing core mandates, networks of interaction, and interests. Although different terms are used to describe postconflict peacebuilding, there are even greater divisions regarding the specific approaches that might achieve it, which is the focus of the second section. Some programs focus on the production of stability and security in the early days of a peace agreement's implementation, while others focus on building vibrant civil societies and furthering development, democracy, justice, and the rule of law. Although there are various reasons for these differing priorities, the prevailing organizational mandates and interests are an important part of the explanation. Thus far, though, programs have focused on the immediate or underlying causes of conflict—to the relative neglect of state institutions. This neglect is a possible artifact of the ingrained belief by wealthy countries that liberalization,

---

4 Stephen Krasner and Carlos Pascual, "Addressing State Failure," *Foreign Affairs*, July/August 2005: 153–163.

5 This is a selective, rather than a comprehensive review. We have drawn from available data on official development assistance (ODA), emergency assistance, and assessed contributions to peacekeeping operations in ten postconflict countries (see Appendix 2, p. 57) to identify a list of the key bilateral and multilateral organizations involved in financing or implementing international "peacebuilding" efforts. Appendix 3 (p. 58) lists the actors included in the survey: the United Nations, World Bank, IMF, European Commission, United States, France, Germany, Japan, UK, and Canada. The list of the dozens of documents we reviewed and that inform our analysis are available from Michael Barnett.

largely defined as the movement toward democracy, markets, and the rule of law, is the best way to develop a positive peace in poor ones. In this respect, international peacebuilders have demonstrated greater concern with the kind of state being built rather than its degree. There is evidence, however, that this neglect is being redressed. Although this greater attention is overdue, to the extent that it is driven by a fear that weak states create a permissive environment for terrorist and criminal networks, it might create a willingness to be more concerned with the degree of the state rather than the kind.

By way of conclusion, we discuss several policy implications. Although we see a lot of interest in peacebuilding, much of it is at the level of rhetoric and not at the level of resources. The danger, therefore, is that while peacebuilding looks highly supported on paper, in fact it receives little meaningful financial and political support relative to the costs of renewed conflict. Second, we need to be very cognizant of the particular version of peacebuilding that is being institutionalized. There are important differences in how various actors see the complex task of peacebuilding and the many priorities it entails. Debates among agencies over how to implement peacebuilding in particular areas must not be settled by bureaucratic power but by the recipient states themselves, with international actors helping inform their choices by access to evidence-based arguments (and an acknowledgment that the evidence is limited and analysis highly provisional). These are critical issues to keep in mind at the UN Peacebuilding Commission. Finally, agencies must focus more attention on creating state institutions that can deliver basic public goods in an equitable manner. Although the state is not the only institution that underpins stability, pursuing peacebuilding without an institutional foundation is a recipe for failure.

1   Peacebuilding and Its Aliases

Peacebuilding is generically understood as external interventions that are intended to reduce the risk that a state will erupt into or return to war. Yet, as captured in Table 13.1, different agencies use a wide variety of terms that are related to but are not necessarily synonymous with peacebuilding. Even more confusing, some use the same term, peacebuilding, in slightly different ways. Different groupings clearly emerge: the UN Secretariat, UN specialized agencies, European organizations, and member states. This differentiation, as we suggest below, owes partly to prevailing organizational mandates and networks. The organization's core mandate will heavily influence its reception to, and definition and revision of, the concept of peacebuilding. Moreover, organizations do not exist in isolation but instead are nested in structured relationships and exchange of resources and information; those that are linked have tended to converge on a consensus definition.[6]

The UN Secretariat continues to build on former UN Secretary-General Boutros Boutros-Ghali's original formulation: "action to identify and support structures which will tend to strengthen and solidify peace in order to avoid relapse into conflict."[7] At the UN, "peacebuilding" complements the organization's peacemaking and peacekeeping functions. In his *Supplement to an Agenda for Peace*, Boutros-Ghali expanded on the basic ideas behind peacebuilding and then defined its essential goal as "the creation of structures for the institutionalization of peace."[8] Since then, other units within the Secretariat have modified and refined this formulation. As Charles Call notes in his review of peacebuilding at the UN, at this point the UN introduced two important clarifications. One, it began to emphasize that peacebuilding is more than the elimination of armed conflict; after all, stability can be achieved by the balance or threat of force. Instead, it involves the creation of a positive peace, the elimination of the root causes of conflict so that actors no longer have the motive to use violence to settle their differences. The other clarification, a logical implication of the first, is that the same technologies that are used to help build peace after war also can be used to help societies avoid war in the first instance. In other words, peacebuilding is conflict prevention by another name and, therefore, "postconflict" often modifies peacebuilding to distinguish it from conflict prevention.[9]

In early 2000 the Brahimi Report on Peacekeeping Reform further refined the definition of peacebuilding: "activities undertaken on the far side of conflict to reassemble the foundations of peace and provide the tools for building on those foundations something that is more than just the absence of war."[10] Although the report stressed how peacebuilding comes after conflict, and thus intentionally bracketed its applicability to conflict prevention, this restriction primarily owed to the commission's mandate to review peacekeeping operations in the main (and to bracket what comes afterwards). The Department

---

6   We also detect moments when tightly networked agencies attempt to distinguish themselves and protect their turf by developing distinctive definitions of peacebuilding and alternative concepts.

7   *Agenda for Peace*, para. 21.

8   "Report of the Secretary-General on the work of the Organization, Supplement to an *Agenda for Peace*: Position Paper of the Secretary-General on the occasion of the fiftieth anniversary of the United Nations," A/50/60-S/1995/1, 3 January 1995.

9   Charles Call, *Institutionalizing Peace: A Review of Postconflict Peacebuilding Issues for DPA*, January 2005, unpublished paper on file with Barnett, pp. 3–4.

10   "UN, Report of the Panel on United Nations Peace Operations," October 2000. Accessed at http://www.un.org/peace/reports/peace_operations/.

TABLE 13.1   Different concepts and definitions across agencies

Agency	Major concepts	Definitions	Other concepts
UN Department of Political Affairs (DPA)	Postconflict peacebuilding	All external efforts to assist countries and regions in their transitions from war to peace, including all activities and programs designed to support and strengthen these transitions.	n/a
UN Department of Peacekeeping Operations (DPKO)	Peacekeeping	Activities to help countries torn by conflict create conditions for sustainable peace, including activities to monitor and observe peace processes that emerge in postconflict situations and assist excombatants to implement the peace agreements.	n/a
UN Development Programme (UNDP)	Conflict prevention and peacebuilding	Activities undertaken on the far side of conflict to reassemble the foundations of peace and provide the tools for building on those foundations, something that is more than just the absence of war (Brahimi report).[a]	Postconflict recovery n/a
World Bank	Postconflict reconstruction	Activities that support the transition from conflict to peace in an affected country through the rebuilding of the socioeconomic framework of the society.	n/a
International Monetary Fund (IMF)	Postconflict recovery	Activities to restore assets and production levels in the disrupted economy.	Postconflict peacebuilding

a   UN, *Report of the Panel on United Nations Peace Operations*, October 2000, available at http://www.un.org/peace/reports/peace_operations.

TABLE 13.1   Different concepts and definitions across agencies (*cont.*)

Agency	Major concepts	Definitions	Other concepts
European Commission (EC)	Conflict prevention and crisis management	Activities aiming not only at easing a situation where an outbreak of violence is imminent (conflict prevention in a narrow sense) but also at preventing the occurrence of such a situation (conflict prevention in a wider sense).	n/a
	Reconstruction and rehabilitation	Reestablishment of a working economy and the institutional capacities needed to restore social and political stability in developing countries that have suffered serious damage through war, civil disorder, or natural disaster.	n/a
US Department of State	Postconflict reconstruction and stabilization	Activities to help postconflict states lay a foundation for lasting peace, good governance, and sustainable development.	Peacebuilding
US Department of Defense (DOD)	Reconstruction and stabilization	Competencies identified for reconstruction include humanitarian assistance, public health, infrastructure, economic development, rule of law, civil administration, and media, whereas stability operations require sufficient security forces, communication skills, humanitarian capabilities, and area expertise.	Conflict prevention

TABLE 13.1   Different concepts and definitions across agencies (*cont.*)

Agency	Major concepts	Definitions	Other concepts
US Agency for International Development (USAID)	Postconflict recovery and transition assistance	Immediate interventions to build momentum in support of the peace process including supporting peace negotiations; building citizen security; promoting reconciliation; and expanding democratic political processes.	Conflict prevention; reconstruction
UK Foreign and Commonwealth Office (UKFCO)	Postconflict reconstruction	An umbrella term covering a range of activities required in the immediate aftermath of conflict.	Postconflict peacebuilding; conflict prevention
UK Ministry of Defence (UKMOD)	Peacebuilding	Activities relating to the underlying causes of conflict and the longer-term needs of the people; requires a commitment to a long-term process.	
UK Department for International Development (DFID)	Conflict reduction and postconflict peacebuilding	Conflict reduction includes conflict management (activities to prevent the spread of existing conflict); conflict prevention (short-term activities to prevent the outbreak or recurrence of violent conflict); conflict resolution (short-term activities to end violent conflict); and peacebuilding (medium- and long-term actions to address the factors underlying violent conflict).[b] Essential postconflict	

---

b   Simon Lawry-White, *Review of the UK Government Approach to Peacebuilding: An Synthesis of Lessons Learned from UK Government Funded Peacebuilding Project 1997–2001* (London: UK Department for International Development, 2003, available at: http://www.dfid.gov.uk/ [accessed March 2005]).

TABLE 13.1   Different concepts and definitions across agencies (*cont.*)

Agency	Major concepts	Definitions	Other concepts
		peacebuilding measures include disarmament, demobilization and reintegration programs, and building the public institutions that provide security, transitional justice and reconciliation, and basic social services.[c]	
German Federal Foreign Office (FFO)	Civilian crisis prevention	The concept of civilian crisis prevention encompasses conflict resolution and postconflict peacebuilding and is understood through a number of strategic leverage points, such as the establishment of stable state structures (rule of law, democracy, human rights, and security), and the creation of the potential for peace within civil society, the media, cultural affairs, and education.[d]	Conflict resolution; peacebuilding
German Federal Ministry of Defense (FMD)	Multidimensional peace missions	Multidimensional peace missions aim to redress the destruction of a country's infrastructure resulting from intrastate conflict. In addition to their military aspect, they undertake a	

c   DFID, March 2005, available at http://www.dfid.gov.uk/.

d   OECD, "Action Plan: Civilian Crisis Prevention, Conflict Resolution, and Postconflict Peace Building," Berlin, 12 May 2004, http://www.oecd.org/dataoecd/32/12/33983678.pdf.

TABLE 13.1   Different concepts and definitions across agencies (*cont.*)

Agency	Major concepts	Definitions	Other concepts
		variety of tasks ranging from reform of the security forces and demobilization of combatants to the rebuilding of the justice system and government structures and preparations for elections.	
German Federal Ministry for Economic Cooperation and Development (BMZ)	Development and peacebuilding	Development policy seeks to improve economic, social, ecological, and political conditions so as to help remove the structural causes of conflict and promote peaceful conflict management. Goals include poverty reduction, pro-poor sustainable economic growth, good governance, and democracy.[e] Peacebuilding attempts to encourage the development of the structural conditions, attitudes, and modes of political behavior that may permit peaceful, stable, and ultimately prosperous social and economic development. As conceptualized in the joint Utstein study, peacebuilding	Peace policy; crisis prevention

e   "Crisis Prevention and Conflict Settlement," Position Paper of the German Federal Ministry for Economic Cooperation and Development, 2002, available at http://www.bmz.de/en/ service/infothek/fach/spezial/spezial018/index.html; and "Development Policy as an Element of Global Structural and Peace Policy," excerpts from the German government's 11th Development Policy Report, 2002, available at http://www.bmz.de/en/service/infothek/ fach/spezial/spezial067/90.pdf.

TABLE 13.1   Different concepts and definitions across agencies (*cont.*)

Agency	Major concepts	Definitions	Other concepts
		activities fall under four main headings: security, socioeconomic foundations, political framework of long term peace, and reconciliation.[f]	
French Ministry of Foreign Affairs (MOFA)	Crisis management	Policy primarily pursued through multilateral organizations: peacekeeping, political and constitutional processes, democratization, administrative state capacity, technical assistance for public finance and tax policy, and support for independent media.[g]	Peace consolidation
French Ministry of Defense (MOD)	Peace consolidation	Activities in support of peace consolidation include monitoring compliance with arms embargoes, deployment of peacekeeping troops, DDR, and deployment of police and gendarmerie in support of the rule of law.[g]	Crisis management
Agence Franpaise de Developpement (AFD)	Crisis prevention	The French government's international solidarity policy is pursued in the areas of humanitarian action and development.[g]	Crisis prevention

f   German Federal Ministry for Economic Cooperation and Development, Joint Utstein Study of Peacebuilding, National Report on Germany, 2003, available at http://www.oecd.org/dataoecd/32/53/33983789.pdf.

g   French Ministry of Foreign Affairs, "Report on the Year 2004," 2004, available at http://www.diplomatie.gouv.fr/en/ministry_158/publications_2288/ index.html.

TABLE 13.1 Different concepts and definitions across agencies (*cont.*)

Agency	Major concepts	Definitions	Other concepts
Canada Department of Foreign Affairs and International Trade (DFAIT)	Conflict prevention	Activities to prevent the emergence of violent conflict through an open, inclusive, coherent, and comprehensive framework that takes into account all phases of the peace and conflict cycle.	Peacebuilding
Department of National Defence and Canadian Forces (DND/CF)	Peacebuilding	Actions to support political, economic, social, and military measures aimed at strengthening political stability, which include mechanisms to identify and support structures that promote peaceful conditions, reconciliation, a sense of confidence and well-being, and support economic growth.	n/a
Canadian International Development Agency (CIDA)	Peacebuilding	Efforts to strengthen the prospects for internal peace and decrease the likelihood of violent conflict in order to enhance the indigenous capacity of a society to manage	n/a
Japan's Ministry of Foreign Affairs (MOFA)	Conflict prevention	Activities to prevent violent conflict by promoting a peace process, securing domestic stability and security, and providing humanitarian and reconstruction assistance.	n/a

TABLE 13.1   Different concepts and definitions across agencies (*cont.*)

Agency	Major concepts	Definitions	Other concepts
Japan Development Agency (JDA)	Reconstruction Assistance	Efforts to prevent a regional conflict from recurring after a ceasefire agreement, which include an engagement in relief and reconstruction activities for victims of conflicts from the viewpoint of stabilizing the situation in affected areas.	International peace cooperation
Japan International Cooperation Agency (JICA)	Peacebuilding	A general approach extending from conflict prevention to reconciliation and postconflict reconstruction, in which peace is pursued through across-the-board endeavors that include development assistance in addition to traditional efforts within military and political frameworks.	n/a

of Political Affairs within the Secretariat was given the lead in peacebuilding policy and UNDP in peacebuilding assistance programs. The Department of Peacekeeping Operations tends to refer to all its operations as peacekeeping. Arguably its abstinence owes less to a principled opposition to peacebuilding and more to the view that peacebuilding is outside its mandate and it has a vested interest in ensuring that these areas are treated as distinctive, if related and sequential, activities. In any event, the definition offered in the Brahimi Report proved highly influential, informing discussions at the UN on postconflict assistance.[11]

---

11   "Statement by the President of the Security Council," 20 February 2001, S/PRST/2001/5. Cited from Call, *Institutionalizing Peace: A Review of Postconflict Peacebuilding Issues for DPA*, unpublished paper on file with Barnett, p. 4.

The UN's specialized agencies have adopted other concepts, a pattern that probably owes to how peacebuilding fits into their broader core mandates. Consider the international financial and development agencies, which introduced postconflict activities and terms in 1995. UNDP uses both peacebuilding and conflict prevention because it has a mandate in both. It adopted the definition used in the Brahimi Report, and then observed how peacebuilding and conflict prevention are virtually synonymous (and uses the two concepts interchangeably). In doing so, it signaled that its real concern is with conflict prevention; therefore, the organization should be as concerned with preventing conflict from returning as with stopping it before it begins. The concept of peacebuilding is less attractive to organizations with no direct mandate in peacekeeping. This is particularly true for the international financial institutions, whose mandates potentially conflict with their charge to be apolitical and not meddle in the domestic affairs of states. The World Bank tends to avoid the concept of peacebuilding and its connotations of active interference in favor of postconflict reconstruction and postconflict recovery; in many respects, this represents a return to its original mandate when its involvement in post-World War II reconstruction in Europe gave it its name—the International Bank for Reconstruction and Development. The IMF prefers postconflict recovery. When it writes joint documents, it tends to adopt the concept of postconflict recovery.

Outside the UN system there is greater terminological diversity. The European agencies are more likely to avoid peacebuilding in favor of alternative monikers such as civilian crisis management. Here the effort appears to distinguish these efforts from military and security-based stabilization and peace enforcement efforts. The European Union favors the concepts of conflict prevention and management, and rehabilitation and reconstruction: the former pertains to the desire to prevent the outbreak of violence that is imminent (management) and the elimination of facilitating a broader peace process (prevention); the latter pertains to the reestablishment of a working economy and institutional capacity.

Different agencies within the governments of the United States, UK, Canada, Germany, France, and Japan use different terms. The defense departments in the UK and the United States use the concepts of stabilization, reflecting their security missions (although NATO does use the term peacebuilding). The US Agency for International Development has an Office of Transition Initiatives focused on postconflict recovery and an Office for Conflict Management and Mitigation focused on prevention. The UK's Foreign and Commonwealth Office and Department for International Development prefer postconflict reconstruction rather than peacebuilding, but also make reference to peacebuilding since peace-related activities clearly fall within their respective mandates. Canada's Department of Foreign Affairs describes its postconflict work as conflict prevention, but the Canadian government uses peacebuilding to describe its actions in support of peace operations and economic development. Similarly, Japan's Ministry of Foreign Affairs uses the term conflict prevention, and the Japan International Cooperation Agency, a lead donor to states recovering from conflict, uses the term peacebuilding. The Japan Defense Agency, with a limited role in security provision, describes its peacebuilding involvement as reconstruction assistance. France and Germany share with the European community a preference for civilian crisis management and conflict prevention.

Peacebuilding's popularity can be attributed to a host of factors. To begin, there is a strong interest from both international and domestic actors to help states emerging from civil wars, societal breakdowns, and a violent past. Certainly there is no shortage of demand from below, as many domestic actors look for international assistance in a variety of areas. International actors increasingly view peacebuilding as instrumental to the broader humanitarian and international peace and security agenda. Peacebuilding's place in this agenda helps to explain why so many international actors believe that they can and should contribute to it; not only do they view peacebuilding as related to their core mandate, but peacebuilding also provides an important opportunity to demonstrate their continued relevance. The willingness of so many diverse constituencies with divergent and sometimes conflicting interests to rally around peacebuilding also suggests that one of the concept's talents is to camouflage divisions over how to handle the postconflict challenge. In this respect, it functions much like a favored political symbol. Symbols are often highly ambiguous. Ambiguity can facilitate collective action because different constituencies can support the symbol without necessarily achieving consensus on the substance. National flags, for instance, are potent symbols because most can get behind the flag, though they may do so for highly different, and potentially even conflicting, reasons. The same might be said for peacebuilding. Almost all agree that building peace after war is a good thing but may not agree on why it is a good thing (i.e., because it alleviates human suffering, generates regional stability, or creates conditions for long-term development efforts to take root). There is widespread agreement, as well, that peacebuilding means more than stability promotion; it is designed to create a positive peace, to eliminate the root causes of conflict, to allow states and societies to develop stable expectations of peaceful change. Consensus breaks down, however, over the substance behind the symbol of peacebuilding. Arguably, when the Bush administration thinks of peacebuilding it imagines building market-oriented democracies, while UNDP imagines creating economic development and strong civil societies committed to a culture of nonviolent dispute resolution. These different interpretations over the operationalization of peacebuilding lead to differences over appropriate strategies and priorities; some organizations might highlight democratic elections, transitional justice, and rule of law programs, while others highlight demobilization and private sector reforms. The critical point is that the growing number of international structures whose mandates include peacebuilding might easily mask essential differences regarding the concept's meaning and practice.

2   The Practices of Postconflict Peacebuilding

Because there are multiple contributing causes of conflict, almost any international assistance effort that addresses any perceived or real grievance can arguably be called "peacebuilding." Moreover, anyone invited to imagine the causes of violent conflict might generate a rather expansive laundry list of issues to be addressed in the postconflict period, including income distribution, land reform, democracy and the rule of law, human security, corruption, gender equality, refugee reintegration, economic development, ethnonational divisions, environmental degradation, transitional justice, and on and on. There are at least two good reasons for such a fertile imagination. One, there is no master variable for explaining either the outbreak of violence or the construction of a positive peace but merely groupings of factors across categories such as greed and grievance, and catalytic events. Variables that might be relatively harmless in some contexts can be a potent cocktail in others. Conversely, we have relatively little knowledge regarding what causes peace or what the paths to peace are. Although democratic states that have reasonably high per capita incomes are at a reduced risk of conflict, being democratic and rich is no guarantor of a positive peace, and illiberal and poor countries, at times, also have had their share of success. Second, organizations are likely to claim that their core competencies and mandates are critical to peacebuilding. They might be right. They also might be opportunistic. After all, if peacebuilding is big business, then there are good bureaucratic reasons for claiming that they are an invaluable partner.

Both of these reasons help explain two patterns regarding the practice of peacebuilding. One, different agencies tend to prioritize different activities. These alternative priorities are shaped not only by their knowledge of how to reduce the risk of conflict but also by a consideration of how they might best and most easily extend their existing mandates and expertise into the postconflict arena. Two, most programs emphasize the immediate and/or long-term demands of peacebuilding, that is, how to reduce the risk that the combatants do not return to war soon after the ink is dry on their peace agreement, and how to create the socioeconomic foundations for a positive peace. Conversely, with few exceptions, they fail to give concentrated attention and resources to state institutions during the critical five-year period when the state is still weak and its authority contested.

2.1   *Prioritizing the Practices of Peacebuilding*

In Table 13.2, we divided peacebuilding activities into the following four sectoral categories: security and military; social, economic, developmental, humanitarian; political and diplomatic; and justice and reconciliation.[12] Two important patterns emerge. The first is that different agencies tend to focus on different activities.

The UN Secretariat's units tend to define their activities in a comprehensive manner. Almost all areas of activity are included. However, there are differences between security-oriented and socioeconomic-oriented agencies, which correlate with when they tend to enter into postconflict settings. The departments of political affairs and peacekeeping operations emphasize the political-diplomatic and security-military aspects of peacebuilding, a logical extension of their mandates. UNDP stresses socioeconomic areas. Although the World Bank and IMF focus on economic development, the former emphasizes reconstruction and infrastructure while the latter describes its activities as recovery and technical assistance. The European Union emphasizes the political and diplomatic aspects of peacebuilding activities with a growing focus on conflict assessment and early warning activities, which can be understood as part of the security and military terrain.

The countries we surveyed exhibit their own patterns. The UK has focused on the security and military sector. The United States began with a strong interest in democratization and economic recovery, but its experiences in Afghanistan and Iraq have caused it to refocus attention on stabilization. Japan tends to focus on broad postconflict reconstruction, while France and Germany have focused their attention on immediate postconflict stabilization

---

12   See Appendix 1 (p. 56) for a list of different areas, activities, and descriptions. Table 13.2 identifies the prioritization of areas of involvement by organizations in their official documentation.

and long-term democracy promotion and economic reconstruction. There are important interagency differences within these countries. The defense departments, predictably, restrict themselves to the security and military sectors, while USAID and DFID are more "full service" units. Canada's agencies focus more on security, political, justice/reconciliation than on socioeconomic, developmental, or humanitarian aspects of peacebuilding. Japan, similarly, focuses on humanitarian assistance and development.

What accounts for this variation? The most straightforward explanation is that organizations have extended their existing mandates and competencies into the postconflict area, reflecting bureaucratic inertia and building on existing areas of comparative advantage. Both factors lead to a supply- rather than demand-driven menu of postconflict peacebuilding activities. Within UN funds and programs, for example, UNICEF emphasizes reestablishing primary education and working to reintegrate child soldiers back into society, FAO and IFAD emphasize the importance of food security, UNHCR focuses on refugee return, and UNIFEM stresses the opportunities to push for greater gender equity during moments of postconflict transition and reform. Also, certainly organizations are likely to favor those strategies and definitions that will most clearly advantage their bureaucratic interests. As the UNDP noted, "Crisis and post-conflict situations present a major challenge to development assistance but also constitute a unique opportunity for UNDP to demonstrate the importance of its own core mandate—that of building national capacity for long-term growth and sustainable development."[13] Relatedly, there is tremendous overlap between specific tasks and programs. A recent survey reveals that disarmament, demobilization, and reintegration (DDR) assistance is provided by six major international agencies, security sector reform and rule of law by the same number, repatriation and resettlement of refugees and internally displaced persons are shared among nine agencies, and six specialized agencies work on health sector issues.[14] This suggests not only the existence of tremendous coordination problems, but also that agencies will attempt to expand when and where possible.

---

13   "Role of the UNDP in Crisis and Post-Conflict Situation" (DP/2001/4).

14   Susan L. Woodward, "Peace Operations: the Civilian Dimension, Accounting for UNDP and the UN Specialized Agencies," Discussion Paper, Copenhagen Seminar on Civilian Capacity for Crisis Management, 8–9 June 2004.

TABLE 13.2   Sectoral activities and focus across agencies

Activity categories	Multilateral institutions						United States		
	DPA	DPKO	UNDP	World Bank	IMF	EC	State	DOD	USAID
Security and military									
Demining	□	□	□	□		□	□	□	
DDR		□	□	□		□		□	
Security sector reform		□	□			□		■	□
SALW			□				□		
Security stabilization	□	■					□	□	
Conflict assessment and early warning	■		■			■			□
Defense diplomacy		□						□	
Social, economic, developmental, and humanitarian									
Reconstruction			□	■		■	□	□	
Infrastructure			□	■		□	□	□	
Economic recovery	□		■	□	■	□	■		□
Financial assistance				□	■	□			□
Policy and technical assistance			■	■	■				□
Health and education			■	■					□
Food and agricultural support			□	□		□			□
Media support						□			■
Repatriation and return	□		□			□		□	
NGO capacity building			□	□					□
Trauma counseling			□						□
Political and diplomatic									
Peace agreement and mediation	■	□							
Democratization	□		□			□	■		■
Decentralization			□	□	□	□	□		□
Good governance			□	□	□	□	□		□
Rule of law		□	□	□		□	□	□	
Institution building			□	■	□	□			□
Human rights	□					□			
Election assistance	■					□		□	□

| United Kingdom | | | Germany | | | France | | | Japan | | | Canada | | |
UKFCO	UKMOD	DFID	FFO	FMD	BMZ	MOFA	MOD	AFD	MOFA	JDA	JICA	DFAIT	DND/CF	CIDA
				□			□		□				□	□
□	□		□	□		■			□		□		□	■
■	■	□	■	□		□			□			□	■	
						■						□	□	□
□														
■		□	■	□										
	□		□											
		□		□		■		■		■		□		
		□		□		□	■		□	■		□		■
		■		■		■					□	□		
		□			■	□					□			□
		□		□	□									
		□		■			□		□	□	□	□		
							□			□	□			
						□			□					□
		□		□					□		□	□		
		□	□	■					□			□		□
□				□		□								
	■	■				■								□
	□	□		■	■							□		□
	□	□		■	■							□		□
□	□	■		■	■									□
	□			□	□				□		□			□
□		□			□				□			□		□
		□			□				□					

TABLE 13.2   Sectoral activities and focus across agencies (*cont.*)

Activity categories	Multilateral institutions						United States		
	DPA	DPKO	UNDP	World Bank	IMF	EC	State	DOD	USAID
Justice and reconciliation									
Leader dialogue			❑						❑
Community dialogue			❑						❑
Bridge building			❑						■
Truth and reconciliation						❑			❑

■ = Core organizational competencies; ❑ = Named activities.

2.2   *Dimensions of Peacebuilding*

For heuristic purposes it is possible to identify three dimensions of postconflict peacebuilding—stability creation, restoration of state institutions, and addressing the socioeconomic dimensions of conflict.[15] The first dimension is the desire to reinforce stability and discourage the combatants from returning to war. In important respects, peacebuilding continues an important function of peacekeeping, the attempt to maintain a cease-fire and stability by monitoring the combatants. Yet peacebuilding goes beyond this feature of peacekeeping in several ways. Peacebuilding activities directly attempt to reduce the means available, and the incentives, for actors to return to conflict. Toward that end, they include disarmament, demobilization, reintegration programs, security sector reform, and arms control for light and heavy weapons systems. The general claim is that if peace is to prevail, then the toys must be removed from the boys. But it is not enough to try to reduce the material means for going to war. The reintegration of former combatants requires alternative avenues for the pursuit of wealth and social recognition.

The second dimension is helping to build or restore key state functions that have the capacity to generate basic public goods and possess a modicum of legitimacy. A basic function of the state is the production of public goods. But many states, especially those emerging from conflict, are hard-pressed to deliver such goods. Accordingly, peacebuilders either replace the state or

---

15   This tracks broadly with what the Secretary-General calls the "stages of recovery," including early and medium-term recovery issues and the transition to development. "Explanatory Note of the Secretary-General," 19 April 2005.

United Kingdom			Germany			France			Japan			Canada		
UKFCO	UKMOD	DFID	FFO	FMD	BMZ	MOFA	MOD	AFD	MOFA	JDA	JICA	DFAIT	DND/CF	CIDA
														■
										□				■
										□				□
						□				□				■

partner with the state to rebuild basic facilities, public administration, rule of law systems, transportation and communication networks, and utilities, and to re-create the educational and health infrastructure. But because international actors do not envisage playing state-like functions long into the future, they also provide some degree of technical and capacity-building assistance for state institutions—even as they support parallel NGO or private sector structures that may operate outside of or duplicate state functions. For instance, international financial institutions typically provide technical assistance so that state institutions can develop the capacity to build, monitor, and regulate basic economic and financial activities. Yet an effective state is not enough. It also is important that the state have legitimacy. Indeed, over half of all the named activities that fall into this dimension of peacebuilding involve programs that are designed to create institutions that are democratic, transparent, accountable, and responsive to local needs—that is, legitimate.

The third dimension is the attempt to build not only the state's but also society's ability to manage conflict peacefully and develop the socioeconomic infrastructure necessary to underpin economic development. Toward that end, peacebuilders are involved in trauma counseling, transitional justice and reconciliation, community dialogue, strengthening civil society organizations, increasing human rights, promoting environmental awareness, assisting with gender empowerment, building bridges between different communities, and promoting economic development. The goal is not only to try to create a culture of peace, but also to try to develop civil society organizations and a viable private sector that have the capacity to represent diverse societal interests and constrain the power of the state.

Frequency

16
14
12
10
8
6
4
2
0

Legend:
☐ Stated priorities
■ Core organizational competencies

Stability Creation:
Security sector reform, DDR, Demining, Repatriation and reform, Security stabilization, Conflict assessment/early warning, Small arms and light weapons, Peace agreement/mediation, Media support, Defense diplomacy

Restoration of State Institutions:
Rule of law, Good governance, Institution building, Democratization, Financial assistance, Election assistance, Policy/technical assistance, Decentralization

Socioeconomic Recovery:
Infrastructure, Economic recovery, Reconstruction, Health and education, NGO capacity building, Human rights, Food/agricultural support, Truth and reconciliation, Community dialogue, Bridge building, Trauma counseling, Leader dialogue

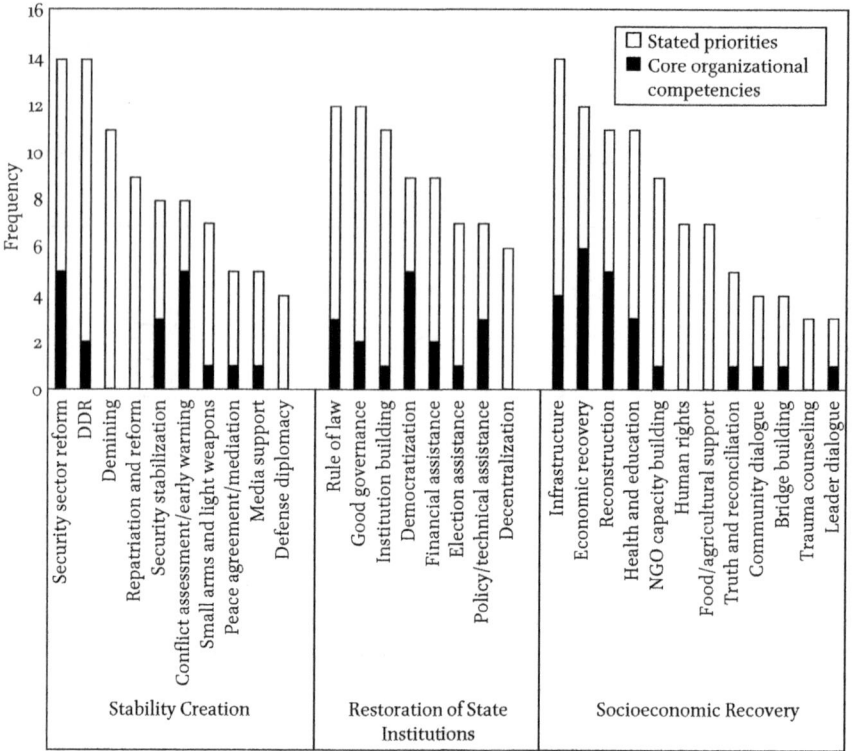

FIGURE 13.1   Name frequency of activities (all agencies)

Do we see any pattern across the categories? At one level, no clear breakdown emerges. Figure 13.1 sets out activities by stages of peacebuilding, as per the data displayed in Table 13.2.

Although it could be that the peacebuilding sector is taking a nonsectarian approach, we suspect that if we weighted indicators or financial data we would see a more discriminatory pattern. While operations suggest that the peacebuilding sector is being equally attentive to all issues, studies of particular operations reveal that it generally gives more priority to one set of activities over another. Also, not all activities cost the same. Investments that fall in the first and third categories (i.e., international provision of security and reconstruction of physical infrastructure) are significantly more costly than investments in the second (public administration).

At another level, though, there is some clustering of peacebuilding activities around the first and third dimensions of peacebuilding to the relative neglect of the second. How do we account for this gap? One explanation is that these patterns reflect a particular image of the state. The modern state "exists when there is a political apparatus (governmental institutions, such as a court, parliament, or congress, plus civil service officials), ruling over a given territory, whose authority is backed by a legal system and the capacity to use force to implement its policies."[16] State building concerns how the modern state comes into existence, that is, how the process of institutionalization is accomplished along two dimensions. One concerns the specific instruments states use to control society. Attention is directed to the monopolization of the means of coercion and the development of a bureaucratic apparatus organized around rational-legal principles with the capacity to regulate, control, and extract from society. The concern, then, is with the *degree* of the state. The other dimension concerns how states and societies negotiate their relationship—that is, the *kind* of state. Attention is directed not only to whether the state has the ability to control society but also to the organizing principles that structure the state's rule over society.

Peacebuilding operations have tended to emphasize the kind of state. Efforts around human rights, transitional justice, and democratization, in contrast, are more concerned about the kind of state rather than degree. Although not neglectful of the need to develop state capacity across a range of functions, traditional liberalization efforts prefer a "small state" and focus on creating mechanisms that limit the state's power, increase societal participation, and hence invest the state with legitimacy. Indeed, many peacebuilding programs attempt to create the liberal state, which respects human rights; protects the rule of law; is constrained by representative institutions, a vigilant media, and periodic elections; and protects markets.[17] This liberal bias has been the subject of considerable commentary in recent years, particularly since it might not promote peace. Several observers have noted that the peacebuilding project, far from eliminating the root causes of conflict, creating the liberal-democratic state, or creating an effective ally in international antiterrorism efforts, has only rekindled the conditions for conflict.[18] Locating the cause of this dysfunctional outcome in the hurried way in which peacebuilding operations attempt to open up competition in a raw atmosphere that is absent of security, trust, or stable institutions, they argue in favor of a more sequenced, slower-paced, and strategic peacebuilding project that emphasizes the

---

16   Anthony Giddens, *Sociology*, 2nd ed. (New York: Polity Press, 1993), p. 309.

17   For related arguments, see Roland Paris, *At War's End* (New York: Cambridge University Press, 2004); Robert Orr, "The United States as Nation Builder," in Robert Orr, ed., *Winning the Peace: An American Strategy for Post-Conflict Reconstruction* (Washington, DC: CSIC Press, 2004), p. 11; and Jens Meierhenrich, "Forming States After Failure," in Robert Rotberg, ed., *When States Fail* (Princeton: Princeton University Press, 2003), pp. 155–156.

18   Roland Paris, *At War's End*; Frances Fukuyama, *International Order and State-building* (Ithaca: Cornell University Press, 2003).

establishment of security and stable institutions before seeking the prize of liberalization and democracy.[19]

Although there is tremendous debate over what the basic functions of the state are (beyond the provision of security) and the minimal degree and kind of state that is required to underpin the peace, several elements are less controversial. To begin, actors must have an incentive to preserve the state and its institutions. What matters, then, is the utility of the state to provide reasonable security guarantees and that powerful actors believe they benefit from a state that can enforce essential rules. In this respect, the test for the emergence of the state is the "appearance of political units persisting in time and fixed in space, the development of permanent, impersonal institutions, agreement on the need for an authority that can give final judgments, and acceptance of the idea that this authority should receive the basic loyalty of its subjects."[20] What is desired, then, is a state that can make credible commitments and deliver on those commitments in a reasonably efficient and impartial manner using rational-legal means (and coercion in the last instance). Although this does not imply the need to neglect the kind of state that is being built, it does suggest the need for more attention to the degree.

This is happening. Various state and nonstate agencies recognize that peacebuilding also is state building and that more attention needs to be directed at building a functional, capable state. Yet this growing interest might also be driven by a concern with ensuring that these states can not only deliver basic services but also contain networks that pose a threat to the international community. Led most prominently by the United States, there is a growing interest in making sure that states, especially those emerging from conflict, have the capacity to maintain stability and counter transnational threats. The degree of the state, then, matters not only because it provides a useful function for domestic society, but also for international society. Yet the desire to make sure that the postconflict state is strong enough to contend with uncivil forces might easily undermine the desire to build a liberal state, one that is accountable to society and fastened by the rule of law. If so, then peacebuilding might prove to be successful to the extent that states do not return to war five years after the peace agreement, but a failure to the extent that it leaves in place authoritarian structures.

---

19 Roland Paris, *At War's End*; Jens Meierhenrich, "Forming States After Failure," in Robert Rotberg, ed., *When States Fail*, pp. 155–156.

20 Joseph Strayer, *On the Medieval Origins of the Modern State* (Princeton: Princeton University Press, 1973), p. 5. Cited in Jens Meierhenrich, "Forming States After Failure," in Robert Rotberg, ed., *When States Fail*, pp. 155–156.

3   Conclusion

Peacebuilding is increasingly institutionalized across the international land-scape. Most major international and regional organizations, states, and non-governmental organizations have a program that either explicitly uses this term, adopts an alternative formulation whose practices overlap with the cur-rent meaning of peacebuilding, or work with an alternative concept whose activities intersect with peacebuilding. Yet there are several outstanding issues that suggest that this institutionalization is not all it appears to be.

To begin, assessing the degree of the institutionalization of peacebuilding requires more than attention to the organizations and units that are actively associated with this agenda—it also demands a consideration of whether states and organizations are putting resources behind their statements. Although such data is difficult to assemble, our casual survey suggests that the peacebuilding agenda is not necessarily gorging on funds and these activities represent small percentages of the overall budgets. Consider the following examples. Since its establishment in 1997, the World Bank Post-Conflict Fund has disbursed a total of $66.7 million, including $10.6 million in 2004.[21] The 2004 budget for the USAID Office of Transition Initiatives was $54.6 million; in 2005 it was $48.6 million, which means that it received only 3.5 percent of a total USAID budget of $9.1 billion.[22] Consequently, while the peacebuilding agenda might look impressive given its recent origins, it remains diminutive when compared to the traditional activities undertaken by these and other organizations.

Second, notwithstanding a consensus definition emerging at the UN, there continues to be considerable variation in the meaning of peacebuild-ing because organizations are likely to adopt a meaning of peacebuilding that is consistent with their already existing mandates, worldviews, and organiza-tional interests. The consequence is that while everyone might support the idea of building peace, they will operate with considerable differences of inter-pretation regarding the meaning and practice of peacebuilding. The impact of existing organizational mandates and worldviews on the variation in the practice of peacebuilding is particularly evident in the actual programs.

This suggests that any consideration of international coordination and collaboration will be more than a technical feat—it also will be profoundly

---

21   World Bank, Post-Conflict Fund, *A Trust Fund for Assisting Conflict-Affected Countries*, August 2004, available at http://lnweb18.worldbank.org/ESSD/sdvext.nsf/67ByDocName/ PCFAnnualReport2004/$FILE/Annual+Report+PCF+04(lowresolution).pdf.

22   USAID Budget, *Transition Initiatives*, 2006, available at http://www.usaid.gov/policy/ budget/cbj2006/ti.html.

political. Different agencies work with alternative modes of operationalizing peacebuilding, which, in turn, are reflective of different strategies for achieving peace after war. These strategies, though, more often than not, reflect unexamined assumptions and deeply rooted organizational mandates rather than "best practices" born from empirical analysis. This suggests that the desire to achieve coordination requires more than simply dividing up the terrain and creating linkage and efficiencies. It also is a political accomplishment that might be settled by bureaucratic and political power. Some might hope that this tendency might be cured by the proposed Peacebuilding Commission at the UN, which is mandated to help coordinate the postconflict activities of the relevant implementing agencies. Although this move can improve the efficiency and implementation of peacebuilding activities, it also is likely to clarify profound differences among these agencies regarding priorities, mandates, strategies, and trade-offs. Although one of the functions of the proposed Peacebuilding Support Office is to provide critical information so that operational agencies can make informed and reasoned choices, it is quite likely that such knowledge will be unavailable for a while. More complicated still is the process of merging this generalized knowledge with specific circumstances on the ground to yield appropriate recommendations.

Consequently, the institutionalization of peacebuilding might emerge from bureaucratic power and political infighting, and not empirical analysis. Scholars and policymakers should, therefore, monitor to see which version of peacebuilding is being institutionalized and attempt to ensure that alternative understandings are kept alive as alternative hypotheses so that reasoned choices are made at critical junctures.

Appendix 1: Peacebuilding Areas, Activities, and Definitions

Activity categories	Explanation and examples
Security and military	
Demining	Mine clearance
DDR	Disarmament, demobilization, and reintegration of excombatants
Security sector reform	Democratic reform and retraining of security, military, police, and correction sectors service with emphasis on efficiency and ethics
SALW	Removal of small arms and light weapons

(cont.)

Activity categories	Explanation and examples
Security stabilization	Clearance of threat and terror after the conflict
Conflict assessment and early warning	Development of conflict assessment system/study and early warning system
Defense diplomacy	Nonoperational activities such as verification of arms control agreement; visits by ships, aircraft, and other military units, and by military and civilian personnel at all levels; staff talks
Social, economic, developmental, and humanitarian	
Reconstruction	Aid for physical reconstruction of buildings, utilities, and structures
Infrastructure	Support for improving economic infrastructure
Economic recovery	Investment in key productive sectors and supporting the conditions for resumption of trade, savings, and domestic and foreign investment, including macroeconomic stabilization, rehabilitation of financial institutions, and restoration of frameworks
Financial assistance	Financial assistance once the situation is sufficiently stable for it to be used effectively
Policy/technical assistance	Assistance to rebuild capacity of key economic institutions responsible for making and implementing fiscal, monetary, and exchange rate policies
Health and education	Rebuilding and maintaining education and health infrastructure including the financing of recurrent costs
Food/agricultural support	Secure the food after the conflict and support and advise on agricultural policy (e.g., releasing land for agricultural purposes)
Media support	Support and development of a free and independent media
Repatriation and return	Support for the repatriation of refugees and return of internally displaced persons
NGO capacity building	Encourage and support networks of nongovernmental organizations and community-based organizations involved with conflict mitigation activities to leverage resources and provide coverage to larger geographic areas

(*cont.*)

Activity categories	Explanation and examples
Trauma counseling	Psychological and trauma counseling
Political and diplomatic	
Peace agreement/ mediation	Negotiation and implementation of peace agreement
Democratization	Support for democratic institutions and activities in the fields of education and culture that have a democratic theme or intention
Decentralization	Support decentralization of political authority
Good governance	Promotion of ethics, transparency, and accountability of government
Rule of law	Establishment of law and order, justice system, and legal reform
Institution building	Help foster the development of democratic institutions and processes including the restoration of local organs of authority
Human rights	Promotion of awareness of international human rights standards and of monitoring and reporting abuses
Election monitoring	Electoral assistance and observation
Justice and reconciliation	
Leader dialogue	Dialogue opportunity between leaders
Community dialogue	Dialogue opportunity between members of antagonistic groups in community
Bridge building	Strengthening and reinforcing interethnic confidence, tolerance, and trust in the state institutions
Truth and reconciliation	Commissions—and/or other means—of inquiry into recent and violent past, using knowledge as basis for reconciliation

Appendix 2: Top Contributors to Current Peacebuilding Operations

Rank	Top donors to 10 countries with ongoing UN peacekeeping missions[a]					Assessed contributions to UN peacekeeping	
	2003 official development assistance			2004 emergency relief		2005 UN peacekeeping budget	
	Millions of $	%		Millions of $	%		%
	Total	10,566		Total	1,806		
1	US	2,879.00	27.2	US	564	31.2	US	26.49
2	France	1,924.00	18.2	EC	288	15.9	Japan	19.47
3	EC	1,280.00	12.1	UK	156	8.6	Germany	8.66
4	Belgium	822.00	7.8	Private	102	5.6	UK	7.38
5	Germany	802.00	7.6	Germany	79	4.4	France	7.26
6	Italy	523.00	4.9	Netherlands	77	4.3	Italy	4.88
7	Sweden	272.00	2.6	Sweden	76	4.2	Canada	2.81
8	UK	203.00	1.9	UN	67	3.7	Spain	2.52
9	Canada	201.00	1.9	Norway	62	3.4	China	2.47
10	Norway	169.00	1.6	Canada	55	3.0	Republic of Korea	1.80
11	Japan	145.00	1.4	Japan	51	2.8	Netherlands	1.69
12	African Development Fund	45.00	0.4	Switzerland	40	2.2	Australia	1.59

a The 10 countries surveyed are Afghanistan, Burundi, Cote d'Ivoire, Democratic Republic of Congo, former Republic of Yugoslavia (and Kosovo), Haiti, Liberia, Sierra Leone, Sudan, and Timor Leste.

SOURCES: OECD DAC DATABASE; OCHA FINANCIAL TRACKING SYSTEM; *2005 ANNUAL PEACEKEEPING REVIEW* (FORTHCOMING)

Appendix 3: List of Organizations Surveyed

Intergovernmental Bodies

European Commission (EC), Conflict Prevention and Crisis Management Unit
International Monetary Fund (IMF)
UN Department of Peacekeeping Operations (DPKO)
UN Department of Political Affairs (DPA)
UN Development Programme's Bureau for Crisis Prevention and Recovery (UNDP)
World Bank (WB)

United States

Agency for International Development (USAID), Bureau for Democracy Conflict and
    Humanitarian Assistance, Office of Conflict Management and Mitigation, and Office of
    Transition Initiatives
Department of Defense (DoD)
Department of State (State)

United Kingdom

Department for International Development (DFID)
Foreign and Commonwealth Office Conflict Prevention Pools (UKFCO)
Ministry of Defence (UKMOD)

Germany

Federal Foreign Office (FFO)
Federal Ministry for Economic Cooperation and Development (BMZ)
Federal Ministry of Defense (FMD)

France

Agence Frangaise de Developpement (AFD-Fr), under Ministry of Economy, Finance and
    Industry, the Ministry of Foreign Affairs, and the Ministry of French Overseas Territories
Ministry of Defense (MOD)
Ministry of Foreign Affairs (MOFA)

Canada

Canadian International Development Agency (CIDA)
Department of Foreign Affairs and International Trade (DFAIT)
Department of National Defence and Canadian Forces (DND/CF)

Japan

Japan Defense Agency (JDA)
Japan International Cooperation Agency (JICA)

CHAPTER 14*

Governance and the Global Water System: A Theoretical Exploration

Claudia Pahl-Wostl, Joyeeta Gupta and Daniel Petry[1]

Water governance can be traced back more than 5,000 years. However, it was only in 1982 and 1997, respectively, that global water agreements like the UN conventions on the seas and watercourses were adopted.[2] Only recently has water become prominent on the global political agenda—for example, with the Mar del Plata conference of 1977, the Dublin conference on water in 1992, the water chapter in Agenda 21 adopted in 1992, the four World Water Forums since 1997, and the Millennium Declaration of 2000. Likewise, scientific work on water has only recently been globalized—for example, with the Global Water System Project of the Earth System Science Partnership and the UN-wide World Water Assessment Programme. Growing political interest in water research and governance raises the questions: What are the appropriate

---

* This chapter was originally published in Global Governance, Volume 14, Issue 4, 2008.
1 Claudia Pahl-Wostl is professor of resources management at the University of Osnabrock. Her research deals with an improved understanding of the complex dynamics of human-environment interactions with emphasis on actor networks, adaptive water management, social learning, and multilevel water governance. She is a representative of the International Human Dimensions Programme on Global Environmental Change (IHDP) in the Executive Scientific Steering Committee of the Global Water System Project, president of the International Society for Integrated Assessment, and coordinator of several EU projects. Joyeeta Gupta is professor of climate law and policy at the Institute for Environmental Studies, Vrije Universiteit Amsterdam, and professor of water law and policy at UNESCO-IHE Institute for Water Education in Delft, the Netherlands. She wishes to acknowledge that her contribution to this article was undertaken in the context of the "Inter-governmental and Private Environmental Regimes and Compatibility with Good Governance, Rule of Law and Sustainable Development" project, which is financially supported by the Organisation for Scientific Research in the Netherlands (contract number: 452-02-03). Daniel Petry was scientific officer at the International Project Office of the Global Water System Project based at the University of Bonn, and currently works at the German Technical and Scientific Association for Gas and Water. His expertise in research and research coordination covers integrated environmental assessment, integrative concepts in environmental planning, and governance and institutions in water resources management.
2 UN Convention on the Law of the Sea, 21 I.L.M. (1982) 1261; UN Convention on the Law of the Non-navigational Uses of International Watercourses (1997), UN Doc. A/51/869; 37 ILM 719.

levels at which research and policy on water governance should be under-taken; and which issues should be addressed at which levels?

In this article, we argue that there are different levels at which water schol-ars and policymakers advocate governance, but the global perspective on water governance needs to be given more importance. We present a concep-tual framework for analyzing governance and conclude that present global water governance (GWG) is a mobius-web form of governance. Regarding the future of GWG, we identify four possible trends in line with scenarios prepared by scholars in related fields. We also consider the implications for water man-agement of these different scenarios.

Why should global governance scholars be interested in GWG? To begin with, huge amounts of financial, administrative, and intellectual resources are being spent in the area of water governance and in related fields of environ-mental governance. A number of new ethical, conceptual, and management approaches are being generated and debated in different political contexts about how water resources can best be managed. These developments need to be recorded and assessed.

Water is a major global public good. Global governance theories that do not actively study the management of global public goods—particularly in the environmental area—will miss the rapidly evolving key issues of the twenty-first century. The contemporary world is extremely competitive, increasingly resource-scarce, and subject to far-reaching environmental change. As sys-temic and cumulative trends indicate global stress in the very resource base of society, including water, there are increasing calls for sustainability science[3] and Earth System Governance theories.[4] Studies of GWG can help to explore these possibilities.

Indeed, research on GWG and comparisons between GWG and other areas of environmental governance may provide valuable insights that could enrich the traditional core of global governance theories. For example, there is con-siderable discussion in the socioecological literature on the need to find transi-tional governance approaches to help society move from current unsustainable governance paradigms to future more sustainable governance paradigms.[5] Notions of adaptive management are being increasingly promoted in the

---

3   R.W. Kates et al., "Sustainability Science," *Science* 292 (2001): 641–642.

4   Frank Biermann, "'Earth System Governance' as a Crosscutting Theme of Global Change Research," *Global Environmental Change* 17, no. 3–4 (2007): 326–337.

5   Per Olsson et al., "Shooting the Rapids: Navigating Transitions to Adaptive Governance of Social-Ecological Systems," *Ecology and Society* 11, no. 1 (2006):18, available at www.ecologyan-dsociety.org/vol11/iss1/art18; Claudia Pahl-Wostl, "Transition Towards Adaptive Management of Water Facing Climate and Global Change," *Water Resources Management* 21 (2007): 49–62.

fields of water management and climate change.[6] Perhaps such ideas could find application in wider areas of global governance such as economy, human rights, and security.

Water also provides a context for exploring the problematic of multilevel governance. Much as with other issue areas, researchers on water policy have tended to focus on one level only: the local, or the national, or the river basin. However, studies on water governance must adopt a multilevel approach to do justice to the complexity of current governance processes and challenges.

Finally, global governance of water provides an occasion for wide-ranging multidisciplinary research. This issue requires collaboration not only among natural scientists, among engineers, and among social scientists, but also across these domains. To date, natural scientists and engineers are providing policy recommendations regarding water management, but this advice so far generally lacks input from global governance academics about how best to translate scientific findings into public policy. This gap needs to be filled.

1   The Need for Global Water Governance

Traditionally, resource governance has essentially been seen as a *local-level* issue. Many anthropologists and others continue to argue that one needs to understand local rights, needs, and stakeholders in order effectively to address governance issues. The driving forces behind this concept are the notions of decentralization and subsidiarity. Since water problems are local, so goes this reasoning, they should be handled at the lowest appropriate governance level.

Another strong school of thought holds that water governance should be regulated at a *national level.*[7] From this perspective, water is a national resource that should be governed for the benefit of the national economy and society: domestic interests come first. Increasingly, this vision is under threat, as many question the basis of the state and its willingness to promote the welfare of the people within it, and the need for international equity. A third approach to governance of water focuses on the *basin level.* This view argues that water-related problems and conflicts are best dealt with within the natural sphere of the system—that is, the hydrologically defined basin, catchment,

---

6   Claudia Pahl-Wostl et al., "Managing Change Towards Adaptive Water Management Through Social Learning," *Ecology and Society* 12, no. 2 (2007): 30, available at www.ecologyandsociety.org/vol12/iss2/art30; Joseph Arvay et al., "Adaptive Management of the Global Climate Problem: Bridging the Gap Between Climate Research and Climate Policy," *Climatic Change* 78 (2006): 217–225.

7   All national water and resource laws, for example, are based on this idea.

or watershed.[8] This concept combines notions of efficiency with a hydrological systems approach. It allows for comprehensive problem analysis and the internalization of otherwise externalized problems as they arise, for instance, from up- and downstream relations. Such research also studies the equitable management of transboundary or international waters (see the articles by Thomas Bernauer and Tobias Siegfried and by Ines Dombrowsky in *Global Governance* 14:4).

A fourth and relatively new school takes a *global* perspective on governance of water. Many water-related environmental and societal problems as well as water use-related conflicts elude appropriate solutions at the local level or within national or basin boundaries. In these cases, it is important to address issues at a global level. Thus, growing attention is being given to multilateralism in the international politics of water[9] and to the recognition that local, national, and basin-level water issues are interlinked within a global water system.[10]

These approaches—local, national, basin, and global—are not mutually exclusive. They indicate that different water issues are dealt with at different levels and that historically different perspectives have dominated. However, the present article and special issue highlight the global level as the relatively least understood and least explored aspect of water governance.

Four arguments underscore the need for a global perspective alongside attention to local, national, and basin dimensions. First, the hydrological system is a global system, and exchange processes occur at the global level over relevant time periods. Examples include climate change impacts and teleconnections

---

8   See, for example, Ludwik A. Tetzlaff, *The River Basin in History and Law* (The Hague: Martinus Nijhoff, 1967). More recent introductions to the concept are Malcolm D. Newson, *Land, Water, and Development: River Basin Systems and Their Sustainable Management* (London: Routledge, 1997); Global Water Partnership (GWP), *Integrated Water Resources Management*, Global Water Partnership Technical Advisory Committee Background Papers No. 4 (Stockholm: GWP, 2000); Bruce Hooper, *Integrated River Basin Governance: Learning from International Experience* (London: IWA Publishing, 2005).

9   Peter H. Gleick and Jon Lane, "Large International Water Meetings: Time for a Reappraisal," *Water International* 30 (2005): 410–414; Ken Conca, *Governing Water: Contentious Transnational Politics and Global Institution Building* (Cambridge: MIT Press, 2006); Robert G. Varady and Matthew Iles-Shih, "Global Water Initiatives: What Do the Experts Think? Report on a Survey of Leading Figures in the World of Water," in Asit K. Biswas and Cecilia Tortajada, eds., *Impacts of Megaconferences on the Water Sector* (Berlin: Springer-Verlag, forthcoming).

10   Claudia Pahl-Wostl, Holger Hoff, Michel Meybeck, and Soroosh Sorooshian, "The Role of Global Change Research for Aquatic Sciences," editorial in special issue, "Vulnerability of Water Resources to Environmental Change: A Systems' Approach," *Aquatic Sciences* 34 (2002): iv–vi; GWSP, *The Global Water System Project: Science Framework and Implementation Activities*, ESSP Report No. 3, Earth System Science Partnership, 2005.

(patterns/phenomena that are related to each other through cause-effect relations across vast distances) between deforestation and precipitation. Second, global environmental change and socioeconomic phenomena at the global level increasingly create situations in which the driving forces behind water-related problems and conflicts lie outside the reach of local, national, or basin-oriented governance regimes. Global trade impacts on water (as illustrated by Yongsong Liao, Charlotte de Fraiture, and Mark Giordano in *Global Governance* 14:4) provide one such example. Third, many local environmental and social phenomena surrounding water are situated in global dynamics—for instance, of erosion, eutrophication, urbanization, and biodiversity loss. Such local phenomena may, cumulatively, imply alarming global trends. For example, the construction of dams leads to a fragmentation and flow alteration of the world's river basins, with major and sometimes irreversible impacts on associated freshwater ecosystems.[11] Fourth, many direct and indirect impacts of reductions in quantities and qualities of water are likely to be global in character (e.g., changed patterns of food production and bird migration).

Each argument is linked with a specific kind of phenomena transforming the contemporary global water system and thus also with a specific kind of policy response.[12] Phenomena occurring in the context of the first argument can only be dealt with efficiently through governance at the global level due to the physical nature of cause-effect relations; however, adaptation to climate change-induced floods or droughts, for example, needs to take place not only at but also within basins, and actions toward mitigating the indirect causes can only be taken at global levels, which then cascade down to national and local levels.[13] Whereas mitigation of impacts in the context of the third argument (globally occurring local phenomena) lies within the range of local- or basin-level governance, finding efficient and effective solutions to problems and conflicts as well as approaching the driving forces call for a greater global understanding of and better coordinated activities on issues.

Having argued that there is a need for GWG, we must also emphasize that global arrangements for water cannot be understood without taking cross-level

11   Crister Nilsson et al., "Fragmentation and Flow Regulation of the World's Large River Systems," *Science* 308 (2005): 405–408.

12   GWSP, *Global Water System Project.*

13   Cf. Joyeeta Gupta, "Analysing Scale and Scaling in Environmental Governance," in Oran R. Young, Leslie A. King, and Heike Schroeder, eds., *Institutions and Environmental Change: Principal Findings, Applications, and Research Frontiers* (Cambridge: MIT Press, 2008); and Claudia Pahl-Wostl, "Polycentric Integrated Assessment," in Jan Rotmans and Dale S. Rothman, eds., *Scaling in Integrated Assessment*, Integrated Assessment Studies series (Lisse, The Netherlands: Swets & Zeitlinger, 2003), pp. 237–262.

interactions into account. Water governance has a multilevel character, and global mechanisms must be incorporated in ways that are complementary to instruments applied at other levels.[14] While some research has analyzed global institutions in the field of water governance,[15] global- and basin-level issues are often treated separately, without considering interplay across levels.[16]

Thus, GWG can be defined as the development and implementation of norms, principles, rules, incentives, informative tools, and infrastructure to promote a change in the behavior of actors at the global level in the area of water governance. Such governance calls for: (1) recognition that water has a global dimension; (2) inclusion of a global perspective on water governance at all other governance levels; and (3) adoption of more dense systems of multilevel governance from global to local level in the water field, because water policies—if they are to be effective—have to be simultaneously designed at global, fluvial, national, provincial, and local levels.

2   A Conceptual Framework for Analyzing GWG

Governance can be viewed as either a normative or an analytical concept for policy research. Normatively, "good" governance relates to a regulatory system that shows qualities of accountability, transparency, legitimacy, public participation, justice, efficiency, the rule of law, and an absence of corruption.[17] In contrast, an analytical approach provides a scientific basis for developing sound policy recommendations. There is an urgent need for analytical assessment of ongoing policy processes and their ability to meet future policy challenges. In particular, the following questions need to be addressed: How well can the present state of GWG deal with current policy challenges; and what future scenarios of GWG could deal effectively with emerging policy challenges?

Recent decades have brought a shift in social-scientific discourse from *government* to *governance*. This change in terminology signals a recognition that

---

14   Pahl-Wostl, Holger Hoff, Michel Meybeck, and Soroosh Sorooshian, "Role of Global Change Research for Aquatic Sciences"; Charles Vörösmarty et al., "Humans Transforming the Global Water System," *EOS* 85, no. 48 (2004): 509–520; GWSP, *Global Water System Project*.

15   Conca, *Governing Water: Contentious Transnational Politics and Global Institution Building*.

16   Ken Conca, Fengshi Wu, and Ciqi Mei, "Global Regime Formation or Complex Institution Building? The Principal Content of International River Agreements," *International Studies Quarterly* 50 (2006): 263–285.

17   Kristen Lewis, ed., *Water Governance for Poverty Reduction: Key Issues and the UNDP Response to Millennium Development Goals* (New York: UN Development Programme, 2004) p. 94.

government is no longer the single decisionmaking authority, with sovereign control over the people and groups making up civil society. Instead, governance involves a multilevel, polycentric condition where many actors in different institutional settings contribute to policy development and implementation.[18] Governance takes into account various governmental and nongovernmental actors and networks that together formulate and implement contemporary public policy.[19] Governance encompasses coordination and steering processes involving formal as well as informal institutions.[20] A major challenge is to understand how all these different processes in complex interrelations with one another determine policy outcomes and how change in governance regimes occurs. With the complexity of governance systems, change results from a combination of formal regulations and informal self-organizing processes among a range of actors.

Although the governance concept has the strength of encompassing the complexity of contemporary policy processes, it at the same time presents a major challenge of encapsulating this complexity within a concise typological framework. One attempt at classification distinguishes between hierarchies, networks, and markets as three principal modes of governance. Thus, the dominating influence in a given governance arrangement may come from governmental control, from specialized networks, or from market-based structures. Or the three modes may intertwine; it is increasingly realized that markets and networks function best within an official regulatory framework where contracts and the rule of law are respected.

The development of GWG is influenced by (1) the tensions between globalization and regionalization; (2) the dominance of centralization or decentralization; (3) the diversity of formal and informal processes and outcomes; and (4) the influence of state versus nonstate actors and processes. These dimensions are reflected in the governance typology of James Rosenau, which focuses on the structures and processes that sustain the flow of authority, whether they are in the form of commands or of requests for compliance (see Table 14.1).[21]

---

18   Renate Mayntz, *New Challenges to Governance Theory*, Jean Monet Chair Papers No. 50, European University Institute, 1998.

19   Rod A.W. Rhodes, *Understanding Governance: Policy Networks, Reflexivity and Accountability* (Buckingham, UK: Open University Press, 1997).

20   Fritz W. Scharpf, *Games Real Actors Play: Actor-Centered Institutionalism in Policy Research* (Oxford: Westview Press, 1997).

21   James N. Rosenau, "Strong Demand, Huge Supply: Governance in an Emerging Epoch," in Ian Bache and Matthew Flinders, eds., *Multi-level Governance* (Oxford: Oxford University Press, 2004), pp. 31–48.

The structural attribute distinguishes between either formal or informal frameworks, as well as a combination of formal and informal structures. The process attribute makes a distinction in terms of the flow of authority in a single direction (up or down) or in multiple directions (both up and down vertically, as well as both back and forth horizontally). This typology takes into account that the common linear models of governance (those in the left-hand column) have to be complemented with models taking into account nonlinear feedback and network processes. These ideal types highlight distinctions between extremes and emphasize the dominant pathways of policy intervention. Governance includes different processes to varying degrees.

The Rosenau typology is helpful in classifying actors and cross-level interactions. It also avoids normative claims and provides the basis for a strictly analytical framework. However, the typology does not offer explicit guidance regarding the relative importance of state versus nonstate actors beyond asserting that states do not play an exclusive role in governance. Likewise, Rosenau's framework does not specify the relative significance of formality versus informality, of centralization versus decentralization, or of globalization versus regionalization. These matters must be assessed separately in each empirical case.

TABLE 14.1   A typology of structures and processes of governance

	Processes	
	Unidirectional (vertical or horizontal)	Multidirectional (vertical and horizontal)
Structures		
Formal	Top-down governance	Network governance
Informal	Bottom-up governance	Side-by-side governance
Formal and informal	Market governance	Mobius-web governance

SOURCE: JAMES N. ROSENAU, "GOVERNANCE IN A NEW GLOBAL ORDER," IN DAVID HELD AND ANDREW MCGREW, EDS., *GOVERNING GLOBALIZATION: POWER, AUTHORITY AND GLOBAL GOVERNANCE* (MALDEN: POLITY PRESS AND BLACKWELL PUBLISHING LTD., 2002), PP. 70–86

3 The Current State of GWG

The characteristics of governance regimes introduced in the preceding section can now be applied to analyze players and policy processes in the current GWG landscape. The discussion that follows identifies who is involved in policy-making around water—states or predominantly nonstate actors. The analysis further considers how far GWG is formal or informal, global or regional, centralized or decentralized. The results of GWG policy processes are also examined, in terms of binding agreements versus nonbinding declarations.

Important aspects of contemporary GWG come in the form of international law. These agreements generally reflect state practice and result from negotiations between states based on strict rules of procedure.[22] They are relatively top-down, centralized global governance arrangements that lack broad involvement of stakeholder groups at different levels. GWG in this traditional statist vein includes the 1982 UN Convention on the Law of the Sea and its subsequent follow-up agreements, which aim to harmonize rules on managing the seas. Another statist construction, the 1997 UN Convention on the Law of the Non-navigational Uses of International Watercourses, aims to develop common norms for the management of watercourses. Although the Watercourses Convention has not entered into force, it has influenced policy regarding many international river basins.[23] Other intergovernmental treaties address specific species (e.g., the Whaling Convention, 1946[24]) and pollution of the seas (e.g., the convention related to dumping from nuclear ships, 1972[25]).

Alongside international law, GWG also encompasses a number of permanent global intergovernmental agencies, particularly through the United Nations system. The UN is a relatively top-down organization, although it does not exclude participation by nonstate actors and does not speak with one voice. Global governance of water involves a number of UN institutions (e.g., the Food and Agriculture Organization [FAO], the UN Educational, Scientific and Cultural Organization [UNESCO], the World Health Organization [WHO], and the World Bank); funds (e.g., the Global Environment Facility [GEF]); and

---

22   See Joseph Dellapenna and Joyeeta Gupta, this issue.
23   Conca, Wu, and Mei, "Global Regime Formation."
24   UNICW 1947, International Convention for the Regulation of Whaling (Washington), 2 December 1946, in force 10 December 1948; 161 UNTS 72 (as amended, 19 November 1956, 338 UNTS 336).
25   London Dumping Convention 1972, Convention on the Prevention of Marine Pollution by Dumping of Wastes and Other Matter (London, Mexico City, Moscow, Washington DC), 29 December 1972, in force 30 August 1975, 1046 UNTS 120.

programs (e.g., the UN Development Programme [UNDP] and the UN Environment Programme [UNEP]). In 2003, UN Water was established as an umbrella mechanism to coordinate UN implementation of the plan of action agreed upon at the 2002 World Summit on Sustainable Development (WSSD) and the Millennium Development Goals (MDGs), which includes reducing by half the proportion of people without sustainable access to safe drinking water and basic sanitation. UN Water endorses activities like the UNESCO-led World Water Assessment Programme (WWAP), which has since 2003 published a triennial World Water Development Report (WWDR). In 2005, the UN launched the Water for Life Decade (2005–2015) to promote the achievement of the MDGs. Other activities fall fully under the aegis of one UN body (e.g., UNESCO's International Hydrological Programme [IHP]) or are jointly led by two or more bodies (e.g., the Global International Waters Assessment overseen by UNEP and GEF).

Other aspects of GWG are organized at the regional level. In the European Union (EU), for example, the European Union Water Initiative (EUWI), launched at the 2002 Johannesburg summit, affirmed, among other things, that the EU would help achieve the MDG 7 and promote national water resources management plans by 2005. The EUWI is not a statist construction, however, as it relies largely on voluntary agreements for the mobilization of financial and other resources from nonstate actors. Thus, EUWI is on the one hand a formal, centralized process and on the other hand an informal arrangement where state actors function side by side with market actors.

The mix of stakeholders in GWG is taken still further in the World Water Council (WWC), established in 1996. The WWC is an international multistakeholder platform that was established to address critical global water issues through, for example, a World Water Forum, held every three years since 1997. The forum involves an intricate mobius web of interactions between state and nonstate actors and networks. Meanwhile the forums attract more than 15,000 participants, ranging from high-level ministerial delegations to local level managers and decisionmakers, from international water industry companies to local farmer irrigation boards, and include a wide range of nongovernmental organizations (NGOs), lobbyists, advocates, and researchers in such diverse fields as drinking water and sanitation, development aid, nature conservation, food security, and energy supply.

Linked to the forum is a ministerial conference that adopts a political declaration. The conference is an informal process with informal outcomes that are nonbinding and arguably ineffective.[26] The proposed alternative of smaller,

---

26   Gleick and Lane, "Large International Water Meetings."

focused UN negotiations might be more effective, but they might arguably also be less legitimate, involving fewer nonstate actors.

Other aspects of GWG go further in the direction of private governance. For example, transnational water corporations (e.g., Suez, Ondeo, Veolia) are key global actors in water supply and wastewater treatment. About 10 percent of former public water services are now in private hands concentrated in urban centers.[27] The privatization trend has supported the emergence of water companies, and the globalization trend has promoted the dominance of global players who are able to outcompete smaller companies. The increasing importance of private companies and their self-governance initiatives is a case of "market governance."

Finally, global communities of scientists and water professionals increasingly shape GWG. The International Law Association (ILA) has been active on water matters since 1873, and in the 1970s UNESCO set up the International Hydrological Programme. At present, the professional community around water includes the Global Water Partnership, the International Water Association, the International Water Resources Association, the International Network of Basin Organizations, the Global Water System Project, the UNESCO-IHE Institute for Water Education, and many others. However, in contrast to other fields of research—such as climate change—professional circles around water do not constitute a well-defined epistemic community with a formal political mandate, nor do the professionals feed advice through formal channels into the governance process.

The preceding overview reveals the diffuse, heterogeneous, and fragmented character of today's GWG. A number of top-down, bottom-up, network, and side-by-side governance elements exist in parallel. The overall picture can be characterized as one of mobius web-type governance. Some initiatives are centralized, while others are decentralized. Some have a strongly global character, while others tend to be predominantly regional. No centralized UN agency is authorized to make policy, and UN Water as a platform for collaboration among UN agencies does not have a strong mandate. There are no indications of an emergent global leadership. Water is thus a rising issue of global governance characterized by comparatively young and immature structures and processes that have slowly evolved over the past two decades.

This immaturity is strange given that global governance has developed relatively more rapidly in other policy fields, such as the depletion of the ozone

---

27   David Hall and Emanuele Lobina, *Pipe Dreams: The Failure of Private Sector to Invest in Water Services in Developing Countries*, PSIRU report for Public Services International and World Development Movement, London, 2006.

layer and climate change. There, formal links with organized epistemic communities have been arranged. This fuller development may have occurred because ozone depletion and climate change were both from the start perceived to be global problems that call for global governance. These challenges could not be addressed unless everyone participated in one way or other. Moreover, both problems called for the reduction of specific emissions—namely, ozone-depleting substances and greenhouse gases. Relative clarity of focus made it easier to generate concentrated governance programs. At the same time, mitigation strategies could focus on relatively simple technological solutions—for example, the phaseout of ozone-depleting substances and the reduction of CO_2 emissions.

Obviously, this characterization oversimplifies both of these cases of global governance. The actual picture is more complex, and these complexities have made climate governance increasingly more diffuse at the global level. Nevertheless, water is different from ozone depletion and climate change. For example, water issues are "creeping problems," having developed into global problems slowly over the centuries, whereas ozone and climate questions have become acute in a matter of decades. Moreover, the global character of water problems is not always evident: local water problems can be addressed locally. Although up to 2 billion people have poor access to potable water and sanitation services, this problem is not seen as dramatic. Nor are matters of water distribution susceptible to "easy" technological solutions. Awareness of the global dimension of water-related problems and the need for global governance processes to address them is only slowly emerging. In addition, the cross-sectoral character of water (across developmental, environmental, economic, and security dimensions) hampers the development of a well-structured and clear-cut global governance system.

4   Future Scenarios for GWG

As seen in the preceding discussion, water is an emergent problem of global public policy whose governance is so far characterized by a mobius-web structure. The various global initiatives developed to date appear to compete for influence rather than move toward coordination.[28] This competition may be appropriate and fruitful in an early stage of developing governance. However, for the longer-term future it becomes necessary to consider different arrangements and their potential for dealing with increasingly urgent challenges of

---

28   Varady and Iles-Shih, "Global Water Initiatives: What Do the Experts Think?"

sustainable global management of water resources. To this end the following paragraphs elaborate scenarios that are alternative projections of the future of GWG. Scenarios are a useful way to understand how driving forces may shape future developments, to assess the associated uncertainties, and to prepare for these circumstances.

Based on current trends, four possible future directions for the development of GWG can be identified. These include (1) global policymaking through informal, decentralized, and market approaches; (2) global policymaking with a focus on formal treaties and centralized agencies; (3) regional, multi-level policymaking; and (4) state-centered regional policymaking. It should be noted here that these are stylized ideal-typical scenarios that cannot take into account all nuances of possible developments. Clearly there may be informal networks that are centralized and formal bodies that are decentralized. The four scenarios are explained in the following paragraphs (see also Table 14.2).

In scenario 1, the future GWG apparatus would be global, informal, decentralized, and privatized, involving multiple competing or complementary multilevel initiatives. This scenario would take forward trends since the 1990s of multiple global initiatives, mostly undertaken by nonstate actors and the UN system. The resulting situation would be one of fragmented governance with partly competing and partly complementary platforms and initiatives. One can conceive of a growing competition between such initiatives (e.g., the World Water Forums, World Water Week, the World Water Council, the International Water Association, UN Water, and the ILA), without the dominance of one process or actor. Alternatively, one (formal) actor could take the lead and support collaboration between complementary efforts. However, such collaboration is unlikely to emerge without leadership.

Scenario 2 also envisions highly globalized governance, but with an emphasis on formal treaty-based regimes. Apart from the UN conventions on the sea and on watercourses, other relevant global treaties cover a range of issues like climate change and trade.[29] Increasing pressures on water resources and increasing unhappiness with the diffuse and unclear nature of mobius web-like approaches could raise the pressure to develop more formal treaty-based global governance.

Scenario 3 would shift the center of gravity in GWG from the global to the regional level, albeit in a context of continuing to develop multilevel arrangements. In a multispeed world, where parts of the globe have advanced systems of regional cooperation while others lack them, some parties may prefer to regulate water issues at a regional level. Regionalists may fear that agreements at

---

29   See Dellapenna and Gupta, this issue, for details.

TABLE 14.2 Scenarios for the development of GWG

Scenario	Description	Examples
1	Global policymaking with informal, decentralized, and market approaches	Much of current GWG phenomena-like platforms (e.g., World Water Forum, World Water Week) and initiatives (e.g., WWC, GWP, IWA, UN Water)
2	Global policymaking with formal, centralized, and regulatory approaches	UN conventions, MDGS
3	Regional policymaking combined with informal, decentralized, multilevel, and market approaches	European Union
4	Regional policymaking with formal, centralized, and regulatory approaches	State-centered regional treaties, possibly reflecting asymmetries of power in transboundary river basins

the global level do not go far enough or that global arrangements may neglect region-specific contexts. An example of a regional, multilevel agreement is the EU, with its harmonized joint legislation on water issues (e.g., the Water Framework Directive).

Scenario 4 would likewise see more region-centered GWG, but this time with greater initiative centered in states. In effect, this would mean returning GWG to the pattern that prevailed before the 1990s, when states would negotiate treaties with neighboring states on the basis of narrow national interests. While a trend since the 1990s has seen moves to consolidate earlier arrangements in global agreements, the rise of terrorism and the return to unilateralism by the United States, as well as fears of the impact of climate change on national water systems, could take the focus back to state-centered management of water issues.[30]

None of these four scenarios for future GWG is by itself sufficient to address global water issues. A combination of global informal networks and markets

---

30   Joyeeta Gupta, "Environmental Multilateralism: Under Challenge?" in Edward Newman, Ramesh Thakur, and John Tirman, eds., *Multilateralism Under Challenge? Power, Normative Structure and World Order* (Tokyo: United Nations University, 2006), pp. 289–307.

(scenario 1) and a global treaty approach (scenario 2) may have the potential to do so, since it combines global coordination with flexibility and adaptive nego-tiation spaces. Formal regulatory approaches at the global level (scenario 3) tend to remain rather vague and face tremendous difficulties in triggering real action, as the experience with the implementation of UN conventions in the water sectors or the MDGs show. However, they create valuable politi-cal commitment as the basis for further multilateral and regional activities. State-centered regional activities (scenario 4) are likely to continue playing an important role in water governance but are not suitable for addressing the GWG challenges at hand.

To embed these scenarios for GWG in a wider context, they can be linked to other scenario work undertaken by the Intergovernmental Panel on Climate Change (IPCC) in 2000, by the Millennium Assessment (MA) in 2005, and by the fourth Global Environment Outlook (GEO) in 2007.[31]

The IPCC developed four scenarios, named A1, A2, B1, and B2. The A1 sce-nario is broadly in line with GWG scenario 1. It assumes a future with rapid economic growth, rapid technological change, a peak in global population in the middle of the twenty-first century, and increased cultural and social con-vergence among regions. The IPCC's A2 scenario visualizes a heterogeneous world where countries and people focus on self-reliance and local identities, rather on the lines of GWG scenario 4. In IPCC's B1 world, regions converge toward a service and information society, there is much focus on environmen-tal impacts, and governance promotes sustainability and equity. The emphasis on global solutions broadly mirrors GWG scenario 2. The B2 scenario focuses on decentralized solutions emphasizing local routes to sustainability, which again goes in a similar direction as GWG scenario 4.[32]

The MA also developed four scenarios for the future. One, dubbed Global Orchestration, is broadly in congruence with GWG scenario 1. It focuses on sus-tainable development and fair trade, with enhancement of global public goods and global education. A second MA scenario, called Order from Strength, shows significant similarities with GWG scenario 4. It focuses on conservation

---

31   An overview of current global environmental assessments can be found in Caroline
      van Bers, Daniel Petry, and Claudia Pahl-Wostl, eds., *Global Assessments: Bridging Scales*
      and Linking to Policy, report on the joint TIAS-GWSP workshop held at the University of
      Maryland, University College, 10–11 May 2007 (Bonn: GWSP Issues in Global Water System
      Research, No. 2, GWSP International Project Office, 2007).

32   Nebojsa Nakiçenoviç and Robert Swart, eds., *Special Report on Emissions Scenarios*, a
      special report of Working Group III of the Intergovernmental Panel on Climate Change
      (Cambridge: Cambridge University Press, 2000); this report is also the basis for the sce-
      narios of the current 4th Assessment Report of the IPCC.

efforts such as reserves, regional trade blocs, security, and protection and is highly regional in character. The third MA scenario, labeled Adapting Mosaic, largely corresponds to GWG scenario 3. It assumes a focus on local and regional comanagement owing to discredited global institutions in a rather fragmented world. The fourth MA scenario, Techno Garden, shows considerable overlap with GWG scenario 1, with its market-oriented and informal character. It emphasizes green technology, tradable rights, free movement of goods, technical expertise, and the like.[33]

The GEO of 2007 explores four scenarios in a somewhat different manner.[34] The scenarios mainly distinguish between different types of interactions between state and nonstate actors and their performance on environment and sustainability issues. The scenario dubbed Policy First relies on top-down approaches to environmental governance. Here, government implements strong policies to improve environmental and human well-being with the support of private and civil society actors. This scenario has similarities with GWG scenarios 2 and 4. The GEO scenario Sustainability First has government, civil society, and the private sector collaborating to improve environmental and human well-being, with a strong emphasis on equity. With its implicit reliance on informal and decentralized processes, this GEO scenario has similarities with GWG scenarios 1 and 3. A third GEO scenario, called Security First, focuses on national and regional actors as is the case in GWG scenarios 3 and 4. It envisions government and the private sector competing for control in efforts to improve, or at least maintain, human well-being, mainly for the rich and powerful in society. Finally, the GEO scenario called Markets First, emphasizes decentralized and informal market mechanisms at the expense of centralized and formalized policy interventions and therefore overlaps with GWG scenarios 1 and 3. Here the private sector, with active government support, pursues maximum economic growth as the best path to improve environmental and human well-being.[35]

Like the GWG scenarios, the IPCC and MA scenarios (but not the GEO scenarios) make more or less clear distinctions between the four opposing trends that were identified earlier in this article: global versus regional, centralized versus decentralized, formal versus informal, and state versus nonstate. The

33   Millennium Ecosystem Assessment (MA), *Ecosystems and Human Well-Being*, vol. 2, Scenarios, chapter 8, Four Scenarios (Washington, DC: Island Press), pp. 223–294.

34   United Nations Environment Programme (UNEP), Global Environment Outlook 4 (GEO-4), Environment for Development (Nairobi: UNEP, 2007).

35   Dale S. Rothman, "The Development of the GEO-4 Scenarios and Their Basic Storylines," in van Bers, Petry, and Pahl-Wostl, *Global Assessments: Bridging Scales and Linking to Policy*, pp. 24–29.

comparison of scenarios shows that the exploratory analysis of GWG scenarios is generally in line with other projections of future global environmental governance. The comparison also shows that global scenarios differ in the kind of emphasis they give to different elements of governance and the kind of development they consider to be plausible. However, further research may reveal more inconsistencies. Perhaps scholars working on scenarios for global environmental governance (including in respect of water) should strive for a more consistent terminology. Such a terminology should not reduce the diversity of approaches but rather allow comparing why and how they differ.

It is unclear how actual future GWG will develop in relation to the different scenarios. What is clear is that a number of activities are taking place on a number of fronts. Each has advantages and disadvantages. A state-centered approach appears to be outdated, but given the crucial importance of water as a politically sensitive resource, many governments will be reluctant to cede control to fluvial or global-level regimes.[36] Yet a state-centered multilateral regime may inhibit the development of cooperative norms and instruments for the global management of water. Since world regions are in different stages of development, it is likely that water will be treated more as a regional issue and that each region will address the problem within its existing capabilities. A pluralist, global, multiactor approach may work well in the developed countries, where institutional processes exist to ensure accountability of the key actors, but there are major doubts about whether such processes can function well in the developing countries.[37]

5   Conclusion

In this article, we have developed a conceptual framework for analyzing global governance of water. Our analysis of GWG, as well as the development of future projections, has identified clear challenges for global governance scholars. Emphasis needs to be given to cross-level interactions, the development of consistent terminologies, and the construction of a framework that allows better comparative analysis.

---

36   Marco Schouten and Klaas Schwartz, "Water as a Political Good: Implications for Investments," International Environmental Agreements 6, no. 4 (2006): 407–421.

37   Daniel Compagnon, "Scaling and the Nation State in the Third World: Theoretical Gaps and Policy Consequences," in Joyeeta Gupta and Dennis Huitema, eds., *Can Theoretical and Practical Insights on Scale Improve Environmental Governance*, IDGEC Final Report (Cambridge: MIT Press, forthcoming).

Our analysis of present circumstances concludes that GWG is currently diffuse and mobius web-like in character. A lack of strong motivation on the part of UN agencies and states to push water management has encouraged the rise of pluralistic bodies that try to deal with these issues. However, it is not clear that these polycentric governance frameworks can be more successful in generating the necessary political will for global action. Some kind of formal global coordination is required in tandem with more decentralized network and market-based approaches.

However, further questions remain that lie beyond the scope of this article. For example, can effective and legitimate global governance systems for water be developed in a world of decreasing social solidarity and increasing economic and environmental stress? What kind of frameworks for global governance of water should be advocated from a normative perspective, as against the purely analytical approach maintained in the present discussion? Hopefully, the theoretical exploration we have undertaken will stimulate further research along these and other lines into this vital question of global resource management.

CHAPTER 15

The John W. Holmes Lecture: Growing the "Third UN" for People-Centered Development— The United Nations, Civil Society, and Beyond

Roger A. Coate[1]

Three decades ago John Holmes argued that the need for having the kind of "international organizations in which to tackle the inescapably complex economic and social issues in an interdependent world need not be restated." Despite these words, ten years later, when Donald Puchala and I presented the first "State of the United Nations Report" to the second annual meeting of the Academic Council on the United Nations System (ACUNS), we found an organizational system teetering and tottering on the verge of crisis.[2] There was a void of leadership, as well as a crisis of capacity precipitated largely by the refusal of the United States to fulfill its legal obligation to fund UN agencies; and staff morale was at a historic low. One of the main themes that we explored in that report was the challenge to the UN system—as intergovernmental institutions—of dealing with the plethora of global problems that confront the world and dominate the global agenda and that cannot be solved by governmental or intergovernmental means alone. Now, after twenty more years, the illusive quest continues for new avenues and directions for making global governance more effective for promoting sustainable human security and development.

In this context, this article explores the current state of the debate over United Nations–civil society/private sector relations and why this relationship is critical to the future of the UN system and its success in dealing with

---

* This chapter was originally published in Global Governance, Volume 15, Issue 2, 2009.

1 Roger Coate is Paul D. Coverdell Chair of Public Policy at Georgia College and State University and Distinguished Professor Emeritus of Political Science at the University of South Carolina. He is author or coauthor of numerous books, including most recently: *United Nations Politics: Responding to a Challenging World* (2007) and *The United Nations and Changing World Politics*, 6th ed. (2009) He is also cofounding editor of *Global Governance*.

2 Donald Puchala and Roger Coate, *The State of the United Nations*, Reports and Papers, No. 2, Academic Council on the United Nations System (ACUNS), Fall 1988.

---

the nexus of complex issues that crowd the global agenda.[3] But one cannot understand the nature and implications of this debate without understanding its history and exploring the various assumptions, logic, worldviews, and intellectual and practical biases that underpin the positions within it.

1   The UN in Holmesian Perspective

The story begins with John Holmes, in whose honor this essay is being written. In his article examining US-UN relations, "A Non-American Perspective,"[4] Holmes argued that it was because the UN was founded on "permanent reality rather than legal fictions" that the system has survived and grown. Understanding the nature of the meanings of that reality and the inherent contradictions and tensions encompassed within them is critical for understanding the past and present as well as future possibilities of civil UN–civil society/private sector relations. He challenged that

> the popular perception of the UN as a failed world government must be corrected. The problem, of course, always has been that the perfervid defenders and malevolent critics have the same misunderstanding. They are concerned with structure rather than with function. What might correct this misunderstanding is the involvement of far more people in the functions for which the UN system exists.... More precise calculation and fewer general slogans are required in determining exactly what is advisable and possible to expect of the UN system.... A better perspective is gained by starting from the agenda rather than by concerning oneself primarily with the preservation or improvement of the structure.[5]

The United Nations, beginning from the 1942 alliance, represented a unique blend of real politic, liberal ideology, idealism, functionalism, and war weariness. John Holmes understood this well. Again quoting Holmes:

> Roosevelt deliberately launched the UN with a conference dealing with the practical question of food. The United States was as much responsible

---

3   This article is from the John Holmes Memorial Lecture, presented at the 2008 Annual Meeting of the Academic Council on the United Nations System, Bonn, Germany, 5–7 June 2008.

4   John W. Holmes, "A Non-American Perspective," *Proceedings of the Academy of Political Science* 32, no. 4, *The Changing United Nations: Options for the United States* (1977): 30–43; available at www.jstor.org/stable/1173989.

5   Ibid., pp. 8–9.

as any country for seeing that agencies dealing with relief, international monetary and financial questions, and civil aviation were tackled before San Francisco. The UN in wartime had to be created in the abstract, but it was no Wilsonian philosopher's dream. Then as now there were things to be done, and institutions were devised or improvised to cope with them.[6]

The UN that Holmes saw and that Don Puchala and I observed and reported on a decade later was one that was being beaten, battered, and abused by its primary creator—the United States. Twenty years later much has happened, but little seems to have changed—the form has remained basically the same despite all the rhetoric on reform. But a focus on institutional form is narrow and misleading. As regards function, the world body has been undergoing slow but important transformation.

1.1   *Putting Things in Contemporary Perspective: The "Third UN"*
In their article "The 'Third' United Nations *Global Governance*, Thomas Weiss, Tatiana Carayannis, and Richard Jolly explore the intermingled and interdependent world of NGO-UN relations.[7] In doing so, they argue that there is a "third" United Nations. Building on Inis Claude's conceptualization of "two UNs"[8]— the intergovernmental bodies made up of member states, and the secretariats composed of international civil servants—they suggest that a "third UN" has evolved consisting of NGOs, academics, consultants, experts, and independent commissions. All three UNs, they suggest, co-exist in symbiotic relationship. In order to understand UN politics, especially as related to institutional reform, all three UNs need to be considered holistically.[9] This essay endeavors to build on this conceptualization and explore this third United Nations and its potential for enhancing global public policy. In doing so, the focus will be on civil society and the private sector, excluding for this task the fifteen or so UN independent commissions on various topics.

---

6 Ibid., p. 9.
7 Thomas G. Weiss, Tatiana Carayannis, and Richard Jolly, "The 'Third' United Nations," *Global Governance* 15, no. 1 (2009), presented as a paper at the 2008 Annual Meeting of the International Studies Association, San Francisco, 26–29 March 2008.
8 Inis L. Claude Jr., "Peace and Security: Prospective Roles for the Two United Nations," *Global Governance* 2, no. 3 (1996): 289–298.
9 Ibid.; John E. Trent makes a similar argument in *Modernizing the United Nations System: Civil Society's Role in Moving from International Relations to Global Governance* (Opladen and Farmington Hills: Verlag Barbara Budrich Publishers, 2007).

Nongovernmental organizations (NGOs) and other civil society actors were present and active at the creation of the United Nations in San Francisco. Today, some 3,000 NGOs have some form of consultative status in the UN system. Numerous scholars, including Chadwick Alger, Leon Gordenker, Thomas Weiss, Cyril Ritchie, and others (several among us today), have presented succinct overviews of the evolution and nature of the roles of NGOs in the UN system, consisting of informal engagements as well as formal consultative status.[10] Civil society organizations are engaged in every aspect of global policy processes in the UN system, including agenda setting, advocacy, rule making, standard setting, promotion, implementation, monitoring, and evaluation.[11] A problem is that there exists tremendous incoherence within this action set and ambiguity regarding the associated role of civil society in relation to the first two UNs.

In 2003, Secretary-General Kofi Annan appointed a distinguished blue-ribbon panel (part of the "third UN"), chaired by former Brazilian president Fernando Cardoso, to examine the relationship between the UN system and civil society organizations and to recommend ways in which UN agencies might better manage and enhance their relations with such organizations and facilitate the involvement of NGOs from developing countries in UN activities. The Report of the Panel of Eminent Persons on United Nations–Civil Society Relations (the Cardoso Report) was issued in June 2004.[12] The final report reflected a series of politically negotiated observations—as might be expected—and offered more than two dozen recommendations for action. It was underpinned by four main principles: the UN needs to (1) become an outward-looking organization; (2) embrace a plurality of constituencies; (3) connect the local with the global; and (4) help strengthen democracy for the twenty-first century. In brief summary, it recommended that UN agencies invest more in civil society partnerships; focus on engagement at the country level; strengthen the Security Council to broaden its engagement with

---

10   Chadwick Alger, "The Emerging Roles of NGOs in the UN System: From Article 71 to a People's Millennium Assembly," *Global Governance* 8, no. 1 (Spring–Summer 2002): 93–117; Leon Gordenker and Thomas G. Weiss, "Pluralizing Global Governance: Analytical Approaches and Dimensions," in Thomas G. Weiss and Leon Gordenker, eds., *NGOs, the UN, and Global Governance* (Boulder: Lynne Rienner, 1996), pp. 17–47; Cyril Ritchie, "Coordinate? Cooperate? Harmonize? NGO Policy and Operational Coalitions," in Weiss and Gordenker, *NGOs, the UN, and Global Governance*, pp. 177–188.

11   Shepard Forman and Derk Segaar, "New Coalitions for Global Governance: The Changing Dynamics of Globalization," *Global Governance* 12 (2007): 205–225.

12   Report of the Panel of Eminent Persons on United Nations–Civil Society Relations (Cardoso Report), *We the Peoples: Civil Society, the United Nations and Global Governance*, UN Doc. A/58/817 (New York: United Nations, June 2004).

civil society; engage with parliamentarians and other elected representatives; and initiate reforms to make accreditation and access by civil society organizations easier.

Cardoso and company argued that "the most powerful case for reaching out beyond its constituency of central Governments and enhancing dialogue and cooperation with civil society is that doing so will make the United Nations more effective." In the language of the report,

> Our starting paradigms also apply to the other panels and are the foundation for the continued relevance of the United Nations: (a) multilateralism no longer concerns Governments alone but is now multifaceted, involving many constituencies; the United Nations must develop new skills to service this new way of working; (b) it must become an outward-looking or network organization, catalysing the relationships needed to get strong results and not letting the traditions of its formal processes be barriers; (c) it must strengthen global governance by advocating universality, inclusion, participation and accountability at all levels; and (d) it must engage more systematically with world public opinion to become more responsive, to help shape public attitudes and to bolster support for multilateralism.[13]

At the core of the panel's recommendations was increasing investment in multilateral partnerships: "They must be viewed as 'partnerships to achieve global goals' ... decentralized to relevant country and technical units and driven by needs, not funding opportunities. To advance this goal necessitates innovations and resources at both the country and global levels."[14] Accordingly, the panel recommended a number of institutional reforms aimed to facilitate and make more effective civil society–UN engagement. Unfortunately, these recommendations were by and large rather ambiguous and underspecified—reflecting undoubtedly the dynamics within the panel on this politically delicate issue.

1.2   Willetts's Critique and Challenge
While to many astute observers it may appear that the Cardoso Report is headed in a constructive direction, Peter Willetts has challenged that the report is intellectually incoherent and displays "little understanding of the existing NGO consultative arrangements" and that it was "poorly received by

---

13   Ibid., p. 12.
14   Ibid., pp. 9–10.

all significant political actors"—by governments, NGOs, and the UN secretary-general.[15] In assessing the report and its recommendations, he argues that the panel's use of three normative arguments—functionalism, corporatism, and pluralism—leads to confusion because they are incompatible with each other. Moreover, "the first two approaches represent a threat to the NGO participation rights that have been operating for the last sixty years at the United Nations. The only morally sound and politically feasible basis for legitimizing wider NGO participation in the UN system is the democratic claim for all voices to be heard in the global policy debates."[16]

From this perspective, Willetts suggests that the report offered little new by way of enhancing UN–civil society engagement. While perhaps this might appear to be the case to the converted advocates of NGO involvement in UN decisionmaking processes, it clearly is not the case with regard to the "first UN." Moreover, however, Willetts's thesis is not on target regarding the priority that he suggests be given to so-called democratic process over outcomes and attainment of organizational missions.

While there are important deficiencies in the Cardoso Report, all is not a wasteland, and the assumptions on which the report is based are not irrelevant or any more incoherent than the assumptions underlying the international norms and institution forms on which the UN system is based. As reflected in John Holmes's observations, the UN from creation was designed to encompass all of the seemingly incoherencies and incompatibilities identified by Willetts—functionalism, corporatism, and liberal democratic ideals. The UN system was designed to create a dynamic synthesis between the Westphalian interstate political legal order and the capitalist world economy, both to be tempered by liberal ideology. Unfortunately for Willetts's thesis, ignoring such foundations or trying to wish them away is not a proper approach for understanding the contemporary situation or discussing future directions for promoting sustainable human development.

2   Civil Society, Private Sector, and the UN

In this context, an aim of the remainder of this essay is to reexamine the nature, evolution, and extent of civil society and private sector involvement in the UN system as it relates to enhancing or diminishing the effectiveness of

15   Peter Willetts, "The Cardoso Report on the UN and Civil Society: Functionalism, Global Corporatism, or Global Democracy?" *Global Governance* 12, no. 3 (July–Sept. 2006): 308.
16   Ibid., p. 306.

UN agencies in dealing with complex global issues. What is the value added by bringing civil society and other nonstate actors more fully into global policy processes? What are the costs and limitations, and are they worth it?

Regarding the role of civil society in the UN, affairs are not as straightforward as Willetts might like us to believe. Again paraphrasing John Holmes's writing over three decades ago,

> UN purists are somewhat unhappy. If one insists, however, on the need to reform the structure of the UN or on a UN mandate for all that is done in the world, one only strengthens the argument for its futility. Instead, concepts must be adjusted to recognize the values of the galaxy. The UN would collapse if it became too pretentious and assumed an overweening authority. International life is managed to a very large extent by private international bodies—grain exchanges and money exchanges, giant regulatory organizations, and corporations with resources far beyond that of the whole UN budget. What is needed is to incorporate a consciousness of these networks into the designs for world order rather than capture them for an international administration that is simply not mature enough to cope—and possibly never will be.[17]

This is the essence of Agenda 21, with its focus on including ten major groups (see "Partnerships" section on page 160). A crucial question for us to confront thirty years later as we move forward in the twenty-first century is the following: Is international administration now mature enough to more fully engage these crucial elements of world society? If not, what reforms are needed to create such an enabling environment?

2.1 What Has UN Practice Taught Us over the Past Decades?

In brief, at least the "second UN" has discovered that directly engaging civil society is essential for carrying out institutional mandates effectively. The forms of such engagements are many.

Alger's work has been enlightening in this regard, especially his analyses of NGOs and people's movements as, what he terms, "tools for peacebuilding" in the UN.[18] Added to his work have been at least four mechanisms (or additional "peacebuilding tools") through which the UN and civil society have become engaged that influence global policy processes. These mechanisms

---

17   Holmes, "A Non-American Perspective," pp. 39–40.
18   Chadwick Alger, "The Emerging Tool Chest for Peacebuilders," *International Journal of Peace Studies* 1, no. 2 (1996): 21–45.

are networking and coalition building; global campaigns; parallel conferencing; and partnerships.[19] They serve to facilitate in varying ways stages of global policy process—information/problem identification, issue framing, agenda setting, decisionmaking, monitoring, evaluation, and feedback. Civil society actors are actively engaged in each functional area and make contributions that are unique to an otherwise intergovernmental process—contributions such as advocacy and lobbying, promotion, information creation and dissemination, research/policy analysis and evaluation, rule making/standard setting, and monitoring.

2.2   *Networking and Coalition Building*
Ruggie has succinctly summarized and underscored the importance of networking and networks in global governance policy processes.[20] Networking and coalition building are inherent in umbrella international nongovernmental organizations (INGOs) like the International Union for Conservation of Nature (IUCN) and the International Council for Science (ICSU). In essence, umbrella INGOs are coalitions of NGOs that network among themselves. The IUCN, for example, represents a network of over 1,000 organizations and 10,000 experts from around the world.[21] Other leading NGO networks actively and effectively involved in UN policy processes include Jubilee 2000, Climate Change Action Network, International Action Network on Small Arms, Coalition for the International Criminal Court, the Coalition to Stop the Use of Child Soldiers, and the International Federation of Red Cross and Red Crescent Societies. Networks and coalitions, when viewed in the larger context of global governance, serve as linchpins, bridging organizations and information clearinghouses. They promote solidarity and capacity building and advocate policies, programs, and harmonization.[22]

While most NGO networks grow up outside the UN, sometimes NGO networks are spawned as a result of institutional change in the UN system. In 1973, for example, as a result of the creation of the United Nations Environmental Programme (UNEP) in Nairobi, a World Assembly of NGOs Concerned with the Global Environment was held, and out of the gathering emerged the Environment Liaison Center International (ELCI). The ELCI represented a

---

19   Roger Coate, "Civil Society as a Force for Peace," *International Journal of Peace Studies* 9, no. 1 (Spring–Summer 2004), available at www.gmu.edu/academic/ijps/vol9_2/Coate _92IJPS.pdf.

20   John W. Ruggie, "The United Nations and Globalization: Patterns and Limits of Institutional Adaptation," *Global Governance* 9, no. 3 (July–Sept. 2003): 315.

21   See http://cms.iucn.org/.

22   Weiss and Gordenker, *NGOs, the UN, and Global Governance*, p. 367.

coalition of over 500 member organizations that linked more than 6,000 NGOs from around the world. Regardless of their origins, these networks help facilitate the operational work of the second UN and serve to support various functions of the first UN—information, normative, rule-creating, and rule-supervising functions.

The first UN (General Assembly) also has come to recognize the importance of engaging such networks. The 2001 UN General Assembly Special Session (UNGASS) on AIDS, for example, launched an ongoing process for engaging civil society in facilitating the UN's implementation of the UNGASS Declaration of Commitment (DoC) on HIV/AIDS. In preparation for the 2006 five-year review of UNGASS, and again in 2008, the Civil Society Coalition on HIV/AIDS UNGASS was formed to strengthen civil society participation in reviewing progress and in promoting accountability and transparency of the review process. Twelve representatives for stakeholder groups were asked to participate on the task force.

2.3   Global Campaigns

The formation of global campaigns is another mechanism used both by international agencies to accomplish their objectives and by civil society organizations to influence global policy processes, especially as related to the normative and rule-creation functions of international organizations and to the promotion of peace and social justice.[23] For example, the International Action Network on Small Arms (IANSA), Amnesty International, and Oxfam joined together in October 2003 to launch the Control Arms Campaign.[24] The campaign has been working aggressively for a global arms trade treaty. Another global NGO campaign that enjoyed much success was the Baby Food Safety Campaign, spearheaded by the International Baby Food Action Network (IBFAN). IBFBAN joined together the International Organization of Consumers Unions (ICU), the Interfaith Center on Corporate Responsibility, and the Infant Formula Action Coalition (INFACT). The campaign was successful in getting the World Health Organization to approve a set of recommended standards for marketing infant formula. Other instructive examples include the International Campaign to Ban Landmines (ICBL), the Global Campaign for Education, and the campaign against the Multilateral Agreement on

---

23   Daphne Josselin and William Wallace, eds., *Non-State Actors in World Politics* (New York: Palgrave, 2001), p. 255.
24   See www.controlarms.org/.

Investment.[25] In their detailed analysis of global campaigns, Daphne Josselin and William Wallace concluded that "together with international conferences and summits, such campaigns are contributing to the emergence of common norms and values."[26]

2.4   Parallel Conferencing

Beginning in the early 1970s, NGOs developed the practice of holding separate "parallel" conferences at the same time and in the same general location as UN conferences. One of the earliest such parallel conferences was held in conjunction with the UN Conference on the Human Environment (UNCHE) in Stockholm in 1972. Although the UNCHE secretariat was proactive in involving scientific NGOs in conference planning, other NGOs found it difficult to break through the Westphalian wall that surrounded the official conference. Thus they initiated their own conference activities in parallel.[27]

As UN conferencing grew and evolved, NGO conferences and parallel conferences became a permanent fixture on the multilateral scene. Conference after conference, issue upon issue, transnational NGOs, acting in concert, carved out a political space of their own in an attempt to influence norm- and rule-creating activities of international organizations. The Westphalian order that characterized the UN system was under siege. Civic-based actors were not only knocking at the door and requesting a seat at the table but were also building their own chairs and tables and developing their own rules of the game. Parallel conferencing provided a venue that member state governments could constrain but not control.[28]

In more recent years, NGOs have been increasingly able to "occupy seats at the table" in the official conferences themselves. This was illustrated at the 2002 World Summit on Sustainable Development:

> The summit reflected a new approach to conferencing and to sustainable development more generally. It was a dialogue among major stakeholders from governments, civil society, and the private sector. Instead of concentrating primarily on the production of treaties and other

---

25   Craig Warkentin and Karen Mingst, "International Institutions, the State, and Global Civil Society in the Age of the World Wide Web," *Global Governance* 6 (Apr.–June 2000): 237–257.

26   Josselin and Wallace, *Non-State Actors in World Politics*, p. 255.

27   Thomas Weiss et al., *The United Nations in a Changing World Environment*, 5th ed. (New York: Westview, 2007).

28   Coate, "Civil Society as a Force for Peace."

outcome documents, participants focused on the creation of new partnerships to bring additional resources to bear for sustainable development initiatives.[29]

The World Summit on the Information Society (WSIS) possessed a similar
venue with civil society organizations participating in the actual conference
decisions.

2.5   *Partnerships*
The new "growth industry" with respect to UN–civil society and private sector engagement is partnership creation and promotion. Such an approach
was inherent in the wake of UNCED. The conference outcome document and
plan of action, Agenda 21, specifically called for the integration of ten major
groups—NGOs, indigenous peoples, local governments, workers, businesses,
scientific communities, farmers, women, children, and youth—in the work of
the newly created Commission on Sustainable Development (CSD). In the context of this mandate, the Economic and Social Council (ECOSOC) authorized
the CSD to bring all 1,400 NGOs represented at the conference into consultative
status with the new body. Thus, integrating "major groups" within civil society into decisionmaking was explicitly embedded in CSD's mandate. In terms
of UN jargon, the CSD currently has over 340 "voluntary multi-stakeholder
partnerships."[30]
    In the context of the entire UN system, however, this represents just the tip
of a very large iceberg. The UN Development Programme (UNDP), the World
Bank, and nearly every other operational agency have evolved elaborate systems of partnerships with NGOs and other diverse elements of civil society. In
its 1999 annual report, for example, the World Bank reported that 50 percent
of its approved projects were run through NGOs.[31] The Bank argues that such
extensive reliance on partnerships makes perfect sense, since NGOs have a comparative advantage in getting the product to the poor.[32] A leading catchphrase
of the era has become "multistakeholder" arrangements/partnerships, as

---

29   Ibid.
30   See http://webapps01.un.org/dsd/partnerships/public/welcome.do.
31   Derk Segaar, *The Evolving Roles of NGOs in Global Governance* (New York: Center on
      International Cooperation, May 2004), p. 3, available at www.worldbank.org/html/extpb/
      annrep99/.
32   World Bank, *NGOs and the Bank: Incorporating FY95 Progress on Cooperation Between the
      World Bank and NGOs* (Washington, DC: World Bank, 1996), cited in Coate, "Civil Society
      as a Force for Peace."

evidenced, for example, in the UN-initiated Global Reporting Initiative, Forest Stewardship Council, and Global Alliance for Vaccines and Immunization.

As reflected in Willetts's stinging critique, the most controversial aspects of such partnership creation have been public-private partnerships and, most especially, the Global Compact initiated by Secretary-General Kofi Annan. Unfortunately, the critique of the Global Compact is all too often conducted on an abstract level and is related to issues of civil society representation regarding UN delegate bodies and not focused on participation—the implications for the effectiveness of UN agencies in fulfilling mandates and dealing with critical global problems. Viewing public-private partnerships in more concrete terms yields a different perspective.

The UN Office for Partnerships (UNOP) facilitates UN relations with the private sector and private foundations. It oversees the UN Fund for International Partnerships (UNFIP), which is an autonomous trust fund that manages UN Foundation relations with UN agencies. As of August 2008, the UNFIP–UN Foundation partnership had yielded more than an additional $1 billion in real resources for over 400 UN-agency projects in 123 countries.[33]

Nearly every UN operational agency, however, has developed its own method for involving the private sector as needed. The UN Office for the Coordination of Humanitarian Affairs (OCHA), for example, partners with the private sector in dealing with humanitarian disasters. The private sector is viewed as being particularly helpful for mobilizing resources rapidly; contributing to relief efforts in sectors that are underresourced, such as agriculture education, health care, and sanitation; providing technical expertise; and assisting with logistics, communications, and the warehousing of goods and equipment. The agency has worked with the International Business Leaders Forum to produce and disseminate a framework for business response for management and planning in case of natural disasters.

Focusing more concretely on the UN's Global Compact with business reveals some interesting programmatic initiatives.[34] The Global Compact's least developed country initiative, for example, works to attract private investment for sustainable development and to identify opportunities for local small and medium-sized enterprises in resource-poor countries. The Global Compact has also launched an initiative, Business in Zones of Conflict, designed to

---

33   "Enhanced Cooperation Between the United Nations and All Relevant Partners, in Particular the Private Sector," Report by the Secretary-General, New York, United Nations, 18 August 2003, available at http://daccessdds.un.org/doc/UNDOC/GEN/N03/461/70/PDF/N0346170.pdf?OpenElement.

34   John G. Ruggie, "global_governance.net: The Global Compact as Learning Network," *Global Governance* 7, no. 4 (2001): 371–378.

provide guidance to the private sector regarding roles that businesses can play in preventing and resolving conflict. In the context of the Global Compact, the Conference of the Parties to the Basel Convention (on the Control of Transboundary Movements of Hazardous Wastes and Their Disposal) has established a very elaborate and formal public-private partnership program, designed to provide governments and stakeholders with more effective means to collectively address and manage waste streams by tapping expertise and knowledge and leveraging scarce resources beyond those normally available to government bodies, especially at subnational levels. Partnership activities include training; information collection and dissemination; development and utilization of practical tools; and capacity building. This multistakeholder arrangement encompasses actors from industry and business, international institutions, environmental and other nongovernmental organizations, academia, and government at all levels.

3   The Cardoso Report Reconsidered

Reflecting on Willetts's critique that the Cardoso Report is intellectually incoherent and displays little understanding of the existing NGO consultative arrangements, it seems a bit harsh to expect a coherent analysis and set of recommendations regarding what is largely a very complex and incoherent phenomenon. Civil society participation in policymaking contains significant aspects of functionalism: UN agencies need and desire NGO expertise. In an environment of declining donor state commitment to providing adequate development financing, new and innovative alternatives are needed to make sustainable development a reality. In order to solve in any sustainable way the kinds of complex social and economic problems that dominate UN agencies' agendas, those most affected need to be involved in the process. Finally, the UN system is committed to enhancing democratic policymaking, and engaging NGOs in every aspect of the policy process is one way of doing so. The problem is how to reform the UN system in order to accomplish all the above without placing an impossible set of burdens on international civil servants.

The panel offered a number of institutional reform recommendations, but because they were unfortunately left underdeveloped, especially with regard to their implications for established NGO consultative mechanisms and arrangements, they were easy targets of criticism. It is important to keep in mind, however, that the Cardoso panel is but one of the many attempts to think through more thoroughly the question of UN–civil society relations systematically. In 1999, for example, the Global Development Network (GDN), sponsored by the

World Bank and other international institutions, brought together over 500 economic policy think tanks to explore ways to improve the capacity of such entities to promote economic development.[35] Participants at this meeting addressed the issue of how UN agencies might best work with the plethora of NGOs that wish to influence and participate in UN policymaking and activities specifically, and how UN agencies can make best use of the potential contributions of the NGOs and how they can coordinate and channel relations with them. They proposed that the transnational research community serve as a "quality check system ... vetting NGOs and their worthiness for interaction with the UN."[36] The group concluded that think tanks could play several main roles in this regard: communicate and translate global values and agreements to regional and local audiences; review international agreements and recommend the formulation of national and regional policy options; convene and build alliances among NGOs and civil society; and educate fledgling NGOs on organizational management, planning, and advocacy.[37]

In the final analysis, it seems that the issue of the democratic deficit in the United Nations and global governance is for many, like Willetts, the core issue. This is inherent in Willetts's complaint that NGOs have no formal status in the main organs of the UN other than ECOSOC and have no formal status with the Bretton Woods Institutions.[38] But who do NGOs, especially those that operate at the global level and make their presence felt in New York, Geneva, and Washington, represent? Paul Wapner has inferred that, on balance, NGOs may be no less accountable to their constituencies than are most national governments or transnational corporations.[39] Yet, it seems important to always keep in mind that NGOs are interest groups underpinned with particular values and interests that they seek to promote. While some may claim to operate in the best collective interests of all humankind, why should other actors automatically assume any degree of legitimacy in such claims? The Quaker Office at the United Nations, for example, has worked hard to promote norms against child soldiers, weapons proliferation, and violations of human rights. So who or what is the foundation for its legitimacy and from where does its authority

---

35 Diane Stone, "The 'Policy Research' Knowledge Elite and Global Policy Processes," in Daphne Josselin and William Wallace, eds., *Non-State Actors in World Politics* (Basingstoke: Palgrave, 2001), p. 119; Overseas Development Council, "Dialogue with Think Tanks: A Report of a Meeting with the United Nations Secretary-General," United Nations, New York, 4–5 May 1999.

36 Ibid., p. 124.

37 Ibid.

38 Peter Willetts, "The Cardoso Report on the UN and Civil Society: Functionalism, Global Corporatism, or Global Democracy?" *Global Governance* 12, no. 3 (July–Sept. 2006): 305.

39 Paul Wapner, "Defending Accountability in NGOs," *Chicago Journal of International Law* 3, no. 1 (2002): 197–205.

to act emanate? The answer, of course, is the set of values and normative convictions on which it operates. Yet, in a multicultural world, is that enough?

The increasing use of collaborative networks has raised accountability issues. Ruggie addresses this issue in two parts: "accountable for what?" and "accountable to whom?" In terms of the "for what" criterion, Ruggie argues that networks are not normally rule based and can only be managed for results.[40] With regard to "accountable to whom," he offers that participants in multistakeholder partnerships may not be, strictly speaking, accountable to anyone but themselves. For example, some NGOs are large membership organizations with transparent governance structures and funding sources, but many others are not.

To what extent does a focus on integrating NGOs into global governance represent cultural bias toward Western liberal ideology? For example, in their edited volume on the role of donor funding of civil society organizations for democratic promotion, Marina Ottaway and Thomas Carothers and their colleagues raise serious questions about the impacts of such practices. They go as far as to suggest that such external civil society aid may actually undermine the legitimacy of the organizations the donors are trying to promote, because "the kinds of NGOs that donors most often select to support are generally not organizations representing a genuine constituency."[41] These NGOs can only speak "on behalf of" but not "for" the constituencies they claim to represent. Moreover, the case studies in this volume illustrate how, especially in the Islamic world and Africa, those types of civil society groups that are most influential in society—professional associations and ethnic and religious groups—are systematically bypassed by major donors (especially the United States).[42] "The organizations ... [that donor funding] helps call into being and develop are the creations of donor funding rather than of social demands for representation and a role in policy-making."[43]

So, in this sober light, what is the answer to the question: What is the value added by bringing civil society, the private sector, and other elements of world society more fully into global policy processes? Well, the answer may or may not be increased democratization of global governance processes, but it is clearly the enhancement of global policy processes in terms of increasing the capacity and competence of international organizations for fulfilling critically

---

40   Ruggie, "The United Nations and Globalization," p. 316.
41   Roger A. Coate, "Review Article: The Promotion of Democracy," *Global Society* 19, no. 4 (Oct. 2005): 446; Marina Ottaway and Thomas Carothers, eds., *Funding Virtue: Civil Society Aid and Democratic Promotion* (Washington, DC: Carnegie Endowment for International Peace, 2000).
42   Ibid.
43   Ottaway and Carothers, *Funding Virtue*, p. 82.

important information, normative, rule-creating, rule-supervising, and operational functions. NGOs, other civil society organizations, subnational governance institutions, and the private sector indeed provide much needed value added but also represent good value for the money in coping with the myriad problems confronting humankind in the early twenty-first century.

Each of the categories of "constituencies," as the Cardoso Report puts it, brings with it disadvantages as well as advantages, constraints as well as capabilities, and costs as well as benefits. As the World Commission on Global Governance cautioned, engaging with a more diverse range of civil society actors means that international civil servants and governments alike are forced to deal with a broader range of interests and operating styles. This, I believe, is more of a virtue than a cost. It reflects more closely the complex world in which international programs, projects, and policies must be carried out.

But still, strong voices ask: Why include the private sector? Of course there are numerous arguments for both excluding and including the private sector in our discussion of UN–civil society partnerships despite the fact that we may not want technically to include it in the definition of civil society. Consider, for example, the first Global Compact rationalization offered by former Secretary-General Kofi Annan. In essence, the aim of this program is to garner wider support for the protection of international norms and standards by bringing international business "inside." The globalizing world of market expansion has led to a growing imbalance in the ability to enforce various kinds of international norms. While substantial progress has been made in globalizing and integrating free-trade and other liberal economic norms into domestic settings, much less movement has occurred in the area of promoting social norms related to such economic processes as human rights, labor standards, and environmental protection.[44] To help redress such an imbalance, Annan proposed a partnership involving the private sector, NGOs, and international agencies—the "global compact." In this compact, corporations were asked to embrace and support nine international principles, drawn from UN human rights, labor, and environmental legal instruments, and accordingly to embrace related "good practices."

As John Holmes reminded us many years ago, much if not most of the real governance in the world through which values become authoritatively allocated is in reality done by private sector institutions and entities. This is part and parcel of the grand compromise/synthesis on which the post-World War II world order has been based—the liberal melding of the Westphalian-interstate order with the capitalist world economy. The UN system was from its inception

---

44   Ruggie, "The United Nations and Globalization."

an amalgamation of these two perceived disparate systems. While the international institutions established were to be based on states and the unit of membership (with all the legal fictions that accompany the concept), the allocation of values within the world politic was to be largely managed by the "invisible hand" of private sector operations, over which the governments of states should place minimalist constraints. Liberal democracy called for civil and political equality as a fundamental principle, while at the same time liberal economics, which serves as de facto political allocator, enshrines inequality as a guiding principle.

Although the Global Compact was a grand scheme, it was not ill conceived. Its creators understood well the nature of the complex interdependent and holistic organic world in which the UN operates. Empowering people for sustainable human security requires providing sustainable livelihoods. It requires empowerment. Empowering people with ideas without providing them with political economic empowerment is a path to conflict, not cooperation. Human rights and democratic ideals are hollow without social and economic security. Is freedom to be constantly hungry, to be malnourished, to live in abject poverty, to live without safe drinking water or adequate sanitation, or to allow all the above to be determined by the invisible hand of supply and demand really freedom? Continuing to operate in a schizophrenic manner that endeavors to promote better governance while at the same time ignoring and excluding from engagement those kinds of forces, as suggested by John Holmes, that have the greatest effect on global, transnational, and national allocation processes seems to some foolhardy. Inclusion of NGOs and other elements of traditionally conceived civil society is not enough. In the words of the Cardoso Report, "Civil society is now so vital to the United Nations that engaging with it well is a necessity, not an option. It must also engage with others, including the private sector, parliaments and local authorities."[45]

In conclusion, as Holmes suggested, effective multilateral diplomacy requires something like "synchronized diplomacy." In a globalizing, highly complex, interdependent world, successful global policy requires that all the instruments and performers necessary for producing harmonious outcomes be engaged constructively in the symphony. Important constructive change has been afoot in the UN system. But the change has been in function, the function of the organic UN, not in form, the form of the "first UN," which remains highly resistant to meaningful reform.

---

45   Report of the Panel of Eminent Persons on United Nations–Civil Society Relations (Cardoso Report), p. 9.

CHAPTER 16

The "Monster That We Need to Slay"? Global Governance, the United States, and the International Criminal Court

Andrea Birdsall[1]

Heated outbursts in the US Senate in 1998, just after the end of the Diplomatic Conference of Plenipotentiaries on the Establishment of an International Criminal Court (the Rome Conference), set the tone for the US position toward the International Criminal Court (ICC). Senator Rod Grams called it "dangerous" and a "monster" that needed to be slayed, and Senator Jesse Helms predicted that "as long as there is a breath in me, the United States will never—and I repeat never, never—allow its national security decisions to be judged by an international criminal court."[2]

Before negotiations for the ICC started in 1998, Congress had expressed general support for a permanent court in principle, arguing that such a court would "serve the interests of the United States and the world community" and that "the United States delegation should make every effort to advance this proposal at the United Nations."[3] This support began to diminish, however, when as the ICC came closer to reality during the negotiations in Rome, the United States was not able to achieve the safeguards it wanted. Under the George W. Bush administration, the United States engaged in a number of hostile actions with the aim to exempt US citizens from the court. More recently, however, there have been signs that such open hostility is fading and

---

*   This chapter was originally published in Global Governance, Volume 16, Issue 4, 2010.

1   Andrea Birdsall is Senior Lecturer in International Relations at the University of Edinburgh. Her main research interests lie in the interplay between international relations and international law with a particular focus on human rights, international criminal justice, and global governance. Her recent publications include *The International Politics of Judicial Intervention: Creating a More Just Order* (2009).

2   "Is a U.N. International Criminal Court in the U.S. National Interest?" Subcommittee on International Operations of the Committee on Foreign Relations, United States Senate, 1998, 105th Congress, 2nd session, 23 July 1998, p. 6.

3   "Calling for the United States to support efforts of the United Nations to conclude an international agreement to establish an international criminal court," S.J. Res. 32, 103rd Cong., 1st session, 28 January 1993.

---

the United States is starting to engage with the court that it could not prevent from being established.

In this article, I analyze the ICC as an instrument of global governance of human rights and the US response to it. The US position toward the ICC is important because the court depends on its member states and would benefit from the support of the remaining superpower in order to be strengthened and be able to operate more effectively.

I start by looking at the main reasons why the United States claims that the court is not in its national interest. I then chart actions taken in opposition to the ICC as well as more recent changes in US attitudes toward the court. I conclude that the United States started to engage with the court because it could no longer afford to ignore an international institution that has 113 member states, including some vital US allies, and it had to acknowledge that the opposition is harmful to its national interests—the very issue it wanted to protect in the first place.

1   Creation of the ICC

The ICC was created during the Rome Conference that took place from 15 June to 17 July 1998. Nearly 160 states met to negotiate a final act for the proposed ICC. The negotiations were complex and, by the end of the conference, some of the key issues still were not resolved to everyone's satisfaction. However, a "package deal" was put to the vote on 17 July 1998 with 120 states voting in favor, 7 against (including the United States), and 21 abstaining.[4] The ICC came into being on 1 July 2002, six months after the sixtieth state ratified the court's statute into its national laws.

The ICC is a permanent and independent court that has jurisdiction over war crimes, crimes against humanity, and genocide.[5] It constitutes a step away from the classic regime of state sovereignty toward integrating a broader framework of global governance to enforce international human rights and administer international criminal justice. The court's statute includes a number of compromises that were necessary to preserve the fundamental principle of state sovereignty but, at the same time, ensure that a functioning global mechanism for enforcing existing human rights laws could be created. Achieving

---

4   It is widely believed that the states voting against the statute were the United States, China, Israel, Libya, Iraq, Yemen, and Qatar.

5   Article 5 of the statute also includes the crime of aggression, but the ICC can exercise jurisdiction over aggression only after a common definition has been agreed on.

such a compromise was possible because the notion of sovereignty changed over the years to include not only rights for states, but also obligations toward a state's own citizens.[6] It can be argued that "there is a widening consensus that the protection of human rights is a matter of collective international concern and a legitimate object of foreign policy."[7] The main problem remains, however, that even though states sign up to a large number of international laws to protect human rights, the laws' enforcement is nevertheless dependent on voluntary state cooperation.

2   The United States and the ICC

The ICC enjoys broad support from a large number of states, but the United States has thus far refused to join the court. This opposition is out of line with US historic support for international criminal courts based on liberal values of human rights and the rule of law. The United States played an active role in the Nuremberg trials and also the creation of the UN ad hoc courts for the former Yugoslavia and Rwanda. Even though the United States engaged actively at the Rome Conference and subsequent meetings, it always maintained that acceptable protection measures had to be built into the statute and was not satisfied with the compromises reached in Rome.

The US position shifted with different administrations. The William J. Clinton administration remained cautiously engaged with the court, demonstrating general support for the idea of a permanent international court. In contrast, the George W. Bush administration took a number of actions to undermine the court, based on a unilateralist focus on national interests and national law enforcement. This initial hostility changed to a more pragmatic approach when the United States recognized that these actions could not stop the ICC from coming into being and were actually harmful to US interests. At the time of this writing, the Barack Obama administration is reviewing its official policy regarding the ICC, but has already stated that it will end the hostility toward the court and continue to cooperate in the investigation currently taking place in the Darfur region of Sudan.

---

6   For a discussion on "sovereignty as responsibility," see G. Evans and M. Sahnoun, "The Responsibility to Protect," *Foreign Affairs* 81, no. 6 (2002): 99–110; and C. Joyner, "The Responsibility to Protect: Humanitarian Concern and the Lawfulness of Armed Intervention," *Virginia Journal of International Law* 47 (Winter 2007): 693–723.

7   J. Mayerfeld, "Who Shall Be Judge?: The United States, the International Criminal Court, and the Global Enforcement of Human Rights," *Human Rights Quarterly* 25, no. 1 (2003): 93–129.

Changes in the US stance toward the ICC reflect differences of what is considered by the respective administrations to constitute the national interest and whether the ICC can be used as a tool to further it. Particularly the George W. Bush administration acted from a realist position of focusing on national interests rather than collective values of a liberal order beneficial to the international community as a whole. State interests are not a static given, but change over time and adjust to changing circumstances. "Rather, national interests are intersubjective understandings about what it takes to advance power, influence and wealth, that survive the political process, given the distribution of power and knowledge in a society."[8] Looking at changes in the US position through such a constructivist lens will help explain how national interests are created and how they influence policymaking.[9] It provides a way of understanding the evolution of the US position over time.

3   Issues of Opposition

The US opposition to the ICC focuses on two main areas: (1) the court's jurisdiction as set out in Article 12; and (2) the fact that the ICC is independent from the UN Security Council and does not recognize the "special" role that the United States plays as a major superpower in international relations.

3.1   *Article 12 and the ICC's Jurisdiction*

The United States opposes Article 12 of the statute, which gives the ICC jurisdiction if an offense is committed on a state party's territory or if the accused is a national of an ICC member state. This means that—at least in theory—the ICC could exercise jurisdiction over US nationals if they were accused of committing an ICC crime on a state party's territory, without the need for US consent.[10] The United States argues that this would in effect give the ICC—as an international institution—universal jurisdiction, which is not part of

---

8   E. Adler, "Seizing the Middle Ground: Constructivism and World Politics," *European Journal of International Relations* 3, no. 3 (1997): 319–363.

9   For a more detailed exposition of constructivism in international relations, see K.M. Fierke, "Constructivism," in T. Dunne, M. Kurki, and S. Smith, eds., *International Relations Theories: Disciplines and Diversity* (Oxford: Oxford University Press, 2007), pp. 167–184.

10   Such action would be possible only in accordance with the complementarity principle, which means that the ICC complements national jurisdiction and can act only if the state in question is genuinely unable or unwilling to investigate or prosecute itself.

customary international law.[11] This view is controversial and rejected by international lawyers "on the simple basis that while a non-party *state* is not itself bound to accept an assertion of jurisdiction over itself unless it has consented, the same is not true of its *nationals* if they commit offenses in the territory of a state that is a party."[12] Individuals are subject to states' territorial jurisdictions, which includes the possibility of extradition to an international court.

The fact that the ICC can exercise jurisdiction over third parties without a need for additional express consent is part of the court's fundamental setup: it empowers the court to investigate and prosecute individuals for the most serious crimes that are already established in international law, independent from states. The United States agreed to such provisions in other treaties, such as the Torture Convention, which allows (and even requires) prosecution or extradition of alleged criminals regardless of their nationality. The ICC is based on precedents set by such conventions and also the ad hoc courts, which similarly do not require express state consent. Given that they enjoy US support, it is evident "that there is no objection in principle to the idea of international courts,"[13] but that the objection is only related to an international court exercising criminal jurisdiction over Americans.

The crimes in the ICC's statute are already established in international treaties and conventions and the statute therefore does not create new laws; it establishes a new collective enforcement mechanism for already accepted universal norms.[14] This means that "the failure of the US to become a party to the ICC does not exempt its citizens from the universality already established."[15] Even though the ICC draws most immediately from territorial and national jurisdiction, it receives added support from the increasingly important notion of universal jurisdiction. This is the point where the ICC adds to existing provisions and where it seeks to fill a gap: it constitutes a global enforcement mechanism for universal values aimed to be largely independent from states.

---

11 D.J. Scheffer, "Staying the Course with the International Criminal Court," *Cornell International Law Journal* 35, no. 1 (2002): 47–100.

12 M. Leigh, "The United States and the Statute of Rome," *American Journal of International Law* 95, no. 1 (2001): 124–131.

13 P. Sands, *Lawless World: America and the Making and Breaking of Global Rules* (London: Penguin; London: Allen Lane, 2005).

14 G. Hafner, K. Boon, A. Rübesame, and J. Huston, "A Response to the American View as Presented by Ruth Wedgwood," *European Journal of International Law* 10, no. 1 (1999): 108–123.

15 M. Weller, "Undoing the Global Constitution: UN Security Council Action on the International Criminal Court," *International Affairs* 78, no. 4 (2002): 693–712.

3.2 Great Power Responsibility and the Security Council Veto

The United States claims that, even though it supports the overall aims of the ICC, it is concerned that the ICC could threaten the independence and flexibility of US military forces. Some argue that, as the only remaining superpower, the United States should be given special protection and that the ICC "fails to recognize [the United States'] unique responsibilities in the world when issues of international peace and security are involved."[16] Others, however, point out that, even though the United States does have unique responsibilities as a great power, "when it claims to act for the common good of international society ... it also has a democratic duty to be accountable to international society for the way it fulfils those responsibilities."[17] The United States is accountable for its actions to the international community in whose name it claims to act, which also means that it cannot impose double standards by exempting its own citizens from acting in accordance with justice norms to which others must adhere.

The ICC is independent from the UN, which is a major concern for the United States because it cannot fully control the ICC through its powers in the Security Council. The Security Council can refer a situation[18] to the ICC prosecutor when acting under Chapter VII of the UN Charter, which makes the establishment of any further ad hoc tribunals unnecessary. This gives the Security Council the power to still be able to intervene judicially in a situation that it deems a threat to peace and security by making use of the ICC as a standing court.

More controversially, however, the Security Council does not have the power to halt proceedings taking place before the ICC. Article 16 of the statute sets out that the Security Council can defer (but not terminate) an investigation or prosecution for a period of twelve months (with the possibility of renewal). To do this, the Council cannot simply veto ICC action, but has to adopt a declaration to postpone proceedings, which requires a minimum of nine affirmative votes. By having to vote in favor of deferring ICC action, the possibility of unilateral veto against the ICC by any one of the Security Council's permanent members is removed.

Article 16 represents a significant development integrated into the statute because it means that no one state (including the five permanent members of

---

16   W.K. Lietzau, "International Criminal Law After Rome: Concerns from a U.S. Military Perspective," *Law and Contemporary Problems* 64, no. 1 (2001): 119–140.

17   J. Ralph, "Between Cosmopolitan and American Democracy: Understanding US Opposition to the International Criminal Court," *International Relations* 17, no. 2 (2003): 195–212.

18   The Security Council is not the only power to do so—states parties and the independent prosecutor can also refer cases to the ICC.

the Security Council) can unilaterally control ICC proceedings. The role of the Security Council in maintaining peace and security remains integrated in the statute (by having the power to refer cases and suspend proceedings if deemed necessary), but the council is awarded only limited powers. This removal of direct Security Council control over the court is an "innovative aspect"[19] of the statute, necessary to make it possible for the ICC to function independently from the UN as a political body. This compromise was important because of the different natures of the two institutions: the UN is a state-centered institution, primarily concerned with protecting the inviolability of state sovereignty, whereas the ICC aims to enforce justice for individuals universally, independent from the national interests of different states.

The United States has criticized this lack of Security Council control because it argues that US soldiers are required in a large number of UN missions to restore or maintain peace and security, which makes them uniquely vulnerable to possible ICC jurisdiction. However, other permanent members of the Security Council that also commit peacekeeping forces to UN missions, such as the United Kingdom and France (and to a degree Russia, which at least signed the treaty), were satisfied with existing safeguards incorporated into the statute. This begs the question: why were they not sufficient for the United States? The answer might lie in the fact that, even though the ICC was created to work alongside the UN and not to undermine it, it also attempted to do indirectly what could not be done directly; namely, to reform the UN by removing direct Security Council control. This challenge to the Security Council can be seen on the one hand as a reason for the US opposition, but on the other as a cause for the enthusiasm and support of such a large number of states that back the idea of equal treatment.[20] As Samantha Power argues, "Many deem the Security Council as the epitome of a politically motivated institution and want an independent ICC precisely because they believe it will not be driven strictly by great power politics."[21]

---

19   A.D. Edgar, "Peace, Justice, and Politics: The International Criminal Court, 'New Diplomacy,' and the UN System," in A.F. Cooper, J. English, and R. Thakur, eds., *Enhancing Global Governance: Towards a New Diplomacy?* (Tokyo: United Nations University Press, 2002), pp. 133–151.

20   W.A. Schabas, "United States Hostility to the International Criminal Court: It's All About the Security Council," *European Journal of International Law* 15, no. 4 (2004): 701–720.

21   S. Power, "The United States and Genocide Law: A History of Ambivalence," in S.B. Sewall and C. Kaysen, eds., *The United States and the International Criminal Court: National Security and International Law* (London: Rowman & Littlefield, 2000), pp. 165–175.

3.3 Staying Engaged: President Clinton Signs the Treaty

The United States did not vote in favor of the ICC in Rome mainly because of the fact that it could not fully control ICC actions in case they went against possible US interests. This meant that the United States attempted to "maintain great power hegemony over international justice."[22] Despite the opposition to the statute as it emerged from the Rome Conference in 1998, the US delegation continued to engage in the Preparatory Commission meetings that followed, which aimed at negotiating further details of the statute such as elements of crimes and the rules of procedure and evidence. David Scheffer, then US ambassador at large for war crimes issues and head of the US delegation, believed that enough progress had been made in the negotiations after Rome to reconsider the US position on whether to sign the statute. He was convinced that the US delegation had achieved

> the most that pragmatically could be achieved in light of all that we confronted, both internally and externally: a sophisticated matrix of safeguards that provided a high degree of protection for US interests and ... additional safeguards that would achieve the best possible relationship for the United States with the ICC.[23]

He argued that some compromises were necessary to achieve a greater good of enforcing universal norms globally, and he also believed that the United States could gain from membership to the court.

There were a lot of divisions within the administration and opposition in the Senate.[24] Jesse Helms, then chair of the Senate Foreign Relations Committee, argued that the court would be "dead-on-arrival" in the Senate, if the treaty

---

22   J. Ralph, "International Society, the International Criminal Court and American Foreign Policy," *Review of International Studies* 31, no. 1 (2005): 27–44.

23   Scheffer, "Staying the Course," p. 63.

24   It is important to note that, in the US system, a dedicated and ideological minority can block ratification of treaties of liberally minded executives in the Senate. For example, this was the case for Woodrow Wilson who faced opposition to the signing of the Covenant of the League of Nations in the Senate. Negotiations surrounding the creation of the ICC are a good example of a two-level game in which the Senate has considerable influence over the bargaining power of the executive branch in international relations between states. For a detailed exposition of the interplay between domestic and international politics see, for example, R.D. Putnam, "Diplomacy and Domestic Politics: The Logic of Two-level Games," *International Organization* 42, no. 3 (1988): 427–460.

did not include United States' veto powers over which cases were brought before it.[25]

> The Senate's opposition to the Court was based on the perception that the Court unduly threatened US sovereignty and its military personnel stationed overseas ... such opposition to the Court represents an electoral logic or political reality in which realist concerns now reproduce domestic political outcomes that are not favorable to international human rights norms.[26]

Despite this domestic opposition, Scheffer was convinced that signing the statute was beneficial for the United States in order to be able "to negotiate further Treaty-friendly proposals and thus protect American interests while pursuing international justice."[27] In line with a constructivist approach of evolving national interests, he emphasized the possible utility of the ICC for US interests and being able to use the court whenever necessary.

On 31 December 2000, the last possible day for signature, President Clinton decided to sign the statute and expressed US "strong support for international accountability and for bringing to justice perpetrators of genocide, war crimes, and crimes against humanity."[28] He argued that the United States signed the treaty in order to "remain engaged in making the ICC an instrument of impartial and effective justice in the years to come" and to sustain the tradition of US "moral leadership" in its commitment to individual accountability. Yet Clinton also made clear that the United States was not satisfied with the Rome Statute in its present form and that "in signing, however, we are not abandoning our concerns about significant flaws in the treaty." He acknowledged existing domestic opposition and did "not recommend my successor submit the treaty to the Senate for advice and consent until our fundamental concerns are satisfied." He concluded that the ICC could make a "profound contribution in deterring egregious human rights abuses worldwide"[29] and that, by signing,

---

25   R. Wedgwood, "The Irresolution of Rome," *Law and Contemporary Problems* 64, no. 1 (2001): 193–214.

26   C.A. Smith and H.M. Smith, "Embedded Realpolitik? Reevaluating United States' Opposition to the International Criminal Court," in S.C. Roach, ed., *Governance, Order, and the International Criminal Court Between Realpolitik and a Cosmopolitan Court* (Oxford: Oxford University Press, 2009), pp. 29–53.

27   D.J. Scheffer, "Restoring U.S. Engagement with the International Criminal Court," *Wisconsin International Law Journal* 21, no. 3 (2003): 599–609.

28   Statement by Bill Clinton: Signature of the International Criminal Court Treaty, 31 December 2000, Camp David, Maryland.

29   Ibid.

the United States wanted to continue to engage in discussion with other governments in order to advance these goals. President Clinton recognized that it was in the US national interest to stay engaged with the ICC and be able to take part in future negotiations. His administration supported the broader goals of the court and hoped that US involvement would eventually lead to changes in the statute more in line with US interests.

3.4   Hostile Opposition: President Bush Unsigns the Treaty

Upon taking over from its predecessor in 2001, the George W. Bush administration did not take a favorable approach to the ICC and did not engage constructively in the Preparatory Commission meetings. John Bolton, under secretary of state for arms control and international security, argued that "America's posture toward the ICC should be 'Three Noes': no financial support, directly or indirectly; no cooperation; and no further negotiations with other governments to 'improve' the ICC."[30] Scheffer criticized the "shortsighted and anaemic approach"[31] of the administration and believed that it resulted in forfeiting opportunities his delegation had initiated in preceding meetings.

On 6 May 2002, President Bush decided to formally withdraw from the Rome treaty and to effectively "unsign" it.[32] Bolton issued a letter to the UN that the United States did not want to become part of the ICC and, therefore, did not have any legal obligations toward the court arising from President Clinton's signature. Bolton, probably the most vocal opponent to the ICC during the Bush administration, once described the ICC as "a product of fuzzy-minded romanticism [that] is not just naive, but dangerous."[33] He maintained that the ICC was "a stealth approach to eroding our constitutionalism and undermining the independence and flexibility that our military forces need to defend our interests around the world."[34]

The move to unsign the treaty was in line with a general shift of the Bush administration's attitude away from multilateralism: "Rather than unveiling new initiatives, the focus of Bush's foreign policy during his first eight months

---

30   J.R. Bolton, "The Risks and Weaknesses of the International Criminal Court from America's Perspective," *Law and Contemporary Problems* 64, no. 1 (2001): 167–180.

31   Scheffer, "Staying the Course," p. 63.

32   According to Article 18 of the Vienna Convention on the Law of Treaties, a signatory to a treaty is "obliged to refrain from acts which would defeat the object and the purpose" of the treaty. The George W. Bush administration therefore had to formally unsign the Rome Statute in order to be able to take action that effectively undermined the functioning of the ICC.

33   J.R. Bolton, "Unsign that Treaty," *Washington Post*, 4 January 2001, p. A21.

34   Ibid.

in office was on extracting the United States from existing ones."[35] In line with a realist approach toward foreign policy, the Bush administration put a stronger focus on national interests and unilateral action. As Secretary of State Condoleezza Rice already set out in 2000, the administration's foreign policy would "proceed from the firm ground of the national interest, not from the interests of an illusory international community."[36]

This position intensified further after September 11, 2001. The National Security Strategy of 2002 set out an agenda for possible unilateral and pre-emptive action in the pursuit of national security that also involved new interpretations of international law to justify such conduct. Public support for Bush's policies increased, and Congress authorized him to "use all necessary and appropriate force" in the "war on terror," giving the president almost unchecked powers to make foreign policy decisions.[37] This move

> partly reflected the enormity of the [September 11] attacks and a principled belief that crises require lawmakers to accede to strong presidential leadership. But Congress's deference also reflected the Democratic Party's weakness on foreign and defense policy.... Worried that their criticisms would at best not be credible with the American people and at worst might sound unpatriotic, most Democratic lawmakers who would have preferred to criticize the White House opted for silence.[38]

Unsigning the ICC statute underlined the US state-centered and unilateralist view that realizing justice for victims of serious human rights abuses was part of individual states' sovereignty and not an issue for global governance (i.e., an international institution intervening in internal affairs). The Bush administration's realist approach toward international relations emphasized the importance of state sovereignty and national interests that questioned the utility of international institutions in general. As Under Secretary for Political Affairs Marc Grossman argued, "states, not international institutions are primarily

---

35   I.H. Daalder and J.M. Lindsay, "Bush's Foreign Policy Revolution," in F.I. Greenstein, ed., *The George W. Bush Presidency: An Early Assessment* (Baltimore, MD: Johns Hopkins University Press, 2003), pp. 100–137.

36   C. Rice, "Campaign 2000: Promoting the National Interest," *Foreign Affairs* 79, no. 1 (2000): 62.

37   Authorization for Use of Military Force, 107th Congress, 2nd Session, 18 September 2001, S.J. Res. 23.

38   Daalder and Lindsay, "Bush's Foreign Policy Revolution," p. 122.

responsible for ensuring justice in the international system."[39] However, by withdrawing from the treaty, the United States also lost any form of control it might have had otherwise in shaping the ICC and its workings and also the possibility of using the ICC for its own interests. This raised concerns for US officials and might be a reason why—after the initial hostile and active opposition—the Bush administration had to change its approach toward the ICC in later years.

Unsigning the treaty was condemned by a number of different groups. Several members of Congress sent a letter to President Bush in which they objected that this action "has damaged the moral credibility of the United States and serves as a US repudiation of the notion that war criminals and perpetrators of genocide should be brought to justice."[40] They argued that the United States had the same values as those intended by the ICC and that reject- ing the institution "now places the United States in the company of notorious human rights abusers like Iraq, North Korea, China, Cuba, Libya, and Burma." The European Union (EU) also formally issued a declaration on behalf of its member states criticizing the US position and stating its "disappointment and regret."[41] It argued that the EU respected the sovereign right of the United States not to sign the treaty, but also believed that "this unilateral action may have undesirable consequences on multilateral treaty-making and generally on the rule of law in international relations."

4   US Actions in Opposition to the ICC

Because the United States could not prevent the ICC from coming into force, it undertook a number of actions to undermine the workings of the court and to exempt US nationals from its reach.

39   M. Grossman, "American Foreign Policy and the International Criminal Court," remarks delivered at the Center for Strategic and International Studies, Washington, DC, 6 May 2002.

40   Congressional Letter to President George W. Bush, 22 May 2002, signed by forty-four Democrats and one Republican, which is further evidence of the division between realist and liberal foreign policy approaches (unilateral focus on national interests vs. multilat- eral engagement with international institutions).

41   Declaration by the Presidency on Behalf of the European Union on the Position of the U.S. Towards the International Criminal Court, 13 May 2002, Madrid and Brussels.

4.1   *UN Resolutions*

In 2002, the United States vetoed the extension of the UN peacekeeping mission to Bosnia and Herzegovina and also threatened to withdraw all of its other UN peacekeeping forces because it claimed that US soldiers were at risk of possible ICC jurisdiction on that territory. Justifying this action, the US ambassador to the UN, John Negroponte, argued that even though it was unfortunate that the United States had to veto the extension of the mission, it was not prepared to ask its peacekeepers "to accept the additional risk of politicized prosecutions before a court whose jurisdiction over our people the Government of the United States does not accept."[42] He maintained that the United States remained committed to contributing to UN peacekeeping missions, but that a compromise to solve this problem needed to be found. The United States proposed complete immunity for UN peacekeepers by adopting a resolution in line with Article 16 of the statute with the prospect of renewing it after twelve months.

Despite criticisms expressed by a number of states (most of which were not allowed to vote), Resolution 1422 was adopted unanimously by the members of the Security Council, exempting peacekeeping personnel from the ICC's jurisdiction for a period of twelve months. The resolution was renewed for another twelve months in 2003.[43]

In May 2004, the United States sought to renew Resolution 1422 for a second time, but it faced stiff opposition from a number of states and eventually decided to withdraw the request. One major argument of the opposition was the growing concern about revelations of abuse against prisoners at Abu Ghraib prison in Iraq by US troops. Then Secretary-General Kofi Annan believed that requesting an exemption for the United States in this situation would seem hypocritical and would impose double standards because the United States was accused of having violated universal standards of justice in the way it treated Iraqi prisoners.[44] US officials interpreted the situation to the contrary, arguing that Abu Ghraib proved that "the United States does stand for justice and will itself impose justice on any members of our services who might undertake things that constitute international crimes.... But it's a matter for us to take care of and not for some court with some jurisdiction that we're not party to."[45] The United States thereby emphasized that, even though

---

42   UN Security Council, Record of the 4563rd Security Council Meeting, 30 June 2002.

43   Resolution 1487 (2003) was adopted with twelve votes in favor and three abstentions (from Germany, France, and the Syrian Arab Republic), UN Doc. no. S/Res/1487.

44   Secretary-General's press encounter on arrival at UN headquarters (unofficial transcript), 17 June 2004.

45   R. Boucher, State Department noon briefing, 23 June 2004.

it proclaimed to be committed to protecting and enforcing justice norms, this could only be achieved through national courts without external intervention. However, then secretary of state Colin Powell admitted that Abu Ghraib had affected the way people looked at the ICC and conceded that it was less likely the United States would be able to achieve another renewal of the resolution under these circumstances.[46] The United States eventually decided to withdraw its request, arguing that it did not want to engage the Security Council in a "prolonged and divisive debate."[47]

This reversal of strict opposition to the ICC is evidence of a constructivist approach toward foreign policy making whereby foreign policy is what elites can make of it in a given context. The United States still acted from the premise of its national interests, which are not static but an ongoing process of practice and interaction, and therefore change over time. The United States was forced to change its position given the circumstances, and had to adjust its policy accordingly. However, it still emphasized the importance of its own interests and therefore issued a statement to the UN in which it argued that failure to renew the resolution would mean that the United States "will need to take into account the risk of ICC review when determining contributions to UN authorized or established operations."[48] A few days later, the Defense Department announced that it would withdraw personnel from peacekeeping missions in Ethiopia and Eritrea and also Kosovo because they were perceived to be at risk of possible ICC jurisdiction. Altogether, nine individuals were withdrawn at the time. This was done to continue US opposition to the ICC, but less radically than what was done previously, which showed that policy had to be adjusted to changing circumstances.

4.2 Additional Measures

Since the UN resolutions only protected US personnel acting as part of UN peacekeeping missions and only for a limited period of time, the United States sought to implement additional measures to permanently exempt all of its nationals from the ICC. The two most important measures implemented by the George W. Bush administration were bilateral immunity agreements (BIAS) and the American Service-Members' Protection Act (ASPA).

---

46   P. Richter, "Iraq Prison Abuse Undermines U.S. Hope for War Crimes Waiver," *Los Angeles Times*, 23 June 2004.

47   Boucher, State Department noon briefing.

48   J. Aita, "U.S. Drops Effort to Secure ICC Immunity for Peacekeepers," 23 June 2004, available at www.usembassy.it/file2004_06/alia/a4062304.htm.

The bilateral so-called Article 98 agreements[49] between the United States and individual states stipulate that US personnel and nationals cannot be detained, arrested, or sent to the ICC. The original intent of Article 98 was to cover so-called status-of-forces agreements (SOFA) between the United States and other countries (mainly NATO states) that give the United States primacy in exercising jurisdiction over US personnel acting on foreign soil. The Bush administration, however, used this provision to seek exemptions from a number of different states, exerting strong diplomatic and financial pressure if states refused to sign with "many of the states approached ... too weak to resist."[50]

At the time of this writing, 102 states have signed BIAs, including 52 ICC member states.[51] Larger and more influential states, such as Canada and states in the EU, have refused to sign BIAs, arguing that doing so would be inconsistent with their obligations as ICC states parties. The European Parliament even issued an official position in which it not only outlines its opposition to these agreements, but also argues that "ratifying such an agreement is incompatible with membership of the EU."[52]

In addition, George W. Bush signed the ASPA into law,[53] authorizing the United States to use "all means necessary, including military force, to rescue a US citizen taken into the court's custody." This provision led the ASPA to be called "the Hague Invasion Act." It limits US cooperation with the ICC, including the ability to collaborate, extradite, support, fund, and share classified information. In addition, the ASPA imposes prohibition of military aid to states parties of the ICC, but allows waivers if it is in the US national interest or if states signed Article 98 agreements. It also allows waivers for NATO states and major NATO allies.

---

49   The United States claims that these agreements are in line with Article 98(2) of the ICC's statute, which states that "the Court may not proceed with a request for surrender which would require the requested State to act inconsistently with its obligations under international agreements."

50   D. McGoldrick, "Political and Legal Reponses to the ICC," in D. McGoldrick, P. Rowe, and E. Donnelly, eds., *The Permanent International Criminal Court: Legal and Policy Issues* (Oxford, UK: Hart, 2004), pp. 389–449.

51   See the American Non-Government Organizations Coalition for the International Criminal Court (AMICC), www.amicc.org.

52   European Parliament resolution on the International Criminal Court (ICC) (2002), P5_TA (2002)0449.

53   The ASPA was already proposed in 2000, but only a heavily modified version that included a number of exemptions allowing for presidential discretion was eventually adopted in August 2002.

5   Changing US Perceptions

Since the ICC's first actions in 2004, however, the United States seems to have adopted a more pragmatic approach toward the court, and a shift is discernible from the initial firm opposition to a fresh assessment of the court.

One reason for this change in attitude is the admission by a number of influential US politicians that BIAS and the ASPA are actually harmful to US interests. Cuts in military assistance to countries that have not signed BIAS mean lost opportunities of military training provided by US troops aimed at strengthening US links to other countries, particularly in its fight against terrorism abroad. The Defense Department severely criticized the effects that these measures have had on military operations and cooperation in strategically important regions (such as Latin America and Africa). In 2006, a US Army commander argued that the restrictions placed on US assistance in such countries gave China the opportunity to fill a void and step up its efforts to gain influence.[54] Furthermore, Condoleezza Rice admitted that the Article 98 agreements are like "shooting ourselves in the foot."[55] In September 2006, Congress passed an amendment that repeals the section of the ASPA that restricts international military education and training (IMET) funds to ICC states parties. By September 2008, the United States waived and retracted a large number of restrictions related to countries refusing to sign BIAS as well as all ASPA sanction provisions. The United States conceded that the policy of Article 98 restrictions had failed and needed to be eliminated "once and for all."[56]

5.1   *US and ICC Action in Darfur*
Contrary to its overall hostility toward the ICC in general, the United States demonstrated its support for ICC action in Darfur from the start. The United States actively engaged in drafting a UN resolution that was eventually put to a vote in March 2005. The United States did not veto this resolution (it abstained) and even declared to be prepared to assist the court if asked. This resolution is controversial, however, because no other nonstate party can be prosecuted without its consent by the ICC. The United States thus ensured that

---

54   Posture Statement of General Bantz J. Craddock, United States Army commander, Senate Armed Services Committee, 109th Congress, 2nd Session, 14 March 2006, p. 26.

55   US Department of State, On the Record Briefing, Secretary of State Condoleezza Rice, en route to San Juan, Puerto Rico, March 10, 2006, http://montevideo.usembassy.gov/usaweb/paginas/2006/06-094aEN.shtml.

56   US Congress, House of Representatives, *Foreign Assistance in the Americas*, House Foreign Affairs Subcommittee on the Western Hemisphere, 110th Congress, 2nd Session, 16 September 2008, p. 12.

its own citizens continue to remain outside the court's jurisdiction. This was important not only from a practical point of view, but also because it meant that the United States was not seen as giving outright support for the ICC and as having abandoned its concerns regarding the court. The abstention can be seen as a trade-off: the US did not want to legitimize the ICC by voting in favor of the resolution but, because it had called the situation in Darfur "genocide," it invoked an obligation to act under international law.

The George W. Bush administration also faced a lot of domestic pressure from its own ranks to act in Darfur. John Danforth, former ambassador to the UN, admitted that the administration labeled the situation as genocide to please the Christian right ahead of the presidential elections. He said that "it was of great interest to Christian conservatives in the United States, a good part of President Bush's base and it was something that was of personal interest to him."[57]

This conflict between public diplomacy toward Darfur and the opposition against the ICC was politically unsustainable. By abstaining, the United States could find a compromise that allowed it to maintain its opposition to the ICC while, at the same time, showing tacit support for the international rule of law against genocide. As J.G. Ralph argues, however, the way "the administration was able to use the Security Council referral process to negotiate exemptions for its own citizens suggests that US policy had not really shifted at all."[58]

A number of US officials acknowledged the role of the ICC in the conflict in Darfur. The State Department's chief lawyer, John Bellinger, conceded that the United States could not delegitimize a court that has more than 100 member states, including a number of major US allies. He argued that, even though the Bush administration would never allow US nationals to be tried by the ICC, "we do acknowledge that it has a role to play in the overall system of international justice."[59] In September 2006, Republican politicians John McCain and Bob Dole agreed that the ICC had jurisdiction to prosecute war crimes committed in Darfur, thereby sending a strong signal that US leaders accepted the existence of the ICC and were willing to prosecute high officials in office.[60]

Overall, it can be argued that the initial active opposition of the Bush administration gradually gave way to a more pragmatic approach toward the ICC as

---

57   "Never Again," interview with John Danforth, *Panorama*, BBC One, 3 July 2005.
58   J.G. Ralph, "Anarchy Is What Criminal Lawyers and Other Actors Make of It: International Criminal Justice as an Institution of International and World Society," in S.C. Roach, ed., *Governance, Order, and the International Criminal Court Between Realpolitik and a Cosmopolitan Court* (Oxford: Oxford University Press, 2009), pp. 133–153.
59   J. Bravin, "US Warms to Hague Tribunal," *Wall Street Journal*, 14 June 2006.
60   J. McCain and B. Dole, "Rescue Darfur Now," *Washington Post*, 10 September 2006, p. B7.

a working global governance institution for some of the most serious human rights abuses. This change was partly due to some vocal opponents leaving the administration, such as Bolton in 2006, and also because of pragmatic considerations over time. Clint Williamson, then ambassador for war crimes issues, argued that there was a need to bridge the divide between the United States and its allies over the ICC: "so what has happened is, you have this quiet change. No statement that policy was changing, and certainly no admission that the initial approach to the ICC was in any way wrong. The change has been incremental.... What we have done is just implement this policy on the working levels."[61] The United States acknowledged that the ICC was an appropriate forum to try some of the most serious human rights abuses in certain cases. It also showed, however, that the United States started to use the court to protect its national interests whenever it suited its policy agenda. It used the resolution on Sudan to protect its own soldiers and also to appease the Christian right and other interest groups that wanted to see action in Darfur. Abstaining meant that the United States could act without having to detract its public opposition to the court. This demonstrates that national interests are not fixed but, in line with a constructivist approach, can be seen as changing: once the Bush administration realized that the ICC could be used to protect its soldiers, it changed its rhetoric to suit its national interests.

The United States maintained that it opposed the ICC because it had the potential to limit state sovereignty by enforcing universal values through an international institution that was unaccountable to the UN and also to the United States. Countermeasures such as the Article 98 agreements, however, started to prevent the United States from exerting influence in strategically important states in its war on terror. Rather than continuing its active opposition, it found the ICC to be a useful element of "coercive diplomacy"[62] against rogue states such as Sudan. The United States could use the ICC as a tool without having to use military force to intervene in a situation it had labeled genocide. As A.L. George argues,

> in employing coercive diplomacy ... one gives the adversary an opportunity to stop or back off before one resorts to military operations [and, further] coercive diplomacy is an attractive strategy insofar that it offers

61   Century Foundation, transcript, "Reassessing the International Criminal Court: Ten Years Past Rome" (Washington, DC: Century Foundation, 13 January 2009).

62   For an in-depth account of the idea and use of coercive diplomacy, see A.L. George, *Forceful Persuasion: Coercive Diplomacy as an Alternative to War* (Washington, DC: United States Institute of Peace Press, 1991).

the possibility of achieving one's objectives in a crisis economically, with little or no bloodshed, fewer political and psychological costs, and often with less risk of unwanted escalation than does traditional military strategy.[63]

This is an attractive strategy for a powerful state like the United States that can influence a weaker state with relatively little costs and risks.

6   The Approach of President Obama's Administration

As George W. Bush left the White House and Barack Obama took the oath of office, it was anticipated that the US policy toward the ICC would continue to be cooperative and less hostile. It is still too early to be certain how the Obama administration will choose to relate to the court, but initial signs point to positive engagement. President Obama outlined the strengthening of international institutions as one of his administration's foreign policy priorities, which signals a rhetoric shift from the Bush administration's unilateral policy-making toward increased multilateralism.

Secretary of State Hillary Clinton laid out the Obama administration's approach by stating that "we will end hostility towards the ICC, and look for opportunities to encourage effective ICC action in ways to promote US interests by bringing war criminals to justice."[64] Indeed, the Obama administration seems to engage in a more multilateral approach toward international human rights in general. Susan E. Rice, US ambassador to the UN, stated that the United States is committed to ending violations of international humanitarian law in conjunction with the UN and other international organizations. She also argued that the ICC "looks to become an important and credible instrument for trying to hold accountable the senior leadership responsible for atrocities committed in the Congo, Uganda, and Darfur."[65]

The United States participated actively in the 2010 Review Conference in Kampala, in which issues such as the definition of the crime of aggression were negotiated. The United States was able to take part as a nonstate party, although joining the ICC would have given it even stronger leverage in the

---

63   Ibid.
64   H.R. Clinton, Questions for the Record, Senator John Kerry: Senate Foreign Relations Committee, 11th Congress, 1st session, 13 January 2009.
65   S.E. Rice, Statement by Ambassador Susan E. Rice on Respect for International Humanitarian Law, in the Security Council, US-UN Press Release 020/09, New York, 29 January 2009.

negotiations. The United States sent a delegation to the ICC's Assembly of States Parties meeting in November 2009, which was the first time that it had attended a meeting of the ICC since 2001. At this stage, however, it is not realistic to expect the United States to ratify the ICC statute, but it is likely that the Obama administration will engage in first steps toward it—such as reinstating the US signature to be able to participate in and support the court's meetings and activities. Arguably, such action would not be a complete change from US policies toward the end of the Bush administration, but it would indicate a further movement toward improving its relationship with the court.

7   Conclusion

US actions in opposition to the ICC were, to a large extent, based on the understanding that human rights law enforcement can be administered only by sovereign states and not through a mechanism of global governance of justice. The United States is predominantly concerned about protecting its national interests and in maintaining its unique powerful position in international relations. Yet the United States is inconsistent in its approach to international justice dispensed through international courts: it showed strong support for the ad hoc tribunals, but engaged in hostile actions against the ICC. The United States opposes the ICC because it is an independent institution not controlled by the UN Security Council, which means that there is at least a theoretical possibility that the ICC can compromise US sovereignty on issues related to universally recognized human rights norms. The United States changed its active opposition toward the court when it realized the utility of such an international regime for genocide and crimes against humanity had been proven in practice. This was both a shift in the US position and a rearticulation of its stance toward the ICC that had been seen since the Rome Conference.

The initial actions taken in opposition to the ICC are problematic because other states are being prevented from cooperating and assisting the court in its operations. These actions were intended to intimidate the court's supporters with the aim of achieving further concessions and exclusions from the ICC's jurisdiction. They were also based on a belief that the United States could prevent the court from coming into being. So far, however, the ICC has proved to be too strong, which is due to the strong foundation on which it is built. Since the end of World War II, a number of developments toward increased global governance of international criminal justice and international law have taken place. The ad hoc tribunals, for instance, were the last in a line of numerous changes in the way human rights are being enforced internationally. The ICC is the latest step toward internalizing enforcement of justice and human rights norms that are incorporated in international law. A large number of states see the ICC as a necessary global governance institution for the enforcement of such laws that includes enough safeguards to prevent a dramatic erosion of state sovereignty. The ICC is only a court of last resort. It is aimed not at changing existing power relations and undermining the predominant position of the United States, but at protecting human rights.

The fact that the United States abstained from the Security Council resolutions related to the ICC action in Darfur is evidence that it is trying to find more practical ways to work with the court and its supporters instead of continuing its active opposition. The US government even began to cooperate with the ICC in calling on the government of Sudan to enforce the ICC's arrest warrant for Sudanese president Omar Hassan al-Bashir for orchestrating genocide in the Darfur region and in acknowledging the ICC's role in the overall system of justice. This is an important step because, in the world following September 11, it is necessary to be consistent with existing fundamental principles of the liberal democratic order, which includes multilateral action and recognizes the importance of universal principles, human rights, and international law. As David Held argues, "what is needed is a movement of global, not American or French or British, justice and legitimacy."[66]

66   D. Held, "Globalization, International Law and Human Rights," public lecture presented at the Human Rights Centre, University of Connecticut (20 September 2005).

CHAPTER 17

Global and Local Policy Responses to the Resource Trap

Gilles Carbonnier, Fritz Brugger and Jana Krause[1]

Energy security ranks among the top priorities of the Organisation for Economic Co-operation and Development (OECD) and emerging economies alike, whose foreign relations agenda is often dictated by a permanent concern to secure oil and gas supplies. Yet there is no such thing as a global governance system for energy. Instead, there is a myriad of regional and sectoral organizations as well as bilateral agreements that address specific concerns between selected producer and consumer states. It is true that the International Energy Forum (IEF) has served as a global platform for dialogue between consumer, producer, and transit countries since the beginning of the 1990s. But the IEF is not an intergovernmental organization and its recommendations are not binding. Investment and trade agreements are negotiated in a piecemeal manner under bilateral and regional agreements or treaties like the Energy Charter Treaty.

Against this background, it is no wonder that industrialized countries do not make poverty alleviation their first priority vis-à-vis resource-rich developing countries. Addressing the resource curse is not a top priority as long as it does not put energy security at risk. Governance and development in fragile, resource-rich states have nonetheless drawn increasingly more attention from rich countries because of the ensuing risks in terms of regional stability and energy supply. Donor governments—many of which are net oil importers and home to multinational extractive industries—have launched and supported several multistakeholder initiatives over the past decade with a view to addressing the resource trap jointly with nongovernmental organizations (NGOs) and businesses. NGOs have become natural partners: they were

---

* This chapter was originally published in Global Governance, Volume 17, Issue 2, 2011.

1 Gilles Carbonnier is professor of development economics at the Graduate Institute of International and Development Studies (GIIDS) in Geneva. He is editor in chief of the International Development Policy series and deputy director of the Centre on Conflict, Development and Peacebuilding. Fritz Brugger is a Senior Scientist at the Centre for Development Studies of the Swiss Federal Institute of Technology in Zurich (ETHZ). Jana Krause is Associate Professor in the Department of Political Science at the University of Oslo.

instrumental in promoting these multistakeholder processes through global campaigns calling for increased transparency, accountability, and respect for human rights in the extractive sector. The rationale for businesses to join in is primarily dictated by a concern to address security, reputation, and legal risks.

There is as yet little evidence of how effective these recent multistakeholder mechanisms are in fulfilling their promise. They have only started to be implemented at field level in resource-rich developing countries over the past few years. It may be premature to assess their effectiveness, which may explain the paucity of rigorous impact evaluation to date. It is nonetheless possible to assess their relevance with regard to the emerging conclusions from the resource-curse literature and the adequacy of their overall design with regard to their objectives. To do so, we resort to regime theory as a heuristic tool and follow the approach of Oran Young and Marc Levy in the case of international environmental regimes.[2] Like them, we focus on the causal connections between the regimes and subsequent behavioral changes, or on the pathways through which multistakeholder regimes in the extractive sector are meant to alter the behavior of state and nonstate actors.

In the first two sections, we show that high expectations are placed on civil society organizations (CSOs), reflecting the neoliberal development model[3] and the general context of weak statehood. They are entrusted with the responsibility to monitor compliance by governments and businesses and are expected to establish effective checks on the otherwise discretionary power of the ruling elite. We then highlight that the very concept of civil society remains fuzzy and the ability of CSOs to live up to the expectations raises serious doubts, particularly in weak but resource-rich states. Finally, we focus on the implementation of the Extractive Industries Transparency Initiative (EITI) in Nigeria and Azerbaijan and examine how far CSOs have been able and willing to play the pivotal role to which they have been assigned.

1   Addressing the Resource Curse

Escaping the resource curse is widely considered as one of the major developmental challenges in resource-rich developing countries. Yet there is no

---

2   Oran Young and Marc Levy, eds., *The Effectiveness of International Environmental Regimes: Causal Connections and Behavioral Mechanisms* (Boston: MIT Press, 1999).

3   Tobias Debiel and Monika Sticht, "Towards a New Profile? Development, Humanitarian and Conflict Resolution NGOs in the Age of Globalisation," Institute for Development and Peace Report No. 79 (Duisburg, Germany: University of Duisburg-Essen, 2005); Christoph Spurk, "Understanding Civil Society," in Thania Paffenholz, ed., *Civil Society and Peacebuilding: A Critical Assessment* (Boulder: Lynne Rienner, 2010), pp. 3–29.

consensus on the precise conditions required to escape the resource curse, let alone if the curse argument is a valid one. As detailed by Jonathan Di John in this special issue,[4] the scholarly literature finds increasing evidence that the quality of institutions is a key determinant of whether a resource-rich developing country is able to avoid the resource curse.[5] The rent-cycling theory highlights that high rent prevents the alignment of the elite interests with those of the majority of the population. It provides incentives for the elites to seek self-enrichment rather than public goods and economic growth.[6] The literature highlights the crucial role of constraints on the power of the ruling elite and of effective accountability mechanisms.

This first widely cited example of resource curse illustrates this well; that is, the rapid decline of early modern Spain in the seventeenth century, which suffered from Dutch disease and the rentier-state syndrome as a direct result of the extraordinary amount of precious metals it extracted from its Latin American colonies.[7] Mauricio Drelichman forcefully argues that the silver windfall eroded Spanish institutions and harmed its nascent industry.[8] Before the extractive boom, the country was evolving in the direction of limiting the power of the king in favor of the Cortes, a quasi-parliamentary body with representatives of the main cities of Castile in which an emerging merchant class was to gain influence.[9] The resource rent, which amounted up to a third of total crown revenue, allowed the king to set policies unchecked by any powerful actor outside the monarchy and to embark in costly war enterprises.[10] Silver revenue diminished drastically at the beginning of the seventeenth century, stretching the tax base to its limit and precipitating Castile's decline for almost three centuries. Mauricio Drelichman and Hans-Joachim Voth contend that

---

4   Jonathan Di John, "Is There Really a Resource Curse? A Critical Survey of Theory and Evidence," in this special issue.

5   Halvor Mehlum, Karls Moene, and Ragnar Torvik, "Institutions and the Resource Curse," *Economic Journal* 116, no. 508 (2006): 1–20.

6   Richard Auty, "Elites, Rent-cycling and Development: Adjustment to Land Scarcity in Mauritius, Kenya and Côte d'Ivoire," *Development Policy Review* 28, no. 4 (2010): 411–433.

7   I.A.A. Thompson and Bartolomé Yun Casalilla, eds., *The Castilian Crisis of the Seventeenth Century* (Cambridge: Cambridge University Press, 1994).

8   Mauricio Drechliman, "The Curse of Moctezuma: American Silver and the Dutch Disease," *Exploration in Economics History* 42, no. 3 (2005): 349–380.

9   Bartolomé Yun Casalilla, "The Castilian Aristocracy in the Seventeenth Century: Crisis, Refeudalisation, or Political Offensive?" in I.A.A. Thompson and Bartolomé Yun Casalilla, eds., *The Castilian Crisis of the Seventeenth Century* (Cambridge: Cambridge University Press, 1994), p. 300.

10   Mauricio Drelichman and Hans-Joachim Voth, "Institutions and the Resource Curse in Early Modern Spain," in Elhanan Helpman, ed., *Institutions and Economic Performance* (Cambridge: Harvard University Press, 2008), p. 30.

this explains why Spain lost out to its main competitors of the time—Britain and the Netherlands—that were relatively resource scarce.

The Spanish example is echoed by a contemporary counterexample: Botswana. The country took advantage of its diamond riches after independence to boost development. It experienced the world's highest per capita growth rate from 1966 to 2000, albeit with raising inequalities. Daron Acemoglu, Simon Johnson, and James Robinson explain this "Botswana miracle" by the existence of precolonial institutions that placed constraints on the political elite. These institutions survived British colonial rule and contributed to the consolidation of the institutions of private property.[11] They argue that Botswana averted the resource curse thanks to the nature of its political system with institutions that constrained rulers and permitted the inclusion of a broad cross section of the society, unlike Spain three centuries earlier. They contrast this with the failure of many resource-rich fragile states like Equatorial Guinea and Turkmenistan to translate extraction into development.

2   Assessing Multistakeholder Initiatives in the Extractive Sector

Scholars are still debating not only the precise interactions between institutions, governance, and the resource curse,[12] but also the drivers of institutional change[13] and the critical factors to improve governance.[14] On the policy side nonetheless, a number of multistakeholder initiatives have been launched to address the institutional dimension of resource-curse dynamics. The most prominent ones on which we focus below are the Extractive Industries Transparency Initiative, the Kimberley Process Certification Scheme for diamond trade (KPCS), and the Voluntary Principles on Security and Human Rights in the extractive sector (VPS). These global public-private partnerships are located in the policy space between states and markets and present several common characteristics. They are voluntary (i.e., based on the self-interest

---

11   Daron Acemoglu, Simon Johnson, and James Robinson, "An African Success: Botswana," Centre for Economic and Policy Research Discussion Paper No. 3219 (London: CEPR, 2001).

12   For example, Halvor Mehlum, Karls Moene, and Ragnar Torvik, "Cursed by Resources or Institutions?" *World Economy* 29, no. 8 (2006): 1117–1131.

13   Paul Stevens and Evelyn Dietsche, "Resource Curse: An Analysis of Causes, Experiences and Possible Ways Forward," *Energy Policy* 36, no. 1 (2008): 56–65.

14   For example, Ivar Kolstad and Arne Wiig, "Political Economy Models of the Resource Curse: Implications for Policy and Research," Chr. Michelsen Institute Working Paper No. 6 (Bergen, Norway: CMI, 2008).

of each stakeholder), they are horizontal and preserve the autonomy of every participant, they are multiactor and participatory with joint governance and decisionmaking mechanisms, and they address global and often intergenerational issues.[15]

These initiatives display regime characteristics as defined by Stephen D. Krasner in that they are based on "implicit or explicit principles, norms, rules and decisionmaking procedures around which actors' expectations converge."[16] Namely, they establish new standards or extend existing norms of international public law to nonstate actors, look at incentive structures to modify actors' preferences and behavior, and typically entrust civil society with monitoring and whistle-blowing in order to constrain the power of the political and economic elite. Table 17.1 lists some of the main policy initiatives displaying regime characteristics that involve nonstate actors.

Most of these initiatives have not been operational long enough to provide solid evidence of eventual success in establishing sustainable accountability frameworks and governance mechanisms in producer states. Yet we can assess the design effectiveness following Young and Levy's evaluation of

TABLE 17.1   Multistakeholder initiatives that address resource-curse dynamics and display regime characteristics

Launched by	Initiative (launch year)
Multistakeholder	Extractive Industries Transparency Initiative, 2003; Kimberley Process Certification Scheme, 2003; Voluntary Principles on Security and Human Rights, 1999
International organization	Chad-Cameroon Oil Pipeline Project, launched by the World Bank, 1998
Business	Sustainable Development Framework, launched by the International Council on Mining and Metals, 2001; Responsible Jewelry Council Certification, 2005
Civil society	Fair Trade Diamond Standard and Certification Scheme, launched by Transfair USA, 2008

---

15   Ingue Kaul, "Exploring the Policy Space Between Market and States: Global Public Private Partnerships," in Inge Kaul and Pedro Conceição, eds., *The New Public Finance* (Oxford: Oxford University Press, 2006), pp. 95–146.

16   Stephen D. Krasner, "Sharing Sovereignty: New Institutions for Collapsed and Failing States," *International Security* 29, no. 2 (2004): 85–120.

environmental regimes looking at six different behavioral pathways through which regimes are expected to affect the behavior and decisions of major players (see Table 17.2).[17] Examining these six complementary channels, Young and Levy's main findings are twofold. First, modifying key actors' utility functions and preferences may be effective channels through which regimes can affect their behavior (regimes as utility modifier or enhancer of cooperation). Second, almost every successful regime deploys "a complex dynamic in which several types of mechanisms operate in tandem to produce the behavioral effects."[18]

For each of the four multistakeholder initiatives in the extractive sector, we briefly outline below how they evolved, analyze the behavioral pathways through which they are designed to effect change, and discuss their effectiveness.

The EITI has shown a remarkable capacity to evolve since its inception. The twelve general principles adopted in 2003 ($EITI_0$) were based on the assumption that transparency over payments made by extractive firms to host governments were critical to avert the resource curse. Two years later, the participants adopted eight implementing criteria ($EITI_1$) and, in 2007, agreed on a validation procedure based on minimum standards that host countries have to fulfill to acquire EITI compliant status ($EITI_2$).

As a regime, $EITI_0$ was meant to effect change through the moral authority of revenue transparency as its founding principle. With $EITI_1$, the regime provided a framework for cooperation to better address the classical collective action problem where utility-maximizing actors fail to reap joint gains or avoid joint losses. $EITI_1$ provides incentives under which rational actors adapt their strategic behavior that results in enhanced recorded government revenue. In order to change the power balance within the members of the regime, CSOs are introduced and entrusted with the task of holding governments and companies to account. As a fourth pathway, the validation scheme introduced in 2007 is meant to influence the cost-benefit calculus ($EITI_2$): governments may find it easier to access development finance and the international capital markets when they can show compliance with the EITI validation requirements.

Yet the results by July 2010 were far below expectations. First, evidence of additional revenue recorded as a result of EITI in the thirty-two implementing countries remained sporadic. Second, the introduction of a rigorous validation process may have strengthened the credibility of the initiative, but made it necessary to extend the final validation deadline for sixteen candidate countries and to expel Equatorial Guinea and São Tome and Principe, which reflected a dramatic lack of sufficient progress on the ground. The situation has since improved with the validation of six more countries at the fifth EITI

---

17   Young and Levy, eds., *The Effectiveness of International Environmental Regimes.*
18   Ibid., p. 261.

TABLE 17.2   Pathways through which regimes influence actors' behavior

Actor assumption	Utilitarist and unitary actors, rational utility maximizers		Unitary behavior but relaxes the rational utility maximizing assumption			Further relaxes the unitary actor assumption
Regime as	Utility modifier	Enhancer of cooperation	Bestower of authority	Social learning facilitator	Role definer	Agent of internal realignment
Effect	Influences actor's costs and benefits calculus	Allows participants to achieve collective outcome that lies closer to the Pareto frontier	Actors regard rules as legitimate and comply without detailed cost-benefit	Changes information, discourses, and values. Alters motives and provides new perspectives	(Re)defines roles and shapes new identities and interests	Creates new constituencies, shifts balance among subgroups, restructures alignment
Behavioral pathways used by	CCP_0, $EITI_2$, $KPCS_0$	$EITI_1$, VP_1, $KPCS_0$	VP_0, $EITI_0$	VP_0	CCP_0, $KPCS_0$	$EITI_0$, CCP_0, VP_0

CCP: Chad-Cameroon Oil Pipeline Project; EITI: Extractive Industries Transparency Initiative; KPCS: Kimberley Process Certification Scheme; VP: Voluntary Principles on Security and Human Rights. The subscript numbers (0, 1, 2) refer to evolution over time: 0 indicates behavioral pathways by the time of the establishment of the multistakeholder initiative; 1 and 2 correspond to behavioral pathways deployed over the medium term and long term, respectively.

SOURCE: ADAPTED FROM ORAN YOUNG AND MARC LEVY, EDS., THE EFFECTIVENESS OF INTERNATIONAL ENVIRONMENTAL REGIMES: CAUSAL CONNECTIONS AND BEHAVIORAL MECHANISMS (BOSTON: MIT PRESS, 1999)

Global Conference, which took place in Paris in March 2011, raising the number of compliant countries to eleven out of thirty-five participating countries. Third, experience in several EITI implementing countries nonetheless shows that local civil society remains too weak to fulfill its watchdog function. It is often either co-opted or marginalized by the government, or simply lacks the capacity to hold governments and business to account,[19] as we show below

---

19   For example, Inge Amundsen and Cesaltina Abreu, "Civil Society in Angola: Inroads, Space and Accountability," Chr. Michelsen Institute Report No. 14 (Bergen, Norway: CMI, 2006).

in the case of Nigeria and Azerbaijan. In addition, civil society should be able to process and react on the information made available through increased transparency in order to put effective constraint on revenue misuse by the ruling elite. It must also be able to rely on independent media and enjoy a space for democratic deliberation,[20] both of which are often lacking in EITI candidate countries.

The Voluntary Principles (VPs) were initiated by the US and UK governments with international human rights NGOs and extractive industries headquartered in these two countries. Launched in 2000, the VP process first focused on establishing the principles and describing how they apply to extractive industries in their relations with public and private security forces (VP_0). Extractive firms supported the process and welcomed the principles as legitimate and authoritative. Yet this proved overly optimistic: international NGOs complained about the lack of progress in implementing the principles on the ground and criticized the absence of clear admission criteria and the lack of significant monitoring and reporting requirements.[21] Under mounting pressure from NGOs that threatened to quit, the initiative addressed strategic behavior by introducing specific accountability mechanisms in 2007 (VP_1). The members collectively agreed to strengthen the minimum requirements for extractive industries' participation in the initiative and established clearer dispute settlement provisions in case of noncompliance. They introduced a new mechanism to exclude noncompliant members with a view to enhancing the VPs effectiveness. They further required participatory companies to publicly report on implementation on a regular basis.

As a regime, VP_0 was conceptualized as a learning facilitator and a bestower of authority. It further relied on NGOs as agents of internal realignment. The latter constituency was instrumental in strengthening the process. The transition from VP_0 to VP_1 deployed a fourth behavioral pathway, establishing the VPs as an enhancer of cooperation between the stakeholders involved.

International NGOs were successful in strengthening the VP process by enhancing the incentives for cooperation over the years, together with some of the more progressive industries that put peer pressure on stragglers. Unlike domestic CSOs in weak states, international NGOs enjoyed the resources, skills,

---

20   Ivar Kolstad and Arne Wiig, "Is Transparency the Key to Reducing Corruption in Resource-rich Countries?" *World Development* 37, no. 3 (2009): 521–532.

21   Bennett Freeman, "The Voluntary Principles at 10: Time to Complete the Work of Construction, Get on with the Job of Implementation," www.institutehrb.org/blogs/board/voluntary_principles_at_10.html (accessed 1 August 2010).

and capacity to make a difference and have been able to successfully use the threat of withdrawal as a bargaining tool.

The Kimberley Process Certification Scheme was established in 2003 to ban conflict diamonds from reaching the (legal) market. Seven years later, sixty-seven countries participate in the scheme together with the diamond industry. The initiators succeeded in establishing a new intergovernmental agreement in just three years with the support of the industry. This success can be explained by the deep concern of industry and producing states about the potential impact of the blood diamond controversy on consumers. Although two NGOs were instrumental in bringing the KPCS into being, civil society enjoys only an observer status in the process, participating in selected working groups.

Unlike the EITI and the VPs, the KPCS as a regime has not seen an accumulation of behavioral pathways deployed over time. Since its inception, it has provided a framework for cooperation in which the member states monitor compliance by their peers. The KPCS also assigned a new task to member states that have to issue certificates for conflict-free diamonds and to allow the import of certified diamonds only. Because of the risk of being excluded from the market, the regime clearly has an influence on exporting states' cost-benefit calculus.

The KPCS faces a free-rider problem against the absence of third-party monitoring and weak accountability mechanisms, which came to undermine the initial success and strong reputation of the initiative. This is exemplified by a disagreement over Zimbabwe where the KPCS proved unable to take remedial action and impose sanctions.[22] In contrast to the VPs and the EITI, international NGOs are not full-fledged members of the regime. NGOs participate in the KPCS peer-review mechanism and can have a say in the recommendations provided. But the latter are not binding. The two main players, Global Witness and Partnership Africa-Canada (PAC), assume a watchdog function without having a formal say in the governing body. Ian Smillie, PAC top representative, left the KPCS in May 2009 arguing that it systematically failed to live up to its initial commitment. He declared, "the KPCS has been confronted by many

---

22   Lucy Koechlin, "Zimbabwe and the Kimberley Process: Just How Effective Are Multistake-holder Initiatives?" Blog of the European Journal of International Law, 24 November 2009, www.ejiltalk.org/zimbabwe-and-the-kimberley-process-just-how-effective-are-multi stakeholder-initiatives (accessed 1 August 2010); Global Witness, "Failure to Suspend Zimbabwe from Blood Diamond Scheme Undermines Efforts to End Abuses and Clean Up International Trade," Global Witness press release, 8 November 2009, www.fatal transactions.org/News/2009/Failure-to-suspend-Zimbabwe-from-blood-diamond -scheme-undermines-efforts-to-end-abuses-and-clean-up-international-trade (accessed 1 August 2010).

challenges in the past five years, and it has failed to deal quickly or effectively with most of them: smuggling and fraud in Brazil, and issues of even greater importance in Côte d'Ivoire/Ghana, Guyana, Venezuela, Zimbabwe and now Guinea and Lebanon. In each case the issue has had to become a media debacle before the KP would deal with it (if at all)."[23] NGOs lacked the clout to effect changes in the regime design whereas the diamond industry and producer states succeeded (temporarily) in protecting the diamond business from damage to its reputation.

The Chad-Cameroon Oil Pipeline Project (CCP) policy framework is presented in detail by John A. Gould and Matthew S. Winters in this special issue.[24] From a regime perspective, the CCP deployed three behavioral pathways: The CCP channeled part of the oil revenues through an escrow account to change the government's utility structure; it redefined roles within the government through the establishment of specific institutions; and introduced civil society as a new actor with a say on oil revenue allocation. More important perhaps, it changed the government's cost-benefit calculus by conditioning access to project finance and restricting discretionary access to oil revenues.

However, the Oil Revenue Law 001 and the allocation mechanisms failed to modify the government's utility structure in the long term, once the typical obsolescing bargain syndrome played out.[25] Covering less than half of oil revenue streams in Chad, it gave increasing room for maneuver over time to the executive once revenue started flowing and the investment in physical infrastructure was completed. The oversight bodies established to instill accountability were not sufficiently insulated from government intrusion, which had both the de facto upper hand in the designation of governmental and non-governmental representatives alike and an influence through funding. This shows again that increasing revenue transparency and giving a say to CSOs is not enough. There was no shortage of information about what was going wrong. Yet civil society had no means to hold the government accountable.[26]

A few patterns emerge when looking at the four regimes above. All of them seek to effect change through multiple behavioral pathways from the very start.

23   "Ian Smillie Quits Kimberly Process," *Africa Files*, 28 May 2009, www.africafiles.org/article. asp?ID=21072 (accessed 1 August 2010).

24   John A. Gould and Matthew S. Winters, "Betting on Oil: The World Bank's Attempt to Promote Accountability in Chad," in this special issue.

25   Lorraine Eden, Stefanie Lenway, and Douglas A. Schular, "From the Obsolescing Bargain to the Political Bargaining Model," in Robert Grosse, ed., *International Business and Government Relations* (Cambridge: Cambridge University Press, 2005), pp. 251–273.

26   Scott Pegg, "Briefing: Chronicle of a Death Foretold: The Collapse of the Chad-Cameroon Pipeline Project," *African Affairs* 108, no. 431 (2009): 311–320.

Regimes tend to evolve over time. Voluntary multistakeholder initiatives like the EITI and the VPs initially focus on agreed principles and later elaborate on the rules of the game by introducing stronger accountability frameworks and participation criteria. Although important, regime effectiveness does not hang only on utility modifier pathways; deploying complementary pathways simultaneously seems to be critical to change behavior. In the case of voluntary, non-binding initiatives, market incentives play a critical role, be it via consumers (KPCS) or access to development finance (EITI) or capital markets.

This gives credence to recent expressive theories of law that recognize that emerging norms structure behavior in a way that may produce some elements of compliance even without legal sanctions, contrary to the standard economic approach to law compliance that views sanctions as a central factor in the decision of rational actors to invest in law compliance.[27] Public information and advocacy tend to play an increasingly important role in regulating behavior. Yet this does not mean that sanctions become irrelevant. To the contrary, in the case of the EITI, NGOs hailed as a major push for effective transparency the adoption by the US Congress in July 2010 of a new law requiring US and foreign energy and mining companies to be registered with the US Securities and Exchange Commission to disclose how much they pay to governments for oil, gas, and mining.[28] This covers twenty-nine of the thirty-two largest international oil companies as well as eight of the ten largest mining companies that will have to report payments disaggregated at the country level.

All four regimes try to strengthen domestic civil society as a key player to shift the power balance to the disadvantage of rent-seeking and corrupt elites and, thereby, counter the absence of sanctions for misbehavior. Civil society becomes a critical actor in shaping the behavior of government elites and economic actors in an era of regulation through information and advocacy. To better explain the potential and challenges of CSOs to become critical agents of internal realignment, we examine the concept of civil society in the next section and then turn to the implementation of the EITI in Nigeria and Azerbaijan.

---

27   Cynthia Williams, "Civil Society Initiative and 'Soft Law' in the Oil and Gas Industry," *Journal of International Law and Politics* 36, nos. 2–3 (2004): 457–502.

28   Revenue Watch, "U.S. Financial Reform Sets New Standard for Energy and Mining Industry Transparency," press release, www.revenuewatch.org/news/news-article/united -states/us-financial-reform-sets-new-standard-energy-and-mining-industry-tra (accessed 1 August 2010).

3   Civil Society

The term *civil society* originates from European models of state formation and
development. It is generally understood as the arena of voluntary, uncoerced
collective action around shared interests, purposes, and values outside of the
family, the state, and the market where people associate to advance common
interests.[29] In practice, the boundaries between these sectors are often complex and blurred. The sector of "voluntary action" comprises classic NGOs
and other forms of civic associations such as trade and labor unions, interest
groups of all sorts, and social movements. The term *voluntary* is not that clear
in practice because many organizations are based on clan, ethnic, or religious
identities and group affiliation into which people are born. Thus, people may
join an association to avoid social and economic disadvantages rather than for
promoting a cause.[30]

Within the academic debate, the concept gained enthusiastic attention subsequent to Robert Putnam's argument that civil society is crucial in "making
democracy work."[31] His simple mantra of "strong society, strong economy;
strong society, strong state"[32] has become the bottom line of many development promotion programs. It is now common sense to assume that robust
democratic institutions need to be underpinned by a network of civil associations as well as by responsible citizenship and political participation.

Civil society has become more prominent in international development
cooperation since the mid-1980s in the context of the good governance and
democratization agendas. Western governments and international organizations increasingly sought to bypass the host state and implement aid programs
and political reforms via nonstate actors. The multiplication of NGOs and
CSOs during the past decade reflects optimistic expectations that national and
transnational civic activism can make important contributions toward democratic governance and development.

In recent years, critical voices have pointed out that civil society may have
demonstrated negative impacts, furthering conflict between groups and

---

29   Wolfgang Merkel and Hans Joachim Lauth, "Systemwechsel und Zivilgesellschaft: Welche
      Zivilgesellschaft braucht die Demokratie?" *Aus Politik und Zeitgeschichte* 6, no. 7 (1998):
      3–12. See also the definition employed by the Civicus project, www.civicus.org.
30   Marina Ottaway, "Civil Society," in Peter Burnell and Vicky Randall, eds., *Politics in the
      Developing World* (Oxford: Oxford University Press, 2005), pp. 166–186.
31   Robert Putnam, *Making Democracy Work: Civic Traditions in Modern Italy* (Princeton:
      Princeton University Press, 1993).
32   See Putnam, *Making Democracy Work*, p. 176.

undermining democratic development.[33] Thus, the impact of civil society may not be solely positive. Civic ties may imply the exclusion of individuals and groups, and civic networks may not necessarily promote democratic and peaceful values. This is particularly evident in weak and fragile developing states. Political liberalization in many African countries contributed to significant growth in the civil society sector,[34] but the latter still suffers from many shortcomings. Chronic weakness and fragmentation across the urban-rural and ethnic divides as well as the lack of cooperation, communication, and sharing of information are characteristic of the sector.

Civil society organizations themselves are also confronted with transparency and accountability challenges; that is, with the very issues that they are supposed to address on a much larger scale in the case of the oil and mining rent. Competition over scarce resources increases fragmentation on the basis of regional, class, ethnic, and religious group interests and loyalties.[35] A study by the World Bank found that CSOs are sometimes exclusionary and reinforce societal divisions.[36] Their organizational structures often reflect an absence of democratic values and procedures. Civil society actors may move between political parties and civil society organizations, thus blurring the lines between state and civil society actors.[37] In Nigeria, some civil society organizations were deliberately created by the Abacha regime.[38] Furthermore, CSO accountability toward local communities is often low, and the relationships between international NGOs and local CSOs tend to entail consultation rather than true partnership.

---

33   See, for example, J. Howell and J. Pearce, *Civil Society and Development: A Critical Exploration* (Boulder: Lynne Rienner Publishers, 2002); Thomas Carothers, "Think Again: Civil Society," *Foreign Policy* 117, (Winter 1999): 18–30; Augustine Ikelegbe, "The Perverse Manifestation of Civil Society: Evidence from Nigeria," *Journal of Modern African Studies* 39, no. 1 (2001): 1–24.

34   Paul Opoku-Mensah, "The State of Civil Society in Sub-Saharan Africa," in Volkhart Heinrich and Lorenzo Fioramonti, eds., *Civicus Global Survey of the State of Civil Society*, vol. 2: *Comparative Perspectives* (Bloomfield, CT: Kumarian Press, 2008), pp. 75–91.

35   Robert Fatton, "Africa in the Age of Democratization: The Civic Limitations of Civil Society," *African Studies Review* 38, no. 2 (1995): 67–99.

36   World Bank, "Civil Society and Peacebuilding: Potentials, Limitations and Critical Factors," World Bank Report No. 36445-GLB (Washington, DC: World Bank, 2006), http://site resources.worldbank.org/EXTSOCIALDEVELOPMENT/Resources/244362-1164107274725/ 3182370-1164110717447/Civil_Society_and_Peacebuilding.pdf (accessed 1 August 2010).

37   Christoph Spurk, "Understanding Civil Society," in Thania Paffenholz, ed., *Civil Society and Peacebuilding: A Critical Assessment* (Boulder: Lynne Rienner, 2010), pp. 3–29.

38   Ebenezer Obadare, "The Alternative Genealogy of Civil Society and Its Implications for Africa: Notes for Further Research," *Africa Development* 24, no. 4 (2004): 1–18; Ikelegbe, "The Perverse Manifestation of Civil Society: Evidence from Nigeria."

Civil society is often presented as a solution to social, economic, and political ills that governments are unable or unwilling to cure. Expectation placed in the concept of civil society clearly "soared far beyond its demonstrated returns."[39] In fact, early modern thinkers primarily stressed the uncivil aspects of groups and associations and the challenge they posed to political stability. Margaret Kohn remarks poignantly that "civil society is not a buffer that limits the expansion of the state," nor is it "a utopia of civic virtue where citizens are exempt from the logic of the market and the oversight of the state;" instead, civil society can only be a "terrain where citizens can organize to contest or defend the existing distributions of power."[40]

Several empirical studies have nonetheless demonstrated the positive impact of domestic civil society activism for a range of specific sectors, during particular phases and in limited cases.[41] Civil society actors may fulfill important functions relating to the protection of citizens, monitoring and advocacy, intermediation between citizens and state institutions, and socialization for democratic values. However, weak and corrupt, but resource-rich states represent a particularly difficult environment for these actors to fulfill such functions.

The Civicus Survey for Sub-Saharan Africa concludes that "the weakest area of civil society's impact is at the level of holding the state and the private sector to account, indicating that the liberal concept of civil society as a bulwark against the state is not strongly supported in the surveyed countries."[42] This is precisely the role that CSOs are meant to fulfill within the framework of multistakeholder initiatives such as the EITI, which states that "citizen and civil society benefit from the increased transparency by being able to hold their government and companies to account when the tax payments are disclosed."[43] There seems to be a fundamental contradiction between the expectations on domestic CSOs and their actual leverage. When CSOs are politically weak in the first place, receiving transparent revenue data does not automatically translate into better performance in the area of political advocacy and monitoring. Consequently, if CSOs have thus far been unable to hold their governments to account, there is no guarantee they can do so once EITI reports on

39   Carothers, "Think Again: Civil Society."
40   Margaret Kohn, "Panacea or Privilege? New Approaches to Democracy and Association," *Political Theory* 30, no. 2 (2002): 289–298.
41   See the case studies in Thania Paffenholz, ed., *Civil Society and Peacebuilding: A Critical Assessment* (London: Lynne Rienner, 2010).
42   Opoku-Mensah, "The State of Civil Society in Sub-Saharan Africa," p. 4.
43   EITI Factsheet, http://eiti.org/document/factsheet (accessed 28 July 2010).

payments by extractive firms are made public. In the next section, we illustrate such difficulties in implementing the EITI in Nigeria and Azerbaijan.

4   The EITI in Nigeria and Azerbaijan

Nigeria, the world's seventh largest oil producer, has come to exemplify the resource curse. Five decades of oil extraction in the country have resulted in failed development, poverty, corruption, environmental degradation, ethnic and gang violence, kidnappings, and the like. The overwhelming majority of oil revenue is concentrated in the hands of a very small part of the population. Nigeria's anticorruption chief claimed, for instance, that 70 percent of the country's wealth was stolen or wasted in 2003.[44]

Nigeria was the first country to sign on to the EITI process in 2003 and was first at the forefront in implementing the initiative, which raised hopes that the EITI would bear fruit in this country plagued by large-scale corruption. It published audit reports for the period 1999–2004 that contributed significantly to transparency in the country's oil industry and went even beyond the basic requirement of the global EITI by providing disaggregated payments. Expectations of improved governance and better resource management were also high because the country had a relatively vibrant civil society. But seven years down the road, Nigeria has not succeeded in being validated as compliant with all the EITI requirements. The Nigerian EITI (NEITI) was established in 2004 amid a political climate of reform and fighting against corruption during the second term of President Olusegun Obasanjo (2003–2007). A National Stakeholders Working Group was established to manage the NEITI, with two civil society representatives and fourteen government officials among its twenty-eight members.[45] As detailed by Nicholas Shaxon, the two civil society representatives were supposed to engage a wider civil society network including trade unions, professional associations, NGOs, and other constituencies.[46] A civil society steering committee was established later to include a broader range of civil society activists. No research into civil society

---

44   Anna Khakee, "Energy and Development: Lessons from Nigeria," European Development Cooperation Policy Brief No. 1 (Bonn: European Association of Development Institute, 2008).

45   See the NEITI Handbook, www.neiti.org.ng/files-pdf/NEITI_Handbook4.pdf (accessed 1 August 2010).

46   Nicholas Shaxon, Nigeria's Extractive Industries Transparency Initiative: Just a Glorius Audit? (London: Chatham House, 2009).

structures or mapping of organizations took place in the course of the NEITI implementation.[47] One respondent described civil society activists in this context as "single person self-promoters" in a highly divided NGO scene where fractures among leading NGOs seriously hampered their capacity to fulfill their monitoring role.[48] (The composition of NEITI has changed recently. Nigeria has since achieved compliant status.)

The NEITI produced two audit reports in 2006 and 2009 that revealed a blatant lack of government oversight over extractive activities and revenues. But the revenue data was too complicated to be used effectively by CSOs and capacity building appears to have been rather ineffective.[49] Alexandra Gillies reports that only the House of Representatives and the National Assembly were able to use the data when questioning certain bids and policies.[50] Furthermore, CSOs had no way of holding their officials accountable due to a lack of transparency on the expenditure side; in particular with regard to federal, state, and local governments.[51] Apart from these difficulties, regional NGOs based in the Niger Delta were more focused on Memorandums of Understanding (MoUs) between oil companies and local communities than the NEITI process because the MoUs directly benefited their local constituencies.[52]

Thus, civil society did not play a key role within the NEITI process and does not appear to have benefited from the initiative in any substantive manner. Former president Obasanjo provided an open space for political reform in order to please the international community and restore trust in Nigeria's oil industry. The NEITI provided tools and helped shape reforms that proved to be beneficial to the country's image as Nigeria managed to receive a large write-off of its debt with the Paris Club in 2005.[53] At the same time, the Obasanjo regime kept feeding oil money into a patronized and highly corrupt system. The actual purpose of the NEITI may rather have been to "restore trust in the

---

47   Ibid.

48   Ibid., p. 25.

49   Ibid., p. 26.

50   Interview with Alexandra Gillies, in Shaxon, *Nigeria's Extractive Industries Transparency Initiative*, p. 27.

51   For a detailed report, see Human Rights Watch, *Chop Fine: The Human Rights Impact of Government Corruption and Mismanagement in Rivers State, Nigeria* (New York: Human Rights Watch, 2007), www.hrw.org/en/reports/2007/01/30/chop-fine (accessed 1 August 2010).

52   Shaxon, *Nigeria's Extractive Industries Transparency Initiative*, p. 25.

53   Ngozi Okonjo-Iweala, "Point of View: Nigeria's Shot at Redemption," *Finance and Development* 45, no. 4 (2008), www.imf.org/external/pubs/ft/fandd/2008/12/okonjo.htm (accessed 1 August 2010).

system"[54] than to improve governance and revenue management. It may have helped NGOs to mobilize on issues related to budget transparency at the subnational level in the states of the Niger Delta, but civil society activists agree that it has yet to prove any significant and sustainable positive impact on revenue management, poverty alleviation, and good governance.[55]

The role of civil society is also precarious in the case of Azerbaijan where the extractive sector accounts for 54 percent of gross domestic product (GDP) and has provided the country with solid GDP growth in recent years.[56] Like Nigeria, Azerbaijan joined the EITI early on in 2003 and established a state committee for the national EITI initiative the same year. The country has also been a poster child for the EITI. But in contrast to Nigeria, it managed to succeed on the entire validation path and become the first EITI compliant country in February 2009. Yet the state of civil society in this former Soviet country is precarious. Even if the country qualified as EITI compliant in 2009, civil society complained that it was not able "to participate on equal terms in the EITI decision making process."[57] The Azerbaijani government had to be forced into accepting CSOs as stakeholders in the EITI process from the beginning. As is the case in Nigeria, civil society activism is hampered not as much because of a lack of transparency over revenues, but due to a lack of information on government expenditures, even if it is true that revenue management per se is not covered by the EITI.

While the EITI did spark some civil society momentum, the initiative was largely implemented without its involvement.[58] In 2009, the Azerbaijani parliament even tried to pass a bill proposing a limit of 50 percent to the funding of domestic NGOs from international sources. This would have effectively terminated the work of most NGOs in the country. After much civil society advocacy and international pressure, a light version of the original bill passed—excluding funding restrictions, but raising requirements for intergovernmental agreement on CSO registration and making civil society activism

---

54   David Goldwyn, in Shaxon, *Nigeria's Extractive Industries Transparency Initiative*, p. 7.

55   Statement by OSIWA country director. See Publish What You Pay Coalition, "PWYP Draws More Attention to NEITI Audit," 9 December 2010, http://publishwhatyoupay.org/en/ resources/pwyp-draws-more-attention-neiti-audit.

56   Publish What You Pay Coalition, "Coalition Spotlight: Azerbaijan," 13 May 2010, www .publishwhatyoupay.org/en/resources/pwyp-coalition-spotlight-azerbaijan (1 accessed August 2010).

57   Ibid.

58   Asadov Farda, "The Public Oversight of Oil Projects in Azerbaijan, 2004–2007," *International Social Science Journal* 57, no. 1 (2005): 93–106.

more difficult overall.[59] The formalization of civil society engagement in the form of a multistakeholder group was long delayed; it was established only in 2010. Since this formalization of the Azerbaijani EITI process, civil society activists have reported some promising changes in the political climate and shown some optimism in its ability to contribute to revenue transparency.[60]

In other EITI candidate countries, the persecution of civil society activists (in Gabon, the Republic of Congo, and Niger[61]) is worrisome as is the weakness of CSOs in many implementing states and their lack of monitoring capacity. International NGOs are offering technical assistance and training modules for domestic civil society actors on revenue monitoring and advocacy. The international NGO coalition Publish What You Pay has played a critical role in contributing to the emergence and strengthening of local CSOs capacitated to focus on extractive revenues.[62] Yet capacity building may not suffice to address the general weakness and fragmentation of civil society in resource-rich, but weak states. And more transparency does not in itself lead to poverty alleviation. The budget allocation process is central in translating extraction into development.[63] If civil society is not in a position to discuss and monitor public expenditure, there is little chance that more revenue transparency will directly translate into significant poverty alleviation.

---

59   "Azerbaijan: NGO LAW Passed," www.eurasianet.org/departments/news/articles/eav06 3009.shtml (accessed 1 August 2010); Publish What You Pay Coalition, "Coalition Spotlight: Azerbaijan."

60   Publish What You Pay Coalition, "Coalition Spotlight: Azerbaijan."

61   In Gabon: Publish What You Pay Coalition, "Gabon Crackdown on Civil Society Groups Prompts Swift Outcry from Publish What You Pay US Coalition," 11 January 2008, www .revenuewatch.org/news/news-article/gabon/gabon-crackdown-civil-society-groups -prompts-swift-outcry-publish-what-you-p (accessed 1 August 2010). In Congo-Brazzaville: Revenue Watch, "Legal Defence Funding for Civil Society Activists," 2008, www .revenuewatch.org/our-work/projects/legal-defense-funding-civil-society-activists (accessed 1 August 2010). In Niger: Revenue Watch, "Harassment of Activists Stalls EITI Process in Niger," 19 August 2009, www.revenuewatch.org/news/news-article/niger/ harassment-activists-stalls-eiti-process-niger (accessed 1 August 2010).

62   Mabel van Oranje and Henry Parham, "Publish What We Learn," 19 November 2009, www.publishwhatyoupay.org/en/resources/publishing-what-we-learned (accessed 7 March 2011).

63   Ivar Kolstad, "Is Transparency the Key to Reducing Corruption in Resource-rich Countries?" World Development 37, no. 3 (2009): 521–532; Shaxon, Nigeria's Extractive Industries Transparency Initiative.

5   Conclusion

Voluntary regimes in the extractive sector are the main global policy response to address the political and institutional dimensions of the resource-curse phenomenon. The rules and procedures presiding over those regimes tend to evolve over time and involve a variety of behavioral pathways. To start with, parties to the regimes often agree over a set of fundamental principles such as revenue transparency (EITI), traceability (KPCS), or the promotion of human rights (VPS). This process facilitates collective learning and raises awareness among participants. Later the regimes tend to introduce tighter participation criteria, which is critical for a voluntary regime to enhance compliance and impact over time. Political and economic incentives are introduced with a view to change the behavior of key players under the unitary, rational actor assumption.

An analysis of the major regimes in the extractive sector shows that the most effective pathway to spur behavioral change is to alter the variables entering in the cost-benefit calculus of producer states and extractive industries. This conclusion echoes the findings of Young and Levy and finds a good illustration in the Kimberly process: the fear that consumers may shy away from so-called blood diamonds enabled the set-up of the KPCS regime within a short period of time with the buy-in of virtually all the major producing and importing countries as well as of industry.[64]

The multistakeholder initiatives examined above have all introduced civil society as an agent of internal realignment and put high demands on CSOs in terms of monitoring and public advocacy. Civil society in resource-rich, but weak states is nascent and divided. It often lacks the capacity, resources, and independence to effectively perform the role to which it has been assigned. Reflecting on the theoretical limitations of the civil society concept and the practical challenges that these actors face in countries such as Nigeria and Azerbaijan, it clearly appears that civil society organizations can only partially fulfill the key functions within the regimes examined here. Even if capacity building and training programs for local CSOs have a significant and positive impact over the long run, the influence of CSOs on unwilling resource-rich states and corrupt elites remains limited.

Alternatives to civil society as the agent of internal realignment are required to enhance regime effectiveness. Market incentives and regulation offer a promising avenue to bring about decisive change in elite behavior in producer states, as recently illustrated by the Kimberly process whose success resulted

---

64   Young and Levy, *The Effectiveness of International Environmental Regimes.*

from a concern over the risk of a consumer boycott. The situation is different in the oil and gas market. Consumers cannot vote with their purse when purchasing fuels because products from diverse origins are often blended at the refining stage. Yet capital markets as well as project and development finance have the potential to send strong signals in favor of enhanced transparency and accountability. This is, for example, the case with the EITI: over eighty investment and institutional funds have issued support statements and officially back the process. A representative of the financial sector even sits in the governing board of the initiative.

Relying only on market incentives and voluntary commitments is not sufficient and bears the risk of governments abandoning their regulatory responsibility. Market regulation keeps playing a central role in dealing with free riders and moving toward better compliance with transparency norms. The EITI received a necessary boost with the adoption of the Dodd-Frank Wall Street Reform and Consumer Protection Act requiring all extractive firms registered with the US Securities and Exchange Commission to report their payments to individual governments for access to oil, gas, and minerals.

The final outcome depends not only on the quality of the regime design, but also on how it interacts with other dimensions of the resource trap; in particular with the rent-cycling and obsolescing bargain dynamics. This deserves further scrutiny.

CHAPTER 18

Principles, Politics, and Prudence: Libya, the Responsibility to Protect, and the Use of Military Force

Paul D. Williams and Alex J. Bellamy[1]

Resolution 1973 (17 March 2011) was the first time the United Nations Security Council authorized the use of military force for human protection purposes against a functioning de jure government. As such, it represents a significant development in the international politics of military force. But what are its likely consequences and how did it come about? We submit that Resolution 1973 and the subsequent enforcement operations, Odyssey Dawn and Unified Protector, were partly facilitated by the developing principle and practice of the Responsibility to Protect (R2P).

Despite an increasing number of rhetorical commitments made by international institutions and many governments to prevent mass atrocities in the post-Cold War era, the use of force for human protection purposes remained severely constrained by principled objections rooted in international law and moral differences, the low political payoffs and potentially grave risks associated with humanitarian war, and the combination of difficult operational dilemmas and an absence of clear guidance about the strategies and tactics most likely to have positive effects in different circumstances.[2]

---

* This chapter was originally published in Global Governance, Volume 18, Issue 3, 2012.

1 Paul D. Williams is Professor of International Affairs in the Elliott School of International Affairs at George Washington University. His books include *War and Conflict in Africa* (2011); *Understanding Peacekeeping*, 2nd edition (coauthored with Alex J. Bellamy, 2010); and *The International Politics of Mass Atrocities: The Case of Darfur* (coedited with David Black, 2010).

   Alex J. Bellamy is Director of the Asia Pacific Centre for the Responsibility to Protect and Professor of Peace and Conflict Studies at The University of Queensland. His books include *Massacres and Morality: Mass Atrocities in an Age of Civilian Immunity* (2012); *Global Politics and the Responsibility to Protect* (2011); and *Understanding Peacekeeping*, 2nd edition (coauthored with Paul D. Williams, 2010).

2 In February 2011, UN Secretary-General Ban Ki-moon defined *human protection* as "a subset of the more encompassing concept of human security. The latter reminds us that the security of 'we the peoples' matters every bit as much as the security of states. Human protection addresses more immediate threats to the survival of individuals and groups." Ban Ki-moon, "Human Protection and the 21st Century United Nations," Cyril Foster Lecture,

Historically, these obstacles coalesced to produce a default policy environment that was strongly averse to the use of force to prevent or end the commission of genocide, war crimes, ethnic cleansing, or crimes against humanity (hereafter, genocide and mass atrocities). We submit that R2P has helped mitigate these three types of constraints, albeit unevenly, making UN-authorized humanitarian military intervention both politically possible in Libya and more likely in other similar cases.[3] First, R2P has largely resolved principled debate about whether international society should become engaged in such crises and replaced it with debates about how to best protect populations from grave abuses. Within international society, this principle is underscored by a widely shared understanding of the need for Security Council authorization for any use of military force. Second, R2P has helped to change international political calculations by establishing shared expectations and common interests, though of course national interests and domestic politics continue to shape decisions about using force. Third, it has provided a catalyst for more creative thinking about operational issues, most notably supporting moves toward using a broader range of measures to coerce and induce behavioral change and deepening understanding of the range of potential military measures and associated pitfalls. Nevertheless, while agreement on principles is important, reaching consensus on how to consistently apply those principles in response to specific cases is far more difficult, as the case of Syria in 2012 demonstrates only too well.[4] Moreover, while the use of force to protect populations from genocide and mass atrocities has become more likely, it is still rare and is likely to remain so for the foreseeable future.[5]

To substantiate these claims, we begin this article by summarizing the road to the use of force in Libya, focusing on the forging of international consensus around Resolution 1973. Next, we contextualize Resolution 1973 by outlining the main principled, political, and prudential obstacles to using force for human protection purposes. In the final section, we revisit these obstacles and explore R2P's role in reshaping the way they are conceptualized and, in turn, the politics of using force to protect populations from genocide and mass atrocities.

Oxford University, 2 February 2011, www.un.org/apps/news/infocus/sgspeeches/search_full .asp?statID=1064.

3 We define *humanitarian military intervention* as the use of military force by external actors without host state consent aimed at preventing or ending genocide and mass atrocities.

4 We emphasize this point in Alex J. Bellamy and Paul D. Williams, "The New Politics of Protection: Côte d'Ivoire, Libya and the Responsibility to Protect," *International Affairs* 87, no. 4 (2011): 825–850.

5 See Alex J. Bellamy, "Military Intervention," in Donald Bloxham and Dirk Moses, eds., *The Oxford Handbook of Genocide Studies* (Oxford: Oxford University Press, 2010), pp. 597–616.

1   Libya: The Road to Humanitarian War

On 19 March 2011, military forces from France, Canada, the United Kingdom, and the United States struck the air defenses and soldiers of Muammar Gaddafi's regime in Libya. These countries led a coalition of states with the expressed aim of enforcing the objectives set out by UN Security Council Resolution 1973, principally the operation of a no-fly zone over Libya, imposition of an arms embargo, and the protection of civilians on the ground.[6] Although Gaddafi's officials declared that they had put in place a cease-fire shortly after Resolution 1973 was authorized, by the morning of 18 March it was clear that this was not the case and that the regime's assault on the rebel stronghold of Benghazi was under way.

The following day, an impromptu summit was convened in Paris in which the initial modalities of Odyssey Dawn were finalized. This involved representatives of eighteen states primarily from Europe and North America, but also including Iraq, Jordan, Morocco, Qatar, and the United Arab Emirates (UAE) as well as officials from the League of Arab States (LAS) and the European Union (EU).[7] Just a few hours after the summit, French aircraft began a series of flights and bombing raids over Libyan territory. Predictably, Gaddafi's regime quickly denounced these strikes as the work of "crusader enemies" and claimed they had targeted civilians and fuel supplies in the rebel-held city of Misrata. On 23 March, NATO leadership took over enforcement of the arms embargo; on 26 March, it assumed responsibility for enforcement of the no-fly zone; and, on 31 March, the alliance assumed full control of operations under what was now called Operation Unified Protector. Not all NATO states deployed forces in harm's way (notably absent were Poland and Germany), but the alliance was joined by several nonmembers, including Sweden, Jordan, Qatar, and the UAE. On 4 April, President Obama withdrew US forces from direct combat, after which the lion's share of combat missions were conducted by France, Great Britain, Italy, Denmark, Belgium, Canada, the UAE, Qatar, and Norway.[8]

The attack on Libya was the first time the Security Council had authorized the use of military force for protection purposes against the will of a functioning de jure government. Although the Council had come close in the past, it had never before crossed the line. For example, in Resolution 794 (December 1992),

---

6   According to US sources, by early March fifteen states had agreed to participate in a US-led coalition to enforce Security Council demands. *Libya: Operation Odyssey Dawn* (Suffolk, VA: Joint and Coalition Operational Analysis, 4 October 2011), p. 2.

7   Paris Summit for the Support of the Libyan People, 19 March 2011, http://blogs.wsj.com/dispatch/2011/03/19/declaration-issued-after-paris-summit.

8   Ben Barry, "Libya's Lessons," *Survival* 53, no. 5 (2011): 6.

the Council authorized the Unified Task Force to enter Somalia to ease the humanitarian crisis, but this was in the absence of a central government rather than against one. Similarly, in Resolution 929 (June 1994), the Security Council authorized the French-led Operation Turquoise, ostensibly with the humanitarian aim to protect victims of the ongoing genocide in Rwanda. Despite many concerns over the French government's motives, Operation Turquoise enjoyed the consent of the interim government in Rwanda as well as its armed forces. In Resolution 940 (September 1994), the Security Council authorized the use of military force to oust the military junta in Haiti. But not only did this mission receive the explicit support of Haiti's de jure authorities (S/1994/905 Annex), it was justified primarily with reference to defending democracy. The protection of Haitian civilians was implied only in the resolution's references to the intervening force maintaining a "secure and stable environment" (operative paragraphs 4 and 9a). More recently, in Democratic Republic of Congo (DRC), Sudan, and Côte d'Ivoire, the Security Council authorized the use of all necessary measures to protect civilians, but the Blue Helmet operations in these countries all operate with the official permission of the state's de jure authorities.[9] This was not the case in Libya. The Security Council has thus entered new political terrain: using military force against a de jure government with the stated aim of protecting civilians.

The roots of Resolution 1973 lie in the political upheavals associated with the protests that spread across the Arab world from late 2010 from Tunisia to Egypt and beyond.[10] In Libya, protests quickly turned violent, partly because of the regime's crackdown and partly because an armed opposition group was quickly established under the Interim National Transitional Council (NTC). The NTC coalesced from a mixture of Libyan diplomats who publicly denounced the Gaddafi regime from their posts abroad and switched their allegiance, segments of the armed forces who also had defected, and leaders of the opposition within Libya, particularly those in Benghazi. While the NTC enjoyed rapid successes in mid-February 2011 declaring its forces had taken control of most of the major cities, in late February and early March Gaddafi's forces tipped the balance back in their favor, and by mid-March they were threatening to crush the rebellion's eastern epicenter in Benghazi.

---

9   See Victoria Holt and Glyn Taylor, with Max Kelly, *Protecting Civilians in the Context of UN Peacekeeping Operations* (New York: UN Department of Peacekeeping Operations and Office for the Coordination of Humanitarian Affairs, November 2009); Siobhan Wills, *Protecting Civilians: The Obligations of Peacekeepers* (Oxford: Oxford University Press, 2009).

10   The best overview of these protests is Marc Lynch, *The Arab Uprising* (New York: Public Affairs, 2012).

Almost from the outset of the crisis, senior UN officials warned of the imminent threat of mass atrocities and framed their responses in R2P terms. On 22 February, the UN's High Commissioner for Human Rights, Navi Pillay, emphasized the need to protect civilians and called on the authorities to stop using violence against demonstrators, which "may amount to crimes against humanity."[11] On the same day, the special advisers to the UN Secretary-General on genocide prevention and R2P also stated that the Libyan regime's behavior could amount to crimes against humanity and that the Libyan regime, which has the primary responsibility to protect its people, must exercise its R2P.[12] On the following day, the Secretary-General framed the ensuing debate as one about the prevention of mass atrocities and protection of vulnerable populations.

The first sign that the international response would be unusual also came on 22 February when the LAS—which now included postrevolution authorities in Egypt and Tunisia—suspended Libya's participation in the organization. On 23 February, the Peace and Security Council of the African Union (AU), of which Libya was a member, condemned "the indiscriminate and excessive use of force and lethal weapons against peaceful protestors, in violation of human rights and International Humanitarian Law" that was used in response to the "legitimate ... aspirations of the people of Libya for democracy, political reform, justice and socio-economic development."[13]

Two days later, on 25 February, the UN Human Rights Council established a commission of inquiry to investigate the situation and urged the General Assembly to suspend Libya from the Human Rights Council—which it duly did on 1 March. On 26 February, the UN Security Council voted unanimously to pass Resolution 1970. Among other things, this condemned "the widespread and systematic attacks" against civilians, which it suspected "may amount to crimes against humanity"; welcomed the earlier criticisms of the Libyan government's actions by the LAS, the AU, and the Organization of the Islamic Conference (OIC); and underlined the Libyan government's responsibility to protect its population. Acting under Chapter VII of the UN Charter, the Council demanded an immediate end to the violence; urged Gaddafi's government to ensure safe passage for humanitarian and medical supplies; referred the situation in Libya since 15 February to the prosecutor of the International

---

11   "Libya Attacks May Be Crimes Against Humanity: UN," Reuters, 22 February 2011, www. reuters.com/article/2011/02/22/us-libya-protests-rights-idUSTRE71L4Z020110222.

12   See www.un.org/en/preventgenocide/adviser/pdf/OSAPG,%20Special%20Advisers%20 Statement%20on%20Libya,%2022%20February%202011.pdf.

13   AU Doc. PSC/PR/COMM(CCLXI), 23 February 2011.

Criminal Court;[14] established an arms embargo on the country; imposed indefinite travel bans on sixteen individuals of the Libyan regime; froze indefinitely the assets of six members of the ruling regime; established a sanctions committee to monitor the implementation of these measures; and called on member states to make available humanitarian and related assistance for Libya. In response, on 2 March, Gaddafi's regime wrote to the UN Security Council declaring that the Council's condemnation of Libya was premature and requesting that Resolution 1970 be suspended until the allegations against it were confirmed.[15]

Three days later, the NTC in Benghazi declared itself Libya's sole representative and requested that "the international community ... fulfill its obligations to protect the Libyan people from any further genocide and crimes against humanity without any direct military intervention on Libya soil."[16] This declaration was given important political support from within the Arab world when, on 7 March, the Gulf Cooperation Council (GCC) released a statement calling for "the UN Security Council [to] take all necessary measures to protect civilians, including enforcing a no-fly zone over Libya" and condemning "crimes committed against civilians, the use of heavy arms and the recruitment of mercenaries" by the Libyan regime.[17] That same day, the Libyan mission to the UN in New York—many of whose members had by now defected from Gaddafi's regime—also urged UN member states to recognize the NTC as Libya's legitimate authorities. At this stage the UN Secretary-General appointed former Jordanian foreign minister Abdelilah Al-Khatib as his special envoy to Libya, and UN Security Council members held informal consultations about possible further measures against Libya, including the option of a no-fly zone.[18]

On 8 March, the OIC echoed the GCC position by calling for a no-fly zone over Libya, although it said this excluded foreign military operations on the ground.[19] On 10 March, the GCC claimed that Gaddafi's regime had lost all

---

14   On 3 March, the International Criminal Court prosecutor, Luis Moreno-Ocampo, said his office was investigating crimes against humanity that may have been committed by Gaddafi's regime.

15   Cited in Security Council Report, Update Report No. 1 Libya, 14 March 2011, www.secur itycouncilreport.org/site/c.glKWLeMTIsG/b.6621881/k.63C4/Update_Report_No_1br Libyabr14_March_2011.htm.

16   Founding statement of the Interim Transitional National Council, 5 March 2011, http:// ntclibya.org/english/founding-statement-of-the-interim-transitional-national-council.

17   Wissam Keyrouz, "Gulf States Back Libya No-Fly Zone," Agence France-Presse, 7 March 2011, www.google.com/hostednews/afp/article/ALeqM5jRu1VXz2KQyUHoqOAAUYFhCg RCkg?docId=CNG.49104d077a72cbffeafe9d3689e92793.ba1.

18   Security Council Report, Update Report No. 1 Libya, 14 March 2011.

19   At www.oic-oci.org/topic_detail.asp?t_id=5031.

legitimacy and urged the LAS to initiate contact with the NTC. That same day, France, Italy, and EU foreign affairs head Catherine Ashton also opened dialogue with the NTC.

In Addis Ababa, however, the AU's Peace and Security Council was rather less generous to the NTC. After defining the situation in Libya as "a serious threat to peace and security in that country and in the region as a whole," the AU condemned "the indiscriminate use of force and lethal weapons ... and the transformation of pacific demonstrations into an armed rebellion." It went on to emphasize its "strong commitment to the respect of the unity and territorial integrity of Libya, as well as its rejection of any foreign military intervention, whatever its form."[20]

In the transatlantic region, Great Britain and France led the call for a tougher international response, a view opposed by Germany and initially regarded with considerable caution by the United States. On 10 March, however, NATO announced that it was moving additional ships into the region to support humanitarian assistance efforts and its ability to monitor the crisis effectively. NATO's secretary-general also revealed the alliance was discussing how an arms embargo or no-fly zone, or both, over Libya might be enforced.[21] But with the United States decidedly uncommitted and without authorization from the UN Security Council, the prospects for military action appeared slim.

On the diplomatic front, Gaddafi's regime rejected the demands set out in Security Council Resolution 1970 and refused to permit humanitarian aid convoys into besieged towns such as Misrata and Ajdabiya. The UN Secretary-General personally contacted the Libyan leader and in a forty-minute conversation tried—and failed—to persuade Gaddafi to comply with the Council's demands. Thus, while the search for a diplomatic solution through the UN special envoy and the AU high-level committee enjoyed widespread support, many governments, commentators, and UN officials alike were coming to the view that diplomacy alone would not prevent the commission of large-scale crimes against humanity should Benghazi fall.

It was the 12 March declaration by the LAS that proved the game changer. Specifically, the LAS called on the UN Security Council "to take the necessary measures to impose immediately a no-fly zone on Libyan military aviation, and to establish safe areas in places exposed to shelling as a precautionary measure that allows the protection of the Libyan people and foreign nationals residing in Libya, while respecting the sovereignty and territorial integrity of neighboring States," and to "*cooperate and communicate* with the Transitional National

---

20   AU Doc. PSC/PR/COMM.2(CCLXV), 10 March 2011.
21   EU Doc. EUCO 7/11, Brussels, 11 March 2011, paras. 6 and 7.

Council of Libya and to provide the Libyan people with urgent and continuing support as well as the necessary protection from the serious violations and grave crimes committed by the Libyan authorities, which have consequently lost their legitimacy."[22]

Inside the Barack Obama administration, the LAS resolution strengthened the hand of the interventionists. On 15 March, senior officials held what was described as an "extremely contentious" White House meeting that resulted in President Obama accepting the case for intervention argued by Hillary Clinton, Samantha Power, Gayle Smith, and Mike McFaul over the more cautious position expressed by Robert Gates, Tom Donilon, Denis McDonough, and others.[23] Having decided to support the use of force, the administration made it a priority to obtain Security Council authorization and brought significant diplomatic pressure to bear on wavering Council members.

It was in this context that the Security Council members debated whether to authorize the use of force to establish a no-fly zone and to protect civilians.[24] One of the central arguments made in the Council, and outside, was that the situation in Libya was both an ongoing threat to international peace and security and a humanitarian crisis that was likely to get significantly worse without urgent and decisive action. From this perspective, Gaddafi's description of the protesters as "cockroaches," his promise to "cleanse Libya house by house," and his threat to attack Benghazi and show its residents "no mercy" provided clear evidence of the regime's intent to commit mass atrocities and supported the view of senior UN officials that the crisis should be viewed through the lens of atrocity prevention.[25]

Within an unusually "heavyweight" Security Council, including not only the Permanent Five but also Brazil, Germany, India, and South Africa, there were a number of sticking points. Most significantly, two permanent members (China and Russia) and several nonpermanent members were unconvinced of the need to use military force. Their rationale was in part principled—for instance, China's long-established "five principles of foreign policy" includes the nonuse of force. But they also presented prudential and pragmatic objections, including that the use of military force might exacerbate an already bad situation and that the decision to impose a no-fly zone could quickly lead to more military commitments and might prolong the conflict. An additional

22   Council of the League of Arab States, Res. No. 7360, 12 March 2011, paras. 1 and 2.
23   Josh Rogin, "How Obama Turned on a Dime Toward War," 18 March 2011, http://thecable
      .foreignpolicy.com/posts/2011/03/18/how_obama_turned_on_a_dime_toward_war.
24   See S/PV.6498, 17 March 2011.
25   "Libya Protests: Defiant Gaddafi Refuses to Quit," BBC News, 22 February 2011, www.bbc
      .co.uk/news/world-middle-east-12544624.

problem identified by China, Russia, and India revolved around procedural and pragmatic questions that were left unanswered in Resolution 1973: How would the no-fly zone be enforced? What assets would be used? What rules of engagement would the coalition adopt? And crucially, what might the end-game entail? The Russian delegation also complained that new provisions (it did not specify which) had been added to the resolution that went beyond the LAS request and opened the door to more large-scale military intervention. India's representative also questioned the timing of the decision to use force before the UN special envoy had delivered his report to the Council. Brazil's representative questioned whether the use of military force by external actors would change the homegrown nature of the rebellion and thereby inhibit long-term conflict resolution. With a highly skeptical domestic audience, South Africa was also deeply concerned about the potential use of force.

Nevertheless, the skeptics were left with little diplomatic room for maneuver because the Council had accepted the legitimacy of international engagement by unanimously adopting Resolution 1970 and was confronted with advice from the UN Secretariat and elsewhere that mass atrocities were imminent. Hence, when a draft resolution calling for political dialogue was presented by Russia it secured little political momentum, in part because it seemed dangerously out of step with the rapidly evolving situation on the ground and in part because of greater support for a draft circulated by France, Great Britain, and Lebanon.[26]

In the end, the vote on 17 March saw Resolution 1973 pass with ten votes in favor (Bosnia and Herzegovina, Colombia, France, Gabon, Lebanon, Portugal, Nigeria, South Africa, the United Kingdom, and the United States), zero votes against, and five abstentions (Brazil, China, Germany, India, and Russia). The eight-page resolution initially reiterated the Council's concern that crimes against humanity may have been committed, deplored the ongoing humanitarian crisis, and took note of the criticisms of Gaddafi's regime made by a variety of international organizations, particularly the LAS call for a no-fly zone and safe areas to protect civilians. Once again, it defined the situation in Libya as a threat to international peace and security and, acting under Chapter VII of the UN Charter, demanded, among other things, an immediate cease-fire and intensified efforts to find a political solution to the crisis. In operative paragraph 4, the Council authorized the use of "all necessary measures ... to protect civilians and civilian populated areas under threat of attack ... while excluding a foreign occupation force of any form on any part of Libyan territory." In operative paragraph 6, it established "a ban on all flights in the

---

26   Lebanon was acting as the representative of the LAS.

airspace of the Libyan Arab Jamahiriya in order to help protect civilians." The only exceptions were those flights necessary to enforce the no-fly zone and those "whose sole purpose is humanitarian" (operative paragraph 7). It also refined the arms embargo and asset freeze detailed in Resolution 1970, in part by creating a panel of experts to assist in their implementation.

Why did these five states abstain rather than vote against the draft resolution? In our view, five major factors stand out. First, a vote against would have undermined the Council's own credibility and authority. This was because the Council had already demanded "an immediate end to the violence" in Resolution 1970, there was clear evidence of continued violence more than two weeks later as well as the threat of mass atrocities, and Gaddafi's regime had consistently refused to comply with its demands. A second factor was that two of the most relevant regional organizations, the LAS and OIC, explicitly called for such a resolution and the three African members of the Council voted in support. Although the AU had rejected the use of force, it was widely believed that the African members of the Security Council were sympathetic to the UK-French-Lebanese draft. In this context, a vote against Resolution 1973 could have been construed as ignoring key regional voices, something that the Chinese in particular were usually keen to avoid. Indeed, without the call for force issued by the LAS, OIC, and GCC, it is highly unlikely that a text similar to what became Resolution 1973 would ever have been voted on. A third factor was the declaration by the United States, the United Kingdom, and France that they would use force only if authorized to do so by the Security Council, a prerequisite for R2P as agreed by UN member states. The Obama administration's obvious reticence about intervention and the insistence on a UN mandate reassured states that might otherwise have been critical of "Western interventionism." The fourth major factor was the lack of good alternative policy options. Gaddafi's public threats against his own population made it difficult to argue that the threat of mass atrocities was not real or that if Benghazi fell mass atrocities would not occur quickly. The fifth factor was Gaddafi's lack of friends. Over the past few decades, Gaddafi had managed to insult and alienate many leaders across the Middle East and Africa; his regime's previous support for international terrorism had alienated the West; and his erratic posturing had eroded his credibility with much of the rest of international society. As a result of these factors, Council members that remained skeptical about the use of force calculated that they could not justify voting against measures designed to halt mass atrocities.

These concerns were evident in the statements of several Council members that abstained on Resolution 1973. Brazil, for example, noted that its abstention "should in no way be interpreted as condoning the behaviour of the

Libyan authorities or as disregard for the need to protect civilians and respect their rights." However, its representative remained unconvinced "that the use of force as provided for in paragraph 4 of the resolution will lead to the realization of our common objective—the immediate end to violence and the protection of civilians." Russia also claimed it was a "consistent and firm" advocate of the "basic principle" of protecting civilians and stressed that it "did not prevent the adoption of this resolution." However, its representative thought "that the quickest way to ensure robust security for the civilian population and the long-term stabilization of the situation in Libya is an immediate ceasefire." Finally, China emphasized that it supported "the Security Council's adoption of appropriate and necessary action to stabilize the situation in Libya as soon as possible and to halt acts of violence against civilians," but that it was "always against the use of force in international relations." China's representative also raised procedural issues by noting that many of China's questions during the "consultations on resolution 1973 ... failed to be clarified or answered." Consequently, China had "serious difficulty with parts of the resolution."[27] Each of these statements exhibited wariness about the use of force but these countries concluded that, on balance, this was better registered via an abstention than a vote against, which for Russia and China at least would have scuppered attempts to prevent imminent mass atrocities.

Interestingly, after the enforcement campaign began, it was South African president Jacob Zuma who was among its most vocal critics. Although South Africa was a member of the AU's Peace and Security Council that had earlier rejected the use of force, its representative had voted in support of Resolution 1973. South Africa's decision about which way to vote was taken at the highest level and at the last possible moment, with its permanent representative to the UN arriving late to the Council meeting because he was receiving last minute instructions from Pretoria. South Africa's statement in support of Resolution 1973 also noted its rejection of "any foreign occupation or unilateral military intervention under the pretext of protecting civilians."[28] Zuma's subsequent criticisms of the enforcement campaign seemed to revolve largely around his concerns that the coalition had overstepped the terms of its mandate, about its lack of support for the AU's road map and its high-level panel of which he was a member, and because of vocal criticism of the campaign by a number of influential domestic groups within South Africa.[29]

---

27   All quotes from S/PV.6498, 17 March 2011.
28   S/PV.6498, 17 March 2011, p. 10.
29   A good indicator of the South African domestic debate on Libya is the public letter released
      in August 2011 and supported by some 300 mainly South African public intellectuals and

With the passage of Resolution 1973, UN-authorized force against a de jure government for human protection purposes is no longer just a theoretical possibility. Although the resolution owes its existence to several political factors that were unique to the situation in Libya—and are therefore unlikely to be repeated often—it is difficult to imagine how it could have passed without the preceding decade of advocacy for the R2P principle. In the next section, we summarize the three main traditional challenges to the use of force for human protection purposes before discussing how advocacy on R2P helped overcome them, thereby facilitating the passage of Resolution 1973.

2   The Challenges of Using Military Force

Historically, the use of force for human protection purposes remains the exception rather than the rule. A study of how nineteen episodes of mass killing ended during the twentieth century identified four primary factors: the perpetrators achieved their goals, local resistance reduced the rate of killing, dissension occurred among the perpetrator's elites, and external military intervention was carried out for primarily self-interested purposes.[30] These external interventions tended to be both more likely and more effective than interventions inspired by humanitarian concerns. Another study examined the role of military force in ending twelve cases of genocidal killing from the early twentieth century to 2008. It found that, with few exceptions, these episodes ended because the perpetrators chose to stop or were defeated militarily by local opponents.[31]

Although the two studies used slightly different sets of cases, they highlighted several common points. First, in more than half of the cases covered by both studies, mass killing ended only when the perpetrators chose to stop, whether because they had achieved their goals, because they had recalibrated their calculations of relative costs and benefits, or because of internal elite dissension. Second, when perpetrators were forced to stop the killing, it was most often a product of local armed resistance by actors working on behalf of the victim group. Third, external military intervention could sometimes prove

---

activists, including Thabo Mbeki. This accused the Security Council of "subverting" and "repudiating" the "rule of international law" and "undermining the legitimacy of the UN in the eyes of the African people" and NATO of "rewriting" resolution 1973 and engaging in a "war of aggression in Libya." The text and details are at www.concernedafricans.co.za.

30   Alex de Waal and Bridget Conley-Zilkic, "Reflections on How Genocidal Killings Are Brought to an End," *Social Science Research Council*, 22 December 2006.

31   Bellamy, "Military Intervention," pp. 599–601.

decisive, but was usually inspired by self-interest rather than humanitarianism. Both studies agreed that external military intervention expressly aimed at protecting populations was among the rarest of endings. Finally, response strategies short of direct military confrontation (e.g., peacekeeping troops, safe havens, economic sanctions, political sanctions, and criminal indictment) did little to deescalate or end mass killing.[32]

What accounts for the rarity of forcible human protection policies? We suggest that the answer lies in three major sets of challenges related to principled disagreements, political objections, and prudential considerations. When combined, these challenges usually make the use of military force an extremely unattractive proposition for policymakers, even those who see some merit in preventing and responding to genocide and mass atrocities abroad.

2.1   *Principled Disagreements*

Principled challenges usually question the legality and/or morality of using military force. The legal debate revolves around whether international law permits a right of military intervention in the absence of Security Council authorization. It tends to be framed around an enduring struggle between states' rights to territorial integrity, political independence, and nonintervention and basic human rights—a tension abundantly evident in the UN Charter. Because many states remain committed to the principle of noninterference, seeing it as an essential legal right that protects them from the arbitrary power of strong states and allows them to determine their own political fate, it has proved difficult to persuade the UN Security Council to authorize the use of military force against governments that perpetrate mass atrocities. In 1979, for example, the Council admonished Vietnam for invading Cambodia, even though it put an end to a genocide that killed 1.5 million people in three and one-half years and would have killed many more.[33] More recently, Pakistan used this line of argument to prevent the UN from employing enforcement measures in Darfur because "the Sudan has all the rights and privileges incumbent under the United Nations Charter, including to sovereignty, political independence, unity and territorial integrity."[34]

Adam Roberts accurately sums up this legal debate as "there is not at present a one-word general answer to this seemingly clear question. Nor is there

---

32   See de Waal and Conley-Zilkic, "Reflections"; Bellamy, "Military Intervention."
33   Nicholas J. Wheeler, *Saving Strangers: Humanitarian Intervention in International Society* (Oxford: Oxford University Press, 2000), pp. 90–91.
34   S/PV.4988, 11 June 2004, p. 4.

any chance of such an answer emerging in the near future."[35] While it is widely acknowledged that the UN Security Council has the right to authorize the use of military force for any purpose deemed necessary to maintain international peace and security, the dispute centers on whether other actors could conduct such an intervention legally without the Security Council's authorization. While a small handful of international legal experts have argued that such action is permissible—largely on the basis of an interpretation of customary international law and a reading of specific treaties and sources of international humanitarian law—the majority view remains that such interventions are illegal.[36] The challenge for those advocating, in certain dire circumstances, for force to be used to protect civilians, was that until Resolution 1973 the Council had never authorized military force to stop genocide and mass atrocities against the will of a de jure government.

In this context, probably the best that interveners could hope for would be to acknowledge the general perception that their action stretched the limits of international legality and to make a plea in mitigation in light of moral necessity in exceptional circumstances.[37] But placing the normative risks firmly on the shoulders of interveners constitutes a powerful deterrent to intervention and encourages states to consider this route only when other vital interests are also at stake.

In addition to the legal problems, the use of military force for protection purposes also faces principled moral objections. These have come in three main varieties related to its potential to encourage *instability*, *abuse*, and *selectivity*. One argument suggests that endorsing a norm of humanitarian intervention within a society of states whose members rarely agree on what counts as just conduct is a recipe for undermining the normative basis of the contemporary international order and provoking instability that will lead to greater levels of human suffering in the long run.[38] From this perspective, other norms, such as the principles of nonintervention and self-determination, are equally, if not more important than the protection of populations from genocide and mass

---

35   Adam Roberts, "The So-called 'Right' of Humanitarian Intervention," *Yearbook of International Humanitarian Law* 3 (Summer 2001): 3.

36   See, for example, the series of articles on the Kosovo crisis in *International and Comparative Law Quarterly* 49, no. 4 (2000): 876–943; Simon Chesterman, *Just War or Just Peace? Humanitarian Intervention and International Law* (Oxford: Oxford University Press, 2001).

37   See Michael Byers and Simon Chesterman, "Changing the Rules About Rules? Unilateral Humanitarian Intervention and the Future of International Law," in J.L. Holzgrefe and Robert O. Keohane, eds., *Humanitarian Intervention* (Cambridge: Cambridge University Press, 2003), pp. 199–200.

38   See Robert Jackson, *The Global Covenant* (Oxford: Oxford University Press, 2000).

atrocities. Indeed, both of these norms have attracted more persistent support within international society as a better basis on which to build a stable international order.[39] Moreover, the concept of humanitarian intervention has been regularly and explicitly rejected by significant numbers of states as an unacceptable breach of sovereignty that, after all, is the last line of defense against imperialism for the world's small states.[40]

A second objection is that, whatever altruistic motives may lie behind the desire to codify a norm of humanitarian military intervention, its practical application in contemporary world politics will always be open to abuse by powerful governments. As the recent cases of the US-led invasion of Iraq (2003) and Russian military action in South Ossetia and Georgia (2008) illustrate, powerful states remain willing to use humanitarian rhetoric as a fig leaf for the pursuit of narrow political interests. From this perspective, it is no coincidence that US military power has led the way in almost all of the most controversial cases of military intervention in the post-Cold War period, including northern Iraq (1991), Somalia (1992), Haiti (1994), Kosovo (1999), Afghanistan (2001), Iraq (2003), and now Libya (2011).

A third challenge stems from the related argument that the moral case for using force would be greatly strengthened if the military instrument was applied in a consistent manner. In practice, however, powerful governments usually make arguments to justify why the suffering of certain groups of humans should be considered more important than others: thus during the 1990s, NATO forces were called on to act in response to the indiscriminate killing of civilians in Bosnia and Kosovo but not those in, for example, Chechnya, Turkey, or Palestine.

In summary, the use of military force for human protection purposes has traditionally faced some serious legal and moral challenges. Although they did not stop determined states or groups of states from using force when it suited them, as in NATO's intervention in Kosovo (1999), they did make intervention unattractive and potentially costly.

2.2 Political Objections

Advocates of using military force to protect populations from genocide and mass atrocities must also overcome a range of tough political objections. First

---

39 See Martha Finnemore, "Paradoxes in Humanitarian Intervention," in Richard Price, ed., *Moral Limit and Possibility in World Politics* (Cambridge: Cambridge University Press, 2008), pp. 197–224.

40 See, for example, Declaration on the Inadmissibility of Intervention and Interference in the Internal Affairs of States, UN General Assembly, A/RES/36/103, 9 December 1981.

and foremost, "saving strangers" (read foreigners) is rarely a priority for any state's foreign policy. As a consequence, in real and potential cases of mass atrocities states can usually point to a range of more important political priorities to justify nonintervention.

The root of these political obstacles is the fact that the appeal of committing military resources to humanitarian enterprises abroad is largely based on cosmopolitan political theories and ideals of global justice.[41] The use of force to protect distant populations makes perfect sense if one subscribes to these starting points and assumptions. However, the most prevalent sentiments held by domestic publics about foreign policy are more nationalistic and communitarian than cosmopolitan. Even in liberal democratic states, most politicians do not see a vote-winning opportunity in sending their soldiers to fight in somebody else's complicated war. In other words, the center of political gravity in most domestic debates about the use of military force for human protection defines politicians' primary responsibility as protecting their own citizens rather than foreigners. Risking "our" soldiers to save "their" people thus requires politicians to make a set of arguments that usually run against the political grain of domestic opinion. Few votes are won by sending soldiers overseas to save strangers, but there are many to be lost if the operation goes badly.

Other political obstacles derive from this basic disconnect. Two of the most commonly asserted relate to financial costs and political capital. Military interventions will inevitably be a costly drain on the state's financial resources so, once again, politicians have to make the case for why intervention is worth the money. In addition, if one is interested in saving strangers, then the military invasion of another country is never likely to be a cost-effective method of going about it. Since literally millions of people around the world die each year from preventable diseases, it makes sense that investing in better international public health programs would save many more lives at a fraction of the cost (it would also probably "not require killing anyone or violating any international laws").[42] Moreover, even when leaders muster the necessary political capital to embark on an intervention, they will be acutely aware that it is a risky venture likely to face various complications along the way that might jeopardize their invested capital.

---

41   See, for example, Mary Kaldor's notion of "cosmopolitan law enforcement" in *New and Old Wars* (Oxford: Polity, 1999), especially chapter 6. See also Simon Caney, *Justice Beyond Borders* (Oxford: Oxford University Press, 2005).

42   See Benjamin Valentino, "The Perils of Limited Humanitarian Intervention: Lessons from the 1990s," *Wisconsin International Law Journal* 24, no. 3 (2006): 734ff.

The result is that domestic politics tends to pull democratic governments away from using force to protect populations from genocide and mass atrocities. Where few national interests are at stake, it takes brave politicians to commit forces to such a campaign.

2.3 *Prudential Considerations*

Prudential considerations appear most acutely once the use of force has been recognized as a legitimate policy option to stop genocide and mass atrocities or protect vulnerable populations. They suggest that, on balance, an intervention is likely to do more harm than good in the theater in question, in relation to wider international political dynamics, or both. Prudential considerations are often framed as calls to engage with the issues raised by mass killing on the assumption that the use of military force will always be a blunt tool to deal with such problems.[43] For example, deploying forces might provoke a wider conflict; jeopardize the search for a political solution by providing incentives for weaker parties to continue to fight; inadvertently empower local warlords; prolong conflict and suffering by increasing the magnitude of violence, thereby dragging external actors into complex wars with no easy exit; and fail to improve conditions on the ground.

Such risks encourage states that are already risk averse (thanks to the principled and political objections discussed above) to judge that they lack the capacity to intervene effectively. Debates in 2004–2005 over potential intervention in Darfur highlighted each of these problems. Opponents argued that it would do more harm than good; might jeopardize other priorities (especially the so-called Comprehensive Peace Agreement between the Government of Sudan and the Sudan People's Liberation Movement, which brought a longer-running and more deadly civil war to an end); and that with ongoing commitments in Iraq, Afghanistan, and the Balkans, Western governments lacked the political capital and military capacity to assist. Thus, one respected commentator concluded that "however attractive it might be from a distance, actually providing physical protection for Darfurians with international troops is not feasible."[44] Likewise, Francis Deng, currently the UN Secretary-General's special adviser

---

43   For example, Ken Booth, "Military Intervention: Duty and Prudence," in Lawrence Freedman, ed., *Military Intervention in European Conflicts* (Oxford: Blackwell, 1994), pp. 56–75; and, in relation to Syria, Marc Lynch, *Pressure Not War: A Pragmatic and Principled Policy Towards Syria* (Washington, DC: Center for a New American Security, 2012).

44   Alex de Waal, "No Such Thing as Humanitarian Intervention," *Harvard International Review*, 21 March 2007, http://hir.harvard.edu/no-such-thing-as-humanitarian-intervention.

on the prevention of genocide, argued that coercive measures would "complicate and aggravate" the crisis by increasing the level of violence.[45]

There is also a real challenge related to the lack of appropriate and tested military doctrine in relevant states and international organizations on how to perform the core tasks of civilian protection.[46] As one recent analysis put it, at the strategic level there has been a lack of systematic "thinking about *how* military forces might respond" to situations of mass killing.[47] Put another way, asking soldiers trained to defeat enemies and capture territory—the basis of most traditional military training—may sometimes be sufficient for responding to episodes of mass killing, but not always.

In sum, even when states are genuinely concerned about the commission of mass atrocities abroad, principled disagreements, political objections, and prudential considerations have elevated the moral, political, and material risks and reduced the potential payoffs of using force to protect populations in danger. It is therefore hardly surprising that the use of military force by outsiders for human protection has been rare. And yet while the civilian bodies kept piling up, the issues raised in these debates would not go away. It was this stubborn fact that spurred R2P's advocates to shift the debate from whether actors had a right to intervene to stop atrocities to how states should exercise their responsibility to protect populations in danger—the central theme advanced by the international commission that first coined the phrase "R2P" in 2001.[48] In the next section, we examine the extent to which the R2P principle changed the prospects for overcoming these challenges and thereby helped enable Resolution 1973.

---

45   *Report of the Representative of the Secretary-General on Internally Displaced Persons: Mission to the Sudan The Darfur Crisis*, UN Doc. E/CN.4/2005/8, 27 September 2004, paras. 36–37.

46   For attempts to overcome this gap, see Victoria K. Holt and Tobias C. Berkman, *The Impossible Mandate? Military Preparedness, the Responsibility to Protect, and Modern Peace Operations* (Washington, DC: Henry L. Stimson Center, 2006); Sarah Sewall et al., *Mass Atrocity Response Operations: A Military Planning Handbook* (Cambridge: Harvard Kennedy School and Peacekeeping and Stability Operations Institute, 2010); Alison Giffen, *Addressing the Doctrinal Deficit: Developing Guidance to Prevent and Respond to Widespread or Systematic Attacks Against Civilians*, A Workshop Report (Washington, DC: Henry L. Stimson Center, Spring 2010).

47   Sewall et al., *Mass Atrocity Response Operations*, p. 5.

48   International Commission on Intervention and State Sovereignty (ICISS), *The Responsibility to Protect* (Ottawa: International Development Research Center, 2001).

3   The "R2P Effect"

In 2005 the world's governments acknowledged their responsibility to protect their populations from genocide, war crimes, ethnic cleansing, and crimes against humanity as well as their incitement.[49] They also said they would assist each other to meet their responsibilities and that, should any state be found to be "manifestly failing to protect their populations" from these four crimes, external actors would "take collective action, in a timely and decisive manner, through the Security Council, in accordance with the Charter."[50] Since then, the R2P principle has been endorsed in Security Council resolutions, General Assembly statements, and several reports of the UN Secretary-General and has generated a new Joint Office of the Secretary-General's Special Advisers on Genocide Prevention and R2P.[51]

But while R2P calls for the strengthening of capacities to prevent and respond effectively to mass atrocities, it does not prescribe appropriate courses of action for specific contexts or resolve political and prudential disputes about the most effective courses of action in particular situations. The challenge for us in this section is to assess the extent to which R2P has overcome the principled, political, and prudential challenges to the use of force discussed above.

3.1   *Principle*

R2P has succeeded in changing the terms of international debates about mass atrocities from questions about whether external actors should be engaged to how they should be engaged. In contrast to the tenor of debates in the 1990s and early 2000s, the statements made by those states that abstained on Resolution 1973 gave no hint of being guided by concerns about the Council's jurisdiction. Indeed, after being such a large part of the debates in the 1990s, it was notable that the phrase "*international* peace and security" was aired only by Colombia, which put forth one of the most robust defenses of Resolution 1973 and pointed specifically to R2P.[52]

This R2P–related shift is significant for two principal reasons. First, by focusing on the prevention of mass atrocities and protection of would-be victims, international actors have become more familiar with a wider range of policy options short of military force and have adopted new tactics such as lending

---

49   The principle was first advanced by the ICISS. Its genesis is discussed in Gareth Evans, *The Responsibility to Protect* (Washington, DC: Brookings Institution Press, 2009).

50   *2005 World Summit Outcome*, UN Doc. A/60/L.1, 24 October 2005, paras. 138–140.

51   See Alex J. Bellamy, "The Responsibility to Protect—Five Years On," *Ethics and International Affairs* 24, no. 2 (2010): 143–169.

52   S/PV.6498, 17 March 2011.

political support to regionally led efforts. Since 2007, these have had some impact, most notably the AU-UN efforts in Kenya (2007–2008), the initiative in Guinea led by the Economic Community of West African States (ECOWAS) and backed by the UN Security Council, and UN and other efforts to prevent the January 2011 referendum in Sudan from sparking a new wave of mass killing. Sometimes, however, a degree of military force was deemed necessary to protect civilians, as reflected in the Council's robust mandates for peacekeepers in eastern DRC, Sudan, and Côte d'Ivoire.

Second, once states accept that international actors have a responsibility to protect foreign civilians from mass atrocities, it is harder—though not impossible—for them to remain indifferent in the face of compelling evidence of such crimes. Of course, real cases are sufficiently complex to allow states to accept the need for action but to demand a response short of military force on prudential grounds. This has been evident in the international debates over how to respond, for example, to mass atrocities in Sudan and Syria. But on rare occasions, the nature of the situation makes it difficult to plausibly sustain such a position. In Libya, the impending fall of Benghazi, the regime's overt threats to commit atrocities, evidence that it had already targeted civilians, and its long track record of abuses left little room to doubt the credibility and the urgency of the threat. In the end, in the absence of plausible alternative policies for preventing a massacre in Benghazi, even those members of the Security Council that remained deeply skeptical about the use of force felt unable to vote against those calling for a forceful response. With this in mind, it is worth noting that neither of the draft resolutions on Syria vetoed by Russia and China (5 October 2011 and 4 February 2012) contained clear pathways to resolve the crisis or specific measures designed to prevent atrocities. Furthermore, on both occasions, Russia and China argued that—in the absence of such clear linkage between Council action and atrocity prevention—the resolution's passage would inflame the situation and increase the overall risk to the population. Indeed, after vetoing the 4 February draft resolution, Russia's permanent representative emphasized that Moscow was actively employing diplomatic means to end the crisis and that its proposed amendments to the text were designed to improve the situation, notably by insisting that Syrian government forces withdraw from cities "in conjunction" with the withdrawal of rebel forces.[53] Thus, one of several key differences between the Libya and Syria cases was that

---

53 See informal comments to the media by Vitaly I. Churkin, permanent representative of the Russian Federation to the UN, 4 February 2012, www.unmultimedia.org/tv/webcast/2012/02/h-e-mr-vitaly-i-churkin-russian-federation-on-the-situation-in-syria-security-council-media-stakeout-2.html.

the former provided little scope for doubting the threat and few alternative strategies while the latter saw Council members disagree on the nature of the problem (especially the role of non-government forces) and the most appropriate way forward.

How do we explain this shift? To be clear, state leaders have certainly not decided to jettison their commitment to noninterference in favor of R2P. Many UN members explicitly reaffirmed the principles of noninterference and territorial integrity even as they supported or acquiesced in decisions to enforce Council resolutions. Instead, the transformation of the principled terrain in the Security Council can be explained by reference to two theories. The first suggests that some governments remain skeptical about R2P and prefer the norm of noninterference, but attempt to conceal this by "mimicking" support for R2P.[54] They do this, so the argument goes, because while they do not support R2P, they are unwilling to publicly argue against the principle's goal of preventing genocide and mass atrocities. Having repeatedly affirmed the R2P principle in the General Assembly and thematic Security Council resolutions, such governments might be expected to offer rhetorical support for R2P in principle but offer a raft of prudential reasons to stymie international activism. Occasionally, however, these states become trapped by their own rhetorical commitments and, in the absence of plausible alternatives, face a choice between either acquiescing in behavior they find deeply uncomfortable or contradicting themselves so obviously as to potentially undermine the credibility of other rhetorical commitments to which they are more wedded.

A parallel process is that of norm localization. From this perspective, the consensus about R2P that led to Resolution 1973 derived from processes of norm localization that are producing an accommodation between the principles of R2P and noninterference.[55] This entails the subtle realignment of each in order to make them compatible. During the process of negotiating R2P at the UN General Assembly, revisions were made that limited its capacity to legitimize coercive interference, excluding entirely the potential for enforcement without UN Security Council approval (i.e., decoupling R2P from efforts to develop a legal norm supporting humanitarian military intervention).[56] On the other hand, the norm of noninterference has also been recalibrated to

---

54   See Alistair Iain Johnston, *Social States: China in International Institutions, 1980–2000* (Princeton: Princeton University Press, 2007).

55   See Amitav Acharya, *Whose Ideas Matter? Agency and Power in Asian Regionalism* (Ithaca: Cornell University Press, 2009).

56   Report of the UN Secretary-General, *Implementing the Responsibility to Protect*, UN Doc. A/63/677, 12 January 2009, par. 3. See, for example, Michael W. Doyle, "International Ethics and the Responsibility to Protect," *International Studies Review* 13, no. 1 (2011): 82.

permit expressions of concern, offers of assistance, and even the application of diplomatic pressure and coercive force in response to major humanitarian crises. This shift was evident within the LAS, OIC, and GCC, but is also evident in other parts of the world.[57] In the Libyan case, the compatibility was evident inasmuch as traditional R2P skeptics acknowledged that international society should adopt measures to prevent mass atrocities while interventionist states conceded that they would use military force only if granted a mandate by the UN Security Council.

One of the lingering problems is that the current version of compatibility between R2P and the principle of noninterference requires that the use of force to prevent or stop genocide and mass atrocities be mandated by the UN Security Council. This leaves in place difficult questions about where the responsibility to protect lies if the Security Council agrees such crimes have been committed, but fails to agree on how to respond. While states were willing and able to find common ground on Libya, this will not always be the case.

3.2   *Politics*

Political will is malleable: it can "be built or destroyed by actions over time."[58] In some states advocacy efforts associated with R2P centers, coalitions, and activists have influenced national politics by subtly shifting the political balance in favor of using military force to protect civilians in certain circumstances. In the United States, for example, R2P has been part of the development of an epistemic community of experts, practitioners, and activists working on atrocity prevention and response. Motivated in large part by the catastrophes in Rwanda and Darfur, these groups have sought to build an antigenocide constituency within US domestic politics—including institutions like the United States Institute of Peace, the US Holocaust Memorial Museum, the Enough Project, and the Genocide Intervention Network—but also to alter the government's decisionmaking structures so that mass atrocity prevention is always given a seat in the key decisionmaking processes. They have recently enjoyed some success. Not only was R2P included in the May 2010 US National Security Strategy, but President Obama established a new position

---

57   For example, regarding Africa and Southeast Asia, see Paul D. Williams, "From Non-intervention to Non-indifference: The Origins and Development of the African Union's Security Culture," *African Affairs* 106, no. 423 (2007): 253–279; Alex J. Bellamy and Catherine Drummond, "The Responsibility to Protect in Southeast Asia: Between Non-interference and Sovereignty as Responsibility," *Pacific Review* 24, no. 2 (2011): 179–200.

58   Edward C. Luck, "The Responsibility to Protect: Growing Pains or Early Promise?" *Ethics and International Affairs* 24, no. 4 (2010): 359.

on the National Security Staff—director for war crimes, atrocities, and civilian protection—who is responsible for coordinating and supporting the administration's policies on preventing, identifying, and responding to mass atrocities and genocide. In August 2011, this was followed up with the creation of an Interagency Atrocities Prevention Board and a corresponding interagency review under Presidential Study Directive 10. This board met for the first time in April 2012.

This epistemic community has at times played an activist role, when its members demand that the government take steps to protect vulnerable populations overseas. Its members have also provided critical commentary about the effectiveness of extant policies and, in some respects, served a policy advising function by identifying practical and plausible steps to alleviate human suffering.[59] It is difficult to know where the call for a no-fly zone in Libya originated, but it appears that experts and activists in the United States and United Kingdom were somewhat ahead of political leaders in this regard.[60] Finally, the US epistemic community serves as a repository of expertise from which governments can draw. Within the Obama administration, two of the principal advocates of military action over Libya were well-known members of the atrocity prevention epistemic community: namely, Samantha Power, senior director for multilateral affairs at the National Security Council, and the US permanent representative to the UN, Susan E. Rice.

All these activities have helped shape domestic expectations and, hence, the context in which political will is generated. It needs to be stressed however that the US antigenocide epistemic community is much more advanced than in most other countries and that its capacity to influence government behavior is likely to vary considerably across cases and administrations. Moreover, it does not alter the fact that domestic politics usually creates powerful incentives for political leaders to be risk averse in the face of mass atrocities abroad. Nevertheless, it has helped insert atrocity prevention into foreign policy deliberations, and centrally so when the threat is obvious and imminent.

---

59   The International Crisis Group and Refugees International were both born of this belief. See Mark Malloch-Brown, *The Unfinished Global Revolution* (Harmondsworth: Penguin Press, 2011).

60   To our knowledge, the first significant reference came on 21 February 2011, when Libya's defecting permanent representative to the UN called for a no-fly zone. On 22 February, the Global Center for R2P preceded both the British prime minister and French president with its "Open Statement on Libya," 22 February 2011, www.globalr2p.org/media/pdf/Open_Statement_on_the_Situation_in_Libya.pdf.

3.3   *Prudence*

Assuming that the various principled and political challenges can be overcome, advocates of using military force to protect populations from genocide
and mass atrocities still confront serious prudential considerations. Even in
Libya, where the threat of mass atrocities was exceptionally clear and imminent, there was considerable uncertainty about what a no-fly zone should
entail and where to draw the line between missions carried out to protect civilians and those to hasten regime change.[61] There was also deep skepticism
about the capacity of aviation operations to protect civilians on the ground—
in part because of the history of previous air campaigns in Iraq, Bosnia, and
Kosovo. It is notable that not only did NATO struggle to maintain the tempo
of sorties it had originally planned (conducting about 150 rather than 300 a
day), but the air campaign was augmented by the delivery of armaments to
the rebels (violating the Security Council's own arms embargo, according to
some members of the Council); the provision of basic training to anti-Gaddafi
forces; and the covert deployment of special forces into Libya, including
by Great Britain, France, Italy, Qatar, and the UAE, first to evacuate foreign
nationals and then to coordinate with the rebels, aid the air campaign, and
secure key installations.[62]

Proponents of R2P must therefore develop more systematic responses to
these questions. Although much work remains to be done, some progress has
been made in (1) identifying and applying a broader continuum of measures
and (2) sharpening doctrinal thinking about the use of military force to protect
civilians. On the first point, it clearly makes no sense to rely exclusively on a
policy (military force) that deals with only the symptoms of mass atrocities
rather than the underlying conditions that make such episodes more likely.[63]
Good policy must begin "with anticipation and prevention, early engagement,
and keeping as many reasonable options open as possible."[64] In other words,
the use of military force tackles only part of the mass killing equation and

---

61   Arguably the most blatant indicator that the coalition had crossed the line between civil-
      ian protection and regime change at the strategic/political level was the op-ed by Barack
      Obama, David Cameron, and Nicolas Sarkozy, "Libya's Pathway to Peace," *New York Times*,
      14 April 2011, www.nytimes.com/2011/04/15/opinion/15iht-edlibya15.html.
62   See Barry, "Libya's Lessons," pp. 8–9; *Accidental Heroes: Britain, France and the Libya
      Operation*, RUSI Interim Campaign Report, (London: Royal United Services Institute for
      Defence and Security Studies, September 2011), pp. 10–11; David Roberts, "Behind Qatar's
      Intervention in Libya," *Foreign Affairs*, 28 September 2011, www.foreignaffairs.com/
      articles/68302/david-roberts/behind-qatars-intervention-in-libya.
63   See Edward Luck, "A Response," *Global Responsibility to Protect* 2, nos. 1–2 (2010): 181.
64   Ibid., p. 181.

represents only one potentially useful instrument among a larger toolbox of policy options aimed at prevention as well as response.

R2P, on the other hand, demands a much wider range of policy tools, including diplomacy, early warning, prevention, peacekeeping, sanctions, and judicial measures as well as coercion.[65] One of the difficulties for any preventive agenda is that R2P crimes can occur in contexts of armed conflict as well as during peacetime, although most occur in the former scenario. This means that policymakers concerned with preventing R2P crimes require an "atrocity prevention lens" to assess which contexts might generate atrocities and to tailor their responses to the different challenges posed by wartime and peacetime environments.[66] To some extent, the UN's newly formed joint office for genocide prevention and R2P reflects precisely these concerns.

While a useful start, policymakers are still in the early stages of understanding, let alone effectively wielding, the full range of preventive instruments. As a consequence, they must continue to try to overcome the difficult prudential questions about the use of military force in circumstances like those in Libya where there were few viable alternatives.

This has stimulated efforts to develop doctrine relevant to civilian protection operations. To date, this has come in two main strands. The first is what has become known as the Protection of Civilians (PoC) agenda within contemporary peace operations. Given its setting within peace operations, this strand relates only to scenarios where forces are deployed with the consent of the host government, are able to operate impartially, and are able to conduct protection tasks with minimum force. This has influenced documents setting out guidelines, principles, and to some extent doctrine within the UN, AU, and EU in particular. In these scenarios the principal threats to civilians usually come from a combination of insurgents, predatory government soldiers, and criminal gangs, and the principal protection activities involve positioning military forces between the civilian population and those that threaten them and taking measures designed to eliminate or restrict the activities of armed groups that threaten civilians.[67]

The second strand has emerged from attempts to develop new doctrine for the US armed forces that might help them function effectively in situations of

---

65   See, for example, the measures proposed in the Report of the UN Secretary-General, *Implementing the Responsibility to Protect*, pars. 14, 17, 22, 24, 27, 30, 32, 38, 42, 43, 45, and 48.

66   See Alex J. Bellamy, *Mass Atrocities and Armed Conflict*, Stanley Foundation Policy Analysis Brief (Muscatine, IA: Stanley Foundation, February 2011).

67   See, for example, Holt and Taylor, *Protecting Civilians*; Giffen, *Addressing the Doctrinal Deficit*.

mass atrocities.[68] Arguably the most useful example of this type of approach has been the Mass Atrocity Response Operations (MARO) military planning handbook. A collaborative effort between the Carr Center for Human Rights Policy at the Harvard Kennedy School and the US Army's Peacekeeping and Stability Operations Institute, this project aims to persuade the US government to enshrine the MARO concept into its military doctrine. A MARO "describes a contingency operation to halt widespread and systematic use of violence by state or non-state armed groups against non-combatants," which is distinguished in military terms by its "primary objective of stopping the killing of civilians."[69] MAROs take place in contexts characterized by multi-party dynamics between victims, perpetrators, and bystanders rather than traditional contexts between enemy and friendly forces, where the intervening force will inevitably be seen as siding with the victims against the perpetrators, and where there is a tendency for the mass killings to rapidly escalate once begun. The handbook has significantly advanced the wider international debate on how to protect civilians through its discussion of seven approaches to direct military intervention: the saturation, "oil spot," separation, safe areas, partner enabling, containment, and defeat perpetrators approaches.

R2P has thus been associated, if sometimes only indirectly, with attempts to address prudential questions about how to operationalize the prevention of mass atrocities agenda and employ military force to protect vulnerable populations when needed. But as Libya demonstrates, policymakers and military planners still have to make difficult decisions with little information about what works, and military commanders have to develop ad hoc operational concepts and strategies.

4   Conclusion

Ultimately, it was the combination of the popular protests across the Arab world, the behavior of Gaddafi's regime, and the unusual international politics surrounding his regime that catalyzed the process that ultimately produced Resolution 1973. But the resolution was made more likely because of a decade of advocacy on R2P that had laid much of the political groundwork by: (1) helping to establish the principle that foreign governments have a responsibility to

---

68   See Genocide Prevention Task Force (GPTF), *Preventing Genocide: A Blueprint for US Policymakers* (Washington, DC: United States Institute for Peace, 2008); Sewall et al., *Mass Atrocity Response Operations.*

69   Sewall et al., *Mass Atrocity Response Operations*, p. 21.

stop mass atrocities; (2) helping to clarify how military means might support humanitarian outcomes; and (3) supporting the development of epistemic communities that are slowly warming domestic politics to the idea of saving strangers. Progress in each of these areas has been uneven and has been subject to a degree of backtracking, partly as a result of events in Libya. But an important threshold has been crossed with the Security Council determining that it will not be inhibited *as a matter of principle* from authorizing the use of force against states that kill and terrorize their own populations. While agreement on principle is an important step, agreeing how to apply that principle in the face of complex crises and competing demands is another matter entirely. Military force should be used only if R2P advocates can also make a persuasive case that the political objections are overstated and the prudential considerations can be overcome.

CHAPTER 19*

Special Representatives of the Secretary-General as Norm Arbitrators? Understanding Bottom-Up Authority in UN Peacekeeping

John Karlsrud[1]

> Of course I met Taliban leaders during the time I was in Afghanistan. Anything else for me would have been unthinkable, given the emphasis I was placing on it myself, and the mandate that we have.
>
> KAI EIDE, *special representative of the UN Secretary-General in Afghanistan*[2]

∴

On 4 and 10 April 2011, Choi Young-jin, special representative of the Secretary-General (SRSG)[3] for the UN Operation in Côte d'Ivoire (ONUCI), authorized air strikes against the troops of President Laurent Gbagbo, using MI-24 attack helicopters to defend civilian populations from attacks with heavy weapons by Gbagbo forces.[4] Russia reacted with strong condemnation,

---

* This chapter was originally published in Global Governance, Volume 19, Issue 4, 2013.

1 Dr. John Karlsrud is Research Professor and Head of the Research Group on Peace, Conflict and Development at the Norwegian Institute of International Affairs (NUPI). He has previously served as special assistant to the SRSG and strategic planning officer to the UN Mission in the Central African Republic and Chad (MINURCAT).

   The author thanks Connie Peck, Giulia Piccolino, and two anonymous reviewers for incisive and helpful comments as well as participants at the European Consortium for Political Research general conference in Reykjavik, 25–27 August 2011; the Millennium conference in London, 22–23 October 2011; the NUPI annual theory seminar in December 2011; and the International Studies Association annual meeting in San Diego, 1–4 April 2012.

2 Julian Borger, "Kai Eide Lashes Out," *The Guardian*, 18 March 2010, www.guardian.co.uk/world/julian-borger-global-security-blog/2010/mar/18/afghanistan-taliban (emphasis added).

3 The term *special representative of the Secretary-General* (SRSG) is used here to refer to the various types of representatives of the Secretary-General who may be titled special representative, personal representative, executive representative, special envoy, or special advisor.

4 "Ivory Coast: Besieged Gbagbo 'in Basement' of Residence," *BBC World News*, 5 April 2011, www.bbc.co.uk/news/mobile/world-africa-12967610.

---

immediately questioning the legality of the attack.[5] One year earlier, Kai Eide had stepped down from his post as SRSG for the UN Operation in Afghanistan (UNAMA) after admitting to having initiated contacts with the Taliban,[6] which challenged the US and UK policy of "sticks and carrots."[7]

Such controversial actions and the relationship between the norms they are affecting are pivotal to UN peacekeeping. In Afghanistan, at stake was the principle of impartiality and whether the UN should provide its good offices to the Taliban, which the UN Security Council had designated as terrorists. In Côte d'Ivoire, the tension was between the principles of impartiality and protection of civilians.

In both instances there was a clash between center and periphery, between UN headquarters and the field, with Security Council members showing diminishing support of the SRSGs involved. In this article, I examine some potentially controversial actions of SRSGs, asking whether such actions can reveal how authority is composed in the UN system and the roles of SRSGs in the norm change processes of that system. What can this indicate about norm change in UN peacekeeping operations and in international organizations more generally? How do new norms arise? Rational theories stress the importance of interests of states and, particularly, those of powerful states whereas constructivist theories have shown how the UN can act autonomously, even against the intent of its member states. The scholarly debate has focused on whether the UN can act autonomously against the intent of member states,[8] the role of the Security Council in developing new norms,[9] and whether the

---

5   Alexei Anishchuk, "Russia Criticises UN Force Role in Ivory Coast," 14 April 2011, www.reuters
    .com/article/2011/04/14/ozatp-russia-ivorycoast-idAFJOE73D0C020110414.

6   Interview with Lyse Doucet, "Afghanistan: A Job Half Done," *BBC News*, 4 December 2006,
    http://news.bbc.co.uk/2/hi/south_asia/6205220.stm.

7   Christina Lamb and Stephen Grey, "UN Chief Scorns Miliband Plan for Taliban Talks," *Times
    Online*, 2 August 2009, www.timesonline.co.uk/tol/news/world/asia/article6736047.ece.

8   See, for example, Michael N. Barnett and Martha Finnemore, "The Politics, Power, and
    Pathologies of International Organizations," *International Organization* 53, no. 4 (1999):
    699–732; Michael N. Barnett and Martha Finnemore, *Rules for the World: International
    Organizations in Global Politics* (Ithaca: Cornell University Press, 2004); Deborah D. Avant,
    Martha Finnemore, and Susan K. Sell, *Who Governs the Globe?* (New York: Cambridge
    University Press, 2010).

9   See, for example, Ian Johnstone, "Normative Evolution at the UN: Impact on Operational
    Imperatives," in Bruce D. Jones, Shepard Forman, and Richard Gowan, eds., *Cooperating
    for Peace and Security: Evolving Institutions and Arrangements in a Context of Changing US
    Security Policy* (New York: Cambridge University Press, 2010), pp. 187–214; Ian Johnstone,
    "Legislation and Adjudication in the UN Security Council: Bringing Down the Deliberative
    Deficit," *American Journal of International Law* 102, no. 2 (2008), pp. 275–283; David Malone,
    The UN Security Council: From the Cold War to the 21st Century (Boulder: Lynne Rienner,
    2004).

Secretary-General can be considered a norm entrepreneur as such.[10] While these approaches have shed some light on norm change processes in the UN, they are marred by a top-down perspective that underestimates the role of the field where actual operations unfold.

Some literature has examined bottom-up perspectives on norm change in international organizations (IOs); for example, Martha Finnemore and Kathryn Sikkink's seminal work on nongovernmental organizations (NGOs) as norm entrepreneurs.[11] And the organizational learning literature has focused on the role that assembling best practices and lessons learned has had for the development of guidelines for action and new norms in peacekeeping.[12] Here, I seek to bring in a bottom-up perspective from the field. In peacekeeping, decisions have to be made on a daily basis in politically charged, fluctuating situations. The SRSG operates under authority delegated from the Security Council and the Secretary-General through a Security Council mandate and general guidelines for action, but there remains considerable room for discretion.[13] Asking whether SRSGs can mediate between conflicting norms as norm arbitrators, I examine controversial decisions where there were no clear directions from UN headquarters in New York and where several principles for peacekeeping clashed with each other or with instructions from headquarters.

I begin with two case studies from Afghanistan and Côte d'Ivoire, both involving situations where tensions between UN headquarters and the field were evident. Existing theory cannot grasp these case studies sufficiently, so I suggest some steps to remedy such shortcomings. I analyze the sources of SRSG authority to explain how SRSGs can operate as norm arbitrators in a field

---

10   See Benjamin Rivlin and Leon Gordenker, *The Challenging Role of the UN Secretary-General: Making "The Most Impossible Job in the World" Possible* (Westport, CT: Praeger, 1993); Simon Chesterman, ed., *Secretary or General? The UN Secretary-General in World Politics* (Cambridge University Press, 2007); Ian Johnstone, "The Secretary-General as Norm Entrepreneur: Secretary or General?" in Simon Chesterman, ed., *Secretary or General? The UN Secretary-General in World Politics* (New York: Cambridge University Press, 2007), pp. 123–138.

11   Martha Finnemore and Kathryn Sikkink, "International Norm Dynamics and Political Change," *International Organization* 52, no. 4 (1998), pp. 887–917.

12   See, for example, Thorsten Benner and Philipp Rotmann, "Learning to Learn? UN Peacebuilding and the Challenges of Building a Learning Organization," *Journal of Intervention and Statebuilding* 2, no. 1 (2008): 43–62.

13   Lise Morjé Howard has examined the relationship between headquarters and the field and found that a peacekeeping mission is most likely to be successful when it receives moderate attention from the Security Council. Lise Morjé Howard, *UN Peacekeeping in Civil Wars* (Cambridge: Cambridge University Press, 2008), p. 13.

generally held to be dominated by member states. Finally, I summarize the findings and outline a further research agenda.

1   Giving Meaning to Peacekeeping Norms through Actions: A Bottom-Up, Practice-Driven Approach?

Peacekeeping operates according to three core traditional principles: impartiality, consent of the parties, and nonuse of force. After the UN failures in Rwanda, Somalia, and Bosnia, the Responsibility to Protect (R2P) and Protection of Civilians (PoC) have been advanced as important norms. However, all of these principles or norms are rarely found coexisting harmoniously in a peacekeeping context. Norms exist in a competitive arena; and, according to the context of the peacekeeping operation, the normative composition is rebalanced each time. Alex J. Bellamy, Paul Williams, and Stuart Griffin argue that there is an ongoing normative battle about what peacekeeping ought to be and do.[14] This indicates that practices and the normative reasoning backing up these practices are significant when tracing how norms for peacekeeping operations wax and wane.

1.1   Côte d'Ivoire: What Does "Robust Peacekeeping" Really Mean?
In an unprecedented move on 4 and 10 April 2011, UNOCI carried out a joint strike with attack helicopters on the residence of former President Gbagbo, together with French Licorne forces. SRSG Choi Young-jin was sharply criticized by Sergei Lavrov, Russian minister of foreign affairs: "We are now looking into the legal side of the issue because peacekeepers had a mandate which requires them to be neutral and impartial."[15] A few days later, President Dmitry Medvedev stated: "The United Nations cannot take sides, but that is de facto what happened."[16]

Only one month earlier, the UN had authorized the use of "all military means" to protect civilians in Libya, noting Libya's responsibility to protect its civilian population.[17] This was the first time the concept of R2P had been directly quoted in a Security Council resolution on a situation in a country. The

---

14   Alex J. Bellamy, Paul Williams, and Stuart Griffin, *Understanding Peacekeeping*, 2nd ed. (Cambridge: Polity, 2010).
15   "Besieged Gbagbo 'in Basement.'"
16   Anishchuk, "Russia Criticises UN Force Role."
17   UN Security Council, Res. S/RES/1970 (26 February 2011), www.un.org/Docs/sc/unsc_res olutions11.htm; UN Security Council, Res. S/RES/1973 (17 March 2011), www.un.org/Docs/sc/unsc_resolutions11.htm.

use of R2P in the mandates on Libya, and the subsequent authorizations to use all necessary means to protect civilians in Libya as well as in Côte d'Ivoire, seemed to set a new standard for mandates and the willingness of the Security Council to authorize robust action, even against strategic-level actors, to protect civilians.

In fact, there have been historical precedents. In 2005 the UN Stabilization Mission in Haiti (MINUSTAH) engaged criminal gangs in Cité Soleil in direct confrontation, with civilian casualties, in Operation Iron Fist. In a matter of hours on 15 August, Peruvian and Brazilian peacekeepers fired more than 20,000 rounds of ammunition, grenades, and mortar fire in a densely populated area, killing the gang leader Emmanuel "Dread" Wilme and many of his followers.[18] Jean-Marie Guéhenno, then UN under-secretary-general for peacekeeping operations, said it was necessary to stand up to armed groups that threaten to undermine peacekeeping missions. But he said that UN commanders had to strike a balance between engaging in all-out warfare and resorting to the passive military posture that characterized UN operations in Srebrenica, where Dutch peacekeepers stood down as Bosnian Serb troops killed thousands of unarmed civilians.[19]

Another precedent was the robust action taken by the UN Mission in Democratic Republic of Congo (MONUC) against rebel groups in eastern Democratic Republic of Congo in 2006.[20] Its support of the national Forces Armées de la République Démocratique du Congo (FARDC) resulted in MONUC being considered as a party to the conflict, even by some of its staff members.[21] Both of these instances have since been cited as examples of robust action to protect civilians.[22]

Back to Côte d'Ivoire, Security Council Resolution 1975 considered the situation in that country by condemning "the attacks, threats, acts of obstructions and violence perpetrated by FDSCI [Defence and Security Forces of Côte

---

18   Colum Lynch, "UN Peacekeeping More Assertive, Creating Risk for Civilians," *Washington Post*, 15 August 2005.

19   Ibid.

20   Jim Terrie, "The Use of Force in UN Peacekeeping: The Experience of MONUC," *African Security Review* 18 (2008): 21–34.

21   Victoria Holt, Glyn Taylor, and Max Kelly, *Protecting Civilians in the Context of UN Peacekeeping Operations: Successes, Setbacks and Remaining Challenges* (New York: UN Department of Peacekeeping Operations and Office for the Coordination of Humanitarian Affairs, 2009), p. 168.

22   Nealin Parker, ed., *Robust Peacekeeping: The Politics of Force* (New York: Center on International Cooperation, New York University, 2009), p. 52; UN, *Draft DPKO/DFS Concept Note on Robust Peacekeeping* (New York: UN Department of Peacekeeping Operations and Department of Field Support, 2010), p. 2.

d'Ivoire]" and stressing "that those responsible for such crimes under international law must be held accountable and calls upon all parties, in particular Mr. Laurent Gbagbo's supporters and forces, to fully cooperate with the United Nations Operation in Côte d'Ivoire (UNOCI)."[23] In this difficult situation, the SRSG was mandated to use all necessary means to protect civilians against the use of heavy weapons. The Security Council recalls "its authorization and stresses its full support given to the UNOCI, while *impartially* implementing its mandate, to *use all necessary means* to carry out its mandate to protect civilians under imminent threat of physical violence, *within its capabilities* and its areas of deployment, including to *prevent the use of heavy weapons against the civilian population.*"[24]

The SRSG was tasked to impartially implement the mandate but, at the same time, use all necessary means to prevent the use of heavy weapons against the civilian population. Previous UN operations had been forced into similar situations, but the UN mission in Somalia in the early 1990s was the only one that had gone into confrontation with one of the principal parties to the conflict and no mission had attacked the forces of an incumbent president. The use of force in Côte d'Ivoire thus seems to run counter to how the UN had outlined the principle of "robust peacekeeping" only one year prior in a concept note presented to the Special Committee on Peacekeeping Operations (C-34) for the February 2010 Substantive Session. Again, it is worth quoting an entire paragraph:

> Robust peacekeeping is not peace enforcement. Robust peacekeeping is distinct from peace enforcement where use of force is at the strategic level and pursued often without the consent of the host nation/and or main parties to the conflict.... Large scale violence or one where the major parties are engaged in violent conflict is no longer a robust peacekeeping context. Robust missions are not configured or intended to address any systemic breakdown in a political process.[25]

This concept note was actually criticized for being too assertive.[26] Morocco, representing the Non-Aligned Movement (NAM), said that peacekeeping was

---

23   UN Security Council, Res. S/RES/1975 (30 March 2011), www.un.org/Docs/sc/unsc_resolutions11.htm, p. 3.

24   Ibid., p. 6 (emphasis added).

25   UN, *Concept Note on Robust Peacekeeping*, p. 3 (emphasis in original).

26   World Federalist Movement, "IGP Matrix of Issues: General Debate of the Special Committee on Peacekeeping Operations (C34) 2010 Substantive Session" (New York:

robust enough, and South Africa said that robust peacekeeping should not be used as a peace enforcement tool.[27]

By the end of March 2011, the situation became intolerable for the UN, according to a senior UN official: "The situation had become very difficult for the UN operation, very difficult for us to have the freedom of movement, and we had to use convoys with armored vehicles…. On 3 March, a group of women supporters of Alassane Ouattara demonstrated against the government. FDSCI fired with a 20 mm cannon from an armored personnel carrier into the crowd."[28] This incident was one of the key reasons that the Security Council gave the mandate to UNOCI to protect civilians against the use of heavy weapons.

By 31 March the Ivory Coast Republican Forces, which were pro-Ouattara forces, were standing outside of Abidjan.[29] With a full-scale civil war imminent, the Security Council took action and gave the mission a robust mandate, bordering on peace enforcement. With the linkage established that the heavy weapons guarding President Gbagbo also were used to attack civilian populations, the ground was prepared for the UN to use force. Finally, "on 10 April French Licorne forces and the UN attacked with heavy weapons and ground forces moved in on the presidential residence and captured Gbagbo."[30]

1.2   *Navigating Uncharted Waters*

ONUCI was equipped with Mi-24 gunship helicopters, which could and indeed did make a serious difference in joint attacks with French Licorne forces on 4 and 10 April. After the two attacks, President Gbagbo's troops were finally conquered and he was taken into custody. The SRSG could have avoided entering the conflict, citing the need for impartiality and the limited capabilities of the mission. He could have argued, as many SRSGs had done before him, that he would need more troops to be able to protect civilians and that the use of helicopters would risk involving the UN in a protracted direct confrontation with Gbagbo's forces.

World Federalist Movement; Institute for Global Policy, 2010), www.betterpeace.org/files/ C34_Matrix_General_Debate_22_23Feb10Final_0.pdf.

27   Permanent Mission of South Africa to the United Nations, "Statement by Ambassador Baso Sangqu, Permanent Representative of the Republic of South Africa to the United Nations at the Meeting of the Special Committee on Peacekeeping Operations 2010 Substantive Session. United Nations, New York, 22 February 2010" (New York: Permanent Mission of South Africa to the United Nations, 2010), www.betterpeace.org/files/c34_ south_africa_22feb10.pdf.

28   Senior UN official, interviewed by the author, Oslo, 15 November 2012.

29   Ibid.

30   Ibid.

Navigating these uncharted waters, the SRSG could well anticipate that his actions would be controversial no matter what. Had he chosen to ignore the continued fighting, he would have joined the list of SRSGs who had been condemned for doing nothing when faced with the killing of civilians. Instead, he was attacked for taking sides to forcibly change the regime of an African country and install a pro-Western president.

Clearly, the actions of this SRSG violated the principle of robust peacekeeping as outlined in the 2010 concept note. Two major parties were engaged in violent conflict at the strategic level, and the use of force was pursued without the consent of the main parties. As the UN is wary of member state skepticism, the concept note took into consideration how practices had evolved over the past decade, with the actions taken to protect civilians against gangs in Haiti and rebels in eastern Democratic Republic of Congo. No one foresaw that the UN would become engaged in peace enforcement in Côte d'Ivoire only one year later. This indicates a time gap between practice and policy, with practice preceding policy and doctrine development at UN headquarters.

The concept note also stressed that "the Security Council should be clearly informed of the risks before the decision is taken."[31] In Côte d'Ivoire, the SRSG warned that he was in the process of using force and that action was imminent, just hours before launching the first attack.[32] There was no time for the Security Council to convene to discuss the potential risks of the action; thus, the SRSG proceeded to authorize the attack without Council intervention.

What emerges from Côte d'Ivoire is a case where the norms of protection of civilians and robust peacekeeping were redefined through actions on the ground. This has a significant impact on the other core principles of peacekeeping—impartiality, consent of the parties, and minimal use of force. To protect civilians and prevent or stop mass atrocities and crimes against humanity, the UN may at times be willing to use force at the strategic level against one of the main parties to the conflict. While the Security Council provides the mandate for action, it is within the prerogative of the SRSG to determine whether the mission has sufficient capabilities to undertake such action.

1.3 Afghanistan: Upholding the Principle of Impartiality, or Undermining the Operation?

After the events of 11 September 2001, the United States launched Operation Enduring Freedom on 7 October 2001 to fight the Taliban and al-Qaeda. With

---

31   UN, *Concept Note on Robust Peacekeeping*, p. 3.
32   CNN, *World Report*, 4 April 2011.

Security Council Resolution 1378 of 14 November 2001,[33] the Council affirmed that the UN would have an important role to play. Following the Bonn Agreement in December 2001, the Security Council established UNAMA on 28 March 2002.

Overnight, the war on terrorism changed the environment in which UN staff operated. In many Middle Eastern countries, interlocutors were now termed "terrorists" by the United States and the Security Council. The Taliban did not participate in the negotiations for the Bonn Agreement in December 2001: at that point, the US-led coalition had control of most of Afghanistan and saw no need to include the Taliban. The Security Council established a special counterterrorism unit to track members of al-Qaeda and the Taliban, effectively designating these groups and their members as "beyond the pale."[34] However, the Taliban proved to be a difficult opponent, and the war in Afghanistan lasted for more than a decade. Engagement proved complicated because of the reluctance of the Afghan government as well as of the United States to engage in talks with the Taliban.

In March 2010 just before leaving his post as SRSG, Eide admitted to regular contacts with Taliban members, including the leadership.[35] In fact, engagement had begun much earlier than this: "We started careful contact with the rebel movement [Taliban] during the autumn of 2008, with a humanitarian focus to provide food and vaccines."[36] Being mindful of the sensitivity of these talks, Eide made sure that he had the support of President Hamid Karzai before engaging the Taliban.[37] Eide underscored that before initiating contact, he also had "warmed up" member states to the idea, particularly the Permanent Five on the Security Council, by talking about the need to engage in public. In the Security Council, Eide brought up the need to talk with the rebel movement, but "both the Russians and Teheran were opposed to such contacts."[38] While the European Union's special representative for Afghanistan Francesc Vendrell and the UK ambassador Sherard Cowper-Coles on a personal basis supported the engagement with the Taliban, the governments they represented were much more reluctant. Ambassador Cowper-Coles was forced to take "extended leave" in 2010 and eventually quit the UK Foreign Service after insisting "that the military-driven counter-insurgency effort was

---

33   UN Security Council, Res. S/RES/1378 (1 November 2001).

34   Term used by Alvaro de Soto, *End of Mission Report* (New York: UN, 2007).

35   Borger, "Kai Eide Lashes Out."

36   Kai Eide, interviewed by the author, Oslo, 4 September 2012.

37   Ibid.

38   Ibid.

headed for failure, and that talks with the Taliban should be prioritized."[39] The engagement was also "supported by Barney [Barnett] Rubin, but he was not yet inside [the US Department of] State."[40] Contacts picked up in 2009 but, on 28 January 2010 in connection with the meeting on Afghanistan held in London, "it was incorrectly leaked to a British newspaper that I [Eide] had had meetings with the Taliban in Dubai early that month. This, together with the arrest of Taliban's number two, Mullah Baradar ruined any possibility for further dialogue."[41] Looking at the talks in retrospect, Eide argues that "we established connections that were important and interesting, and later we also had confirmation that these went all the way to the top."[42]

In Afghanistan, there was considerable pressure from UN headquarters and the Security Council against engagement with the Taliban but, as shown in the epigraph, operational imperatives and the long-term goals of the UN, as interpreted by SRSG Eide, dictated another approach. Secret talks and low-profile engagement continued, the argument being that all parties had to be involved if sustainable peace and security were to be established—particularly since the Taliban represented a significant part of the population in Afghanistan.

1.4 *Operating between Conflicting Imperatives*

What can the UN engagement with the Taliban and Hamas reveal to us about how norms develop in the UN, and the influence of powerful states like the United States with regard to the autonomy and influence of the UN itself? Over the past twenty years, the UN has carved out a role for itself in some of the world's most intractable conflicts. It has established a tradition of talking with everyone, even those deemed beyond the pale. That practice has been central to peacemaking and mediation in conflicts in Latin America, Central Africa, and the Middle East, and the organization has engaged in contact with groups such as the Lord's Resistance Army in Uganda, the Revolutionary United Front in Sierra Leone, Hezbollah and Hamas in the Middle East, and the Revolutionary Armed Forces of Colombia—all frequently labeled as terrorist organizations.

After 9/11, engaging with these groups has proven more difficult. In the Middle East, Alvaro de Soto resigned from his post because of the restrictions

---

39   Declan Walsh and Jon Boone, "UK Special Envoy to Afghanistan Who Called for Talks with Taliban Quits," *The Guardian*, 21 June 2010, www.guardian.co.uk/world/2010/jun/21/uk-special-envoy-afghanistan-quits.

40   Eide interview. Barnett Rubin was later appointed senior adviser to the special representative of the president for Afghanistan and Pakistan in the US Department of State.

41   Eide interview; see also Borger, "Kai Eide Lashes Out."

42   Eide interview.

on engaging with Hamas and Syria. In his *End of Mission Report*, he warned against establishing a new precedent for UN officials of talking only with those actors seen to be in the clear: "Since the late 1980s the UN has become rather adept dealing with groups that most governments can't or won't touch. If this ability is removed we would seriously weaken our hand as a peace-making tool."[43]

What can the UN engagement with the Taliban and Hamas reveal about how norms develop in the UN, and the influence of powerful states like the United States with regard to the autonomy and influence of the UN itself? On the surface, SRSG Eide's engagement with the Taliban seems to contradict the views of several key members of the Security Council. Eide, according to his own interpretation, had been given a political mandate to work for the long-term peace and stability of Afghanistan. For him, not talking with the Taliban was not an option since it had to be an integral part of a sustainable and long-term solution. Here, it was not a new norm that was being generated, but rather the interpretation of the norm of impartiality that was used as the main argument for engagement. Like de Soto, Eide stressed the importance of being able to meet with everyone so that he could execute the political mandate of the mission: "We met senior people in the Taliban leadership and we also met people who have the authority of the Quetta Shura to engage in that kind of discussion. I have always believed in an engagement policy. I have always believed that it is better to try to talk than to refrain from talking."[44]

Here, Eide was drawing on the moral authority of the established norm of impartiality—like de Soto, he underscored the importance of being able to engage and talk with all involved parties. This comes in conflict with the newer post-9/11 norm of not talking to terrorists. Through his practices, Eide thus reaffirmed the traditional norm of impartiality and knowingly risked conflict with UN headquarters and key member states. Eide is today convinced that "the way we handled this had an effect on the way the international community viewed the issue of negotiating.... When asked whether I was prepared to talk with Mullah Omar, my answer always was 'You have to talk with relevant people to get relevant results!'"[45]

---

43 De Soto, *End of Mission Report*, par. 91, p. 34.
44 Borger, "Kai Eide Lashes Out."
45 Eide interview.

2   SRSG Autonomy: The Composition of Authority in UN Peacekeeping

The case studies I have presented show instances where the SRSGs have navigated in difficult normative environments. The norms guiding peacekeeping have not been in concordance, and the SRSGs have been forced to make choices. The ensuing actions have been controversial, stirring the waters in the UN Secretariat, in the Security Council, and among member states.

The literature on the role of SRSGs and their relative authority vis-à-vis UN headquarters has been evolving.[46] Some claims have already been made regarding the responsibility of SRSGs to make difficult choices in tight situations when civilians are at risk. Victoria Holt, examining implementation of the PoC concept in MONUC, asserts: "The authorization for civilian protection is clear, but the Council's resolution leaves the decision to protect civilians up to the Special Representative of the Secretary General (SRSG), the force commander or another actor further down the chain to "deem" it to be within the scope of 'its capabilities.'"[47]

Lise Howard has similarly argued that UN peace operations that attract high interest from the Security Council tend to be less successful, and that the success of UN peace operations hinges on the relative autonomy of the operation vis-à-vis headquarters as well as the degree to which SRSGs interpret their mandate independently.[48] However, there is no doubt that the SRSG needs the support of the Security Council and the Secretary-General to maintain credibility with the main actors on the ground.[49]

---

46   See, especially, "Special Focus: Postwar Mediation in UN Peace Operations," *Global Governance* 16, no. 2 (2010). See also Donald J. Puchala, "The Secretary-General and His Special Representatives," in Benjamin Rivlin and Leon Gordenker, eds., *The Challenging Role of the UN Secretary-General: Making "The Most Impossible Job in the World" Possible* (Westport, CT: Praeger, 1993), pp. 81–97; Cyrus R. Vance and David A. Hamburg, *Pathfinders for Peace: A Report to the UN Secretary-General on the Role of Special Representatives and Personal Envoys* (New York: Carnegie Commission on Preventing Deadly Conflict, 1997); Fafo Institute for Applied Social Science, *Command from the Saddle: Managing United Nations Peace-Building Missions* (Oslo: Fafo Institute for Applied Social Science, 1999); Connie Peck, "Special Representatives of the Secretary General," in David Malone, ed., *The UN Security Council: From the Cold War to the 21st Century* (Boulder: Lynne Rienner, 2004), pp. 325–339; Connie Peck, *On Being a Special Representative to the Secretary-General* (Geneva: UN Institute for Training and Research, 2006).

47   Victoria K. Holt, *The Responsibility to Protect: Considering Operational Capacity for Civilian Protection. Discussion Paper* (Washington, DC: Henry L. Stimson Center, 2005), p. 14.

48   Howard, *UN Peacekeeping in Civil Wars*.

49   See, for example, Fafo Institute for Applied Social Science, *Command from the Saddle*; Cedric de Coning, "Mediation and Peacebuilding: SRSGs and DSRSGs in Integrated Missions," *Global Governance* 16, no. 2 (2010): 281–299.

Benjamin de Carvalho and Jon Harald Sande Lie argue that the PoC concept has been made deliberately vague so as to decentralize intent and responsibility for interpreting the mandate to the SRSG in the field: "The ambiguous protection language recognises the case-by-case applicability, as it lacks clearly demarcated thresholds and criteria for what constitutes a protection situation, and its decentralised intent, that the mission head is responsible to deem the when and what of protection activities."[50]

It may be argued that SRSGs can have some relative autonomy to implement Security Council mandates and Department of Peacekeeping Operations (DPKO) policies with a certain level of discretion. But what if this brings them into conflict with the Security Council or the Secretary-General? What other sources of authority can SRSGs invoke that can explain this form of anomalous behavior? I argue that SRSGs have access to several forms of authority in decisionmaking processes. Drawing on some of the extant literature on authority and the UN system, I distinguish five such sources of authority: (1) delegated authority from the Security Council and the Secretary-General; (2) expert authority; (3) moral authority; (4) charismatic authority; and (5) prestige.[51]

2.1   Delegated Authority

Member states create IOs, delegating authority to them to solve various tasks, including the maintenance of peace and security. The Security Council can deem a situation in a country to be a threat to international peace and security, and delegate to the Secretary-General appropriate tasks for tackling this threat; in turn, the Secretary-General can delegate these tasks to an SRSG. The delegated authority of the SRSG can be subdivided into two components—operational guidance from the Secretary-General and the Secretariat, and strategic guidance from the Security Council.

The Secretary-General has delegated executive responsibilities to the SRSGs, and they carry out their assignments under authority given to the Secretary-General to appoint his staff in Article 101 of the UN Charter: under Article 99, which gives the Secretary-General the opportunity to open good offices and

---

50   Benjamin de Carvalho and Jon Harald Sande Lie, "Chronicle of a Frustration Foretold? The Implementation of a Broad Protection Agenda in the United Nations," *Journal of International Peacekeeping* 15, no. 3 (2011): 350.

51   Barnett and Finnemore list only three sources of authority in *Rules for the World*: delegated, moral, and expert authority, pp. 20–29. I include also charismatic authority and prestige due to the particular nature of the role of the SRSG as both an official within the UN system and one who draws on his or her personal experience.

have an independent political role; and under Article 33, which invites the parties to select mediators of their own choice.[52]

Donald J. Puchala argues that, because of staffing constraints at the Secretary-General's office, the ad hoc nature of special representation, and their history of relative autonomy, SRSGs have been granted wide latitude for personal initiatives, critical thinking, and inventiveness.[53] While this has permitted swift action on the ground, it has also "tempted special representatives to ignore or go beyond their mandates and instructions, thus creating tensions in center-mission relations or otherwise raising questions about the structure of authority. *Sometimes it becomes unclear who is the tail and who is the dog.*"[54]

To adapt to the changing circumstances on the ground, the SRSG needs to keep the Security Council abreast of developments through regular reporting. This practice, instituted by Secretary-General Kofi Annan, has been greatly appreciated by the Council.[55] Moreover, members of the Council often make field visits to get their own impressions of the situation. Besides briefing the Security Council, many SRSGs also choose to brief a selection of ambassadors at regular intervals. This can reinforce messages that an SRSG wants to send to garner support for a particular strategy.[56] The SRSGs depend on Council support to maintain a strong standing and the respect of the parties in the field.

2.2 Expert Authority

Delegated authority can be further divided into the expert authority conferred on the SRSG on behalf of the UN system, the collective experience and guidelines established for the role to be executed, and the moral authority conferred on the SRSG by executing the will of the member states according to the established principles and values of the UN. SRSGs have expert or rational-legal authority that draws on personal experience, knowledge of previous cases, and established precedence. Further, SRSGs have the aid of their offices, technical sections and units, and the senior management team, forming a minibureaucracy with expertise at their disposal.[57] The expanding body of lessons learned and formal guidance is also part of the repository of expert authority.

---

52   UN, *Charter of the United Nations* (New York: Office of Public Information, United Nations, 1945).

53   Puchala, "The Secretary-General and His Special Representatives."

54   Ibid., p. 94 (emphasis added).

55   Peck, *The UN Security Council*, p. 331.

56   See SRSG Aldo Ajello, quoted in Peck, *The UN Security Council*, p. 333.

57   See also Peter M. Haas, "Epistemic Communities and International Policy Coordination: Introduction," *International Organization* 46, no. 1 (1992): 1–35.

2.3   Moral Authority

SRSGs are to execute their mandates according to the established principles and norms for peacekeeping. As noted above, the traditional norms are consent of the parties, minimal use of force, and impartiality; after the failures in Bosnia, Somalia, and Rwanda, protection of civilians has been established as an important new norm. However, these principles do not always form a coherent framework for action, but can instead conflict with each other. Which norm is paramount, and who is to decide? The SRSGs, through years of experience, are inculcated with these norms and have personal views on how they should be interpreted and weighed against each other.

SRSGs are vested with moral authority as representatives of the UN. They are to embody the values of the UN and act "as agents of the international community and purveyors of UN norms."[58] In the course of years as a UN official or career diplomat, SRSGs have developed personal views on how the values of the UN should be interpreted and implemented. Not violating these personal views about UN values may be more important than actually keeping the position as a special envoy for the UN, as seen in the case of de Soto.

2.4   Charismatic Authority

Max Weber differentiates between bureaucratic and charismatic authority, arguing that the modern bureaucracy has advanced beyond charismatic authority as expressed through the patriarchal structure. While this is an important distinction, I argue that SRSGs draw on both forms of authority in executing their roles. Weber defines "charismatic authority" as "a rule over men, whether predominantly external or predominantly internal, to which the governed submit because of their belief in the extraordinary quality of the specific person."[59] SRSGs are often charismatic personalities, frequently top diplomats of their country or high in the ranks of the UN.

The UN can be vested with extraordinary powers in a postconflict country, and it is the job of the SRSG to execute these powers. Many missions have been given executive mandates, effectively instituting the SRSG as a "viceroy," as in Kosovo and Timor-Leste.[60] Even where the UN mission has only a mandate to support what may be a fledgling state, the SRSGs have influential roles

---

58   Puchala, "The Secretary-General and His Special Representatives," p. 89.

59   H.H. Gerth and C. Wright Mills, trans. and ed., *From Max Weber: Essays in Sociology* (New York: Oxford University Press, 1946), p. 295, emphasis in original.

60   See, for example, Max Boot, "Paving the Road to Hell: The Failure of UN Peacekeeping," *Foreign Affairs* (March–April 2000): 143–148; Simon Chesterman, *You, the People: The United Nations, Transitional Administration, and State-building* (Oxford: Oxford University Press, 2004). Various other articles have made the same point.

vis-à-vis national politics and dynamics. The influence they are able to wield is impacted not only by the relative degree of executive power included in the mandate, but also by the support of important states. SRSGs form the focal point for sources of power of potentially formidable size. Their position at the intersection as a medium between the international and the national confers charismatic authority, akin to the authority that Weber argues that the monarch wielded over his subjects.[61] Compared to the leader of the country to which the mission is deployed, an SRSG often controls and coordinates vast financial, material, and human resources, and can have significant influence on how the situation in the country is portrayed internationally (e.g., through his or her regular briefings to the Security Council and through contact with international media, NGOs, and the research community).

2.5   Prestige or "Revolving Doors" Authority

We have seen that SRSGs are sometimes willing to go out on a limb, making controversial decisions that the member states may not support or indeed may oppose. What source of authority do SRSGs draw on in instances where they risk losing significant political capital and support from the Security Council and the Secretary-General? SRSGs draw on the moral authority vested in the position, balancing the various guiding norms of peacekeeping against each other. Perhaps more importantly, SRSG are enabled to make controversial decisions because of their prior career backgrounds, through a combination of articulate and background knowledge.[62]

SRSGs have normally developed long and distinguished careers in the service of their country or as UN staff members. Some SRSGs have also come from national parliaments or NGOs. While they are required to be managers of a peace operation, they are first and foremost diplomats with a keen sense of politics. Over the years they may have built up considerable political capital and prestige, which they may be willing to risk, at least in part, in defending a controversial decision. Breaking norms creates stigma[63] but, in these cases, one norm is broken to uphold another. The prestige of an SRSG is composed of the reputation for integrity and accountability built up through a lengthy career. Prestige grows on investment—by making a controversial decision that involves exposure to risk, an SRSG may actually gain more prestige and credibility if the decision proves correct. In arbitrating between the different norms,

---

61   Gerth and Mills, *From Max Weber.*
62   Vincent Pouliot, "The Logic of Practicality: A Theory of Practice of Security Communities," *International Organization* 62, no. 2 (2008): 257–288.
63   Finnemore and Sikkink, "International Norm Dynamics and Political Change," p. 892.

SRSGs thus risk their credibility, but they may also increase their prestige. The relationship between credibility and prestige is flexible: SRSGs may be willing to lose their credibility and their post to uphold their values and, ultimately, their prestige.

Moreover, most SRSGs have some sort of exit option. On finishing their assignment or being relieved of their duty, they may be able to return to the diplomatic service at home, to a distinguished fellowship position at a prestigious university, or to serve as senior fellow at a think-tank. In these posts they continue to engage with the issues they have worked with as SRSGs, and may act as advisors to the Secretary-General (e.g., participating in a senior advisory panel). Throughout their careers, they may have moved back and forth between these various roles—a "revolving doors" phenomenon in the field of peace operations. This leads to exit options—if disagreement arises because of differences of opinion in how to interpret the UN Charter and the norms guiding peace operations, an SRSG can choose to go elsewhere without losing his or her pride, understanding of UN values, and prestige.

3   Autonomous Behavior of IOs: The Role of SRSG Norm Arbitration

The UN has several sources of agenda and agency. It consists of a range of bodies, each with its particular dynamics, membership, and staff. The Security Council is the most important actor, and volumes have been written about the role of the Council with regard to peacekeeping.[64] The General Assembly and the C-34 meet each year to discuss matters pertaining to peacekeeping. Further, the General Assembly has plenary discussions on peacekeeping matters from time to time. In addition to these various centers of agency at UN headquarters, the SRSG adds another layer of agency in the organization.

According to Finnemore and Sikkink, new norms in the international system are formed through the persuasion of member states by norm entrepreneurs.[65] Norm entrepreneurs call attention to and frame issues by applying new terms and reinterpreting issues and putting them into new contexts. During an emergence stage they use their organizational platform, as well as their expertise and knowledge, to promote the norm vis-à-vis member states, IOs, and networks of professionals. Using the analytical framework developed by Finnemore and

---

64   See, for example, Malone, *The UN Security Council*; Mats R. Berdal and Spyros Economides, *United Nations Interventionism, 1991–2004* (New York: Cambridge University Press, 2007); Howard, *UN Peacekeeping in Civil Wars*.

65   Finnemore and Sikkink, "International Norm Dynamics and Political Change."

Sikkink, Ian Johnstone argues that the Secretary-General can act as a norm entrepreneur as when Annan helped push the norm of R2P to a "tipping point" at the 2005 World Summit.[66]

The SRSGs in the case studies above were navigating in difficult normative waters, seeking to balance and arbitrate between different peacekeeping principles and norms—always with a view to the context, their interpretation of UN values and norms, their experience, and the risks to their own credibility and position vis-à-vis local stakeholders, the Secretary-General, and the Security Council. SRSGs Choi and Eide took actions for which they were criticized, but also received support. Talking with the Taliban has become the main line from Presidents Barack Obama and Karzai, and Côte d'Ivoire has now reached a calmer period where the economy can restart and normal life can return.

SRSGs have to take risks, and sometimes it is better to ask for forgiveness than permission. The need to trust the discretion of the SRSG to take the right action in pressed circumstances has major implications for the selection process. An SRSG must be well versed in the intricacies of UN politics and bureaucratic procedures, intimately familiar with international diplomacy, and able to build and nurture relationships with the main powers that have vested interests in a particular conflict as well as be perceived by the host-state stakeholders— from top to bottom—as a legitimate, credible, and accountable partner.

As SRSGs, they must juggle a series of roles. In UN integrated missions, the SRSG is the top political representative of the Secretary-General and the Security Council, serving to provide the good offices of the Secretary-General, as the eyes and ears of the Secretary-General in the field, as overall coordinator of the UN system, and as general manager of the peace operation. Puchala, quoting Cyrus Vance and David A. Hamburg, argues that the SRSG must be "a bona fide surrogate" of the Secretary-General.[67] The SRSG is often expected to play a coordinating role outside of the UN, interacting with national counterparts, bilateral development donors, and the humanitarian community in addition to chairing coordination efforts in these widely varying domains.

Making strategic decisions, with a mandate from the Security Council, involves considerable discretion. SRSGs interpret the mandate (delegated authority) in light of their own interpretation of the UN Charter (expert and moral authority) and in terms of personal gain or loss of prestige (revolving

---

66   Johnstone, "The Secretary-General as Norm Entrepreneur," p. 134; Alex J. Bellamy, *Responsibility to Protect: The Global Effort to End Mass Atrocities* (Cambridge: Polity, 2009), pp. 27–28.

67   Puchala, "The Secretary-General and His Special Representatives," p. 83.

doors authority). The sources of authority guiding SRSG action are inherently complex, offering a range of different arguments and solutions. This in turn opens up the application of discretion and contextualized responses by SRSGs, depending on the personal analysis of the political economy on the ground, the personalities involved, the guidance given from headquarters, and the personal experience and fallback options of the SRSG.

4   Conclusion

Overnight, the war on terrorism changed the normative framework for senior UN staff in Afghanistan. Established practices of talking with everyone had to yield to a more restrained mode of operation where some groups were considered beyond the pale. However, as senior staff realized their loss of freedom, they set about regaining lost territory through assertive practices in the field. De Soto argues for this principled approach in his *End of Mission Report*: "The UN is not in the business of recognizing governments; we deal pragmatically with whoever are the authorities. In good offices, we deal with the players who need to be part of peace agreements. We should practice *realpolitik* in the purest sense, by removing *politik* and dealing with reality."[68]

The role of the good offices of the Secretary-General was developed during the Cold War, when the Security Council was deadlocked between East and West. The Secretary-General, through his special representatives, mediated in various conflicts, gradually establishing a mechanism for peaceable settlement that also enhanced the authority and autonomy of the Secretary-General with regard to the General Assembly and the Security Council. The SRSGs are an extension of this authority and, by being deployed in the field, they enjoy considerable discretion in strategic questions as well as in their day-to-day activities.

The cases of Côte d'Ivoire and Afghanistan show how SRSGs have engaged in controversial practices that could give impetus to important doctrinal developments and change. These have been clear examples of tension between center and periphery where the SRSGs have chosen to take initiatives to controversial actions, stepping out of the comfort zone and actively interpreting their mandates. This is a necessary feature of their role, if SRSGs are to be relevant and useful to the countries where they are deployed. In every peacekeeping operation, the relationship between the core principles of peacekeeping is contested

---

68   De Soto, *End of Mission Report*, par. 82, p. 32.

again and again, particularly with the addition of protection of civilians as a staple ingredient in most mandates today.

The actions of the SRSGs in Côte d'Ivoire and Afghanistan showed a certain level of decentralized authority and relative autonomy of the SRSGs in the UN system. The concept of prestige can help to explain why SRSGs engage in potentially controversial practices. Further research should examine the various sources of authority that SRSGs draw on.

The literature has reported on how the UN occasionally acts counter to its rules and mandates, but only in a negative way, focusing on dysfunctions and pathologies and organized hypocrisy. I argue that the gap between theory, doctrine, and practice is often of a positive nature, one that can create a *generative ambiguity* within which senior field staff can operate. The literature has dealt with these ambiguities in a simplistic manner: the real world is highly complex and differentiated. The rules and norms of an organization are more than bounded rationality, distinct from the environment—they shape the rationality of the organization's actors and guide individual action. The relationship between rules and bureaucrats is mutually constitutive and dynamic and, at any given time, several rules may be applicable. I argue that there is a need for considerable leeway for senior leaders in field, and caution against a too fine-grained and detailed normative framework that limits the freedom of action of special representatives and envoys. The drive to conceptualize and codify peacekeeping experience may, at times, be counterproductive. Using their local knowledge and previous experience, UN special representatives and envoys can utilize the generative ambiguity of mandates and guidelines that do not spell out rules for all forms of behavior.

Examining the practices of senior leaders of the UN, not just the Secretary-General, may offer a promising new avenue for theorizing norm change in IOs. Norm change is constant and nonlinear, and norms wax and wane through decisionmaking at the Security Council as well as through practices in the field. However, the latter often precedes the former, with a temporal-spatial lag between periphery and center where practices in the field and codified norms at headquarters may differ. Practices precede and lead to codification of norms—and that has important consequences for how we understand norm change processes in the UN.

The literature has dealt with these contradictions simplistically: the real world is more complex and differentiated. Senior managers in the field rely on their prestige and experience when they perform actions apparently in contradiction of established norms and rules, and they enjoy relative safety in challenging the central authority through their own networks and exit options. SRSGs are norm arbitrators—arbitrating the relationship between conflicting norms in each case. In arbitrating between the different norms, SRSGs risk their credibility but may also increase their own prestige and the relevance of the UN to host populations.

SRSG practices in the field form a prism where central issues concerning IOs converge. By examining the practices of SRSGs, we can learn more about how new practices are formed; about how norms and rules are arbitrated and maintained, but also broken; and, ultimately, about bottom-up influences on norm change in IOs. The relationship and evolving practices involve important, perhaps crucial, insights and implications for the evolving and changing principle of sovereignty.

CHAPTER 20

Latin American Countries as Norm Protagonists of the Idea of International Human Rights

Kathryn Sikkink[1]

As the discipline of international relations is moving away from the study of "international relations" and toward the study of "global governance," it has generated a greater interest in the social construction of what is to be governed—that is, how a problem becomes defined and gets placed on the agenda.[2]

Scholars looking at who sets the global human rights agenda often argue that attention to human rights issues is the result of the dominance of powerful states. Others argue that Northern-based nongovernmental organizations (NGOs) continue to be powerful gatekeepers who frequently block or reshape issues from NGOs and social movements based in the Global South.[3] Scholars of diffusion suggest that ideas and policies often diffuse vertically from the Global North to the Global South via processes of coercion or emulation.[4]

There is a need for scholars of international norms to pay greater attention to the potential agency of states outside the Global North despite important structural inequality in the international system. But the very binaries of North/South or West/non-West may obscure the process we hope to illuminate. Latin America, for example, complicates these binaries that associate the Global North with the West. Because Latin American scholars and politicians are from the Global South, and yet as Louise Fawcett argues, are neither fully

---

*   This chapter was originally published in Global Governance, Volume 20, Issue 3, 2014.

1   Kathryn Sikkink is the Ryan Family Professor of Human Rights Policy at Harvard Kennedy School and the Carol K. Pforzheimer Professor at the Radcliffe Institute for Advanced Study.

2   Michael Barnett and Kathryn Sikkink, "From International Relations to Global Society," in Christian Reus-Smit and Duncan Snidal, eds., *The Oxford Handbook of International Relations* (New York: Oxford University Press, 2008), pp. 62–83.

3   Clifford Bob, *The Marketing of Rebellion: Insurgents, Media, and International Activism* (Cambridge: Cambridge University Press, 2005); Charli Carpenter, "Governing the Global Agenda: 'Gatekeepers' and 'Issue Adoption' in Transnational Advocacy Networks," in Debra Avant, Martha Finnemore, and Susan Sell, eds., *Who Governs the Globe?* (Cambridge: Cambridge University Press, 2010), pp. 202–237.

4   Beth Simmons, Frank Dobbins, and Geoffrey Garrett, "Introduction: The International Diffusion of Liberalism," *International Organization* 60, no. 4 (2006): 781–810.

"Western" nor "non-Western," the West/non-West dichotomy in some international relations scholarship has neglected Latin American contributions.[5]

Southern protagonism arguably increases the legitimacy of global governance projects, including the human rights project. Amitav Acharya, for example, critiques the study of normative change for ignoring the appeal of local and regional norms and for failing to locate agency in local and regional actors. He then develops the concepts of norm "localization," a process through which local actors actively reconstruct global norms to create a fit between those norms and prior local norms, and the related concept of norm "subsidiarity," whereby states and regional actors from the Global South can create new norms or new understandings of existing global norms.[6] Acharya's concept of localization is related to the concept of norm "vernacularization" proposed by anthropologist Sally Engle Merry. Merry points to social movements as human rights "intermediaries" that help "vernacularize international human rights discourses,"[7] negotiating between "the language of international human rights preferred by international donors, and cultural terms that will be acceptable to at least some of the local community."[8]

Elsewhere I have made the case for the historical normative agency of Latin America with regard to democracy promotion and human rights, and more recently for Argentina as a "global human rights protagonist" through an exposition of the country's innovations in the field of transitional justice.[9] Another way to talk about these processes of norm diffusion is to think of "norms entrepreneurs" in and from the Global South.[10] In his contribution to this special section, Eric Helleiner discusses Southern agency for the norm that international

5   Louise Fawcett, "Between West and Non-West: Latin American Contributions to International Thought," *International History Review* 34, no. 4 (2012): 679–704.

6   Amitav Acharya, "How Ideas Spread: Whose Norms Matter? Norm Localization and Institutional Change in Asian Regionalism," *International Organization* 58, no. 2 (2004): 239–275; Amitav Acharya, "Norm Subsidiarity and Regional Orders: Sovereignty, Regionalism, and Rule-making in the Third World," *International Studies Quarterly* 55, no. 1 (2011): 95–123.

7   Sally Engle Merry, "Transnational Human Rights and Local Activism," *American Anthropologist* 108, no. 1 (2006): 38–51.

8   Ibid.

9   Kathryn Sikkink, "Reconceptualizing Sovereignty in the Americas: Historical Precursors and Current Practices," *Houston Journal of International Law* 19, no. 3 (Spring 1997): 705–729; Kathryn Sikkink, "From Pariah State to Global Protagonist: Argentina and the Struggle for International Human Rights," *Latin American Politics and Society* 50, no. 1 (2008): 1–29; Kathryn Sikkink, *The Justice Cascade: How Human Rights Prosecutions Are Changing World Politics* (London: Norton, 2011).

10   Martha Finnemore and Kathryn Sikkink, "International Norm Dynamics and Political Change," *International Organization* 52, no. 4 (1998): 887–917.

institutions should support economic development of poor countries.[11] In a related vein, Jorge Dominguez stresses that Latin American regional organizations have been "international rule innovators" rather than simply "price takers."[12] In particular, Dominguez shows how Latin American states pioneered the defense of sovereignty and nonintervention, and later modified such doctrines to permit international intervention on behalf of democracy.[13]

Here, I argue that Latin American countries were protagonists of the idea of "international human rights"; that is, the idea that there should be international involvement in formulating and enforcing international human rights norms and law, and the related idea that there should be international involvement in democracy promotion. I illustrate this argument by looking at the role of Latin American states in promoting these international human rights norms in the post-World War II period, especially in the drafting of the first intergovernmental declaration of rights—the American Declaration of the Rights and Duties of Man, a full eight months before the Universal Declaration of Human Rights (UDHR) was passed in the UN General Assembly on 10 December 1948. The UDHR is usually seen as the starting point of the global human rights regime, and the American Declaration has been largely ignored outside of the hemisphere. While this argument relates to debates about Latin American and the "new regionalism," it goes beyond it in stressing Latin American contributions to the global normative and legal order, and not only to regional orders.[14]

Latin American countries have a strong tradition of support for the doctrines of sovereignty, sovereign equality, and nonintervention as a means by which weaker countries might find refuge from the less law-like interventions of the more powerful, especially the United States.[15] These arguments about

---

11 See Eric Helleiner, "Southern Pioneers of International Development," in this issue.

12 Jorge Dominguez, "International Cooperation in Latin America: The Design of Regional Institutions by Slow Accretion," in Amitav Acharya and Alastair I. Johnston, eds., *Crafting Cooperation: Regional International Institutions in Comparative Perspective* (Cambridge: Cambridge University Press, 2007).

13 Dominguez, "International Cooperation in Latin America."

14 See, for example, Amitav Acharya and Alastair I. Johnston, eds., *Crafting Cooperation: Regional Institutions in Comparative Perspective* (Cambridge: Cambridge University Press, 2007); Louise Fawcett and Monica Serrano, eds., *Regionalism and Governance in the Americas: Continental Drift* (London: Palgrave Macmillan, 2005); Pia Riggirozzi and Diana Tussi, eds., *The Rise of Post-hegemonic Regionalism: The Case of Latin America*, United Nations University Series on Regionalism, vol. 4 (New York: Springer, 2011).

15 See, for example, Fawcett, "Between West and Non-West." See also Ivan I. Jaksic and Andrés Bello, *Scholarship and Nation-building in Nineteenth-Century Latin America* (Cambridge: Cambridge University Press, 2001), on the role of Andrés Bello in international law, in particular.

the importance of sovereign equality, for example, were important for leading to participation of all countries in international conferences, which is
the theme of the article by Martha Finnemore and Michelle Jurkovich in this
special section. Latin American countries saw international law as one of the
"weapons of the weak" to balance US power.[16]

At the same time as they defended sovereignty, however, Latin American
legal scholars, policymakers, and activists also have long been at the forefront of
the struggle for international human rights and democracy.[17] One reason why
they promoted the international protection of human rights is that it would
"eliminate the misuse of diplomatic protection of citizens abroad," especially
by the United States.[18] But these Latin American diplomats and legal scholars were also committed to the ideal of rights: they were part of the Western
and enlightenment intellectual tradition even as they operated from what we
would now call the periphery or the Global South. Paolo Carozza, for example,
has traced the origins of Latin American concern with human rights to the
work of Bartolomé de las Casas in the colonial period and to Latin America's
embrace of enlightenment writers during the wars of independence.[19] Latin
American revolutions of independence, like that in the United States, were
motivated by enlightenment ideas of rights, present at the very moment of
state creation, rather than as a result of a later export or diffusion of ideas.[20]
But although informed by enlightenment ideas, Latin America scholars and
politicians were neither fully "Western" nor "non-Western."[21] Liliana Obregón
has traced the origins of a "creole" legal consciousness that blended elements
of a unique Latin American experiences and concerns with the international

16   Dominguez, "International Cooperation in Latin America."
17   Sikkink, "Reconceptualizing Sovereignty in the Americas"; G. Pope Atkins, *Latin America
      in the International Political System*, 2nd ed. (Boulder, CO: Westview, 1989); Dominguez,
      "International Cooperation in Latin America."
18   From Resolution 40, "International Protection of the Essential Rights of Man" of the
      Final Act of the Inter-American Conference on Problems of War and Peace, as cited in
      Inter-American Juridical Committee, "Draft Declaration of the International Rights and
      Duties of Man and Accompanying Report" (Washington, DC: Pan-American Union,
      March 1946).
19   Paolo Carozza, "From Conquest to Constitutions: Retrieving a Latin American Tradition
      of the Idea of Human Rights," *Human Rights Quarterly* 25, no. 2 (2003): 281–313.
20   Christian Reus-Smit, *Individual Rights and the Making of the International System*
      (Cambridge: Cambridge University Press, 2013); Paulina Ochoa Espejo, "Paradoxes
      of Popular Sovereignty: A View From Spanish America," *Journal of Politics* 74, no. 4
      (October 2012): 1053–1065.
21   Fawcett, "Between West and Non-West."

legal traditions of the time.[22] The Latin American jurists and diplomats who promoted rights came from the periphery of the global system, but they were not at all peripheral to global debates on international law and institutions during their lifetime.[23]

It is important to keep these precursors in mind when considering the current situation of the promotion of human rights and the defense of democracy. In this sense, we can see the developments of the late twentieth and early twenty-first centuries not as an unusual break with the past, but rather as a resurrection of ideals and concerns that had been present in inter-American debates for many years and had not yet received majority support.

1   Historical Background

Before World War II, human rights were not considered an appropriate topic for international scrutiny and rule formation. The international precursors to the human rights issue included the movement for respect of human rights during armed conflict, the campaign for the abolition of the slave trade and slavery, the work within the League of Nations for the protection of minority rights, the early work on the rights of workers in the International Labour Organization, and the movement for women's suffrage. But each of these limited issue areas fell far short of a full-fledged demand for attention to human rights as a legitimate topic for international action.

Some Latin American politicians also called very early for international efforts at what we would name "democracy promotion" today.[24] Like the United States and France, Spanish America was a laboratory for early experiences in democratic rule, and was the first to experiment with universal male suffrage.[25] But countries in the region suffered more frequent interruptions of these democratic experiments, and thus began to think early about how international pressures might enhance democracies in neighboring states. For example, Juan Bautista Alberdi, framer of the Argentine constitution of 1853, proposed an American court with the right of collective intervention to

---

22   Liliana Obregón, "Between Civilization and Barbarism: Creole Interventions in International Law," *Third World Quarterly* 27, no. 5 (2006): 815–832.

23   See Liliana Obregón, "Noted for Dissent: The International Life of Alejandro Alvarez," *Leiden Journal of International Law* 19, no. 4 (2006): 983–1016.

24   See Sikkink, "Reconceptualizing Sovereignty in the Americas."

25   Ochoa Espejo, "Paradoxes of Popular Sovereignty."

oppose tyranny.[26] Ecuadorian diplomat, Carlos Tobar proposed in 1907 a policy of collective nonrecognition of governments coming to power by other than democratic means.[27] In the 1940s, the Betancourt government in Venezuela used and advocated a related Betancourt Doctrine, whereby diplomatic relations with military regimes were severed.[28] None of these proposals led to any internationally agreed on policies of nonrecognition of authoritarian regimes, but they illustrate the early concern in the region with measures to promote democracy.

By the end of World War II, a consensus began to emerge that human rights and democracy would need to be an essential part of the postwar order. This consensus was particularly strong in Latin America, where an unprecedented wave of democratization had taken place in the mid-1940s, bringing to power various governments of the center left with strong support from labor unions.[29] Most scholars are familiar with the initiatives taken by the Allies during the war to stress the importance of human rights: in particular, Roosevelt's "Four Freedoms" speech and the inclusion of human rights language in the Atlantic Charter. But with the important exception of work by Johannes Morsink and Mary Ann Glendon, scholars are much less aware of the important role Latin American delegations and NGOs played in promoting the idea of international human rights, first at the San Francisco meeting where the UN Charter was drafted and later in drafting the UDHR.[30]

Although the Allies stressed human rights in their war aims, there were deep divisions within the US and UK governments about including human rights in

---

26   G. Pope Atkins, *Latin America in the International Political System*, 2nd ed. (Boulder: Westview, 1989), p. 228. See also Pablo Rojas Paz, ed., "La Omnipotencia del Estado es la Negación de la Libertad Individual," in Juan Bautista Alberdi, *El Pensamiento de Alberdi* (Buenos Aires: Editorial Lautaro, 1943), pp. 11, 35.

27   Atkins, *Latin America in the International Political System*, p. 228.

28   Steve Ellner, "Venezuela," in Leslie Bethell and Ian Roxborough, eds., *Latin American Between the Second World War and the Cold War, 1944–1948* (Cambridge: Cambridge University Press, 1992).

29   Leslie Bethell and Ian Roxborough, "Introduction: The Postwar Conjuncture in Latin America: Democracy, Labor, and the Left," in Leslie Bethell and Ian Roxborough, eds., *Latin American Between the Second World War and the Cold War, 1944–1948* (Cambridge: Cambridge University Press, 1992), pp. 1–32; Hernan Santa Cruz, *Cooperar o Perecer: El Dilema de la Comunidad Mundial* (Buenos Aires: Grupo Editor Latinoamericano, 1984), p. 57.

30   See Sikkink, "Reconceptualizing Sovereignty in the Americas"; Johannes Morsink, *The Universal Declaration of Human Rights: Origins, Drafting, and Intent* (Philadelphia: University of Pennsylvania Press, 1999); Mary Ann Glendon, "The Forgotten Crucible: The Latin American Influence on the Universal Human Rights Idea," *Harvard Human Rights Journal* 16 (2003): 27–39; also see Carozza, "From Conquest to Constitutions."

the postwar order. US secretary of state Cordell Hull had been willing to use human rights during the war as part of the articulation of war aims, but he opposed any efforts to promote human rights that would undermine national sovereignty.[31] Other members of the US government, especially Under Secretary of State Sumner Welles, were more deeply committed to incorporating human rights into US foreign policy and into a new international organization. Welles chaired one of the most important subcommittees of the Advisory Committee on Postwar Foreign Policy. Under his leadership, the group produced an international bill of human rights in 1942, but the State Department never published or used the document. Hull eventually carried the day, and Welles was forced to resign in 1943. The US delegation to the Dumbarton Oaks meeting was instructed to avoid any detailed discussion of human rights.[32]

The initial US drafts of the UN Charter contained no reference to human rights, while the proposals that emerged from the Big Four meeting at Dumbarton Oaks to prepare for the San Francisco conference contained only one reference to human rights.[33] The failure of the great powers to include human rights language in the Dumbarton Oaks draft mobilized both the community of NGOs and a group of less powerful states, particularly in Latin America, but also including New Zealand and Australia. Latin American countries felt betrayed because they had not been involved in the Dumbarton Oaks discussion about a postwar organization, and also because the Dumbarton Oaks draft did not incorporate various ideals they supported, including human rights.[34] To promote their concerns and formulate a collective policy, Latin American countries called an extraordinary meeting at the Chapultepec Castle in Mexico City in February 1945, the Inter-American Conference on Problems of War and Peace, which ended just weeks before the opening of the San Francisco conference. Delegates at the meeting raised a series of important issues about great-power dominance, the importance of international law, regional agreements for security, and economic and social problems. Human rights issues figured prominently in the speeches and resolutions.[35]

31   Cited in Paul Gordon Lauren, *The Evolution of International Human Rights: Visions Seen* (Philadelphia: University of Pennsylvania Press, 1998), p. 165.

32   Lauren, *The Evolution of International Human Rights*, pp. 162, 164–165, 167.

33   Jacob Robinson, *Human Rights and Fundamental Freedoms in the Charter of the United Nations* (New York: Institute of Jewish Affairs, 1946), p. 17.

34   Lauren, *The Evolution of International Human Rights*, pp. 174–179; Sumner Welles, *Where Are We Heading?* (New York: Harper & Brothers, 1946), p. 34.

35   "Final Act of the Inter-American Conference on Problems of War and Peace, Mexico City, February–March, 1945," in *Report of the Delegation of the United States of America to the Inter-American Conference on Problems of War and Peace, Mexico City, Mexico, February 21–March 8, 1945* (Washington, DC: US Printing Office, 1946).

At the 1945 conference in Mexico City, many Latin American states argued that World War II had created a worldwide demand that rights should be recognized and protected at the international level.[36] At an earlier meeting of the Inter-American Bar Association in Mexico City in 1944, resolutions had also emphasized the "necessity" of a declaration of rights of man, and the importance of international machinery and procedures to put the principles in the declaration into action. Acting on these concerns, the delegates at Mexico City instructed the Inter-American Juridical Committee to prepare a draft declaration of the rights and duties of man.[37]

One key element of the creole legal consciousness that motivated many early Latin American advocates of rights was a doctrine of popular sovereignty in which sovereignty ultimately rested with the people.[38] For this reason, early Latin American advocates of both nonintervention and international protection of human rights did not necessarily see a contradiction in their positions. Sovereignty was essential to protect states from the unlawful intervention of outsiders, but was not always conceived of as a justification for the government to abuse the rights of citizens.

"The Uruguayan foreign minister Alberto Rodriguez Larreta recognized this in 1945 when he wrote ... [N]on-intervention is not a shield behind which crime may be perpetrated, law may be violated ... and binding obligations may be circumvented."[39] The Chilean delegation to the San Francisco conference made the relationship clearer. When discussing sovereignty, the Chileans clarified, "The State is lord of its territory, can grant itself whatever *democratic* form of government it may desire *within standards which respect the inalienable rights of man.*"[40]

Latin America delegations—especially, Uruguay, Chile, Panama, and Mexico—brought these arguments in favor of the international protection of rights to the San Francisco conference in 1945. There, they were supported

---

36   *Report of the Delegation of the United States of America to the Inter-American Conference on Problems of War and Peace, Mexico City, Mexico, February 21–March 8, 1945* (Washington, DC: US Printing Office, 1946); Morsink, *The Universal Declaration of Human Rights*, pp. 130–131.

37   Inter-American Juridical Committee, "Draft Declaration of the International Rights and Duties of Man and Accompanying Report" (Washington, DC: PanAmerican Union, March 1946), pp. 57–58.

38   Ochoa Espejo, "Paradoxes of Popular Sovereignty."

39   Alberto Rodriguez Larreta, "Inter-American Solidarity: Safeguarding the Democratic Ideal: Note from Uruguayan Foreign Minister to Secretary of State," *Department of State Bulletin* (25 November 1945): 865–866.

40   *Documents of the United Nations Conference on International Organization, San Francisco, 1945* (New York: UN Information Organizations, 1945), p. 293, emphasis added.

by a number of US-based NGOs present at the conference. Latin American countries made up twenty of the fifty states present at the San Francisco conference.[41] Because there were many democratic countries with a shared worldview at this historical moment in Latin America, they became the most important voting bloc at San Francisco.[42] The British government gave this Latin American bloc credit for changing the US government's position on human rights at San Francisco.[43] They were able to do this in part because they supported and reinforced a position already held by a minority faction with the US government that had lost influence in the drafting of the Dumbarton Oaks proposal. But without Latin American protagonism, it is unlikely that the Charter would have contained references to human rights.

The record of the success of the NGO lobbying effort and the efforts of Latin American delegations in favor of human rights find testimony in the Charter itself. The final UN Charter has seven references to human rights, including key amendments whereby promotion of human rights is listed as one of the basic purposes of the organization, and the Economic and Social Council (ECOSOC) is called on to set up a human rights commission, the only specifically mandated commission in the Charter. In particular, the initiatives of the Latin American countries helped extend the economic, social, and human rights objectives in the Charter, in particular Articles 55 and 56, on which so much later human rights work of the organization rested.[44]

If the Charter, adopted at a high point of postwar collaboration, had not contained references to human rights and specifically to a Human Rights Commission, it is quite likely that the Universal Declaration of Human Rights would not have been drafted in 1948. The inclusion of the human rights language in the Charter of the United Nations was a critical juncture that channeled the history of postwar global governance in the direction of setting international norms and law about the promotion of human rights. This language was not the language of the great powers, and it was finally adopted by the great powers only in response to pressures from small states and civil society.

The initial unwillingness of the great powers to include references to human rights in the UN Charter calls into question both a realist and a critical theory

---

41   Lauren, *The Evolution of International Human Rights*, p. 193; "Opinion of the Department of Foreign Relations of Mexico Concerning the Dumbarton Oaks Proposals for the Creation of a General International Organization," *Documents of the United Nations Conference on International Organization, San Francisco, 1945:* Volume 3 (New York: UN Information Organization, 1945), pp. 71–73.

42   Morsink, *The Universal Declaration of Human Rights*, p. 130.

43   Lauren, *The Evolution of International Human Rights*, p. 337, footnote 86.

44   Santa Cruz, *Cooperar o Perecer*, p. 69.

explanation for the origins of human rights norms. If human rights emerged primarily from the goals and needs of powerful states, as realists claim, then why did these powerful states not include human rights language in the Dumbarton Oaks draft?[45] Only China, the weakest of the four, pressed for inclusion of some human rights language. But China's effort to include an explicit statement against racial discrimination was rejected by the other great powers.

The two other key governmental actors, the USSR and the United Kingdom, shared the US concern to limit possible infringement on domestic jurisdiction.[46] Although the human rights provisions did not carry teeth at this early stage, states were wary of the sovereignty implications of the human rights issue. If human rights policy was the result of powerful states, as realist theory suggests, it simply cannot help us understand why these powerful states came to support international human rights norms so reluctantly.

If, as critical theorists suggest, human rights was a discourse that powerful states used to reaffirm their identity as superior to the weaker nations, and to promote monitoring and surveillance, why did more powerful states resist the adoption of human rights discourses and less powerful states promote it?[47] I believe that both realist and critical theory accounts have misunderstood and misrepresented the history of human rights ideas and human rights policies. Reading the history of the human rights policies reveals that these policies, especially multilateral policies, have often been embraced by the less powerful to try to restrain the more powerful. These less powerful groups are more likely to succeed, however, when they also have allies within powerful states.

Both states and NGOs demanded an international organization that would have more far-reaching power to enforce international human rights norms. The Uruguayan delegation, for example, proposed that the Charter itself should contain a "Declaration of Rights," and "a system of effective juridical guardianship of those rights."[48] Uruguay proposed to make it possible to suspend from

---

45   See, for example, Stephen D. Krasner, "Sovereignty, Regimes, and Human Rights," in Volker Rittberger and Peter Mayer, eds., *Regime Theory and International Relations* (New York: Oxford University Press, 1993).

46   M. Glen Johnson, "The Contributions of Eleanor and Franklin Roosevelt to the Development of International Protection for Human Rights," *Human Rights Quarterly* 9, no. 1 (February 1987): 24.

47   See, for example, Roxanne Doty, *Imperial Encounters: The Politics of Representation in North-South Relations* (Minneapolis: University of Minnesota Press, 1996), pp. 127–144.

48   "New Uruguayan Proposals on the Dumbarton Oaks Proposals," *Documents of the United Nations Conference on International Organization, San Francisco, 1945:* Volume 3 (New York: UN Information Organization, 1945), p. 34.

the organization countries that persistently violated human rights.[49] The final language, however, called on the UN only to promote, encourage, and assist respect for human rights.

As a result, the Charter mandate on human rights is less firm than many states and NGOs desired because it calls on the UN to promote and encourage respect for human rights, rather than to actually protect rights.[50] More far-reaching alternative visions were presented and articulated at the San Francisco conference, and the NGO consultants and a handful of democratic Latin American states were among the most eloquent spokespeople for them. These alternative visions continued to be further elaborated in the drafting of the American Declaration of the Rights and Duties of Man, which began as soon as the San Francisco conference ended.

2   The American Declaration of the Rights and Duties of Man
       and the UDHR

Most histories of human rights in the world emphasize the Universal Declaration of Human Rights, passed by the UN General Assembly on 10 December 1948, as the founding moment of international human rights.[51] The dramatic story of the drafting of the UDHR has been told well and at length elsewhere.[52] I do not repeat that history here, but rather stress a much less well-known story—the ways in which the drafting of the American Declaration of the Rights and Duties of Man preceded the drafting of the UDHR.

The American Declaration was first approved by the Ninth International Conference of American States at Bogotá, Colombia, in April 1948, eight months before the passage of the UDHR. The Organization of American States (OAS) did not yet exist at time of the Bogotá meeting, and so the America Declaration

---

49   "Statement of Uruguayan Delegation of Its Position with Reference to Chapters I and II of the Charter as Considered by Committee I/1," 15 June 1945, *Documents of the United Nations Conference on International Organization, San Francisco, 1945:* Volume 6 (New York: UN Information Organization, 1945), pp. 628–633.

50   "Report of Rapporteur, Subcommittee I/1/A (Farid Zeineddine, Syria), to Committee I/1," *Documents of the United Nations Conference on International Organization, San Francisco, 1945* (New York: UN Information Organization, 1945), p. 705.

51   Lynn Hunt, *Inventing Human Rights: A History* (New York: Norton, 2007); Mary Ann Glendon, *A World Made New: Eleanor Roosevelt and the Universal Declaration of Human Rights* (New York: Random House, 2001); Morsink, *The Universal Declaration of Human Rights.*

52   See, in particular, Lauren, *The Evolution of International Human Rights*, chaps. 6–7; Morsink, *The Universal Declaration of Human Rights*; Glendon, *A World Made New.*

was formally adopted later by a unanimous vote of the newly formed OAS, but still some three months before the General Assembly acted on the UDHR.[53]

Because Latin American states adopted the American Declaration of the Rights and Duties of Man before the General Assembly passed the UDHR, the American Declaration was in fact the "the first broadly detailed enumeration of rights to be adopted by an intergovernmental organization."[54] But because the two documents were being drafted around the same time, these two processes were overlapping and complementary, so it is useful to discuss them together.

But what I want to stress here is that the process of drafting the American Declaration of the Rights and Duties of Man was always a step ahead of the drafting of the UDHR. Because the American republics had requested a draft declaration of rights from the Inter-American Juridical Committee at the Mexico City conference in 1945 before the San Francisco conference, the American Declaration process had a head start over the process of drafting the UDHR that had to wait to get started until after the San Francisco meeting and after ratifications of the UN Charter. The Inter-American Judicial Committee worked rapidly to produce this complete draft declaration, including twenty-one articles and another fifty pages of full commentary, by 31 December 1945, only six months after the San Francisco conference had concluded. The document was published in March 1946, before the UN Preparatory Committee tasked with drafting the UDHR had even held its first meeting.[55] The American states expanded the final American Declaration beyond this draft declaration, adding eight additional articles on rights and ten additional articles on the duties of states, but all the core civil, political, economic, social, and cultural rights of the American Declaration were present in the draft. The Juridical Committee's justifications for rights in this document gives an idea of how some Latin American jurists were thinking about the relationship between sovereignty and human rights in this period:

> In view of the widespread denial of these political rights by totalitarian governments in recent years it may be well to reinstate the basic theory underlying them. The state is not an end in itself, it is only a means to an

53   Tom Farer, "The Rise of the Inter-American Human Rights Regime: No Longer a Unicorn, Not Yet an Ox," in David Harris and Stephen Livingstone, eds., *The Inter-American System of Human Rights* (New York: Oxford University Press, 1998), p. 35.

54   Ibid.

55   Inter-American Juridical Committee, "Draft Declaration of the International Rights and Duties of Man and Accompanying Report" (Washington, DC: PanAmerican Union, March 1946). The UN Nuclear Preparatory Committee held its first meetings in April and May 1946. Morsink, *The Universal Declaration of Human Rights*, p. 4.

end; it is not in itself a source of rights but the means by which the inherent rights of the individual person may be made practically effective.... Not only, therefore, are particular governments bound to respect the fundamental rights of man, but the state itself is without authority to override them.[56]

This is as clear a statement as possible of the doctrine of popular sovereignty that was part of the legal tradition in Latin America. The Inter-American Judicial Committee then went on to say that the broad principles of distributive justice provide a justification for the inclusion of economic and social rights in the draft declaration as "the complicated economic lives of modern states has made the old doctrine of laissez-faire no longer adequate."[57]

The American Declaration was completed before the second round of drafting of the UDHR, and it was influential in the text of the UDHR, particularly in the articles on social and economic rights. In his detailed book on the drafting of the UDHR, Morsink wrote that the American Declaration "heavily influenced the drafting process and product of the universal one."[58]

The American Declaration includes thirty-eight articles, of which twenty-eight are devoted to an enumeration of rights and ten to duties. This attention to duties sets the American Declaration apart from the UDHR, which does not enumerate specific duties, although it does mention them in Article 29. Of the twenty-eight articles on rights, approximately two-thirds of the articles address civil and political rights, and approximately one-third address economic, social, and cultural rights, including the rights to health, education, work and fair remuneration, culture, leisure, social security, and property. All of the rights in the UDHR also appear in the American Declaration, although the UDHR sometimes elaborates on these rights in greater detail. The American Declaration has a single right—that of petition—as well as the nine additional articles on duties that are not in the UDHR.[59]

This heavy influence of the American Declaration on the UDHR is not surprising because they had similar sources. When John Humphrey, the Canadian who served as the head of the UN Secretariat's Human Rights Division, wrote

---

56   Inter-American Juridical Committee, "Draft Declaration of the International Rights and Duties of Man," p. 21.
57   Ibid.
58   Morsink, *The Universal Declaration of Human Rights*, p. 130.
59   "Estudio Comparativo de la Declaracion Americana de los Derechos y Deberes del Hombre y la Declaracion Universal de Derechos del Hombre," unnumbered mimeographed document in file "human rights," archives of the Columbus Library, Organization of American States, Washington, DC.

the Secretariat outline (a draft bill of rights) for the Human Rights Commission to use its deliberations in producing the eventual UDHR, he used for models the score of drafts the Secretariat had collected from law professors and legal and social NGOs as well as from other intergovernmental organizations, including the Pan-American Union.[60] Although the Secretariat outline was modified significantly during the debates, the influence of these diverse nongovernmental and intergovernmental sources are clearly seen in the final version of the Universal Declaration of Human Rights. Cuba, Panama, and Chile were the first three countries to submit full drafts of bills of rights to the commission. Each of these contained references to rights to education, food, and health care, and other social security provisions.[61] Humphrey, a social democrat, used these drafts extensively in preparing the Secretariat's draft for the commission to consider. "Humphrey took much of the wording and almost all of the ideas for the social, economic, and cultural rights from his first draft from the tradition of Latin American socialism by way of the bills submitted by Panama and Chile."[62] The research showing the impact of Latin American countries on the inclusion of economic and social rights in the UDHR corrected a long-held belief that the economic and social rights in the UDHR were primarily the result of Soviet pressure.[63]

   In addition to their contributions to the economic and social rights in the UDHR, Latin American delegates made other important contributions. Latin American delegations, especially Mexico, Cuba, and Chile, almost single-handedly inserted language about the right to justice into both the American Declaration and the UDHR. The probable source for Latin American proposals on the need for accountability in the American Declaration and the UDHR are the *amparo* laws that existed in some, but not all, Latin American countries.[64] Since there is no equivalent of a full *amparo* law in common-law countries, it is difficult to translate. Habeas corpus is related, but it is only for protection against unjust detention, while *amparo* or *tutela* laws offer protections for the full range of rights violations that may occur as a result of "acts of authority." So, habeas corpus is like a "species" in a broader "genus" of protections, many

60   John P. Humphrey, *Human Rights and the United Nations: A Great Adventure* (Dobbs Ferry, NY: Transnational, 1984), pp. 31–32.

61   The Panamanian draft was prepared by the American Law Institute and the Chilean draft was prepared by the Inter-American Juridical Committee of the OAS. Morsink, *The Universal Declaration of Human Rights*, p. 131.

62   Morsink, *The Universal Declaration of Human Rights*, p. 131.

63   Glendon, *A World Made New*; Morsink, *The Universal Declaration of Human Rights*; Humphrey, *Human Rights and the United Nations*.

64   Pan-American Union, *Human Rights in the American States* (Washington, DC: OAS, Department of Legal Affairs, 1960).

of which are covered by *amparo* laws.[65] This is a clear example of normative innovation where Latin American delegations took legal procedures from their own constitutional tradition, one that was not present in the constitutions of the large common-law countries, and used it to craft an essential article of the new human rights declarations. Far from an example of norm localization or even vernacularization, this is a clearer case of norm protagonism or innovation from countries in the Global South. This idea of a right to justice would later serve as the backbone of Latin American efforts to secure accountability through the inter-American system. In this sense, there is genuine continuity from the normative and legal contributions that Latin American states made to the UDHR and the American Declaration and the later work of the Inter-American Commission and the Inter-American Court of Human Rights on behalf of accountability for past human rights violations.

3   Conclusion

Why has Latin America's important role in the emergence of global human rights norms and law not been more broadly perceived or understood by international relations scholars, including even at times scholars from the Latin America region? There are a number of possible explanations. First, there was a paradox at the heart of Latin America defense of human rights that may have undermined its effectiveness. At the same time as many Latin American countries were advocating international human rights norms, practices on the ground in many countries fell far short of the human rights ideal. This paradox was graphically present even at the Ninth Inter-American Conference where the American Declaration was first approved by the American states.

In the midst of the conference, an important populist political leader in Colombia, Jorge Eliécer Gaitán, was assassinated on the streets of Bogotá, leading to intense protests and violence that temporarily suspended the conference proceedings. Gaitán, a leader of the left wing of the Liberal Party, was an eloquent speaker greatly admired by the poor of the city who responded to his murder with riots, looting, and killings, which in turn led to a violent response by the state security forces. This riot is known as the Bogotazo (Bogotá attack), in which thousands were killed and a large part of the city burned to the ground. The Bogotazo is now seen as the start of the period in Colombia known as La Violencia (the time of violence), in which hundreds of thousands of ordinary Colombians died.

---

65   Ibid.

So, we have this juxtaposition of a conference to set up a new regional organization and to proclaim the rights and duties of man and the importance of democracy in the region at the same time as the host government of the conference and the people in the streets are trampling on the rights of man. The response of the world community, and indeed many in the region, may have been to dismiss the noble words inside the conference that would appear to be contradicted by the practices outside of it. Or perhaps the events simply foreshadowed the pressing problems of security and violence that would dominate the Cold War period and lead to the disregard of general declarations.

But a second reason, and this is much more critical for IR scholars, is that many scholars of international relations have neither the training, the knowledge of other languages, nor the inclination to conduct field research in the developing world. So, they turn to sources in the Global North. There is yet a new paradox here: even scholars that critique how the Global North imposes norms on the Global South often do so on the basis of research conducted almost solely in the Global North, using sources available there. The research design of these scholars reproduces the very situation they critique. In their efforts to stress how the countries of the Global North have silenced voices in the developing world and imposed Northern values on them, they too have silenced the past by not carefully investigating sources from the developing world itself. Thus, this short article is a plea of sorts for attention to the possibility of Southern protagonism at many stages of global norm development and global governance.

This historical work tracing the origins of international norms helps shed light on current developments. In the case of Latin America, various developments on the international supervision of human rights and democracy in regional and international organizations can be seen as manifestations of the ideas presented by Latin American states at the San Francisco conference and articulated in the American Declaration of the Rights and Duties of Man. Developments in the inter-American system that now allow the OAS to suspend from membership governments that come to power through military coups are the concrete realization of proposals that countries like Uruguay and Guatemala made in San Francisco in 1945. The International Criminal Court is the embodiment of the idea that the international system not only should promote rights, but also should provide actual enforcement and juridical protection of those rights. Latin American involvement in these recent initiatives therefore is not a puzzle or a result of great-power leadership, but a continuation of much longer traditions and activism on behalf of the international protection of human rights and democracy.

CHAPTER 21

Between Doctrine and Practice: The UN Peacekeeping Dilemma

Mateja Peter[1]

... to prevent the expansion of all armed groups, neutralize these groups, and to disarm them.

> *UN Organization Stabilization Mission in the Democratic Republic of the Congo (MONUSCO) list of tasks, UN Security Council Resolution S/RES/2098 (28 March 2013)*

• • •

... to stabilize the key population centres, especially in the north of Mali and, in this context, to deter threats and take active steps to prevent the return of armed elements to those areas.

> *UN Mission in Mali (MINUSMA) mandate, UN Security Council Resolution S/RES/2100 (25 April 2013)*

• •
•

In spring of 2013, the UN Security Council expanded the mandate of a long-standing peacekeeping mission in the Democratic Republic of Congo (DRC) and established a new operation in Mali. Both of these missions are operating in highly challenging environments, environments where the Security Council and the UN Department of Peacekeeping Operations would traditionally be reluctant to deploy. More important, both missions have unprecedentedly

---

* This chapter was originally published in Global Governance, Volume 21, Issue 3, 2015.

1 Mateja Peter is Lecturer in International Relations at the University of S. Andrews. Her research centers on global governance, peace operations, international organizations, and studies of the Balkans and sub-Saharan Africa.

    The author thanks Morten Boas, Cedric de Coning, Ingvild Magnæs Gjelsvik, John Karlsrud, Karli Osland, Randi Solhjell, and the three anonymous reviewers for their comments.

robust mandates, further expanding and drawing attention to the range of activities that UN peacekeepers have recently been engaging in and supporting. Authorization of an intervention brigade, references to unmanned aerial vehicles (drones) in mission mandates, invocation of explicit links between terrorism and organized crime, and support for extension of state authority in the midst of open conflicts are all changing the nature of peacekeeping. Moreover, in practice, peacekeeping operations have started to rely on new capabilities such as the use of strategic communication and, more recently, military intelligence. UN peacekeeping is increasingly bearing a resemblance to the stabilization missions in Afghanistan and Iraq. It is erasing the line between peacekeeping and peace enforcement, opening questions about future developments and repercussions. UN peacekeeping seems to be going down the path not only of enforcing military solutions through offensive action, but also of presuming and precluding particular political solutions by siding with (often contested) governments.

Recent UN peacekeeping practice is not aligned with its doctrine. This tension has not escaped informed observers[2] or the UN itself. Both the member states and the UN Secretariat through the Department of Peacekeeping Operations are cognizant that they are encountering a range of new problems. Concerns about nonstate actors and nontraditional threats top the list. Consequently, the UN is engaging in major efforts to strengthen its capability-driven approach to peacekeeping with an aim to respond to the challenges of the twenty-first century. However, while these reform initiatives attempt to address many of the practical concerns arising out of increasingly robust missions (including growing budgets and troop commitments),[3] these endeavors have endorsed, advocated, and been underpinned by the basic principles of UN peacekeeping as developed through the Brahimi Report and the Capstone Doctrine: consent, impartiality, and nonuse of force.[4] They heavily invoke the Capstone principles in what amounts to almost a collective denial of the mismatch between the doctrine and practice.

---

2 Challenges Forum, "The Death of Doctrine? Are 'Fit-for-Purpose' Peace Operations the Way Forward?" Policy Brief 2013:2 (Stockholm: Challenges Forum, 2013); Richard Gowan, "The Changing Face of Peace Operations: New Mandates and Risks for Peacekeeping and Political Missions," in Center on International Cooperation, *Annual Review of Global Peace Operations 2013* (Boulder: Lynne Rienner, 2013).

3 Alex J. Bellamy and Paul D. Williams, eds., *Providing Peacekeepers: The Politics, Challenges and Future of United Nations Peacekeeping Contributions* (Oxford: Oxford University Press, 2013).

4 United Nations, "Report of the Panel on United Nations Peace Operations" (hereafter Brahimi Report), UN Doc. A/55/305–S/2000/809 (August 2000); United Nations, "United Nations Peacekeeping: Principles and Guidelines" (hereafter Capstone Doctrine), (UN Department of Peacekeeping Operations, 18 January 2008), www.unrol.org/files/Capstone_Doctrine_ENG.pdf, pp. 31–35.

The argument presented here proceeds in two parts. First, I demonstrate that the recent innovations in peacekeeping fundamentally challenge the Brahimi Report, the Capstone Doctrine, and their understanding of what peacekeeping is. Second, I argue that such fundamental challenges, when not properly acknowledged, create a wall between operational activities and strategic/doctrinal considerations. Thus, they preclude a proper debate on the problematic externalities of the new peacekeeping reality. In this article, I address the repercussions of expanding mandates on political processes and longer-term peacebuilding activities. I argue that the lack of acknowledgment of a doctrinal shift complicates developments and planning in host states and regions in the long run.

This article is structured into four sections. First, I look at the reality of contemporary peacekeeping, highlighting that UN peacekeeping practice is learning from stabilization missions in Iraq and Afghanistan. Second, I outline the doctrinal mismatch and the UN responses to it. I show that these responses have not recognized the extent of a gap between the reality and the doctrine. Third, I explore implications of these changes for UN peacekeeping and international efforts. Fourth, I address repercussions for political processes and peacebuilding in the host state and region. In the conclusion, I reflect on what this new era of enforcement peacekeeping means for the UN and its role in conflict resolution and management.

1   New Realities of UN Peacekeeping

After a period of steady growth from the late 1990s on, the UN peacekeeping expansion seemed to have started contracting toward the end of the past decade. Three large-scale operations in Kosovo, Timor-Leste, and Liberia were slowly drawing down, planning their exits, and transitioning to peacebuilding activities. In addition, the global financial crisis of 2008 presented a sobering moment for international peacekeeping, putting substantial pressures on any and all proposals to reduce budgets and curtail tasks. Experiences with the stabilization missions in Iraq and Afghanistan contributed to this broad disillusionment over large-scale and potentially protracted international interventions. Peacekeeping was seemingly in less demand. However, this development did not last long. Not only has the Security Council authorized a deployment of 12,000 troops and police to Mali[5] and 10,000 to the Central African Republic (CAR)[6]—the scale of missions we have not seen since before the financial

---

5   UN Security Council, Res. S/RES/2100 (25 April 2013).
6   UN Security Council, Res. S/RES/2149 (10 April 2014).

crisis—but the types of activities that the new missions and the newly enhanced missions are mandated to perform substantially expand and change the nature of UN peacekeeping. After traditional and multidimensional peace-keeping, we are now entering a new era of enforcement peacekeeping.[7]

Enforcement peacekeeping manifests itself both in enforcement of politi-cal solutions through support of a government's state-building ambitions and its attempts to extend state authority in the midst of conflict and in enforce-ment of military victories through offensive use of force. This is connected to the fact that the targets of peacekeeping actions are nonstate actors that enjoy little international legitimacy due to their appalling human rights or war crimes records. As a result, no comprehensive peace agreements with them are sought before peacekeepers are deployed, something that is in stark contrast to both traditional and multidimensional peacekeeping. As outlined below, these missions bear resemblance to the stabilization missions in Iraq and—even more starkly—Afghanistan. Unlike UN operations, the mission in Afghanistan was Security Council-mandated but carried out by a US-led coali-tion of mostly Western states, with the UN footprint being light in the form of a special political mission.[8] While the missions in Iraq and Afghanistan could hardly be described as successful, the UN is emulating them as it is confronting actors seemingly similar to al-Qaeda and the Taliban (e.g., Al-Shabaab, M23, Boko Haram, and al-Qaeda in the Islamic Maghreb). However, as the appetite for unilateral or coalition-led interventions has decreased among the Western powers, these operations are now conducted on a smaller scale in the context of UN peacekeeping, with an intention to manage and contain these conflicts. The following paragraphs provide an illustration of some of these new activi-ties and hint that a seismic change is under way.

---

7   The UN distinguishes between two generations of peacekeeping: traditional and multidi-mensional. *Traditional peacekeeping* focuses on monitoring cease-fires; in *multidimensional operations*, peacekeepers support the implementation of a comprehensive peace settle-ment. Scholars have pointed to a possible third generation focusing on employment of mili-tary means to implement a humanitarian mandate. See Connie Peck, *The United Nations as a Dispute Settlement System: Improving Mechanisms for the Prevention and Resolution of Conflict* (The Hague: Kluwer Law International, 1996); Oliver Ramsbotham, Hugh Miall, and Tom Woodhouse, *Contemporary Conflict Resolution* (Cambridge: Polity, 2011). Others have contended that the UN has developed another generation of peacekeeping—international administrations. See Christine Gray, *International Law and the Use of Force: Foundations of Public International Law* (Oxford: Oxford University Press, 2000).

8   For more, see Blanca Antonini, ed., *Security Council Resolutions Under Chapter VII: Design, Implementation and Accountability—The Cases of Afghanistan, Côte d'Ivoire, Kosovo and Sierra Leone* (Madrid: FRIDE, 2009).

One of the more striking innovations in UN peacekeeping is the intro-duction of targeted combat operations and the switch from defensive to offensive peacekeeping. Most noticeably, this has been the case in the DRC, where the Security Council authorized the inclusion of a "force intervention brigade" within an existing UN Organization Stabilization Mission in the Democratic Republic of the Congo (MONUSCO) mission structure. This is the "first-ever 'offensive' combat force" in UN peacekeeping.[9] The brigade was set up with an intention to "neutralize and disarm"—a euphemism widely used by the military when engaging in offensive operations—the Tutsi March 23 (M23) militia in the eastern parts of the DRC. This group had previously put increasing pressure on both the Congolese forces and UN peacekeepers and, in November 2012, even managed to seize the regional center of Goma. At the same time, while the expansion of the mission was prompted by recent activities of M23, the Security Council resolution is framed considerably more broadly. It mandates UN peacekeepers to assist Congolese forces in fighting all armed groups, listing the Democratic Forces for the Liberation of Rwanda (FDLR) and the Lord's Resistance Army (LRA) as two other examples. This is the first time in the history of UN peacekeeping that the Security Council has created a list of enemies that UN peacekeepers are supposed to neutralize. The language of the resolution and the types of activities that UN peacekeepers are mandated to perform imply that the UN is engaged in a battle in coalition with the Congolese government, the same government that the UN and other international actors have repeatedly criticized for condoning serious abuses by its military against civilians.[10]

---

9   UN News, "'Intervention Brigade' Authorized as Security Council Grants Mandate Renewal for United Nations Mission in Democratic Republic of Congo," SC/10964, press release (28 March 2013); UN Security Council, Res. S/RES/2098 (28 March 2013).

10   For example, UN Security Council Meeting Record S/PV.6400 (14 October 2010); Human Rights Watch, "World Report 2012: Democratic Republic of Congo, January" (New York: Human Rights Watch, 2012). For more on the recent developments in the DRC and how they are connected to the expansion of MONUSCO mandates, see J. Arthur Boutellis, "From Crisis to Reform: Peacekeeping Strategies for the Protection of Civilians in the Democratic Republic of the Congo," *Stability: International Journal of Security and Development* 2, no. 3 (2013): 1–11; Naomi Kok, "From the International Conference on the Great Lakes Region-led Negotiation to the Intervention Brigade: Dealing with the Latest Crisis in the Democratic Republic of Congo," *African Security Review* 22, no. 3 (2013): 175–180; Sandra Adong Oder, "Understanding the Complexities of the Democratic Republic of Congo at the Turn of the Decade," *African Security Review* 20, no. 2 (2011): 51–55; Theodore Trefon, "Uncertainty and Powerlessness in Congo 2012," *Review of African Political Economy* 40, no. 135 (2013): 141–151.

While the Congolese experience has not been entirely replicated in other missions (yet), it does conform to a wider trend in UN peacekeeping. MINUSMA, the UN operation in Mali, does not have a mandate that is as explicitly offensive as the mission in the DRC. While some Security Council member states were flirting with such an idea, in the end the mandate does not directly authorize UN offensive actions. This is partly because of the Secretary-General's concerns about the inability of UN troops to engage in desert combat, and partly due to reluctance of emerging powers to authorize such a mandate under UN control.[11] However, when the UN mission was established, it assimilated the extant Economic Community of West African States (ECOWAS) mission AFISMA. And AFISMA had previously been authorized by the Security Council to support the government of Mali, an ECOWAS member nation, in its fight against Islamist rebels in the northern Mali conflict.[12] Moreover, the resolution establishing MINUSMA also authorized French troops conducting Operation Serval to use all necessary means to intervene within the limits of their capacities and areas of deployment in support of elements of MINUSMA when under imminent and serious threat and on request of the Secretary-General. Operation Serval, which has been in Mali since the end of 2012, was deployed following an official request by the Malian interim government. Its aim is to oust Islamic militants in northern Mali. By associating MINUSMA with Operation Serval, the Security Council in essence authorized an intervention brigade, just not under the UN command.

Similarly, in Somalia, the Security Council established a political mission with a mandate to support the government and African Union Mission in Somalia (AMISOM) peacekeepers.[13] These are in essence fighting a war against Al-Shabaab, which means that the UN is associated with those activities. Richard Gowan further writes that an African Union regional intervention force, currently under development, "could potentially conduct aggressive military operations not only in parts of the DRC patrolled by UN troops, but also in South Sudan and the Central African Republic."[14] The deployment of offensive combat troops is thus far-reaching, and even when the UN is not deploying these forces itself, it is supporting regional organizations and states in ways that their actions are not clearly detached.[15]

---

11   See, for example, Aljazeera, "Ban Proposes Mali Peacekeeping Force," 27 March 2013.

12   UN Security Council, Res. S/RES/2085 (20 December 2012).

13   UN Security Council, Res. S/RES/2102 (2 May 2013).

14   Gowan, "The Changing Face of Peace Operations," p. 16.

15   In the past, the UN has also deployed a UN–African Union hybrid mission in Darfur. See Thierry Tardy, "Hybrid Peace Operations: Rationale and Challenges," *Global Governance* 20, no. 1 (2014): 95–118.

At the same time, the UN not only engages in military action against particular targets, in coalition with the host state, but also assists these states in their state-building attempts. In the case of Somalia, the UN Assistance Mission in Somalia (UNSOM) is supporting the government in the development of a federal system.[16] Both MINUSMA in Mali and MONUSCO in the DRC have extension of state authority as part of their mandates. Support for particular state structures is occurring without a comprehensive peace agreement in place.

In parallel, UN peace operations have seen an increasing deployment of regional actors that are part of the conflict dynamics. For the entire peacekeeping history, there has been a strong reluctance to deploy peacekeepers to areas where they could be seen as acting as instruments of their governments' policies.[17] When regional actors have been deployed as part of a UN mission, for example, Australia in Timor-Leste (UN Transitional Administration in East Timor, UNTAET) or Nigeria in Sierra Leone (UN Assistance Mission in Sierra Leone, UNAMSIL), this has been with the consent of all main parties to the conflict and after a comprehensive peace agreement was in place. As discussed below, the rationale for excluding regional actors with interest in the conflict outcome not only has to do with obtaining consent, but also with making sure that UN peacekeeping is not used as a political tool. The policy is intended to protect the credibility of operations as well as to protect peacekeepers themselves from attacks.

In the African context, where sovereign borders are a result of a colonial logic, such cross-border interests are even more apparent. While UN peace operations as a rule have a single-state mandate, the conflicts in Mali, Somalia, the DRC, the CAR, Sudan, and South Sudan, to mention only some, are all *regional* conflicts. Their neighboring states are part of the conflict dynamics. However, prohibition against deployment to areas where states have interests is now changing.[18] UN operations increasingly rely on regional contributions, not least because only highly interested states are willing to risk the lives of their troops in increasingly robust operations. That is, regional states are interested in conflicts that affect their security and political interests, therefore they are willing to contribute to high-risk situations.

A prime example of this development is MINUSMA, which by incorporating AFISMA became ostensibly a mission composed of regional troops. The

---

16   UN Security Council, Res. S/RES/2102.

17   Marrack Goulding, "The Evolution of United Nations Peacekeeping," *International Affairs* 69, no. 3 (1993): 451–464, at 454.

18   See, for example, Jonah Victor, "African Peacekeeping in Africa: Warlord Politics, Defense Economics, and State Legitimacy," *Journal of Peace Research* 47, no. 2 (2010): 217–229.

largest troop contributors to the Mali mission are Chad, Burkina Faso, Niger, Togo, and Senegal, all regional states.[19] Regional troops are also the ones primarily deployed to the most volatile northern parts of Mali. In the DRC, the primary contributors to the intervention brigade are South Africa, Tanzania, and Malawi, while the rest of the MONUSCO mission is composed mainly of South Asian troops. Similarly, the UN-supported African Union mission in Somalia consists mostly of regional troops from Kenya, Uganda, Burundi, Ethiopia, and Djibouti. Such a composition has already shown to be problematic, with Kenyan peacekeepers profiteering in the local charcoal trade and Ethiopian troops, which have a long history of invasions of Somalia, being extremely unpopular among the local population.[20] Likewise, the presence of Chadian soldiers in the African-led International Support Mission to the Central African Republic (MISCA) has been highly polarizing due to Chad's perceived backing of the Muslim rebel group Seleka, which overthrew the CAR government. In one incident, peacekeepers fired on a crowd protesting the presence of the Chadian troops. As a result, to diffuse the tensions, these troops were redeployed outside of the mostly Christian capital.[21] The plan of the UN Multidimensional Integrated Stabilization Mission in the Central African Republic (MINUSCA) is to incorporate these troops akin to MINUSMA in Mali.[22]

As these examples aptly demonstrate, the Security Council is increasingly becoming more willing to deploy peacekeepers where there is no peace to keep. The short-lived UN Supervision Mission in Syria, which had to terminate its activities after only four months, is a good recent example of the Security Council deploying operations to a war zone. The mission was scrapped due

---

19   "UN Mission's Contributions by Country," February 2014, www.un.org/en/peacekeeping/
        contributors/2014/feb14_5.pdf.

20   For recent controversies related to the AMISOM mission, see *The Economist*, "Somalia's
        Civil War: Pushing It Across the Borders," 8 February 2014. For background on Ethiopian
        involvement in Somalia, see Ismail I. Ahmed, "The Heritage of War and State Collapse in
        Somalia and Somaliland: Local-level Effects, External Interventions and Reconstruction,"
        Third World Quarterly 20, no. 1 (1999): 113–127; John Prendergast and Colin Thomas-Fensen,
        "Blowing the Horn," *Foreign Affairs* 86, no. 2 (2007).

21   Aljazeera, "Chad Troops in CAR Accused of Pro-Seleka Bias," 26 December 2013; Celeste
        Hicks, "Chad: Déby's Misstep in the Central African Republic," *Think Africa Press*,
        27 January 2014.

22   UN Security Council, Res. S/RES/2149. For more on the role of regional players in peace-
        keeping, see Gray, *International Law and the Use of Force*, pp. 370–425; Judith Vorrath,
        "When the Neighbors Keep a Foot in the Door: Regional Interventions and Peacekeeping
        Missions in the Democratic Republic of Congo and Somalia," in Thierry Tardy and Marco
        Wyss, eds., *Peacekeeping in Africa: The Evolving Security Architecture* (London: Routledge,
        2014).

to the accumulation of obstacles to its mandate's implementation that had "rendered operational activities unworkable."[23] However, its mere deployment highlights that the Security Council is willing to use peacekeepers in increasingly risk-prone areas. Moreover, not only are such deployments into conflict areas intended to monitor cease-fires and protect civilians and humanitarian aid, but the peacekeeping tasks in the midst of conflict zones are expanding. Peacekeepers are now often protecting states. In Somalia, the UN is engaging in disarmament, demobilization, and reintegration (DDR), an activity normally conducted after the peace agreement has been signed.[24] The peacekeeping mission in the CAR is entering into the conflict with the same mandate. How one is supposed to effectively demobilize and reintegrate former combatants, when their fellow fighters have not laid down their arms, has not been sufficiently addressed. But experiences in Afghanistan demonstrate that not properly acknowledging political realities of an ongoing conflict largely undermines the DDR process.[25] As mentioned above, the UN political mission in Somalia is also asked to support "the development of a federal system"[26]— while the government and AMISOM are fighting a war against Al-Shabaab, and the future of the country is highly uncertain.

The reality that UN peacekeepers are increasingly involved in enforcement of political and military solutions is also seen in the types of capabilities that these missions are relying on. The UN has advocated the use of surveillance drones in the eastern DRC, on the border between Côte d'Ivoire and Liberia, in South Sudan, and in Mali.[27] In Mali, peacekeepers have openly been relying on strategic intelligence, an activity causing such unease for decades among the Global South nations that in 1960 then Secretary-General Dag Hammarskjold categorically rejected a possibility for a UN intelligence agency on the grounds that the organization "must have clean hands."[28] The Brahimi Report advocated for the incorporation of field intelligence in peace operations so that they could

---

23   Report of the Secretary-General on the implementation of UN Security Council Res. S/2012/523 (6 July 2012).

24   United Nations, Integrated Disarmament, Demobilization and Reintegration Standards (2006), http://pksoi.army.mil/doctrine_concepts/documents/UN%20Guidelines/IDDRS .pdf.

25   Antonio Giustozzi, "Bureaucratic Facade and Political Realities of Disarmament and Demobilisation in Afghanistan," *Conflict, Security, and Development* 8, no. 2 (2008): 169–192.

26   UN Security Council, Res. S/RES/2102.

27   John Karlsrud and Frederik Rosen, "In the Eye of the Beholder? The UN and the Use of Drones to Protect Civilians," *Stability: International Journal of Security and Development* 2, no. 2 (2013): 1–10.

28   Colum Lynch, "Dutch Double Down in Mali," *Foreign Policy*, 30 November 2013.

better respond to complex situations,[29] but these recommendations were not favorably viewed by the member states. While the UN has always relied on some tactical intelligence and information from other sources' intelligence activities, an outright and open incorporation of strategic intelligence into UN peacekeeping missions is new and setting precedents.[30] In a similar development, in Somalia the UN is engaged in strategic communication campaigning and has hired a consultancy firm that, according to its statements, "runs a fully integrated campaign to counter the radicalising effect of Al-Shabaab and engage Somalis in building a positive future for their country."[31] Drones, intelligence, and strategic communication all evoke ideas of stabilization missions. The major difference is that the UN peacekeeping activities as a rule are conducted on request of governments in target states.

2   The Delusion of a Doctrine

UN peacekeeping is underpinned by three key principles: consent, impartiality, and the nonuse of force. In this section, I briefly explore their meaning as defined by the Capstone Doctrine and demonstrate that recent practice is not in line with these principles. I further examine how the UN has been responding to this mismatch.

2.1   *Consent*
UN peacekeeping operations are supposed to be deployed with the consent of the main parties to the conflict. This distinguishes them from enforcement operations. Consent requires a commitment by the parties to a political process. As the Capstone Doctrine argues, "In the absence of such consent, a United Nations peacekeeping operation risks becoming a party to the conflict; and being drawn towards enforcement action, and away from its intrinsic role of keeping the peace."[32] This is not just for normative reasons, but also for purely practical ones. Consent is sought to make the work and tasks of UN

---

29   United Nations, Brahimi Report, par. 51.

30   For more on the UN's history with intelligence, see A. Walter Dorn, "The Cloak and the Blue Beret: Limitations on Intelligence in UN Peacekeeping," *International Journal of Intelligence and Counterintelligence* 12, no. 4 (1999): 414–447; A. Walter Dorn, *Keeping Watch: Monitoring, Technology and Innovation in UN Peace Operations* (Tokyo: United Nations University Press, 2011).

31   Albany Associates, "Somalia: AU/UN Information Support," www.albanyassociates.com/projects/somalia.

32   United Nations, Capstone Doctrine, p. 32.

peacekeepers more achievable. It is usually obtained through a peace agreement among main parties to the conflict. While peacekeepers are deployed to volatile situations, they are not intended to conduct their activities in the midst of open conflicts.

The examples above show that consent is missing in contemporary operations, mainly because comprehensive peace agreements are lacking. While the problem of spoilers has always existed in peacekeeping, the new operations take an additional step away from seeking consent of the main parties.[33] Missions such as the ones in the DRC, Mali, and Somalia are deployed to empower the state's government and help it defeat one of the parties to the conflict. "Expansion of state authority" is now often part of a mission's mandate. Importantly, the targeted parties possess enough political and military power that governments are unable to defeat them by themselves. These groups therefore cannot be thought of as anything else but a main party to the conflict. Such peacekeeping operations disregard the practical considerations for why UN peacekeepers are not supposed to conduct enforcement operations. However, their deployment happens not just for security reasons, but to a large extent also for a moral one. The latter often tips the scale toward the Security Council's willingness to deploy. Al-Shabaab in Somalia, al-Qaeda-affiliated groups in northern Mali, and to a large extent also the LRA, the FDLR, and M23 militias in the eastern DRC are not considered legitimate participants to the conflict; therefore, their consent is not sought. These groups often find themselves on terrorist lists of Northern states, making members of the Security Council as a whole even less willing to allow them any legitimate claims. But the lack of legitimacy among interveners does not mean a lack of legitimacy among the local population or a lack of political agency.

2.2   *Impartiality*
According to the Capstone Doctrine, UN peacekeeping missions must implement their mandates without favor or prejudice to any party. Furthermore, impartiality is seen as "crucial to maintaining the consent and cooperation of the main parties, but should not be confused with neutrality or inactivity."[34] It is clear that the cornerstone of impartiality is actually consent to peacekeeping activities; impartiality is intended to ensure the continued cooperation

---

33   See, for example, Kelly M. Greenhill and Solomon Major, "The Perils of Profiling: Civil War Spoilers and the Collapse of Intrastate Peace Accords," *International Security* 31, no. 3 (2007): 7–40; Stephen John Stedman, "Spoiler Problems in Peace Processes," *International Security* 22, no. 2 (1997): 5–53.

34   For more, see David Malone and Ramesh Thakur, "UN Peacekeeping: Lessons Learned?" *Global Governance* 7, no. 1 (2001): 11–17.

of all key political players so that the operation can successfully implement its mandate. In addition, the Brahimi Report clearly argues that "the United Nations does not wage war," and continues that when such action is required it is entrusted to coalitions of willing states with the authorization of the Security Council.[35]

The new peacekeeping operations are far from being impartial to main parties to the conflict. In this context, the lack of consent makes it impossible for these operations to be impartial even in principle—the missions are mandated to be partial. We have seen this not only in enforcement missions like the ones in the DRC and Mali, but also in South Sudan and more recently in Somalia, where the UN is building new states in collaboration with the government and against the interests of other political players. It is thus producing a specific partial reality. But not only are UN peacekeeping operations mandated "to side with the government" against interests of other parties; these missions are also staffed by personnel from parties that have vested interests. As discussed in the previous section, many new missions are composed of troops sent by regional states that are part of the conflict dynamics. The Great Lakes region, the Horn of Africa, and the Sahel have long been recognized as regional conflicts (e.g., the European Union now has regional strategies on all three). However, when composing missions to these areas, the consideration of impartiality is trumped by the need to acquire a sufficient number of personnel. It thus is not entirely clear whether troops participating in these missions are deployed to uphold the peacekeeping mandate or to protect immediate interests of the states contributing them. Their impartiality is suspect.

2.3   Nonuse of Force

The principle of nonuse of force except in self-defense is one of the cornerstones of peacekeeping and dates back to the first deployments of armed UN peacekeepers.[36] Despite this principled prohibition, it is widely understood that peacekeepers may use force at the tactical level, with the authorization of the Security Council and if acting in self-defense or defense of the mandate. A move toward more robust mandates in the post-Cold War era led to the Security Council's willingness to authorize UN peacekeepers to use all necessary means to "deter forceful attempts to disrupt the political process, protect civilians under imminent threat of physical attack, and/or assist the national

---

35   United Nations, Brahimi Report, par. 53.
36   For more on the use of force in UN peacekeeping, see Trevor Findlay, *The Use of Force in UN Peace Operations* (Solna: Stockholm International Peace Research Institute, 2002).

authorities in maintaining law and order."[37] Beginning in the 1990s, there has been a continuously increasing tolerance for the use of force in peacekeeping.

However, the new mandates present a further qualitative shift, moving from defensive toward offensive use of force. The UN not only is using force to protect the peace agreement, civilians, or itself—all established reasons for the use of force—but also to protect and assist the host state and its government. In this respect, the intervention brigade in the DRC is particularly telling. While past operations could use force to protect their mandates, now the use of force is an important part of the mandate itself. Not only do the objectives of the mission need to be protected through the use of force, but they cannot be achieved without it. As with the abrogation of consent and impartiality, such use of force is connected to the lack of legitimacy of the groups being targeted. These groups operate outside the traditional international system of collective security, allowing for exceptional measures.[38] However, as argued above, that does not deprive these groups of political agency or legitimacy among the local population. Of the three key principles, the Security Council is the least comfortable abrogating the nonuse of force. The Security Council resolution establishing an intervention brigade as part of MONUSCO even clearly states that such brigade is created "on an exceptional basis and without creating a precedent or any prejudice to the agreed principles of peacekeeping."[39] Based on experience from other theaters, it is clear that the Security Council is more comfortable in relying on regional groupings and interested parties (e.g., France in Mali, AMISOM in Somalia) to perform these tasks, even if the UN mission is directly supporting them.

2.4   Responses

These changes in the practice of peacekeeping have been met with some reluctance, particularly by states from the Global South. When discussing establishment of an intervention brigade as part of MONUSCO in the DRC, the representative of a nonpermanent Security Council member, Guatemala, worried that the mission was bordering on a peace enforcement one.[40] The

---

37   United Nations, Capstone Doctrine, p. 34.
38   Mateja Peter, "The Politics of Self-defence: Beyond a Legal Understanding of International Norms," *Cambridge Review of International Affairs* 24, no. 2 (2011): 245–264.
39   UN Security Council, Res. S/RES/2098.
40   Similar discussions were had about the interventions in Somalia and Bosnia and Herzegovina in the early 1990s. See Ramesh Thakur, "From Peacekeeping to Peace Enforcement: The UN Operation in Somalia," *Journal of Modern African Studies* 32, no. 3 (1994): 387–410; Shashi Tharoor, "Should UN Peacekeeping Go 'Back to Basics'?" *Survival: Global Politics and Strategy* 37, no. 4 (1995): 52–64.

ambassador reasoned that the UN should always be seen as an "honest broker" and that, while his country understood the logic behind the proposed deployment, it would have preferred the brigade to be a self-standing unit with specific duties distinguishable from those of MONUSCO's other work.[41] This communicated the unease about long-term implications of a new type of activity for broader missions. In the same debate, the representative from Argentina supported this sentiment. He claimed that, although the text clearly stated that the brigade would not set a precedent, the idea of "enforcing peace rather than keeping it" required deep reflection, not just a week of negotiations. The Argentinian representative also argued for a better consultation process with troop contributors, so that they could be better apprised of the new activities.[42] He hinted at the potentially problematic consequences of separating political considerations at the Security Council level from practical realities on the ground. Similarly for the MINUSMA mission in Mali, Argentina, Guatemala, Pakistan, and Russia pushed for a clear mention in the preamble of the basic principles of peacekeeping—consent of the parties, impartiality, and nonuse of force.[43] A number of member states, particularly the emerging powers, are showing resistance to the direction that peacekeeping is moving into.

While the reality on the ground is changing and the Security Council is becoming more willing to authorize robust missions, the official UN responses to these challenges have not acknowledged the extent of the mismatch between doctrine and practice. The resolutions establishing these missions characterize their activities as exceptions, despite practical evidence to the contrary. Moreover, the last peacekeeping review process was silent on the extent of these challenges. The New Horizon process, as the review was called, was designed to "assess the major policy and strategy dilemmas facing UN Peacekeeping today and over the coming years" and "reinvigorate the ongoing dialogue with stakeholders on possible solutions to better calibrate UN Peacekeeping to meet current and future requirements."[44] However, while the process was supposed to adjust and adapt UN peacekeeping to meet new and emerging challenges, it only reinforced previous review documents. The Secretary-General's Report to the Special Committee on Peacekeeping Operations identified four reform priorities—policy development, capability

---

41   UN News, "'Intervention Brigade' Authorized as Security Council Grants Mandate Renewal for United Nations Mission in Democratic Republic of Congo."

42   Ibid.

43   "Resolution Establishing a UN Mission in Mali," What's in Blue: Insights on the Work of the UN Security Council, 24 April 2013, www.whatsinblue.org.

44   United Nations, "UN Peacekeeping: The 'New Horizon' Process," www.un.org/en/peacekeeping/operations/newhorizon.shtml.

development, global field support strategy, and planning and oversight—all very practically, capability oriented.[45]

The nonpaper that kicked off this peacekeeping review process addressed the question of robustness in UN missions, but phrased it narrowly: "The concept of 'robustness' in UN peacekeeping is a political and operational strategy to signal the intention of a UN mission to implement its mandate and to deter threats to an existing peace process in the face of resistance from spoilers."[46] Robustness is intended to describe defensive aspects of the use of force, not offensive ones. Moreover, the nonpaper also limited the space for possible discussions about doctrinal implications in further debates by providing that robustness "is rooted in the guiding principles that are the foundations of UN peacekeeping: nonuse of force except in self-defence and defence of the mandate, consent of the main parties and impartiality in implementation."[47] There was no discussion of any possible doctrinal changes or challenges.

At the June 2014 open debate of the Security Council on "new trends in UN peacekeeping operations," Secretary-General Ban Ki-moon announced that he had asked the Secretariat to initiate work on a review of UN peacekeeping. While his speech focused on new threats and needed capabilities and steered away from discussing the doctrine, it did offer a possibility for such a debate by asking what the limits of UN peacekeeping are.[48] The ongoing review process consists of two parallel but interrelated efforts on the part of the High-Level Independent Panel on UN Peace Operations, chaired by Nobel Laureate José Ramos-Horta, and the UN Secretariat. This process presents another opportunity to openly address where the UN peacekeeping practice does not fit its doctrine anymore. A continued denial of the mismatch has potentially negative implications for what these missions can achieve and how places where they intervene can be transformed.

3   Implications for UN Peacekeeping and Humanitarian Efforts

Abrogation of peacekeeping principles is bound to carry unintended consequences. While the full extent of these is difficult to foresee, considering the

---

45   United Nations, "Report of the Secretary General, Implementation of the Recommendations of the Special Committee on Peacekeeping Operations," UN Doc. A/64/573 (22 December 2009).

46   UN Department of Peacekeeping Operations and Department of Field Support, *A New Partnership Agenda: Charting a New Horizon for UN Peacekeeping, July* (New York: UN, 2009).

47   Ibid.

48   UN Security Council Meeting Record S/PV.7196 (11 June 2014).

stakes involved for both the hosting states and the future of UN peacekeeping, this kind of an assessment is needed as part of strategic considerations. In this section, I examine a series of repercussions of expanding mandates for execution of peacekeeping operations and for other international engagements, highlighting that both security and implementation of mandates could become complicated.

It is not unreasonable to expect that peacekeepers taking sides in a conflict will result in increased resistance from disenfranchised groups. We have seen this in the CAR, where deployment of Chadian peacekeepers resulted in protests, and even more clearly in the DRC, where on establishment of a UN intervention brigade the president of the rebel group M23 vowed, "If UN forces come and attack us they will find us here and if they [are] against us, we will fight."[49] Although there was a spike in the number of fatalities caused by malicious acts in 2013 and early 2014, the time line is too short for the data to conclusively confirm an increased risk associated with more robust mandates. However, Alex J. Bellamy notes that in the past "mandates have not been interpreted as requiring the adoption of greater risks by peacekeepers."[50] With an increasing pressure to move the strategy from defensive to offensive thinking, it is reasonable to expect that fatalities will increase.

Offensive mandates also expose to harm other parts of the peacekeeping mission. UN peacekeeping has been continually moving toward greater complexity. Individual mission mandates now cover a broad range of issues and involve political, security, humanitarian, refugee, gender, and other components. Any offensive parts of the operation thus inevitably form only a small part of the overall mission. For example, the intervention brigade in the DRC consists of roughly 3,000 troops, out of around 22,000 total MONUSCO staff. However, activities of offensive components could have negative spillover effects on other parts, in particular, as these are less prepared for combat and thus more vulnerable to attacks. Displaying a UN mission symbol, which historically provided peacekeepers with an invisible layer of protection, could come to mean exactly the opposite. It could be an invitation for retaliation. It is for this reason that some member states, as discussed above, wanted offensive components of the DRC mission to be separated from the broader peacekeeping operation.

However, separating combat elements from the rest of the mission or assigning such tasks to non-UN actors that are tightly knit with the peacekeeping

---

49   Aljazeera, "M23 Says It Will 'Fight Back' Against UN," 6 April 2013.
50   Alex J. Bellamy, "Are New Robust Mandates Putting UN Peacekeepers More at Risk?" *Global Observatory* (2014), http://theglobalobservatory.org.

operation (e.g., France in Mali, AMISOM in Somalia) addresses only the legal aspects of the problem. It does not resolve how these operations can end up being perceived by potential retaliators. The UN itself has been moving toward an integrated model of operation on the ground. Such an approach was introduced to ensure coherence of UN action across security, development, and governance in conflict and postconflict zones.[51] Although individual components remain functionally separate, their operation in the field takes place within integrated teams.[52] Integrated missions make it more difficult to distinguish one part of the operation from the other, thus potentially implicating all components of UN activity into problematic activities of one of its parts.

The humanitarian community has been raising concerns over an integrated approach to UN presence. Many aid actors are opposed to increasing integration on principle, as it blurs the distinction between military, political, and humanitarian action and subordinates humanitarian priorities to political agendas. It also changes the nature of aid activities by pushing humanitarian actors into compounds and, thus, further away from aid recipients.[53] Studies indicate that closer cooperation among international actors can have both positive and negative effects.[54] However, UN political support for highly contested governments and an increasing robustness of operation are likely to further politicize international peacekeeping and exacerbate negative effects on the aid community. Aid actors' ability to act independently and impartially could be severely challenged.

Finally, the increasing robustness of missions and their state-building mandates in the midst of conflicts are likely to complicate their success and extraction. Consent of the main parties has been established as a necessary

---

51   A UN *integrated mission* is defined as "one in which there is a shared vision among all UN actors as to the strategic objective of the UN presence at country level." United Nations, "Integrated Missions Planning Process (IMPP), Guidelines Endorsed by the Secretary-General on 13 June 2006," https://docs.unocha.org.

52   International Forum for the Challenges of Peace Operations, *Consideration for Mission Leadership in United Nations Peacekeeping Operations* (Stockholm: Edita Vastra Aros AB, 2010).

53   Mark Duffield, "Risk-management and the Fortified Aid Compound: Everyday Life in Post-interventionary Society," *Journal of Intervention and Statebuilding* 4, no. 4 (2010): 453–474; Lisa Smirl, "Building the Other, Constructing Ourselves: Spatial Dimensions of International Humanitarian Response," *International Political Sociology* 2, no. 3 (2008): 236–253.

54   Victoria Metcalfe, Alison Giffen, and Samir Elhawary, "UN Integration and Humanitarian Space: An Independent Study Commissioned by the UN Integration Steering Group" (London: Overseas Development Institute and Stimson Center, 2011), p. 1; Oliver Ulrich, "Integration: Recent Developments and Consistent Misperceptions," *Humanitarian Exchange Magazine* 46 (2010): 39–41.

condition for a mission's success.[55] It is difficult to foresee how involvement of UN peacekeepers in combat could completely alter political realities in host states. While a particular armed group might be defeated, in conflicts that have been lasting for decades—such as the ones in the Great Lakes region or the Sahel—other groups with similar agendas and similar motivations are likely to emerge. This could involve combat forces in protracted engagements that are difficult to end. Lessons from Afghanistan, Iraq, and Syria apply here if on a smaller scale. However, what is more likely is that the Security Council will terminate combative elements of those missions that are not considered of high interest to the Security Council members, before a proper political settlement is reached. This would inevitably leave the rest of the mission with more difficulties in completing its mandate. Similarly, it is also highly problematic that the Security Council is assigning state-building tasks to missions operating in the midst of conflicts. How these tasks are supposed to be successfully completed, so operations do not remain trapped, has not been sufficiently considered. Without a peace to keep, there is no state to build.

4   Implications for Conflict Dynamics and Peacebuilding

When UN peacekeepers side with one side in a conflict, whether by helping it extend state authority or defeat enemy combatants, this substantially affects conflict and political dynamics at a particular time. It confers legitimacy on one set of actors while delegitimizing the claims of others. It also empowers specific actors against others in ways that might be unsustainable in the long run. Here, I provide a broader assessment of likely implications of expanding mandates for host states and regions, focusing on political processes, peacebuilding, and regional conflict dynamics.

Conflict parties against which the government and now UN action is directed are key players in a conflict. Why else would a government need international assistance in countering them and their influence? Regardless of their international legitimacy, these armed groups or their political reincarnations will need to be included in peace settlements if these are to become sustainable. Such was the practice in the past. The UN undoubtedly is cognizant of this. However, trying to be an impartial broker in a peace process, while at the same time attempting to neutralize and disarm one of the parties, creates internal contradictions. Although it is not unusual for negotiating parties to be

---

55   Lise Morje Howard, *UN Peacekeeping in Civil Wars* (Cambridge: Cambridge University Press, 2008), p. 8.

suspicious of the impartiality and benevolent intents of outside brokers, when a broker openly takes sides in a conflict such a claim acquires more credibility.

The Congolese developments are already exposing a number of difficulties in trying to pursue negotiations simultaneously with enforcement mandates. In December 2012 and under heavy international pressure, M23 agreed to pull out from Goma in exchange for the start of negotiations with the Kinshasa government. Less than four months later, the Security Council authorized a UN intervention brigade. At the time, the UN envoy for Africa's Great Lakes region, Mary Robinson, reiterated her support for the stalled Kampala talks between the DRC government and the M23 group, and she urged Congolese president Joseph Kabila "to remain committed to this process with a view to expediting it as soon as possible."[56] In response to the UN's decision to deploy an intervention brigade, M23 representatives walked out of negotiations.

When they returned to the negotiating table a couple of months later, the talks were marred with problems and accusations. However, while the motivations and commitment of M23 to a diplomatic solution are highly suspect, the military and political backing of the international community also empowered the DRC government to assume a maximalist take-it-or-leave-it position in the negotiations. DRC government spokesperson Lambert Mende Omalanga told IRIN by phone, "It depends on whether M23 is ready to accept ... what has been decided in Addis Ababa and [in the] UN for them to disarm. If they accept, we are ready to finalize the Kampala process."[57] With support from UN peacekeepers, the DRC government was more likely to defeat M23 militarily, thus improving its negotiating position. The M23 rebels were defeated in November 2013, leading to the completion of the Kampala process a month later. While both sides agreed to a number of commitments, their implementation is experiencing serious setbacks.

The UN's support for the central government politically or militarily empowers one side and can result in a peace settlement that fails to reflect the political reality on the ground. This complicates longer-term peacebuilding and reconciliation processes. Armed groups against which the new UN peacekeeping mandates are directed often hold little legitimacy in the eyes of the outside world. They do, however, either enjoy popular support of wide segments of the local population, such as Al-Shabaab in Somalia, or more commonly, raise real concerns and grievances that the local population has against

---

56 UN News, "UN Envoy Tells Security Council There Is 'Renewed Opportunity' for DR Congo Peace Efforts" (6 May 2013), www.un.org/apps/news/story.asp?NewsID=44836.

57 IRIN News, "Briefing: North Kivu Sees Fresh Clashes as Peace Talks Stall in Kampala," 18 July 2013.

the government. More than half a year after M23's military defeat, the former M23 spokesperson highlighted a number of concerns that the group had been raising, but that had not been addressed by the government: "the need to return assets of the Congolese people that were confiscated, stop discrimination against Congolese in eastern part of the country and return of refugees who are scattered in the neighbouring countries."[58] Despite the undoubtedly political motivations of the source, these are serious and legitimate concerns that are crucial to any peacebuilding and reconciliation effort. However, with the defeat of the party airing such grievances, these do not need to be comprehensively addressed in a peace agreement. This makes it more likely that a reincarnation of the defeated group will emerge in one form or another, making peace unsustainable.

Finally, there is a need for a broader consideration of how enforcement peacekeeping could impact regional dynamics. The conflicts in Mali, Somalia, the DRC, the CAR, Sudan, and South Sudan, among others, are all regional conflicts. At the same time, UN peacekeeping operations, as a rule, have a single-state focus. Militarily defeating an armed group in a particular state, such as Al-Shabaab in Somalia or al-Qaeda-affiliated groups in northern Mali, could move some of their operations to neighboring states. We have seen this in the past in the Middle East and in Africa. In their introduction to a special journal issue on how the intervention in Libya influenced the conflict dynamics in the Sahel, Morten Bøås and Mats Utas argue that, while in the Mali conflict "recapturing large parts of northern Mali from the Islamists may have been a relatively easy military operation, controlling this vast territory will be much more difficult and time-consuming."[59] Spillover to neighboring states can be expected when underlying conflicts remain unresolved.

5   Conclusions

The UN is moving toward a new era of enforcement peacekeeping. This has manifested itself both in enforcement of political solutions through support of governments' state-building ambitions in the midst of conflicts and in enforcement of military victories through offensive use of force. These changes demonstrably challenge all three key peacekeeping principles: consent, impartiality, and nonuse of force. Such a shift in UN peacekeeping opens the door

---

58   Risdel Kasasira, "Kabila Signs Amnesty for M23 Rebels," *Daily Monitor*, 3 May 2014.
59   Morten Bøås and Mats Utas, "Introduction: Post-Gaddafi Repercussions in the Sahel and West Africa," *Strategic Review for Southern Africa* 35, no. 2 (2013): 3–15.

to a number of unintended, but problematic, consequences. In contemporary peacekeeping, the targets of peacekeeping actions tend to be nonstate actors that enjoy little international legitimacy. As a result, no comprehensive peace agreements with them are sought before the international community takes sides in a conflict. UN peacekeeping is bearing a startling resemblance to the stabilization missions in Afghanistan and Iraq, whose mixed short-term results and unaccomplished longer-term objectives should hold lessons for UN peacekeeping.

Recent developments raise dilemmas that are similar to those of mid-1990s peacekeeping. Two decades ago the international community was engaging in robust operations (Somalia), establishing safe havens (the former Yugoslavia, Rwanda), and creating protracted transitional administrations merging peace-keeping with state building (Cambodia, Timor-Leste, and Kosovo). UN peace-keeping suffered many setbacks during that era, leading some to speculate on its demise. In the end, these developments led to reaffirmation of the founding principles of UN peacekeeping through the Brahimi Report. Importantly for the argument here, developments in the 1990s were occurring ad hoc and in parallel to the peacekeeping doctrine. This resulted in a number of problem-atic consequences that were not addressed in strategic preparations. Similar developments are occurring with more recent peacekeeping expansions and risk analogous failures.

The future of peacekeeping is at stake. There is a need to acknowledge the trap brought by the merger of peacekeeping and peace enforcement and task-ing peacekeepers to assist governments to build states in the midst of con-flict. It is unlikely that the nature of challenges emanating from contemporary conflicts will change substantially in the near future. It thus is not enough to reaffirm the doctrine through another strategic review and then continue to ignore it in practice. In trying to resolve the tension between doctrine and practice, the UN and member states are faced with two options. They can align the peacekeeping practice more closely with the doctrine, reaffirming the UN's role in defensive and impartial tasks in the midst of conflict (e.g., protection of civilians) and refocus on postconflict processes and mediation. Or, they can embrace the new practices and provide for a new strategic or doc-trinal underpinning. A series of exceptions constitutes a new norm. While a new doctrine would fundamentally challenge the nature of UN peacekeeping, it would at least provide for an open reappraisal of longer-term consequences of new peacekeeping practices. Sticking with the current inconsistency merely tarnishes the reputation of UN peacekeeping and undermines future deployments.

CHAPTER 22

Asian Infrastructure Investment Bank: Governance Innovation and Prospects

Gregory T. Chin[1]

On 29 June 2015, the leaders of China and representatives of fifty-six nations gathered in Beijing to sign the Memorandum of Understanding for the creation of the Asian Infrastructure Investment Bank (AIIB). According to its Articles of Agreement, the purpose of the bank is: first, to "foster sustainable economic development, create wealth and improve infrastructure connectivity in Asia by investing in infrastructure and other productive sectors"; and, second, "promote regional cooperation and partnership in addressing development challenges by working in close collaboration with other multilateral and bilateral development institutions." The creation of this new bank is the latest in a wave of new global initiatives that China has promoted, alongside the Group of 20 Leaders Summits (G-20); the internationalization of the renminbi (China's national currency); the New Development Bank (NDB) of the "BRICS" grouping (Brazil, Russia, India, China, and South Africa); and the Silk Road Economic Belt and Twenty-first Century Maritime Silk Road (One Belt & One Road).

The AIIB will be headquartered in Beijing, with an initial capital stock of $100 billion. China is contributing the largest share for the new bank, by a large measure ($29.8 billion). According to its fifty-seven "founding members," the AIIB "grew from the recognition of the importance of infrastructure to the development of Asia, and the need for significant additional long-term financing" for infrastructure and development in the region and beyond the region.[2] The other motivation is that China and many developing countries have grown frustrated with what they perceive as the often slow and overly bureaucratic

---

* This chapter was originally published in Global Governance, Volume 22, Issue 1, 2016.
1 Gregory T. Chin is associate professor of political science at York University (Canada). He was first secretary (development) in the Canadian embassy in Beijing (2003–2006) and was responsible for liaising with multilateral and bilateral donors, including the World Bank, Asian Development Bank, and the special agencies of the United Nations.
2 The "Articles of Agreement" of the Asian Infrastructure Investment Bank can be accessed at www.aiib.org/html/2015/NEWS_0629/11.html.

ways of the traditional lenders and their slow pace of representational and operational reform.[3]

The fact that it has been a quarter-century since the last major multilateral development bank was created (the European Bank for Reconstruction and Development, founded in 1991),[4] and that the new bank is championed by China (and not by the traditional Western powers or Japan), signals a shift in the balance of world economic power. The lack of precedence of the People's Republic sitting at the center of the table, setting the agenda, defining priorities, and rethinking rules means that rules could emerge in the AIIB-funded projects that differ from those of the liberal international economic order. That a number of the allies of the United States, including Australia, South Korea, Britain, Germany, and France, decided to join the AIIB, even though the United States had discouraged them, suggests that geopolitical calculations among followers are also shifting.[5] Thus, *People's Daily*, the official newspaper of the Chinese Communist Party, observed wryly that "the expanding Asian Infrastructure Investment Bank shows China's growing global influence. AIIB is attracting international attention."[6]

The points above suggest that the creation of the AIIB is an important development in global governance and reflects key shifts in the balance of world economic power. It further suggests that China has made the transition to global leadership, including building new multilateral organizations, after decades where it mainly learned the established norms.[7] In this essay, I examine whether and how the AIIB represents innovation in global governance. I further provide a critical appraisal of the prospects for the new China-backed multilateral bank. My main findings are that the AIIB reflects both continuities

---

3 See also in this issue, Miles Kahler, "The Global Economic Multilaterals: Will Eighty Years Be Enough?" *Global Governance* 22, no. 1 (2016): 1–9.

4 The Chiang Mai Initiative (CMI) was created in 2001 by the ASEAN+3 nations in East Asia; however, the CMI is geared to providing emergency liquidity, or crisis liquidity, to deal with balance of payments crises rather than capital for medium- to long-term development.

5 Ramesh Thakur, "A Lesson in the Geopolitics of Infrastructure Finance," *Japan Times*, 21 June 2015, www.japantimes.co.jp/opinion/2015/06/21/commentary/japan-commentary/lesson-geo politics-infrastructure-finance/#.VhvC5flVhBc; Ramesh Thakur, "Asia's New Banking Muscle," *Asia & the Pacific Policy Society (APPS) Policy Forum*, July 2015, www.policyforum.net/ asias-new-banking-muscle/.

6 People's Daily Online, "Asian Infrastructure Investment Bank Is Expanding," 20 March 2015, http://en.people.cn/n/2015/0320/c98649-8866152.html.

7 See Gregory Chin and Ramesh Thakur, "Will China Change the Rules of Global Order?" *Washington Quarterly* 33, no. 4 (October 2010): 119–138. On China learning global norms, see Alastair Iain Johnston, *Social States: China in International Institutions, 1980–2000* (Princeton: Princeton University Press, 2007).

and innovations in global governance. So far, most of the innovations are in the governance structures of the bank and its overarching legal frameworks. What is significant about the AIIB's governance innovations is that they are aimed at unlocking the creative potential for the new bank to make breakthroughs in decisionmaking, management, and staffing, and, most importantly, in the lending practices and business models of the bank. One of the key goals that the creators of the bank have set for themselves is to establish new organizational arrangements that give adequate voice to emerging and developing countries, the main borrowers, and more effective and even-handed lending practices compared to the incumbents. At the same time, the proponents of the AIIB must ensure that the new bank can deal adequately with the environmental and social impacts of its projects and avoid corruption. Environmental protection, social responsibility, and corruption avoidance have become broadly accepted global norms in the international system. To the extent that the AIIB achieves success in these areas, and China is willing and able to exercise restraint in providing multilateral leadership within the bank, followership and buy-in for the new bank can be fostered and sustained.

1   **Continuity and Innovation**

The new bank is fast taking shape. By early summer 2015, the Multilateral Interim Secretariat for the AIIB had worked out many of the governance arrangements and had completed drafting the legal provisions for the new bank. The Articles of Agreement[8] (henceforth, Articles) were signed in May 2015 by the fifty-seven founding members, and the Interim Secretariat also issued the staff recruitment procedures for the new bank. The Articles set out a three-level governance structure for the new bank, with a Board of Governors to review and approve, modify, or reject key decisions; a Board of Directors; and a bank president and "one or more" vice president(s). "Officers and staff" of the bank will execute the decisions.

1.1   *Balance of Authority*
Although there is clear intention to do things differently with this new bank, there are continuities with established norms of the World Bank or the Asian Development Bank (ADB) (the main incumbents). The *first* relates to the balance of representation and authority structure of the AIIB. The first decision was whether the main capital contributor to the bank—China—would hold veto power over important decisions at the Board of Directors level of the bank.

---

8   www.gov.cn/foot/site1/20150629/14931435546625843.pdf.

In the case of the International Monetary Fund (IMF) and the World Bank, the centrality of the United States is built into the "DNA" of the board structures of each institution. For the World Bank, it is further secured by the United States' hold on the presidency of the bank. In the run-up to the final decision on the balance of representation in the board of the AIIB, Beijing had reportedly offered to forgo the veto power and reduce its voting rights to less than one-quarter if Japan or the United States had been willing to join the new bank as founding members. Neither joined, and Beijing decided to secure the veto. The other members supported the decision, given China's initial $29.78 billion contribution to the bank's $100 billion capital base.

The initial subscription, listed in the Articles, set China as the largest shareholder (30.34 percent); India, with an $8.37 billion contribution, as a distant second; Russia third at $6.53 billion; and South Korea fourth at $3.74 billion. Based on a voting formula that is apportioned according to each member's capital contribution, the size of its economy, basic votes each member receives equally, plus another 600 votes for each founding member, the shareholding translates into China having 26.06 percent of the votes, India 7.5 percent, Russia 5.92 percent, and South Korea 3.5 percent. Under Article 28(2), decisions involving structure, membership, capital increases, and other significant issues require a "super majority" of "not less than three-fourths of the total voting power of the members," thus giving China a de facto veto.

Germany is the largest capital contributor among the non-Asian members,[9] with a $4.48 billion contribution over the next three years, which is more than South Korea. Berlin holds 4.1 percent of the votes. The German ambassador to China, Michael Clauss, suggests that although China holds veto power over important decisions, it would be against China's interests to actually use the veto,[10] as it will affect outside perceptions about Chinese influence over the new bank. Jin Liqun,[11] the Chinese head of the Interim Secretariat, says that China will not dominate the operations and is not looking to politicize the decisions or activities of the bank.[12] The Chinese Foreign Ministry says that the goal is to create a bank that is "inclusive and transparent" and that the

---

9   Behind Germany, among non-Asian members, are France's contribution of $3.37 billion and Brazil's contribution of $3.18 billion.
10   Caixin online, "China Fleshing Out AIIB for Asia and the World," 29 March 2015, http://english.caixin.com/2015-04-29/100804954.html.
11   Jin Liqun is a former Chinese vice minister of finance, and former vice president of the Asian Development Bank, the first appointed from the People's Republic of China. Jin has also held board and senior management positions in Chinese financial institutions.
12   Izumi Nakagawa and Manoj Kumar, "China's Influence over AIIB a Concern Ahead of Founders' Meeting," 13 April 2015, http://in.reuters.com/article/2015/04/13/asia-aiib-shareholding-idINKBN0N40T620150413.

"important idea is to achieve common development" and to "build a new model of international cooperation."[13] In brief, both the Chinese and the partners in the AIIB are aware that it is essential for the future success of the bank that China exercises restraint in the use of its power and influence in the bank (discussed further below).

Unlike the ADB, the Articles of the AIIB limit the shares of nonregional members to less than one-third, with the aim of preserving the influence of the Asian regional member states in the bank or the bank's regional feel. This is similar to the African Development Bank (AfDB). In the AIIB, at least 75 percent of the votes have been reserved for Asian members. In contrast, in the ADB, non-Asian members such as Canada, for example, have maintained their influence in the bank due to the relative size of their original financial contribution at the start of the organization.

1.2 *Management*

The *second* (likely) continuity relates to the selection of the managerial head. As of the time of writing, the president for the new bank has yet to be appointed. The fact that the president of the World Bank has always been an American, the director of the IMF a European, and the governor of the ADB from Japan has generated controversy, questions about the fairness and transparency of the selection process (merit vs. nationality of the candidate), and the evenhandedness of the senior management in carrying out their duties. Experienced commentators hope that the AIIB's appointment process can be more open and transparent than the established pattern to date. David Dollar, former China country director for the World Bank, former emissary of the US Treasury to China, and an (unpaid) adviser on the AIIB's Interim Secretariat, has said, for example, "Someday, I hope that all these important posts will be competitively filled by the most capable people, regardless of nationality."[14] In fact, Article 29(1) states that "the Board of Governors, through an open, transparent and merit-based process, shall elect a president of the Bank by a Super Majority.... He shall be a national of a regional member country." Most commentators, including Dollar, agree, however, that it would be "fair" for the AIIB's first president to be from China, considering that China has championed the bank and has the largest financial stake in the new bank (China's $29.8 billion contribution is more than the combined contributions of India, Russia,

---

13   Mark Magnier, "How China Plans to Run AIIB: Leaner, with Veto", 8 June 2015, http://www.wsj.com/articles/how-china-plans-to-run-aiib-leaner-with-veto-1433764079.

14   Wang Ling, Zhang Yuzhe, Wang Liwei, and Li Qing, "China Fleshing Out AIIB for Asia and the World," 29 April 2015, http://english.caixin.com/2015-04-29/100804954.html.

South Korea, and Australia).[15] Former ADB China country director, Robert Wihtol, says, "It's reasonable" to expect that someone from China would be appointed as the first president of the AIIB, considering that China has taken the lead in establishing the bank.[16]

The AIIB's Board of Governors will formally announce the inaugural president at its first board meeting, planned for late 2015. Since late 2014, Jin Liqun, an experienced hand, has served as the secretary general of the Interim Secretariat for establishing the AIIB. Beijing nominated Jin for the first AIIB president, and he was appointed president-designate on 1 September 2015.[17] In turn, Jin has brought in former World Bank staff from Washington, DC, and its offices around the world to help work out the governance issues and provide the key frameworks for the new institution, which help to foster the new bank's credibility with Western governments. The Indian media reports that "an Indian" is likely to get the vice president's post.[18] It appears that the appointment of the first AIIB president will follow the established pattern; however, the Articles establish the intention to be innovative and this could happen as early as the appointment of the second president.

1.3   The Boards

Where the AIIB is an innovator (from its inception) is with its dual board arrangement, and delegated authorities from a larger Board of Governors (fifty-seven governors) to a smaller Board of Directors (twelve directors), with the latter "responsible for the direction of the general operations of the Bank" (Article 26), including delegating further authorities to the bank president. Article 24(3) states:

> The Board of Governors shall by regulation establish procedures whereby the Board of Directors may obtain a vote of the Governors on a specific question without a meeting and provide for electronic meetings of the Board of Governors in special circumstances. The Board of Governors, and the Board of Directors ... may establish such subsidiary entities, and

---

15   It is worth noting here that the first president of the "companion" BRICS New Development Bank, headquartered in Shanghai, is Indian.

16   Wang, Zhang, Wang, and Li, "China Fleshing Out AIIB for Asia and the World."

17   The Bank's founding members had until July 2015 to nominate their candidates for president. A short list was finalized at a negotiators meeting in mid-August 2015.

18   *Economic Times*, "Indian Likely to Get VP's Post in China Floated AIIB," 22 April 2015, http://articles.economictimes.indiatimes.com/2015-04-22/news/61417274_1_aiib-brics-bank-asian-development-bank.

adopt such rules and regulations, as may be necessary or appropriate to conduct the business of the Bank.

The Board of Governors will meet regularly once a year ("annual meeting") and at other times as requested by the Board of Governors or the Board of Directors. The Board of Directors will "function on a non-resident basis" (except as otherwise decided by the Board of Governors). The above allows the two boards of the new Beijing-based AIIB to be nonresident, unlike the World Bank, the ADB, and the AfDB. Another noteworthy difference is that the AIIB directors (and alternate directors) are to be unpaid ("shall serve without remuneration from the Bank, unless the Board of Governors decide otherwise").

In contrast, in the World Bank and the IMF, the most influential member states are represented by resident executive directors, on a single executive board, who are actively involved in the institutions and vote on new policy and major program and project decisions. The in-residence board representatives act as a check on management and can influence the lending decisions of the global multilaterals at the Country Program level. The idea of a nonresident board was first posed in the early AIIB discussions, as early as 2011, by China's minister of finance Lou Jiwei.[19] Lou suggested that the new bank should be informed by the good practices of the existing multilateral lenders in the areas of environmental policy, governance structure, and loan assessment; however, the new bank should also strive to go a step further, by improving on these practices, cutting costs, and improving on efficiency.

Skeptics have derided Beijing as trying to give the bank's management more unchecked power over the institution. For example, Edward Truman, a former senior US treasury official, remarked that "I understand why the [United States] or other advanced countries prefer the resident board.... We do not trust the likely management."[20] However, other observers, with senior management experience in multilateral development banks, have highlighted that resident boards often slow down decisionmaking, sometimes unnecessarily, and that having nonresident boards may help to streamline decisionmaking processes. Dollar notes that the resident board of the World Bank costs some $70 million annually, and that, when he worked at the bank, "there was often a certain tension between the management and the board members,

19   Wang, Zhang, Wang, and Li, "China Fleshing Out AIIB for Asia and the World."

20   Lingling Wei and Bob Davis, "China Forgoes Veto at New Bank to Win Key European Nations' Support," 23 March 2015, http://www.wsj.com/articles/china-forgoes-veto -power-at-new-bank-to-win-key-european-nations-support-1427131055.

whose resident staff wanted to find out about projects at an early stage."[21] Moreover, the Zedillo Report, the product of the High Level Commission on Modernization of the World Bank Group, chaired by the former Mexican president, and including China's Central Bank governor among emerging market representatives, is also critical of the current World Bank arrangement of a resident board that approves all major loans. The report concurs that the extra layer of management slows down project preparation and makes the bank less efficient. Dollar suggests that the enthusiastic response of developing countries to the AIIB reflects their belief that a new bank can have good safeguards and still be quicker and more efficient than the existing multilaterals.[22] Forgoing a resident board could save friction and governance costs for the AIIB and allow the money to be redirected for loans, investment, technical assistance, policy advisory, or training purposes.

Most ironic is that the idea of the nonresident board seems to have originated in the United States.[23] In November 2008, US treasury secretary Henry Paulson said in a speech at Washington, DC:

> The IMF, the World Bank, as well as the regional development banks should consider how to reform their executive boards to make them more accountable, streamlined and effective. We should also consider whether these institutions could benefit from non-resident boards. This proposal could free-up resources and enable management to focus on issues of more strategic importance.[24]

As early as 2006, in a report on the AfDB, Dennis de Tray and Todd Moss noted that the idea of nonresident boards for the World Bank and the IMF came originally from John Maynard Keynes but was rejected at the time due to the limits of international travel and communication in the 1940s.[25] However, much has changed with video conferencing technology and modern air travel. AIIB Article 27(4) states that "the Board of Directors shall establish procedures

---

21   Magnier, "How China Plans to Run AIIB."

22   David Dollar, "Lessons for the AIIB from the World Bank," 27 April 2015, www.brookings
     .edu/research/articles/2015/04/27-china-on-global-stage-dollar.

23   I thank Kevin Carmichael for this observation.

24   US Department of the Treasury, "Remarks by Secretary Henry M. Paulson Jr. at The Ronald
     Reagan Presidential Library," 20 November 2008, http://www.treasury.gov/press-center/
     press-releases/Pages/hp1285.aspx.

25   Dennis de Tray and Todd Moss, "Fixing International Financial Institutions: How Africa
     Can Lead the Way," Center for Global Development, 22 September 2006, http://www.cgdev
     .org/publication/fixing-international-financial-institutions-how-africa-can-lead-way.

whereby the Board can hold an electronic meeting or vote on a matter without holding a meeting." This suggests that there are rational organizational reasons for proposing a nonresident board that are not about a Chinese attempt to undermine international oversight. The nonresident board ought to be tried if the management team can be held accountable using a combination of modern communications technology and periodic gatherings in person; if millions can be saved in salaries, travel, and residency expenses and reallocated to the bank's main purposes; and if the ecological footprint of the bank can be lessened. Such is the spirit (of innovation) behind Jin's statement that, "unlike existing multilateral banks," the goal behind the nonresident board for the AIIB is to be "lean, clean and green."[26] This objective also guides the new bank's aim to maintain a lean staff ("as needed"), compared to the over 12,000 staff and consultants employed by the World Bank.

To the extent that the AIIB dual nonresident board arrangement is effective, it will have a demonstration effect and create pressure on the World Bank, the ADB, and perhaps even the IMF to adjust their governance arrangements. It is likely not coincidental that the World Bank has recently started a "fundamental review" of its governance structure.[27]

2   Prospects and Determinants

Two elements seem key to determining the future prospects of the AIIB. First is China's ability and willingness to exercise multilateral forms of leadership, including, importantly, showing restraint in the use of its dominant power inside the new bank. China will need to be able and willing to provide a large share of the international public goods and, at times, even be willing to sacrifice its own national interests for the greater good while forgoing random, arbitrary, or excessive use of the power it holds in the institution. In settling disputes, China will need to demonstrate that it is willing to subject itself to the rules of the collective, including when it may go against its national interest. It will need to exercise its influence in a manner that is evenhanded and balanced and, equally important, perceived by others as such. Second is whether the new bank is effective; that is, whether its loans and advice are seen as useful by its membership and, especially, its borrowers. The latter will also determine

---

26   Lean Alfred Santos, "Deviating from the Norm: AIIB Moves Away from Country Strategies," 15 July 2015, http://www.devex.com/news/deviating-from-norm-aiib-moves-away-from-country-strategies-86544.

27   Wei and Davis, "China Forgoes Veto at New Bank to Win Key European Nations' Support."

the degree of ownership that the others (non-China) take in the bank, which, in turn, will affect its performance and longevity.

The real significance of the AIIB's governance arrangements lies in its effects on whether the bank is well managed and, most importantly, whether it can actually meet the developmental needs of its clients—whether it can deliver loans effectively, especially compared to the incumbents. Similar to the existing multilaterals, at a minimum, the future of the AIIB will be decided by whether its clients find it useful, and this, in turn, will have a great bearing on whether it has the support of its member states. Much will ride on the effectiveness of the new bank; that is, its performance legitimacy.

2.1   *Demand*

There are real infrastructure needs in Asia. The ADB has estimated the infrastructure needs of the Asian region during the current decade (2011–2020) as $8 trillion. The ADB has a capital base of about $160 billion, and the World Bank has $223 billion. For many years, Chinese officials have urged the World Bank to put more focus and resources into infrastructure (and industrial development).[28] Indian officials have pointed to the "tremendous problem" of rising delays in the approval of World Bank-financed infrastructure projects; project appraisals often exceed two years.[29] The Indian government tried to spur the World Bank to clear up the "clutter" and move more quickly on infrastructure projects. The lack of infrastructure finance is further compounded by the reality that private finance for infrastructure has fallen off sharply since the 2008–2009 great financial crisis. Private bank financing is reportedly at one-third of the amount before the crisis and, although there is around $75 trillion of new assets in sovereign wealth funds and pension funds, it has proven difficult to get these fund managers to invest in infrastructure, especially in the developing world.[30]

China's willingness to contribute to, and kick-start, cost-sharing on infrastructure financing and public-private partnership, via the AIIB—and to move rapidly—has been embraced eagerly by potential recipient governments in Asia. They have lauded the focus on infrastructure and the fact that, unlike

---

28   Dollar, "Lessons for the AIIB from the World Bank."

29   Subhomoy Battacharjee, "Post AIIB, India to Reduce Banking on World Bank Infra Arm," 3 July 2015, http://indianexpress.com/article/business/banking-and-finance/post-aiib-india-to-reduce-banking-on-world-bank-infra-arm/.

30   Amar Bhattacharya and Mattia Romani, "Meeting the Infrastructure Challenge: The Case for the New Development Bank," presentation at the Group of 24 Technical Committee meeting, Washington, DC, 21 March 2013; Gregory T. Chin, "The BRICS-Led Development Bank," *Global Policy* 5, no. 3 (September 2014): 367–368.

the World Bank, the new bank will not also try to cover agricultural development, health, and education. Bangladesh minister of finance and planning
M.A. Mannan highlighted, supportively, that the entire focus of the AIIB will
be on physical infrastructure, especially loans for big infrastructure projects,
such as roads, railways, ports, and power, and that "we'll need huge capital in
physical infrastructures and we'll have to go a long way since we're building
the second Padma Bridge and even more."[31] Hoping to borrow from the new
China-backed bank, Bangladesh authorities agreed to contribute $660.50 mil-
lion as capital subscription to the AIIB, over five years, in return for 0.8348 percent of the voting share. Cambodian prime minister Hun Sen suggests that "the
lack of capital is a main obstacle for countries in the development of infrastructure, so China's initiatives for the AIIB [and the Silk Road Fund] are very
useful."[32] The Cambodian National Strategic Development Plan for 2014–2018
states that the country needs $1.6 billion during the period, with the majority
going to roads, railways, power and electricity, and postal and telecom services
($1.3 billion), and some to urban water and sanitation projects.[33] In Central
Asia, officials in Kazakhstan, where China is one of the largest foreign investors, lauded the creation of the bank, saying that "Kazakhstan is in urgent
need of developing infrastructure."[34] A senior policy analyst of the National
Economy Research Institute, Azamat Nurseytov, emphasized (November 2014)
that President Nursultan Nazarbeyev highlighted the country's infrastructure
needs as the core element of the new economic policies and that the AIIB is
"so attractive to us ... especially in the construction of railways, highways, the
energy sector and airports."[35] When applying to join the AIIB in May 2015,
Alymbek Orozbekov, representative of the Investment Department of the
Ministry of Economy of Kyrgyzstan, the smaller and less developed neigh-
bor to Kazakhstan, highlighted that "Kyrgyzstan needs huge investment in

---

31   The Daily Observer, "Dhaka Set to Sign AIIB Agreement in Beijing," 27 June 2015, http://
      www.observerbd.com/2015/06/27/96508.php.
32   Xinhua News Agency, "Cambodian PM Hails China for Initiatives on AIIB and Silk Road
      Fund," 12 January 2015, http://news.xinhuanet.com/english/china/2015-01/12/c_127380575.
      htm.
33   Anath Baliga, "Concerns New China-Backed Global Lender Could Be Hurdle to Self-
      Reliance," 4 April 2015, http://www.phnompenhpost.com/post-weekend/concerns-new
      -china-backed-global-lender-could-be-hurdle-self-reliance.
34   CCTV News Content, "AIIB Established at Right Time for Kazakhstan: Economist,"
      13 April 2015, http://newscontent.cctv.com/NewJsp/news.jsp?fileId=291499.
35   Ibid.

infrastructure if it is to maintain economic growth and development for the next five to seven years."[36]

However, the demand is not only coming from the less developed or smaller economies in Asia. Indonesian finance minister Bambang Brodjonegoro emphasized: "We have more than $450 billion of infrastructure financing needs for the next five years. With that kind of need, I don't think a single multilateral agency like World Bank or ADB can fulfill that kind of requirement."[37] India also has massive domestic infrastructure needs. In May 2015, the current government of Narendra Modi stated that the country needs about $1 trillion in infrastructure investment over the "next few years," to fulfill its reform agenda and return the nation to 9 percent growth (the World Bank puts the total closer to $1.7 trillion).[38] Massive investment is needed to improve roads, rail, ports, power, and other infrastructure (not to forget the basic infrastructure needs of the poor in India, including clean water, sewage, sanitation, and basic electricity).[39] Meanwhile, India's infrastructure conglomerates are struggling, hampered by high debt levels and weak balance sheets.[40] With deeper motivations to borrow, India was among the first nations to join the AIIB; New Delhi stepped up to pledge $8.37 billion to the capital stock of the AIIB, as the second-largest shareholder, and gained the second-largest voting share at 7.5 percent.

For the immediate term, New Delhi and Jakarta are each looking at AIIB to help with coal power projects, which the World Bank has largely frozen, seemingly in response to the policy line of the US administration. In 2013, President Barack Obama announced restrictions on financing coal-fired electricity generation abroad, to limit global warming. One month later, the World Bank stated that only in "rare circumstances" would it lend for coal-fired electricity projects.[41] Indian authorities criticized the World Bank's decision, saying

---

36   China Ministry of Industry and Information Technology (Zhenwei Group Corporation, Information Department), "AIIB to Be Important Creator for Regional Development," 3 April 2015, http://www.xjice.com/en/shown.asp?newsid=767.

37   Sri Jegarajah and See Kit Tang, "AIIB Vital to Meet Asia's Funding Needs: Indonesia FinMin," 30 June 2015, http://www.cnbc.com/2015/06/30/aiib-vital-to-meet-asias-funding-needs-indonesia-finmin.html.

38   The Economic Times, "India Needs $1 Trillion for New Infrastructure: Nirmala Sitharaman," 28 May 2015, http://articles.economictimes.indiatimes.com/2015-05-28/news/62765618_1_asia-pacific-asia-pacific-new-infrastructure.

39   Henry Sender, "India Infrastructure: Built on Debt," 22 June 2015, http://www.ft.com/intl/cms/s/0/7b101156-f310-11e4-a979-00144feab7de.html.

40   Ibid.

41   J. Vasuki, "For India, AIIB Can Be a Game Changer in Coal Energy Sector," 28 June 2015, http://www.theopendigest.com/news/news-india/india-aiib-coal-energy-sector/.

the restriction on funding coal projects amounts to denying a country (India) access to cheap power, a country that is already struggling to provide for 1 billion electricity-starved people—and yet has the first-largest coal reserves in the world, and is already using coal to generate three-fifths of the nation's power supply. India is looking to the AIIB for $100 billion in financing for coal energy projects. Indonesia is asking the AIIB to fund a 2,000-megawatt coal-fired power plant, which the ADB has shown little interest in funding. The Indonesian finance minister suggested that this is one example of how the AIIB will complement the other multilateral banks; that is, they will each focus on "different projects [of] different scale."[42] In Asia, the hope is that AIIB will focus on large-scale infrastructure projects and power plants and leave basic infrastructure, such as irrigation systems and arterial and rural roads, to the ADB and the World Bank.

2.2   *New Model*

Jin has responded to the comment that China will dominate the new bank by saying that the "AIIB is a bank, not a political organization or a political alliance."[43] His remark speaks to the reality that the most important factor in determining the prospects of the AIIB is its ability to fulfill its raison d'être as a "bank"—though one that provides development finance. The AIIB's prospects will be determined, and the bank ultimately judged, by the details of its lending and the results that are achieved. Can the AIIB allocate its credit on a programming and project basis to meet the needs of its clients by supporting transformative and sustainable change, in a timely manner, and secure repayment to ensure the bank's own sustainability? Observers, such as one Australia and New Zealand Bank (ANZ) representative, suggest that the bank has a unique opportunity to "offer a new approach for Asia's infrastructure financing."[44]

The Chinese and their partners in the AIIB have set for themselves the ambitious goal of learning from and borrowing some of the experiences and established practices of the multilateral and bilateral donors, but not simply copying the so-called best practices. Rather, the goal is to improve on the existing norms and to exceed current standards, not only in areas of policy, but also

---

42   Ben Otto, "China-Led Bank to Focus on Big Ticket Projects, Indonesia Says," 10 April 2015, www.wsj.com/articles/china-led-aiib-to-focus-on-big-ticket-projects-indonesia-says -1428647276.

43   Nakagawa and Kumar, "China's Influence over AIIB a Concern Ahead of Founders' Meeting."

44   Enda Curran, "China's New Bank Offers Fresh Approach to Old Problems," 26 March 2015, http://www.bloomberg.com/news/articles/2015-03-26/china-s-new-bank-offers-fresh -approach-to-old-problems.

on procurement systems and technical matters of programming. Furthermore, Chinese finance minister Lou Jiwei emphasized, while on a panel with ADB governor Takehiko Nakao in Beijing in March 2015, that the AIIB (read: unlike the ADB) will be "mainly led by developing countries, and we must consider their appeals—some rules proposed by Western countries may not be best, in my view."[45]

At a media briefing in Beijing in mid-July 2015, Jin said that the new infrastructure-focused bank will follow a "more business-like approach" in its operations. Exactly what this means is still to be seen. The details need to be worked out for the bank's lending objectives, project design, approval, implementation and evaluation processes, and terms and conditions for its loans. So far, Jin has said that the AIIB will not take the country-focused approach of the traditional donor agencies. He noted that, in developing projects, the AIIB will "follow business lines like private companies" but still keep in mind the needs of countries. Jin noted that a "special department" will be designated in the new bank to forge the consensus for programs and projects. Chinese deputy finance minister Shi Yaobin added that the AIIB "will mobilize all resources, including private capital, to fund its infrastructure investment missions."[46]

It is to be seen whether, or how, the Chinese reticence for the existing rules will carry into the bank's handling of "conditionality" for its loans, and for the avoidance of "moral hazard" on loan repayments. In establishing the new bank, China and its partners face the same challenge as the existing multilaterals in figuring out how to allocate the bank's funds to the most appropriate projects, in the least amount of time, and to ensure repayment. So far, Chinese officials involved in the creation of the bank have indicated only that the AIIB will have some features of a commercial bank—where emphasis is focused on the business case for a loan rather than on poverty reduction alone.[47] The Articles indicate that the new bank may offer new opportunities for market actors and that a broader range of private sector actors could be involved in the delivery of AIIB programs and projects. The Articles note that English will be used as the operating language. The Articles state the AIIB will open bidding for procurement to all, unlike the ADB, which restricts contracts to member countries. Banking sector analysts suggest that by including developed countries in its membership (including from Western Europe), the banks and firms

---

45   Ibid.

46   Xinhua News Agency, "China Focus: AIIB Preparation in Full Swing," 16 April 2015, http://news.xinhuanet.com/english/2015-04/16/c_134156867.htm.

47   Ibid.

from those nations will likely compete for AIIB projects and, to the extent they are successful, this should raise the overall standards of the new bank.

For its infrastructure project financing, and if the AIIB is to fund the afore-mentioned coal power projects, it will need to work out its position on "sustain-ability"; that is, environmental protection and social impact safeguards.[48] In addition to high level frameworks, standards for environmental impact review and social impact safeguards need to be developed and institutionalized at the project level. Here, the World Bank and the ADB have achieved major gains dur-ing the past two decades and have already set the standard that the new bank must either meet or try to exceed. Environmental protection, preventing cli-mate change, and the need to consult local stakeholders have become broadly accepted *global norms* that require serious handling by the new AIIB. A Task Force between the Global Economic Governance Initiative (GEGI) at Boston University and Brookings Institution is highlighting the importance of devel-oping guidelines, innovative business models, and financing arrangements for "sustainable infrastructure."[49] A lot of attention from nongovernmental orga-nizations and international nongovernmental organizations will be focused on this element in the new bank's programs. So far, the Articles pledge to heed environmental risk and social impact (Article 13[4]), but the details of the spe-cific mechanisms that will safeguard against environmental degradation, bid-rigging, and other potential risks in huge infrastructure projects are still to be worked out. The AIIB Interim Secretariat issued a draft "Environmental and Social Framework" on 3 August 2015, offered three-months of consultation, and invited comments to be submitted online to an AIIB email address. During the month of September 2015, the Secretariat held rounds of consultations on the document with "interested stakeholders," using video and audio links, provid-ing "opportunities for questions, comments and discussion." The time frame for the consultations was then extended to 23 October 2015 to allow for further feedback. One academic researcher suggested that the extension showed the seriousness that the AIIB is assigning to the safeguards, while another observer suggested that the delay showed the difficulty that the new bank is experienc-ing in reaching consensus on its new environmental and social impact norms. Additionally, the creators of the AIIB must ensure that the new bank adheres

---

48   Daniel Bradlow similarly highlights the importance of developing environmentally and socially responsible infrastructure projects for the AIIB. See D. Bradlow, "Global Support for Asian Bank May Hand South Africa Benefits," *Business Day* (Johannesburg), 24 April 2015.

49   The Task Force on Sustainable Infrastructure is co-led by Kevin Gallagher at Boston University and Rogerio Studart and Amar Battacharya at The Brookings Institution.

to strict guidelines on corruption prevention. Chinese officials emphasize that the AIIB will aim for "clean governance," with a "zero tolerance" stance.[50]

For the potential recipients, even if the AIIB realizes only a part of its promise, it will make a marked difference. It therefore is noteworthy that Indonesia's finance minister has already defended the governance of the AIIB, in public, saying that the members of the new China-backed bank will ensure that its projects are "high quality" and delivered with appropriate standards. Brodjonegoro noted that Indonesia has been, and continues to be, involved in the discussions regarding the establishment and governance of the AIIB, and that "so far, we are satisfied.... In fact, we're trying to improve on what the World Bank and ADB have been doing well, in order to make the AIIB better." He emphasized that the AIIB is adhering to "best practices."[51]

The above shows that Beijing and the creators of the AIIB are exploring new ways to provide multilateral finance for infrastructure development and fostering connectivity—trying to improve on existing practices—even while they also anchor the new bank on a rich reservoir of experience. Much of the attention so far has been on the governance structure and managerial arrangements for the new bank. The creators of the AIIB are "banking" on their new governance arrangements to unlock the creative potential of the bank's members, management team, and staff for devising improved modes of development lending and new business models. Ultimately, however, the key factor in determining the prospects of the AIIB is whether the new China-backed bank is effective, over the medium-term, as a bank that supports infrastructure modernization and sustainable development—especially compared to the incumbents. Duvvuri Subbarao, former governor of the Reserve Bank of India, captures the essence of the challenge: "The AIIB has the challenge of showing that it can deliver a different business model and add value to economic growth and poverty reduction. It is a good experiment to try. At this time, there is no evidence or basis to say it is negative."[52]

To the extent that the AIIB succeeds, it will secure the buy-in of its clients and member states, and the new bank may even exert pressure on the established multilateral lenders to change. However, much of the hard work lies ahead. One should not underestimate the scale of the challenge in staffing the bank adequately and appropriately, especially given the ambitious mission that has been set. One source (a former senior manager of a multilateral development bank, who has advised the AIIB's interim secretary-general) noted to

---

50   Xinhua News Agency, "China Focus."
51   Jegarajah and Tang, "AIIB Vital to Meet Asia's Funding Needs."
52   Curran, "China's New Bank Offers Fresh Approach to Old Problems."

the author that the hiring process has already started and that by October 2015 more than 30 staff had already been hired.[53] Observers will rightly be watching whether the AIIB is run by professional staff who are hired on the basis of merit rather than citizenship or political leanings, with the necessary talent and skills, and are from around the world (including nonmember countries[54]). As Johannes Linn, a former World Bank vice president, suggests, the bank's hiring practices could go a long way in defusing concerns about excessive political influence within the bank's operations.[55] Expectations have been raised, and the pressure is on, especially if the bank is to be open by early 2016.

53   The author has promised to maintain the anonymity of the source.
54   Wang, Zhang, Wang, and Li, "China Fleshing Out AIIB for Asia and the World."
55   Ibid.

CHAPTER 23

Emerging Powers and Emerging Trends in Global Governance

Matthew D. Stephen[1]

In the 1990s, the global system entered a new phase. The United States reigned supreme after the collapse of the Soviet Union discredited alternatives to liberal capitalism and removed the only global counterweight to Western influence. Attention turned to international institutions, human rights, democracy promotion, and economic liberalization. Infused with the liberal zeitgeist of the time, "global governance" began to emerge as a perspective on world politics as well as a new approach to managing international affairs.[2] It represented an ambition to manage the world by collaboratively "solving problems," the major political questions having already been resolved in the West's favor.

Today, this project appears to be in trouble. In Crimea and Syria, in the corridors of the World Trade Organization (WTO) in Geneva, in the backrooms of the United Nations in New York, universal multilateralism has taken a hit and power politics appears to be on the rise. China, India, and the three other BRICS countries (Brazil, Russia, South Africa) have experienced rapid economic growth and are increasingly challenging Western dominance. The legitimacy of the rules and leadership roles of global governance is in dispute. China and Russia appear to offer political alternatives to liberal democracy while economic growth in the developing world has been greatest not under neoliberal regimes, but under varieties of state capitalism. In developed democracies, new right-wing political movements have emerged that challenge outward-oriented pro-globalization policies. Meanwhile, the BRICS criticize the biases

---

*   This chapter was originally published in Global Governance, Volume 23, Issue 3, 2017.
1   Matthew D. Stephen is a research fellow at the WZB Berlin Social Science Center. He has published in *European Journal of International Relations, Millennium, and Review of International Studies*, among other journals.
2   Klaus Dingwerth and Philipp Pattberg, "Global Governance as a Perspective on World Politics," *Global Governance* 12, no. 2 (2006): 185–203; Henk Overbeek, Klaus Dingwerth, Philipp Pattberg, and Daniel Compagnon, "Forum: Global Governance: Decline or Maturation of an Academic Concept?" *International Studies Review* 12, no. 4 (2010): 696–719.

of the existing order and have begun to build their own international institutions. What is the impact of emerging powers on the constellation of multilateral institutions, norms, and rules that guide and constrain behavior at the global level? What remains of the ambition to govern the globe?

In this article, I argue that as a result of the rise of new powers, the heterogeneity of preferences weighted by power in the international system has increased over the past two decades. The great-power club of systemically significant countries has become more diverse. But international institutions are sticky, and existing institutions privilege established powers and largely reflect their preferences and ideas. As a result, new conflicts are emerging that are generating novel forms of institutional adaptation and change. I survey the nature and extent of these conflicts and outline the trends in global governance that are developing as a result. My main conclusion is that a combination of exacerbated collective action problems and divergent preferences means that the kinds of major achievements of global governance in the 1990s are unlikely to be repeated. Instead, a "new global governance" is materializing that is strongly contested, less universal, less liberal, and more fragmented.

1   The Emergence of Global Governance

When we look back at the 1990s, we see an explosion of liberal optimism that permeated the study and practice of international politics. In the context of a deepening world market and the denationalization of policy fields such as trade, investment, health, and the environment, global governance appeared as the only path "through which conflicting or diverse interests may be accommodated and cooperative action may be taken."[3] For the first time since the Russian Revolution, capitalism reigned practically unchallenged across the globe. Resources previously denied to the investor were integrated into the world market: in the former Soviet bloc under shock therapy, in China as a result of socialism with Chinese characteristics, and in Latin America under the tutelage of the International Monetary Fund (IMF) structural adjustment programs. Even a social democratic addendum to capitalism began to appear anachronistic, and "third way" social democracy, largely adapted to neoliberal economic prescriptions, emerged.[4] This was the context for the emergence of a governance system that was, for the first time, truly global. Thus began a phase

---

3   Commission on Global Governance, *Our Global Neighbourhood: The Report of the Commission on Global Governance* (Oxford: Oxford University Press, 1995), p. 2.

4   Perry Anderson, "Renewals," *New Left Review* 1 (January–February 2000): 5–24.

of multilateral institution building that is only comparable in its scope and ambition with the foundation of the UN system after World War II.

The pooling of economic clout enabled the United States and Europe during the Uruguay Round to push through the creation of the WTO, bringing into existence a nearly universal legal regime formally committed to the liberalization of world trade.[5] Developing countries were forced to take on new obligations to protect the "intellectual property" of big Northern corporations and to commit new economic sectors such as services and investment to the multilateral liberalization agenda. In return, developing countries got the incorporation of agriculture and textiles into the multilateral regime—but not much in the way of liberalizing them. The launch of the WTO Millennium Round in 1999 heralded the ambition to extend and deepen liberal globalization as a quasi-constitutional feature of the world economy.[6]

The creation and consolidation of the WTO represented only the most ambitious attempt to constitutionalize the creation of a liberal global economic order. In the same year the WTO came into force, more ambitious developed countries began exploring the prospect of extending the multilateral approach to investment liberalization, backed up by an effective dispute settlement mechanism. The failure of Organisation for Economic Co-operation and Development (OECD) governments to agree to the Multilateral Agreement on Investment in 1998 did not prevent the rapid proliferation of bilateral investment treaties (BITs) and the inexorable rise of international investment arbitration tribunals.[7] Meanwhile, global governors in the IMF, the World Bank, and the US Treasury had already converged on the correct recipe for economic reforms. The Washington Consensus reflected liberal principles of neoclassical economics, providing a powerful and coherent set of policy prescriptions centered on privatization, trade and financial liberalization, and fiscal conservatism. Lending conditionalities and political pressure diffused this policy paradigm around the developing world and contributed to the perception that economic policy could be standardized into a "best practice."[8] In the European

---

5   Richard H. Steinberg, "In the Shadow of Law or Power? Consensus-based Bargaining and Outcomes in the GATT/WTO," *International Organization* 56, no. 2 (2002): 339–374.

6   Nitsan Chorev, "The Institutional Project of Neo-liberal Globalism: The Case of the WTO," *Theory and Society* 34, no. 3 (2005): 317–355.

7   In the thirty years after the first BIT in 1959 until 1989, 400 BITs were signed. From 1990 until 2000, this increased by more than 1,600. Calculated from the International Centre for Settlement of Investment Disputes, "Database of Bilateral Investment Treaties," https://icsid. worldbank.org/en/Pages/resources/Bilateral-Investment-Treaties-Database.aspx (2017).

8   Sarah Babb, "The Washington Consensus as Transnational Policy Paradigm: Its Origins, Trajectory and Likely Successor," *Review of International Political Economy* 20, no. 2 (2013): 268–297.

context, the Maastricht Treaty (1992) paved the way for one of the most ambitious supranational institutions in history, creating a "European Union" based on common liberal economic criteria and leading to the creation of a single European currency.

The aspiration to deliver on cosmopolitan notions of universal justice was realized through the entrepreneurial diplomacy of a coalition of middle powers and civil society groups, culminating in the Rome Statute of 1998 that established the legal basis for the International Criminal Court.[9] The Ottawa treaty on landmines (1997) had already demonstrated the capacity for multilateral action even where some major powers reject it.[10] The North Atlantic Treaty Organization (NATO), the core geopolitical alliance of the liberal democratic states, was expanded through the decade and by 2004 incorporated a total of twenty-six countries, stretching deep behind the former Iron Curtain. US air power could be used in the service of not only upholding the territorial integrity of states (as in the Gulf War of 1991), but increasingly in the service of putatively humanitarian imperatives (as in the former Yugoslavia). In a gradual process of increasing normative ambition, the concept of "humanitarian intervention" gave way to the "responsibility to protect."[11]

The operation of a globalized economy and the expansion of modern industry would of course generate its share of externalities, especially for the earth's biosphere. The UN Framework Convention on Climate Change (UNFCCC) was consecrated in 1992 and the Kyoto Protocol adopted in 1997 as the most ambitious attempts of global governance to limit the prospects of runaway global warming. The worst social and environmental effects of profit-driven multinational corporations could, it was hoped, be blunted through voluntary initiatives like the Global Compact (2000), providing a "framework of reference and dialogue" rather than regulatory codes of conduct such as the failed UN Code of Conduct on Transnational Corporations.[12]

In sum, the 1990s witnessed a burst of multilateral treaty making and a flourishing of new global initiatives to deepen economic liberalization, expand human rights, and take care of some of the most egregious externalities of global capitalism. The international system became heavily institutionalized

---

9   Nicole Deitelhoff, "The Discursive Process of Legalization: Charting Islands of Persuasion in the ICC Case," *International Organization* 63, no. 1 (2009): 33–65.

10   Ramesh Thakur and William Maley, "The Ottawa Convention on Landmines: A Landmark Humanitarian Treaty in Arms Control?" *Global Governance* 5, no. 3 (1999): 273–302.

11   Carsten Stahn, "Responsibility to Protect: Political Rhetoric or Emerging Legal Norm?" *American Journal of International Law* 101, no. 1 (2007): 99–120.

12   Georg Kell and Gerard Ruggie, "Global Markets and Social Legitimacy: The Case of the 'Global Compact,'" *Transnational Corporations* 8, no. 3 (1999): 101–120.

and, for the first time, these initiatives were truly global. Moreover, in most instances, states and social forces from the Global North were in the driving seat. By 2012, an observer such as Robert Keohane could look back on two decades of "the dominance of the view that cooperation in world politics can be enhanced through the construction and support of multilateral institutions based on liberal principles."[13] Global governance could be made not only in the common interest, but in the pursuit of a better society.

2   The Emergence of New Powers

Into this mix have come the emerging powers. Recent years have not been kind to the BRICS. Since 2014, Russia's economy has been hit by low oil prices and Western sanctions. Domestic factors and the end of a commodities supercycle have undermined Brazil's economic trajectory, and even China's red-hot growth rates have cooled. Only India has bucked the trend.[14] While growth in the BRICS has slowed (and even reversed in some cases), the distribution of power in the international system has already been fundamentally altered since the 1990s phase of institution building. Between 2004 and 2014, China's gross domestic product (GDP) grew from $6.6 trillion to $17.2 trillion (an increase of 159 percent) while India's expanded from $3.4 trillion to $7.0 trillion (109 percent). US GDP grew from $14.2 trillion to $16.6 trillion (16.8 percent).[15] China is no longer a peripheral underdeveloped country but is beginning to rival the United States. India is fast catching up.

The power shift goes beyond China and India or even the BRICS. Take, for example, the current members of the Group of 20 (G-20). Today, OECD and non-OECD members are evenly split in terms of total GDP.[16] Just one decade ago, the split was 63 percent to 37 percent. Two decades ago, it was 71 percent to 29 percent.[17] The attention currently lavished on stalling growth in

---

13   Robert O. Keohane, "Twenty Years of Institutional Liberalism," *International Relations* 26, no. 2 (2012): 125.

14   For an overview, see World Bank, *Global Economic Prospects: Spillovers Amid Weak Growth* (Washington, DC: World Bank, 2016).

15   Figures are in purchasing parity terms and come from the World Banks' *World Development Indicators*, 4 May 2016, http://databank.worldbank.org/.

16   OECD, *OECD Data*, 4 May 2016, https://data.oecd.org/gdp/gross-domestic-product-gdp .htm. Note that OECD G-20 members include three countries (Mexico, South Korea, and Turkey) sometimes associated with emerging economy status. Data are missing for Argentina.

17   Figures are in purchasing parity terms and come from World Bank, *World Development Indicators*, 4 May 2016, http://databank.worldbank.org/.

emerging markets is a sign of their importance for the global economy, not their peripherality.[18] Moreover, growth in emerging economies is expected to remain stronger than in high-income countries.[19] The power relations that underpinned the burst of multilateral institution building in the 1990s are gone.

How will global governance change as a result? Some authors, primarily but not exclusively realists, foresee global governance being undermined, a return to great-power rivalry, and a resurgence of geopolitical competition.[20] International institutions, which reflect US hegemony, will wither and decline.[21] Conversely, neoliberal institutionalists emphasize the mutual interests that new and old powers have in maintaining the global governance system and the limited ambitions of new powers to change it.[22] Although clearly in tension, both of these perspectives capture important parts of the story, but they remain fundamentally incomplete to the extent that they ignore or downplay two important features of contemporary global governance.

First, contemporary global governance in many important respects reflects the preferences and social purposes prevalent among dominant social groups in Western, developed, and liberal democracies.[23] Since the 1980s, this social purpose has taken on a distinctly neoliberal dimension.[24] By externalizing features of their domestic societies into international institutions and other transnational actors, Western states have shaped global governance in their own image. In contrast, new powers are economically, politically, and culturally

---

18   "The simultaneous slowing of four of the largest emerging markets—Brazil, Russia, China, and South Africa—poses the risk of spillover effects for the rest of the world economy." World Bank, *Global Economic Prospects*, p. xv.

19   Ibid., p. 4.

20   Giovanni Arrighi, *Adam Smith in Beijing: Lineages of the Twenty-first Century* (London: Verso, 2007); John Mearsheimer, "The Gathering Storm: China's Challenge to US Power in Asia," *Chinese Journal of International Politics* 3, no. 4 (2010): 381–396.

21   Christopher Layne, "This Time It's Real: The End of Unipolarity and the Pax Americana," *International Studies Quarterly* 56, no. 1 (2012): 203–213.

22   G. John Ikenberry, "The Future of the Liberal World Order," *Foreign Affairs* 90, no. 3 (2011): 56–62 Miles Kahler, "Rising Powers and Global Governance: Negotiating Change in a Resilient Status Quo," *International Affairs* 89, no. 3 (2013): 711–729.

23   In theoretical terms, see Robert W. Cox, "Social Forces, States and World Orders: Beyond International Relations Theory," *Millennium* 10, no. 2 (1981): 126–155; John G. Ruggie, "International Regimes, Transactions and Change: Embedded Liberalism in the Postwar Economic Order," *International Organization* 36, no. 2 (1982): 379–415.

24   Steven Bernstein, "Ideas, Social Structure and the Compromise of Liberal Environmentalism," *European Journal of International Relations* 6, no. 4 (2000): 464–512; Nitsan Chorev, "The Institutional Project of Neo-liberal Globalism," pp. 317–355; Charles Kupchan, "The Normative Foundations of Hegemony and the Coming Challenge to Pax Americana," *Security Studies* 23, no. 2 (2014): 219–257.

different from established powers. Economically, the emerging powers remain poorer in per capita terms and much more unequal than the established powers; their forms of capitalism are more organized, less "free," and generally less liberal than those of the established powers. Far from seeking neoliberal economic credentials, most emerging economies have developed pragmatic alliances with local and foreign investors that have breathed new life into economic regimes that hardly approximate Washington Consensus norms.[25] Emerging powers are also politically different from established powers: China is governed by a one-party regime defined in its constitution as "a socialist state under the people's democratic dictatorship," and Russia has developed a personalized form of rule that has been theorized as "sovereign democracy."[26] While countries such as India and Brazil are committed to multiparty democracy, their political systems are characterized by weaker rule of law and weaker voice and accountability than established powers (see Table 23.1). It is interesting to note that these differences appear to extend into the cultural sphere. According to survey data, "survival values" prevail among the citizens of emerging powers, as opposed to the "postmaterial" self-expression values characteristic of the developed West (see Figure 23.1). This suggests that societal attitudes toward issues such as environmental protection, social diversity and out-groups, and political participation are very different in emerging countries.

Because new powers are economically, politically, and culturally different from established powers, they are likely to have different preferences regarding international rules and to pursue different social purposes in their foreign policies.[27] Due to a more diffuse distribution of state power, these preferences are more readily translated into international outcomes. In short, the rise of new powers increases the heterogeneity of preferences weighted by power that underpins the international system. Following the logic of collective action, even where established and emerging powers share common interests, the addition of new powers to the international system can be expected to make common agreements more difficult. The fact that they are also quite different

---

25   Christopher A. McNally, "Sino-capitalism: China's Reemergence and the International Political Economy," *World Politics* 64, no. 4 (2012): 741–776; Andreas Nölke et al., "Domestic Structures, Foreign Economic Policies and Global Economic Order: Implications from the Rise of Large Emerging Economies," *European Journal of International Relations* 21, no. 3 (2015): 538–567.

26   Viatcheslav Morozov, "Sovereignty and Democracy in Contemporary Russia: A Modern Subject Faces the Post-modern World," *Journal of International Relations and Development* 11, no. 2 (2008): 152–180.

27   Matthew D. Stephen, "Rising Powers, Global Capitalism and Liberal Global Governance: A Historical Materialist Account of the BRICs Challenge," *European Journal of International Relations* 20, no. 4 (2014): 912–938.

from established powers suggests that these difficulties of collective action will be exacerbated.

Second, international institutions are sticky and do not adapt perfectly to new distributions of power and preferences.[28] Institutions and practices will take time to adjust to the new constellation, and some may never do so.

Established powers retain their privileges in existing institutions as emerging powers may find it increasingly attractive to explore exit options. The

TABLE 23.1   Political and economic characteristics of major powers

	Rule of law (0–100)	Voice and accountability (0–100)	GDP per capita (US dollars, PPP)	Economic liberalism (0–100)
BRICS				
Brazil	55	61	15,518	57
Russia	26	20	23,561	52
India	54	61	5,244	55
China	43	5	11,805	53
South Africa	64	68	12,454	63
Average	49	43	13,717	56
G5				
United States	90	80	51,282	76
United Kingdom	94	92	36,908	76
Japan	89	79	35,614	73
Germany	93	96	42,887	74
France	88	89	37,309	63
Average	91	87	40,800	72

GDP, gross domestic product; PPP, purchasing power parities; BRICS, Brazil, Russia, India, China, and South Africa; G5, Group of 5.
SOURCES: WORLD BANK, WORLDWIDE GOVERNANCE INDICATORS, 2014 DATA, HTTP:// INFO.WORLDBANK.ORG/GOVERNANCE/WGI/INDEX.ASPX; WORLD BANK, *WORLD DEVELOPMENT INDICATORS*, 2015 DATA, HTTP://DATABANK.WORLDBANK.ORG/DATA/; HERITAGE FOUNDATION, ECONOMIC FREEDOM INDEX, 2015 DATA, WWW.HERITAGE.ORG/ INDEX/DOWNLOAD

28   Tine Hanrieder, "Gradual Change in International Organisations: Agency Theory and Historical Institutionalism," *Politics* 34, no. 4 (2014): 324–333; Bernhard Zangl et al., "Imperfect Adaptation: How the WTO and the IMF Adjust to Shifting Power Distributions Among Their Members," *Review of International Organizations* 11, no. 2 (2016): 171–196.

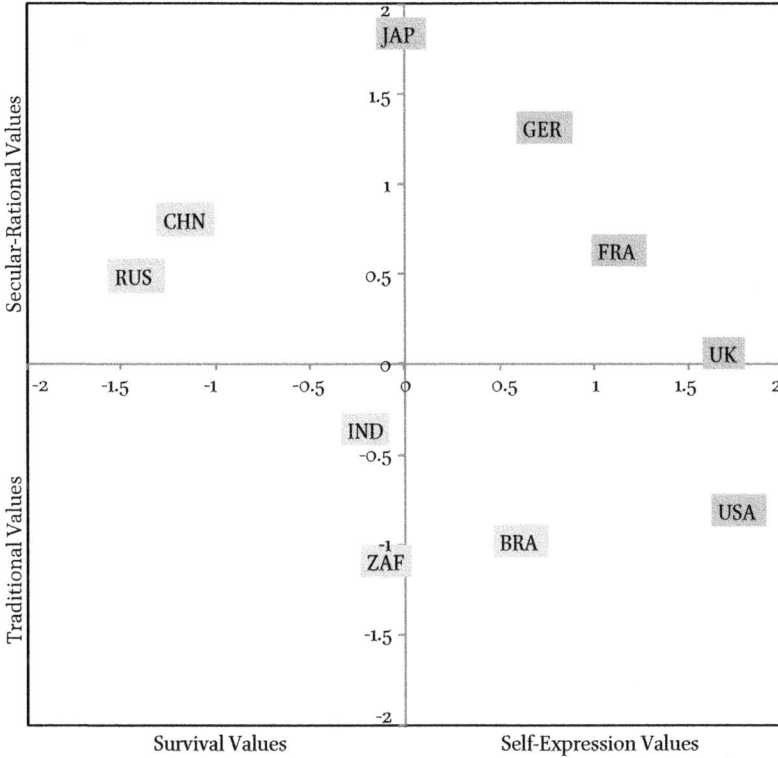

FIGURE 23.1   Cultural values in major powers
JAP, Japan; CHN, China; RUS, Russia; GER, Germany; FRA, France; UK,
United Kingdom; IND, India; ZAF, South Africa; BRA, Brazil; USA, United
States.
SOURCES: RONALD INGLEHART AND CHRISTIAN WELZEL, "CHANGING
MASS PRIORITIES: THE LINK BETWEEN MODERNIZATION AND
DEMOCRACY," *PERSPECTIVES ON POLITICS* 8, NO. 2 (2010): 551–567;
DATA FROM THE *WORLD VALUES SURVEY*, HTTPS://WEB.ARCHIVE.ORG/
WEB/20131019112321/HTTP://WWW.WORLDVALUESSURVEY.ORG/WVS/
ARTICLES/FOLDER_PUBLISHED/ARTICLE_BASE_54

impact of emerging powers on global governance will be an outcome not
only of a new heterogeneity of power and preferences, but also of the path-
dependent development of the existing order.

3   The New Global Governance: Six Emerging Trends

The liberal global governance project that took off in the 1990s—uniting the
world under multilateral institutions wedded to liberal ideas and principles

under Western leadership—is encountering increasing challenges. The creation of strong and encompassing international institutions means that emerging powers are pursuing their interests in a system not of their making but which they cannot ignore. Under the pressure of increased systemic heterogeneity and their own path dependency, many existing regimes cannot adapt. The new global governance is a product of both increased systemic heterogeneity and the path-dependent trajectory of the status quo. By observing the processes currently manifest within various multilateral institutions, it is possible to identify the trajectories of change that have emerged and appear likely to continue in the near future: (1) global governance is here to stay, but is increasingly contested; (2) a struggle is ensuing for leadership and privilege within global governance; (3) the liberal social purpose of global governance is taking a back seat; (4) existing multilateral institutions are facing increased deadlock; (5) informalization is likely to increase; and (6) global governance is becoming more fragmented.

3.1   *Global Governance Is Here to Stay, but Is Increasingly Contested*

Despite the turmoil of global governance in recent years, there are strong reasons to believe that the challenges posed to existing institutions are taking place within certain limits, that opposition is selective rather than total, and that conflicts are internal to the existing order rather than existential. In contrast to liberal optimists, emerging powers are unlikely to simply accept the existing rules.[29] But contrary to realists fixated on great-power conflict, they also have strong incentives to use rather than oppose global governance to achieve their goals.[30] Emerging powers are rendering parts of global governance dysfunctional, layering onto it and complicating it, but not overthrowing it. The emerging global governance order is growing out of the existing one.

A major reason for global governance's durability consists of the global economic context within which current conflicts are being played out. This is usually referred to as "globalization" and designates the processes of social and economic denationalization that have taken place especially since the 1970s. This is reflected in an exponential increase of trade, investment, and financial flows. The emerging economies are strongly—but selectively—integrated into these global flows, which have surpassed all previous historical periods in their

---

29   Ikenberry, "The Future of the Liberal World Order."
30   Randall L. Schweller, "Emerging Powers in an Age of Disorder," *Global Governance* 17, no. 3 (2011): 285–297.

geographic extent and intensity.[31] This economic environment, unleashing the deterritorializing and disciplinary effects of a world market, has several concrete effects.

First, it has become unnecessary for emerging powers to obtain and hold foreign territory to secure the material conditions of their rise. In a competitive mercantilist or imperial system, established powers can monopolize market access and the raw materials necessary to sustain a modern industrial economy. In a system of liberal multilateralism, where goods can be bought rather than conquered, conflicts shift gear.[32] Second, neoliberal globalization dramatically increases the opportunity costs of autarkic economic development. Whether emerging powers like it or not, there is little alternative but to seek to exploit the opportunities afforded by transnational production, trade, and knowledge transfer. Today, each of the BRICS hosts substantial foreign direct investments, accounting for between 10 percent and 42 percent of their GDP.[33] Likewise, the BRICS economies on average are almost as dependent on international trade as the Group of 7 (G7) industrialized economies.[34] By becoming dependent on international trade and investment, emerging powers are forced to collaborate with other states to secure access to international markets. This increases their incentive to participate in global governance but also raises the stakes involved. Third, by opening up to global capitalism, the domestic social structures of emerging powers have also changed. This involves not only the self-reinforcing formation of pro-integration social constituencies at home (the winners of opening up), but the possibility of transnational class linkages forming with elites from the developed core.

The combined effect of this economic denationalization is to increase the reliance of emerging powers on global capitalism and the multilateral institutions that enable and regulate it. Revived systemic war seems profoundly unlikely in light of this and other factors such as nuclear deterrence, the prohibitive costs of foreign occupation (Iraq and Afghanistan cost the United States around $2 trillion dollars each),[35] and the widespread acceptance of

31   Philip McCann, "Globalisation, Multinationals and the BRIICS," in Raed Safadi and Ralph Lattimore, eds., *Globalisation and Emerging Economies* (Geneva: OECD, 2008), pp. 71–117.

32   Erik Gartzke and Dominic Rohner, "The Political Economy of Imperialism, Decolonization and Development," *British Journal of Political Science* 41, no. 3 (2011): 525–556.

33   UN Conference on Trade and Development (UNCTAD), *UNCTAD Stat*, 24 October 2016, http://unctadstat.unctad.org/ReportFolders/reportFolders.aspx, citing 2014 data.

34   Stephen, "Rising Powers, Global Capitalism and Liberal Global Governance," p. 927.

35   Daniel Trotta, "Iraq War Costs U.S. More than $2 trillion: Study," Reuters, 14 March 2013, www.reuters.com/article/2013/03/14/us-iraq-war-anniversary-idUSBRE92D0PG20130314.

the norm of territorial integrity.[36] Given the strong functional incentives to preserve international institutions and to manage the global economy, combined with the advantage of incumbency that existing institutions enjoy, it seems unlikely that international institutions will simply fade away. But if the material context of globalization furnishes incentives for emerging powers to collaborate in the existing global governance order, it does not prevent the formation of new conflicts, nor can it prevent these conflicts from resulting in institutional change.

3.2 A Struggle Is Ensuing for Leadership and Privilege within Global Governance

Precisely because all major powers need to use international institutions to achieve their goals, the rise of new powers has unleashed a contest over leadership and privileges within global governance. The demand for a heightened say over global governance is central for rising developmental states for whom traditional Listian autonomy has become unfeasible.[37] But securing leadership and privileges within global governance is important not just for economic reasons. As the regulatory reach and enforcement capacity of international institutions has expanded, it has increased the constraints on autonomous sovereign decisionmaking and increased the salience of value conflicts between diverse societies. The purview of international institutions, international nongovernmental organizations (NGOs), and other global governors has expanded beyond the functional cooperation of standard setting or foreign economic policy coordination. It now includes issues of fundamental ethical value such as human rights, domestic political and economic orders, and minority rights. These principles, norms, and rules then become the common standards to adjudicate who is worthy of praise or blame, who is to be named and shamed, and who is to be deemed morally superior or inferior. As such, global governance has become critical in the allocation of fundamental social recognition such as prestige, status, and respect.[38]

While the world economy has become multipolar, the keystone global economic multilaterals remain dominated by the United States, Europe, and

---

36   The reaction to Russia's annexation of Crimea shows the norm to be alive and well.

37   Gerard Strange, "China's Post-Listian Rise: Beyond Radical Globalisation Theory and the Political Economy of Neoliberal Hegemony," *New Political Economy* 16, no. 5 (2011): 539–559.

38   Philip Nel, "Redistribution and Recognition: What Emerging Regional Powers Want," *Review of International Studies* 36, no. 4 (2010): 951–974; Reinhard Wolf, "Respect and Disrespect in International Politics: The Significance of Status Recognition," *International Theory* 3, no. 1 (2011): 105–142.

Japan.[39] The IMF and the World Bank, pivotal institutions of monetary and financial governance, still have voting rules that privilege developed countries and even afford the United States unique privileges as a de facto veto power. To add insult to injury, their management positions are also duopolized by the United States and Europe. Integration into this financial oligarchy has been a major priority for the emerging powers, even though it is becoming increasingly clear that they are unlikely to be sufficiently accommodated into it.[40] Another key privilege of global governance is the United States' capacity to mint the world's major international currency.[41] The status of the US dollar has allowed it a vast line of credit for which it does not have to pay interest and made it effectively immune to market disciplines that shape the policies of other states. Dedollarization in international transactions and the internationalization of the renminbi is one path by which emerging powers, especially China and Russia, have attempted to contest this dimension of US privilege.[42] At the UN Security Council, excluded emerging powers like India, Brazil, and South Africa have joined forces with Germany and Japan to seek leadership positions as new permanent members, however unsuccessfully.[43] In all of these areas, emerging powers are calling for a redistribution of leadership positions and positional advantages within these institutions and an end to Western domination, in part by pursuing their own special rights and privileges within the existing hierarchy.

3.3   The Liberal Social Purpose of Global Governance Is Taking a Back Seat

While emerging powers seek to extend their influence over the various mechanisms of global governance, they remain significantly different from established powers in their social, political, and cultural traditions. The differing contours of emerging powers' state-society relations provide the foundations for conflicts with Western powers over the features of global governance that

---

39   Miles Kahler, "The Global Economic Multilaterals: Will Eighty Years Be Enough?" *Global Governance* 22, no. 1 (2016): 1–9.

40   Jakob Vestergaard and Robert H. Wade, "Still in the Woods: Gridlock in the IMF and the World Bank Puts Multilateralism at Risk," *Global Policy* 6, no. 1 (2015): 1–12.

41   Jonathan Kirshner, "After the (Relative) Fall: Dollar Diminution and the Consequences for American Power," in Eric Helleiner and Jonathan Kirshner, eds., *The Future of the Dollar* (Ithaca: Cornell University Press, 2009), pp. 191–215.

42   McNally, "Sino-capitalism," pp. 757–764.

43   Jonas von Freiesleben, "Reform of the Security Council," in Lydia Swart and Estelle Perry, eds., *Governing and Managing Change at the United Nations* (New York: Center for UN Reform Education, 2013), pp. 1–22.

most explicitly embody its liberal and neoliberal social purpose.[44] The kinds of capitalism emerging are very different than those of the developed countries; moreover, countries such as China, India, and Russia are deeply suspicious of the ways in which liberal political demands have been used to criticize their domestic political systems and human rights practices.[45]

The fallout of the global financial crisis and the simultaneous growth of emerging powers pursuing nonliberal roads to capitalist development have challenged neoliberal ideas of economic management and development (privatization, autonomous markets, and open capital accounts). This has reinvigorated the pursuit of export-oriented interventionism (managed currencies and active industrial policies) as the standard road to capitalist catch-up development in the emerging world. It is not only the Chinese but also social groups in several emerging powers who "see virtue in a strong state, a disciplined society, stable economic growth, and national security over 'imported' notions of human rights, democracy, and unregulated markets."[46] Although hardly a rival package of counterhegemonic ideas, the improvised muddling through pragmatism of emerging varieties of capitalism suggests a new pluralism of ideas for economic development.[47] In light of the lessons learned from the uncontrolled liberalization experiments of the 1990s, and given strong domestic interests vested in statist institutions,[48] emerging power convergence along the lines of the Washington Consensus seems unlikely. This has already had implications for the WTO, where emerging powers have contributed to the deflection of the liberalization thrust that was supposed to be one of its raisons d'être.[49] Novel forms of state-capitalist interlinkages also pro-

---

44   Daron Acemoglu and James A. Robinson, "Is State Capitalism Winning?" Project Syndi-
      cate, 31 December 2012, www.project-syndicate.org/commentary/why-china-s-growth
      -model-will-fail-by-daron-acemoglu-and-james-a-robinson; Stephen, "Rising Powers,
      Global Capitalism and Liberal Global Governance."

45   Nölke et al., "Domestic Structures, Foreign Economic Policies and Global Economic
      Order"; Matthew D. Stephen, "India, Emerging Powers and Global Human Rights: Yes,
      but ...," in Doutje Lettinga and Lars van Troost, eds., Shifting Power and Human Rights
      Diplomacy: India (Amsterdam: Amnesty International, 2014), pp. 55–64.

46   Gregory Chin and Ramesh Thakur, "Will China Change the Rules of Global Order?"
      Washington Quarterly 33, no. 4 (2010): 122.

47   Cornel Ban and Mark Blyth, "The BRICs and the Washington Consensus: An Introduc-
      tion," Review of International Political Economy 20, no. 2 (2013): 241–255.

48   Benjamin L. Liebman and Curtis J. Milhaupt, eds., Regulating the Invisible Hand? The
      Institutional Implications of Chinese State Capitalism (Oxford: Oxford University Press, 2016).

49   Kristen Hopewell, Breaking the WTO: How Emerging Powers Disrupted the Neoliberal
      Project (Stanford: Stanford University Press, 2016); Amrita Narlikar, "New Powers in the
      Club: The Challenges of Global Trade Governance," International Affairs 86, no. 3 (2010):
      717–728.

vide the foundations for new conflicts over international trade and investment law.[50] The greater emphasis of emerging powers on pragmatic economic interventionism has also had implications for multilateral projects such as capital account liberalization, which was championed by established powers as a new international norm and commitment at the IMF.[51]

The conflict line over global governance's social purpose is reflected in deep disagreements over the operational implementation of human rights and the cosmopolitan concept of "conditional sovereignty."[52] Emerging powers express an affinity for hard conceptions of sovereignty as the basis for international relations. This challenges the liberal cosmopolitan assumption that human rights concerns trump the sovereign's prerogative over domestic affairs. The almost obsessive fascination of Western politicians and academics with the Responsibility to Protect (R2P) is not reciprocated by elites in emerging powers who are wary of neoimperial discourses and tend to interpret the R2P's three pillars in a sovereignty-reinforcing manner.[53] For these reasons, the further deepening of the liberal dimension of global governance has slowed down and may grind to a halt. In the face of a new heterogeneity of preferences, its extension in the near future appears unlikely.

3.4   Existing Multilateral Institutions Are Facing Increased Deadlock

Although multilateral institutions are clearly more durable than the US hegemony that sponsored many of them, one virtue of hegemonic stability theory is that it emphasizes the difficulty of collective action in the absence of a dominant state powerful enough to bring the others into line.[54] As a result of the international diffusion of state power, the number of major international players has increased, and the interests of the group of systemically significant countries have become more diverse. This narrows the win set of overlapping interests. International institutions have become more intrusive

---

50   Mark Wu, "The WTO and China's Unique Economic Structure," in Benjamin L. Liebman and Curtis J. Milhaupt, eds., *Regulating the Invisible Hand? The Institutional Implications of Chinese State Capitalism* (Oxford: Oxford University Press, 2016), pp. 313–350.

51   Sacha Dierckx, "After the Crisis and Beyond the New Constitutionalism? The Case of the Free Movement of Capital," *Globalizations* 10, no. 6 (2013): 803–818.

52   Richard Gowan and Franziska Brantner, *A Global Force for Human Rights? An Audit of European Power at the UN* (London: European Council on Foreign Relations, 2008).

53   Philipp Rotmann, Gerrit Kurtz, and Sarah Brockmeier, "Major Powers and the Contested Evolution of a Responsibility to Protect," *Conflict, Security and Development* 14, no. 4 (2014): 355–377.

54   Charles P. Kindleberger, "Dominance and Leadership in the International Economy: Exploitation, Public Goods, and Free Rides," *International Studies Quarterly* 25, no. 2 (1981): 242–254.

and authoritative than they were in the past, raising the stakes of international cooperation.[55] Simultaneously, the major multilateral institutions have become more inclusive, and more diverse positions need to be accommodated.[56] The major result is that global agreements are much harder to achieve than in the past. In the absence of the G7 countries' capacity to cajole major developing states into agreeing to new common rules, as they have done in the past, one outcome for existing institutions is a tendency toward stalemate and deadlock. That is, established institutions are likely to have difficulty adapting to the new constellation of preferences weighted by power. While they continue to function (deadlock does not imply paralysis), it is becoming increasingly difficult to update them in the face of new demands and circumstances.

Deadlock has already manifested in the keystone institutions of liberal global governance. Despite the declared intentions of the G-20 major economies in 2009, the protracted refinancing and quota and voice reforms at the IMF have exacerbated differences between established and emerging powers. The agreements reached have hardly been enough to satisfy emerging and developing countries.[57] The protracted and open-ended negotiations to reform voting quotas, combined with diverging policy preferences on substantive issues such as policy advice, lending conditionalities, and multilateral surveillance, make it difficult to conclude that "accommodation with the incumbent powers" will be the full story.[58] In trade, despite more than a decade and a half of sporadic multilateral negotiations, the WTO Doha Round remains largely in a stalemate with no end in sight.[59] It is now twenty years since the last major multilateral trade agreement in the Uruguay Round. The climate change negotiations to renew the Kyoto Protocol have also exhibited a tendency toward deadlock of existing institutions, leading to a far less demanding compact in Paris in 2015.[60] Although still highly active in the deployment of peacekeeping operations, the Security Council remains interminably deadlocked on the issues of both institutional reform and geopolitical high politics. Deadlock appears to

---

55   Michael Zürn, Martin Binder, and Matthias Ecker-Ehrhardt, "International Political Authority and Its Politicization," *International Theory* 4, no. 1 (2012): 69–106.

56   Kahler, "The Global Economic Multilaterals," p. 3.

57   Vestergaard and Wade, "Still in the Woods," pp. 1–12.

58   Kahler, "The Global Economic Multilaterals," p. 6.

59   Paul Collier, "Why the WTO Is Deadlocked: And What Can Be Done About It," *World Economy* 29, no. 10 (2006): 1423–1449.

60   Wolfgang Obergassel et al., *Phoenix from the Ashes—An Analysis of the Paris Agreement to the United Nations Framework Convention on Climate Change* (Wuppertal, Germany: Wuppertal Institute for Climate, Environment and Energy, 2016).

be a major obstacle to the integration of emerging powers through internal institutional reform.

Deadlock often results in what historical institutionalists refer to as institutional drift: if an institution fails to change in tandem with a changing environment, its real role will change and its effectiveness may erode.[61] Institutional stasis becomes a form of institutional change when the broader environment is changing. WTO rules are thus much less developed in the major growth areas of the global economy where deepening trade integration would require common regulatory standards rather than exchanging tariff concessions.[62] Likewise, the failure to comprehensively recapitalize the IMF is eroding its centrality to the international financial system—despite acknowledgment of its need to evolve.[63] In the longer run, deadlock increases the incentive to pursue alternative avenues to realize international policy goals, such as informal outside options, and alternative institutional arrangements.

3.5   Informalization Is Increasing

Informalization denotes a move away from codified norms and explicit rules, away from formal legal agreements and contracts, and toward loose agreements, common understandings, implicit rules, flexibility, and pragmatism.[64] Informalization is likely to increase in response to a more even international distribution of power, as binding agreements become harder to reach, even if there may be countervailing tendencies in particular areas. A wink and a nudge between the great powers may replace the binding resolution. Because informalization reduces certainty and erodes the level of obligation and precision of formal rules, it is likely to be more favored by the larger, more powerful states than the smaller powers. The reinvigoration of "G-groups" is one of the most prominent traits of informalization in global governance today,

---

61   Wolfgang Streeck and Kathleen Thelen, "Introduction: Institutional Change in Advanced Political Economies," in Wolfgang Streeck and Kathleen Thelen, eds., *Beyond Continuity: Institutional Change in Advanced Political Economies* (Oxford: Oxford University Press, 2005), pp. 3–39.

62   Richard Baldwin, "21st Century Regionalism: Filling the Gap Between 21st Century Trade and 20th Century Trade Rules," Staff Working Paper No. ERSD-2011-08 (WTO, 2011).

63   David Dodge and John Murray, "The Evolving International Monetary Order and the Need for an Evolving IMF," *Global Governance* 12, no. 4 (2006): 361–372.

64   Christopher Daase, "Die Informalisierung internationaler Politik: Beobachtun- gen zum Stand der internationalen Organisation," in Klaus Dingwerth, Dieter Kerwer, and Andreas Nölke, eds., *Die Organisierte Welt: Internationale Beziehungen und Organisationsforschung* (Baden-Baden: Nomos, 2009), pp. 289–307; Joost Pauwelyn, "Is It International Law or Not, and Does It Even Matter?" in Joost Pauwelyn, Ramses A. Wessel, and Jan Wouters, eds., *Informal International Lawmaking* (Oxford: Oxford University Press, 2012), pp. 125–161.

with the G-20 representing an expanded Aereopagus designating itself as the major forum for economic collaboration among the biggest countries.[65] The suspension of Russia's membership in the G7/8 has led to the consolidation of two informal great-power clubs: the G7 of established and largely satisfied countries, and the BRICS grouping of emerging and dissatisfied countries.[66] By restricting the participation of smaller powers and leaving implementation up to individual members, groups such as these represent the reassertion of a great-power system in the new global governance—in practice, also eroding the norm of sovereign equality and marginalizing forums such as the UN General Assembly.

The softening of existing agreements is another facet of informalization that overlaps with institutional drift, such as the agreement between the major powers not to adopt a successor agreement to the Kyoto Protocol and to revert instead to voluntary pledges in the Paris Agreement. Informalization can also take the form of unspoken rules and common understandings that may be imprudent to speak of in public, such as major states recognizing in practice the spheres of interest of the others. As new powers consolidate their international influence and seek a greater role in global governance, the trend toward informalization is likely to continue. Informalization can also involve the creation of new informal institutions and clubs—in which case it overlaps with the process of fragmentation in global governance.

3.6   *Global Governance Is Becoming More Fragmented*
Because existing international institutions tend to be sticky, the changes and challenges currently affecting global governance are of a gradual nature. New powers are coming into an already institutionalized order. Neither emerging nor established powers can simply wipe the slate clean. Because of this, new initiatives are likely to be "layered" on top of existing ones,[67] contributing to institutional complexity and fragmentation. The creation or strengthening of alternative venues may be an attractive prospect for emerging powers because they can get around the vested interests and veto players of existing institutions. Creating new institutions, however, can be a costly exercise and may diminish the utility of established institutions. Along with informalization, fragmentation may arise in response to persistent deadlocks that block

65   Robert H. Wade, "Emerging World Order? From Multipolarity to Multilateralism in the G20, the World Bank, and the IMF," *Politics and Society* 39, no. 3 (2011): 347–378.

66   Ramesh Thakur, "How Representative Are BRICS?" *Third World Quarterly* 35, no. 10 (2014): 1791–1808.

67   Streeck and Thelen, "Introduction."

emerging powers from achieving their goals through existing institutions. The same is true for established powers.

The most developed form of fragmentation in the existing global governance order is the creation of new formal institutions alongside, and partly competing with, established ones. With the WTO Doha Round being a victim of persistent disagreement between emerging and established powers, initiatives to further liberalize international trade have shifted to regional and interregional integration projects. The United States has pursued a bioceanic strategy of deep integration in the pursuit of a bilateral Transatlantic Trade and Investment Partnership (TTIP) with the European Union and a Trans-Pacific Partnership (TPP) with countries it sees as being at risk of getting sucked into the China orbit.[68] The Chinese response has come primarily in the form of an Association of Southeast Asian Nations plus China, India, Japan, South Korea, Australia, and New Zealand (ASEAN+6) megaregional free trade agreement called the Regional Comprehensive Economic Partnership. Fragmentation into partially overlapping spheres of influence backed up by rival institutional projects shows that geopolitical rivalries and international institutions are compatible and increasingly intertwined.

In development finance, the pursuit of a New Development Bank (NDB) by the BRICS countries has been widely interpreted as a result of their frustration with the reform deadlock at the IMF. A similar story might be told about China's creation of the Asian Infrastructure Investment Bank (AIIB), which signaled China's growing capacity to provide financial firepower, mobilize political leadership, and attract a rather undignified scramble of close US allies.[69] Emerging powers have no intention of repeating their 1990s experiences with Washington-dominated institutions and would prefer to create their own than remain subordinated.[70]

Creating new informal clubs alongside established institutions also fragments global governance. The formation of emerging power clubs such as the India, Brazil, and South Africa (IBSA) Forum and the BRICS Forum is an example of fragmentation through the creation of informal clubs. In some cases, these new forums may spur reform of existing institutions, such as the G-20's directive to reform the IMF or IBSA's efforts to reform the Security Council. In other cases, they may represent obstacles by diverting political capital from

---

68 Daniel S. Hamilton, "America's Mega-regional Trade Diplomacy: Comparing TPP and TTIP," *International Spectator* 49, no. 1 (2014): 81–97.

69 Gregory T. Chin, "Asian Infrastructure Investment Bank: Governance Innovation and Prospects," *Global Governance* 22, no. 1 (2016): 11–26.

70 Chin and Thakur, "Will China Change the Rules of Global Order?" pp. 125–126; Kahler, "The Global Economic Multilaterals," p. 2.

more inclusive institutions, such as megaregional agreements that detract from the WTO's Doha Round. Fragmentation in the form of institutional layering is likely to provide states with increased forum shopping opportunities and to erode the universal character of global governance.

As a result of institutional fragmentation, the Western-led institutional order is no longer the only game in town. A new Eurasian forum for security cooperation has emerged (the Shanghai Cooperation Organisation); new clubs for collaboration between non-Western emerging powers have been established (BRICS and IBSA); and new banks complement and compete with older ones and with each other (the AIIB and NDB). Even interinstitutional competition to host informal gatherings to foster transnational elite exchanges has emerged, with the Boao Forum for Asia (explicitly modeled on the World Economic Forum) hosting annual gatherings of governmental, business, and academic elites since 2001. Naturally, it is based in China.

To the extent that these institutions hasten the emerging countries' rise and embody different priorities and ideas for how global governance should proceed, the plurality and complexity of global governance will be enhanced at the expense of its universality and coherence. In most cases, however, these instances of "contested multilateralism"[71] highlight not just the conflicting interests driving institutional change, but also that global governance is being used rather than opposed by emerging powers to pursue their goals.

4   Conclusion

The emergence of new powers with different multilateral preferences has diminished the tendency toward consolidation of a universal liberal global governance project and raised questions about the adaptability of existing institutions. A new introspection appears to have affected the exponents of liberal global governance; its further deepening can no longer be taken for granted. Instead, a new global governance is emerging: existing institutions face conflicts over positions of leadership and privilege and are more prone to deadlock, while the dimensions of global governance that externalize the liberal social purposes of established powers are facing increased challenges. In addition, informalization is playing a central role in adapting global governance to new circumstances of power and interest, and the creation of new institutions alongside others is contributing to the fragmentation of global

---

71   Julia C. Morse and Robert O. Keohane, "Contested Multilateralism," *Review of International Organizations* 9, no. 4 (2014): 385–412.

governance. Western-dominated global institutions are facing competition from new centers of power.

The risk for global governance is not that emerging powers will disengage from or seek to overthrow the existing order. It is more likely that the pursuit of competing multilateral projects with different social purposes and different leading states will fragment the institutional landscape and lead to new forms of geoeconomic-institutional rivalry. In this respect, the new global governance is likely to be more institutionally diverse and polycentric, with more signs of overt conflict compared to the recent past as emerging powers are able to afford to openly disagree with established powers. In any case, "problem solving" and "cooperation" cannot adequately describe the central dynamics of the new global governance—politics is back.

CHAPTER 24

Banning the Bomb: Inconsequential Posturing or Meaningful Stigmatization?

Kjølv Egeland[1]

On 7 July 2017, 122 states adopted a treaty declaring nuclear weapons illegal under international law: the UN Treaty on the Prohibition of Nuclear Weapons (NWPT). On 20 September, the treaty was formally opened for signature.[2] In contrast to the Nuclear Non-Proliferation Treaty (NPT) of 1968, which permits five major powers to possess and use nuclear weapons,[3] the new and more comprehensive prohibition enshrines the attitude that there are "no right hands for wrong weapons."[4] Given that none of the states that actually possess nuclear weapons are likely to sign the treaty anytime soon, some have dismissed the process as an exercise in inconsequential posturing by insignificant actors. But the adoption of the ban treaty is momentous. Not only does the prohibition constitute a plausible means of delegitimizing nuclear weapons and thus facilitating their eventual elimination, but the treaty has deep historical significance: the adoption of the ban signifies that most of the world's states are no longer prepared to accord certain states special entitlements under international law, at any rate not to possess nuclear weapons.[5]

---

* This chapter was originally published in Global Governance, Volume 24, Issue 1, 2018.

1 Kjølv Egeland is Marie Skłodowska-Curie Postdoctoral Fellow in Security Studies at Sciences Po, and focuses on the dynamics of multilateral disarmament diplomacy and international security. He has contributed commentary and research articles inter alia to the *Bulletin of the Atomic Scientists*, the *Nordic Journal of International Law*, *Peace Review*, *New Internationalist*, *European Leadership Network*, and several Norwegian dailies.

2 As of 23 September 2017, the treaty has been signed by fifty-three governments and ratified by three states.

3 The NPT does not explicitly give the nuclear weapons states a "right" to possess nuclear weapons. Rather, the NPT withdraws the non-nuclear weapons states' supposed "natural right" to develop nuclear weapons without doing the same for the states that had already exercised theirs.

4 Ban Ki-moon, "'There Are No Right Hands that Can Handle These Wrong Weapons,' Secretary-General Says of Mass Destruction Weapons, at 1540 Event, Urging Their Total Elimination," 22 April 2013, www.un.org/press/en/2013/sgsm14968.doc.htm, accessed 9 July 2017.

5 Compare Hedley Bull, *The Anarchical Society: A Study of Order in World Politics*, 2nd ed. (London: Macmillan, 1995).

The hierarchical nature of one of international society's last explicitly unequal legal regimes—the nonproliferation regime—is being powerfully contested.

1   Banning the Bomb

The mandate for the ban treaty negotiations was secured by the adoption of a resolution calling for the negotiation of a "legally binding instrument to prohibit nuclear weapons" at the UN General Assembly in December 2016. Reflecting widespread disillusionment among nonaligned states[6] with the cautious "step-by-step approach" to disarmament favored by the nuclear armed, the idea of negotiating a treaty unconditionally prohibiting nuclear weapons has been the main talking point in the multilateral forums concerned with nuclear nonproliferation and disarmament in recent years. Proponents of the idea of a ban argued that the vision of a world free of nuclear weapons has been undercut by the simple fact that politicians and defense experts in many states continue to see nuclear arms as legitimate and even prestigious instruments of statecraft.[7] The ban treaty, proponents hope, will stigmatize nuclear weapons as unacceptable weapons of mass destruction with no place in civilized international relations.[8] The ban treaty movement was orchestrated by the International Campaign to Abolish Nuclear Weapons (ICAN), the International Committee of the Red Cross (ICRC), and an evolving coalition of non-nuclear weapon states (Mexico, South Africa, Brazil, Nigeria, Austria, and Ireland being the original sponsors of the resolution to mandate negotiations in 2017). While ICAN and other civil society actors played a crucial role in placing the idea of a ban on the international community's agenda from 2012 onward, governments took greater ownership of the cause during the latter phase of the process.

The ban treaty is not intended as a substitute for careful negotiations on verifiable stockpile reductions or incremental changes to military postures; nobody expected the nuclear-armed states to join the ban treaty right away or even in the medium term. What proponents do hope, however, is that, over time,

---

6   In lower case, "nonaligned" refers to any state not formally allied to any of the established major powers, not just members of the (upper case) Non-Aligned Movement.

7   See, for example, Nick Ritchie, "Valuing and Devaluing Nuclear Weapons," *Contemporary Security Policy* 34, no. 1 (2013): 146–173.

8   International Campaign to Abolish Nuclear Weapons (ICAN), "Stigmatize, Ban and Eliminate: A Way Forward for Nuclear Disarmament," 1 October 2017, www.icanw.org/campaign-news/stigmatize-ban-and-eliminate-a-way-forward-for-nuclear-disarmament/, accessed 6 April 2017.

the ban treaty will nudge the nuclear-armed states to pursue disarmament—
unilaterally, bilaterally, or multilaterally—with greater intensity than before.
Thomas Doyle, who in a Global Forum essay in *Global Governance* argues
that banning nuclear weapons is "morally and politically responsible only if
undertaken in conjunction with other actions that address the security and
status dilemmas that have long motivated the NWS [nuclear weapons states]
and their allies to maintain a reliance on nuclear weapons,"[9] may take comfort from the fact that the ban treaty, in a nutshell, simply demands that the
nuclear-armed states pursue these other actions with much greater urgency
than they have over the past decades. More than seventy years after the United
Nation's first call for nuclear disarmament, and almost three decades after the
end of the Cold War, none of the states defined by the NPT as "nuclear-weapon
states" have moved "even nominally toward a policy of actual disarmament."[10]

Not surprisingly, the nuclear-armed states and most of their allies have vig-
orously opposed the ban treaty movement since its emergence in 2012. These
states have for decades resisted every initiative with the capacity of challenging the status quo and, by extension, their own dominance of the global
nuclear order. The Russian government, for example, postulated in 2016 that
the adoption of the ban treaty could be "catastrophic" and "thrust the world
into chaos and instability."[11] Around the same time, US undersecretary of
state Frank Rose referred to the proposed ban as a "pie in the sky," claiming
it could "harm disarmament efforts within the NPT framework"—not men-
tioning that not a single nuclear warhead has ever been dismantled through
the NPT framework.[12] On 27 March 2017, the day the ban treaty negotiations
opened at the UN headquarters in New York City, a group of government officials representing members and affiliates of NATO staged a curious protest
against the proposed treaty in the hallway outside the UN conference room
where the negotiations were to take place. Flanked by representatives of
Albania, Hungary, Romania, and a handful of other states, the UN ambassadors
of Britain, France, and the United States contended, somewhat confusingly,
that a treaty banning nuclear weapons would be both dangerously disruptive

---

9   Thomas Doyle, "A Moral Argument for the Mass Defection of Non-Nuclear-Weapon States
      from the Nuclear Nonproliferation Treaty Regime," *Global Governance* 23, no. 1 (2017):
      15–26, at 18.

10   Campbell Craig and Jan Ruzicka, "The Nonproliferation Complex," *Ethics and International
      Affairs* 27, no. 3 (2013): 329–348, at 341.

11   Kingston Reif, "UN Approves Start of Nuclear Ban Talks," Arms Control Association,
      November 2016, www.armscontrol.org/print/7815, accessed 6 April 2017.

12   Institutt for Forsvarsstudier, "Strategic Stability," 6 September 2017, https://www.forsvaret.
      no/ifs/us-perspectives-on-strategic-stability, accessed 5 July 2017.

and utterly insignificant. No NATO governments bar that of the Netherlands, which had been forced to attend by the Dutch parliament, sent delegations to the negotiations. The boycotting states asserted that the international security environment was not presently conducive to negotiate a global ban, contending that nuclear arms are not like other weapons.

From the perspective of most nonaligned states, however, these arguments rung hollow. Most of the states opposing the NWPT, after all, had for years argued that the core values underpinning the laws of war were universal. Most of these states had ratified the conventions against other indiscriminate weapons such as chemical and biological weapons and often branded holdouts from those treaties as moral laggards and "barbarians."[13]

The nuclear-armed states and their allies received considerable backing from several academics. Funding structures as well as the revolving door between Western governments and top think tanks has ensured that many members of the nuclear expert community take great care not to stray too far from the major powers' policy line. It is not that every nuclear policy wonk is bankrolled by Whitehall or wants a job in the US government, but nuclear weapons have, as Campbell Craig and Jan Ruzicka point out, given rise to a powerful "non-proliferation complex" that sets the tone in the debate. While those who buy in to the arms control paradigm promoted by the United States "enjoy funding, political support, and 'policy relevance'; those who deviate from it do not." Those ideas that "more squarely tackle the nuclear danger are crowded out."[14] Several members of the nonproliferation complex have accordingly spent the past few years arguing that a ban on nuclear weapons would be catastrophic for strategic stability, for disarmament efforts, and for the world.

In 2014, following a change of government in Oslo, the NATO-allied Norwegian government (which had hosted the first humanitarian impacts conference in 2013) cut its political and economic support for ICAN, the most vocal supporter of a prohibition treaty, just as the idea of a ban was starting to gain traction in the diplomatic community. Finances depleted, ICAN had to let most of its staff in Geneva go. The campaign for a ban, in other words, had a lot working against it. But the humanitarian case was compelling. In addition, the idea that no state should enjoy special entitlements—that sovereign states should bear the same rights and duties—resonated strongly with many

---

13   See, for example, "Susan Rice Speaks on Syria, Full Text," Politico, 9 September 2013, www
      .politico.com/story/2013/09/susan-rice-syria-full-speech-text-096484, accessed 8 July
      2017.
14   Craig and Ruzicka, "The Nonproliferation Complex," p. 341.

nonaligned states. The remaining ICAN campaigners' argument that nuclear weapons should be placed in the same category as chemical and biological weapons—that is, as fundamentally unacceptable weapons—accordingly found attentive audiences across the world. Increasingly, sympathetic governments joined the campaign by explicitly demanding the negotiation of a prohibition treaty. Eloquent diplomats, such as Jamaica's Shorna-Kay Richards and Costa Rica's Maritza Chan, provided persuasive interventions in New York and Geneva. On 10 December 2017, the Norwegian government faced the visual embarrassment in its capital of the glittering annual Nobel Peace Prize ceremony that recognizes a treaty it opposed and honors a nongovernmental organization (NGO) it defunded.

The use by nuclear-armed states and allies of hard-line tactics of opposition only seems to have strengthened the resolve of nonaligned governments to push ahead with the ban. In particular, the decision of the five states defined by the NPT as "nuclear-weapon states" to collectively boycott the first two ad hoc conferences on the humanitarian impact of nuclear weapons, convened by the Norwegian and Mexican governments in 2013 and 2014 respectively, appears to have been a serious tactical mistake on their part. By boycotting these conferences, the nuclear weapons states seemed to signal that they did not take seriously either the humanitarian consequences of nuclear weapons or the concerns of less powerful states.[15] As longtime student of nuclear politics Ramesh Thakur has pointed out, the claims of the nuclear-armed states and their apologists that a ban treaty would make nuclear war more likely, cause a cascade of proliferation, or deepen the rift between nuclear and non-nuclear states simply came across as disingenuous and self-serving.[16] The supporters of the ban treaty pointed out that the possession and use of nuclear weapons seems irreconcilable with the fundamental precepts of international humanitarian law; namely, the principles of noncombatant immunity, avoidance of unnecessary suffering and superfluous injury, and proportionality between the ends and means of war.[17] Almost any conceivable use of nuclear weap-

---

15   See Alexander Kmentt, "Development of the International Initiative on the Humanitarian Impact of Nuclear Weapons and Its Effect on the Nuclear Weapons Debate," *International Review of the Red Cross* 97, no. 899 (2015): 681–709.

16   Ramesh Thakur, "Don't Obstruct Efforts to Ban Nuclear Weapons," *Japan Times*, 29 March 2017, www.japantimes.co.jp/opinion/2017/03/29/commentary/japan-comment ary/dont-obstruct-efforts-ban-nuclear-weapons/#.WOYCbhhh1p8, accessed 6 April 2017. See also, for example, the Indonesian delegation's statement to the UN General Assembly First Committee on 21 October 2015, UN Doc. A/C.1/70/PV.11 (2016).

17   See Gro Nystuen, Stuart Casey-Maslen, and Annie G. Bersagel, eds., *Nuclear Weapons Under International Law* (Cambridge: Cambridge University Press, 2014).

ons would kill innumerable civilians and cause enormous harm to the natural environment. The consequences of nuclear war cannot be contained either in space or in time. Emergency services would have no adequate response. The use and possession of nuclear weapons, in short, is uncivilized and should be declared explicitly illegal.[18] Humanitarian principles and environmental protection arguments are powerfully affirmed in the preamble to the NWPT.

2   Standards of Civilization and the Universalization of the Laws of War

And here we come to the crux of the matter, the real reason for the nuclear-armed states and their allies' resistance to the ban: by declaring the possession, use, and threat of use of nuclear weapons contrary to international law, the international community has branded the practice of nuclear deterrence, a pillar of the nuclear-armed states' and the North Atlantic community's military postures, as morally unacceptable in civilized international society. Hitherto, legal standard setting has been largely a prerogative of major powers and, to the extent that the system of great powers was eurocentric, of the European major powers. It is noteworthy that of all the continents, the biggest concentration of opponents of the NWPT is in Europe. The periphery states (whether judged by material assets or by membership in the North Atlantic community) are asserting themselves as standard setters on an issue on which the very survival of humanity is at stake.

"Law," Erik Ringmar argues, "provides a standard by which political entities may be recognized as entities of a certain kind."[19] Emerging as an element of the European "standard of civilization" in the nineteenth century, the laws of war were meant, in part, to distinguish "civilized" Europe from the "uncivilized" rest of the world.[20] Membership in international society as a civilized state depended, in part, on a perceived capacity of adherence to the developing codes of international humanitarian law. When outsiders wished to join the European family of nations, they were held to the standard of civilization. Polities found to fall short were duly opened to the conquest, subjugation, and

---

18   This is not to say that the nuclear-armed states are in violation of the NWPT; since they have not signed the treaty, they cannot be held to its commands.

19   Erik Ringmar, "The Relevance of International Law: A Hegelian Interpretation of a Peculiar Seventeenth-century Preoccupation," *Review of International Studies* 21, no. 1 (1995): 87–103, at 87.

20   See Antony Anghie, *Imperialism, Sovereignty and the Making of International Law* (Cambridge: Cambridge University Press, 2013), p. 4.

"civilizing mission" of the Europeans.[21] The result, Andrew Linklater has argued, was a form of "collective humiliation" of many of the states that today form the nonaligned bloc at the UN.[22]

The distinction between "civilized" and "uncivilized" states lives on in contemporary international legal discourse. The Statute of the International Court of Justice—the closest thing that modern international law has to a constitution—identifies as sources of international law not just treaties and customs, but also the "general principles of law recognized by civilized nations" (Article 38). The discourse of civilization was expertly instrumentalized by Western leaders to justify sanctions and use of force against the states of the "axis of evil" in the first years of the new millennium (initially Iraq, Iran, and North Korea, later expanded to also include Cuba, Libya, and Syria). But the discourse of civilization has also been instrumentalized for pacific purposes: when NGOs and liberal do-gooder states such as Belgium, Canada, and Norway promoted conventions against cluster munitions and landmines in the 1990s and 2000s, they were broadcasting the following message: sign or be recognized as an uncivilized militarist without concern for civilian lives and suffering!

The campaign for a ban on nuclear weapons was deliberately built on a similar rhetorical platform to those to ban landmines and cluster munitions. The very idea of the ban, as put by the Austrian government in its "Humanitarian Pledge," is to accelerate the elimination of nuclear weapons through stigmatization.[23] As in the cases of the landmine and cluster munition campaigns, the weapon in question was presented as a danger to human security just as much as national security.[24] Like the Ottawa landmine treaty and the Oslo Convention on Cluster Munitions, the NWPT resembles an instrument of humanitarian law more than a traditional arms control agreement in that its main purpose is to promote a normative shift, not regulate a specific process.[25] As in previous humanitarian disarmament campaigns, the

---

21   See Erik Ringmar, "Recognition and the Origins of International Society," *Global Discourse* 4, no. 4 (2014): 446–458.

22   Andrew Linklater, "The 'Standard of Civilisation' in World Politics," *Human Figurations* 5, no. 2, July 2016, https://quod.lib.umich.edu/h/humfig/11217607.0005.205?view=text;rgn= main, accessed 15 November 2017.

23   Austria, "Humanitarian Pledge," delivered at the Third Conference on the Humanitarian Impact of Nuclear Weapons, Vienna, 9 December 2014.

24   See Denise Garcia, *Disarmament Diplomacy and Human Security: Regimes, Norms, and Moral Progress in International Relations* (London: Routledge, 2011).

25   See Ramesh Thakur and William Maley, "The Ottawa Convention on Landmines: A Landmark Humanitarian Treaty in Arms Control," *Global Governance* 5, no. 3 (1999): 273–302.

NWPT process was encouraged and aided by a transnational advocacy network of NGOs, parliamentarians, mayors, labor unions, religious institutions, and scholars.[26] And also as in previous humanitarian disarmament campaigns, the ban movement saw close cooperation between like-minded governments and civil society actors. The NWPT recognizes the crucial role of civil society by declaring that the ICRC, the International Federation of Red Cross and Red Crescent Societies, and "relevant non-governmental organizations" will be invited to attend meetings of states parties (Article 8(5)).

The only significant difference between the ban treaty campaign and previous humanitarian disarmament campaigns is that the ban treaty movement draws the bulk of its support from nonaligned states. The vast majority of these states, in turn, are located in the Global South. While the majority of the ban treaty's supporters may be found in Latin America, Africa, and Asia Pacific, most European and North Atlantic states oppose it (Austria, Ireland, Lichtenstein, and New Zealand being notable exceptions).[27] Somewhat simplified, the ban treaty represents an effort by the states formerly classified as "uncivilized" at turning the norms of humanitarian law against its creators.

Non-European states have been active participants in the development of international humanitarian law and disarmament agreements in the past. The Treaty of Tlatelolco, which denuclearized the entire Latin American continent, was negotiated and adopted before the NPT, the latter coming into being one year later. States such as Mexico, Nigeria, and Indonesia can point to long records of deep engagement in multilateral diplomacy, including nuclear disarmament advocacy. When the NPT was negotiated in the 1960s, Mexico in particular played an instrumental role in transforming the proposed treaty from a limited agreement that would simply prohibit non-nuclear weapon states from acquiring nuclear arms into a more encompassing bargain that would also formally commit the nuclear weapons states to negotiate toward disarmament.[28] Mexico was arguably also the international community's strongest and most persistent proponent of a Comprehensive Nuclear Test-Ban Treaty, spending significant diplomatic capital over several decades on the struggle to end nuclear testing. Even norms that are widely considered "Western" or "Northern" have in reality been supported, or even spearheaded,

---

26   See Margaret Keck and Kathryn Sikkink, "Transnational Advocacy Networks in International and Regional Politics," *International Social Science Journal* 51, no. 159 (1999): 89–101.

27   Sweden and Switzerland have been more cautious in their support for the prohibition treaty. The last formally neutral country in Europe, Finland, opposed it.

28   See Mohammed I. Shaker, *The Nuclear Non-Proliferation Treaty: Origin and Implementation, 1959–1979* (London: Oceana, 1980).

by states of the Global South.[29] International human rights law, for example, was staunchly promoted by Latin American states.[30] South Africa and the Philippines were key members of the core group of states that led the push for a ban on cluster munitions.[31] China, India, Brazil, and South Africa have been central to the shaping of the international climate regime.[32]

Yet the nuclear ban treaty movement does mark the first time an instrument of international humanitarian law has been forced into existence against the fierce opposition of the major powers and the majority of European states. The big European powers may not have been at the forefront of all initiatives aimed at deepening humanitarian or disarmament law, but never has a contribution to the laws of war been adopted with such opposition. States such as Britain, France, Germany, Japan, and Italy have signed all multilateral disarmament treaties in existence plus all the Geneva Conventions and their two additional protocols. Now, they find themselves having to explain why they cannot support a treaty declaring nuclear weapons—a technology developed to level whole cities and vaporize civilians—taboo as well.

Conventional theories of international relations conceptualize institutions as expressions of the interests of major powers. While realists and Marxists view institutions and law as a moralistic guise or superstructure overlaying the most powerful players' true Machiavellian interests, neoliberals are prepared to offer institutions at least some causal power of their own (institutions may, e.g., affect actors' preferences by reducing transaction costs). Constructivists, for their part, view institutions not only as expressions of their creators' interests, but also of their identities. Common to most approaches to international relations, however, is their assumption that institution building is the domain of major powers. This assumption reflects the simple fact that the major powers, in most cases, have the greatest capacity to solve the cooperation problem in question (they are "critical states"[33]). But the assumption that institution building is for the great powers often also rests on a normative expectation that,

---

29   See the special section, "Principles from the Periphery: The Neglected Southern Sources of Global Norms," *Global Governance* 30, no. 3 (2014): 359–417.

30   Kathryn Sikkink, "Latin American Countries as Norm Protagonists of the Idea of International Human Rights," *Global Governance* 20, no. 3 (2014): 389–404.

31   See John Borrie, *Unacceptable Harm: A History of How the Treaty to Ban Cluster Munitions Was Won* (Geneva: UN Institute for Disarmament Research, 2009).

32   Kilaparti Ramakrishna, "The UNFCCC—History and Evolution of the Climate Change Negotiations," in Luis Gómez-Echeverri, ed., *Climate Change and Development* (New Haven: Yale University, 2000), pp. 47–62.

33   Martha Finnemore and Kathryn Sikkink, "International Norm Dynamics and Political Change," *International Organization* 52, no. 4 (1998): 887–917.

with great power, comes great responsibility. Hedley Bull, for example, believed the great powers bear "managerial responsibilities" for international society.[34]

The theory that institutions are children of major powers has significant empirical backing. Over the past two centuries, a relatively small group of (mostly Western) major powers have spun a vast web of rules and institutions governing the use of force between states, diplomatic and cultural relations, global trade, and environmental protection. The project of creating a liberal world order, first conceived by British statesmen during the nineteenth century, accelerated under American post-World War II hegemony. The United States has been directly involved in creating most of the international institutions that have sprung into being over the past seven decades. In the rare cases where the United States has declined to take leadership, leading powers of the old world have been quick to fill the vacuum. The United Kingdom's leadership of the process that culminated with the adoption of the Arms Trade Treaty in 2013 is a case in point.

But no major powers supported the nuclear ban process. All five permanent members of the UN Security Council plus India, Germany, and Japan opposed the ban with varying degrees of vigor. The closest the ban treaty came to a major power supporter was Brazil—a country that ranks eighth on the list of the world's largest economies. South Africa, Nigeria, and Indonesia are also important regional powers, but hardly register among the most influential actors on the global stage. The ban treaty, in other words, was secured by the many small (and nonaligned) against the wishes of the few and powerful (and nuclear dependent).

The nuclear ban treaty is not the first legal instrument championed by small- and medium-sized states. The campaigns for the establishment of the International Criminal Court and for the conventions on landmines and cluster munitions are often pointed to as paradigmatic examples of "new diplomacy"—coalitions of small states and civil society actors leveraging moral suasion to induce change.[35] But all three campaigns were supported by at least some of the major powers and were not actively opposed like the nuclear ban. Britain, Germany, Japan, and France all signed the conventions on landmines and cluster munitions at the earliest possible date. France also signed the Statute of the International Criminal Court on the very day that treaty was opened for signature.

---

34   Bull, *The Anarchical Society*, p. 196.

35   Andrew F. Cooper, John English, and Ramesh Thakur, eds., *Enhancing Global Governance: Towards a New Diplomacy?* (Tokyo: United Nations University Press, 2002).

A process that resembles the ban treaty movement in that it was promoted by relatively disempowered states against the opposition of international society's most powerful actors was the campaign by a group of developing countries launched in 1974 for a New International Economic Order (NIEO). But in contrast to the movement for a NIEO, which was aimed broadly at changing the relation between the Global South and North, the ban initiative has been singularly aimed at introducing a specific piece of international legislation. The ban treaty declares as illegal what is arguably one of the major powers' defining characteristics: the possession of nuclear weapons. The supporters of the ban are aiming to replace the NPT's distinction between nuclear haves and have-nots with a distinction between nuclear civilizers and barbarians.

It remains to be seen whether the ban treaty will have a noticeable impact on efforts to reduce and eliminate nuclear dangers. It is certainly possible that the ban treaty will have less of an impact than its supporters hope. But the changing legal landscape is at any rate significant. It signals that states such as France and Britain no longer enjoy what Bull identified as a central component of status as a great power: "Great powers are powers *recognized by others* to have ... special rights and duties."[36] The major powers' once special "right" to possess nuclear weapons, codified by the 1968 Nuclear Non-Proliferation Treaty, has been withdrawn by the international community.

---

36   Bull, *The Anarchical Society*, p. 196 (emphasis added).

CHAPTER 25

Dispensing with the Indispensable Nation?

Multilateralism Minus One in the Trump Era

Caroline Fehl and Johannes Thimm[1]

1 Introduction

US president Donald Trump has repeatedly characterized his approach to the world as "America first." What this means for the multilateral global order was already apparent in his nomination speech at the Republican National Convention in July 2016: "Americanism, not globalism, will be our credo. As long as we are led by politicians who will not put America first, then we can be assured that other nations will not treat America with the respect that we deserve."[2] In his 2017 and 2018 speeches at the UN General Assembly, he vowed to "defend America's interests above all else"[3] and "choose independence and cooperation over global governance, control, and domination."[4] His repeated warnings that the United States would "no longer be taken advantage of"[5] illustrate that Trump perceives international politics in narrow "transactional" terms,[6] governed by a zero-sum logic. One country's gain comes at the loss of another country, with few possibilities of mutual benefit. This sentiment runs counter to the logic of multilateral institutions, which are intended to foster cooperation by providing benefits to all participants.

Two years into Trump's presidency, it is evident that he has sought to put his rhetoric into practice by reversing key multilateral achievements of his predecessors. Under Trump, the United States has withdrawn from climate and trade agreements, multilateral arms control initiatives and UN bodies such as the Human Rights Council and the UN Educational, Scientific and Cultural

---

* This chapter was originally published in Global Governance, Volume 25, No. 1, 2019.
1 Caroline Fehl is Senior Research Fellow at the Peace Research Institute Frankfurt. Johannes Thimm is Deputy Head of Research Division "The Americas" at Stiftung Wissenschaft und Politik, German Institute for International and Security Affairs.
2 Bump and Blake 2016.
3 White House 2017.
4 White House 2018.
5 White House 2017; see also the near-identical formulation in White House 2018.
6 Zenko and Lissner 2018.

Organization (UNESCO); it has cut down funding for UN peacekeeping and UN agencies dealing with Palestinian refugees, population control, and global warming; and it has threatened key multilateral organizations including the North Atlantic Treaty Organization (NATO), the World Trade Organization (WTO), and the International Criminal Court (ICC). During his first year in office, Trump made foreign policy headlines with declarations of intent, but did not always follow up on his unilateral statements with actual policies. However, since John Bolton was appointed as national security adviser, the pace of treaty withdrawals has picked up and the unilateral direction of the administration is no longer in doubt. For the rest of the world, this has posed increasingly difficult problems.[7] US hegemony and support for multilateral institutions used to be a cornerstone of the international order. As the most influential country retreats from or even undermines global institutions, other governments that have an interest in maintaining and advancing the multilateral agenda have been facing hard questions: What, if anything, can and should be done to accommodate Washington's concerns and keep it engaged in multilateral fora? Failing a compromise, how effective are global institutions without US participation? What are the political costs of cooperating without or even against the United States? Who can fill the leadership vacuum left by the United States?

In this article, we analyze the prospects and limitations of advancing global governance in the Trump era through a "multilateralism minus one."[8] To assess the effectiveness and political feasibility of this approach, we compare the present situation to earlier periods of US opposition to multilateral cooperation. Despite Trump's unusual presidency, US governments questioning multilateral institutions are nothing new—and neither are doubts about the United States' ability to exert effective leadership in the face of global power shifts. International relations (IR) scholars have debated the possibility of "nonhegemonic cooperation" since the 1980s. This literature provides some clues about the circumstances under which a multilateralism minus one can be successful.

In Section 2, we therefore review earlier research on nonhegemonic cooperation, situating the scholarly debate in the historical context of repeated ups and downs in the US commitment to the multilateral order. Rather than subjecting the propositions in this literature to a new test, we use its findings to derive key factors that have helped or hindered nonhegemonic cooperation

---

7 Jentleson 2017; Lake 2018; Stokes 2018.

8 The term is adopted from Krause 2004, 43–59, especially 53. We understand it as referring to the attempt to build new multilateral institutions or to maintain the functionality of existing ones without the participation or leadership of the United States.

in past instances. In Section 3, we use these factors as analytical guidance in evaluating both the political feasibility and the likely effectiveness of ongoing and potential nonhegemonic cooperation initiatives in the Trump era, compared to earlier historical periods. We focus on three key issue areas of global governance where the Trump administration's challenge to multilateral frameworks has been particularly critical: arms control, climate change, and trade.

Our analysis suggests that, despite some variation across policy areas, the prospects for "cooperating without America"[9] have generally improved. New actors such as emerging powers from the BRICS club and China in particular,[10] as well as nongovernmental organizations (NGOs), have acquired stakes and influence in multilateral negotiations. At the same time, many countries are turning to minilateral, informal, and ad hoc arrangements, which are increasingly replacing universal, formal, legally binding commitments. Both developments are heightening flexibility among participants and enabling new constellations of like-minded actors to cooperate on global issues. And yet, the task of managing the resulting fragmentation of the global order and the fluidity of new coalitions are increasing the demands on political leadership, suggesting that nonhegemonic cooperation will be neither easy to orchestrate nor necessarily successful.

2   IR Theory and the Question of Nonhegemonic Cooperation

2.1   *The Debate in Historical Context*
The US relationship with the global multilateral order has long been ambivalent.[11] After World War II, the United States took the leadership in setting up the institutional pillars of the present multilateral order: the United Nations, the Bretton Woods regime, the General Agreement on Tariffs and Trade, the Nuclear Non-Proliferation Treaty (NPT), and (within its sphere of influence) NATO.[12] Following this phase of hegemonic institution building, global power shifts and repeated phases of US disengagement cast doubt on the United States' willingness and ability to exert multilateral leadership—and prompted IR scholars to discuss under what conditions states might cooperate in the absence of an order-creating hegemon.

Reflecting the postwar experience, scholarly thinking was initially dominated by "hegemonic stability theory," which attributed the creation and

---

9   Brem and Stiles 2009.
10   The BRICS include Brazil, Russia, India, China, and South Africa.
11   Luck 1999.
12   Patrick 2009.

maintenance of a liberal (economic) order to US hegemony.[13] This changed when, in the 1970s, contemporaries began to observe signs of US economic decline while postwar economic regimes remained relatively stable. IR scholars now argued that institutionalized cooperation could outlast the decline of a hegemon, and that coalitions of middle powers might even create new institutions.[14] In this period, arguably the greatest disruption of the postwar multilateral system came in the field of monetary governance with President Richard Nixon's 1971 decision to give up on the US dollar's convertibility to gold. The decision was taken after the US role of guaranteeing the Bretton Woods system of fixed exchange rates came increasingly under strain due to falling US shares of global economic output and growing US budget and balance of payments deficits.[15]

It thus was the perceived US weakness in the 1970s, rather than the unilateralist turn of US foreign policy that would follow under President Ronald Reagan in the 1980s, which triggered the first IR discussion of nonhegemonic cooperation. Reagan engaged in unilateral interventions, questioned multilateral arms control, withheld US dues to the UN, and withdrew from UNESCO.[16] Yet he also accepted new multilateral commitments such as the UN Convention against Torture.

The early debate about nonhegemonic cooperation ended with the United States' economic and military resurgence late in the Cold War, which exposed the "myth of lost hegemony"[17] and led to the proclamation of a "unipolar moment" after the Cold War had ended.[18] Both President George H.W. Bush and his successor Bill Clinton used the new US preponderance to reinvigorate the United States' commitment to existing multilateral institutions and to contribute to a new wave of institution building that produced, inter alia, the UN Framework Convention on Climate Change (UNFCCC) and the WTO. This new multilateral turn led IR scholars to draw comparisons between US hegemony in the postwar and post-Cold War periods.[19] The analogy turned out to be short-lived, however.

---

13   Kindleberger 1976.

14   Keohane [1984] 2005; Snidal 1985.

15   As Keohane notes, however, despite the disintegration of explicit regime rules there was a "continuity in regime principles" that testified to the potential for continued cooperation in the face of hegemonic decline, see Keohane [1984] 2005, 187.

16   Johansen 1986.

17   Strange 1987.

18   Krauthammer 1990.

19   Ikenberry 2001.

Under pressure from bureaucratic infighting and a unilateralist Congress, the Clinton administration became reluctant to enter ambitious new agreements, most notably the ICC and the Ottawa Convention on antipersonnel landmines.[20] When both treaties were concluded over US objections, observers heralded the beginning of a "non-hegemonic diplomacy."[21] The successive embrace of aggressive unilateralism under George W. Bush intensified the debate. Agreements such as the Kyoto Protocol continued without US support whereas others, such as the proposed verification protocol to the Biological Weapons Convention, were dropped in the face of US opposition. These developments prompted fresh analyses of the conditions under which nonhegemonic cooperation is feasible and effective.[22] Thus, the second IR debate about nonhegemonic cooperation evolved against the background of a unilateral United States that appeared to be bursting in strength rather than declining.

President Barack Obama reembraced multilateralism, although strong domestic opposition denied him some achievements. He led his country into the Paris Agreement on climate change, but at the price of making the latter less binding. While his administration cooperated with the ICC, the prospect of the United States formally joining the court remained as elusive as Obama's aim of ratifying the Comprehensive Nuclear-Test-Ban Treaty (CTBT). He concluded the bilateral New Strategic Arms Reduction Treaty (New START) with Russia, but could only persuade Congress to ratify it by promising a modernization of US nuclear weapons that deepened divisions within the multilateral arms control regime.

Despite these limitations, most observers during Obama's presidency saw the greater challenge to the multilateral order in a new global power shift, which became particularly visible in the global financial crisis. Echoing the 1980s debate, scholars now pondered whether and in what shape US- and Western-built institutions would survive the rise of China and other new powers.[23] Mounting reform pressure on the International Monetary Fund and the World Bank and deadlock at the WTO, as well as rising powers' initiatives to set up new institutions, such as the BRICS Development Bank and the Asian Infrastructure Investment Bank (AIIB), all indicated challenges to established, Western-dominated multilateral institutions.[24]

---

20   Thimm 2016,51–97, 143–183.
21   Cooper 2002, 1–18, especially 1.
22   Bower 2017; Brem and Stiles 2009; Cooper 2002; Fehl 2012.
23   Ikenberry 2011.
24   Stephen 2017.

2.2   *Lessons Learned*

President Trump has inherited these challenges to US and Western dominance. At the same time, he and key figures in his administration do not share
President Obama's instinct to compensate for the loss of US power by locking
US policy preferences into multilateral rules. Thus, for the first time in postwar history, US unilateralism coincides with declining US power, making both
the first and the second debate about nonhegemonic cooperation relevant to
the present situation. Contributions to both debates highlight a range of factors that make cooperation without the United States effective and politically
achievable. These factors can be used as points of reference to assess the prospects and limitations of this approach in the Trump era.

The first group of factors, highlighted in the more recent debate about US
unilateralism and nonhegemonic cooperation, concerns current and future
US policies and their likely impact. To judge the effectiveness of a multilateralism minus one approach in a given policy area, other governments must take
into account the relevance of the United States to the specific problem at stake
and to its multilateral solution and weigh the cost of losing US support—as
well as any cost that the United States could impose on them to block their
initiatives—against the potential alternative: Is it feasible to accommodate US
objections to keep it on board, what would be the *cost of such a compromise*,
and would it be honored by the US government?[25] In addition, they must consider the likelihood of future US administrations reversing current US policies.

A second group of variables central to both debates about nonhegemonic
cooperation concerns potential *alternative leaders*. Are other key players in the
policy area interested in preserving or advancing existing multilateral institutions, or do they prefer unilateral action or alternative institutions that could
challenge or undermine existing fora?[26] Are they willing to challenge US hegemonic leadership? And if so, are they able to form a coalition that is large and
stable enough to fill the leadership vacuum left by the former hegemon?[27]

A third cluster of factors, highlighted particularly in the second debate,
concerns the role of *private actors* in facilitating or obstructing nonhegemonic
cooperation. In the 1990s and 2000s, transnational civil society organizations
successfully pushed for the new nonhegemonic diplomacy. Domestic industry
representatives, worried about their competitiveness, opposed many multilateral commitments without US participation.[28]

---

25   Stiles 2009; Fehl 2012, 3–27.
26   Morse and Keohane 2014.
27   Snidal 1985; Brem 2009; Vabulas and Snidal 2014.
28   Cooper 2002; Anderson 2000.

In the next section, we apply these theoretical insights to understand the challenge of nonhegemonic cooperation in the evolving Trump era, and to compare the effectiveness and political feasibility of a multilateralism minus one across policy areas and historical experiences. We use the above list of factors as a heuristic tool for our analysis, yet remain open to identifying additional relevant factors that have not featured prominently in past discussions of nonhegemonic cooperation.

3   Nonhegemonic Cooperation in the Trump Era

3.1   *Nuclear Arms Control*
As both the most powerful nuclear-weapon state and a historical leader on nonproliferation and disarmament, the United States has been pivotal to the nuclear arms control regime. The regime's core treaty, the NPT, restricts the possession of nuclear weapons to five official nuclear weapon states, while also committing them to pursuing "negotiations in good faith" on their eventual disarmament (Article VI). President Obama initially declared his support for nuclear disarmament, but agreed to the modernization of US nuclear weapons in exchange for Senate ratification of the New START treaty. Progress therefore was already limited; nonetheless, Trump has begun to undermine even Obama's hard-won successes.

3.1.1   US Policy and Impact
In October 2018, the Trump administration announced that it would withdraw from the bilateral Intermediate-Range Nuclear Forces (INF) Treaty, which prohibits the United States and Russia from developing and deploying ground-launched midrange nuclear (and conventional) missiles. While the US intelligence community has long accused Russia of violating the treaty, Trump's plans to abandon it and develop new midrange missiles risk triggering a new nuclear arms race. The administration has also turned down Russian offers to renew New START, which limits the number of US and Russian deployed strategic nuclear weapons, after its expiry in 2021.[29] Both steps could soon leave the world's largest nuclear arsenals without any legal constraints. The 2018 Nuclear Posture Review (NPR) further aggravates the situation by upgrading the role of nuclear weapons in US strategy and envisaging new "low-yield options."[30] All of these policies not only will endanger bilateral strategic stability, but also will

29   Reif 2018.
30   Mount 2018.

further weaken the NPT's crumbling disarmament pillar. Ultimately, this will also undermine the treaty's nonproliferation pillar, which is politically tied to disarmament in a "grand bargain."

More immediately, global nonproliferation efforts have been set back by Trump's attempts to undo the Joint Comprehensive Plan of Action (JCPOA), a seven-party agreement designed to prevent Iran from developing nuclear weapons. After announcing the US withdrawal from the pact in May 2018, Trump not only has reinstated previous US sanctions on Iran, but also has threatened aggressive secondary sanctions against foreign companies doing business with Iran.[31] Should this pressure push Iran to revive its nuclear program or take hostile counteractions, a new regional arms race or even a US-Iranian war could follow.[32]

3.1.2   Feasibility and Cost of Compromise

While the cost of losing US support for nuclear arms controls is consequently high, there are few indications that Trump is—or would have been—open to compromises on any of the disputed issues. With regard to Iran, his declared aim of obtaining a "better deal" is neither realistic nor earnest. The maximalist demands raised by his administration are unacceptable not just to Iranian hard-liners.[33] Even European efforts to increase pressure on Iran and negotiate possible side agreements to the JCPOA could not sway the president—although State Department diplomats were close to agreeing on a strategy with their European counterparts.[34]

On the greater cause of preventing the next nuclear arms race, much depends on the United States' rivals China and Russia. But if New START is any indication, Trump is less interested in substantive proposals for compromise than in broader great-power relations.

Despite Trump's extreme attitude, obstacles to effective arms control go beyond his administration. Congress has been a driving force behind plans for new missiles and the INF crisis,[35] and Trump's confrontational Iran policy has solid support among congressional Republicans (and some Democrats). Given this state of affairs, it seems unlikely that a future administration will champion nuclear disarmament and arms control beyond the status quo before Trump. Unlike in other policy areas, arms control advocates cannot

31   Geranmayeh 2018.
32   On a possible US attack on Iran, see Cirincione 2018.
33   Kahl 2017.
34   Borger 2018.
35   Stowe-Thurston 2018.

hope that any ambitious new initiatives will be embraced by the United States in the not-too-distant future.

3.1.3   Private Actors
This does not bode well for the Treaty on the Prohibition of Nuclear Weapons that was concluded in 2017 at the United Nations. While NGOs generally play a lesser role in nuclear arms control than in other policy fields, the initiative for the ban treaty goes back to civil society activists frustrated about the lack of progress on nuclear disarmament in the NPT framework. Inspired by the success of the antipersonnel landmines ban, NGOs coalesced with like-minded states to push for the negotiation of a new disarmament treaty outside of established fora, preventing nuclear powers from exercising a veto. The idea, which won the 2017 Nobel peace prize for the NGO campaign, is to shame nuclear powers into action. In the landmines case, this "new diplomacy" was successful in setting a moral standard that even states who refused to join have followed: with the exception of the Korean peninsula, the United States has complied with the treaty's prohibition of mines even as a non-member of the mine ban treaty. However, it is improbable that this success can be repeated with strategically more important (nuclear) weapons. Even modest moves toward disarmament are unlikely as long as the ban treaty lacks support from the most influential states.

3.1.4   Alternative Leaders
Prospects for nonhegemonic cooperation vary across the different issues discussed above. Other countries are only bystanders to the US-Russian New START and INF discussions. The nuclear weapons ban is opposed by all (official and unofficial) nuclear powers; Europe has been deeply split about this new treaty, with small countries like Austria leading the pro-ban coalition and NATO members opposing it. Yet the policy of ignoring the prohibition agreement altogether—all NATO members except the Netherlands abstained from the negotiations—risks making future efforts to prevent nuclear proliferation more difficult. At the least, Europeans should acknowledge the legitimacy of the effort and engage with its supporters to prevent the rift in the nuclear arms control regime from getting wider.

   Prospects for nonhegemonic leadership are best regarding the JCPOA. The European Union (EU) in particular has been working hard to save the deal, which it perceives as its most important diplomatic success to date. The regional bloc not only revived its older Blocking Statute to counter potential US sanctions on European companies, but it also is taking the unprecedented step of directly undercutting US sanctions by setting up a Special Purpose

Vehicle (SPV), designed to enable continued Iranian exports. While it remains unclear at the time of this writing what goods the SPV will cover and who will have access to it, it is unlikely to substantially soften the blow of US sanctions on Iran's economy.[36] Still, the European initiative sends an important political signal that Europe is willing to spend political capital on rescuing the JCPOA.[37] This signal could help Iran's moderates to defend the deal against hard-liners perhaps long enough for a more conciliatory US president to win office.

3.2   *Climate Change*

On climate policy, tensions between the United States and multilateral regimes long preceded Trump. At first sight, Trump's announcement on 1 June 2017 to pull out of the Paris Agreement on climate change mirrors George W. Bush's decision to withdraw from the Kyoto Protocol to the UNFCCC sixteen years earlier. As in 2001, the US withdrawal threatens the regime's effectiveness and raises the issue of how to advance efforts to fight global warming without US participation and leadership. And yet on close examination, the differences between the two episodes are more instructive than the similarities.[38]

3.2.1   US Policy and Impact

In 2001, the United States was the world's largest emitter of greenhouse gases, accounting for 39 percent of global emissions. By 2013, it had been surpassed by China, which now accounted for 26 percent of global emissions (with the United States ranking second at 14 percent).[39] The fact that China has no commitments under the Kyoto Protocol, but is a key participant in the Paris Agreement, makes clear that the US contribution to the problem of climate change is relatively less significant today. Many state-level and local emissions reduction initiatives in the United States are continuing even without federal support. The US withdrawal from the global regime is still painful, but not as detrimental as it was in 2001.[40]

Despite the shrinking US share of global emissions, its nonparticipation could endanger the effectiveness of the Paris Agreement by weakening others' implementation of the agreement. This risk relates to a broader global trend toward softer multilateral governance, which has also affected climate

---

36   Geranmayeh and Batmanghelidj 2018.

37   Irish and Emmott 2018.

38   Pickering et al. 2018.

39   World Resources Institute 2014.

40   Urpelainen and Van de Graaf 2018 argue that US emissions are likely to decline in spite of Trump's lenient climate policies.

negotiations.[41] While both Kyoto and Paris are legally binding treaties, targets, time tables, and measures are voluntary under the Paris approach, in contrast to Kyoto's binding regime of commitments enforced by sanctions. This softening up of the climate regime helped to bring the United States on board—but it also means that to develop a "compliance pull" comparable to that of hard international law, the Paris Agreement must rely on "naming and shaming" and on financial incentives.[42] For both mechanisms US participation would have been a major advantage. In the Pledge and Review Process through which voluntary commitments are monitored under the Paris Agreement, the United States could have led by example in setting a high standard of implementation, increasing the moral pressure on others.[43] Washington also would have paid for about one-third of the $10 billion Green Climate Fund (GCF) until 2020, and would have contributed even more to the $100 billion per year that developed countries have vowed to mobilize to help developing countries reduce emissions and adjust to climate change.[44]

3.2.2   Feasibility and Cost of Compromise
In light of the nonbinding nature of the Paris Agreement, Trump's repeated offers to renegotiate its terms appear as empty rhetoric. Although the accord does not allow states to unilaterally weaken their nationally determined contributions (NDCs), noncompliance remains unsanctioned, which implies that changes in the Paris deal would not benefit the United States in substance. Symbolic concessions could help if the Trump administration actually *wanted* to remain inside Paris, but this seems doubtful.[45]

However, there are reasons to hope that the United States may reverse its decision to shun the Paris Agreement even without further compromises at this stage—under a new president. In 2001, a key reason for Kyoto supporters to move ahead was the hope that a future US administration would reengage in global climate negotiations. With President Obama taking the leadership on the Paris Agreement, their calculus paid off. Today's domestic opposition to Trump's climate policy—business leaders, Democrats, states, and cities—is even more vocal than back then, providing even more grounds for optimism regarding a future US policy shift.

---

41   Vabulas and Snidal 2013.
42   Bodansky 2015, 155–165, especially 161.
43   Victor 2017.
44   Urpelainen and Van de Graaf 2018 see the loss of the US contribution to climate finance as the most problematic consequence of the US withdrawal.
45   Wirth 2017.

3.2.3   Alternative Leaders

In 2001, there was a real danger that other major emitters would follow the US decision to leave Kyoto in a "domino effect." To save the protocol, European diplomats had to engage in extensive shuttle diplomacy.[46] In contrast, the global reaction to the Paris withdrawal was much prompter and more unanimous. Again, European governments took the lead in declaring that Paris was "irreversible,"[47] but other key players also quickly signaled their determination to stick with the agreement. Media attention has focused on China's forceful reaffirmation of its commitment to the climate regime, but the continued support of Brazil, India, and South Africa is equally important. Since 2009, these emerging economies have formed an alliance with China, the so-called BASIC bloc, which has become increasingly influential in UN climate negotiations.[48] This established coalition could facilitate the task of building a new nonhegemonic leadership group. Already, the EU, Canada, and China have convened a new Ministerial on Climate Action attended by thirty-four governments to replace the US-led Major Economies Forum—an informal grouping that had played a key role in preparing the Paris Agreement.[49]

The striking difference in reactions to the 2001 and 2017 US withdrawals is partly explained by the more advanced institutional stage of today's climate regime. The Paris Agreement has been in force since November 2016 and, at the earliest, allows parties to exit the treaty four years after that date—a procedure that even the Trump administration has vowed to respect. The Kyoto Protocol had not reached that stage when George W. Bush withdrew in 2001.

More importantly, unlike in 2001, the EU and other key players such as China have a vested interest in battling climate change and advancing green energy. In addition, emerging economies are eager to preserve the climate finance system established as part of the Paris Agreement, from which they stand to benefit as major recipients.[50]

And yet all of these key players will need to do more to make Paris not only lasting, but also effective. A key question is whether they will be able to lead by example under the Pledge and Review Process. Currently, neither the EU nor BASIC members are on track to meet their Paris commitments. The one exception is India, which has made strides toward its renewable energy goals.[51] However, sustaining progress in the developing world will hinge on developed

---

46   Vogler and Bretherton 2006.
47   Stefanini and Oroschakoff 2017.
48   Hochstetler and Milkoreit 2015.
49   Chemnick 2018.
50   Seetharaman 2017.
51   Erickson 2018.

nations keeping their financial promises—including by shouldering the financial commitments shed by Washington. At the time of writing, it was still uncertain whether the rest of the developed world will collectively step up to this task. After Trump's withdrawal, Germany's environment minister declared that "no country that refuses joint international solidarity can expect that others just step in to fill the gap."[52] Yet filling the gap is exactly the kind of leadership that would be required to overcome conflicts over climate finance, which have proved a major stumbling block at the 2018 Bonn and Bangkok climate meetings.[53] While Germany itself recently announced its intention to increase its contribution to the GCF, others such as Australia have followed Trump's lead in ruling out any further donations.[54]

3.2.4   Private Actors

A bolder approach by European and other Paris supporters would also unlikely receive the same kind of private sector opposition that Europeans faced in 2001. After George W. Bush's Kyoto withdrawal, energy lobbyists (and policymakers) in Europe and elsewhere feared that their adherence to the climate accord would provide an advantage to US competitors. In 2017, the few voices expressing this sentiment—for instance within the German Christian Democratic Union (CDU) party—were met with public condemnation.[55] In stark contrast to 2001, even in the United States leading energy companies urged Trump to remain in the Paris Agreement, reflecting the massive green energy investments by the private sector despite US nonparticipation in Kyoto.[56]

3.3   *Trade*

The most radical departure from traditional US foreign policy under Trump has happened on trade. The criticism that the liberal trade order and past US support for it had not served US interests well is central to Trump's international agenda. Since entering office, he has reversed his predecessor's decision to join the Trans-Pacific Partnership (TPP), threatened to leave the North American Free Trade Agreement (NAFTA) and the WTO, and undermined the multilateral trade order by pressuring countries into bilateral negotiations and by imposing tariffs against allies and rivals alike. Because of the traditional US commitment to free trade, there was little need for nonhegemonic cooperation

---

52   Yeo 2017.
53   Carr 2018.
54   "Germany to Double Donation for UN Climate Change Fund" 2018; Karp 2018.
55   "Berliner Kreis erntet Kritik" 2017.
56   Raphelson 2017.

in the past. Now that this is changing, nonhegemonic cooperation could help to mitigate the effect of US protectionist measures on others.

3.3.1   US Policy and Impact

It is still not clear if Trump wants to reform WTO rules or do away with the organization altogether. The administration has used various provisions under US law to impose a range of tariffs on imports, ostensibly not to disrupt free trade but to protect US security and to counter others' "unfair" trade practices.[57] In January 2018, Trump announced antidumping measures against foreign solar panels and washing machines. In March, his administration implemented tariffs of 10 percent on steel and 25 percent on aluminum imports based on a national security exemption to WTO rules. After a temporary suspension of these tariffs with respect to some allies expired, Canada and the EU implemented countervailing measures, as did China. In June, based on charges of unfair practices relating to technology transfer, intellectual property, and innovation, Washington imposed tariffs on a long list of Chinese imports. China responded in kind, prompting two more rounds of additional US tariffs and Chinese retaliations.

While technically the United States is not in violation of WTO regulations as long as no ruling by the organization's dispute settlement body has been issued, its justifications for protectionist measures—especially the exemptions claimed on national security grounds—are questionable.[58] Furthermore, even as the United States is filing complaints against others' retaliating measures, it is blocking the appointment of judges to the WTO's appellate body. US representatives claim that they are using the veto to force WTO reform, but have shown little interest in Canadian and European proposals to that effect. The administration's real goal thus seems to be to undermine the multilateral trade regime's system of centralized dispute settlement—arguably *the* central function of the WTO at a time when new global trade rounds are out of reach anyway. If the seats remain unfilled, the number of appellate judges will fall below three in 2019, in which case the panel would no longer meet the quorum for dispute resolution decisions.[59] The measures already implemented and the uncertainty about the future are depressing global economic growth.[60]

---

57   Brown and Kolb 2018.

58   Lawrence 2018.

59   "America Holds the World Trade Organization Hostage" 2017.

60   Freund et al. 2018.

3.3.2 Feasibility and Cost of Compromise

Because Washington's ultimate goals are unclear, identifying potential compromises remains elusive. This problem is most pronounced in the escalating tit-for-tat application of protectionist measures between the United States and China. Despite the many legitimate grievances about China's trade practices—foremost the lack of transparency about connections between state and private enterprises with all its implications—the specific accusations from the United States keep shifting.[61] Add to this the fact that trade issues are mixed with security issues concerning the long-term strategic rivalry between the two countries, and it becomes unclear what concessions would bring the United States to scale back tariffs. The criticisms leveled against others, like Trump's economically misguided focus on bilateral trade deficits, are just as confusing. This represents a challenge: on the one hand, Washington's protectionist measures outside the WTO should be met with unified resistance, as they would undermine the multilateral trade system at a fundamental level; on the other hand, where US criticisms are justified, countries in the crosshairs would do well to take a conciliatory approach. For instance, although Germany's current account surplus is arguably more to the disadvantage of its European neighbors than the United States, taking measures to address it may be a way to signal willingness to compromise.[62]

3.3.3 Private Actors

Despite some opportunistic support for specific protectionist measures, the private sector in the United States generally advocates against tariffs.[63] Protectionism hurts companies with international supply chains and the retail sector. The United States has a trade surplus in the services, not least because of the global dominance of internet giants such as Google, Amazon, Facebook, and Apple. Their importance to the global economy presents its own challenges for regulators, but their business model is the antithesis to protectionism. Furthermore, the globally active US service industry—even beyond the tech giants—wants to avoid becoming a target of countermeasures. In some instances, the private sector has been able to exert a moderating influence; for example, by averting plans for a border adjustment tax or preventing the president from exiting NAFTA without a replacement. Yet Trump's willingness to take risks and his disregard for the consequences of his decisions limit the influence of the private sector while he is in office.

---

61   Frankel 2018.
62   Coricelli 2017.
63   Higgins 2018.

3.3.4   Alternative Leaders

Power relations between the main actors are more balanced on trade than on other issues: the EU's single market is comparable in size to the US economy and European investment in the United States is strong. China is becoming more assertive, illustrated by the fact that it launches its own initiatives such as the Regional Comprehensive Economic Partnership, sometimes viewed as a TPP competitor. The countermeasures of those targeted by US tariffs—whether China, Canada, or the EU—attest to this new confidence.

In addition, the emergence of alternative leaders is aided by the rise of bilateral, regional, and megaregional trade agreements. The United States itself has championed these formats, valued for their flexibility and ability to circumvent veto players from blocking progress in the WTO's long-stalled Doha Round. Now, this very flexibility could enable others to circumvent a protectionist United States. For instance, the EU is concluding bilateral agreements with Japan, Canada, Mexico, and others. TPP participants are moving ahead without the United States under the leadership of Japan. These efforts promise to mitigate the fallout from protectionist disruptions to international trade and indicate a potential for nonhegemonic cooperation. At the same time, they highlight the challenge for free traders in coordinating an increasingly fragmented global trading system while pushing back against US protectionism. In particular, it has proven difficult to resist US pressure to negotiate bilateral deals to avoid punitive measures. Mexico struck a deal on a successor agreement to NAFTA, leaving Canada scrambling to be included. Under this deal, the United States was granted benefits that it would have enjoyed under TPP while imposing restrictions on a future Canadian-Chinese trade agreement. The EU has thus far managed to hold off tariffs against European car imports by reportedly agreeing to buy more US agricultural products. Within the WTO, one concrete measure to signal continued support for the multilateral trading system in the face of US pressure, and thereby cooperating without the hegemon, would be to approve new appellate judges by majority vote if Washington continues to hold their appointments hostage to its demands.

4   Conclusion

For the first time in postwar history, a period of US unilateralism is coinciding with increasing challenges by other powers—most notably China and other BRICS states—to US dominance. The relative decline of the United States across various issue areas is turning cooperation without its leadership or even participation into a more realistic prospect. This trend has resulted not only from the shifting balance of power in the state system, but also from the rising importance of new nongovernmental actors in global governance. Transnational civil society networks often advocate "leaving America behind." While some business actors can gain from the fragmentation of regulatory regimes that results from US unilateralism, for many the benefits of harmonization through multilateral means outweigh the costs.

Although these factors work together to improve the prospects for nonhegemonic cooperation, concrete initiatives have remained limited to date. There is no single country or region that can replace US leadership. The EU, with its experience with supranational governance and its professed commitment to advancing the multilateral order, would be one important piece to the puzzle, but it keeps punching below its weight. The selective engagement of China and its (also selective) willingness to accept more responsibilities on the international stage open up possibilities for new coalitions, as does the increasingly prominent role of nongovernmental actors in multilateral diplomacy. However, alliances among these very different players will be easier to create and sustain in areas such as climate change than in policy fields such as human rights or Internet governance, where China opposes the liberal agenda of global institutions, or nuclear disarmament, where China sides with the United States and other nuclear powers while the EU is split. Political linkages across these issue areas could further complicate the task of assembling multilateralist coalitions. The increasing diversity of multilateral formats—including minilateral, informal, and ad hoc arrangements—enhances flexibility among potential coalition partners and can thus facilitate nonhegemonic cooperation. And yet this development is not without risks. The shift from global to regional and bilateral trade agreements threatens to fragment the global trading system and disadvantage those too weak to defend their interests. Softer forms of global governance—for instance, in climate policy—mean that agreements are no longer self-executing and require sustained political leadership to be effective.

In addition to both general trends and issue-specific configurations of contemporary global governance, the case for nonhegemonic cooperation is strengthened by the Trump administration's unwillingness to compromise, which is on display across all issue areas. One consequence is that supporters of multilateral regulation do not have to ponder the difficult question of how much substance they are willing to sacrifice to keep the United States on board—a dilemma they repeatedly faced with the Clinton and Obama administrations. Another possibility is that the Trump administration's bullying tactics, while paying off in the short run, will work to unify other countries and generate a policy backlash further down the line. Indications of such a development—which was already visible to some extent under the

George W. Bush administration—can be seen not only in public opinion surveys, but also in recent voting patterns at the United Nations[64] and in calls for challenging the dominance of the US dollar as international currency.[65]

This opens a window of opportunity to make global governance less dependent on US leadership and more resilient against attempts to undermine it. Contemporary political decision-makers could draw inspiration from the proposal made by Swedish foreign minister Olof Palme in 1985 to cap national contributions at 10 to 12 percent of the total UN budget so as to reduce the organization's dependence on its biggest donor countries. At the time, President Reagan's secretary of state George Schultz opposed the proposal for fear of losing US influence. Today, Trump actively calls for the rest of the world to shoulder a greater share of the burdens of multilateralism, opening a window of opportunity to make institutions less susceptible to US blackmail.

The challenges of nonhegemonic coalition building sketched above make plain that the task will not be an easy one. Although today's global governance landscape offers more options for circumventing the "reluctant hegemon" United States,[66] realizing them and achieving effective outcomes will require sustained political commitment by supporters of the global multilateral order, in Europe and beyond.

Bibliography

"America Holds the World Trade Organization Hostage." *The Economist*, 23 September 2017. https://www.economist.com/news/finance-and-economics/21729462-rules-based-system-trade-faces-threats-beyond-trumps-tariffs-america-holds.

Anderson, Kenneth. "The Ottawa Convention Banning Landmines, the Role of International Non-Governmental Organizations and the Idea of International Civil Society." *European Journal of International Law* 11 (1) (2000), 91–120.

"Berliner Kreis erntet Kritik: CDU-Spitze hält an Klimaschutzzielen fest." NTV, 5 June 2017. http://www.n-tv.de/politik/CDU-Spitze-haelt-an-Klimaschutzzielen-fest-article19874934.html.

Bodansky, Daniel. "Legally Binding versus Non-Legally Binding Instruments." In *Towards a Workable and Effective Climate Regime*, eds. Scott Barrett, Carlo Carraro, and Jaime de Melo (London: Centre for Economic Policy Research, 2015), 155–165.

---

64   Lynch 2018.
65   Khan and Brunsden 2018.
66   Fehl 2012.

Borger, Julian. "Friends without Benefits: How Europe Was Wrongfooted by Trump over Iran." *The Guardian*, 14 May 2018. https://www.theguardian.com/world/2018/may/14/the-myth-of-trumps-european-allies-shows-of-friendship-dont-signal-influence.

Bower, Adam. *Norms without the Great Powers: International Law and Changing Social Standards in World Politics* (Oxford: Oxford University Press, 2017).

Brem, Stefan. "Conclusion: Is There a Future for Non-Hegemonic Cooperation? Explaining Success and Failure of Alternative Regime Creation." In *Cooperating without America: Theories and Case Studies of Non-Hegemonic Cooperation*, eds. Stefan Brem and Kendall Stiles (London: Routledge, 2009), 173–186.

Brem, Stefan, and Kendall Stiles, eds. *Cooperating without America: Theories and Case Studies of Non-Hegemonic Cooperation* (London: Routledge, 2009).

Brown, Chad P., and Melina Kolb. "Trump's Trade War Timeline: An Up-to-Date Guide" (Washington, DC: Peterson Institute for International Economics, 24 September 2018). https://piie.com/blogs/trade-investment-policy-watch/trump-trade-war-china-date-guide.

Bump, Philip, and Aron Blake. "Donald Trump's Dark Speech to the Republican National Convention, Annotated." *The Washington Post*, 21 July 2016. https://wapo.st/29X0dPA.

Carr, Mathew. "UN Climate Talks Stalled as Developing Countries Demand Long-Promised $100 Billion Aid from Richer Nations." *The National Post*, 11 May 2018. http://nationalpost.com/wcm/01eb9908-d17f-46ab-8a97-3c037792abae.

Chemnick, Jean. "How the World Is Coping 1 Year after Trump Abandoned Paris Climate Pact." *Scientific American*, 31 May 2018. https://www.scientificamerican.com/article/how-the-world-is-coping-1-year-after-trump-abandoned-paris-climate-pact/.

Cirincione, Joe. "Trump's March to War with Iran." *The New Arab*, 4 October 2018. https://www.alaraby.co.uk/english/comment/2018/10/4/trumps-march-to-war-with-iran.

Cooper, Andrew F. "Like-Minded Nations, NGOs, and the Changing Pattern of Diplomacy within the UN System: An Introductory Perspective." In *Enhancing Global Governance: Towards a New Diplomacy?* eds. Andrew F. Cooper, John English, and Ramesh Thakur (Tokyo: United Nations University Press, 2002), 1–18.

Coricelli, Fabrizio. "Surmounting the German Surplus" (Prague: Project Syndicate, 8 September 2017). https://www.project-syndicate.org/onpoint/surmounting-the-german-surplus-by-fabrizio-coricelli-2017-09.

Erickson, Amanda. "Few Countries Are Meeting the Paris Climate Goals. Here Are the Ones that Are." *The Washington Post*, 11 October 2018. https://www.washingtonpost.com/world/2018/10/11/few-countries-are-meeting-paris-climate-goals-here-are-ones-that-are.

Fehl, Caroline. *Living with a Reluctant Hegemon: Explaining European Responses to US Unilateralism* (Oxford: Oxford University Press, 2012).

Frankel, Jeffrey. "Trump Renews Charges of Chinese Currency Manipulation" (Cambridge, MA: Belfer Center for Science and International Affairs, 24 September 2018). https://www.belfercenter.org/publication/trump-renews -charges-chinese-currency-manipulation.

Freund, Caroline, et al. "Impacts on Global Trade and Income of Current Trade Disputes." MTI Practice Note No. 2 (Washington, DC: World Bank Group, 2018). http://documents.worldbank.org/curated/en/685941532023153019/Impacts-on -Global-Trade-and-Income-of-Current-Trade-Disputes.

Geranmayeh, Ellie. "Trump's Iran Sanctions: An Explainer on Their Impact for Europe" (London et al.: European Council on Foreign Relations, 12 September 2018). https://www.ecfr.eu/article/commentary_trumps_iran_sanctions_an_explainer_on _their_impact_for_europe.

Geranmayeh, Ellie, and Esfandyar Batmanghelidj. "Bankless Task: Can Europe Stay Connected to Iran?" (London et al.: European Council on Foreign Relations, 10 October 2018). https://www.ecfr.eu/article/commentary_bankless_task_can _europe_stay_connected_to_iran.

"Germany to Double Donation for UN Climate Change Fund." DW.com, 28 November 2018. https://www.dw.com/en/germany-to-double-donation-for-un -climate-change-fund/a-46488796.

Higgins, Sean. "Business to Trump: End Steel and Aluminum Tariffs in Wake of US-Canada-Mexico Trade Deal." *The Washington Examiner*, 4 October 2018. https:// www.washingtonexaminer.com/policy/economy/business-to-trump-end-steel -and-aluminum-tariffs-in-wake-of-us-canada-mexico-trade-deal.

Hochstetler, Kathryn, and Manjana Milkoreit. "Responsibilities in Transition: Emerging Powers in the Climate Change Negotiations." *Global Governance* 21 (2) (2015), 205226.

Ikenberry, G. John. *After Victory: Institutions, Strategic Restraint, and the Rebuilding of Order after Major Wars* (Princeton: Princeton University Press, 2001).

Ikenberry, G. John. "The Future of the Liberal World Order: Internationalism after America." *Foreign Affairs* 90 (3) (2011), 56–68.

Irish, John, and Robin Emmott. "As U.S. sanctions Near, Europe Fails to Protect Iran Deal." Reuters, 24 September 2018. https://www.reuters.com/article/us-iran-nuclear -eu/as-u-s-sanctions-near-europe-fails-to-protect-iran-deal-idUSKCN1M41UO.

Jentleson, Bruce W. "Global Governance, the United Nations, and the Challenge of Trumping Trump." *Global Governance* 23 (2) (2017), 143–149.

Johansen, Robert C. "The Reagan Administration and the U.N.: The Costs of Unilateralism." *World Policy Journal* 3 (4) (1986), 601–641.

Kahl, Colin. "The Myth of a 'Better' Iran Deal." *Foreign Policy*, 26 September 2017. http:// foreignpolicy.com/2017/09/26/the-myth-of-a-better-iran-deal/.

Karp, Paul. "Morrison Says Australia Won't Provide More Money for Global Climate Fund." *The Guardian*, 7 October 2018. https://www.theguardian.com/environ ment/2018/oct/08/scott-morrison-resists-calls-to-withdraw-from-paris-climate -agreement.

Keohane, Robert O. *After Hegemony: Cooperation and Discord in the World Political Economy* (Princeton: Princeton University Press, [1984] 2005).

Khan, Mehreen, and Jim Brunsden. "Juncker Vows to Turn Euro into Reserve Currency to Rival US Dollar." *The Financial Times*, 12 September 2018. https://www.ft.com/content/7358f396-b66d-11e8-bbc3-ccd7deo85ffe.

Kindleberger, Charles P. "Systems of International Economic Organization." In *Money and the Coming World Order*, ed. David Calleo (New York: New York University Press, 1976), 15–39.

Krause, Joachim. "Multilateralism: Behind European Views." *Washington Quarterly* 27 (2) (2004), 43–59.

Krauthammer, Charles. "The Unipolar Moment." *Foreign Affairs* 70 (1) (1990), 23–33.

Lake, David. "International Legitimacy Lost? Rule and Resistance When America Is First." *Perspectives on Politics* 15 (1) (2018), 6–21.

Lawrence, Robert Z. "How the United States Should Confront China without Threatening the Global Trading System." PIIE Policy Brief No. 18–17 (Washington, DC: Peterson Institute for International Economics, 2018).

Luck, Edward C. *Mixed Messages: American Politics and International Organization 1919–1999* (Washington, DC: Brookings Institution Press, 1999).

Lynch, Colum. "Nikki Haley's Loyalty Test Backfires." *Foreign Policy*, 30 April 2018. https://foreignpolicy.com/2018/04/30/nikki-haleys-loyalty-test-backfires/.

Morse, Julia C., and Robert O. Keohane. "Contested Multilateralism." *Review of International Organizations* 9 (4) (2014), 385–412.

Mount, Adam. "Trump's Troubling Nuclear Plan." *Foreign Affairs*, 2 February 2018. https://www.foreignaffairs.com/articles/2018-02-02/trumps-troubling-nuclear-plan.

Patrick, Stewart. *The Best Laid Plans: The Origins of American Multilateralism and the Dawn of the Cold War* (Lanham, MD: Rowman and Littlefield, 2009).

Pickering, John, Jeffrey S. McGee, Tim Stephens, and Sylvia I. Karlsson-Vinkhuyzen. "The Impact of the US Retreat from the Paris Agreement: Kyoto Revisited?" *Climate Policy* 18 (7) (2018), 818–827.

Raphelson, Samantha. "Energy Companies Urge Trump to Remain in Paris Climate Agreement." NPR, 18 May 2017. http://www.npr.org/2017/05/18/528998592/energy -companies-urge-trump-to-remain-in-paris-climate-agreement.

Reif, Kingston. "Republican Senators Back New START." *Arms Control Today*, October 2018. https://www.armscontrol.org/act/2018-10/news/republican-senators -back-new-start.

Seetharaman, Ganesan. "India among the Largest Recipients of Climate Change Assistance, but a Few Questions Remain Unanswered." *The Economic Times*, 25 November 2017. http://www.ecoti.in/_n3Toa.

Snidal, Duncan. "The Limits of Hegemonic Stability Theory." *International Organization* 39 (4) (1985), 579–614.

Stefanini, Sara, and Kalina Oroschakoff. "France, Germany and Italy: Paris Deal 'Cannot Be Renegotiated.'" *Politico*, 1 June 2017. http://www.politico.eu/article/france-germany-and-italy-paris-deal-cannot-be-renegotiated/.

Stephen, Matthew. "Emerging Powers and Emerging Trends in Global Governance." *Global Governance* 23 (3) (2017), 483–502.

Stiles, Kendall. "Introduction: Theories of Non-Hegemonic Cooperation." In *Cooperating without America: Theories and Case Studies of Non-Hegemonic Cooperation*, eds. Stefan Brem and Kendall Stiles (London: Routledge, 2009), 1–20.

Stokes, Doug. "Trump, American Hegemony and the Future of the Liberal International Order." *International Affairs* 94 (11) (2018), 133–150.

Stowe-Thurston, Abigail. "The Wrong Response to Russia's INF Treaty Violation." *Bulletin of the Atomic Scientists*, 31 August 2018. https://thebulletin.org/2018/08/the-wrong-response-to-russias-inf-treaty-violation/.

Strange, Susan. "The Persistent Myth of Lost Hegemony." *International Organization* 41 (4) (1987), 551–574.

Thimm, Johannes. *The United States & Multilateral Treaties: A Policy Puzzle* (Boulder: FirstForum Press, 2016).

Urpelainen, Johannes, and Thijs Van de Graaf. "United States Non-Cooperation and the Paris Agreement." *Climate Policy* 18 (7) (2018), 839–852.

Vabulas, Felicity, and Duncan Snidal. "Organization without Delegation: Informal Intergovernmental Organizations (IIGOs) and the Spectrum of Intergovernmental Arrangements." *Review of International Organizations* 8 (2) (2013), 193–220.

Vabulas, Felicity, and Duncan Snidal. "Rising Powers and Forum Shopping: The Use of Informal IGOs to Bypass Formal Institutional Constraints." Paper prepared for the Workshop on Informal Governance, Annual Meeting of the International Studies Association, Toronto, Ontario, Canada, March 2014.

Victor, David. "America Heads to the Exit: What Trump Got Wrong about Paris." *Planetpolicy*, Brookings Institution, 6 June 2017. https://www.brookings.edu/blog/planetpolicy/2017/06/06/america-heads-to-the-exit-what-trump-got-wrong-about-paris/.

Vogler, John, and Charlotte Bretherton. "The European Union as a Protagonist to the United States on Climate Change." *International Studies Perspectives* 7 (1) (2006), 122.

White House. "Remarks by President Trump to the 72nd Session of the United Nations General Assembly." New York, 19 September 2017. https://www.white house.gov/the-press-office/2017/09/19/remarks-president-trump-72nd-session -united-nations-general-assembly.

White House. "Remarks by President Trump to the 73rd Session of the United Nations General Assembly." New York, 25 September 2018. https://www.whitehouse.gov/ briefings-statements/remarks-president-trump-73rd-session-united-nations -general-assembly-new-york-ny/.

Wirth, David A. "While Trump Pledges Withdrawal from Paris Agreement on Climate, International Law May Provide a Safety Net." *Lawfare*, 2 June 2017. https://www .lawfareblog.com/while-trump-pledges-withdrawal-paris-agreement-climate -international-law-may-provide-safety-net.

World Resources Institute. "CAIT—Country Greenhouse Gas Emissions Data." April 2014. http://www.wri.org/resources/data-sets/cait-country-greenhouse-gas -emissions-data.

Yeo, Sophie. "Michael Bloomberg's Millions Can't Compensate for Trump's Climate Policies." *The Washington Post*, 5 June 2017. https://wapo.st/2qYAXPf.

Zenko, Micah, and Friedman Lissner. "Trump Is Going to Regret not Having a Grand Strategy." *Foreign Policy*, 13 January 2018. https://foreignpolicy.com/2017/01/13/ trump-is-going-to-regret-not-having-a-grand-strategy/.

Index

Page numbers in **bold** refer to tables; page numbers in *italics* refer to figures; 'n' after a page number indicates the footnote number.

.